JAPANESE LITERATURE
IN THE
MEIJI ERA

Compiled and Edited by
OKAZAKI YOSHIE
Translated and Adapted by
V. H. VIGLIELMO

ŌBUNSHA

1955

謹呈

Tōsei Shosei Katagi by Tsubouchi Shōyō
(cover and frontispiece)

Takekurabe by Higuchi Ichiyō
(a sample page and frontispiece)

Konjiki Yasha by Ozaki Kōyō
(illustration)

Wakanashū
by Shimazaki Tōson
(cover)

Midaregami
by Yosano Akiko
(cover)

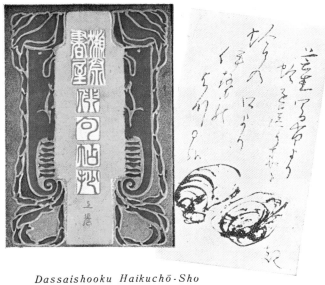

Dassaishooku Haikuchō-Sho
by Masaoka Shiki ; (cover) and sample of Shiki's writing

Wagahai wa Neko de Aru by Natsume Sōseki
(cover and illustration)

Sora Utsu Nami by Kōda Rohan
(cover and frontispiece)

Inaka Kyōshi by Tayama Katai
(illustration)

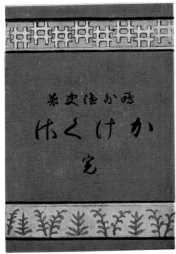

Kagegusa by Mori Ōgai
(cover)

Gakumon no Susume by Fukuzawa Yukichi
(cover and a sample page)

Ukigumo by Futabatei Shimei
(cover and illustration)

Bungakkai

Kiri Hitoha
by Tsubouchi Shōyō
(cover)

Ummeironja by Kunikida Doppo
(illustration)

Ichiaku no Suna
by Ishikawa Takuboku
(cover)

Tsubouchi Shōyō
(1859–1935)

Mori Ogai
(1862–1922)

Natsume Sōseki
(1867–1916)

Ozaki Kōyō
(1867–1903)

Masaoka Shiki
(1861–1902)

Kōda Rohan
(1867–1947)

Higuchi Ichiyō
(1872–1896)

Shimazaki Tōson
(1872–1943)

Yosano Akiko
(1878–1941)

Ishikawa Takuboku
(1885–1912)

FOREWORD

Modern Japan was born with the Meiji Restoration in 1868. But the true genesis of the Restoration occurred when Commodore Perry arrived at Uraga with his squadron in 1853, and the country was opened as the result of the conclusion of the American-Japanese Treaty in the following year. The rapid progress thereafter was often called "The Marvel of the Century," and prepared the way for the further development of national prosperity, which eventually brought Japan to the rank of a world power.

The Centenary Cultural Council, which was established to commemorate the centenary of the opening of the country, has undertaken to compile and publish a series on the cultural history of the Meiji Era, together with a history of American-Japanese cultural relations during the last hundred years, under the editorship of leading authorities in their respective fields of study. In order to realize this project, the councillors have met frequently and have carefully chosen competent editors and their collaborators for each section. Several volumes have already been published, and the remaining ones will appear at short intervals. Moreover, the Council is very happy to announce that it has planned the English translation of the series, and a group of British and American scholars now staying in Japan to pursue their research in Japanese history and culture have begun their task of translation. As the Council plans to supply a readable history to the general public, copious notes or detailed discussions of disputed problems are omitted, though it is founded on the solid basis of scientific investigation.

With regard to the English translation of the series, a committee made up of Mr. Matsumoto Shigeharu, Dr. Takagi Yasaka, Dr. Gordon Bowles, Mr. Tōgasaki Kiyoshi, Mr. Glenn W. Shaw, Professor Ishida Mikinosuke and Dr. Sakanishi Shio has been meeting to select the translators and supervise their work.   At the same time that the Council is sensible of the labors of the translators, it hopes that through these translated volumes the modern culture of Japan will come to be understood by the people of foreign countries.

The Council sincerely wishes to gain the interest and assistance of scholars as well as that of the reading public in general, and hopes that the series will be read widely at home and throughout the world.

HANEDA TŌRU

Centenary Cultural Council President

Tōkyō, July 1954

TRANSLATOR'S PREFACE

This volume is a translation of a history of one aspect of Japanese culture of the Meiji Era (1868–1912), namely literature. Inasmuch as this is the first time such a complete history has appeared in any Western language, it has necessitated the adoption of certain policies with regard to the translation.

1. Almost all dates are given in accordance with the Western calendar. However, I have occasionally referred to the Meiji twenties (1887–1896), thirties (1897–1906), and forties (1907–1912). I have used the terms " Meiji Era " and " Meiji Period " interchangeably ; indeed, for variety I have even used the term " Meiji " alone to mean the era, *e.g.*, " in Meiji " or " during Meiji."

2. All Japanese names are given in the Japanese order of surname first. Where the author has a pen-name, I have employed it, putting his real name in brackets, *e. g.*, Mori Ōgai (Rintarō). The second time and thereafter that an author's name is mentioned, I have used only the pen-name, *e. g.*, Ōgai. Almost all of the authors discussed in this volume had such pen-names, although there are some notable exceptions, such as Tanizaki Jun'ichirō.

3. The first time the title of a book appears I have used the Romanized transcription followed by the English translation in brackets. Thereafter I have used only the Romanized transcription. However, if a book is not mentioned for many pages and then appears again, I have once again given the translated English title. In some instances it has been impossible to translate a title, and it has therefore been given only in the Romanized transcription. This has occurred rather often in the section on the drama, where the play titles are frequently puns or have some special symbolic significance which cannot be conveyed by translation. Names of magazines and literary or dramatic organizations have been treated in the same way as book and play titles.

4. Capitalization of titles in all languages is in conformity with common English usage.

5. Titles of books in languages other than Japanese have, for the most part, been given only in English translation, *e. g.*, *Crime and Punishment*. In the case of certain very well-known French and German books, I have given only the original title, *e. g.*, *Les Misérables*.

6. I have endeavored to avoid footnotes as much as possible, and thus even the sources of quotations are given in the body of the text.

7. All Japanese terms that have not yet been fully assimilated into the English language appear in italics. I have used the Hepburn system of Romanization throughout the work.

8. All translations of the poetry and of the excerpts from novels and critical writing which appear in this work are my own.

While I have striven for consistency, it has not always been possible to achieve it. For example, the reader will note that the definite article appears before the names of certain periodicals and anthologies, and not before others. In the matter of capitalization, too, there are many difficulties, and consistency is well-nigh impossible. For instance, I have capitalized literary movements which I consider to have a certain fixed character, such as Naturalism, but not others, such as realism or idealism. I request the reader's indulgence on this matter.

I feel I must also apologize for the fact that the dates of birth and death do not appear after the first mention of each author. My only excuse is that they are not given in the original of this work. And yet had I not been under such pressure of time, I should have rectified this omission.

The plates which appear in this work will, I trust, give the Western reader some idea of what actual Meiji literature, and the men and women who created it, looked like. I have endeavored to make a representative selection.

If, after reading this volume, anyone should wish to know

more about Meiji literature, he is referred to the section on literature of the most recent bibliography on Japan, *A Selected List of Books and Articles on Japan in English, French and German*, by Hugh Borton, Serge Elisséeff, William W. Lockwood, and John C. Pelzel, Harvard University Press, 1954. He is also urged to read the excellent anthology of Japanese literature edited by my good friend and colleague, Dr. Donald Keene, and published by the Grove Press, 1955.

If this work succeeds in arousing the interest of the West in a significant body of literature that it has too long neglected, I shall consider my efforts to have been amply rewarded.

V. H. VIGLIELMO

Tōkyō, Japan
Spring 1955

TRANSLATOR'S ACKNOWLEDGEMENTS

First of all I wish to express my gratitude to the Centenary Cultural Council for having selected me to translate this volume. It was with sadness that I learned of Dr. Haneda Tōru's very serious illness, for it was he, who as President of the Council, was largely instrumental in my undertaking this work.

I next wish to express my appreciation to Professor Okazaki Yoshie of Tōhoku University, the editor of the original work, and to all those who worked under him in its compilation, for their encouragement and support in this translation. Unfortunately, the distance between Sendai and Tōkyō is such that frequent consultation has proved impossible.

My acknowledgements are due to Professor Hirabayashi Takeo of Meiji Gakuin University, and Messrs. Kobayashi Noritake, Kojima Noboru, Kudō Yukio, Miyakawa Tsuyoshi, and Yoshida Kazuto for their assistance in the first draft of certain sections of this translation.

In the typing of the manuscript I am indebted to the staff of International House of Japan, Inc., who gave liberally of their time and effort. For help in solving the numerous specific problems that arose in the course of the translation I am indebted to many people. However, I particularly wish to mention Professor Itō Sei of Kōgyō University for his advice in the interpretation of certain difficult *haiku* and *tanka*. My very special thanks go to Miss Tsutsui Yoshiko for her invaluable assistance in the last feverish weeks of preparation of the manuscript for publication. I am grateful also to Miss Motoko Fujishiro, Miss Frances Weinberg, and Mr. Ernest Young, who in this same period rendered great service in the painstaking task of proof-reading. I wish to thank Professor Shiota Ryōhei of Keiō University for having kindly lent the photographs which appear in this volume.

I am indebted to the staff of Ōbunsha too for their patience and understanding in dealing with the many difficulties that arose in the course of publication.

V. H. V.

CONTENTS

PART ONE A GENERAL SURVEY OF MEIJI LITERATURE

CHAPTER I THE POSITION OF MEIJI LITERATURE IN JAPANESE LITERARY HISTORY

1. *The Position of the Meiji Era as a Period in Japanese Literature*

The literature of Japan, like that of many other countries, did not begin as a fixed form but rather was transmitted orally. The orally transmitted myths, legends, and folk songs were recorded only after Chinese characters had been introduced from the Asiatic mainland. The officially compiled *Kojiki* (Records of Ancient Matters) (712), the *Nihonshoki* (History-Book of Ancient Japan), completed in 720, and the *Manyōshū* (Anthology of a Myriad Leaves), which is believed to have been compiled in the latter half of the eighth century, are the first noteworthy works. Thereafter, until the present, through almost twelve and a half centuries, Japanese literature has developed its traditions under relatively favorable conditions in its island home. There are many points of comparison with English literature, which, since *Beowulf*, believed to have emerged in the first half of the eighth century, has maintained a steady course to the present day.

Since the Edo Era (1600–1868), there have been various attempts at dividing into periods this vast span of Japanese literary history. In the Edo Era, Fujitani Shigeaya and his son, in connection with the changes in *waka* (indigenous Japanese poetry), made the following divisions: *Kamitsuyo* (The Era of the Gods); *Nakamukashi* (Mid-Antiquity); *Nakakoro* (The Middle Era); *Chikamukashi* (Near-Antiquity); *Ototsuyo* (The Era of

the Recent Past); *Ima no yo* (The Present Era). Motoori Norinaga recognized only four periods: *Jōko* (Upper Antiquity);
Chūko (Mid-Antiquity); *Geko* (Lower Antiquity); *Konji* (The
Present). Ban Kōkei employed only three periods, *Kotai* (An-
cient Form), *Chūkotai* (Mid-Ancient Form), and *Kintai* (Recent
Form), in tracing the changes in prose literary style. Among
the scholars of the Meiji Era also there were those who made
the divisions on the basis of the nearness or remoteness of the
periods. Ōwada Tateki's *Wabungakushi* (A History of Japanese
Literature), which appeared in 1892, used *Jōko, Chūko, Kinko*
(The Recent Past), *Kinsei* (The Recent Era), and *Kondai* (The
Present Era), while Haga Yaichi in his *Kokubungakushi Jikkō*
(Ten Lectures on the History of Our National Literature), which
was published in 1899, used the same categories except that he
called the last period *Gendai* (The Modern Era). Both of these
men made five periods, but nowadays there are many who,
copying Western historical methods, make only three: *Kodai*
(The Ancient Era); *Chūsei* (The Medieval Era); and *Kindai* (The
Modern Era).

There is another method of division based on the political
and cultural centers, which has been used since the appearance
in 1890 of Mikami Sanji's and Takatsu Kuwasaburō's *Nihon
Bungakushi* (A History of Japanese Literature). This work is
divided into six sections: The Origin and Development of
Japanese Literature; The Literature of the Nara Period; The
Literature of the Heian Period; The Literature of the Kamakura
Period; The Literature of the Northern and Southern Courts
and of the Muromachi Period; The Literature of the Edo Period.
Some scholars since then have called the period before the
Heian Period the Yamato Period and the period since the
beginning of Meiji the Tōkyō Period, and there have been many
who mix the political divisions with those based on the distance
in time from the present.

Since the Taishō Era (1912–1926), there has been much research in cultural history, with the result that divisions based

on the changes in the ruling class, such as the Period of Aristocratic Literature, the Period of Warrior Literature, and the Period of Popular Literature, or even those based on changes in intellectual history came to be used as well. Such divisions were already attempted by Europeans like Aston, who in his *A History of Japanese Literature* calls the Nara Period " Poetry Cultivated," the Kamakura Period " Decline of Learning," and the Edo Period " Revival of Learning." In the case of the Heian Period he calls it the " Heian or Classical Period," thus adding a word to indicate the main characteristic of the literature of that period. Florenz in his *Geschichte der Japanischen Literatur* employs a similar method. It can be thought that both men brought to bear on their studies of Japanese literature results acquired in research on Western literature, and Japanese scholars from Taishō on also have been applying Western methodology.

Thus, while there have been many attempts to divide the history of Japanese literature, almost all of them have employed either three or five periods. The three-period division method is the above-mentioned Western system of Ancient, Medieval, and Modern Eras; the five-period division method subdivides the Ancient Era into Remote Ancient (or the Primitive) Era and the Ancient Era, and subdivides the Modern Era into the Recent Past and the Present Era. The following table shows the interrelation of all of these methods of division.

According to the Three-Period Division Method

Ancient		Medieval	Modern	
Remote Ancient (Primitive) Pre-Nara	Ancient (Classical) Nara & Heian	Medieval Kamakura & Muromachi	Recent Past Edo	Present Meiji, Taishō & Shōwa

According to the Five-Period Division Method

However, this table merely presents the usual divisions, and there are some scholars who separate the Kamakura from the

Muromachi, and the Nara from the Heian Periods. The greatest problems arise in attempting to fix the upper and lower limits of the Medieval Era. Some say it should begin with Heian, some with Kamakura, and some with Muromachi. We intend to take the position that since Japanese literature begins in the seventh and eighth centuries when Western history is already in the Medieval Era, in Japanese literary history it is difficult to find any period which one can call an Ancient Era. When it comes to fixing the lower limit of the Medieval Era and the starting point of the Modern Era there are also many theories. Should it be placed at the end of Muromachi (Azuchi-Momoyama), or at the beginning of Edo, or at the beginning of Meiji, or even at the end of Meiji with the rise of Naturalism?

Since Meiji literature is the subject of this work, the upper limit of the Medieval Era is not of immediate concern. Instead, we wish to dwell on the problem of the lower limit. The lower limit of the Medieval Era is the upper limit of the Modern Era, and if one makes comparisons with Western history, one must seek therein manifestations of a Japanese Renaissance. With regard to the beginning of the Modern Era, in Western history too there are various theories, some placing it at the fall of the Eastern Roman Empire in 1453, others at the discovery of America in 1492, and still others placing it at the beginning of the Reformation in 1517, but the differences are not so great. In Japan, however, there is a considerable difference in time between the Azuchi-Momoyama and early Edo Periods on the one hand and the Meiji Restoration (1868) and late Meiji Periods on the other. If the early Edo Period is made to correspond to the Renaissance in the West, which is placed at about the fifteenth century, there is no great difference in time, but since the Edo Period represents the maturity of the feudal system, and since there were deep traces of the medieval order, the content of the culture was greatly different from that of the West. Nevertheless, on the significant point of the development of a popular culture, the modern West and Japan of the Edo Period are not incomparable. The culture, and particularly the literature, of the Genroku Period (1688–1704), with the emergence of Saikaku, Bashō, and Chikamatsu, almost demands comparison with the Italy of the Renaissance.

If one makes the complete destruction of the feudal system and the establishment of a modern state the standard, then there is no doubt that the Meiji Restoration presents these characteristics. Therefore, present-day historians largely employ this method. According to this, however, Saikaku must be counted among the medieval authors; but since his erotic works and those with the *chōnin* (tradesman) as the prime figure are actually more modern in spirit than the works of Boccaccio, such inclusion is clearly absurd. The novelists of the late Edo Period also, when compared with European authors of the seventeenth and eighteenth centuries, cannot be said to be medieval. When one looks at the problem from this viewpoint, then Japan's Modern Era begins with the Edo Period, and the Genroku Period corresponds approximately to the Renaissance. The essence of the culture was modern, but in the political and economic realms feudalism long persisted, so that complete modernization begins only with the Meiji Restoration. Therefore, the Edo Period should be called the Early Modern Period to distinguish it from the Meiji and post-Meiji Periods. There are some who distinguish the two by calling the Edo Period *Kinsei*, but actually there is little difference in meaning between *Kinsei* and *Kindai*, the word used to denote the period from 1868 to the present.

Thus, the Meiji Restoration means the emergence of a true modern spirit in Japanese culture, but since it was impossible to catch up with Western modern culture immediately, the whole period was one of confusion, wherein the past was being sloughed off at the same time that elements of the Ancient, Medieval, and Modern Eras of the West were introduced. The Meiji Restoration corresponds to the time in Europe when

Naturalism was already established, signalling the maturity of the Modern Era. If one refers to the chronological tables, one will observe that in the year before the first year of Meiji (1868) Baudelaire died, and the first volume of *Das Kapital* appeared. In the previous year Dostoevsky's *Crime and Punishment* appeared, and in the year prior to that, the first volume of Tolstoy's *War and Peace* was published. In 1871 Zola's *Rougon Macquart* series began to appear. Ibsen's *A Doll's House* followed five years later, while Nietzsche's *Thus Spake Zarathustra* began to be published in 1882. Thus, in the years immediately preceding and following the Meiji Restoration, in the West the modern spirit had reached its peak, while in Japan a modern state had barely been established and Western civilization had only begun to be introduced.

A generation after its first introduction, in late Meiji, this transplanted culture was flourishing, and it was not until then that a truly modern aspect appeared in literature. To trace the course of Meiji literature then is to provide a solution to the problem of the extent to which the writers who with difficulty had extricated themselves from feudalism and who had rapidly assimilated Western literary ideas, were able in the course of one generation to achieve modernization.

In order to ascertain the place of Meiji literature in the current of Japanese literature as a whole, one must first look at the past. The very first literary work in Japan is the *Kojiki*, which purports to be a work of history but which is actually an epic containing many songs and heroic tales. The songs of the *Kojiki* developed into the lyric poems of the *Manyōshū*, while its epic elements, by the addition of certain lyric qualities, developed into such works as the *Ise Monogatari* (The Tale of Ise) and *Taketori Monogatari* (The Tale of the Bamboo-Hewer), and ultimately attained the greatness of the *Genji Monogatari* (The Tale of Genji). This latter work would certainly be put in the Western category of the novel. It is a detailed and realistic account of court life written in a pure Japanese prose almost devoid of Chinese influence. This type of novel later degenerated and disappeared entirely, to be replaced by the epic war tales of the following period, which in turn degenerated and were replaced by the modern realistic novel. The form of the realistic novel was perfected by Saikaku, and it persisted into early Meiji, although accompanied unfortunately by elements of a lower order of fiction.

The stream of lyric poetry passed from the *Manyōshū* to the *Kokinshū* (Anthology of Poems, Ancient and Modern), and with the establishment of the *tanka* (short verse of thirty-one syllables) form, there began a long and unbroken tradition continuing to the present day. Indeed it is not too much to say that the *tanka* is the very backbone of Japanese literature. From the *tanka* emerged the *renga* (linked verse), and through further refinement of the latter form emerged the *haiku* (seventeen-syllabled verse) which is still being written today. Songs and ballads represent another stream of literature.

Dramatic literature appeared very late in Japan. The *nō* (Noh drama), a lyric drama that depends heavily on music and the dance, emerged in the latter half of the fourteenth century. In the Edo Period the *kabuki*, which combines pure dramatic elements with those taken from the *jōruri*, the puppet drama, and the *jōruri* itself were established and continued into Meiji. Both the *nō* and the *kabuki* were closer to the romantic drama or the opera than they were to the Greek-type classical drama.

In addition to these three forms (the novel, poetry, and drama), diaries, travelogues, and miscellaneous writings achieved an aesthetic excellence that cannot be disparaged, although it is difficult to say that they developed in any consistent manner.

From the point of view of literary form these various currents constituted a tradition that continued into the Meiji Era. When one looks beyond form to content, the following observations can be made.

Since primitive characteristics of Japanese literature are present to a high degree in the *Kojiki*, there are still many expressions of naive instinct, but in the *Manyōshū* for the first time the Japanese people through lyric poetry express their simple admiration of the universe and its wonders. From the *Kokinshū* on is developed a method wherein, by a refined sensibility, the relationship between the subtle human psychology and the atmosphere of a mysterious nature is transmuted into art. Concomitant with poetry, the development of the tale or the story form enabled the Japanese to make detailed observations on love and other aspects of the human psychology, and with the aid of the sensibility nurtured in poetry, enabled them to achieve the first real novel ever produced in the world.

Such prose and poetry represent the literary maturity of the court life through the Heian Period, and Aston, Florenz, and others are justified in considering it Japan's Classical Era. It is certainly true that the crude and primitive myths, legends, and songs were polished into an elegant and sophisticated form, and that we can see in it the artistic culmination of those purely Japanese sentiments of *mono no aware* and *miyabi*, which defy translation. However, this period chronologically extends from the seventh and eighth to the twelfth and thirteenth centuries, corresponding to the Middle Ages in the West and to the period from T'ang through Sung in China; therefore, looked at in the light of world history, the period acquires a medieval romantic coloring. Furthermore, one can clearly perceive the emergence of a lyric spirit based on love and the Buddhist concept of the evanescence of life. When compared with Western medieval literature, it is not impossible to make the interpretation that, together with that of the T'ang, Heian literature represents the first efflorescence of medieval literature in the world.

However, the period when the Buddhist faith controlled the spiritual and intellectual world and when literature too under its influence became largely an instrument of religion is the time when literature truly acquired a medieval cast. This period, extending from about the thirteenth to the sixteenth century, is the Kamakura-Muromachi Era when the warrior controlled the political and economic worlds, and the Buddhist priest was the leader of the intellectual world. There are startling resemblances to the Western Medieval Era. The refined aristocratic sentiments of *mono no aware* and *miyabi* gave way to loftier and more masculine sentiment, appropriate to a warrior and priest-centered culture. Japanese medieval tastes are also remarkably similar to those of the Sung and Yuan cultures of China, and indeed in painting we can see direct influences.

In the Edo Period we find many traces of the medieval aesthetic ideals in Bashō, but men like Saikaku and Chikamatsu sought to create a new type of beauty through popularization of the aristocratic ideals. *Mono no aware* and *miyabi* become *ninjō* (human feeling), *sui* (gracefulness), and *iki* (smartness, almost synonymous with *sui*). These were the ideals of the merchant's life in the market-place and in the gay quarters, and they found artistic expression in the *ukiyozōshi* (genre novels) and puppet plays. To replace the medieval Buddhist doctrine of salvation there appeared a new ethical code appropriate to the times. The emphasis on *giri* (ties of obligation) by Chikamatsu and the *kanzen chōaku* (promoting virtue and reproving vice) of Bakin are the best examples. At the same time that this was the fixed ethical code of a feudalism, it was also a part of Confucian teaching. Toward the end of the Tokugawa Shōgunate these ideas degenerated and became fixed, losing the vitality they possessed in the Genroku Era. In this weakened form they continued into early Meiji.

When one considers the problem of the extent to which the Meiji Era changed these traditional ideas, one finds that in its early years there were many traces of the Edo Era, and that the spirit of the new age was hardly felt. The ways in which the Meiji reformation was spurred on by the advance of Western civilization are many, but since Japan had not yet fully awakened from its long dream of isolation, there was not the proper atmosphere to effect at once a complete transformation of every aspect of culture. It seems as if Japan from the very beginning of Meiji hastily embarked upon a program of Westernization, but this is true only of the external, material realms of politics and economics; there was not sufficient time for Westernization to penetrate the intellectual world.

Of course it is true that the influences of Western rationalism, democracy, and materialism are considerable in the investigation of natural laws in science, in the emphasis on the people's rights in politics and law, and in the utilitarianism which permeated the whole Meiji intellectual world, but in the realm of art Western influence is not so readily discernible. Furthermore, early Meiji literature, if it was not nostalgically pursuing the departed Edo Era through its old style, lower order fiction, was content to be annexed to those writings which expressed the new scientific ideas and political theories of the day. Twenty years later in the mid-Meiji Period the situation changed considerably. A literature was born which could keep pace with that of the West, and a new type of poetry, together with the realistic novel, were successfully transplanted to Japan. In late Meiji, with the establishment of Naturalism in the novel and Symbolism in poetry, the process was almost completed.

When looked at in this fashion, it would seem that Meiji literature implies Westernization and that the current of Japanese literature was interrupted and tradition was destroyed. The relationship between continuing tradition and outside influence is a particularly important subject in Meiji literary history. Of course, before, during, and after the Nara Period a great influence was exerted on the course of Japanese literature by the spread of continental culture, but since at that time Japanese culture was not highly developed and in the realm of literature there was as yet no strong tradition, there did not emerge anything like the conflict and ultimate harmonization of Shintō and Buddhism in the realm of religion. While submissively accepting continental influences, the Japanese endeavored to assimilate them gradually and build a Japanese-style structure. In the Meiji Era, however, since a strong body of tradition already existed, a sharp conflict developed when waves of foreign influence were exerted against it. This can be seen in every area of culture, but in literature especially such conflict is difficult to overlook.

And yet actually, to a certain extent, the outside influences of the Meiji Era were accepted only after they had been Japanized, and the traditional spirit which accepted them is a part of the stream of literature from earliest times. This fact is very frequently overlooked by people who study only the literature since Meiji, and yet it is of no small importance. Tradition was not only preserved but was further developed. In the case of the *tanka* and *haiku* this is quite clear, but in the novel and in miscellaneous writings, too, the tradition of Saikaku, Bakin, Shunsui, and Tanehiko was continued, and even that of the *Genji Monogatari* did not die out. In the drama the continued existence of the *kabuki* is even more remarkable. Of course all of these forms have continued to exist to the present day with a certain amount of Westernization, but the distinctive literary spirit of the past still is at its core.

In conjunction with this, we cannot deny the existence of the traditional spirit which entered into and permeated the literary forms introduced from the West and Japanized them from within. The spirit of the *waka* and the *haiku* which concealed itself in the *shintaishi* (New Style poetry), and the Oriental symbolism embodied in the pantheistic view of the world in Symbolist poetry and that of later date, are the best examples. There is also that intrinsic desire for lyricism which transformed the Naturalistic novel into the *shishōsetsu* (personal novel) and the *shinkyō-shōsetsu* (mental life novel). Moreover, the fact that the modern drama, while originating in translations of modern Western drama, succeeded in the one-act form common to the indigenous *nō*, *kyogen* (short farces), and *kabuki* is further evidence.

Thus, although one must emphasize the influence which

modern Western literature exerted on Japan when looking at Meiji literature from the vantage point of world literature, one must also note how such Western literature was Japanized when tracing the whole stream of Japanese literature.

Since Meiji literature includes both the Westernization of Japanese literature and the Japanization of Western literature, the subject of our research becomes the problem of how the two were synthesized and how they became a part of the Japanese culture in the Meiji Era.

2. *The Development of Meiji Literature and Its Division into Periods*

By means of the Meiji Restoration Japan emerged from its previous isolation, and through its policy of opening the country it came to accept freely the foreign culture. Thereupon the modern culture of Europe, which just at that time was reaching the peak of its maturity, entered like a flood, and the structure of Japan as a modern state was gradually established. Of course the modernization of Japan was not completed so suddenly. It met with considerable difficulties, and it presented, in a certain sense, an incomplete and, in another sense, a warped aspect. Perhaps it would be best to say that Japan selected its own course of modernization, peculiar to itself. Thus, while Japan acquired features somewhat different from those of European and American modern culture, nevertheless it proceeded in the general direction of modernization.

The Meiji Era which began its new course under the guidance of European and American culture was an era of unprecedented innovation with regard to Japanese culture. The Meiji Era, together with that period from the reign of the Empress Suiko through the beginning of Nara, when a new culture developed from the introduction of that of the continent, represent the greatest upheavals in Japanese civilization. Neither the rise to power of the warrior and the priest in the Kamakura Era nor the rise and flowering of a popular culture in the early Edo

Era represents so great a change. Furthermore, the Meiji and Nara Periods were the times when the zeal for cultural attainment was at its height. Although it included much confusion and immaturity, the Meiji Era was filled with an ardent spirit and was a period of extreme vitality.

Meiji literature, availing itself of the temper of the times, attempted to transform itself. One facet of this may have been the nationalistic desire to resurrect all the old traditions, but even more than that was the desire to expand in order to form itself anew. The impatient striving to grow to the stature of European and American culture continued. The course of Meiji literature had as its very core this self-transformation for the purpose of growth. When one looks at the development of Meiji literature, one notes that the course and stages of this transformation mark the divisions of the period as a whole. However, inasmuch as the course of this transformation is variously conceived, we shall next mention several noteworthy viewpoints and give a cursory look at the main trends of Meiji literature. There will be many instances when this will necessitate touching upon the over-all development of Meiji culture.

In the process of the development of Meiji culture, the first thing one thinks of is the various periods created by the rivalry and alternate flourishing of that nationalism which sought to preserve tradition (Traditionalism) and that Europeanizing force which sought to expand itself through outside influence (Exoticism). The Meiji Restoration, as the restoration of imperial authority would imply, can be thought of as a vigorous return-to-the-past movement, but it can also be thought of as a Europeanization movement based on its ideas of opening the country. It is the special characteristic of the Meiji Restoration that it should have within it at the same time two such conflicting movements, and the course of the culture which followed it was always in the direction of repeating this pattern of the meeting and reconciliation of these two conflicting movements.

Generally speaking, the twenty-year period after the Meiji Restoration was one of Europeanization, and the longing for a new way of life, as shown by the flourishing of translation, the popularity of elementary works introducing Western civilization, the currency of ideas on the people's rights and freedom, and the balls at the Rokumeikan (which means the Mansion of the Baying Stag), best indicates the trend of the times. Of course traces of Edo literature were still strong, but the pro-foreign spirit which sought to overwhelm them was welcomed as the progressive force. Those who have discussed Meiji literature heretofore have called this early period one of acceptance of (Western) civilization, or of propagation of the new civilization, or simply the period of enlightenment or of Europeanization, but it was also one of instruction and of confusion. Or we can also say that, in the very essence of the culture, it was a kind of period of translation. This new life was not founded on a complete awakening, but rather the people sought to create it by imitation of the West. In this sense the period can also be called one of imitation. During this time there was nothing produced worthy of being considered literature, and almost all of the works were of an elementary, instructive kind. Nishi Amane, Fukuzawa Yukichi, and Nakamura Keiu (Masanao) were the guiding lights of this period. The Meirokusha, begun in 1873 by Mori Arinori, is a part of this general trend of popular enlightenment as is the group belonging to Tokutomi Sohō's (Iichirō) Min'yūsha (Friends of the People Society). Nakae Chōmin (Atsusuke) and others who propounded the doctrines of freedom and equality also stood on the side of Europeanization.

It is a problem as to when this first period ends, and there are those who feel the second period already begins in 1878 with the translated novel *Ōshū Kiji : Karyū Shunwa* (A Strange Event in Europe : A Spring Tale of Flowers and Willows). Others see the dawn of a new age in Meiji literature beginning with the revolution in the world of poetry caused by the appearance in 1882 of the *Shintaishishō* (A Collection of New Style Poetry). We must consider, however, that it was still the confused period of the Enlightenment.

Most scholars are now agreed in dating the second period of Meiji literature, the period of the emergence of a new literature, from the publication in 1885 of *Shōsetsu Shinzui* (The Essence of the Novel) and *Ichidoku Santan : Tōsei Shosei Katagi* (Once-Read Thrice-Admired : The Character of the Modern Student) and the establishment of the Ken'yūsha (Friends of the Inkstone Society), but we must not think that at this time Europeanization was already ended. It was two or three years later that the people awakened to the extreme Europeanization of early Meiji, and that the nationalistic movement became prominent. In 1887 the Min'yūsha was formed with Tokutomi Sohō at its head to guide the progressive youth toward democracy, and in the same year the magazine *Kokumin no Tomo* (The Nation's Friend) was first published. This group and its periodical favored Europeanization, but it also urged reconsideration of mere superficial Westernization. Again in the same year the Buddhists of the Nishi Honganji sect, with the slogan "Abolition of Drinking and Promotion of Virtue," attempted to bring about a revival of Buddhism, and published the *Hanseikai Zasshi* (The Magazine of the Society of Introspection) (later the *Hansei Zasshi*, The Magazine of Introspection, and still later, the *Chūō Kōron*, Central Review), and this was clearly a movement with a pronounced conservative trend. In the following year Miyake Setsurei (Yūjirō) and Shiga Shinsen (Jūkō), among others, formed the Seikyōsha (The Political Teaching Society) and published the nationalistic magazine *Nihonjin* (The Japanese People) (later *Nihon oyobi Nihonjin*, Japan and the Japanese People) which tried to direct the future of Japan toward Japanism, and Setsurei wrote such books as *Shinzembi Nihonjin* (The True, Good, and Beautiful Japanese People) and *Giakushū Nihonjin* (The False, Evil, and Ugly Japanese People), while Shinsen extolled Japanese-type beauty in his *Nihon Fūkeiron* (A Study of

Japanese Landscapes). Furthermore, in 1889 Kuga Katsunan (Minoru) began publishing the newspaper *Nihon* (Japan) to resurrect and exalt the nationalistic spirit of Japan which had been lost.

Later, through the period of the debate on nationalism which arose between Inoue Tetsujirō and the Christians, and after the Sino-Japanese War, the awakening of the people was increasingly advocated, and in 1897 the Dai Nihon Kyōkai (The Greater Japan Society), an ultra-nationalistic group, was formed, and *Nihonshugi* (Japanism) was first published. Inoue Tetsujirō's and Takayama Chogyū's extreme nationalistic views appeared in this periodical. In the literary world, Ochiai Naobumi, Ōwada Tateki, and Konakamura (Ikebe) Yoshikata urged the revival of classicism, and the activity of the Myōjō-Ha (The Morning Star Group) in the *tanka* and Masaoka Shiki's movement to reform the *haiku* in the newspaper *Nihon* appeared. The rise of Romanticism was concomitant with that of nationalism.

We can consider that this nationalistic awakening lasted approximately fifteen years. From about 1900 the influx of Naturalism, together with the trend toward individualism, became prominent, and with the publication of *Hakai* (The Breaking of the Commandment) in 1906 and *Futon* (The Quilt) in the following year, the period of Naturalism had clearly arrived. Thereafter, modern European literary ideas flooded the country to the extent that we can call it the second period of Europeanization, and the trend toward realism, which *Shōsetsu Shinzui* and *Ukigumo* (The Drifting Clouds) began at the end of the first period of Europeanization in early Meiji and which had been interrupted, rapidly came to the forefront of the literary scene.

Thus, when we look at Meiji literature as the alternation of the two currents of nationalism and Europeanization, we can divide it into three periods, the first period of Europeanization from 1868 to about 1886, the second period of nationalism until about 1906, and the third period, that of the second Europeanization or modernization, from 1906 through the subsequent Taishō Era (1912–1926).

We can see in some degree the alternation of the two currents of nationalism and Europeanization in the world of literature, but it is rather a problem of general culture, and we can see it to a high degree in areas of spiritual culture, such as science, religion, and morality, as well as in the area of material civilization. Since nationalism aimed at a revival of those ideas on morality peculiar to Japan, the revival of religion, specifically Shintō and Buddhism, accompanied it. Since the Europeanization movement principally endeavored to transplant completely those scientific ideas which form the base of Western civilization, from the investigation of natural law of early Meiji to the application of science to literature at the end of Meiji, there is consistency. In the realm of religion, Christianity accompanied this movement, and in the realm of morality, individualism and freedom based on the awakening of a modern type of personality were prized.

When we come to consider the course of progress of literature itself in this general cultural context, we first think of the alternation of Romanticism, or Idealism, with Realism, and this is not an invalid approach, but Meiji literature was formed by the constant mingling and opposition of these two ideas rather than by a mere alternation of them.

In connection with the idea that Classicism and Romanticism, or Realism and Idealism, are two mutually opposed literary ideas, it is also said, when discussing European literature, that such opposition and alternation serve to advance literature. Meiji literature also can be looked at in this way. Since the historical method which disposes in this way of the stages through which modern European literature, particularly that since the Renaissance, has passed, has already become commonly accepted, it is possible to apply it to Meiji literature; and indeed many attempts have already been made. And yet such alternation has not come in an orderly process, for we frequently find that both ideas coexist and intermingle in the same period.

For the first twenty years of Meiji, as we have said before, there was much superficial imitation, introduction, and admiration of Western civilization, and since even when this was not the case, there were efforts to bring Japan abreast with the times in some degree, while preserving the old atmosphere of the previous era, we can call this period generally one of education or enlightenment. When we compare it with the European period of the Enlightenment, of course we realize that it did not emerge from the depths of our culture but was rather imposed from without.

Thus, the force to enlighten every area of the spirit from within was weak and it ended in superficiality, but we must not overlook the fact that there was the will to depart from the conventions of the previous era and to build a new culture, and that there was an attempt to seek practical methods for realizing it.

Nishi Amane, who in 1870 began his lectures on his *Hyakugaku Renkan* (Chain of a Hundred Studies) and who later wrote *Chisetsu* (Theory of Knowledge), *Bimyōgakusetsu* (Theory of Aesthetics), and *Hyakuichi Shinron* (A Hundred and One New Discourses), stood at the forefront of this first period, together with Fukuzawa Yukichi who through his *Kummō : Kyūri Zukai* (To Enlighten : An Explanation of Natural Law), *Seiyō Jijō* (Institutions of the West), *Sekai Kunizukushi* (All About the Countries of the World), *Gakumon no Susume* (Encouragement of Learning), *Dōmō Oshiegusa* (Didactic Tales for the Enlightenment of Youth), and *Moji no Oshie* (The Teaching of Characters) fulfilled his function of enlightenment. Apart from such crude introductions to the West as *Bankoku Kōkai : Seiyō Dōchū Hizakurige* (Voyage to Myriad Countries : A Hiking-Tour in the West) and *Ushiya Zōdan : Agura Nabe* (Idle Talk at a Sukiyaki Shop : A Cross-Legged Session), the numerous works of translation completely performed this function of enlightenment in literature. Moreover, we can consider that the political novels such as *Saibu Meishi : Keikoku Bidan* (A Noble Tale of Statesmanship) and *Kajin no Kigū* (The Chance Meeting with Two Beauties) also had the aim of arousing the people from the delusions and fallacies of the feudal period.

The period of Enlightenment in modern European culture was in the mid-eighteenth century, and it was followed first by Classicism and then by the flowering of Romanticism. Of course it is possible to consider that Classicism arose in the sixteenth century and that enlightenment also was inherent in this long classic tradition. In France the seventeenth century was the height of Classicism, and we can also think that the Enlightenment was its destructive process. In Germany, however, since at the end of the Enlightenment the study of ancient Greece was begun and the Classicism of men like Goethe appeared, the period of Classicism lasted from the eighteenth to the middle of the nineteenth century. Meiji Classicism, following the German pattern of appearing after the Enlightenment, continued for about ten years after 1887.

It is doubtful whether anything that we can truly think of as Classicism existed in Meiji, but even if there was something resembling it, perhaps it was nothing more than a revival of the classics or what we must call pseudo-Classicism. Nevertheless, beginning in 1885 with the *Shiseki Shūran* (A Collection of Historical Works), reprints of the classics such as the *Nihon Bungaku Zensho* (The Complete Works of Japanese Literature) (from 1890 on) and the *Nihon Kagaku Zensho* (The Complete Works of Japanese Poetry) (also from 1890 on) continued to appear, and in the works of Ozaki Kōyō, Kōda Rohan, and Mori Ōgai written in an elegant prose style, there was a striving in content as well to achieve classic perfection. Since at this time perfection of form was indeed considered the highest goal of literature, Kōyō and others, while still concerned about plot and content, were equally concerned about polishing their prose.

The most significant group which strove to create a neo-classical style from the study of classical literature was the Asakasha (The Faint Perfume Society) founded in 1893 by Ochiai Naobumi, and it did not restrict its activity to *waka* poetry, but in prose as well, in such works as *Bibun Imbun : Hana Momiji* (Prose and Poetry : The Flowery Red Leaves of Autumn) which appeared in 1896, is to be found a form that is a recreation of that of the classical world. In Ōgai's novel *Maihime* (The Dancing Girl), in his translated novel *Sokkyōshijin* (The Improvisator), and in the Ōgai-directed translations of poetry collected in a work entitled *Omokage* (Vestiges), he is deeply aware of endeavoring to reconstruct the Heian style. Of course it is possible to say that these works of Ōgai merely represent the influence of Naobumi's style. At any rate, this style persisted into the period of Romanticism, and by the time Naturalism arose, had permeated every area of literature. The revival of old words on the part of Susukida Kyūkin and Kambara Ariake and the mysterious and restrained qualities of the verse of *Miotsukushi* (Channel Markings) and *Kaichōon* (The Sound of the Tide) represent an after-effect of this same movement. Even if we cannot say that the revival of Saikaku which early appeared in the works of such men as Kōyō and Rohan was definitely a classical trend, the influence of the *Genji Monogatari* on Kōyō and the formation of the Chikamatsu Kenkyūkai (The Chikamatsu Research Society) in 1896 with Tsubouchi Shōyō at its head do ornament the end of this period.

After 1885, which is the year of transition between the Enlightenment and Classicism, Shōyō's *Shōsetsu Shinzui* and *Tōsei Shosei Katagi* and Futabatei Shimei's *Ukigumo* and his translation from Turgenev under the title *Aibiki* (Rendezvous) successively appeared. Since these works were part of a kind of enlightenment movement to introduce Western realism to Japan, we can consider the predominantly classic style of the Ken'yūsha group and Rohan to be a reaction against the movement. However, a considerable Romantic element can also be seen in the style of Kōyō and Rohan who dominated the scene at this time, and in 1891 while Rohan's *Gojū no Tō* (The Five-Storied Pagoda) clearly manifested Romanticism and Idealism, Ōgai raised the flag of Idealism in the periodical *Shigarami-Zōshi* (Tangled Tales) and challenged Shōyō's *botsu-risō* (Submerged Idealism) thesis which appeared in another periodical, *Waseda Bungaku* (Waseda Literature). In the following year Ōgai's brilliant translation from Andersen, *Sokkyōshijin* (The Improvisator), began to appear in *Shigarami-Zōshi* and aided the Romantic trend. The leader of Romanticism, Kitamura Tōkoku, was also active at this time, and in the year that *Gojū no Tō* appeared so also did his *Hōraikyoku* (The Song of Fairyland).

We notice, therefore, that this Romantic tendency was already increasing in importance during the period of Classicism. In 1894 Tōkoku committed suicide, and Chogyū arrived on the literary scene through his *Takiguchi Nyūdō* (The Lay Priest Takiguchi). With the death of the pioneer of Romanticism we feel more keenly the emergence of the main body of the movement. Actually Tōkoku, with his extreme Romantic character, appeared when the Enlightenment and Classicism still dominated the scene, and literally destroyed himself by standing in this exposed *Sturm und Drang* pioneer position. It is possible for us, therefore, to consider the year in which Tōkoku died as the year of the establishment of Meiji Romanticism.

In the novel, however, the following year, 1895, saw the emergence of the *kannen shōsetsu* (ideological novel), the *hisan shōsetsu* (tragic novel), and the *shinkoku shōsetsu* (profound novel) with Izumi Kyōka's *Yakō Junsa* (The Night-Duty Policeman) and *Gekashitsu* (The Surgery), and several works by Kawakami Bizan and Hirotsu Ryūrō. Since the same year saw the publication of Higuchi Ichiyō's *Takekurabe* (Comparing Heights) and *Nigorie* (The Muddied Stream) and clearly marks a period, this year is also taken by some as the beginning of the Romantic Era. At any rate, from this time on the Romantic coloring became deeper, and we are able to compare it to the time from the end of the eighteenth through the nineteenth century when in every country of Europe Romanticism flourished. The popularity of the New Style poetry, the emergence of the two major poets, Shimazaki Tōson and Tsuchii (Doi) Bansui, and the activity of the Myōjō group centering around Yosano Tekkan and Yosano Akiko are among the many things which testify to this trend. In the world of literary criticism there were Chogyū, Ueda Bin, Ōgai, and Shimamura Hōgetsu.

This Romanticism represented the rather prominent trend of the times, and it is possible to consider that in this movement the modern aspect of the Japanese literary scene clearly appeared; but there are those who, from another point of view, do not think of this as a period of Romanticism. They consider rather that it was a period of Realism, or the second period of Realism, when those realistic elements of *Tōsei Shosei Katagi* and *Ukigumo* finally bore fruit. There are also some who say that this is a period of the opposition of Idealism and Realism. It is certainly true that in the midst of this Romantic trend there was another strong one working against it, as shown by the advocacy of Zolaism by Kosugi Tengai and Nagai Kafū, and by the emergence of Oguri Fūyō's realistic novels. Although those forms called *shinri shōsetsu* (psychological novel), *shakai shōsetsu* (social novel), and *katei shōsetsu* (domestic novel) began to flourish, it cannot be said that these too do not represent a Realism in the guise of Romanticism. From another point of view, it is not impossible to form the theory that this Romanticism was the cultivation period of Naturalism.

In addition to the various works of those pioneers of Naturalism, Tengai, Fūyō, and Kafū, we are able to mention Katai's *Jūemon no Saigo* (The End of Jūemon) (1902) and Tōson's *Kyūshujin* (The Old Master) (1902) and *Suisai Gaka* (The Water-Color Painter) (1904), and it is the accepted theory today that the realization of Naturalism came with Tōson's *Hakai* (1906) and Katai's *Futon* (1907). But when it comes to the problem of fixing the exact year when the Naturalistic Period begins, it is difficult to make the various theories accord. It is variously placed anywhere between 1902 and 1907. Since there is no one who places it any later than 1907, it is generally believed that *Futon* determines the firm establishment of Naturalism ; moreover, in the same year a considerable number of naturalistic novels and critical works appeared, and Kunikida Doppo from that time on clearly approached Naturalism. The beginning of Naturalism can be placed in 1902 because in that year, in addition to Katai's *Jūemon no Saigo*, there appeared Tengai's *Hayariuta* (A Popular Song), Fūyō's *Ryōen* (The Cool Flame) and *Numa no Onna* (The Marsh Woman), Kafū's *Jigoku no Hana* (The Flowers of Hell), Tokuda Shūsei's *Shunkō* (Spring Light), Tōson's *Kyūshujin*, and Doppo's *Shuchū Nikki* (Wine-Soaked Diary).

At any rate, since from 1907 on we clearly enter the Naturalistic Period, the few years prior to that date represent the advance to realism from romanticism, corresponding to the period in France when Balzac and Stendhal were active. At this time both romantic and realistic works appeared and also a great number that combined elements of both movements. The realistic trend gradually advanced and finally Naturalism was established. Of course this observation is based on the novel, and poetry and the drama merely received its after-effects, while in those genres the romantic trend still remained strong. At about the same time that Naturalism appeared in the novel, Symbolism was introduced in poetry and drama, heralding the early establishment of Neo-Idealism and Neo-Romanticism.

We can find the beginnings of Neo-Romanticism and Symbolism already in 1905. In that year we can see the introduction of French Symbolism in Ueda Bin's *Kaichōon* and in Ariake's symbolistic poetic étude, *Shunchōshū* (The Spring Bird Anthology). In the novel, Natsume Sōseki created a fresh romantic style with his *Wagahai wa Neko De Aru* (I Am a Cat), *Rondon Tō* (The Tower of London), *Maboroshi no Tate* (The Phantom Shield), and *Kairokō* (The Song of Evanescence). In the following year he brought out *Botchan* and *Kusamakura* (The Grass Pillow) while one of his protegés, Suzuki Miekichi, brought out *Chidori* (The Plover). In the year that *Kusamakura* appeared, in the world of criticism there appeared Shimamura Hōgetsu's *Torawaretaru Bungei* (The Captive Literature) and Iwano Hōmei's *Shimpiteki Hanjūshugi* (Mystic Semi-Animalism). It is better to consider these works as a manifestation of post-Naturalistic Romanticism and Mysticism rather than as a continuation of Romanticism. Since in Europe too at this time the Naturalistic Period was drawing to a close and Neo-Idealism and Neo-Romanticism were gaining strength, men like Hōgetsu during their stay abroad were infused with this new spirit, and after their return to Japan tried, through such works as *Torawaretaru Bungei*, to depart from the naturalistic intellectualism and move forward to a religious subjectivism.

However, since in Japan at the very time that Naturalism was finally establishing itself, the post-Naturalistic ideas which had matured in Europe were introduced, the confusion and complications were great, and they were embodied in such men as Hōmei. Hōgetsu from the first was a man with pronounced subjective tendencies, and even though for a while he concealed the assertions of *Torawaretaru Bungei* and, as a supporter of Naturalism, became editor of *Waseda Bungaku* and kept pace with the prevailing literary trend, he was unable to become a theorist of pure Naturalism.

Kafū also in the beginning appeared to be an exponent of Naturalism, but he too is essentially a romantic and lyricist, and when in 1908 he returned from abroad, he became one of the leaders of the anti-Naturalism movement. He led the young romantics, hedonists, and decadents through such magazines as *Subaru* (first published in 1909), *Okujō Teien* (The Roof Garden) (also first published in 1909), and *Mita Bungaku* (Mita Literature) (first published in 1910), and for a time appeared to dominate the whole literary scene. Ōgai, Bin, and others assisted, and the young men of the Sōseki school had a common bond, so that the anti-Naturalism trend became conspicuous. Kyōka's second period of activity can be seen in his *Shirasagi* (The Snowy Heron) (1909) and in his *Uta Andon* (Song and the Lamp) (1910). This trend became decisive with the appearance in 1910 of Tanizaki Jun'ichirō's *Shisei* (The Tattooing) in the first issue of the second *Shinshichō* (The New Current of Thought) edited by Osanai Kaoru. Yoshii Isamu's *waka* anthology *Sakahogai* (The Drinking-Party) and his play *Kawachiya Yohei* appeared in the same year, and the poetry and plays of Kinoshita Mokutarō charmed the younger generation at about this time. The establishment of the Symbolist poetry of Kitahara Hakushū and Miki Rofū also took place at this time.

Thus, a new romantic trend, somewhat later than but almost concurrent with Naturalism, appeared, and the Meiji Era closed while still in the midst of this brilliant modern movement. Already at this time, however, the humanitarianism of the Shirakaba-Ha (The White Birch Group), and the activity of the Neo-Idealist critics surrounding Sōseki had begun, so that the literary scene made yet another turn, heralding the era of anti-Naturalistic Idealism. Thus, there are many who consider the Taishō Period and later to be the period of Neo-Idealism. We can think of these Neo-Romantic, Hedonist, and Decadent schools as performing the function of destroying Naturalism and guiding the way towards a new idealism. In this sense, the schools are of a transitional character and resemble the realism of the Romantic Period which heralded Naturalism. And yet, since Meiji literature in an extremely short period of time sought to rush through its course of modernization, it was never able to avoid overlapping and confusion.

In modern Western literature too we cannot say that the Enlightenment, Classicism, Romanticism, Realism, Naturalism, Neo-Romanticism, and Neo-Idealism always followed that sequence ; we must recognize a considerable amount of overlapping. But since modern Western literature progressed over about three centuries, such overlapping as did exist did not lead to utter confusion. Since Meiji literature passed through these stages in less than half a century, and since it followed for the most part the course of the importation of Western ideas, it was absolutely impossible for it to have an orderly development. Some men like Sōseki felt that this rapid course of development was productive of a nervous breakdown in the Japanese national character, but is not Meiji literature, as the development of modern literature in microcosm in a corner of the Far East, thereby the more worthy of the attention of the world ?

When we look at Meiji literature as keeping pace with the advance of modern European literature, we are able to make the following period divisions : prior to 1886, the Enlightenment ; the era of Classicism until about 1894 ; from then until about 1905, the transitional period from Romanticism to Realism ; thereafter until 1912, the period from Naturalism to Neo-Romanticism and Decadence ; the era of Neo-Idealism after the entry into Taishō. Yet we must remember that because of considerable overlapping, we cannot avoid inaccuracy. These changes in literary ideas and the afore-mentioned period divisions based on the alternate flourishing of nationalism and Europeanization almost coincide, and the periods of Classicism and Romanticism are included in the period of Nationalism.

When we examine the above method of division, we are made to realize the extent to which the Sino-Japanese (1894–1895) and Russo-Japanese (1904–1905) Wars changed the ideas of the times, becoming the lines of demarcation between periods. If we make our viewpoint fit the general historical one, it is possible to make three periods with the two wars as the dividing lines, and then further to subdivide the time before the Sino-Japanese War into two periods.

Thus, for the most part it is convenient to divide Meiji literature into either three or four periods, but there are some who make only two periods, pre-Naturalism and post-Naturalism, and there are others who make more precise divisions into five, six, and even seven periods. There is some reason in making only two periods based on Naturalism, but still this means an over-emphasis on the modern significance of this movement. Again, to make many divisions is to consider the novel, the poetry, and the drama separately, and to dwell on the small changes in each genre. Of course it is possible to make many small divisions in each genre, but since these apply only to that genre, and only large changes apply to the whole area of literature, we are able to make only large divisions. Just as literature does not necessarily keep pace with art and music, so also within literature each genre possesses its own particular pace, and they all are not necessarily coordinated with one another. For the over-all order, it is necessary to make comparatively large periods.

With regard to the divisions within each genre, there are still many things to discuss, but we shall touch upon them in the chapters devoted to those genres. For the study of all of Meiji literature, we think that either the three or four-period method of division is suitable. The four-period division method is perhaps the most convenient. The Manyō Era is rather appropriately divided into four periods, and in the extent of time it is rather like the Meiji Era. But since this work treats of Meiji literature in a detailed fashion and seeks to trace the changes in thought of every area of that literature, we have made merely a cursory examination of the over-all period divisions, and we intend not to be unduly restricted by such categorization.

3. *The Characteristic Features of the Meiji Literary World*

The emergence of specialized writers of literature is a comparatively recent phenomenon in Japan. In ancient times literature was the secondary occupation of court aristocrats or retired priests. Ō no Yasumaro, the compiler of the *Kojiki*, and the great poets of the *Manyōshū*, Hitomaro, Akahito, Okura, and Yakamochi, were all officials serving at the court. Hitomaro and Okura did not have a very high rank as officials, but they were not men who had as their profession the writing of poetry. Tsurayuki and Kintō also, the great writers of the Heian Era, were rather high-ranking officials, and Murasaki Shikibu and Sei Shōnagon too were court ladies serving either the second consort of the Emperor or the Empress herself. Without such rank, they would have had neither the opportunity to make their works public, nor would they have found a method of acquiring the materials for them.

From the Kamakura Period on, mendicants like Saigyō, and recluses like Chōmei and Kenkō, left imperishable works, but they too had as their main vocation the Buddhist priesthood. From among the warrior class too poets emerged, but their interest in literature was an avocation or else desire for cultural refinement. Among the fictitious tales, war tales, and historical tales there are many anonymous works, but they probably represent the secondary occupation of some aristocrat or priest, and we cannot think that there were specialized writers. Of course we can imagine that among them there were those for whom the subsidiary occupation had become primary, and yet they never declared themselves writers of literature. Shunzei was hailed as one of the greatest poets of his day, and on the occasion of his ninetieth birthday there was a great celebration in the court, but in the *Shinkokinshū* (The New Anthology of Ancient and Modern Poems) his official rank is still given as Chamberlain of the Empress Dowager.

When we come to the Muromachi Period, however, such *nō* actors and authors as Kan'ami, Seami, and Zenchiku can be considered to be almost specialists, and such *renga* masters as Sōgi, Shinkei, and Shōha, although they were priests, can also be considered to be practically professionals. In the Edo Period the writers of first rank like Saikaku, Bashō, and Chikamatsu established themselves as specialists, and made their living by writing. The Edo *haiku* poets, authors of lower order fiction, and *jōruri* and *kabuki* writers were also for the most part professionals. Among the *waka* and Chinese-style poets, however, while there were some professionals, there were also those who wrote in their scholarly leisure and cannot be considered as such. And yet there were those for whom the writing of *waka* and Chinese poetry was the prime vocation and scholarship secondary.

The strict professionalization of writers of literature in Meiji can be thought of as a natural development from their social position in the Edo Era. Because of the establishment of a modern economic system in the early Edo Era, such a literary occupation became possible, and by means of printing, works could be marketed easily. Therefore, the extension of the publishing business and the professionalization of writing which took place during Meiji can certainly not be said to be a result of European influence. In the Edo Era, however, since books were printed only by the wood-block method, and large-scale publication by means of movable metal type was impossible, it was not at all easy to make one's living as a writer. Thus it was that writers led a very uncertain existence, were frequently in need, and had an extremely low social position.

In the Meiji Era the social position of writers of literature was raised considerably, and a social unit, which wielded a kind of cultural pressure and which came to be a factor of great importance in society, was formed out of the groups of writers. We must recognize this new social unit as one of the main features of the Meiji literary world. The raising of the social position of literature itself can be thought of as the factor which led to the raising of the position of the writers. This development doubtless owes much also to the high social position of literature in Europe.

In the East also from ancient times there has existed the idea that " Literature is the essential part of statecraft, the imperishable grand enterprise," but literature in this sense has a very broad meaning, and is not necessarily restricted to literature as art ; moreover, this idea of the Emperor of the Wei must be thought of as rather exceptional in China in its respect for literature. In Japan also expressions of praise for literature are to be found in the prefaces of the *Kojiki* and the *Kokinshū*, but underlying such praise is the attitude that simply as an expression of the national consciousness literature was difficult to disparage. Also, in "The Glow-Worm" chapter of the *Genji Monogatari* and in Bashō's views on poetry, there are instances of valuing highly the place of literature in life, but such statements did not necessarily receive social approval, and there are no indications that the social position of either Lady Murasaki or Bashō rose because of them. Rather, from the Kamakura Period on, literature was considered by Buddhism as either an evil that had to be shunned, or else merely as a vehicle for the propagation of its faith. In the Edo Era, from the standpoint of Confucian morality, literature was looked upon either as a pastime or as an instrument for promoting virtue and reproving vice, and it was seldom, if ever, that the worth in life of literature for its own sake was recognized.

The main reason that in Meiji the social position of literature was suddenly elevated is that Japan was influenced by Europe, where literature and the other arts are valued highly and considered significant in life. This elevation of the position of Meiji literature was first performed by politicians. When it became known that such statesmen as Bulwer-Lytton and Disraeli were participating in literature, in Japan too the political novel which recognized the relation between literature and politics, and literature which expounded political ideas came into importance. Accompanying this was the emergence, among politicians and scholars, of the idea of reforming the drama, and of providing national facilities for its development comparable to the theatres of Europe and America. This led later to the establishment of the Committee on Literature in 1911, and to such events as the invitation of prominent literary figures to a party held by Prince Saionji's Useikai (The Voice of the Rain Society) in 1907. In the realm of art also this European influence can be seen in the opening of exhibitions under government auspices.

Yet such activities were primarily for political objectives, and even though the value of literature was recognized, its autonomy was not allowed, and it was considered merely as one of the roads to national cultural achievement. Thus, at the same time, with government authority, works were censored and their sale frequently forbidden, and public performances or art exhibitions were obstructed. The political literature of the early political theorists was unable to perform the function of truly elevating the position of literature ; it merely prepared the way. Since the later policy of the government with regard to literature was a combination of encouragement and oppression, its merits and demerits offset each other. Men like Ōgai resolutely opposed the interference, for the purpose of suppression, of government in the realm of literature.

We must realize that the elevation of the social position of literature in Meiji originated very largely in the cultural elevation of the people as a whole. Since the course of Meiji culture was founded on the principle that " all measures of government shall be decided by public opinion," as is expressed in the Five Articles of the Imperial Oath, it was not allowed that one group of politicians should decide all policy. As it is also written in the Five Articles of the Imperial Oath " seek knowledge from the world," so indeed did the Meiji intellectuals strive to acquire learning from every country of the world. Above all, they endeavored to learn from Europe, to assimilate as rapidly as possible its system of artistic values, and to perfect its theories. Such activity was carried on very largely by those leading spirits among the scholars who had studied at the universities. Men like Shōyō, Ōgai, Chogyū, Hōgetsu, and Sōseki are representative. The *Shintaishishō* was the work of five scholars, and *Kaichōon* was written by a man who later became a professor at Kyōto University. These men are to be considered the leaders of the world of Meiji poetry. Tōson and Bansui also were teachers of English, and it is not impossible to consider them too as scholars. When *Shōsetsu Shinzui* and *Tōsei Shosei Katagi* appeared, the fact that they were the works of a scholar was important in their receiving popular approval. It also cannot be denied that the rise of Romanticism was aided by *Teikoku Bungaku* (Imperial Literature), a magazine published at the then Tōkyō Imperial University, and that the establishment of Naturalism was assisted by *Waseda Bungaku* (Waseda Literature), a magazine published at Waseda University. Those two universities were significant forces in the development of Meiji literary thought. Later, *Mita Bungaku* (Mita Literature) of Keiō University appeared on the literary scene and added to this trend.

However, this elevation of the position of literature by scholars had some attendant evils, and it cannot escape the criticism that such an academic tone caused the formalization of the production of literature. The fact that the group around Kōyō through its *Garakuta Bunko* (Library of Miscellany) espoused fiction of a lower order and was able to satisfy the yearnings of the age reflects the temper of that section of the literary world which disliked the overly academic. Rohan, a foe of the Ken'yūsha, was himself a competent scholar and later lectured at Kyōto University, but he took the side of the non-academic layman, and together with Kyōka, who stood at the forefront of the group of Romantic writers, identified himself completely with the people. Kafū and Jun'ichirō continued this trend. Furthermore, among the writers in the Naturalistic tradition, even those with considerable learning opposed the academic literature of the universities, and led a life of economic hardship. Moreover, the world of the *tanka* and *haiku* that centered around Shiki and Tekkan felt it was voicing, through its poetry, the aspirations of the people. The statement in a *tanka* of the poet of the Araragi school, Itō Sachio, that "when the cowherd composes a poem, a great new poem appears in the world" indicates the state of Meiji literature that was unable to popularize itself to the point where a cowherd could compose poetry. It also indicates the will to seek for the poetry of the cowherd. This also accorded with the purport of the Five Articles of the Imperial Oath which stated that "the civil, the military, and even the commoners, should carry through their objectives."

We cannot say that the elevation of the position of literature in Meiji, which was assisted by the stimulation of the desire for art on the part of the people, was wholly a result of the influence of Western literary ideas. It is possible to think that the development of Japanese culture inevitably brought this to pass, and that even though the policies of the Meiji government had a somewhat reactionary slant, basically they were founded on the principle of respect for human rights. This desire on the part of the people themselves to have a literature meant that they sought a genuine people's literature, and not one merely for the aristocracy, the priests and warriors, the merchants, or the scholars alone. This desire was the source of the strength of the literary world. Thus, the spirit of the Imperial Oath which states that "the evil customs of the past should be destroyed, and that everything should be based upon the just and equitable principle of nature" extended to the *literati*.

There were various social bases which made possible this popularization of literature, but the most significant of these was the successive emergence of literary or intellectual groups which through group pressure were able to propagate their ideas, while the progress in publishing further facilitated their dissemination. If it had not been for this special phenomenon of the spread of publications in Meiji, literature would never have been able to become so rapidly the possession of the people as a whole. We shall clarify these facts further in the next chapter when we discuss the social background of Meiji literature. Now we shall consider the artistic awakening of the literary world as seen in the establishment of the social position of the Meiji writers.

The elevation of the social position of both literature itself and the writers of that literature is one of the special features of the Meiji Era, but at its base we must not overlook the fact that the artistic awakening of those who contributed to literature was great, and that the trend to place a high value on art in life became prominent. In early Meiji the old ideas of lower-order fiction, of literature for amusement, or for promoting virtue and reproving vice, still remained, and in the period of the political novel the tendentious literary trend, with politics all-powerful, became strong, but after the appearance of *Shōsetsu Shinzui* belief in the independent value of art emerged, and writers sought to realize this primarily in the realistic form. Yet at the same time there were also those who sought artistic values in an idealistic form through the Idealism and the Romanticism of Ōgai, Chogyū, Tōkoku, and others. While the realistic and idealistic streams intermingled, the writers advanced toward one aesthetic objective. Since Meiji literature before the rise of Naturalism was largely classical and romantic, its artistic goal was beauty (the very word for art was *bijutsu*, which has the character for beauty in it), and the aestheticians discussed its theoretical basis. Even Shōyō in his early period discussed the realistic novel under the name of *bijutsu*.

Shōyō and Ōgai had different standpoints, but they both recognized that literature was an art that had beauty as its objective. Even Shiki, who was a realistic writer, shared this view. While Shōyō's *Shōsetsu Shinzui* admitted the secondary significance of literature in refining man's sensibilities, it also recognized that literature had a significance in and of itself. Ōgai opposed judging literature by standards of moral goodness and truth, and vigorously supported the position that the literary value of tendentious art is not to be determined by the virtues it espouses. This idea of recognizing the autonomy of art was by no means swept away after the rise of Naturalism, but rather the Naturalistic authors, too, at the same time that they set a value on coming to grips with human existence, emphasized the fact that in art there are unique worlds according to the point of observation, and they held a position close to that of art-for-art's-sake.

The motto which appeared on the cover of Hōgetsu's *Kindai Bungei no Kenkyū* (Research in Modern Literature) (1909) to the effect that " the world of observation which, facing reality as it is, strives to discover the significance of all life, and the life that has penetrated to taste, this state of mind is art " indicates approximately the point of arrival of the Meiji literary awakening, and foreshadows the point of departure of that of the Taishō. From this we are able to perceive the situation wherein Meiji literature, having passed through a romantic and a classical stage, arrived at the *shinkyō* (mental life) novel and delineation from life, as the point of fusion of Realism and Idealism, and of the combination of Western and Japanese thought. Furthermore, this situation was based on the attitude which recognized the autonomy of art as " the world of observation," and which endeavored to link art as closely as possible to the life of reality. Moreover, art as " life that has penetrated to taste " is a form of life, and as something which " strives to discover the significance of all of life " was thought capable of taking the place of religion and philosophy, and of possessing even the qualities of a kind of *Weltanschauung*. The point of " facing reality as it is " indicates that there was no lack of relationship to scientific truth and practical behavior. At any rate, it is clear that this position emphasized the significance of art in life, and possessed the spirit of reliance on art.

It is true that at the beginning of the Taishō Era, in the period of maturity of Naturalism, such a literary awakening was agitated by the emergence of nihilistic thought, and by the rise of humanitarianism acquired the tendency of dissolving into even broader values of life, but the Meiji Era was a relatively happy one in which the unique importance of art in life was believed. There were no basic misgivings with regard to art. Of course there were those like Futabatei Shimei who doubted whether literature was a worthy occupation for the whole of man's life, but even though he said that art, science, and thought existed for life's sake, he also said that life too was nothing more than an idea, and that he belonged to the sceptic school. There were also those like Bizan and Tōkoku who, though they possessed extraordinary talent, ended their own lives. However, even though they felt keenly their own inability to find a course of their own in the midst of a general trend which sought to recognize the high value of literature in life, they were not ones who basically had contempt for art.

We are also able to learn of the idea of treating literature seriously from the words of Chogyū in the fourth chapter, " The Seriousness of Literature," of his book *Bungei Zatsudan* (Literary Conversations) (1902) : " Literature is definitely not a pastime. Its seriousness is in no way inferior to that of life itself." At the same time, however, that he and others like him were trying to find in the realm of literature the same seriousness which exists in life, of necessity they came to emphasize those works which portray life realistically. Particularly when, like Hōgetsu, they came to esteem " the world of observation," " facing reality as it is," it was natural that they should turn toward those works having the intellectual and objective form of the novel. This is indeed a general tendency of modern literature, and Japan also was included in it, but there is also the significant fact that the serious atmosphere of the Meiji Era which sought to place literature in a high position in life, and which demanded a link between art and life, should have turned to the novel for the realization of these aims.

Shōyō's attempt to open the way for a new literature by his study of the novel in his *Shōsetsu Shinzui*, or " The Essence of the Novel," suggests the destiny of all of Meiji literature. Later, Shōyō ceased to write novels, turned to playwriting, and through his " Submerged Idealism " position came to value the drama highly. It must also be borne in mind, however, that by his contact with Futabatei he sensed his weakness as a novelist, and that through his study of Shakespeare he came to delve more deeply in the drama. His having begun as a novelist is indication of his having discerned the trend of the Meiji Era. Furthermore, by the *Waseda Bungaku* group which Shōyō founded, there later were lit the signal-fires of the Naturalistic novel. Ōgai also showed great interest in the drama, and there is the view that he was in the position of leadership in the new dramatic movement, but his actual work in the drama was small, and he produced his masterpieces in the novel and the historical biography. Men with a pronounced poetic bent like Rohan, Kafū, and Jun'ichirō, too, succeeded as novelists, and others like Kōyō, Katai, and Tōson of a definite lyrical nature also attained greatness in the same way. Such a born poet as Tōkoku showed great talent in his lyrical and dramatic poetry études, but there are no complete works, and he achieved only a small measure of success in his literary criticism.

In the Meiji Era it was rather difficult to succeed as a pure poet or playwright. Whatever the reason, the Meiji literary world was one in which the novelist reigned supreme. For economic reasons it was thought difficult to make one's living as a writer unless one were a novelist. The phenomenon of the dominant position of the novel determines the character of Meiji literature. It was only in the Romantic Period between the Sino-Japanese and the Russo-Japanese Wars that there was the flowering of the New Style poetry, and only after the establishment of Naturalism that the New Drama movement arose and that the drama too achieved a certain brilliance. Furthermore, literature in the traditional form, such as the *tanka* and the *haiku*, continued unbroken as before. Such a conservative form as Chinese-style poetry also was not discontinued, and Sōseki in his later years employed this form directly to express his ideal of *sokuten kyoshi* (to follow Heaven, and to depart from the self). However, when compared to the zenith of prosperity of the novel, other forms are certainly outshone.

Even though one must admit the overwhelmingly dominant position of the novel, it is also not impossible to say that the various literary forms rivalled each other. The activity of criticism which went hand in hand with the novel is particularly noteworthy, and by performing the new task of intellectualizing literature, its position is also remarkable in the Meiji literary world. For the most part the novel was in the most important position. The poetry of the New Style and criticism followed it, and the *tanka* in turn followed that. These constituted the mainstream of literature and were greatly influenced by Western literary ideas. The *haiku* was looked upon as almost another world, and despite efforts at its modernization, and also despite the fact that it received surprising popular support, there was a tendency on the part of the leaders of the literary world to look down upon it. When we come to Chinese-style poetry, it was considered only as a very special form, and as not being qualified for a place in the Meiji literary world. The clear-cut distinctions of the position of these literary forms can also be said to be a characteristic of the Meiji Era.

4. *The Changes in Literary Style*

We are able to see both in the view of art which formed the basis of Meiji literature, and in the thought and emotional content which it expressed, how the literature of the previous era was startlingly reformed, and in the form of the expression also we can see how tremendous was the change. In the first half of Meiji, literary style was not very different from that of the Edo Period, and at the beginning, the style of the late Edo lower order fiction writers and the translation of European literature in Chinese style prevailed. It seems that at that time Bakin's style was considered the best, but later an elegant pseudo-classical style and one imitative of Saikaku appeared, and it developed in the direction of a compromise between the classical and the colloquial, the Japanese and Chinese styles. This in essence was the literary style movement, and it continued right up until the rise of Naturalism.

The most noteworthy point in Meiji literary style, however,

is that in opposition to *bungotai* (literary language style), *kōgotai* (colloquial language style) and *gembun itchitai* (style unifying the written and spoken language) were advocated, and there were conscious efforts to colloquialize literary expression. This movement began with Maejima Raisuke's (Hisoka) *Plan for the Abolition of Chinese Characters* in 1866. He thought that " we must use as simple a writing system as possible " as the method of bringing education to all of the people, and he further stated that he wished " to eliminate the distinction between the spoken and the written language." And yet the petition to Tokugawa Keiki itself employed the traditional epistolary language as before. After the beginning of Meiji, men like Maejima Hisoka, Fukuzawa Yukichi, Nishi Amane, and Watanabe Shūjirō exerted their efforts toward the simplification of the language and liberation from Chinese characters, while in works like Nakamura Masanao's *Saikoku Rissi-Hen* (Biographies of Self-Made Men of the Western Nations) (1871) a translation into the colloquial language was placed to the left of the Chinese characters.

Accompanying the educational reforms of the Meiji government, the movement for language reform gradually developed, and its goals were partially realized in the establishment of an agency for the investigation of the language and for the reform of the language textbooks. In 1882 Yatabe Ryōkichi's (Shōko) plan for making the Tōkyō dialect standard and Tagusari Tsunanori's Japanese shorthand system appeared ; in 1884 Miyake Yonekichi's plan for the investigation of dialects and San'yūtei Enchō's shorthand version of *Botan Tōrō* (The Peony Lantern) emerged, while in 1886 Mozume Takami's *Gembun Itchi* (The Unification of the Spoken and Written Language) was published. *Gembun Itchi* is the text of the addresses made before the Society for the Adoption of the *Kana* Syllabary as the National Language. He contended that a conversational style was more alive than any imitative one. " I truly think that it is better if I write down the lively, animated speech as it naturally comes out of my mouth." He thus believed that by writing exactly as one speaks, the language would become unified and more beautiful. This work employed both the *de aru* and the *de arimasu* forms, and at the end of the book the author translated into the modern colloquial style of the *de aru* form each first sentence of twenty-one classics, beginning with *Ise Monogatari* (The Tales of Ise).

Thus the tendency of the new literature which arose in the Meiji twenties (1887–1896), with such a movement for language reform on the part of politicians, government officials, journalists, scholars, and educators as the background, was toward the final realization of the *gembun itchi* movement in literary works. Futabatei Shimei in his *Ukigumo* (1887) used the *da* form and tried to express as much as possible in the colloquial language, but there are many places where sentences end with nouns or contractions, and he was not able to avoid a certain comical effect; moreover, with Shōyō's approval, he did not break away completely from the classical and Chinese style. In his translated work *Aibiki* (1888) he came much closer to a free colloquial style, and by continuing to produce works in it he exerted a great influence on the literary world. At about the same time, Bimyōsai used the *de atta* form in his *Fūkin Shirabe no Hitofushi* (An Organ Melody) (1887) which appeared in the periodical *Iratsume* (The Maiden), and the *desu* form in the works which were collected in *Natsu Kodachi* (The Summer Grove) (1888). He thus began a fresh *gembun itchi* style, and by using European type rhetoric and punctuation, he made a new departure in literary style; while this created a considerable sensation, there was the feeling that the style was somewhat frivolous, and it did not have sufficient power to dominate the literary world for very long.

The *gembun itchi* style which Meiji literature finally adopted was the *de aru* form begun by Kōyō and employed in part in his *Futari Nyōbo* (Two Wives) (1891), and also in his *Murasaki* (Purple) (1894), and which achieved its greatest success in his *Tajō Takon* (Tears and Regrets) (1896). Kōyō, however, was unable to dispense with the literary language style and returned to it again in his *Konjiki Yasha* (The Gold Demon), but the number of people who used his *de aru* form gradually increased, and after acquiring considerable strength in the Meiji thirties (1897–1906), it brought about almost a complete change in the forties (1907–1912) in the literary style of the novel and critical writing. The *de aru* form had already been employed in Mozume Takami's *Gembun Itchi*, but this was only a fragmentary and childish thing, and it was not until *Tajō Takon* that it received its artistic consummation.

However, that the *gembun itchi* style truly arrived at unifying literary terms at the end of Meiji is due in large measure to the reform in language expression which accompanied Naturalism, namely the movement to eliminate artifice from literature which Katai and others advocated. On the other hand, it is difficult to forget the service performed by the *shaseibun* (sketching style) group, which arose around Shiki, in polishing the colloquial style. With Sōseki it achieved utter perfection. Again, Ōgai read orally many Western plays and translated them, and as a result of such training was able to write novels in a uniquely pithy, logically consistent colloquial style. The writing of children's novels and fairy tales in an easy colloquial style by Wakamatsu Shizuko and Iwaya Sazanami and others also aided in maintaining the spoken language style.

The *de aru* form of the colloquial style is certainly not the spoken word exactly the way it is. In everyday conversation we do not use *de aru* to end our sentences. And yet this form is one which at once made the colloquial language precise and which succeeded in creating a literary language as close as possible to the spoken. The so-called unification of the spoken and written language then is not the exact reproduction of speech in writing such as Mozume urged; rather, we can think of it as a movement in the direction of a transformation of the spoken language into literature.

The colloquialization of prose exerted an influence on verse, and in 1888 Hayashi Mikaomi published a *gembun itchi* poem in the *Tōyō Gakugeikai Zasshi* (The Magazine of the Society of Oriental Arts and Sciences); thereafter, from the Naturalistic Period on, the colloquial language *tanka* movement arose, but such a form proved very difficult and to date has not achieved much success. The colloquialization of the New Style poetry made steady progress and today we almost see its perfection. During Meiji, however, the movement for a spoken language free verse was still just beginning, and with the exception of Hakushū's folk-songs such as *Omoide* (Recollections), it did not produce any very outstanding works.

The process whereby the style of Meiji literature advanced in the direction of a free prose which expressed actual speech was accompanied by a realism in content, but the reason that the style was different from everyday speech and was indeed unable to be completely natural can be said to be the influence of various traditional elements and those new ones brought in from abroad. The former were the Chinese and indigenous Japanese styles which for so long had dominated Japanese literature, and the latter was for the most part the European style which was introduced after the beginning of Meiji. While these two styles intermingled and continued through Meiji, the former was stronger in the early years and the latter in the later years of the era.

The Chinese style was originally introduced from the continent, but in the Edo Period Chinese studies flourished and it constituted the mainstream of literary style. From ancient times it was even thought that Chinese style prose was the only elegant, orthodox form, and this attitude continued into early Meiji. The Chinese style possessed much the same authority that Latin did in medieval Europe. Even after the beginning of Meiji, the Min'yūsha disputants like Tokutomi Sohō, Takegoshi Sansha, and Yamaji Aizan, and the writers of the Seikyōsha group like Miyake Setsurei, Shiga Jūkō, and

Kuga Katsunan employed a supple form of a simplified Chinese style, and created the Meiji essay and critical style. Sohō, by his critical essays in *Kokumin no Tomo*, and Setsurei, by his polemical articles in *Nihon* and *Nihonjin*, both contributed particularly to the spreading of the Chinese style throughout the nation.

When we come to mention those works which have a closer relation to the literary world, the early novels like *Kajin no Kigū* were of course written in a pure Chinese style; yet while men like Chogyū and Ōmachi Keigetsu included elements of the Chinese style in their critical essays and miscellaneous writings, they also included other elements. In Chogyū's *Getsuya no Bikan ni Tsuite* (Concerning the Aesthetic Feeling of a Moonlit Night) and *Heike Zakkan* (Miscellaneous Impressions of the Taira Clan) there is a considerable admixture of the pure Japanese style, and in such purely literary works as his *Wagasode no Ki* (Notes of My Sleeves) and *Takiguchi Nyūdō* it becomes even stronger. Keigetsu is known as an elegant prose writer in the Japanese style, but he included some colloquial language and developed a unique kind of simple style. Moreover, even in such purely literary works as the colloquial language novels like Futabatei's *Ukigumo* and Kōyō's *Tajō Takon*, the Chinese style appears from time to time, and when we come to Kōyō's *Konjiki Yasha* there is the effect of a mixed Chinese and Japanese style. In Rohan's *Gojū no Tō*, too, a simplified Chinese style is employed in the description of the terrible storm, while Sōseki consciously enchases the beauty of the Chinese style in his *Kusamakura*. Both Rohan and Sōseki, and Ōgai too, for that matter, had a profound knowledge of Chinese prose and poetry, and it is but natural that they should have composed Chinese poems and that the Chinese element should have remained in their style for a long time.

In poetry, also, Bansui's *Boshō* (The Evening Bell), *Hoshi Otsu Shūfū Gojōgen* (The Stars Fall and the Autumn Wind Blows on the Field of Gojō), and *Banri Chōjō no Uta* (The

Song of the Great Wall) preserved completely the rhythms of Chinese poetry and received great praise ; even after the rise of Symbolist poetry he continued to exploit the special visual charm of Chinese characters. In the *tanka*, also, men like Tekkan loved the vigor of the Chinese style ; in the early *haiku* in the Buson tradition too, the Chinese element is conspicuous, and poets like Naitō Meisetsu achieved a unique style in it.

In the tradition of the purely Japanese style, scholars of the national literature like Ōwada Tateki and Ochiai Naobumi attempted a new elegant style, while Keigetsu, Shioi Ukō, and Takeshima Hagoromo who studied under Naobumi became famous for their New Style poetry and elegant prose in the Japanese style. Ōgai's early works too are mainly in the Naobumi-type elegant style, and not only in his translated poetry collection, *Omokage,* and his translated prose, *Umoregi* (The Fossil Wood) and *Sokkyōshijin,* but also in his novels, *Maihime, Utakata no Ki* (The Record of a Transient Life), and *Fumizukai* (The Messenger), he added a European style and elements of the Chinese to his essentially elegant Japanese style, and thereby created an exceedingly fresh one.

Kōyō held the Saikaku-type mixed elegant and colloquial style as his ideal, but this also was an off-shoot of the Japanese (as opposed to the Chinese) style, and particularly under the influence of the *Genji Monogatari* he wrote his excellent work *Iwazu Katarazu* (Neither Word nor Speech) in the pure elegant style. The core of his masterpieces like *Tajō Takon* and *Konjiki Yasha* is also in the pure Japanese style. Rohan has many Chinese and some European elements, but like Kōyō he held the Saikaku-type mixed elegant and colloquial style as his ideal. His *Futsuka Monogatari* (The Tale of Two Days) (completed in 1898), particularly since Saigyō is the main character in it, approaches a pure elegant style, and possesses a special beauty when read aloud. Ichiyō also entered prose from her training in Japanese poetry. There are traces of her having studied both the Saikaku style and the *Genji Monogatari,* and her realistic

— 44 —

method also is closer to that of the realistic prose of the Heian court ladies than it is to any imitation of the West. Tōson, through the influence of Bashō and *waka*, created a soft, Japanese-style effect not only in his New Style poetry but also in his novels. Katai also was originally a New Style poet, and he attempted to create a *gembun itchi* style out of a purely Japanese one. In addition, the New Style poetry, *tanka*, and *haiku* of course belonged mainly to the traditional Japanese style.

The European style entered via translation in such principally Japanese-style works as Watanabe On's *Isoppu Monogatari* (The Tales of Aesop) (1873), Miyajima Shunshō's *Ōshū Shōsetsu: Teremaku Kafuku Monogatari* (A European Novel: The Tale of the Vicissitudes of Télémaque) (1879), and through the seven-five syllable *jōruri* style of Shōyō's *Shiizaru Kidan: Jiyū no Tachi Nagori no Kireaji* (The Adventures of Caesar: The Final Sharpness of Freedom's Sword) (1884). Moreover, Niwa Jun'ichirō's translation of Lytton's *Ernest Maltravers* under the title *Karyū Shunwa* (A Spring Tale of Flowers and Willows) was in the Chinese style, and many translated novels appeared in imitation of it. Among them there were some with traces of a literal translation from the original European languages, but most conspicuous was the attempt at Japanization. Later with the rise of a new literature, this changed into a movement to express in Japanese style the detailed descriptions of the original, and it produced the superb style of Futabatei's *Ukigumo*, *Aibiki* (Turgenev's *Rendezvous*), and *Meguriai* (A Chance Meeting). The description of nature in the first section of *Aibiki* expresses particularly admirably the flavor of the original. Ōgai's translations such as *Sokkyōshijin* (Andersen's *The Improvisator*), the various works collected in his *Minawashū* (The Water-Spray Anthology), and *Umoregi* are in the elegant style, but a fresh note pervades them, and we sense the exotic charm of the European style which is subtly interwoven.

Apart from Futabatei's attempts, Bimyōsai, at the time when

he was advocating *gembun itchi*, included many European elements in his works, employing liberally not only metaphors, personifications, and inversions, but also Western punctuation such as the exclamation point, question mark, and series of dots. Yet they were but superficial rhetorical flourishes and did not survive. Shōyō liked to include English in his *Tōsei Shosei Katagi* and Ōgai used French in his novels and German in his non-fiction, but although this produced a temporary sensation, it did not become a common practice as was previously the case with the inclusion of Chinese in a Japanese text.

And yet the formation of a harmonious new style from the fusion of European elements into the *gembun itchi* style really occurred after the rise of Naturalism, and it was nurtured very largely by the Western-type *shaseibun* of such works as Tōson's *Chikumagawa no Suketchi* (Chikuma River Sketches) and the *haibun*-like *shaseibun* of Shiki and Sōseki. We must give particular credit to Tōson and Sōseki for their great contribution in the assimilation of European style. Both men had studied English literature and, in contradistinction to this, Ueda Bin's *Miotsukushi* and *Uzumaki* (The Maelstrom), together with the various works of Kafū, included elements of the French style, while we must not forget the German element included in Ōgai's numerous translations and original works. The fresh style of the younger writers of the Shirakaba school and the elaborate style of the Neo-Romantic group appeared later. We also must not overlook the influence exerted on the poetic world by Bin's translated poetic anthology, *Kaichōon*.

Furthermore, such members of the Shirakaba school as Arishima Takeo arrived on the literary scene with a thorough knowledge of the natural sciences and Christianity, and their literary style and language were startlingly European. This was not a forced exoticism, but rather we feel that it was something which came from within. Such assimilation came only at the end of Meiji, and when we come to the beginning of Taishō, these new European elements found their place very naturally in the spoken language style and came to pervade the entire literary world.

What we have said above about Meiji literary style relates largely to prose. It is one of the features of Japanese literature that prose too should have been traditionally versified and that the distinctions between it and poetry should not be clear. Both the style of the *jōruri* and that of Bakin's *tokuhon* (reader) and Saikaku's *haikai* style were of that type. Thus, until the Meiji colloquialization of prose, a simplified seven-five syllable metre prevailed. After the rise of Naturalism this was swept away, and at the same time that content became realistic, a perfect prose art was established. This tendency of the literary world was responsible for the prosification of poetry, and at the end of Meiji, with the dominance of Naturalism, attempts at spoken language free verse were made ; this process extended to the *tanka* and *haiku*, too, where a group emerged that favored a free style. However, since poetry differs from the art of prose, through Meiji and Taishō it could not be completely prosified, and particularly in the *tanka* and *haiku* the group that wishes to maintain the traditional verse forms even today is overwhelmingly the greater.

Thus the problem of poetic form was one of considerable difficulty throughout the Meiji Era and it was widely discussed, but there was still a very lively production of poetry. We do not have the space to trace now all the achievements in the discussion of poetic form, but when we look at the poems themselves, we see that the New Style poetry was at first satisfied with the standard seven-five and five-seven poetic forms ; later the poets felt that since there is a diversity of poetic form in the West, they should be able to find a similar diversity in Japan, and by drawing on the *yōkyoku* (songs used in the *nō*) and *jōruri*, they attempted a new poetic form employing a five-five, seven-seven, eight-six, eight-seven, eight-eight, and even three or four syllable patterns. At the same time that Iwano Hōmei in his *Shintaishi no Sakuhō* (The Method of Writing New Style

Poetry) showed the fruits of this research, he also made several attempts in actual practice. At about the same time as this, Kambara Ariake, in the opening of his *Dokugen Aika* (A Single-Stringed Elegy), wrote a sonnet-like poem of fourteen lines with each line of either a four-seven-six or a seven-four-six syllable-pattern, and this showed the influence of the translated Christian hymns. In additon to this, he attempted another sonnet-like poem of alternate seven-five-seven and five-seven-five syllable lines, modelled after Ueda Bin's *Kaichōon* and succeeded in creating a new effect.

This new kind of poetic form was further refined by the prose-poetry effects of Hakushū and Rofū and became established in the composition of a free verse style based on the seven-five and five-seven syllable form. On the other hand, pure free verse was attempted, and by the end of Meiji, Japanese poetic form appeared to have undergone a complete transformation. However, since the metre construction of the Japanese language differs so greatly from that of European languages, the establishment of a new Japanese poetic style did not end in complete success, and the poets turned in the direction of mere theorizing about free verse. Since free verse was already only a little removed from prose, the very vexing problem of a new poetic form was discussed in vain.

On the other hand, the bold attempts at composing free verse *tanka* and *haiku* took place, but these were even less successful. The endeavors of Ariake, Kyūkin, Hakushū, and Rofū at the end of Meiji to transform traditional verse forms into free verse remain as new attempts in Meiji poetic form, and of the rest we can say that they were either a preservation of traditional poetic forms or projects for simple prosification. The method of Takuboku and others of dividing the *tanka* into three lines does not derive from this. And yet the various ways in which the New Style poets strove to develop a long poetic form that possessed metres such as had never existed in Japan before make Meiji literature unique from the point of poetic form also.

Even though the metre construction did not have sufficient power to survive very long thereafter, and even though the metric theory was incomplete, the project of reform based on the influence of Western poetic form is worthy of being called a characteristic of the Meiji literary world.

CHAPTER II   THE POSITION OF LITERATURE
IN MEIJI CULTURE

1. *The Social Background of Meiji Literature*

There are many significant aspects of the Meiji Restoration, but in the political realm the most significant are the overthrow of the feudal system which had been perfected by the military families and the attempt to build a modern state based on an urban society. However, the Meiji leaders did not immediately try to build a thorough democratic state modeled after Europe and America, but sought rather to revive tradition and to resurrect the ancient monarchical system. In order to modernize such a system they introduced such new forms as a constitution and a national assembly. In the early years of Meiji, with ideas of freedom and people's rights as the background, great strides were made toward political modernization. Thus, literature, too, through the political novel of the early period, acquired a tendentious aspect as it turned toward this objective.

But after the constitution and the national assembly (the Diet) were achieved, and with a general decrease of interest in political discussion, the people's concern began to turn toward problems of success and advancement in this urban-dominated society. The establishment of the Meiji government meant also the training of the bureaucracy and the military. It is not impossible to think of this as a revival of the feudal ideals which existed in the previous warrior-centered society. When we look at such works as Shōyō's *Tōsei Shosei Katagi, Imotose Kagami* (Mirror of Marriage), *Saikun* (The Wife), Futabatei's *Ukigumo,* and Roka's *Hototogisu* (The Cuckoo), we can understand how important the social position of the bureaucrat and the professional soldier actually was. However, we are unable to overlook the fact that in this interval the economic power of the capitalist class which was joined to the bureaucracy was also gradually heightening.

In the economic realm the Meiji Restoration was an era of the establishment of modern capitalism. This was part of a world-wide trend, but in Japan in the Edo Period already the economic power of the merchant class had been rising gradually, and by the end of Edo had actually overwhelmed the military caste and had advanced to the point of attempting to build its own world. Thus, together with the establishment of the Meiji government, the urban upper class, which was linked with both the bureaucracy and the military, rapidly strengthened the economic organs of capitalism, so that the government was unable to accomplish anything if it overlooked the power of this class.

This relationship of the political power of the bureaucracy and the military to the economic power of the urban upper class can be thought of as a continuation of the Edo Period relationship between the military caste and the merchant class. Literature found its motivation very largely in the struggle and fusion of these two forces. The writers of the Edo Period extolled the Confucian virtues of loyalty, filial piety, constancy, and integrity which formed the morality of the warrior class, and yet at the same time that they did not forget to display constantly on the surface such ideas as "the promoting of virtue and reproving of vice," they attempted to escape from the extremes of such a position by zealously giving voice both to that natural human feeling which cries out at the evanescence of life, and to instinctive love. The former answered man's desire for the sublime and the latter his desire for beauty. The Meiji writers also, at the same time that they devoted themselves to the national objective, certainly did not discard the will to strive to satisfy their individual desires.

Literary writers, as they had in the Edo Period, rather than to that lofty moral spirit which praised the national and collective objectives, devoted themselves to the individual goals which were overshadowed by it. At any rate, there were many more valuable works of art produced under this latter motivation. The new literary movement, which began to flourish from about 1887, for the most part took this direction. In the sense that this represented a liberation of the city-dweller's life, it resembles rather closely the spirit of Genroku, and indeed at this time a revival of Saikaku and Chikamatsu was advocated, while Bakin, who in the late Edo Period was the representative of that fossilized, military caste-supported policy of "the promoting of virtue and reproving of vice," was pushed into the background.

From this time on, modern European literature increasingly entered the country. Together with the extension of power of the bureaucracy and the military through the Sino-Japanese and Russo-Japanese Wars, the economic power of the capitalistic class which acquired world markets gradually attained stability, while the Western ideas of individualism and liberalism which flooded the country, finding suitable hothouse conditions in the urban upper class, dominated the Japanese intellectual world, and came to determine the main current of the literary world. Of course this is not to say that there was not a growth of socialism, as evinced by the Kōtoku Shūsui case. With the establishment of capitalism, the livelihood of the worker became an important social problem, and the social novel and socialistic poetry began to make their appearance. However, it was only after the entry into the Taishō Era that this new force emerged prominently in literature and that clearly defined Marxist and Communist works appeared under the name of Musan-Ha (The Propertyless Group), Socialist, and Proletarian literature, and that we are able to witness writers who had as their main theme the necessity of a revolution to overthrow capitalist society. During Meiji, however, individualism and liberalism which proclaimed the maturity of the capitalistic urban society still formed the basic spirit of literature.

At about the time that this urban individualism reached its peak, Naturalism appeared, and with regard to its establishment, we must consider the place in Meiji society of the high regard for science and the almost blind belief in the powers of the intellect. The Meiji Restoration was based on the principle of opening the country, and since on every point it strove to do away with the policy of isolation, it was freed from the ancient Confucian attitude of " making the people trust the government and yet keeping them in ignorance," and it took the position of encouraging broadly the search for knowledge. Thus, scientific knowledge, which until then had been lacking in the Japanese tradition, was emphasized above all else, and it was considered the duty and privilege of that urban upper class which had raised its social position to acquire that knowledge. In early Meiji this process was called *kyūri* (investigation of natural law), in mid-Meiji the search for *shin* (truth), and later simply the development of *chisei* (the intellect). Those who had achieved such an education, as members of the intelligentsia, were believed to be the ones who should become the cultural leaders. The Imperial universities were considered to be the highest seats of learning, while the private universities were thought to follow them in importance, and it was thought necessary for those who wished to work in literature to pass through the portals of these institutions.

Of course many Meiji authors, as represented by Kōyō and Shiki, were forced to break off their academic training in order to devote themselves to literature. There were those also who like Rohan worked hard to educate themselves. But we are unable to deny that to have been graduated from one of the highest seats of learning, as were Shōyō, Ōgai, and Sōseki, was the most orthodox way to get on in the world, and that it was the short-cut to social approval for authors, too.

The fact that such scientific and academic knowledge was made a social ideal meant the transforming of literature into a science, and by the scientific observation of life the content of literature was also improved. As a result of the maturity of this scientific view of the world and of literature, it was inevitable that the birth of a scientific literature such as Naturalism should have been hastened. Yet the support of science on the part of the Meiji government certainly did not anticipate the establishment of Naturalism, but rather was for the purpose of bringing about the nation's prosperity. The support by the capitalist class, too, had as its objective the advancement of material civilization. The intellectual class which was thus nurtured in society, however, soon created its own independent society, and therein set up its own goals. This class held an independent view of life based on the intellect, and it urged the emergence of a natural scientific art which would look upon human life as a part of that broader life, specifically that of instinctive animals, which is the object of research of the natural sciences.

We are able to see in this that the course of modern European literature was very largely transplanted to a corner of East Asia, and yet uniquely Japanese features are not entirely absent. This can be seen at various points, since the establishment in Japan of a *Weltanschauung* based on the natural sciences in imitation of the European pattern took place so rapidly that the Japanese people with their scant scientific tradition were unable to assimilate, exactly the way it was, the perfected European Naturalism. Thus, the fact that Japanese Naturalism was acclimatized and traditionalized, and came to present a startlingly Japanese aspect has been already amply noted.

A conspicuous feature of this Japanization was, first, the emotionalization, and particularly the susceptibility to the local atmosphere, of the intellect. Such a process had its foundation in the Japanese national consciousness. The national tendency was rather toward the emotional and the subjective than the intellectual and the objective, so that this *Weltanschauung* based on the natural sciences came to be an aesthetic view of life, while realism was twisted into romanticism.

In the second place, individualism was something linked closely to the personal life, and this also as a national characteristic was reflected in Meiji society. Although Naturalism deals with the problem of the destiny of the individual life, it does not deal with the problem of the author's own individual life but rather with the individualism in mankind in general, and tries to grasp experimentally its significance for the human race. The individual is the place of experiment, and consequently his social position becomes a problem. In the later Zola, for instance, this social factor is extremely important. Since the Japanese writers, however, took the attitude of a lyric poet in delving into their own personal lives, such universality and social consciousness are conspicuously absent, and they turned from society to their own subjective world.

In the third place, in order to investigate scientifically the truth about man, Japanese Naturalist writers did not take the true scientific position of putting the individual life on the laboratory table; instead of such a scientific approach they gave birth to a religious and artistic one wherein they sought events exactly as they are reflected in the world of instinct. Thus, they constructed their works more on impression than on observation, more on trust than experimentation, and the world they depicted came closer to being a fruit of history than of science. This has its basis in the national consciousness, but the incompleteness of the Meiji scientific training can also be considered a cause. Ōgai in his *Mōsō* (Strange Fancies) laments the lack of a scientific atmosphere in Japan. It was but natural that the truth which was sought in such an atmosphere should be transformed into a semi-artistic type of history, and even Ōgai himself in his later years was able to indicate the perfected form of this type of work in his historical biographies.

Since the ideals of Meiji society which were thus made to conform to science were actually merely a rapidly constructed imitation of modernization, they were unable to bear sufficient fruit, and a method of intellectualization was discovered to fill this gap. This was a German-type philosophy. In the early period the intelligentsia was not too conscious of it, but after the establishment of a philosophy department in the Imperial universities and the introduction of German idealistic philosophy, it was gradually fascinated by the subtle, logical construction of it, and such cultural leaders as Ōgai, Chogyū, and Hōgetsu, who were endeavoring to form a theoretical foundation for literature from aesthetics, dissatisfied with the truth of the natural sciences, introduced *rinen*, the German *Idee*. After the middle of Meiji this became the main pillar of idealism, in sharp contrast with the natural sciences which formed the main pillar of realism. Such a philosophical trend was the illegitimate offspring of Meiji society, and even though there had been nothing like it in Japan before, we might compare it to the Buddhism of the Kamakura and Muromachi Periods and to the Sung philosophy, particularly that of the Chu Hsi school, of the Edo Period. Doubtless there were many possibilities for the natural sciences and Naturalism to become closely linked to the capitalistic spirit of urban society, and likewise many possibilities for philosophy and idealism to fuse with the nationalistic spirit of the bureaucracy and the military, but in any case, the formation of a particular independent world in the society of the Meiji intelligentsia has points of similarity to what the priests of the Kamakura and Muromachi Periods and the scholars and *literati* of the Edo Period accomplished.

At any rate, even though Meiji society came thus to nurture writers of literature, the bureaucracy, the military, and the capitalists who dominated that society were not necessarily those who understood such literature. Many gifted writers felt, in varying degrees, an antipathy toward this dominating class. They were constantly trying to escape from such domination, and to seek a free world in the realm of the spirit. And yet we are unable to say that this is not the attitude that artists have always taken throughout history. There were Meiji authors, too, who were dissatisfied with the dominant class of this materialistic society, and who strove to depict the tragedy and comedy of the authors themselves who were placed in such a society. They did not, however, in any way show a positive will to reform that society, but rather they set up as a literary objective the building of a spiritual freedom so that they would not be enslaved by it. Shōyō's *botsurisō* (submergedidealism), Hōgetsu's *kanshō no sekai* (the world of observation), Tōkoku's *naibu seimei* (the interior life), Ōgai's *teinen* (resignation), and Sōseki's *sokuten kyoshi* (to follow heaven, and depart from the self) all seemed to be expressing this sort of thing.

That so-called Propertyless Class which was already emerging gradually in the Meiji Era did not in any way try to bring about cooperation with the dominating class, and since it felt that the only course for literature was to dispose of this dissatisfaction as a problem of social reality, it urged that literature become the tool of social reform ; but since this was a period when Meiji society was advancing in the direction of the establishment of a national state and a capitalistic society, the force to destroy these social organs did not have too much room to appear. The mass of the people, for the most part, were trying to build a new life in the midst of this new society, and even though they did not go so far as to sacrifice themselves for consummation of this society, they strove to work in harmony with it.

Meiji society was thus bolstered by the desire for progress on the part of the mass of the people ; even in the midst of confusion there was a marked will toward unity ; even in the midst of dissatisfaction there was a great feeling of contentment. Since the society was in the stage of unity and formation, the necessary factors for destruction and degeneration were very few. Even literature was not a thing that was monopolized by a part of the intellectual class or by the *literati*, but the people tried to come as close as possible to the literary works, and writers also could emerge from among the mass of the people. Indeed, it was not a society wherein the people and literature were separated.

In order to realize this will of the people to have a literature of their own, it was necessary to establish organs to allow the people to participate in literature. One of these organs was the literary society, and an other was the diffusion of printed matter. We shall speak about the activity of the literary societies later ; here let us take a glance at the situation of publishing. The force which nurtured the writers of literature was based to a great extent on the society of writers, but the diffusion of printed matter was necessary in order that there might be readers for that literature from among the mass of the people. Among the printed matter which performed this function of satisfying this desire in the Meiji Era there were the periodicals, such as newspapers and magazines, and also books and series of volumes.

The emergence of newspapers in Japan began in 1862 with the *Kampan Batabiya Shimbun.* In 1871 the *Yokohama Mainichi Shimbun* and, in the following year, the *Tōkyō Nichinichi Shimbun*, both dailies, appeared. But these were small newspapers, mainly for announcements and entertainment, and they did not carry political discussion columns which were the breeding ground of literature. In 1874 the *Yomiuri Shimbun* appeared as the first newspaper of this type, and in 1879 the *Asahi Shimbun* was published in Ōsaka. At this same time many small second-rate newspapers also appeared. The *Kokumin Shimbun*, first published in 1890, was later suppressed by the government as an organ of a political party. It then separated itself from political parties and appeared as a popular newspaper with the editorial policy of a smaller newspaper, and in this new form it carried many literary works. The *Yorozu Chōhō*, which first appeared in 1892, also nurtured literature as a small newspaper.

Before newspapers began to carry novels, such literary magazines as the *Tōkyō Shinshi* (first published in 1876), *Kagetsu Shinshi* (first published in 1877), and the *Marumaru Chimbun* (Anonymous and Curious News) (first published in 1877) carried lower order fiction of the novel type serially in each issue, but in 1877 Kubota Hikosaku's *Torioi O-Matsu no Den* (The Story of O-Matsu the Strolling Singer) (later published under the title *Torioi O-Matsu Kaijō Shinwa*, The New Sea Tale of O-Matsu the Strolling Singer) began to appear in the *Kanayomi Shimbun*, and in 1878 Maeda Kōsetsu's *Kinnosuke no Hanashi* (The Tale of Kinnosuke) began to be serialized in the *Tōkyō E-iri Shimbun* (Tōkyō Illustrated Newspaper), so that the serial newspaper novel emerged. Since these popular smaller newspapers employed lower order fiction writers in order to build up circulation with their novels, Takabatake Ransen became connected with the *Yomiuri Shimbun*, Maeda Kōsetsu and Tamenaga Shunsui II with the *Tōkyō E-iri Shimbun*, the group around Kanagaki Robun with the *Kanayomi Shimbun*, Shinoda Senka with the *Hana no Miyako Onna Shimbun*, and Utagawa Bunkai with the *Naniwa Shimbun*. At that time newspaper novels were called *tsuzukimono* (serials) just as was the general news which appeared in instalments. They were slightly Meijified works of the "promote virtue and reprove vice" lower order fiction type and not yet worthy of being called works of the new era. From about 1880 on, the political novel began to enliven the newspapers, and beginning with Sakazaki Shiran's *Kanketsu Senri no Koma* (The Swift Pony) (serialized in 1883 in the *Doyō Shimbun*, The Earth and Sun Newspaper) and Miyazaki Muryū's *Ki Shūshū* (The Muttering of the Demon) (serialized in 1884–1885 in the *Jiyūtō*, Freedom's Lamp), such famous works as Sudō Nansui's *Ryokusadan* (The Tale of the Green Straw Raincoat) and *Shinsō no Kajin* (The Newly Adorned Beauty) began to appear after 1886 in the *Kaishin Shimbun* (The Newspaper of Reform and Progress).

Shōyō's *Shōsetsu Shinzui* and *Tōsei Shosei Katagi* appeared in 1885, marking a new period in the Meiji novel, and thereafter newspapers emerged which carried this new type of novel serially. Through three months after January 1886 the *Yomiuri Shimbun* carried Katō Shihō's translation of Georges Ohnet's *Les Batailles de la Vie* (The Battles of Life) under the title *Shura Ukiyo : Dantetsujō no Shujin* (The Field of Death, the Floating World : The Master of the Forge). Later it carried the works of Aeba Kōson ; finally Shōyō became the chief of its literary section, and with the employment of the two great authors, Kōyō and Rohan, this literary trend became conclusive. The *Yomiuri Shimbun* further carried the major works of Bimyōsai, Ryokuu, Shiin, Sazanami, Otsuu, Baika, and Kaho, and later introduced to the world such important works as *Tajō Takon* (1896), *Teriha Kyōgen* (The Farce of Teriha) (1896), *Konjiki Yasha* (1897), *Makaze Koikaze* (The Winds of Demons and Love) (1903), *Sora Utsu Nami* (The Heaven-Striking Waves) (1903), and *Seishun* (Youth) (1905). After the beginning of the Naturalistic period it also carried such works as *Sei* (Life) (1908), *Ie* (A Family) (1910), and *Ashiato* (Footprints) (1910). These Naturalistic works were not necessarily designed for the popular taste, and yet they had a great success among the people.

Following the pattern of the *Yomiuri Shimbun*, *Kokkai*, which began publication in 1890, welcomed Rohan, Ningetsu, Ryokuu, Shiken, Tetchō, and Tengai as contributors, and by carrying many novels of a high artistic quality, came to have even a rather intellectual aspect. *Gojū no Tō* (1891) and *Futsuka Monogatari* (the first half of *Kono Ichinichi*, This One Day) (1892) appeared in this newspaper. The *Kokumin Shimbun*, which began publication in 1890, also carried such works as *Hototogisu* (1898), *Omoide no Ki* (A Record of Memories) (1900), *Kuroshio* (The Black Current) (1902), *Fūryūsen* (Elegant Line) (1903), *Arajotai* (The New Household) (1908), and *Uzumaki* (1910), while the *Tōkyō Asahi Shimbun*, which in 1888 changed its name from *Mesamashi Shimbun* (The Awakener), after the beginning of the period of Naturalism also serialized many full-length novels of a high artistic value and gained public acclaim. The most prominent of these novels were *Sono Omokage* (Its Vestiges) (1906), *Gubijinsō* (The Red Poppy) (1907), *Heibon* (Mediocrity) (1907), *Haru* (Spring) (1908), *Sanshirō* (1908), *Baien* (Soot and Smoke) (1909), *Sore Kara* (And Then) (1909), *Shirasagi* (The Snow Heron) (1909), *Reishō* (The Sneer) (1909), *Mon* (The Gate) (1910), *Tsuchi* (The Soil) (1910), *Kabi* (Mold) (1911), and *Higan Sugi Made* (Until After the Spring Equinox) (1912).

When in 1907 Sōseki left his teaching position at the Tōkyō Imperial University to join the staff of the *Tōkyō Asahi Shimbun* and in the following year became head of its literary column, this had a very great effect on the course of the literary world.

In addition to these, the *Miyako Shimbun, Ōsaka Mainichi Shimbun, Niroku Shimpō, Yorozu Chōhō, Shimbun Nihon, Yamato Shimbun,* and *Ōsaka Shimpō* also carried many full-length novels which appealed to the popular taste, but that is not to say that there did not also appear in these newspapers works of a high artistic content. At any rate, the fact that newspapers thus carried long novels over several months was a characteristic of the Meiji Era. Most of these novels also had an illustration in every day's section to attract the reader visually. This can be said to be an extension of the illustrated scroll which is a special feature of Japanese art.

Just as the newspaper was primarily responsible for nurturing the full-length novel, so too did the magazine become the main organ for publication of the short story and poetry. Magazines also, like the newspapers, learned from the West, and the *Seiyō Zasshi* (The Western Magazine), which appeared in 1867, is considered to be the oldest, but it was merely a translation of a Dutch magazine. Articles on Japan were included in it, but they did not have any special connection with literature. The *Meiroku Zasshi,* which was first published in 1874, is noteworthy as the scholarly magazine of the Meirokusha scholars, but it was not an organ for the publication of literary works. The *Dōjinsha Bungaku Zasshi,* edited by Nakamura Keiu and first published in 1876, also merely carried a few Chinese poems and *waka.* When we come to the *Kagetsu Shinshi* of Narushima Ryūhoku which appeared in 1877, the comic magazine *Marumaru Chimbun,* and the contributors' magazine *Eisai Shinshi,* the relationship with literature is somewhat closer, and the latter magazine became the guiding force of Katai and Keigetsu.

In 1885 Shōyō's *Shōsetsu Shinzui* and *Tōsei Shosei Katagi* appeared, the group around Kōyō formed the Ken'yūsha, the *Chūō Gakujutsu Zasshi* which became the organ for the scholarly opinions of Shōyō and others was first published, and so also was the *Jogaku Zasshi*. In the following year the *Ōyashima Gakkai Zasshi* and, in the year after that, the *Hanseikai Zasshi* appeared, all of which strengthened the literary movement. In 1887 the *Kokumin no Tomo*, which was the organ of the Min'-yūsha, appeared, and it too is not without significance as a vehicle for the publication of works of literature. In the following year there appeared in it Futabatei's translation of Turgenev's work *Rendezvous* under the title *Aibiki* which exerted great influence on the literary world. In 1889 Bimyōsai's *Kochō* (Butterfly) won public attention with its accompanying illustrations of a beautiful nude woman, while Shōyō's *Saikun* (The Wife), Saganoya's *Ruten* (Impermanence), and Shiken's translation, *Tantei Yūberu* (The Detective Hubert), were also much discussed. In 1890, with the appearance in the magazine of Ōgai's *Maihime* and Rohan's *Ikkōken* (One Sword), it became the focus of public attention.

It was in May of 1885 that the *Garakuta Bunko* of Kōyō, Bimyō, and Shian appeared as a privately circulating magazine, but in May of 1888 it was put on sale. In the previous year Bimyō had joined the staff of the woman's magazine *Iratsume* (first published in 1887), when he became head of its literary section, and produced many outstanding works. The *Garakuta Bunko* had the appearance of a literary coterie magazine, but it gradually broadened in scope, and when the Ken'yūsha became the center of the literary world, the name was shortened to *Bunko*, or simply "Literary Storehouse."

In the same year that the *Garakuta Bunko* first appeared publicly, such magazines as the *Miyako no Hana* (The Flower of the Capital) and the *Shōsetsu Suikin* (The Novel Collection Brocade) which carried only novels and short stories also first appeared, and thereafter many similar ones, such as the *Yamato Nishiki* (The Yamato Brocade), *Shinshōsetsu* (The New Novel),

Ashiwakebune (The Reed-Parting Boat), *Bunko*, *Edo Murasaki* (The Edo Purple), *Senshi Bankō* (A Thousand Purples, Ten Thousand Scarlets), *Shincho Hyakushu* (A Hundred Varieties of New Works), *Kozakura Odoshi* (The Small Cherry Armor Thread), *Nihon no Bunka* (The Literary Flower of Japan), and *Shincho Gekkan* (The New Book Monthly) also were published.

Shigarami-Zōshi (first published in 1889), edited by Ōgai, and *Waseda Bungaku* (first published in 1891), edited by Shōyō, were magazines with a unique emphasis which did not specialize in fiction but dealt broadly with literary problems in general, and they gave a new tone to this period of the rise of a new literature. These magazines reflected the opposing views of idealism and realism of their respective editors, and the very first edition of *Waseda Bungaku* began the Submerged Idealism discussion which attracted the attention of the literary world. *Waseda Bungaku* later discontinued publication, but in the period of Naturalism it was published again, and at the end of Meiji it stood in a position of leadership in the intellectual world, although it was rivalled by Katai's *Bunshō Sekai* (The World of Writing) (first published in 1906). *Shigarami-Zōshi* later changed its name to *Mesamashigusa* (The Grasses of Awakening), and for a long time was in the camp of idealism. Ueda Bin's *Geien* (Garden of Art) (1902–1906) and his *Geibun* (Art and Literature) (1902) also supported this position.

Bungakkai (The Literary World) (first published in 1893), which took the Romantic position in opposition to the lower order fiction tastes of the *Garakuta Bunko*, but which shared with that periodical the aspect of a literary coterie magazine, sent Tōkoku, Tokuboku, and Tōson into the world, and was one of the guiding lights of the Romantic period which followed. *Bungakkai* is similar to the *Garakuta Bunko* in the fervor with which it espoused literature, while *Teikoku Bungaku* (first published in 1895) with its academic background took the Romantic position of *Shigarami-Zōshi* and was in opposition to that of *Waseda Bungaku*. Men like Chogyū, Chōfū, Bansui, Ukō, and

Hagoromo had their start in this magazine.

All of these magazines still had somewhat the aspect of literary coterie magazines, but *Taiyō* (The Sun) (first published in 1895) was born as a general magazine and was on an extremely large scale. When Chogyū became active in its columns as a critic, however, it came to exert a great deal of pressure on the literary world, and not a few novels were also carried. *Bungei Kurabu* (The Literary Club), which was first published in the same year, seemed to be a magazine of entertainment, but actually it had many of the qualities of a literary magazine which specialized in fiction, and it carried many of the representative works of the Romantic period, such as those of Ryūrō, Bizan, Kyōka, and Ichiyō. In 1899 the *Hansei Zasshi* changed its name to *Chūō Kōron*, and after the Russo-Japanese War it swiftly acquired strength, overwhelming *Taiyō*, and gaining the rank of *Bungei Kurabu* and *Shinshōsetsu*. It came also to carry first-rate works, and after the beginning of Taishō it almost had the authority of a literary magazine that specialized in fiction. *Shinchō* (The New Tide) (first published in 1904) also acquired strength with Naturalism, and has the record of having introduced famous novels to the world; it, too, continued after the beginning of Taishō. The fact that these large magazines emphasized the novel can be said to be a result of popular opinion, but at the same time they raised the level of literature and contributed greatly to its diffusion.

These large magazines, however, welcomed only the major writers who had an established reputation, and they did not concern themselves with the new and not yet famous authors. This meant that new literary movements appeared in the form of literary coterie magazines as before. The several *Shinshichō*s (The New Current of Thought) (the first one was published in 1907 and the second in 1910), which appeared at the end of Meiji, throughout Taishō, and into Shōwa, were brought out by the students of Tōkyō Imperial University under the editorship of Osanai Kaoru, while *Shirakaba* (White Birch) (first published

in 1910) was the organ of publication of the young writers of
the nobility under the leadership of Mushakōji Saneatsu, and
led the humanitarian movement of the Taishō Era. It is difficult to mention all of these literary coterie magazines. *Mita
Bungaku* (first published in 1910) of Keiō University, under the
guidance of Nagai Kafū also had somewhat this aspect, and
Subaru (first published in 1909), under the leadership of Ōgai,
was the organ of the young Decadent and Hedonist writers,
while *Seitō* (The Blue Stocking) (first published in 1911), under
the direction of Hiratsuka Raichō, was the organ of " the new
woman." We cannot deny that these magazines during the
transition period at the end of Meiji operated with considerable
force on the literary world.

The literary coterie magazines appeared particularly prominently in the area of poetry, which had little market value. It is
not that *Bungakkai, Teikoku Bungaku, Taiyō, Bunshō no Sekai,*
and *Waseda Bungaku* did not carry poetry, but they were overwhelmed by novels, short stories, and critical writing, so that
they had the tendency to give it rather poor treatment. Thus,
there was the trend toward the formation of groups of poetry
enthusiasts and also to the issuing of periodicals, which of
necessity was a part of the activity of these societies. We can
see feudal traces in this process, and these publications were
more the vehicles for the propagation of the views of a particular
group or society than they were magazines in any strict sense.
We can further mention *Myōjō, Shirayuri* (The White Lily),
Bunko, Shinsei (The New Voice), *Shiika* (Poetry), *Okujō Teien,*
and *Zamboa* as vehicles of the New Style poetry, *Ashibi, Akane*
(The Crimson), *Araragi* (The Orchid), *Kokoro no Hana* (The
Flower of the Heart), *Sōsaku* (Creative Writing), and *Shazensō*
(The Plantain) as those of the *tanka,* and *Aki no Koe* (The
Voice of Autumn), *Hototogisu, Haisei* (The Haiku Star), *Haisei*
(different Chinese characters from the preceding one) (The Haiku
Voice), *Takarabune* (The Treasure Ship), *Hammen* (Profile),
Uzue, Kakeaoi (The Hanging Hollyhock), *Sōun* (Piled Clouds),

and *Shisaku* (Étude) as those of the *haiku*. We shall touch further on these magazines later when we come to discuss the activity of the literary societies.

Since the drama was directly connected with the actual theatrical performance, there were few independent organs of publication, but *Kabuki Shimpō* (The Kabuki New Report) (first published in 1879), *Kabuki* (first published in 1900), and *Geki to Shi* (Drama and Poetry) (first published in 1910) performed valuable service in this area.

As organs for the publication of Meiji literature and as a means for its diffusion, we must finally mention the various types of independent volumes, series of volumes, and complete collections. The books of early Meiji were of the *kusazōshi* (illustrated story-book) type, and even *Tōsei Shosei Katagi* was introduced to the world on Japanese paper with Ch'ing Dynasty-type print and with illustrations scattered throughout. Even those works which were not quite of the illustrated story-book type were very often bound in Japanese style. In 1878, however, Kawashima Chūnosuke's translation of Jules Verne's *Eighty Days Around the World* and Niwa Jun'ichirō's translation of Bulwer-Lytton's *Ernest Maltravers* appeared in a hard cover and in Western-style binding, and thereafter there were many works which imitated them. *Tōsei Shosei Katagi*, too, was later re-published in a Western-type binding.

Whether the books were paper-bound or more permanently bound, they were largely in Western style, although the paper-bound novels with wood-block prints on the covers and with colored illustrations still retained the flavor of Japanese-style bound works. Both the format and the illustrations gradually became more and more Western, and particularly after the beginning of Naturalism, books came to have a purely Western appearance. The two types that emerged were the cheap paper-bound edition and the *de luxe* edition. The former enlarged the area of readership while the latter raised the standard of literature.

With regard to the printing of series of volumes and complete collections, the Meiji Era, in a certain sense, can be thought of as a Renaissance. Reprinting of the classics flourished, and we see the publication of such series as the *Shiseki Shūran, Nihon Bungaku Zensho, Onchi Sōsho, Nihon Bunko, Hyakumantō, Nihon Kagaku Zensho, Haikai Bunko, Haikai Sōsho, Kokka Taikan, Kokubun Taikan, Kokushi Taikei, Hyakka Setsurin, Shin-Gunsho Ruijū, Gosan Bungaku Zensho, Kokubun Chūshaku Zensho, Kokumin Bunko, Kinsei Bungei Sōsho,* and *Kabuki Sōsho,* while the works of Meiji authors also were often brought out in this form. *Miyako no Hana, Shincho Hyakushu,* and *Shincho Gekkan* were more series of works than actual magazines, and Kōson's *Muratake* (A Clump of Bamboo) took the form of a complete collection from its twenty volumes, while in his *Shinsaku Jūniban* (Twelve New Works) there was one work for each author, with the Number One position going to Kōson himself. The *Akatsuki Sōsho* (Dawn Series) (1902) also published the works of several authors in succession, and *Jūemon no Saigo* (The End of Jūemon), which was the starting point of Katai's Naturalism, appeared as its fifth volume. When Tōson's *Hakai* appeared, it was as the first volume in the *Ryokuin Sōsho* (The Green Shade Series); later his *Haru* (Spring) made up the second, *Ie* (A Family) the third, and *Bifū* (A Breeze) the fourth volume in the series.

These works appeared as part of a series at the time of first publication, but, in the case of reprints, series were even more numerous. The *Kinkōdō Shōsetsu Sōsho, Kokumin Shōsetsu, Shōnen Bungaku, Shūhō Jisshu, Bungaku Sekai, Meiji Bunko, Shōsetsu Hyakkasen, Taiyō Shōsetsu, Shūchin Shōsetsu, Meiji Shōsetsu Bunko,* and *Meika Shōsetsu Bunko* had some new works in them, but most of them were reprints.

Moreover, already in the Meiji Era complete collections and selections of an author's work were published, such as the *Tōkoku Zenshū, Ichiyō Zenshū, Ryūhoku Zenshū, Fukuzawa Zenshū, Rohan Sōsho, Hakuhyō Ikō* (The Posthumous Works of Hakuhyō), *Chogyū Zenshū, Tōson Shishū* (The Collected Poems of Tōson), *Kōyō Zenshū, Shiki Ikō, Shiken Zenshū, Bizan Zenshū, Kōyō-Shū* (The Kōyō Anthology), *Kyōka-Shū, Doppo Zenshū, Ryokuu-Shū, Seiko-Shū, Bimyō-Shū, Futabatei Zenshū, Rohan-Shū,* and *Ōchi Zenshū,* and after the beginning of Taishō even larger scale plans were made to present to the general reader, in as nearly complete a form as possible, works of the major authors ; thus, there was realized a diffusion of literature such as never took place in the pre-Meiji period. The study of these authors based on their complete works spurred on other writers to display their talent and to strengthen their positions as artists. Especially the publication shortly after their death of the complete works of Chogyū and Kōyō in a splendid format was responsible for making heroes of these two men who died so young, and made their works the object of public admiration. The Taishō Period saw the publication of superb editions of the complete works of Sōseki and Ōgai which were worthy monuments to the labors of these two great men, but the way toward their publication had already been prepared in Meiji. Such publication, together with the care of his grave and relics, was a major way of showing respect for a great author.

Since newspapers and general magazines had the tendency to seek contributors from among the established general writers, there was relatively little possibility for them to be linked with the activity of the literary associations, but when we come to the literary coterie magazines, we note that they performed the function of acting as organs for the publication and propagation of the activities of these societies. Even the general-type magazines sometimes took on the functions of an intellectual organization. In the Meiji Era freedom of thought was more widely recognized than in the feudal regime, and social literary movements were fostered by the banding together of like-minded people. As in the West, the tendency to emphasize a literature with a considerable intellectual content grew, and since a criticism based on the intellect came to penetrate the very core of literature, it was but natural that literary writers should join organizations of intellectuals and that the intellectuals in turn should join literary groups, so that very often it was difficult to distinguish between an intellectual group and a literary association.

As we have already mentioned, among the intellectual groups of the Meiji Era, those on the progressive side were the Dōjinsha (Nakamura Masanao, *et al.*, founded 1873), Meirokusha (Nishi Amane, *et al.*, founded 1873), and Min'yūsha (Tokutomi Sohō, *et al.*, founded 1887), while the conservative groups included the Dai-Hasshū Gakkai (founded 1886), Seikyōsha (founded 1888), and Dai-Nihon Kyōkai (The Greater Japan Association) (founded 1897). Most of these had their own periodicals to spread their views. Among them there were those with only a slight relation to literature, but *Kokumin no Tomo* of the Min'yūsha, and *Nihonjin* (later *Nihon oyobi Nihonjin*) of the Seikyōsha made not inconsiderable contributions to literature.

As purely literary groups, we first must mention the Ken'yūsha, composed of Kōyō, Kyūka, Shian, and Bimyō, which published *Garakuta Bunko* and was a powerful social force. From its very establishment it had an " art-for-art's-sake," realistic, and urban character. Kōyō was the best representative of this, who by his depiction, in his elaborate style, of the beguiling world of the emotions, attacked the then powerful political novel writers with their crude, inartistic, and tendentious literature. We must recognize the social significance of this attack, and since the political novel writers did not have the power to form literary societies, the control of the literary world passed temporarily to the Ken'yūsha. The Negishi group of Kōson and Shiken (founded about 1887) resembled this latter society, and was similar to it in its delight in the witty and elegant turn of phrase.

In opposition to these numerous light-minded, pleasure-seeking groups, there were the lyric poetry groups, such as that of

Saganoya and Koshoshi, and the Sendagi group which centered around Ōgai, but none of these had any formal organization. The former groups were made up of young Romantics who were enraptured of the beauties of nature and who wished to sacrifice themselves to "pure emotion," while the latter was made up of solemn, idealistic transcendentalists standing in lofty isolation, and they advanced together with their pure spirit. Ōgai formed the Shinseisha (S. S. S.) and published his collection of translated poems, *Omokage*, in 1889, but his major activity was in *Shigarami-Zōshi* (later *Mesamashigusa*, The Grasses of Awakening); these publications were part of the activity of the literary associations, and as such they were of considerable social significance.

This idealistic trend can be said to have been continued by the group that brought out *Bungakkai* (1893). This group emerged from Iwamoto Zenji's *Jogaku Zasshi* (1885), and even though there was no formal organization, since among Tōkoku, Tenchi, Shūkotsu, Tokuboku, Tōson, Kochō, and Bin there was the same purely Romantic and aesthetic tendency and the same earnestness and zeal which occasionally took on a note of misanthropy and pessimism, we are justified in thinking of them almost as an organized society, one which was the true starting-point of Meiji Romanticism, occupying somewhat the same position that Rousseau and others do in French Romanticism. The Sanraisha, headed by Matsumura Kaiseki, also brought out a strongly Romantic magazine, *Sanrai* (1893), and it carried the poetry of Tōkoku.

The Ken'yūsha and the Sendagi group were strongly opposed to the *Bungakkai* group, and this can be thought of as the opposition of realism to Romanticism. We can find a similar opposition existing between Shōyō's Waseda group (1891) and Ōgai's Sendagi group, and we can recognize much the same sort of thing existing also between the Waseda and *Teikoku Bungaku*, or Akamon (which means Red Gate, the symbol of Tōkyō University) groups. The Akamon group was maintained by such idealists as Chogyū, Chōfū, Bansui, Seisetsu, and Rimpū, and by such Neo-Classic poets as Ukō, Hagoromo, and Keigetsu, who held forth in their magazine *Teikoku Bungaku* (first published in 1895).

With the rise of Naturalism, the Waseda group began publishing *Waseda Bungaku* again, and under the leadership of Hōgetsu it developed greatly, while *Bunshō no Sekai*, edited by Katai, became one of the strong pillars of Naturalism even though it was not published by any highly organized group. Moreover the Ryūdokai was founded by Kunio, Doppo, Tōson, Katai, Ariake, Hōmei, Rinsen, Kaoru, and Musōan, and it too became powerful in the Naturalistic era, acquiring such members as Tenkei, Shūsei, Kisan, and Tengen. The position of the *Waseda Bungaku* group in the center of the literary world of the Naturalistic era is similar to that occupied by the Ken'yūsha in the early Meiji Period, and yet there are points of difference. The literary section of the *Asahi Shimbun* was not controlled by any one group, but nevertheless the young men who surrounded Sōseki, the literary editor, had the unity of a salon coterie, and there were some who felt it extended throughout the newspaper. It is true that as a powerful anti-Naturalistic group it possessed considerable social backing. The *Subaru* group led by Ōgai, the *Okujō Teien* (first published in 1909) group of Hakushū and Mokutarō, which is often considered to be merely a detached force of the *Subaru* group, *Mita Bungaku* of Keiō University, edited by Kafū and supported by Ōgai and Bin, and the coterie magazine *Shinshichō*, brought out by the students of Tōkyō Imperial University under the editorship of Osanai Kaoru, all can be thought of as vehicles of the anti-Naturalistic movement. Furthermore, the Shirakaba group which emerged at about the same time, even though it did not have the unity of an organized society, was a gathering of earnest, idealistic young men of the aristocracy. It occupied a position diametrically opposite to that of the Ken'yūsha, and though it differed somewhat from the *Bungakkai* group in taking a purely humanistic position, it resembled the latter in its group solidarity. In the Taishō Era it came to acquire considerable power in society.

When we come to look at poetry, we find that the most in- fluential society was the largely romantic Tōkyō Shinshisha (Tokyo New Poetry Society) of Tekkan, founded in 1899, while the *Bunko* (1895) and *Shinsei* (1896) groups followed it in im- portance. In the Naturalistic era the Waseda Shisha (Waseda Poetry Society) (1907) and the Jiyūshisha (The Free Verse Society) (1909) became the breeding ground of free verse. The *Subaru* and *Okujō Teien* groups in December 1908 organized the Pan no Kai (The Society of the Devotees of Pan) together with the artists and poets of *Hōsun*, which was first published in 1907, and these young men developed a new urban and somewhat hedonistic poetic style. *Okujō Teien* emerged as the organ of the Pan no Kai. Hakushū's *Zamboa* (1911) performed the func- tion of preparing the way for Symbolist poetry. These various poetry societies were largely of the coterie type, and even though they did not have the social standing of those groups concerned with the novel and criticism, they did provide a vehicle for publication of the poems of their members, who would not otherwise have been able to publish them.

In the *tanka*, Shiki's Negishi Tanka Kai was organized in 1899 in opposition to the Romantic trend of the Tōkyō Shin- shisha which continued the tradition of Naobumi's Asakasha (1893), and it nurtured the realistic poets whose poems appeared in *Ashibi* (1903), *Akane* (1908), and *Araragi* (1908). Ōgai's Kanchōrō Kakai (The Poetry Society of the Pavilion of the Observers of the Tide) was a significant attempt to fuse the two traditions, but it was not entirely successful. Centering around these two great traditions, there are the Chikuhaku Kai (The Bamboo and Oak Society) (1899), which Nobutsuna in- herited from his father Hirotsuna, Kun'en's Shiragiku Kai (The White Chrysanthemum Society) (1903), Saishū's Shazensōsha (The Plantain Society) (1905), Utsubo's Jūgatsu Kai (The October

Society) (1905), Yūgure's Hakunichisha (The White Sun Society) (1907), and Bokusui's Sōsakusha (The Creative Writing Society) (1911).

In the *haiku*, those poets who centered around Shiki are called the Nihon group, the Negishi group, or the Hototogisu group, and in opposition to them there are Kōyō's Murasaki Ginsha (Purple Poetry Society), also called the Tochimandō group (1890), Chikurei and Shōu's Shūsei Kai (The Voice of Autumn Society) (1895), and Shachiku and Seisetsu's Chikuba Kai (1894). Later, as the Naturalistic era approached, there appeared Hekigotō's Haisammai group (1904) and Seisensui's Sōun (The Piled Clouds) group (1911). *Hototogisu* (The Cuckoo) was continued by Kyoshi, and it became an exceedingly influential publication.

All of the Meiji societies were free from the medieval and feudal practice of transmitting tradition uncritically and of observing hereditary descent in their members, and yet while they gave the appearance of being artistic groups assembled for the purpose of furthering a particular system or artistic method, they often were actually controlled by the opinions of their leader; especially in the *tanka* and the *haiku* did this trend remain. However, when compared to the *nō*, *kabuki*, and the schools of flower arrangement, traditional music, and dancing, they were far freer societies, where the individuality of the writer was often emphasized and it was not compulsory to adhere strictly to the methods of that particular school. Yet because of this they did not have the strength to continue very long, and there developed the habit of organizing and disbanding with the rise of every new idea or method. Only such societies as the Hototogisu and Araragi, which were societies in the traditional sense, as schools which strictly preserved the realistic method, had the strength of unity, like that of a religious body, necessary to continue for a long time, but this feature became prominent in society only after the beginning of the Taishō Era.

2. *The Position of Literature in the Moral Culture of the Meiji Era*

The Meiji Restoration gave the impetus to a reformation of every aspect of life, but in the early years the efforts to approximate European and American civilization in the material sphere were dominant, and the term *bummei kaika* (introduction of civilization) applied mainly to this material aspect. Thus, the thought of this first Meiji generation turned toward utilitarianism, and in order to achieve its utilitarian objectives, practical science was highly valued, and the study of the natural sciences was emphasized. However, once this material culture was achieved, the interest of the people began to turn also to the development of a moral culture.

Generally speaking, since the attitude with regard to the introduction of Western culture in the Meiji Era and the basic policy on education were undoubtedly in the direction of raising the level of material culture to meet that of the West, there was the tendency to place the primary emphasis on such practical learning as applied science, and political science, jurisprudence, and economics; the basis of all of this, however, was the spirit of the positivistic natural sciences and the inevitable growth of a pure scientific spirit. Of course this was an imperfect thing, but gradually it was able to attain a certain stage of development.

Thus, Meiji literature found its ideological foundation very largely in scientific positivism and rationalism, and on this foundation was established the literary form of realism. The development of realism is the basic characteristic of Meiji literature, and it was concomitant with the development of the scientific spirit. The reason that Shōyō came to write *Shōsetsu Shinzui* is that from his youth he had the intention of clarifying literary theory; the immediate reason, however, is that while at Tōkyō University, during a final examination in an English literature course, he was asked by the professor, who was an Englishman, to write a character analysis of Queen Gertrude in *Hamlet*, but because he wrote primarily a moral critique, he received a low grade. He profited by this experience, and under the guidance of Takada Hampō he began to read criticism of Western novels. Such reading resulted in his later introducing a new style into the Meiji novel.

But Shōyō's scientific position, as we know from his Submerged Idealism controversy with Ōgai, was an Anglo-American type of rationalism and practicality. Thus it was that he was unable to advance directly to the strict scientific method of Zola, and the first *Waseda Bungaku* was merely a vehicle for the introduction of Shakespeare, criticism of events in the literary world, and announcements of various artistic activities.

This transformation of literature into a science, which was begun by Shōyō, was assisted by Futabatei through his introduction of ideas on the nature of society and through the precision of his descriptions, but the stage of Naturalism was not attained, and even the Zolaism of Tengai, Fūyō, and Kafū was more theory than practice. When *Waseda Bungaku* was revived under Shōyō's successor, Shimamura Hōgetsu (Rōtarō), since the literary world was aflame with Naturalism, the magazine took advantage of the trend and became the center of literary activity; however, Hōgetsu was a student of German aesthetics, and since he went to Europe at a time when Neo-Idealism was already on the rise, he was not necessarily qualified to introduce into Japan the scientific ideas of Naturalism. In like manner, the members of the Waseda group, such as Hasegawa Tenkei (Seiya), Katagami Tengen (Shin), and Kaneko Chikusui (Umaharu), appear to have been greatly concerned with the scientific spirit but actually were not men of true intellect. Thus, Japanese Naturalism, without ever receiving sufficient theoretical support, rapidly passed over into idealism.

Before Meiji, scientific culture in Japan was extremely undeveloped. One of the reasons may have been that it also did not exist in China, which until then was considered by Japan to be its cultural guide, but another reason was that the Japanese national spirit has always been intuitive and emotional rather than one that delights in a scientific rationalism. Thus it was that the realism of Meiji did not quite succeed in transforming literature into a science. A German-type idealistic philosophy entered the literary world to fill this gap. The foremost proponent of this philosophy was Ōgai, who in addition to pursuing his studies in medicine, was completely proficient in the German language, and at the same time that he introduced much modern European literature into Japan, gave a new aesthetic foundation to literature based on the newest theories of such German philosophers as Hartmann, Volkelt, and Wundt.

Ōgai's literary criticism was based on truly precise logic, and this was reflected in the construction of his plays and novels; even in the *tanka* we can say that he began a new style of poetry with intellectual content. His logical philosophical method and idealist position aided the intellectualization of Meiji literature and its transformation into a science, while aestheticians like Chogyū and Hōgetsu, who, even though they were more emotional than Ōgai still were trained in German conceptual philosophy, can be considered as succeeding to the Ōgai tradition. Ningetsu and Sōsan (Shuku) were critics who were also influenced by German ideas. Sōseki was a student of English literature, and he introduced a new psychological approach in his *Bungakuron* (A Study of Literature); also, as the title of his *Bungei no Tetsugakuteki Kiso* (The Philosophical Basis of Literature) indicates, he was concerned with philosophical problems, and since the intellectual content of his novels was for the most part an idealistic rationalism, he occupies a position near Ōgai.

This idealistic, scientific spirit, then, flowed in two great streams, with Ōgai and Sōseki as the sources, and that literature of intellectual content in the Meiji, Taishō, and Shōwa Eras was largely in the Ōgai-Sōseki tradition rather than in the Naturalistic tradition. Thus, we must say that idealism, and Romanticism too, were reinforced by conceptual philosophy in the Meiji Era and were largely transformed into a science, or rather into a philosophy. At the end of Meiji, when Neo-Idealism emerged, critics like Ikuta Chōkō, Abe Yoshishige (Nōsei), Abe Jirō, Komiya Toyotaka (Hōryū), and Watsuji Tetsurō were all steeped in German philosophy, and many of them as young students at Tōkyō University had received the influence of the revered Professor Koeber. During Taishō and later, these philosopher-critics were joined by such pure philosophers as Nishida Ikutarō, Kuwaki Gen'yoku, and Hatano Seiichi, and together they introduced a trend into literature of introspective analysis.

Of course English, American, and French philosophy also exerted considerable influence on Meiji literature. Tōkoku and Doppo were deeply affected by Emerson's transcendentalism, and Carlyle and Ruskin were also emphasized by the men of *Bungakkai*. Roan, Sohō, Roka, Ruikō, and Tenshin also were men who were nurtured by Anglo-American ideas. French learning was not sufficiently strong to have a tradition of its own in the Meiji literary world, but it appears prominently in such men as Chōmin, Reiun, Kogan, Bin, and Kafū, and it must not be underrated.

Thus, while the literary currents of the Meiji Era have a philosophical background, there are also natural scientists who became famous : Ōgai and Mokutarō were doctors, Terada Torahiko was a physicist, and Rinsen was a student of electricity. It is said that Sōseki also at first intended to become an architect. The literary works of these scientists were not mere hobbies, although in their style we can see reflected the gleam of a scientific intellect. Particularly Ōgai's apollonian character attained a stage of development that would have been impossible if he had not passed through an intermediate period of scientific discipline ; in Japan a man who possessed such a well-organized intellect was indeed a rarity. This intellectualization of Meiji literature, when compared to that of Europe, does not loom so very large, but nevertheless for Japan it was an unprecedented development.

This revolution in literature caused by the introduction of scientific rationalism, as has been said before, stimulated the development of realism in the direction of the natural sciences and empiricism, and advanced to the point of nurturing a Naturalism that centered mainly around the Waseda group. Also in the philosophical and conceptual direction it fostered idealistic and Romantic humanitarianism and aestheticism, centering largely around the Akamon group. Indeed, we can generalize and say that the progress of Meiji literature took the form of the opposition, mingling, and fusion of these two main streams.

It is possible also to find two streams in the general area of moral thought. Since in the prevailing mood of realism a grasp of material culture and the nature of society was emphasized, the ethical attitude which emerged had the tendency to determine the nature of existence according to the practical effects of any given doctrine on actual life. The utilitarianism of early Meiji clearly indicated this tendency, and the literature of that period had to be something which cooperated with the political objectives. The intellectual background of the political novel included a certain amount of Romantic reverie and was not devoid of a longing for a vague utopia, but generally speaking, unless the political novel was related to the practical political aims of promulgating the constitution, or establishing the Diet, or reforming a specific institution, it was unable to interest people.

This utilitarianism and enlightenment were in opposition to the Confucianism and " foster-virtue, reprove-vice " ideas of the Edo Era ; they glowed rather with the spirit of the Five Articles of the Imperial Oath which pledged the " destroying of the evil practices of the past," but they had not yet reached the point where they were " based upon the just and equitable principle of nature." Instead there was the urgent practical objective of catching up with the material culture of the West. And yet the writers were able to leave the restrictions of a narrow, tendentious form and were awakened to the autonomy of art. A realism emerged which had as its objective the reflection of the prevailing social conditions, as laid down in *Shōsetsu Shinzui*, but this was still merely a superficial imitation, and it did not go beyond the childishness of a naive empiricism. Futabatei's *Shōsetsu Sōron* (A General Discussion of the Novel) showed the influence of Belinsky and possessed some depth, and yet even this was a superficial imitation of the early thought of the Russian critic and a simple fusion of Hegelian conceptualism and realism.

When we come to the question of how the realistic position of Shōyō and Futabatei was reflected ethically in actual works, it seems that Shōyō did not depart from the generally accepted idea of the empiricists of the time, which was the holding of worldly achievement as the ideal. In his *Tōsei Shosei Katagi* (The Character of the Modern Student) he urges the youth of that time who wished to become officials not to become entangled by love but to acquire culture and become fine gentlemen ; in a later work it seems he even intended to describe their development into *shinshi* (gentlemen). We can imagine that *Yūgaku Hachi Shōnen* (Eight Youths in Pursuit of Knowledge), the first draft of this work, was intended to be an account of worldly achievement of Meiji youth. Shōyō's ethical ideal, then, was largely the English-type gentleman, and he took the characters in Bulwer-Lytton's novels as his models. In his *Imotose Kagami,* or "Mirror of Marriage," in order to indicate the ideal relationship between husband and wife he makes references to Bulwer-Lytton's *Ernest Maltravers* and tries to teach the correct way of marriage ; the work is an extremely sensible exhortation to the gentlemanly way of respect for the personality of the individual. *Saikun*, or "The Wife," and his other translations and adaptations also do not go much beyond this.

In Futabatei's case, to the extent that he received the stimulus from the Russian social novel, he supported the new ideas that were in conflict with the old, and rejected trickery and flattery for the purpose of worldly success ; he seems to have based his attitude on the ideal of justice, but the basic ethical feeling within him was nothing more than an old-fashioned morality which valued simple honesty. However, Futabatei noticed the self suffering in the midst of the social environment, and, in the matter of making the thorough investigation of that self one of his objectives, he went far beyond Shōyō's practicality. We are even able to say that Futabatei was a pioneer of the Romantic awakening of the self. But this awakening of the self did not go beyond the limits of a foetal movement until the emergence of an unmistakable Romantic spirit with the men of *Bungakkai*. Since the Zolaism of Tengai and Kafū also was nothing more than a superficial imitation of realism and had not yet passed through a Romantic awakening, it did not bear much fruit in actual works.

This empirical, positivistic spirit of the natural sciences, and the utilitarianism and practicality which accompanied it, had completed its development by about the end of the Sino-Japanese War, and in the period of the Russo-Japanese War we see the growth of a spiritual attitude, which, together with the rise of Romanticism, caused the literary world to form a new ethic.

Of course this spiritual attitude had begun much earlier in Meiji, and it is not entirely unknown even before 1887, the year that marks the peak of utilitarianism and materialism. It existed primarily in the form of the opposition of the nationalism which centered in Shintō to the Christian spirit which had been brought in from abroad. Since the Restoration was on the one hand a return to the past, at the same time that it gave birth to Europeanization, it fostered chauvinism. Thus, even while the desire for Europeanization was intense, there emerged a nationalism as a reactionary force that attempted to quell it. While Europeanization had as its objectives the freedom of the individual and the betterment of society, nationalism opposed it with its respect for the state and its worship of the Imperial household. Similarly in actual life these two opposing movements clashed constantly.

However, this movement toward Westernization which opposed nationalism had a much more significant spiritual aspect. This was Christianity. After the opening of the country, Christianity gradually came to receive better treatment, and in 1873 finally the proscription was lifted, and it became possible publicly to follow the teachings of the new religion. From the end of the Shōgunate to about 1887 there was still considerable persecution, and many books attacking Christianity appeared, such as *Yaso Benwaku* (An Exposition of the Errors of Christianity) by Sotoyama Seiichi in 1883 and *Ikyō no Gai* (The Evils of the Foreign Religion) by Kurita Hiroshi in 1886, and yet gradually in that interval the religion came to permeate the culture. When the study of English became prominent, the spirit of Christianity was especially implanted in the youth by Englishmen and Americans who had come to Japan as teachers of their language. Such Meiji writers as Tōson, Roka, Tōkoku, Doppo, and Arishima Takeo, who introduced into the world of literature a frank discussion of the basic problems of life, received the influence of Christianity in their youth. Of course it is true that these writers also left the church as their egos grew, but they were never able to eliminate completely the influence which they had received in their early years. The influence of Dōshisha University, founded by Niijima Jō in 1875, and that of such Christian leaders as Uchimura Kanzō and Uemura Masahisa was particularly difficult to overlook. Furthermore, the translation of the Bible and hymns exerted a clear influence on a great number of writers, and there were many like Ariake, who in his *Dokugen Aika* (Single-Stringed Elegy), consciously employed the rhythms of the hymns in his poetry.

Christianity in its physical aspect of church buildings and in its organization had an attractive force, and as a religious system it had a marked effect on literature. It exerted religious influence on many literary-minded young men and women through its excellent system of mission schools. Also, the doctrines of Christianity possess a strong social quality, and it was this which nurtured the Christian socialist literature of Kinoshita Shōkō and others. It was also responsible for the creation of novels and plays describing the domestic, social, and spiritual struggles that accompanied the new occupation of minister, such as Nakamura Shun'u's (Yoshizō) *Ichijiku* (The Fig) (1901) and *Bokushi no Ie* (The Minister's Home) (1910). Furthermore, it gave rise to such religious literature as *Jūni no Ishizuka* (The Twelve Stone Mounds) (1885), a poem derived from Jewish history, by Yuasa Hangetsu (Yoshirō), a Dōshisha-educated Christian, and Tsunashima Ryōsen's (Eiichirō) *Byōkanroku* (The Record of an Illness) (1905). Roka's various works have a distinct Protestant flavor, and since Koshoshi was himself a minister, his works are filled with Christian faith. The various writers of the Shirakaba school assimilated the Christian spirit in their own experience. It should be mentioned, however, that in almost every case the influence which Meiji Christianity exerted on writers was through the medium of Tolstoy's works.

In the area of Catholicism, together with the trend to study *Kirishitan-mono* and *Namban-mono* (works relating to the Jesuit mission in Japan in the late Ashikaga and early Tokugawa Periods), in the late Meiji Period there flourished works which treated in a Romantic manner this nostalgia for the Christianity of the feudal era. In the summer of 1907 Hakushū and Mokutarō visited Nagasaki, crossed over to Amakusa, and talked with the Roman Catholic priest in the church at Ōemura; from these experiences there emerged two poetical works, Hakushū's *Amakusa Gaka* (Elegant Songs of Amakusa) and Mokutaro's *Amakusa Kumi* (An Amakusa Collection). Mokutarō also wrote such a play as *Nambanji Monzen* (In Front of the Gate of the Southern Barbarian Temple) in 1909. Since these works looked upon Christianity of the feudal period more as the symbol of a Romantic yearning, they do not have any real religious significance. They are undoubtedly a manifestation of the influence which Christianity exerted on Meiji literature, but they resurrected the Japanese attitude that prevailed at the time of its first introduction that it was a strange foreign creed, and substituted for its doctrines a sensuous charm, so that perhaps they should be considered as a manifestation of a kind of anti-Christian spirit. However, when we come to Rofū, a true Catholic spirit emerges in poetry.

Christianity had already entered before the Meiji Era, but at that time it had been considered to be an evil foreign creed. After Meiji, however, it was accepted as a world religion, and the influence it exerted on Meiji literature was in the direction of universalizing it. Perhaps its universalizing influence was slight when compared to the intellectualization of Meiji literature and its transformation into a science, but still it should not be overlooked. The above-mentioned Roman Catholic works consisted of an introduction of medieval elements from world literature into Japanese literature, but we must not forget that, in the contrary sense of modernization, Protestantism's profound self-introspection and sense of sin accelerated the awakening of the modern spirit of individualism in Japan. The latter has a very close relation with the Romantic spirit in modern literature. Tōkoku is unique in having testified to the awakening of a Romantic ego in the Japanese literary world, and in his consciousness of *naibu seimei* (the interior life) we can see that he tried to approach the God of Christianity.

When compared to Christianity, the connection of Shintō and Buddhism with literature is slight. As we shall see later, the literary expression of these religions was largely based on the individual religious consciousness of the writers, and it had little relation to social religious groupings or institutions. Of course Shintō acquired considerable strength through the return-to-the-past movement of the Restoration, and it achieved a position of almost a state religion, replacing the Buddhism that was subjected to attack in early Meiji; thus, socially it was of extraordinary importance. Intellectually it was linked with chauvinism and had considerable popularity, and yet this was not reflected in literature. The epic poems of Kyūkin and Ariake drew on old legends for their material, but we cannot say that the ideas of Shintō were expressed in a religious way. In Hōmei there is praise for the ideas of the ancient past, but he was seeking his own particular kind of instinctivism and life-worship (*seimeishugi*) in the simple life of the prehistoric era.

Buddhism, when compared to Shintō, made its appearance in the works of many writers, particularly those with a Romantic tendency. But this was more the Buddhist spirit itself, which is such an important component of Japanese tradition, emerging, and did not mean that it accompanied a revival of Buddhism. Rohan and Kyōka both expressed Buddhist ideas. In Ōgai and Shikō the life of Nichiren, one of the important Japanese religious leaders of the early feudal period, formed the main theme of their plays, and Hakusei wrote an epic poem dealing with the life of Sakyamuni, but again this was merely a taking of the material from Buddhism. Chogyū's Nichirenism alone was based on a conscious conversion to the spirit of Nichiren, but even this was not Buddhism so much as a response to the individual doctrines and personality of Nichiren, for Chogyū found in this intense priestly personality an adequate philosophy after having left Japanism and having become interested in Nietzsche's Superman.

Buddhism, unlike Shintō which became a state religion, and unlike Christianity which advanced from a Western religion to a world religion, found difficulty in securing a strong position in Meiji society; although it did produce a few men with a burning faith, such as Kiyosawa Mitsuyuki in Jōdoshū (The Pure Land Sect) and Tanaka Chigaku in the Nichiren Sect, it was not a religion to move men of literature by the force of its social doctrine. We shall touch on the deep-rooted traditionalism of Buddhism when we later come to speak about the universalization of Meiji literature, but there is nothing particularly significant to say about its social content. This stems of course from the degeneration of Buddhism's social position.

Thus, the rise of Romanticism and spirituality (*seishinshugi*) in mid-Meiji, from after the Sino-Japanese War until the Russo-Japanese War, although accompanied by somewhat of a revival of traditionalism, was nevertheless maintained by the Christian faith and a creed of aestheticism. Looked at from the ethical point of view, it advanced from the awakening of the individual in the direction of humanism, and in certain instances, it took a religious direction from there in an approach to God. This humanism had as its goal the acquiring of a love for all mankind, and this was to be arrived at through the freedom of the individual. Men like Roka sought for this spirit in the land of its birth, went to Jerusalem, and visited Tolstoy in his home in Jasnaja Poljana. This current of thought was somewhat obstructed by the rise of Naturalism, and once again there emerged a world dominated by a materialistic, natural scientific, and mechanistic view of life, but even in this period this spirituality certainly did not die.

When Neo-Idealism arose in late Meiji, the Nietzsche-type existentialism (*seimeishugi*), which had a Romantic direction, grew into a new kind of Bergson-Eucken-type life philosophy (*seimei-tetsugaku*) and religious philosophy, and the Tolstoy-type humanism began to emerge as the humanitarianism of the Shirakaba group. Concurrently, the art-for-art's-sake movement tried to find a new ethic in decadence and hedonism, and this caused either the development toward a religious mysticism or symbolism, or else an attempt to taste the mystery of a forceful modern life in the midst of a Satanism that praised the beauty of evil. Herein a new *fin-de-siècle* ethic and religion were sought, and a way of life for the new century was discovered. From the end of Meiji into early Taishō a second period of Europeanization appeared, as in early Meiji, and while on the surface it seemed to be a world dominated by nationalism, actually, ideas praising the liberty of the individual penetrated to the deepest levels of society, and the literary world received their influence and became the place where the new ethic and religion were espoused. The group of writers who gathered in the Ryūdokai, the new women's group which joined the Seitōsha (The Bluestocking Society), the young Hedonists who feasted in the Pan no Kai (The Society of the Devotees of Pan), the aristocratic idealists of the Shirakaba, the Neo-Idealist writers and scholars around Sōseki, all took upon themselves this new spirit, and *Subaru* and *Shirakaba* became the magazines that were eagerly read by the young intellectuals, while such novels as Sōhei's *Baien* (Soot and Smoke) and Sōseki's *Sanshirō* attempted to depict the new type of love according to the new type of woman. Fūyō, Tengai, and Katai tried to resolve the problems of a morality of love and marriage which had previously formed the starting-point of such men as Shōyō and Futabatei, in a Naturalistic way, as problems in the world of heredity and instinct, but Sōseki, Ōgai, Saneatsu, and Naoya looked on them from an idealistic viewpoint as problems in humanity. In either case, this indicates that the awakening of the self gave rise to the treating in literature of the serious problems of life, and that this trend was reflected in society and changed its ethical position.

We have seen above how Meiji literature maintained its relationship with such areas of spiritual civilization as science, morality, and religion. Now let us look for awhile at what relationship it had with the various areas of art itself.

First of all, the works which employ the lives of various artists as literary material are rather numerous. When we look at the area of the plastic arts, Rohan's *Gojū no Tō* (The Five-Storied Pagoda) uses the building of a five-storied pagoda as its main theme, his *Fūryūbutsu* has a sculptor of Buddhist statues as its main character, and *Fūryūma* a metal-carver, while Ichiyō's *Umoregi* (The Fossil Wood) has a ceramist painter as its main character; indeed, we certainly cannot say that there are few examples. In these works the spirit of the artist is expressed, and there are many where this takes the form of a complete giving of oneself to an Oriental art. And yet it is not merely an expression of a traditional spirit, for we are able to consider the selection of this kind of material as the result of a general deepening of interest, under Western influence, in various areas of art. Indeed this interest in various arts arose largely when, after the introduction of Western aesthetics and studies of art, it became known that in the West there was a great respect for art. In the case of such men as Rohan this is perhaps not so significant, but Ōgai's translated work *Umoregi* (The Fossil Wood) (not to be confused with Ichiyō's short novel of the same title) describes the life of a musician of genius, and in the way in which it shows how music touches the soul of man it undoubtedly had considerable influence. The principal character of another of his translations, *Sokkyōshijin*, is a poet, and Meiji writers may have derived from it the idea of making an artist the protagonist of their novels.

From the fact that the main character of Ōgai's *Utakata no Ki* is an art student named Kyosei and that of Sōseki's *Kusamakura* (The Grass Pillow) is also an artist, we can understand to what extent the spirit of painting mingled and fused with that of literature. In some ways Kyosei is modeled after the painter in the Western style, Harada Naojirō, and he is a character who has embraced the spirit of a Western artist, but the painter of *Kusamakura* can be considered as modeled after Sōseki himself, who went from the production of water colors to that of the Southern school of Chinese painting, and while he is to a certain extent Western, he very largely tries to create an Oriental elegance; by the comparison of only these two characters, we are able to learn of the introduction of the artistic spirit of East and West into Meiji literature.

In the area of music and acting, the actress of Kyōka's *Teriha Kyōgen*, or "The Farce of Teriha," and the *nō* actor of *Uta Andon* are significant and indicate the understanding of this realm by the author whose mother was a younger sister of a *nō* master. This also forms an interesting contrast with the Western-style dancer of Ōgai's *Maihime*, or "The Dancing Girl." Fūyō's *Rembo Nagashi* (A Flood of Affection) treats of love between a noted violinist and a genius of the *shakuhachi*, and his *Katsura Shimoji* (Beneath the Wig) has as its main theme the loves of an actress, and in both of these novels the flavor of the musical and dramatic worlds emerges. These works largely treat of these artistic worlds in a realistic manner. This is true also of the treatment in Tengai's *Hatsusugata* (The New Year's Dress) of the main female character who is an expert of the *kiyomoto* ballad drama.

We note that generally the novels that have artists as the main characters or have their theme in the pursuit of art or in an affection for aesthetic ideals are works with a Romantic tendency. Even if realistic works do use such characters, they look merely at the aspects of everyday or social life, and the artistic spirit is not an important object. The works of Japanese Naturalism rather have the tendency to make the writer himself the main character, and the external and intellectual life of the novelist is always treated, but since he is also a realist, there is no particular emphasis on the aesthetic and artistic levels; there is the tendency, therefore, to treat the protagonist as simply another human being, or rather as another animal or creature of instinct. Tōson's *Suisai Gaka*, or "The Water-Color Artist," makes use of the life history of Maruyama Banka, and while there is still some fervor for painting, the spiritual content of the novel is practically a confession of Tōson himself, and describes how the sexual life tramples art underfoot.

Thus, from the art and artists that were used as material we can detect the existence of romantic and aesthetic elements in Meiji literature. In Jun'ichirō's *Shisei* (The Tattooing) the author seeks for an aesthetic element even in a tattoo artist. Furthermore, these works that have an artistic beauty as their main theme mostly have an interest in things Japanese and Oriental; later Akutagawa Ryūnosuke came to describe this mystical artistic impulse in his *Jigoku-Hen* (Hell Screen), where he tells of a painter of the Heian Period, and in his *Shūsanzu* where the main character is a painter of the Ch'ing Dynasty.

In poetry and the drama of the Meiji Era the Romantic tendency forms the mainstream, and the spirit of reverence for art is to be found everywhere. Beginning with several poems of

Tōson in his *Wakanashū* (Young Greens Anthology) and *Ichi-yōshū* (One Small Craft), and with long poems of Kyūkin such as *Kokyōfu* (Song of an Old Mirror) in his *Botekishū* (The Evening Flute Anthology) and *Ishibori Shishi no Fu* (Song of a Stone Lion) in his *Yuku Haru* (The Departing Spring), there is in Meiji poetry a strong conversion to art; in the drama there are Haiya Shōyū and his son Saburōbei in Gekkō's *Sakura Shigure* (Rain at Cherry Time), the mask maker Yashaō in Kidō's *Shuzenji Monogatari* (Shuzenji Tales), and Kakiemon of Enomoto Torahiko's *Meikō Kakiemon* (The Famous Artisan Kakiemon). In the field of Western art, too, there is the appeal of the painters of the Pre-Raphaelite Brotherhood to the members of *Bungakkai*, the affection of the *Shirakaba* members for Klinger, Rodin, and Western art in general, and the influence of these plastic arts can be felt in their literary works. Ōgai gave his opinion freely on every kind of art and is the literary figure who had the broadest artistic interest. Aestheticians like Chogyū and Hōgetsu also approach Ōgai, and in Chogyū the study of the history of Japanese art is noteworthy.

When we consider next the utilization of literary material in art apart from literature itself, there is the example in 1902 of Kaburagi Kiyokata's *Ichiyō Joshi no Bozu* (A Drawing of Ichiyō's Grave), where a young girl who reminds one of Midori of Ichiyō's *Takekurabe* is sketched in a sentimental pose leaning on the gravestone, but it is very difficult to find many paintings that drew on Meiji literary works for their subject. There are the additional examples of the scroll paintings by Kiyokata of Kyōka's *Chūmonchō* (The Order-Book) and by Eikyū of Sōseki's *Kusamakura*, but these were produced during and after the Taishō Period. As for the filming of literary works, this truly flourishes today, but during the Meiji Period itself it was not significant.

We shall next indicate the most significant aspects of the union of painting and literature as expressed in the binding, design, and illustrations of works of literature. From the beginning of Meiji on, in newspapers, magazines, and books, it became the practice to insert illustrations and frontispieces in novels and plays, and thus a type of professional illustrator emerged. Actually this was a Japanese tradition from the Heian Period, and in the West we do not see this practice to this extent.

In early Meiji the *ukiyoe* woodblock prints of the previous era prevailed, but various aspects of the Enlightenment became the subject of color prints and began to be sold ; this movement extended into the realm of illustrations, and such men as Hōki and Kiyochika particularly distinguished themselves. In translated works and in the political novels, lithographs also appeared, and even a few Western-type copperplate prints were introduced. The cover of *Tōsei Shosei Katagi* was a color print, and there were a colored frontispiece by Kokuhō and illustrations by Kokuhō, Keishū, and Nagahara Kōtarō (Shisui). It is said that the illustrations of the Western-style painter, Nagahara, were included at his request but that they were not well received. Thereafter illustrations of novels became the work of painters in the traditional Japanese style. For example, in *Ukigumo* there were the illustrations of Hōnen and Gekkō (different Chinese characters from the author of *Sakura Shigure*), in *Ninin Bikuni Iro Zange* (Two Nuns' Love Confessions) those of Hōnen and Shōtei, in *Fūryūbutsu* those of Fūko, in *Konjiki Yasha* of Keishū, and in *Sora Utsu Nami* (The Heaven-Striking Waves) of Hanko. Kōyō was particularly fastidious about the illustrations for his novels, and in the last volume of his *Sanninzuma* (Three Wives) he had the three great artists, Keishū, Eisen, and Nempō, collaborate to draw the three wives, Kōbai, O-Sai, and O-Tsuya, while in his *Tajō Takon* there were twenty-six illustrations by Takeuchi Keishū, Watanabe Shōtei, Hashimoto Chikanobu, Toshiyoshi, Toshimine, Ogata Gekkō (the illustrator of *Ukigumo*), Kajita Hanko, Migita Nen'ei, Mishima Shōsō, Watanabe Kinshū, Suzuki Kason, Tomioka Eisen, Toyohara Kunichika, Yamada Keichū, Kubota Beisen, Kobori Tomone, Kobayashi Kiyochika, Terasaki Kōgyō, Murata Tanryō, and Shimomura

Izan, and they each had an interesting title. In addition to the illustrators mentioned above, there were Hirafuku Suian, Shō-getsu, Utagawa Kunimatsu, Inano (Nenkō) Toshitsune, Matsumo-to Senji, Ichijō Seibi, Miyagawa Shuntei, Ryokusui, Kobayashi Eikō, Yamanaka Kodō, and Kaburagi Kiyokata. One of the rea-sons that Tengai's *Makaze Koikaze* (The Winds of Demons and Love) had such an unprecedented reception in the *Yomiuri* was said to have been the force of Kajita Hanko's illustration of a girl student in clear, beautiful lines.

The insertion of Western-style illustrations in novels is said to have begun formally with those of Nakazawa Hiromitsu in the book version of this same *Makaze Koikaze*, and from this time on both in content and in illustrations the novel became Western. The frontispiece of *Futon*, which was serialized in *Shinshōsetsu* (The New Novel), was the work of Kobayashi Shōkichi, and the illustrations in *Hakai* were by Kaburagi Ki-yokata, but they were done in the Western style. Among the Western-style painters, Kuroda Kiyoteru, Koyama Shōtarō, Shimomura Izan, Nagahara Kōtarō, Nakazawa Hiromitsu, Hashi-moto Kunisuke, Nakamura Fusetsu, and Fujishima Takeji strove to transform all of literature into a vehicle for painting. After the rise of Naturalism, however, the intellectual content of the novel became foremost, and since description of the faces and dress of the characters was no longer emphasized, there grad-ually developed the tendency to eliminate both illustrations and frontispieces. In Sōseki's works also, there were at first Hashi-guchi Goyō's lavish bindings and frontispieces, but later his work consisted of only the cover design. It was only when novels were serialized in newspapers that the custom of daily insertion of illustrations remained, and indeed still prevails today.

Anthologies of New Style poetry and of traditional Japanese verse forms also had illustrations, but the format of the book was especially emphasized. In *Wakanashū* there are many illustrations by Nakamura Fusetsu, in *Nijūgogen* (The Twenty-Five Strings) there are seven heliotype illustrations by Okada

Saburōsuke, and in *Shunchōshū* there are a frontispiece and illustrations by Aoki Shigeru. In *Jashūmon* (The Evil Faith) (*i. e.*, Christianity) are included many illustrations and cuts by Ishii Hakutei and illustrations by Mokutarō. And yet the gold-on-dark-green cover design of *Nijūgogen*, the exotically beautiful covers of *Jashūmon* and *Omoide* (Recollections), and the novel bindings patterned after Dehmel's poetic anthology *Haien* (The Abandoned Garden), attracted the eye much more than the frontispieces and the cuts.

The noteworthy thing about bookbinding in the Meiji Era is that it was of considerable artistic merit, on a par with the art of mounting Japanese prints. Of course it made an advance under the influence of Western bookbinding, but we must not forget that it was also in the long tradition of the illustrated scroll tales, the *nara-ehon* of the Muromachi and early Edo Periods, and the Edo woodblock books.

The relationship of Meiji literature with painting, then, is as traced above. As far as sculpture, architecture, and the industrial arts are concerned, there is no direct connection with literature. However, as stated above, these areas of art were used as subject matter in the novel and poetry. Of course bookbinding itself is a kind of industrial art, but in its direct relation to literature there is nothing important to say.

In the realm of music, New Style poetry was often set to music, but in its early period there are many more examples of its having been used as songs. The setting to music of Naobumi's *Kōjo Shiragiku no Uta* (The Song of the Filial Daughter Shiragiku), *Sakurai no Ketsubetsu* (Sakurai's Farewell), and *Mutsu no Fubuki* (The Mutsu Blizzard) took place rather long after the poems already existed. The words for Bansui's *Kōjō no Tsuki* (The Moon on the Ruined Castle) were written in 1898 when the Tōkyō Music School was compiling an anthology of songs for secondary schools; Taki Rentarō added the music, and it was later included in *Chūgaku Shōka* (Middle School Songs) (1901). It is thought that Ōwada Tateki's *Tetsu-*

dō Shōka (Railroad Songs) and numerous other songs were, from the beginning, written to be sung. In the New Style poetry, contrary to what one might expect, there are few instances in Meiji of composers setting poems to music, and the addition of artistic scores to the works of Hakushū and Rofū took place after the beginning of Taishō, while the setting to music of Tōson's *Yashi no Mi* (The Cocoanut) and Ariake's *Matsurika* (The Flower of the *Matsuri*) was even later. In traditional Japanese music there is the example of Ōgai's writing by request the words for a *satsuma biwauta, Chōsokabe Nobuchika* (1903), and it is difficult to mention all of the *biwauta, kotouta, yōkyoku, sokkyoku,* and *naniwabushi* for which words were written.

There is of course an exceedingly close relationship between literature and drama and the dance, as evinced by the dramatization of novels and the writing of plays for stage representation, but we shall touch upon it in a later chapter when we discuss the drama itself. Although the relationship between painting and literature is very close, it is doubtful whether it is close enough to make a new synthetic art. In the Meiji Era it was realized, however, that the simple drama, or the dance and musical drama, together with literature and the other arts, do form a synthetic art. In the staging of the new *kabuki* and in the stage effects of the *shimpa-geki* (the New School drama) there are features, undreamed of in the Edo Era, which are worthy of world notice. Such plays as *Shinkyoku Urashima* and *Nambanji Monzen* (In Front of the Gate of the Southern Barbarian Temple) were first conceived of as impossible dreams and yet were later realized.

3. *The Universalization of Meiji Literature*

We can consider the introduction of Western literature in the Meiji Era as a manifestation of the heartfelt desire to universalize Japanese literature. Let us first look at the situation with regard to translation. Translation is a distinctive feature of the literary activity of this period, and its vicissitudes for the most part kept pace with those of the literary world in general. We are able to divide this translation activity into four periods.

Until about 1887 there was no fixed objective, and since it was a period of utterly disordered translation, there was very little idea of selecting works of a literary value ; thus, such translations as Nakamura Masanao's *Saikoku Risshi-Hen* (Biographies of Self-Made Men of Western Countries) of Samuel Smiles' *Self-Help*, published in 1871, can be considered representative of the tendencies of this period. It was only after the popular adaptation of such works as *Robinson Crusoe* and *The Arabian Nights* and with the appearance of Oda (Niwa) Jun'-ichirō's free translation of Bulwer-Lytton's *Ernest Maltravers* and *Alice* under the title *Karyū Shunwa* (A Spring Tale of Flowers and Willows) (the first three sections were published in October 1878 and the fourth section in January 1879) that we see translations of purely literary works. However, since Bulwer-Lytton, the author of this latter work, had studied law and was active in the political world, there was the tendency to think of this work as a political novel, and this attitude continued until much later.

Of course it is not to be thought that the translator necessarily carried out his work with a political motive, and Shōyō's translations which followed these earlier works, in particular, had a literary objective. And yet, generally speaking, these works were not received from a purely artistic standpoint. Furthermore, apart from the works of Shakespeare, those that occupied the central position were the novels of such politicians as Bulwer-Lytton and Disraeli and the science novels of Jules Verne. Also, despite the fact that at this time in Europe it was already the period of the maturity of Naturalism, there was hardly any attempt made to introduce the most recent literary currents of thought. Instead, works of every period of English and French literature were introduced in the most indiscriminate manner. There was no established method of translation either, and extracts and adaptations were numerous, while the style was either that of *kambun* (Sinico-Japanese) or of *gesaku* (light, or lower order fiction), and there were few attempts at anything new. Only the *Shintaishishō* (1882) was the starting-point of a new poetic form, although the style of the translation was still somewhat awkward and the contents consisted of rather out-dated English and American poems.

In 1888, with Futabatei's translation of a section of Turgenev's *Sportsman's Sketches* under the title *Aibiki* (Rendezvous) and of Turgenev's *Three Encounters* under the title *Meguriai* (Chance Meetings), there was the first introduction of literature, particularly modern literature, in a fresh colloquial style. At about the same time, Morita Shiken published successively translations of Jules Verne's *Michael Strogoff* under the title *Mekura Shisha* (The Blind Envoy) and the section entitled "Hubert" from Victor Hugo's *Choses Vues* under the title *Tantei Yūberu* (The Detective Hubert) (1889). Even though his style was not entirely free from *kambun* influence, he was thorough-going in his method, and it was a brilliant translation of high literary value.

Concurrently, the members of Ōgai's Shinseisha translated the lyric poetry of various nations and published it in 1889 under the title of *Omokage*; in the drama this same group brought out translations of Lessing's *Emilia Galotti* under the title of *Ori Bara* (The Plucked Rose) (1889-1892) and Calderón's *The Mayor of Zalamea* under the title of *Shirabe wa Takashi Gitarura no Hitofushi* (A Guitar Song with High Notes) (1889); and also at the same time it brought out translations of European (primarily German) and American short stories, beginning with Hoffmann's *Fraulein von Scudéry* under the title *Tama o Idaite Tsumi Ari* (There Is a Sin in the Cherishing of Jewels) (1889). All of these works were published in 1892 in the collection *Minawashū* (The Water Spray Anthology). In that year, too, Ōgai began his translation of Andersen's *The*

Improvisator and charmed many readers with the beauty of his style. And yet Ōgai in his work of translation did not necessarily select literary masterpieces, but rather works that are commonly not even listed in the literary histories; he appears to have selected them at will from various areas, and without being restricted by a concern for linguistic accuracy, created a beautiful and elegant style which gave his work the highest literary value and which, together with Ueda Bin's translations of poetry, constitute an art form higher than the original. Indeed we must largely credit Ōgai with exciting the desire for and interest in foreign literature in the first half of the Meiji Era. However, this interest was fostered by the partial Japanization of Western works.

From this year until the following year, 1893, Uchida Fuchian (Roan) translated Dostoevsky's *Crime and Punishment* from an English translation and published the first two volumes. In the same year of 1893, Takayasu Gekkō translated Ibsen's *The Doll's House* and *The Enemy of the People* and Dostoevsky's *Injury and Insult*. In the following year, 1894, Koganei Kimiko translated a chapter of Lermontov's *Modern Heroes* under the title *Yokusenki* (Record of Bathing in a Spring), Shioi Ukō translated Scott's *The Lady of the Lake*, and the biographies of authors entitled *Jūni Bungō* (Twelve Literary Giants) began to be published by the Min'yūsha. Thus, by the time of the Sino-Japanese War we must recognize that the first phase of the introduction of modern European writers had ended. Many of the translated works of this period, looked at even from today's standpoint, are worthy of consideration.

In 1896 Futabatei began his translation of Turgenev's *Unrequited Love*, and Shōyō's translation of Shakespeare's *Hamlet* began to appear serially in *Waseda Bungaku*. Shiken, also, in the same year published his translation of Jules Verne's *A Two-Year Vacation* under the title *Jūgo Shōnen* (Fifteen Youths), and thereby created the first great work of children's literature in the Meiji Era. From this time on, we can say we enter the third period, if we consider the first period as lasting until 1887 and the second until 1896. This third period is really a continuation of the second, but the translation of literary works was carried on with even greater discrimination and care. If we mention the major works, they are as follows : Hugo's *The Last Day of a Condemned Man* by Shiken in 1896, Turgenev's *Rudin* by Futabatei in 1897 ; Burnett's *Little Lord Fauntleroy* by Wakamatsu Shizuko in 1897 ; a collection of translations and short original works under the title *Miotsukushi* by Ueda Bin in 1901 ; Hugo's *Les Misérables* by Kuroiwa Ruikō in 1902 ; and Dumas' *La Dame aux Camélias* by Osada Shūtō (Tadaichi) in 1903.

Furthermore, Tozawa Koya (Seiho) and Asano Hyōkyo (Wasaburō) collaborated on a plan for the translation of Shakespeare's complete works and published ten volumes before Tsubouchi Shōyō began his translation. Koya also did translations of Lafcadio Hearn (known in Japan as Koizumi Yakumo) and Rossetti, while Hyōkyo produced translations of Goldsmith, Irving, and Dickens. We should also mention the translation work of Hirata Tokuboku, Baba Kochō, Togawa Shūkotsu, Hara Hōichian, Tayama Katai, Matsui Shōyō, Kimura Takatarō, and, somewhat later, that of Tobari Chikufū.

In 1905, the year that the Russo-Japanese War ended, Uchida Roan began to publish his translation of Tolstoy's *Resurrection* in the newspaper *Nihon*, and as a brilliant translation of a modern Russian novel it is considered second only to that of Futabatei. Moreover, Ueda Bin collected his translations of modern French poetry which had appeared from time to time in *Teikoku Bungaku*, and published them in one volume under the title *Kaichōon* where they became the agency which changed the whole course of the world of poetry. There were further excellent translations of Russian novels such as Futabatei's of Andreev's *A Record of Blood and Laughter* in 1908, and in the field of modern French poetry there was Nagai Kafū's *Sangoshū* (A Coral Anthology) in 1913.

We can call the period from the Russo-Japanese War until the Taishō Era the fourth period of translation. This was a time when, in the realm of the novel and poetry, there was an attempt to cull only the best from modern Western literature, and this work of translation kept pace with the rise of Naturalism in the literary world. However, an even more noteworthy characteristic of this period is the rapid introduction of the modern Western drama that accompanied the establishment of the modern drama in Japan; this work did not stop at translation, but rather the plays were presented successively on the stage, and most of the translations were done with that goal in mind.

Ōgai was the central figure in the translation of modern drama, and through the medium of the German language he translated many new plays of almost every country of Europe. Such translations of his as that of Hauptmann's *Einsame Menschen* (Lonesome People) and Ibsen's *John Gabriel Borkmann* were performed by the Jiyū Gekijō (The Free Theatre). These were all plays with many acts, but Ōgai also translated many one-act plays by means of dictation, and these were collected in *Hitomaku-Mono* (One-Act Plays) (1909) and *Zoku Hitomaku-Mono* (One-Act Plays, Continued) (1910).

Shōyō, who ranks with Ōgai, presented his Shakespearean plays, *Hamlet* and *The Merchant of Venice*, on the stage of the Bungei Kyōkai, but the association, in order to satisfy modern taste, also presented such plays as Ibsen's *The Doll's House*, translated by Hōgetsu, in 1911, and Sudermann's *Heimat* in 1912. Kusuyama Masao of the Waseda group also was active in the translation of plays, as well as in their production and in drama criticism, and he brought out such plays as Gogol's *The Inspector-General* in 1911, and Shaw's *Man of Destiny* in the same year. Further details of the translation and presentation of plays will be given in the later section on drama.

Among the translations mentioned above, those of the earlier period particularly were almost adaptations, and the translator did his work freely on the basis of his own plan. This practice of consciously producing adaptations continued for a long time. In the early half of Meiji the idea of introducing Western works faithfully was not yet developed and the tendency was overwhelmingly toward Japanization. For example, in such works as Suematsu Kenchō's and Ninomiya Kumajirō's translation, *Tanima no Himeyuri* (Lily of the Valley) (1888), both the characters' names and the place-names are presented in Japanese. With the passage of time, however, we see the gradual appearance of efforts to give a faithful introduction of the Western taste. But, at the same time, efforts were being made in another direction, that is, to write stories patterned after Western works in a rather intangible way.

This latter tendency was most strikingly displayed by the adaptations. For example, Kōyō searched far and wide for material and used it to write numerous adaptations. His *Natsu Kosode* (Summer Sleeves) (1892), *Koi no Yamai* (The Malady of Love) (1893), and *Yaedasuki* (The Double Sash) (1898) were adaptations from Molière's works, while *Reinetsu* (Cold Fever) (1894), *Taka Ryōri* (Hawk Dishes) (1895), *Sankajō* (Three Commandments) (1895), and *Tebiki no Ito* (The String of Guidance) (1898) were adapted from *The Decameron*. In addition to these, Kōyō adapted the stories *Yamato Shōkun* (Princess Yamato) (1899) and *Tōzai Tanryo no Yaiba* (The Short-Sighted Sword of East and West) (1900) from *The Arabian Nights* and derived *Muki Tamago* (The Peeled Boiled Egg) (1891) and *Tonari no Onna* (The Woman Next-Door) (1894) from the works of Zola. Katai relates in his memoirs, *Tōkyō no Sanjūnen* (Thirty Years in Tōkyō), that Kōyō had shown great admiration for the concise description displayed by Zola in *La Faute de l'Abbé Mouret*. There are indications that Kōyō borrowed material from Zola's *L'Oeuvre* in writing his *Muki Tamago*.

There are numerous other examples which, though not genuine adaptations, indicate quite clearly that they were written with material borrowed from Western literature. Bimyō's *Tategoto-Zōshi* (The Tale of the Harp) (1885), published in the first and second volumes of *Garakuta Bunko*, employed material obtained from the biography of Alfred the Great. There are reasons to believe that he was influenced by Shakespeare, Milton, Chaucer, and Thackeray in writing *Fūkin Shirabe no Hitofushi* (1887). Though the origin of the material is unknown, Rohan's *Tsuyu Dandan* (Immaculate Dewdrops) was based on descriptions of scenes near New York City. Tengai's *Hatsusugata* (The New Year Dress) (1900) and Fūyō's *Seishun* (Youth) (1905) were influenced by, or rather, as explained in later paragraphs, were imitations of foreign works. The former was based on *Nana* and the latter on *Rudin*. Also, it is a widely accepted fact that Katai's *Futon* (The Quilt) (1907) and Tōson's *Hakai* (The Breaking of the Commandment) (1906) were written respectively under the influence of *Einsame Menschen* and *Crime and Punishment*, while Sōhei's *Baien* (Soot and Smoke) (1909) was influenced by *Il Trionfo della Morte*.

Although in Ōgai we do not see direct signs of adaptations in his novels, it was different with his dramas. For example, Ōgai based *Tamakushige Futari Urashima* (The Two Urashimas of the Jewelled Box) (1902) on *Faust*, and borrowed the historical episodes concerning the Indian province of Sind in writing *Purumūra* (Prumoula). Among Sōseki's earlier works, *Maboroshi no Tate* (The Phantom Shield) (1905) and *Kairokō* (The Song of Evanescence) (1905) were written on the basis of legends of King Arthur's days or of the author's own imagination. Also, in writing *Wagahai wa Neko de Aru* (1905), Sōseki was betraying the influence of the English eighteenth century satirical works. And in writing *Sanshirō* (1908), the author himself confessed that he was influenced by Sudermann's *Es War*.

Turning to the field of poetry, it is needless to say that the so-called New Style poets were greatly influenced by Western poetry. Yuasa Hangetsu's *Jūni no Ishizuka* (The Twelve Mounds of Stones) was an epic dealing with the legends of the Old

Testament. Tōson, in his adolescent days, was influenced by the lyric poets of the English Romantic school, and modern English literary figures like J. A. Symonds, as well as by the classic poets, Shakespeare and Milton. Through English translations, he came in contact with the works of Dante, Boccaccio, Goethe, and Heine. It is almost unnecessary to say that his brilliant poem *Akikaze no Uta* (The Song of the Autumn Wind) was born under Shelley's influence. The romantics gathered around *Bungakkai* were all well-versed in the works of the Western Romantic school and made conscious efforts to recreate this school on native grounds, the typical example being Tōkoku, who borrowed his material from Byron's *Manfred* in writing the poem *Hōraikyoku* (The Song of Fairyland) (1891). Among later poets, the Symbolist Ariake was deeply influenced by Rossetti. It is needless to say that the establishment of the Symbolist school beginning with Ueda Bin was the result of the transplantation of French Symbolism on native ground.

In the foregoing paragraphs we have merely given a rough summary of the conspicuous examples. If we were to make a detailed research of all of the influences of foreign literature, however minor, this alone would constitute a separate book on comparative literature of considerable length.

That there was a striking inflow of foreign literature in the Meiji years is illustrated by the fact that the histories of Japanese literature written by foreign scholars like Aston, Florenz, and Gundert classify the whole period from Meiji onward as the period of European influence. In contrast with this impressive inflow of foreign literature, the export of native literature, though not very great, still comprised a considerable amount. For example, the histories of Japanese literature written by foreigners, to which we referred a moment ago, devoted space to the introduction and criticism of works written in the Meiji Era and later. In addition to these, there were not a few translations of Japan's classic poetry, and some of them, of necessity, overlapped into the Meiji Period. And yet translations of works exclusively of the Meiji Period also were numerous.

In the list of these translations the most important position naturally was occupied by novels. But in these translations of Japanese novels, the emphasis was not on works which were based on peculiar native taste but on those which could be easily understood by foreigners. Thus, translations of Kunikida Doppo's novels numbered more than ten, including *Men I Shall Never Forget* (*Wasureenu Hitobito*), *Fatalist* (*Ummeironja*), *Spring Bird* (*Haru no Tori*), *Driven To Death* (*Kyūshi*), *A Friend on Horseback* (*Bajō no Tomo*), *Der Biedermann* (*Shōjikimono*), and *Musashino*. Doppo was not directly influenced by native classics but, on the contrary, was a writer who developed under the influence of Christianity and poets like Wordsworth. His literary method was to penetrate directly into the serious problems of life and as such had a universal appeal. These were the chief reasons that the essence of his works could be communicated through translations.

For a similar reason, Tokutomi Roka's works also became the object of numerous translations. There are about ten different ones of his *Hototogisu*. In addition to these, about three or four of his other novels were translated, including *Kuroshio* (The Black Current) and *Omoide no Ki* (A Record of Recollections). As a matter of fact, Roka even became an object of research in China.

Natsume Sōseki was another writer whose works, especially the earlier ones written in the Meiji Period, became the object of numerous translations. These included *I Am a Cat* (*Wagahai wa Neko de Aru*), *Botchan*, *Unhuman Tour*** (*Kusamakura*), *Nihyakutōka*, *Red Poppy* (*Gubijinsō*), *Sanshirō*, and *La Porte* (*Mon*). Among them, there were four different translations of

---

* *Translator's Note*: This awkward and almost meaningless title was undoubtedly intended to convey the sense of Sōseki's philosophy of *hi-ninjō*, or non-human feeling, which is the theme of the work. *Kusamakura* literally is "a grass pillow" and means a travel or a journey.

Botchan. In addition to his novels, his essays were also translated freely.

Besides these three writers, the translation of works of Shimazaki Tōson, Mori Ōgai, and Ozaki Kōyō amounted to a considerable number, while there were scattered translations of works of such writers as Kōda Rohan, Futabatei Shimei, Higuchi Ichiyō, Oguri Fūyō, Hirotsu Ryūrō, Kinoshita Shōkō, Tayama Katai, Masamune Hakuchō, Nagai Kafū, Suzuki Miekichi, Ogawa Mimei, and Mushakōji Saneatsu. A surprising number of translations were made of works of a popular fiction writer like Murai Gensai. Numerous translations have been made of works of Tanizaki Jun'ichirō, Shiga Naoya, and Arishima Takeo, but, in the case of these writers, the emphasis was on those written in the subsequent Taishō Era. Akutagawa Ryūnosuke was another writer whose works were widely translated but, in his case, they belonged strictly to the Taishō Period.

In the drama, there were some translations of plays in the *kabuki* tradition, such as Tsubouchi Shōyō's *Shinkyoku Urashima* (The New Urashima) and *Kiri Hitoha* (One Leaf of Paulownia), and Okamoto Kidō's *Shuzenji Monogatari* (Shuzenji Tales). But the major emphasis was rather on the one-act plays of playwrights like Mushakōji Saneatsu and Kikuchi Kan. These translated dramas belonged largely to the Taishō Era ; among those of the Meiji Period were plays by Mori Ōgai, Tanizaki Jun'ichirō, and Nakamura Kichizō (Shun'u), but the number was negligible when compared to their translated novels. It is exceedingly rare to find separate translations of poetry. There were, however, translations of epics like Ochiai Naobumi's *A White Aster* (*Kōjo Shiragiku no Uta*), Rohan's *Leaving the Hermitage* (*Shutsuro*), and of *tanka* anthologies like Takuboku's *A Handful of Sand* (*Ichiaku no Suna*).

Also, there were relatively few translations of criticism and essays, but we do find an occasional one such as that of Chogyū's *Getsuya no Bikan ni Tsuite* (Concerning the Beauty of a Moonlit Night), Roka's *Nature and Men* (*Shizen to Jinsei*), and Tōkoku's *In Eulogy of Mt. Fuji* (*Fugaku no Shishin o Omou*). Most of them, however, were published in English magazines.

Most of the translations mentioned above appeared after the Meiji Era and were largely the work of Japanese translators. Naturally, it was too much to expect foreigners to undertake translations of contemporary literary works. However, Ōgai's *Maihime* was translated by F. W. Eastlake under the title *The Lady of the Dance* as early as 1907. The following year, translations of Futabatei's works were carried by a Russian magazine *Vostok* (East), published in Yokohama. In 1925, A. and M. Lloyd translated Kōyō's *Konjiki Yasha* under the title *Gold Demon*. Works of Sōseki and Roka were also translated by foreigners. Deserving special attention is the French translation of Sōseki's *Mon*, *La Porte* (*Traduit de Japonais avec un avant-propos par R. Martinie*, 1927).

The translation of native literary works of Meiji and later still continues today. Each year works are being translated and introduced abroad. Therefore, the examples we have given in the foregoing paragraphs are merely a small part of the literary translations made during the course of the years. Furthermore, we can suppose that not a few of these translated works have gained a warm reception in foreign countries.

As summarized in the foregoing paragraphs, the Meiji years saw a tremendous inflow of Western literature, which seemed to overflow its banks and flood the native literary circle. Although negligible when compared to this inflow, a certain amount of native literature was also introduced abroad. But, from this exchange of literature with the Western world, we must now shift our attention to the course of the currents of Oriental literature in the Meiji Period.

Naturally, this current was a feeble one when compared to the flood of Western literature, but still it cannot be ignored. The beginning of the modern age saw a cultural decline in China as well as in India, for these countries were being overwhelmed by the inflow of Western civilization, with the result that the transmission of new culture from these countries to Japan was almost nil. Although from the subsequent Taishō Period there were efforts to introduce the new literature of China into Japan, in the Meiji Period the Oriental cultural current appeared merely in the form of traditional culture and could only influence the native cultural world as such. Let us then examine the role played in Meiji literature by the Oriental spiritual culture which in the long course of years had been transfused into the blood of the native culture.

During Meiji of course Chinese characters were, as now, still employed, and Chinese poetry and prose were still written. Confucianism, Taoism, and Buddhism were still playing a living role in the formation of the national spirit. The Meiji writers, in this sense, were unable to eliminate the influence of these factors from their writings. This is indicated by the prominent display of a Chinese literary style in the writings of Kōyō and Rohan, and by the fact that both Ōgai and Sōseki were authors of skilful Chinese poems. During his study in Germany, Ōgai in fact wrote his diary in Chinese. Sōseki also employed Chinese in writing *Mokusetsuroku* (A Record of Wood Shavings). Even if we set aside these superficial aspects, we cannot deny that Meiji literature is still threaded through with the Oriental tradition.

The Oriental ideas were most richly displayed, and at the same time expressed in superior artistic form, by Rohan. His maiden work *Tsuyu Dandan* (Immaculate Dewdrops) seems to treat of a love affair between two Americans, but actually we can consider the Japanese *haiku* poet Ginchōshi as the true hero of the story. As the story unfolds, Ginchōshi impersonates a Chinese and comes to live in the suburbs of New York, where he enjoys a life bathed in an Oriental atmosphere of Zen-like detachment. Prior to this work, Rohan wrote a novel *Fūryū Zen Temma* (The Romantic Zen Demon of Heaven), but it was never fully realized. The hero of this novel is a man who arrives at the point of spiritual detachment where he is able to practise contemplation in a brothel. Parallel with his advocacy of the spirit of love of Christianity in his *Fūryū Satori* (Elegant Enlightenment) and other works, Rohan showed his inclination toward the spiritual emancipation of Buddhism in *Fūryūbutsu* (The Elegant Buddha) and *Taidokuro* (Facing the Skull). Besides, many suggestions are seen in his works of the influence of the Confucian concept of Heaven (*ten*) and of Taoist nihilism. In Rohan's works the Oriental sense of elegance (*fūryū*) takes the forms of eroticism (*kōshoku*), unworldliness (*shadatsu*), and refinement (*gashu*). It might be said that Rohan's series of elegant pieces (*fūryū-mono*) was actually a systematization of his *Weltanschauung*. Thus, the presence of this great author is excellent proof of the fact that the tradition of the East was the pillar of Meiji literature.

Kyōka, who comes next to Rohan in creating a romantic atmosphere in Meiji literature, although he lacked the idealism of Rohan, had a profound faith in the Kannon (the Goddess of Mercy), and in his stories such as *Kōya Hijiri* some Buddhist thought is discernible. In this regard, we cannot rightly comprehend Kyoshi's *Fūryū Sempō* (The Elegant Confession) or Sōseki's *Kusamakura* (The Grass Pillow), without reference to this faith. Zen philosophy is the most important element in Sōseki's literature. *Yume Jūya* (Ten Nights of Dreams) written in his early period, includes an account of a dream of Zen contemplation (*zazen*), and the character of Dokusen in the novel *Wagahai wa Neko de Aru* (I Am a Cat) represents Taoist philosophy in conjunction with that of Zen. Even the Naturalist Katai reveals an attitude of Mahāyāna Buddhism in his interpretation of Saikaku. Furthermore, in the Taishō Era his peculiar Buddhistic attitude of resignation is obvious in such works as *Zansetsu* (Remaining Snow) and *Aru Sō no Kiseki* (The Miracle of a Bonze).

Nichiren, perhaps the most significant religious figure in the Kamakura Era, was often introduced into literature because of his ardent and colorful character worthy of attention. There are Yamazaki Shikō's long epic *Nichiren Shōnin* (The Buddhist Saint Nichiren), and Ōgai's drama *Nichiren Seijin Tsujizeppō* (Nichiren's Wayside Preaching), and also an article in Nichiren's homage by Takayama Chogyū and Anezaki Chōfū. Another famed Buddhist priest, Shinran, did not become the subject of a literary work until the publication of *Shukke to Sono Deshi* (The Priest and His Disciples) of Kurata Momozō in the Taishō Era, but the spirituality of Kiyosawa Manshi, one of Shinran's followers, undoubtedly exerted much influence on the literary circle indirectly. Other than these, Hiraki Hakusei's drama in verse *Shaka* (Sakyamuni) and Kambara Ariake's lyric poem *Shingyō* (Absolute Faith) may be regarded as Buddhist works. To cite other examples, we have Ōgai's drama *Ikutagawa*, where in the last scene a priest reads Buddhist prayers, suggesting the spiritual emancipation of the heroine. As for *tanka*, there are Itō Sachio's serial work *Horobi no Hikari* (The Light of Death), Saitō Mokichi's *Shakkō* (Red Light) and Aizu Yaichi's *Nankin Shinshō* (The New Song of Nanking), all of which are a reflection of Buddhist philosophy; Kinoshita Mokutarō, known for his *namban* (literally, Southern Barbarian, referring to the Spaniards and Portuguese who came to Japan in the sixteenth century) taste, or romantic longing for things Occidental, had also a liking for Indian culture, and wrote *Indo-Ō to Taishi* (The King of India and the Prince) and other works showing his appreciation of Buddhist thought.

In our examination of the Oriental tradition in Meiji literature, we have seen mainly the influence of Buddhism. However, we also find the enduring influence of the ancient Chinese poets Tu Fu, Tao Yüan-ming, and others in those authors of the magazines *Bungakkai* and *Sanrai*. These Oriental philosophers did not make any systematic infiltration comparable to that of realism, humanism, Christianity, and socialism which were introduced into this country from the West. Although the influence may appear fragmentary, these schools of Oriental philosophy can be defined as undercurrents of Japanese literature which from time to time rose to the surface.

We have already referred to the traditions of Japan when we mentioned the style of Meiji literature and also to the relationship between nationalism (*kokusuishugi*) and the trend toward Westernization (*ōkashugi*). We should like to point out here simply that the traditional literature of Japan had deep roots in Meiji literature. Revaluation of the classical heritage was made in this period in various fields of literature, and this had a significant effect upon modern literary works. Such studies of great authors of the past and their works included the following: the revival of Saikaku through the efforts of Kōyō, Rohan, and Ichiyō; the study of Chikamatsu by Chogyū and the members of the Waseda group; the modernization of the *Genji Monogatari* by Kōyō and Akiko; recognition of Buson by Shiki and the *Hototogisu* group; revaluation of the *Manyō-shū* by the *Ashibi* and *Araragi* poets; the liking for the *Shin-kokinshū* on the part of poets in the Shinshisha tradition; and Chogyū's reappraisal of the *Heike Monogatari* and the writings of Nichiren. The revival of traditional literature was significant in that it enabled the authors to display the substance of it unawares, having the deepest roots in Meiji literature. As compared with this literary inheritance, most imported styles or views of literature from the Occident were significant in Meiji literature only in so far as they provided the impetus for the sloughing off of burdensome tradition and stimulated rapid progress.

This allows us to say, therefore, that it is clear that the Western literary trends, though essential to the modern literature of Japan, once imported, became mingled with the philosophy of the East which already had become part of the flesh and blood of the Japanese people. This naturally led to an eventual mixture of Oriental and Occidental thought. The antagonism between the two different philosophies developed in the form of the rivalry of nationalism and Westernizationism, but such antagonism actually made each concede to the other. We can easily discover that almost every great writer in the Meiji world was in his person a mixture of both thoughts in one form or another. Few were purely Japanese or purely Oriental, and few were categorically Occidental in their outlook. Ōgai, who did much in introducing the West to this country and himself acquired a European intellectual approach, devoted himself in the latter part of his life to research into the names of the eras (*gengō*) and the posthumous names of emperors, and came to hold the opinion that historical research in the Oriental fashion was the only field of activity where the originality of Japanese scholars could fully be displayed. It is almost superfluous to say that Shōyō, who first introduced Western realism as early as 1885 and thus opened the way for Westernization and modernization of Meiji literature, profoundly appreciated the traditional literature and realized the unification of these two elements in a number of his works.

We cannot but feel that the works of any great writer of the Meiji Era, be he Kōyō, Rohan, or Tōson, were after all essentially Japanese, despite obvious influences of Western thought upon them. It also is undeniable that Naturalism, which appeared in the closing years of the Meiji Era at the peak of the influence of Western literature, once in Japan became a Japanese Naturalism with its own peculiar characteristics, and also that the Symbolist poetry of the West was totally Japanized and acquired a direction characteristically Japanese. In this regard, we should point out that the pioneer in this field, Ueda Bin, was a man with a profound understanding of Western literature, as well as a poet-scholar who gave excellent expression to peculiarly Japanese feelings. Was the poetry in *Kaichōon* essentially Western or of a Japanese style ? It is difficult to decide, and we consider the best answer is that it was neither one nor the other but a perfect mixture of both. Similarly, if asked whether Shūsei, the master of Japanese Naturalism, or Sōseki, the greatest author of philosophical novels, was essentially Japanese or Western, the most appropriate answer would be that he was the symbol of the unification of the West and Japan. Thus, Meiji literature indicated the possibility of a complete fusion of the literary currents of East and West, and, if it is not erroneous to call the result of such a fusion universal literature, Meiji literature then was the experiment for establishing it in the modern world. Indeed, we can further say that the experiment was to a large extent a success.

This assertion leads us to the conclusion that from our present vantage-point this Meiji literature of ours was the most remarkable microcosm of universal literature conceivable. In the following chapters we should like to cast light upon how this microcosm of such significance was created in this land of the Far East.

PART TWO THE MEIJI NOVEL

CHAPTER I THE TWILIGHT OF *GESAKU* WRITING
AND THE DAWN OF POLITICAL NOVELS

1. *The Remnant of* Gesaku-*Style Writers and Their Adaptation to the New Era*

The Edo-style *gesaku* writers were still on the scene during the period from the end of the Edo regime to the beginning of the Meiji Era.

If we check through the list of *gesaku,* we find that the following works appeared between 1852 and the early years of Meiji.

yomihon :
(storybooks)

Ehon Asakura Nikki (Asakura Pictorial Diary) by Shōtei Kinsui, 1852 ; *Seigetsu Kōki : Chiba Gunki* (The Brightness of the Stars and Moon : The Chiba Conspiracy) by Nisei Shunsui, 1861 ; *Sano Hōgiroku* (A Record of Revenge in the Sano Family) by Chisokkan Shōkyoku, 1861, etc.

kokkeibon :
(humorous books)

Myōchikurinwa : Shichihenjin (A Tale of the Wonderful Bamboo Forest : The Seven Eccentrics) by Baitei Kinō, 1857 ; *Kokkei Fuji Mōde* (The Amusing Trip to Mt. Fuji) by Kanagaki Robun, 1860, etc.

ninjōbon :
(love stories)

Shunshoku Koi no Somewake (The Crossroad of Love in Spring) by Jōno Saigiku, 1860 ; *Shunshoku Edo Murasaki* (Spring in Hazy Edo) by Sansantei Arindo, 1864 ; *Hana-Goyomi Fūjibumi* (Flower Calendar and Sealed Letters) by Sansantei Arindo, 1864, etc.

gōkan :
(collected volumes)

Hokusetsu Bidan : Jidai Kagami (A Noble Tale of the Snowy North : The Mirror of the Time) by Nisei Shunsui, 1855–1885 ; *Shiranui Monogatari* (Tales of White Thread) by Tanekazu, Nisei Tanehiko, and Tanekiyo, 1849–1885 ; *Shaka*

Hassō : Yamato Bunko (Tales of the Eight-Faced Buddha : A Home Library) by Mantei Ōga, 1845–1871 ; *Jiraiya Gōketsudan* (The Heroic Tales of Jiraiya) by Shōgan, Tanekazu, Tanekiyo, and others, 1839–1868, etc.

sharehon :   *Sunaharai* (The Sunaharai Story) by Ippen, 1857, (gay-quarter   etc.
novelettes)

In addition to these, Kanagaki Robun wrote *Bankoku Kōkai : Seiyō Dōchū Hizakurige* (Hiking Through the West on Shanks' Mare) (1870), *Ushiya Zōdan : Aguranabe* (Idle Talks in the Sukiyaki House) (1871), and *Kappa Sōden : Kiurizukai* (Imps' Talks on Science : How to Use Cucumbers) (1872), works which belong to the genre of *kokkeibon*. However, since the theme of these works was based on the new Meiji Era, they cannot be regarded as genuine Edo-style *gesaku* writing. For this reason, we shall refer to them in later paragraphs.

Virtually all of the works listed above were written in the Edo *gesaku* style. *Shiranui Monogatari*, for example, was published in serial form, comprising seventy-one parts in 1885, and upon completion was to be composed of ninety parts. It is regarded as the largest among *gōkan* (collected volumes). Almost all of the *gesaku* writers who took part in this kind of work were unable to make a living with the opening of the Meiji Era, and thus were forced to give up their *gesaku* style and adapt their literary life to the new age.

Let us trace the last remnants of *gesaku* writing until 1877. It seems that here the central figure was Robun.

Kanagaki Robun (Nozaki Bunzō) first earned his literary reputation by writing *Kokkei Fuji Mōde* in 1860. However, this work lacked originality and was a mere imitation of the writings of Samba and Ikku. In his subsequent works, *Osana-Etoki Bankoku-Banashi* (Children's Picture Book of the World) (1861) and *Yamato-Gana Seiyō Bunko* (Bookshelf of the West), also entitled *Naporeon Ichidaiki* (The Life of Napoleon) (1872),

Robun tried to introduce Occidental manners and customs to this country in a way similar to that of the scholars of Western studies. However, his works were nothing more than *gesaku*, and the fact that his historical writings lacked authenticity in certain points proved that he was not particularly well-versed in foreign affairs. Robun lacked the real ability to become an enlightenment writer. His true field, rather, was in making jokes and drawing caricatures—in short, in giving a light *gesaku* treatment of the new Meiji Era. The following two works are good examples.

Ushiya Zōdan : Aguranabe (Idle Talks in the Sukiyaki House) (1871), bearing another title *Doronken* (derived from a Dutch word meaning drunkard), was a piece set in the days when Western civilization was just beginning to enter Japan, effecting change in every phase of life. It deals with a change in one important aspect of life, namely that of diet. In the olden days it was not the custom to eat meat. But with the coming of the new age, people gradually became accustomed to adding beef to their diet, which resulted in the increasing popularity of sukiyaki houses. The novel purports to show life in a typical sukiyaki house, and in the chapters " The Opening of the Ports " and " Report on Foreign Ways " we learn that people of the time had already come to recognize the nutritional value of eating beef. The sukiyaki house is a meeting place of a variety of characters, including idlers, country warriors, dullards, merchants, etc. Assembled around a steaming meat pot, they talk idly about the old days and the new era just beginning. This plot is similar to that employed by Shikitei Samba in his *Ukiyoburo* (The Up-to-date Public Bath) and *Ukiyodoko* (The Up-to-date Barbershop). The satirical effect of the story is slight, and the whole thing is nothing more than old-fashioned *gesaku* writing. The only thing of note is that the author borrowed theme and material from the new age.

Bankoku Kōkai : Seiyō Dōchū Hizakurige (Hiking Through the West on Shanks' Mare) (Part I published in 1870 and Part

XV in 1876; Parts XII to XV were the work of Sōseikan) was no doubt an imitation of Jippensha Ikku's *Hizakurige*. In this imitation, Robun sends the heroes, Yajirobei and Kitahachi, on a trip to London, where in this unfamiliar foreign capital they find themselves in numerous embarrassing situations. The story ends with their return to their native country. Robun himself never traveled abroad. Apparently he wrote this story partly with the help of material collected from the reports of those who had actually traveled there and partly through sheer imagination. When compared with old *gesaku* pieces, this work is singular in at least one respect. It had a strong undertone of ridicule and mockery of the contemporary society, and in adopting this attitude Robun was following the only literary route left open for *gesaku* writers brought face to face with the emergence of a new civilization.

In the foregoing paragraphs we have touched upon the major works of Robun. However, there remains the problem of the extent to which he was bound to the ideology of the past and the extent to which he showed interest in the things of the new age. Robun does not exactly fit into the category of Edo *gesaku* writers when we consider that he wrote *Osana-Etoki Bankoku-Banashi* before the Meiji Restoration and, later on, such a work as *Guranto-Shi-Den Yamatobunshō* (General Grant's Biography) (1879). He was to a certain degree indoctrinated by the thinking of the modern age. In spite of this, he lacked the calibre to become a great writer, and his literary activities came to a close about 1875. After that, he participated in the founding of the *Kanayomi Shimbun* in 1875, of the *Iroha Shimbun* in 1878, became chief editor of the *Konnichi Shimbun* in 1884, and in 1886 transferred to the *Tōkyō E-iri Shimbun*. This career is not very different from that of the other *gesaku* writers.

Takabatake Ransen (Heizaburō, Kyūtoku, Naoyoshi, or Tadasu) was deeply devoted to Ryūtei Tanehiko as shown by his assumption of the name Nisei Tanehiko, or Tanehiko II, in 1882.

His *kusazōshi* (illustrated story-book) works, however, are nothing more than mere imitations of the original Tanehiko. His first work dealing with the new era is regarded as the *Kaige Hyaku Monogatari* (Tales of a Hundred Ghosts) (1875). The author depicts the gradual disappearance of common belief in ghosts as the new civilization spread scientific knowledge. In the chapters entitled " The Warlord's Ghost," " The Bathmaid's Ghost," " The Young Merchant's Ghost," " The Geisha's Ghost," "The Amateur Connoisseur's Ghost," and " The Ruffian's Ghost," he exposes the contradiction of people who have failed to free themselves from the past and adapt their lives to the new age. The ghosts here are the symbol of the shadows of the past. In this sense, although there is some similarity between this work and *Aguranabe,* the former belongs to a more advanced literary genre inasmuch as the satire is stronger.

Ransen's activities become more conspicuous after 1877. He was rather of the journalist type from the very beginning. His career included participation in the founding of the *Tōkyō Nichinichi Shimbun* in 1872, of the *Hiragana E-iri Shimbun* in 1875, and, after working as printing chief with the *Yomiuri Shimbun* in 1879, he entered the *Daitō Nippōsha* in 1883. This journalistic course helped his writing, and he was able to introduce the innovation in *kusazōshi* of inserting color illustrations as a result of his knowledge of newspaper printing.

The most striking feature of his works is that they are didactic. *Okayama Kibun : Fude no Inochige* (Queer Tales from Okayama) (1882) deals with a conspiracy in the Okayama clan, and the plot is that goodwill finally wins over evil. *Chōtori Tsukuba no Susomoyō* (Tsukuba Patterns) (1884) concerns the assassination of a patriotic samurai of the Mito clan and the orphaned sons' successful revenge against the assassins. *Kandan Shinkeibyō* (Weird Tales for the Bedchamber) (1884) sounds like a collection of ghost stories from its title, but actually it describes the sufferings of a guilty conscience, and is rather closer to the genre of *yomihon.* This characteristic can be perceived in varying degrees in his other works such as *Kōsetsu Konotegashiwa* (A Tale of the Streets: An Oak Leaf like a Child's Hand) (1879), *Umeyanagi Harusame-Banashi* (Tales of Spring Rain on Plum and Willow Trees) (1881), *Shunshoku Koganebana* (Gold Flowers in Spring) (1884), *Kokubyaku Some-wake Tazuna* (Reins of Black and White) (1885), and others. It is interesting to note, in passing, that there are indications that his works *Chōtori Tsukuba no Susomoyō* and *Shunkoku Koganebana* were adapted from the *Genji Monogatari*. Apparently he was following in the footsteps of his master, the original Tanehiko, who wrote *Inaka Genji* (The Provincial Genji).

The *gesaku* writers of the early Meiji Period are usually divided into three groups: the Kanagaki school led by Kanagaki Robun, the Ryūtei school centering around Takabatake Ransen, and the Tamenaga school headed by Somezaki Nobufusa. The Tamenaga school, however, did not have much influence. The Kanagaki school included such authors as Nisei Hanagasa Bunkyō (*Na mo Hiroki Sawabe no Ukigusa*) (The Drifting Grasses at the Side of the Marsh) (1880), Saikaen Ryūka (*Mushirobata Gumma no Inanaki*) (The Neighing of the Horse Herd) (1881), and, although they were not direct disciples of Robun, Kōtō Midori (Saitō Ryokuu), Itō Senzō, and Oka Takeki were close to this group.

Ryūjōtei Hanahiko and Ryūsuitei Tanekiyo belonged to the Ryūtei school. The leader of the Tamenaga school was Some-zaki Nobufusa (Nisei Tamenaga Shunsui), known for the volu-minous work *Kinsei Kibun* (A Record of the Recent Past) (1874–1878), and his disciples included Furukawa Kaitō. Another writer close to Nobufusa's literary circle was Jōno Dempei (Saigiku, or Sansantei Arindo). However, compared to the first two groups, this circle did not have much influence. Nobufusa established himself as a *gesaku* writer through the *Iroha Bunko* (ABC Library) before the beginning of the Meiji Era. Although he revived the *ninjōbon* form by writing newspaper serials after 1877, he was not endowed with the sensibility to grasp the full meaning of the new age.

Among the writers who did not belong to any of these groups were Okamoto Kisen and Yoshikawa Shuntō. Also to be noted here is Matsumura Shunsuke, who wrote *Fukko Yume Monogatari* (Dreamy Tales of the Past), *Kaimei Shōsetsu : Harusame Bunko* (A Novel of Enlightenment : The Library of Spring Rain), and other historical pieces.

If we classify *gesaku* writings by their themes, the works which came out about and after 1877 fall into the following groups : those dealing with the Imperial Restoration, *e.g.*, *Kaimei Shōsetsu : Harusame Bunko* by Shunsuke, adaptations of newspaper human interest stories, *e.g.*, *Torioi O-Matsu Kaijō Shinwa* (The New Sea Tale of O-Matsu the Strolling Singer) by Kubota Hikosaku, *Fuyu Kaede Tsuki no Yūbae* (Winter Maple Trees in the Evening Moonlight) by Zōga Ryūkō, and *Kamuri no Matsu Mado no Yoarashi* (The Evening Storm) by Takeda Kōrai, and works depicting human sentiment, *e.g.*, *Asao Iwakiri : Makoto Kurabe* (The Race to Truth) by Shōtei Kakusen.

Most of these were published in serial form in newspapers before 1886, and it is true that these *gesaku* pieces were quite different from those written before 1877. We notice that *gesaku* writing now was dealing with incidents which actually happened, or were based upon important stories in the newspapers. In other words, we perceive a tendency towards realism. In contrast with previous *gesaku* writers who relied upon sheer imagination, jokes, and caricature, as was the case in *Bankoku Kōkai : Seiyō Dōchū Hizakurige* and *Kappa Sōden : Kiurizukai*, the writers were now turning to documentary novels. In this connection, we must admit that although the literary style and form of these works were of the same old *gesaku* type, they helped considerably in disseminating the literature of the new age, chiefly because they were published as newspaper serials.

On the other hand, we must not overlook the fact that this lingering influence of *gesaku* was still strongly felt in the translation of foreign literature and in political novels. And yet the emergence of a new literature peculiar to the Meiji Era meant at the same time the gradual eradication of this *gesaku* influence.

It is commonly accepted that the appearance of *Ukigumo* (The Drifting Clouds) marked the beginning of the modern novel in Japan. This period was a complicated one in which the traditional literature and the new literature under foreign influence fought and mingled with each other, and one which saw the birth of a multitude of literary theories. It would be somewhat hasty to conclude that the appearance of *Ukigumo* completely ended *gesaku* writing. Although this traditional literary genre was severely shaken at this time, paradoxically, for this very reason it was able to exert such a strong influence over writers of this and later periods. We shall now attempt a brief survey of the course followed by *gesaku* writing between 1887 and 1897.

In the foregoing paragraphs we examined the main activity of *gesaku* writers. After 1877, *gesaku* writing still flourished in the form of documentary pieces published in newspapers. The *gesaku* writers themselves were leaving traditional forms and were moving towards realism.

However, writers like Nansui, Kōsōn, Shōyō, Kōyō, and Ryokuu still showed respect for the old genre and seemed to be working towards its restoration. This attitude was partly a reaction against the awkward style of the translations of foreign literature and the prevailing tendency of political novels. At any rate, these new *gesaku* writers treated literature as a serious matter, at least when compared with the early writers of that genre.

Tsubouchi Shōyō was deeply devoted to Bakin from childhood through his school-days. He also had a passion for *kusazōshi* pieces such as *Jiraiya Gōketsudan* and *Shaka Hassō : Yamato Bunko*. However, his contact with Western literature finally prompted him to bid farewell to the *gesaku* world. The reason he was able to launch such a violent attack on Bakin's didacticism in his *Shōsetsu Shinzui* (The Essence of the Novel) (1885) was mainly that he was so well-versed in Bakin's works. *Ichidoku Santan : Tōsei Shosei Katagi* (Once Read, Thrice Admired : The Character of the Modern Student), written in the same year, purported to be an example of the literary theory and realism expounded in *Shōsetsu Shinzui*. Actually, the material was still of the old *gesaku* genre, and his literary expression on many points resembled Bakin's style. But this defect is counteracted by the fact that the work exerted a strong influence over Futabatei and also over the writers belonging to the Ken'yūsha. In his inability to put into practice the theory expounded in *Shōsetsu Shinzui*, we see how deeply the traces of *gesaku* writing were rooted in this author. Shōyō at this time was still groping in the dark, but he was acting as the pioneer of the reformists, and in this sense playing a highly significant role.

The same year that saw the appearance of *Shōsetsu Shinzui* and *Tōsei Shosei Katagi* saw the formation of the Ken'yūsha by a group of writers including Ozaki Kōyō. The *raison d'être* of this literary movement lay in its dissatisfaction with the political novels and translations of foreign literature which were in vogue at this period, and in its effort to treat literature only as literature. The basis of this movement was found in the restoration of the literary fashion of the Bunka-Bunsei Periods. The fact that the organ circulated by this group, the *Garakuta Bunko* (The Storehouse of Literary Miscellany), was first hand-written gives us an idea of the attitude of the members. This attitude is also reflected in the passages of the introductory articles of its first issue which stated, " We come together to enjoy ourselves, to read as many books as possible in the coming months. We prepare this edition which we hope may pass the time. Nothing is more pleasant than this ! "

Among the circle members, Kōyō and Bimyō played leading roles, but the latter soon left the group. Bimyō was to walk a separate road as a founder of an original literary style. As to Kōyō, following études published in the *Garakuta Bunko*, he wrote *Ninin Bikuni : Iro Zange* (Confessions of Love of Two Nuns) and *Kyara Makura* (The Perfumed Pillow) which brought him closer to the Genroku style. In a sense, these works emerged as a purification of *gesaku* writing. The remaining influence of *gesaku* can be perceived in his later works such as *Tajō Takon* (Tears and Regrets) and *Konjiki Yasha* (The Gold Demon). The same thing can be said about his disciples, all of whom were colored by the *gesaku* style in the better sense of the word.

Another writer representing the *gesaku* writing of this period was Aeba Kōson (Yosaburō). His ambition was to edit a history of the modern novel, and although he failed in this ambitious enterprise, his effort in this direction gave him a deep comprehension of Edo literature. By collecting works he had contributed to newspapers and magazines, he published *Muratake* (A Clump of Bamboo) (1889–1890) which comprised twenty volumes. This work deals with various phases in the lives of connoisseurs. Another major work is *Tōsei Akiudo Katagi* (The Character of the Modern Merchant) comparable to the works of Saikaku dealing with the life of townsmen. In his writings we discover plots and a literary style which are similar to those of Ejima Kiseki and Jishō. The fact that didacticism was the key-note of his works leads us to presume that even at this period he had already become an outdated writer.

Sudō Nansui (Kōki) first wrote serials such as *Ibaragi Otaki Midare no Shiraito* (The Entangled White Thread) (1883). His literary fame was established in 1886 when he wrote *Usō Mampitsu : Ryokusadan* (Random Jottings Like Rain on the Window : The Tale of the Green Straw Raincoat), a political novel. Unlike Kōson, he emerged from the *gesaku* circle and developed an original technique for objective description. Rohan has labeled Kōson and Nansui as " the two great literary luminaries " of the mid-Meiji period. However, it seems to us that this is too great praise.

Saitō Ryokuu (Ken) (he had the additional pen-names of Shōjiki Masadayū and Kōtō Midori) may be regarded as a more accomplished *gesaku* author than those previously mentioned. He was representative of the generation after that of Robun and Ransen. However, his cultivation was only appropriate to the *gesaku* world. *Kakurembo* (Hide-and-Go-Seek) (1891) and *Aburajigoku* (The Hell of Oil) (1891), two of his typical works dealing with life in the prostitute quarter, were merely Meiji versions of *sharehon* which had described the prostitute life of the Bunka-Bunsei Periods. However, his philosophy of human nature is original, his position being that men merely make playthings of the female. This attitude is reflected even in his miscellaneous writings such as *Oboechō* (A Memorandum) and *Hikaechō* (A Notebook), which are included in *Ararezake* (Saké). His active period lasted until about 1900 when the *gesaku* movement as a whole came to a temporary halt.

2. *Enlightenment Writing and Translation of Foreign Literature*

During the years between the end of the Edo regime and the beginning of the Meiji Era, when the *gesaku* writers were being forced to adapt themselves to the changing world, there was a group of persons who actually traveled abroad, absorbed new knowledge, and returned to their native country to assume leading positions in launching an enlightenment movement in various fields. Fukuzawa Yukichi can be singled out as a typical champion of this group. This author is known for such works as *Seiyō Jijō* (Western Affairs) (1866), *Sekai Kunizukushi* (All about the World) (1869), *Bummeiron no Gairyaku* (Outline of a Critique of Civilization) (1875), and *Tsūzoku Minkenron* (Comments on Democratic Rights) (1878), which were either introductions of the ways, customs, and state of the Western world, or textbooks concerning Western civilization and its basic political ideas. Also, in such writing as *Gakumon no Susume* (Encouragement of Learning) (1872), he attempted to introduce the ideas of utilitarian pragmatism, in which we see a strong influence of H. Spencer. *Kummō : Kyūrizukai* (To Enlighten : An Introduction to Science), written in 1868, is a science textbook dealing with subjects corresponding to modern astronomy or geophysics. This was one manifestation of his pragmatism.

The significance of his pioneering efforts lay in the fact that they were directed in every field, and he rightly deserves the name of an enlightenment writer. Even his sole work of fiction, *Katawa Musume* (The Deformed Daughter) (1872), can be considered as enlightenment writing, although it cannot be regarded as a novel in the strictest sense of the word. If included in the category of the novel, it belongs rather to the genre of satirical novel. A similar situation exists in the case of *Sekai Kunizukushi*, which cannot be called a New Style poem, although it was written in strict seven-five-syllable stanzas (*shichigo-chō*). The theme of *Katawa Musume* is explained by the author at the beginning of his collected works. He says, " This work may appear childish, but there was a circumstance which made me write it." In other words, he had the motive, or rather the urgent desire, of putting an end to the effeminate custom, common among the nobility serving in the Kyōto Imperial Palace, of dyeing the teeth black. However, on second thought, he decided that he first should try to stop this same practice among women in general. The story goes like this : In a certain rich family a daughter is born without eyebrows, and she later grows black teeth. The author then explains the scientific advantages of having eyebrows, which, he says, are effective in protecting the eyes from intense light. By the word " deformed " he means the unnatural state of the human body. The " deformed " daughter in his story grows up, but once she reaches the age of twenty, nobody comes to think she is " deformed," and she is happily married. This occurs because it was the common practice to shave off a girl's eyebrows and dye her teeth black when she came of age. Thus, the deformed girl was no longer an unusual sight. The author concludes his story with the old saying, " We owe our body to God. It would be a grave sin wantonly to harm this body." The aim of the author was scientifically to advise Japanese women to abandon the evil practices which had been transmitted for centuries.

It is interesting to note that Nishimura Setsudai wrote *Katawa Musuko* (The Deformed Son) in 1874, but the work was just an imitation of *Katawa Musume.*

Among other writers, Kanagaki Robun, Mantei Ōga, and Takabatake Ransen wrote some pieces which could be called enlightenment writing. However, their main activity was in the *gesaku* field. None of them expressed bold opinions such as was the case with *Katawa Musume.*

Translation of foreign works, such as *Saikoku Risshi-Hen* (Biographies of Self-Made Men of Western Countries) by Nakamura Masanao and *Min'yakuron* (*Social Contract*) by Hattori Toku, also helped in cultivating the enlightenment ideas, but they cannot be regarded as novels. Although we see numerous publications of translations or articles on philosophical, social, and political subjects, the number of works which can be called enlightenment novels is limited. Thus, it may be said that the early period in the history of the modern novel centered on the activity of the *gesaku* writers.

However, at the same time we must not overlook the fact that the introduction of foreign literature was bringing a change to the character of the novel itself. The influence Yukichi and similar authors had on the literary world is negligible when compared with that of translations. To us, rather, the fact that foreign literary works were translated and that they served as a spur in shaping Meiji literature is of a greater importance. Therefore, in the following paragraphs we shall look at the list of early translated works.

The history of translation of foreign literature dates back to 1549 when Christianity was first introduced into this country.

Already in the Edo period we see publication of translations of *Robinson Crusoe* and *Gulliver's Travels.* Thus, the people of that day already had the chance to come in contact with real foreign literature. Most of these translations, however, were not from the original writings but via Dutch translations.

Interest in translation mounted with the coming of the new Meiji Era, but it is quite difficult to say which was the first true translated novel to appear in this period. In the preface of the translation of Lytton's *Night and Morning* (translated by Masuda Katsutoku in 1889), Morita Shiken says, " The history of our country's literature reached a turning-point when Oda gave us our first translated novel, *Karyū Shunwa* (A Spring Tale of Flowers and Willows)." Morita appears to hold that *Karyū Shunwa*, together with *Keishidan* (Lytton's *Kenelm Chillingly*) and *Yoru to Asa* (*Night and Morning*), composed the three big peaks of early translation. He backed up this opinion by citing the orderliness of the sentences in these translations. Although we do not necessarily agree with this argument, we must admit, from various considerations, that *Karyū Shunwa* ranks as the first foreign novel to appear as a translation. The translation of this work came out in 1878. However, during the several years preceding this publication, there were other translations such as *Robinson-Zenden* (*Robinson Crusoe* translated by Saitō Ryōan, 1872), *Tsūzoku Isoppu Monogatari* (*Aesop's Fables*, translated by Watabe Yutaka (On), 1873), and *Kaikan Kyōki : Arabiya Monogatari* (*The Arabian Nights* translated by Nagamine Hideki, 1875). These were not direct translations of the original works but were rather free translations or adaptations. If we add to these, several translations of Shakespeare's dramas, we find that there were more than ten translated works published in this period. The translators were doing their work either in the hope that it would serve in the enlightenment of the era or merely out of curiosity. This is obvious from the introductory chapters or prefaces the writers inserted in their translations. *Ōshū Kiji : Karyū Shunwa*

(Curious Tales of Europe) (we shall refer to this work as *Karyū Shunwa* from now on) was a translation by Oda (Niwa) Jun'ichirō of Lytton's *Ernest Maltravers* and *Alice* which were written in 1837. It is well known that Lytton was an important figure in England's political circles. The translator Oda also was a political speaker and was well versed in foreign affairs through his studies in England. The fact that both the author and translator were political figures invited criticism that their work was a political novel. However, apparently there was no such deliberate motive on the part of the translator.

This story concerns an English youth named Maltravers, who, on his travel home from studies in Germany, meets and falls in love with Alice, the daughter of a villain by the name of Derwill. By the whim of fortune, the lovers are separated for twenty years, and the hero falls in love with several other women during that period. However, the two are finally brought together again in a happy ending. Although the story was a simple one, the translation had a great success. This occurred because, in the first place, the days of strife had then ended, and with the coming of a peaceful life the readers were asking for fresh material. The second reason is that this translated work was neither of the didactic type nor documentary writing but dealt chiefly with human sentiments and the glorification of human nature. As Narushima Ryūhoku states in the preface, the translation showed that the desire for material gain did not occupy the entire mind of the Western people, and that these people also enjoyed a spiritual life. This attitude apparently appealed to the time. *Karyū Shunwa* exerted considerable influence over later translations. We discover traces of its influence in such works as *Shumpū Jōwa* (translated from *The Bride of Lammermoor* by Tachibana Kenzō—actually by Tsubouchi Shōyō, 1880), *Ōshū Jōfu : Gunhō Kiwa* (translations of seven stories from *The Decameron* by Ōkubo Kanzaburō, 1882), *Taisei Katsugeki : Shunsō Kiwa* (*The Lady of the Lake*, translated by Hattori Seiichi—actually by Shōyō, 1884), *Ōshū*

Kibun: Kagetsu Jōwa (translation of *Romeo and Juliet*, by Kikutei Kōsui, 1884). Incidentally, *Ernest Maltravers* and *Alice* (*Karyū Shunwa*) were first translated in a Chinese style, but later were re-written in a style reminiscent of Bakin's, which made them easier to read.

Five months before the publication of *Karyū Shunwa* there appeared the first part of *Shinsetsu: Hachijūnichikan Sekai Isshū* (a translation of Jules Verne's *Around the World in Eighty Days* by Kawashima Tadanosuke). This is a scientific novel as well as being an adventure story. In the hero Fogues, who overcomes every obstacle with the help of money, we see the image of a Western capitalist. The fact that translation of Verne's works became popular, such as *Kyūjūnanaji Nijippunkan: Gessekai Ryokō* (*From the Earth to the Moon*, translated by Inoue Susumu, 1880), *Hokkyoku Isshū* (*Around the North Pole*, by Inoue Susumu, 1881), *Afurika Naichi Sanjūgonichikan: Kūchū Ryokō* (*Thirty-Five Days over the African Wilderness*, 1883, also translated by Inoue Susumu), and *Godaishūchū: Kaitei Ryokō* (*Twenty Thousand Leagues Under the Sea*, translated by Taihei Sanji, 1884), offers ample evidence that the people of the time were thirsty for new knowledge.

We shall now give a list of other significant translations which appeared by about 1885. Since Shakespeare's works will be treated in a later chapter on the drama, we shall limit our list to essays and novels which have not appeared so far in the foregoing paragraphs.

1879 *Ōshū Kiwa: Kisō Shunshi* (Lytton's *The Last Days of Pompeii*, translated by Oda Jun'ichirō); *Ōshū Shōsetsu: Teremaku Kafuku Monogatari* (Fenelon's *Les Aventures de Télem'aque*, translated by Miyajima Shunshō)

1881 *Fukkoku Jōwa: Gojūku-Sessōshi* (Dumas' *Les Quarante-cinq*, translated by Matsuoka Kameo); *Iyaku: Tenro Rekitei* (Bunyan's *Pilgrim's Progress*, translated by Satō Kihō)

1882 *Fukkoku Kakumei Kigen*: *Nishinoumi Chishio no Yoarashi* (Dumas' *Mémoires d'un Médecin*, translated by Sakurada Momoe); *Furansu Kakumeiki*: *Jiyū no Gaika* (Dumas' *Anje Pitou*, translated by Miyajima Muryū); *Ennō no Shimoto* (a story translated by Muryū, dealing with a woman revolutionist of Russia named Sashuritch); *Kyomutō Taiji Kidan* (presumed to be the work of Paul Vernier; translated from the English version, *The Chase of the Nihilists*, by Kawashima Tadanosuke); *Ryōseifu-Dan* (Moore's *Utopia*, translated by Inoue Susumu).

1883 *Zensekai Ichidai-Kisho* (Selected translations from *The Arabian Nights* by Inoue Susumu); *Zessei Kidan*: *Robinson Hyōryūki* (*Robinson Crusoe*, translated by Inoue Susumu); *Rokoku Kibun*: *Kashinchō Shiroku* (Pushkin's *The Captain's Daughter*, translated by Takata Harusuke).

1884 *Seitō Yodan*: *Shun-Ōten* (Disraeli's *Coningsby*, translated by Seki Naohiko); *Doitsu Kisho*: *Kitsune no Saiban* (Goethe's *Reinecke Fuchs*, translated by Inoue Susumu).

During this period translation was undertaken chiefly for enlightenment purposes, but from 1881 or 1882 it took on a new significance. In other words, under the stimulation of the prevailing social conditions, the emphasis of translation was now put on political works, a tendency which must not be overlooked.

Public taste was for Dumas' works dealing with the French Revolution, translations of works concerning the Nihilist party of Russia, and the like. It was precisely this situation that made way for the successive publication of translations from Disraeli's political works.

In addition to these, the list above shows that, with the exception of Shakespeare's dramas, the majority of translations were from the works of Scott and Lytton, followed by those of French writers including Jules Verne and Dumas. Most of them were free or selected translations, or, in some cases, re-translations.

The Japanese versions were written in a variety of styles, some being *gesaku* style, others being direct translation or using Chinese-style prose. In some extreme cases, the original work was rendered into *jōruri*-type writing. There existed no clear thinking as to the method of translation.

In this sense, *Keishidan*, published in 1885, marked a new epoch in translation. The translator in his preface states that "Efforts have been made to preserve the original form of the sentences as far as is allowed by syntax. For this reason, on some trivial points, I have allowed myself the liberty of disregarding Japanese grammatical rules." This work was translated from Lytton's *Kenelm Chillingly*, the title being the phonetic transcription of the original one. Although it is listed as the joint translation of Fujita Mokichi and Ozaki Yasuo, the actual translation is said to have been the work of Asahina Chisen. The hero of this story, Kenelm, is a youth educated according to the spirit of the new age. After numerous experiences, he finally becomes aware that this new spirit is only an empty idea, and decides to live according to tradition. Although this was accepted by the public as a political work, the novel bore the strong influence of " *Wilhelm Meister.* Actually the significance of this translation lay not in its content but in its literary style. Although we know of previous cases of direct translation, such as we see in *Saikoku Risshi-Hen* and *Around the World in Eighty Days*, this was the first time that a translation was intended to be a direct translation of the original.

Listed below are more of the translations published during this period.

1885 *Kaikan Hifun : Gaiseishi-Den* (Lytton's *Rienzi*, translated by Shōyō)

1886 *Bokkasu-Ō Tōka Monogatari : Sōfuren* (Seventh story

in the fifth day of *The Decameron,* translated by Sano Naoshige) ; *Kyūka Enryū : Hokuō Kessen Yojin* (Tolstoy's *War and Peace,* translated by Mori Tai) ; *San'ei Sōbi : Seikai no Jōha* (Disraeli's *Endymion,* translated by Watanabe Osamu) ; *Seiji Shōsetsu : Bairai Yokun* (Scott's *Ivanhoe,* translated by Ushiyama Kakudō).

1887   *En'ō Kikan* (Third story in the third day of *The Decameron,* translated by Kondō Tōnosuke) ; *Kaikan Kyōki : Seiyō Fukushūkidan* (Dumas' *Le Comte de Monte Cristo,* translated by Seki Naohiko).

If we make a rough survey of the situation in about 1890, we find that the number of translations published in 1886 doubled from that of the previous year and increased as much as several-fold in the following year. However, the number starts to decrease after 1887. This, we think, occurred because a correct understanding had been reached by this time concerning the merits of translation. In his preface to the *Gaiseishi-Den* (Lytton's *Rienzi*), Shōyō expresses opinions similar to those he outlined in his previous work, *Shōsetsu Shinzui.* This deserves special attention here because it shows that realism was now becoming the dominant note in the whole literary movement. Based on the consciousness of the true merits of literature, translations which previously had been done as part of the enlightenment movement or out of curiosity, were now being polished in the light of a true modern literature. *Tanima no Himeyuri* (Bertha M. Clay's *Dora Thorne,* translated by Suematsu Kenchō and Ninomiya Kumajirō), which was published in 1888 and through the following year, is probably the last foreign work to be translated by politicians. Yet the story is not political and rather approaches a domestic novel. The psychological description has become considerably detailed, and the work is written in a colloquial style that is easy to understand. In this work, which doubtless marks the end of the early translation period, we see signs of a tendency toward something new. It was at this propitious moment that there appeared Futabatei's epoch-making translations.

As mentioned in previous chapters, Futabatei's *Aibiki* (Rnedezvous) was translated from a chapter of Turgenev's *Sportsman's Sketches* and published in the 25th and 27th issues of the magazine *Kokumin no Tomo* (The Nation's Friend), which appeared on July 3 and August 3, 1888 respectively. The influence of the previously published *Karyū Shunwa* can be regarded as negligible when compared to that of this new work of Futabatei. The significance of Futabatei's translations lay primarily in his genuine artistic approach to the original work. He was able to make an almost complete reproduction of the artistic expression of the Western philosophy of nature. Thus, he stimulated the Japanese people to reconsider their attitude on seasonal tastes (*kidai shumi*) and, at the same time, to teach them that the beauty of nature must be respected in the light of human life and arts. Futabatei's influence was to be felt in marked degree by such authors as Katai, Tōson, and Doppo.

The second significance of Futabatei's work may be found in his utilization of the colloquial style in his translations. Since Futabatei had started to write his original story *Ukigumo* (The Drifting Clouds) the year before, we may say that he was merely applying his own style to that of *Aibiki*. At any rate, the general tendency in translation of this period was, despite the opinions professed in *Keishidan*, to rely on the use of a rigid Chinese style. Futabatei, however, rejected this tendency, and the style he used in *Aibiki* meant, in a sense, the actual application of the ideas expressed in *Keishidan*. In this respect, we can imagine that Futabatei was also under the influence of the ideas expressed by Shōyō in his *Shōsetsu Shinzui*.

In the same year, Futabatei translated Turgenev's *Three Encounters* and, giving it the title *Meguriai* (Encounter), published it in the *Miyako no Hana* (The Flower of the Capital). He gave an excellent translation of the romantic sentiment expressed in the original piece, and his work was warmly received by the public.

While Futabatei was doing such significant work, most of the other men engaged in translation, on the other hand, were clinging to the style of such authors as Shiken and Ruikō. The complete reorganization of translation had to await the appearance of Ōgai and Fuchian.

The same years that saw the appearance of Futabatei also witnessed the rise of a tendency among translators to avoid random selection of original works. Political works were being taken up in smaller number. The general tendency was that in about 1888 the translation of classics decreased and emphasis shifted to modern literature. English and American works were neglected in favor of Continental writing. This situation made way for the appearance of translation experts, and Ōgai commenced his magnificent work in 1889. Another expert, Shiken, as he notes in his preface, translated *Night and Day* completely in the colloquial style and utilized stenography in his work. Although this is a noteworthy effort, it has slight significance when compared with that of Ōgai.

If we classify the translations published until about 1890 on the basis of the authors' nationality, we find that English works were headed by those of Shakespeare, followed by Lytton, Disraeli, and Scott. French works were headed by Verne, followed by those of Hugo, Dumas, and Fénelon. These English and French works head the list, followed by Russian, German, Italian, and Spanish works.

In summing up the whole situation, we can state that the early translation activity made great contributions in that it prepared the way for an evaluation of literary works according to artistic standards, helped in introducing the Western theories of the novel and in disseminating the methods of Western literature, and finally that it served as a major weapon in eliminating the *gesaku* style of writing.

3. *The Political Novel*

Political novels of the early Meiji Era unfold during the

years between 1880 and 1890. There are a number of reasons why political stories flourished during this period.

The most important one probably is that the movement for democratic rights which grew out of the ideas disseminated by the Enlightenment thinkers provided a hotbed for them to develop. This was the proper time, and politicians were now offered a chance to express their political ideas through the medium of the novel.

Another reason for the popularity of political novels was the stimulus provided by the introduction of foreign literature. The principal foreign works introduced in the early years were mostly of English origin and, with exception of the classics, the majority of translations were from the works of Lytton and Disraeli. These translations resulted in informing the Japanese that politicians themselves were capable of becoming writers, and this in turn served in destroying the common belief that novel writing was not a man's proper vocation. In this connection, further stimulus was obtained from Dumas' works dealing with the French Revolution and from the novels treating the Russian Nihilists.

The third reason was the stimulus provided by the renovation of literary ideas. The peak of political novels corresponds to the period which saw the vogue of the literary theories expounded in *Shōsetsu Shinzui*. Therefore, we can say that the ideal of realism also entered the political ideology.

Lastly, there were strong traces of traditional literature in the political novels. A *gesaku* style was especially widely employed, and this we might say was part of the reason for the rapid dissemination of this genre.

And yet the question remains : what in essence is a political novel ? The definition is not easy. We think that we can accept, with slight reservation, the common concept that a political novel is a work dealing with the propaganda of a specific party, or with the improvement of society, or one depicting the life of people supporting the government, or one exposing the factions composing the government. In this sense, political novels must be regarded as belonging to the category of "tendency novels." At any rate, the political novels of this period were special by-products of the age.

The political novel was still in chaos until about 1880. The period prior to that year was a confused one which saw the formation of the Aikoku Kōtō (Patriotic Public Party) (1874), the presentation of a petition for creation of a publicly elected Diet, one which still reflected the aftermath of the Seinan civil war, and which witnessed the subsequent suppression of the democratic rights movement, the clamoring for natural rights of man, and the emergence of an active political movement.

From about 1877, numerous documentary writings appeared dealing with the Meiji Restoration and the peasant uprisings. Although these writings did not espouse any specific or clear-cut political theories and consequently were not full-fledged political novels, they indicated the possibility of the emergence of such a genre.

It is commonly accepted that the forerunner of the political novel was *Minken Engi : Jōkai Haran* (In the Stormy Political Sea), published in 1880. The author, Toda Kindō, became a Christian while he was abroad, and upon his return to Japan, engaged in a movement for social reform. In this work Kindō attempted to satirize the world in the fashion of "the ancient Chinese writer Chuang-tzu or Aesop of the West." It is evident that the word *jōkai* (tempestuous seas) used in the title referred to the political world. A strong political motive is apparent in the names he used for his heroes. The name of the heroine Sakigakeya O-Ken, meant "First-Right," while the hero was named Wakokuya Minji, meaning "Peaceful Nation-People," and the third major character was named Kokubu Masabumi, whose name was composed of four Chinese characters meaning "nation," "government," "justice," and "culture."

The climax of the story sees the hero, Minji, or Peaceful-

Nation-People, wed happily to O-Ken, or First-Right, in a scene entitled "The Banquet of Ryōgoku," which literally translated would be "The Banquet of Two Nations."

In short, the author here tacitly refers to the idea that the democratic rights movement corresponds to the interests of the people, and that this movement would lead to the formation of the National Diet.

Although this work was not first-rate writing, artistically speaking, it had a special significance in that it furnished a specific pattern for political novels. The ideological content is almost nil, and for this reason it was in the true sense a forerunner of the political story. Kindō wrote another work, *Kaorukochi Hanabusa Gunki* (East Winds over the Army) (1882), which provided the original pattern for the later author Yamada Bimyō's *Tategoto Sōshi* (The Tale of the Harp). Both stories deal with Alfred the Great's adventures in his battles against the Danes.

In addition to Kindō, authors like Ueda Shūsei (Hidenari) (*Jiyū no Shiori : Kochōkidan*, The Memo of Liberty, 1882), and Miyazaki Shōfushi (*Tōyō Kidan : Hōen Jōwa*, Strange Tales of the East, 1881) may also be regarded as pioneers of the political novel.

The political novel was born in this way and gradually matured during the years prior to 1885. This period saw the formation of the Jiyūtō (Liberal Party) in 1881 and the Kaishintō (Progressive Party) in 1882. In the meantime, the Emperor issued an edict calling for the convocation of the first National Diet in 1890. As a result, Itō Hirobumi and Itagaki Taisuke successively went abroad to study the constitutions of foreign countries. The Liberal Party was dissolved in 1884. During these years politicians who took active part in writing belonged mostly to the Liberal Party. Typical examples were Sakurada Momoe and Miyazaki Muryū.

Sakurada Momoe (Hyakkaen) published *Okuni Tamizō : Jiyū no Nishiki* (Brocade of Liberty) in 1883. In this work, the author hinted that the people would be freed from the tyranny of clan politics and would be able to enjoy a peaceful life through the establishment of democratic rights. The characters of the story and the development of the plot are similar to those of the aforementioned *Jōkai Haran*. He also published *Nishinoumi Chishio no Yoarashi* (Bloody Tempest in Western Seas), which was carried by the *Jiyū Shimbun* (Liberal Newspaper) in 1882, and exerted a profound influence on the younger generation. This, as mentioned in previous paragraphs, was a translation of Dumas' *Mémoires d'un Médecin* and dealt with the origin of the French Revolution. It played an indirect role in boosting the popularity of political writing. Although he employed the *ninjōbon* style in his work, it deserves special mention in that he was the first to declare openly and assume a conscious attitude that he was a political novelist.

Miyazaki Muryū (Fuyō) was another writer belonging to the Liberal Party who published his works chiefly through the *Jiyū Shimbun*. He was known for works based on loose translation of Western political stories. *Furansu Kakumeiki : Jiyū no Gaika* (Stories about the French Revolution) (1882) was a selected translation of Dumas' *The Battle of the Bastille*, but the translator inserted his own political opinions in various parts of the story. *Kyomutō Jitsudenki : Kishūshū* (Tales about the Nihilists) was adapted from Stepniak's *Underground Russia*, but here also the translator expressed his own political views. The original works of the translations mentioned above were brought back to this country by Itagaki Taisuke, who, during his travel abroad, made the selection under the personal advice of Victor Hugo. Itagaki turned over the materials for translation to his followers in his own party.

Another political novelist who belonged to the Liberal Party was Sakazaki Shiran, known for such works as *Kanketsu Senrigoma* (The Bloodshed of the Thousand-League Colt), *Jiyū no Hanagasa* (The Flower Hat of Liberty), and *Rokoku Anna Monogatari* (Tales of the Russian Anna), all published in 1883.

Komuro Angaidō was a writer who belonged to the Nippon
Rikken Seitō (Japan Constitutional Party) which followed the
policy of the Liberal Party. His political novels included
Shimpen Yamato Nishiki (A Japanese Brocade of New Tales)
(1883), *Kōa Kidan : Yume Renren* (Tales of Rising Asia)
(1884), and *Jiyū Enzetsu Onna Bunshō* (Women's Talk on
Freedom) (1884).

On the other hand, the Progressive Party also boasted of a
political novelist in Yano Ryūkei (Fumio). This author published
his famous work *Saibu Meishi : Keikoku Bidan* (Statesmanship
Stories) in 1883, and through this work, helped in establishing
a pattern for political novels. Since Yano occupied an important
post in his party, the public paid great attention to his writing.
According to the preface of this book, Yano became ill in 1882,
and, to pass the time on his sickbed, started reading Japanese
and Chinese novels. These works did not satisfy him, and,
turning to other reading material, he happened to find a Greek
historical piece dealing with the rise of Thebes. He was
impressed with this work because "it did not attempt any
deliberate interpretation of historical facts and adopted a strict
attitude in telling right from wrong, and good from evil."
This, he explained, was the principal motive in his decision
to edit a Greek history.

He lists eight books as the reference material he used in
writing his work. Almost all of them are works on Greek
history by English writers of the nineteenth century.

The story starts from the period when Thebes frees itself
from the shackles of the Spartans, and it traces its uphill
struggle to become the ruler of Greece. The story deals with
the Herculean efforts of Epaminondas, Pelopidas, and other
heroes. Consequently, this work must be regarded as a historical novel or as an *engitai-shōsetsu* (commentary-type novel).

The motive of the author was apparently to show that the
ideas of the Liberal Party could be likened to the democratic
ideals of Athens, and to hint, on the other hand, that the ideal

of his own Progressive Party lay in its respect of domestic politics and in the maintenance of a high standard of living. Generally speaking, the Progressives, as compared to the radicalism of the Liberals, advocated a moderate approach to political problems. This kind of thinking apparently played an important role in shaping the character of this political novel.

Stimulated by the success of Yano, other Progressive Party members started to engage in writing political novels. One of them was Sudō Nansui, who, after writing romances turned to political novels under the strong influence of *Shōsetsu Shinzui* and the writings of the English politician Disraeli. His novels which enjoyed wide popularity included *Usō Mampitsu : Ryokusadan* (The Tale of the Green Straw Raincoat) (1886), *Ippin Isshō : Shinshō no Kajin* (One Frown, One Smile : The Newly-Adorned Beauty) (1887), *Inkunshi* (The Unknown Nobleman (1888), *Gaisei Hika : Teru Himawari* (The Song of Lament) (1888), and *Karamatsu Misao* (The Pines of Virtue) (1889). Another Progressive, Fujita Meikaku, was the author of *Saimin Igyōroku* (The Noble Rescue of the People) (1887), which, although set in the days of the Ming Dynasty, actually was an attack on the Meiji government. Ozaki Yukio's *Shin-Nippon* (New Japan) (1886) was an ambitious work, but as a novel was childish writing. Shōyō also did some writing in the field of the political novel. Such works included *Keimō Kakumin : Seichitō Kōshaku* (Enlightenment Stories and Lectures) (1882), *Fūkai : Kyōwarambe* (Satires of the Lad from the Capital) (1886), *Naichi Zakkyo : Mirai no Yume* (Looking in the Future from a Crowded Country) (1886), and *Gaimu Daijin* (Foreign Minister) (1888). His translations, such as *Gaiseishi-Den* and *Jiyū no Tachi Nagori no Eihō* (*Julius Caesar*), also had a political coloring.

During this period of development of the political novel, there were some authors who engaged in writing which transcended the interests of the prevailing political parties. One example was Kikutei Kōsui (Satō Kuratarō), who, in his *Geppyō Kigū : Ensai Shunwa* (Spring Tales of Flower of Talents) (1882) proclaimed the necessity of promoting education. This can be regarded as a kind of political novel. It was given another title, *Sampū Hiu : Seiro Nikki* (An Ill Wind and Sad Rain : The Story Route of Life), and published in 1884. This was the forerunner of new-style writing and the new intellectual content of later years. Indeed, it was the leading favorite of the literary-minded youth about the year 1897.

Another political novelist who was now swayed by the interests of specific parties was Tōkai Sanshi (Shiba Shirō) whose representative work *Kajin no Kigū* (Strange Encounters with Beauties) (Part I published in 1885, Part VIII in 1897) was ranked in the class of *Keikoku Bidan*. It has been said there was a ghost-writer by the name of Takahashi Taika and also that some parts of the story were rewritten by Nishimura Tenshū, but neither story has been verified. Tōkai Sanshi (this *nom de plume* meant The Wanderer of the Eastern Sea) spent the years between 1879 and 1885 in the United States where he studied economics at several colleges. In later years, he went abroad again in the accompaniment of Tani Kanjō.

The novel he wrote was based on his observation and the facts he collected during his overseas trips. The story begins on the day when the hero Tōkai Sanshi, exiled as a result of the Meiji Restoration, goes up to the top of Independence Hall in Philadelphia to look up at the cracked Liberty Bell. The action takes place in America until Part IV, and from here the scene shifts to Europe. The other characters appearing in the story are mostly exiles from conquered countries. From Part VI, the author places emphasis on the introduction of Western affairs, and his writings assume the character of political talks. However, he does not bind himself to a specific party or faction, and his arguments are based on the necessity of elevating the international status of the nation.

In places he inserts episodes concerning his strange meeting with a certain Irish beauty, also an exile, and his encounter with a mysterious young lady from Spain, as means of giving a story-like effect to the writing.

Tōkai Sanshi subsequently wrote *Tōyō no Kajin* (An Oriental Beauty) (1888) and *Hanekawa Rokurō* (Stories about Hanekawa Rokurō) (1903), but these works failed to enjoy much popularity. Incidentally, *Kajin no Kigū* was translated into Chinese by Liang Ch'i-ch'ao, and is said to have played an important role in launching the literary revolution in China.

We believe that the political novel reached its peak between the years 1886 and 1890. This period saw in the political field the coalition of political forces (mainly from 1887–1890), with Gotō Shōjirō playing the leading role. The first National Diet was convoked in 1890, which meant the end, at least temporarily, of the democratic rights movement. The political novelist representing this period is Suehiro Tetchō, who is regarded as the writer who put the finishing touches on early political writing.

Suehiro Tetchō (Shigeyasu), from Uwajima in southern Japan, came to Tōkyō and found work in government service. However, he changed to journalism and assumed editorship of the *Akebono* (The Dawn) and the *Chōya* (The Government and People) newspapers. While with the *Chōya* he launched a violent attack on the government's press laws and accordingly was imprisoned together with Narushima Ryūhoku. From this period, we see him as an enthusiastic campaigner in the popular political movement. In 1881, he joined the Liberal Party but later moved closer to the Progressive line. He played an active and enthusiastic role in the movement for a coalition of political parties in 1886, but, since his efforts ended in failure, he went abroad. Following his return to Japan, he left the *Chōya* and worked strenuously for the politician Gotō. He was elected to the first National Diet and assumed the important post of Chairman of the Assembly.

Although he was the author of such novels as *Nijūsannen Miraiki* (An Account of Twenty-Three Years in the Future)

(1886), *Kokkai Kaisetsu no Zengo* (Before and After the Convocation of the National Diet) (1890), and *Tōyō no Daiharan* (Tempest in the Orient) (1891), Tetchō's reputation was based on *Setchūbai* (Plum Blossoms in the Snow) and *Kakan'ō* (The Nightingale among the Flowers).

The opening episode (Part I) of *Seijishōsetsu : Setchūbai* (A Political Novel : Plum Blossoms in the Snow) (1886) is the discovery of an old epitaph of Professor Baikei, a pioneer of the democratic rights movement, and that of his wife on March 3, "National Diet Day," in the fictitious "173rd year of Meiji" (which would correspond to 2040 A.D.). Against this fictitious background, the author tells us that he discovered a biography of the professor, entitled *Setchūbai*, and that of his wife, entitled *Kakan'ō*, in the Ueno Museum, and decided to use these biographies as the basis of his story.

There are four principal characters, Kunino, Kawagishi, Ta-keda, and a woman named O-Haru. The author confesses that he derived his idea for the plot of the story by reading *San'ei Sōbi : Seikai no Jōha*, a work translated from Disraeli's novel by Watanabe Osamu. The title of this translated work means, roughly, "Three Talented Men and Two Beautiful Girls in the Stormy Political Sea." The "three talented men" in Tetchō's version correspond to the three characters, Kunino, Kawagishi, and Takeda, while the "two beautiful girls" are O-Haru and O-Yū (she appears only in the second part of the story, namely in *Kakan'ō*). The story is as follows : Kunino comes to Tōkyō with the ambition to become a politician, and becomes a house-boy of a family named Tominaga. This family attempts to force him into marriage with the daughter, with the result that he runs away from the capital. Later, adopting the false name of Fukaya, Kunino returns to Tōkyō again, and by chance comes to know the heroine O-Haru. However, the hero's senior, Ka-wagishi, is also in love with this girl, and to make the matter more complicated, the girl's uncle is being supported by Kawa-gishi.

The story takes a new turn when the girl's uncle reforms his conduct, and through his efforts, Kunino is able to wed O-Haru. He is also able to make a successful career with the help of a huge fortune inherited by his wife. In the second chapter of the first part of the story, Kunino delivers a speech which strongly reflects the political ideal of the author, who was an advocate of a coalition of political forces. The concluding chapters, in which the hero achieves success with the money of his wife, reflect the bourgeois thinking that success can be erected only on the foundation of intellectual strength and monetary power. This is rather close to the views espoused by the Progressives. This work shows a distinct progress over political novels of the early period, as indicated by the fact that Shōyō held it in high regard.

Seiji Shōsetsu: Kakan'ō (A Political Novel: The Nightingale among the Flowers) (1888–1889) was the sequel to *Setchūbai*, and urged cooperation between the government and the people. The story deals with the consolidation of political forces, the tremendous victory of the Liberals, headed by Kunino, in the elections for the first National Diet in 1890, and the assumption of the hero of an important post, through which he takes an active part in directing the country.

The characters of the story are the same as in the previous one. O-Haru does a commendable job in helping her husband's political activities. Takeda, who belongs to the radicals, takes an active part in politics with the help of O-Yū, a woman of spirit, but at last is forced to seek political refuge in Shanghai. The other male character, Kawagishi, is also forced to succumb to Kunino's power. In his previous novel, *Setchūbai*, the author had restricted himself merely to warning the government. But in this sequel he becomes more aggressive, having arrived at the stage of putting his political beliefs into practice and of exposing corruption. This latter work is interesting, and as a novel it is in a more polished form.

In addition to Tetchō and the previously mentioned Sudō

Nansui, this period also had such political novelists as Hisama-tsu Yoshinori, Fukuchi Ōchi, Komiyama Tenkō, Udagawa Bunkai, and Ushiyama Kakudō.

After this period, the stream of political novels gradually be-came intertwined with the Ken'yūsha movement and the literary realism stemming from Tsubouchi Shōyō. The mission of the political novel was accomplished by about 1890, and it made way for the opening of an era which saw the emergence of full-scale modern novels. In this connection, we see signs of a movement towards the true literary novel in an article published in 1887 by Tokutomi Sohō in the sixth issue of *Kokumin no Tomo*, wherein he launched an attack against political novels and listed five reasons for his severe criticism.

In summary, the political novel was an unusual literary genre which was born out of necessity during the early years of the Meiji Era. From a purely artistic standpoint, we can say that its significance lay in its role of preparing the way for the emergence of the true literary writing which followed.

CHAPTER II THE CLASSIC AND ROMANTIC STYLE OF WRITING

1. *The Classic Style of Writing*

We should acknowledge the historical significance of the translated novel and the political novel in that they helped to eliminate the *gesaku* view of literature and awakened the intellectuals' interest in literature. At the same time, however, it cannot be denied that their rigid expression and political inclination militated against the new trend toward a poetical quality in literature. In a sense, the reform of the Meiji novel was motivated by the urgent desire to give to literature its due position among the arts. It is of course also true that Shōyō's *Shōsetsu Shinzui*, or "The Essence of the Novel," denying didacticism and attaching importance to man's natural feelings, gave strong support to this new trend.

It is true that *Shōsetsu Shinzui* predicted the establishment of modern realism and that this realism had its forerunners in the creative works of Shōyō himself and in Futabatei Shimei's *Ukigumo*. But one decade was needed yet before it actually bore fruit. On the other hand, the realism advocated in *Shōsetsu Shinzui* was, in a certain sense, the modernization of Norinaga's *mono no aware* and Shunsui's mentality in his *ninjōbon*. This new interpretation of the traditional view of literature became united with the nationalistic and retrospective trends in the early Meiji twenties. As a result, the Meiji novel thereafter began to show a tendency toward classicism and sentimentality. In this connection, it was the literary movement of the Ken'yūsha that in actual practice promoted such a reformatory trend and made it the main current of the world of literature.

The Ken'yūsha was a society of amateur writers organized in February 1885, its members being youths with an interest in literature, all of whom were students in the preparatory course of Tōkyō University. They included Ozaki Kōyō, Ishibashi Shian, Yamada Bimyō, and Maruoka Kyūka. At first the organization had no specific principle or opinion to unite it. However, in the process of its development the Ken'yūsha gradually formed its own peculiar opinions and manner of writing. As is well known, Ozaki Kōyō became its leader, both in name and reality.

In May of that year, the Ken'yūsha members came to have their own magazine, the *Garakuta Bunko*, which was handwritten and circulated among them. As symbolized by its title, the magazine was more or less influenced by the *gesaku* way of thinking. Kōyō even chose the pseudonym of Gesakudō and devoted himself to reading *gesaku* writings of the Bunka-Bunsei Periods (1804–1829) of the Tokugawa Era. Such an attitude of the Ken'yūsha was not accompanied by self-depreciation and obscurantism common among old *gesaku* writers. Rather, it indicated the youthful passion of the members in the enjoyment of literature, and it concealed genuine appreciation of the artistic value of literature and a rejection of the utilitarian view of it. This is apparent when one reads Kōyō's *Garakuta Bunko Hirō* (The Announcement of the *Garakuta Bunko*) (*Garakuta Bunko*, first issue) written in a *gesaku* manner. And yet whatever their true spirit was, the *gesaku* attitude alone prevented a work from achieving literary value. Thus, with the development of a consciousness toward literature on the part of the public, this playful *gesaku* attitude of the Ken'yūsha was abandoned. In a certain sense, the literary movement of the Ken'yūsha may be said to have been a necessary step in the process of abandonment of this traditional *gesaku* taste.

Later the magazine *Garakuta Bunko* came to be printed instead of handwritten and, as the members increased, the first official issue was "published" in May 1888. Meanwhile, the society received Kawakami Bizan and Iwaya Sazanami as new members, and they were followed by Emi Suiin, Hirotsu Ryūrō, Ōhashi Otoha, and others. This official publication of the

Garakuta Bunko was undoubtedly prompted by the trend toward a new literature, and under its stimulus the members could no longer remain satisfied with the private character of their organization as a circle of amateur writers. Parallel with this move, some of the members, such as Shian, Kōyō, and Bizan, one after another, left the university, resolved to devote themselves to literature with a fresh ardor. Beginning with the first issue, the magazine carried a few serial novels, Bimyō's *Jōshijin* (The Sentimental Poet), Sazanami's *Satsuki Koi* (The May Carp), both in colloquial style (*gembun itchitai*), and Kōyō's *Fūryū Kyōningyō* (The Elegant Kyōto Doll) written in a style half classic and half colloquial. The romantic content and elaborate form of expression of these works show that the playful attitude had apparently been abjured by the authors. In February of the following year, 1889, the *Garakuta Bunko* changed its title to *Bunko* (Library), and in this erasure of the playful word *garakuta* one can see how the Ken'yūsha writers had changed in their approach to literature.

In such a situation, Yamada Bimyō, one of the most influential members since the foundation of the organization, leaped into literary eminence by publishing a collection of his stories, *Natsu Kodachi* (The Summer Grove), in August 1888, and a novel *Kochō* (Butterfly) in the following January, both of which were highly regarded for their fresh, romantic style. Shortly thereafter he departed from the Ken'yūsha and became its strong rival by writing for the magazines *Iratsume* (The Maiden) and *Miyako no Hana* (The Flower of the Capital). The departure of Bimyō actually stimulated the group members to increased activity. Among others, Kōyō's novel *Ninin Bikuni Iro Zange* (The Amorous Confession of Two Nuns), of which the publication in 1889 made him famous, was a challenge directed against Bimyō's colloquial style in Kōyō's particular style, a blend of the classical and spoken languages. Furthermore, in the trend of the revival of classic works, Kōyō studied the style and taste of Saikaku and established the classical and sentimental style which became characteristic of the Ken'yūsha and which was quite different from Bimyō's manner of writing.

The *Bunko* discontinued publication shortly after its appearance, and although there followed several magazines as semi-official organs of the Ken'yūsha, none of them lasted long. They were *Shō-Bungaku* (Little Literature) (1889–1890), *Edo Murasaki* (Edo Purple) (1890), *Senshi Bankō* (A Thousand Purples and Ten Thousand Scarlets) (1891–1892), and *Kozakura Odoshi* (The Cherry-Colored Armor Thread) (1892–1893). After the failure of these magazines, no periodicals having a direct connection with the Ken'yūsha appeared again. However, the fact that the Ken'yūsha had its own medium of publication in its initial stage and that it had a background of a special relation between Kōyō and journalism facilitated the literary advancement of its member writers and strengthened their movement for a new literature.

Thus, until Kōyō's death in 1903, the Ken'yūsha, through the unity of its members, did not lose its influence, but during this period it faced a crisis in about 1893, when *Bungakkai* (The Literary World), the contributors to which constituted another new group of authors, raised a flag of revolt against it, and the same antagonistic trend came to be seen also in other literary movements. At that time Kōyō was already in a decline and was groping for a new course of development for his talent, while Bizan and Ryūrō broke through the limitation of the Ken'yūsha style. At the same time, Kōyō's pupils of the younger generation, such as Kyōka, Fūyō, Shun'yō, and Shūsei, began successfully cultivating their own fields of activity beyond the reach of their master. In this situation the Ken'-yūsha style could no longer be regarded as the main current of the literary world. Thus, it was during the period between 1889 and 1892 that the movement was most fruitful. In these years, historically called the Kō-Ro Jidai (the period of Kōyō and Rohan), Kōyō was one of the two eminent authors, side by side with Rohan, and the style of the Ken'yūsha was actually represented by his works.

Ozaki Kōyō (Tokutarō) is an author who represents not only the Ken'yūsha, but also the whole world of Meiji literature. As mentioned before, Kōyō gained his reputation by his first novel *Ninin Bikuni : Iro Zange.* An elaborate work in an elegant style where both classical and colloquial languages were blended, it was a sad story of which the subject was "the tears of humanity." (From the preface to the work). In writing this work the author emancipated himself from that *gesaku* atmosphere which had restricted him in his initial stage. The story is as follows : Two nuns, both in the bloom of youth, meet at a mountain hermitage ; each confesses her longing for her dead husband, and subsequently it becomes clear that each of the two in the past happened to love the same man. Although the theme of "love and duty" treated here is a traditional one, the author, unlike feudal writers, gives priority to love. This world of faith and pure love, depicted in an elaborate style, is rich in the refined sentiments of an elegy.

Kōyō's elaboration in style in this work was the natural result of his antipathy toward Bimyō and the latter's colloquial style. On the other hand, however, it also stemmed from the author's delicate sensitivity to beauty of style, a sensitivity typical of a master of literature ; indeed, his extraodinary attention to form never changed throughout his career as a novelist. This was a distinguishing feature of Kōyō's writing but at the same time made his works superficial. Although he studied Saikaku, Kōyō did not try to emulate this great writer in the stern attitude of grasping reality ; he was attracted rather by his style which was versatile, witty, colorful, and flexible. This fact proves his over-evaluation of technique and the consequent superficiality in expression. In spite of this, the exquisite quality of Kōyō's works was undeniably one of the elements indispensable to his classical manner of writing.

Kōyō's works that followed *Ninin Bikuni : Iro Zange* include

Nenge Bishō (The Smile of the Twisted Lotus) (1890), *Oboro-bune* (A Boat in the Haze) (1890), *Natsuyase* (Loss of Weight in Summer) (1890), *Uzumagawa* (Uzuma River) (1890), *Muki-tamago* (A Peeled Boiled Egg) (1891), and *Futari Nyōbō* (Two Wives) (1891). Freeing himself from the dreamy fantasy seen in *Ninin Bikuni : Iro Zange*, the author in these works pursued the purity of love of urban women. *Nenge Bishō* is a story of the pitiful love of a man and a woman who see each other every morning on their way to work but who do not marry because of an insignificant misunderstanding, although they love each other in their hearts. *Oborobune* treats of a girl who dies longing for her lover. A daughter of a ruined samurai family, the heroine is obliged because of poverty to become a secret mistress. She comes to love the man, however, only to have him abandon her. In lonesomeness she dies, still loving him. A timid girl is described in *Mukitamago*. To support her poor family, she begins working as an artist's model. At first she is too ashamed to pose unclothed before the painter. However, as time goes on, she finds herself in love with him. The author depicts the psychological process of her relation with him. The heroine of *Natsuyase* self-sacrificingly adopts her husband's illegitimate child born of a daughter of the master's family. A congenital leper woman has to choose death, refusing her lover, in *Uzuma-gawa*, while the sister of *Futari Nyōbō* pursues happiness in spiritual love and a life of sincerity rather than in materialistic pleasures. Thus, these heroines are equally pure-hearted women who arouse the compassion of the reader.

Further deepening his observation of human beings, in addition to an ethic of purity of heart, Kōyō attempted to seek the substance of man in his instincts, carnal desire and passion. He learned this from Saikaku. With such intention, he wrote *Kyara Makura* (The Perfumed Pillow) (1890), a work resembling Saikaku's *Kōshoku Ichidai Onna* (The Life of a Voluptuous Woman) in its style as well as its taste. Once a very famous courtesan, Sadayū, now sixty years old, confesses her past life of indulging in sensual pleasures from the age of fourteen to twenty-eight. Such is the plot of the story. The work draws the characteristics of a true geisha, *nasake* (compassion), *iki* (stylishness), and *hari* (pride), in the person of the heroine Sadayū, who " desired no gold, loved no man, however handsome, and was known as the most unmanageable girl in the quarter." In this respect, the author seems to admire the sincerity of a woman who is not degraded by the wanton life she lives, and this corresponds, in a sense, to the world of purity in his preceding works. But, in another sense, by relating the life of Sadayū who wantonly changes her lovers one after another, the author actually unrolls before us a picture-scroll of the sensual world. And yet the scroll is full of posed scenes of the life of prostitutes, and thus lacks that thorough contemplation of human life seen in Saikaku's works. However, he ostensibly succeeded in representing the world of eroticism of the gay quarters through his exquisite style and redolent sensuality similar to that of Saikaku. In other words, the erotic, sensual world of Saikaku is diluted by Kōyō's commonplace and limited view of humanity.

The old-fashioned amorous life in the gay quarters described in *Kyara Makura* is transplanted into modern urban life in *Sanninzuma* (Three Wives), published in 1892. This work, usually regarded as Kōyō's greatest masterpiece in the first half of his literary life, is really a condensation of all of his preceding pieces. The first part of the story concerns a parvenu, Katsuragi Yogorō, who leads astray three beautiful women of different status and character, while in the second part is related the deceitful lives of those women, each employing her own particular wiles behind the back of the lawful wife. Here again one may, to a certain extent, find instinctive and sensual passions in the portrayal of the desires and actions of Katsuragi, who always relies upon the power of money as well as exploits the coquetry of women. However, the author fails to reproduce the real world of eroticism, for he merely brings together a proud woman, O-Sai, purehearted O-En, and a common morality binding the feudalistic home life, thereby reducing this work to nothing more than a beautiful illustrated scroll of human manners. In Kōyō some touches of this attitude toward coquetry are discernible in his earlier works beginning with *Ninin Bikuni : Iro Zange* through *Oborobune, Mukitamago,* and *Natsuyase,* but he took up this subject directly in *Kyara Makura* and *Sanninzuma.* In these latter works, Kōyō never attained that quality of aesthetic maturity, which we sometimes call decadence, for there was a definite limit beyond which he could not go.

After he concluded his stories of women by writing *Sanninzuma,* Kōyō turned to treat the life of men systematically in his works *Otoko-Gokoro* (A Man's Heart) (1893), *Kokoro no Yami* (The Darkness of the Heart) (1893), and *Tajō Takon* (Tears and Regrets) (1896). Of course we have other works published during this period, such as *Tonari no Onna* (The Woman Next-Door) (1893), *Reinetsu* (Cool Fever) (1894), and *Iwazu Katarazu* (With Neither Words Nor Speech) (1895), all of which were adapted from Western works. In these works a man was not necessarily the main character, but in Kōyō's treatment of all the characters, there is something in common with the other works of this later period.

While in his stories of women Kōyō represented a world of classical beauty characterized by naiveté (*junjō*), stylishness (*sui*), pertness (*kyan*), and pride (*ikiji*), Kōyō in the works after *Otoko-Gokoro* depicted men of eccentric and obstinate character. As a result, the stories became more serious, and there are even some that have an eerie quality. Interestingly enough, as he employs a more realistic method, in content the stories become more romantic. For instance, in *Otoko-Gokoro* we find something dark and demoniac in the destiny of three generations of a family obsessed with the desire for gain and in the monomania of these unsociable people who cannot adapt themselves to their environment. Similarly, a weird atmosphere fills *Kokoro no Yami,* a story of a blind man, Sanoichi, who, tormented by the agony of unsuccessful love, wanders through life like a walking corpse. The same monomania may be recognized in *Iwazu Katarazu*. The reason for the difficulty between Mrs. Kasahara and her husband is left as an enigma until their reconciliation, when it is solved. Abnormal mentality and behavior are treated again in *Tajō Takon* whose hero Ryūnosuke, like Sanoichi, longs for his dead wife.

However, in Kōyō's case, such abnormality and monomania are not pursued to the utmost, and for this reason the eccentric behavior of Mrs. Kasahara and the abnormal psychology of Ryūnosuke toward his friend's wife, for example, are regarded from his viewpoint of common sense morality as problems of minor importance, although he was able at least to represent in their treatment certain demoniac or frivolous factors. This leads us to think that Kōyō's ideal was actually nothing more than a naive and simple ethic.

Kōyō's last masterpiece is *Konjiki Yasha* (The Gold Demon) (1897–1903), the ultimate fruition of his literary talent. In order to take revenge for having lost his love because of the wealth of his rival, the hero, Hazama Kan'ichi, becomes a cruel and malicious usurer. In spite of this seriousness of theme, the love of Kan'ichi and O-Miya prevails, and consequently, the " Gold Demon " remains, after all, a good-natured paramour without any true demoniac character. The coquetry of the voluptuous Akagashi Mitsue presents nothing different in substance from the feminine eroticism manifest in his preceding works on women. When one considers these things, *Konjiki Yasha* is just an overblown classical romance of sensuality, narrated in an elegant style and with a grandeur of construction.

In summary, Kōyō's romanticism cannot compare with either the mysticism of Kyōka or the decadence of Kafū and Jun'ichirō, and it was unable to emerge from the traditional world of *mono no aware*. As regards Kōyō's later work, we shall treat it in the following section, " The Development of Realism."

Of the Ken'yūsha writers centering around Kōyō, only a few were successful, although they attracted considerable attention at the beginning of their careers. Ishibashi Shian (Sukesaburō) was not able to free himself from the *gesaku* mood in his few romances such as *Otome-Gokoro* (A Maiden's Heart) (1889) and *Kyō Kanoko* (The Dappled Cloth of Kyōto) (1890). Ōhashi Otoha (Matatarō) retired from the literary world to engage in the publishing business shortly after his talent in writing was acknowledged through his works *Tsuyu Kosode* (The Dew-Dampened Sleeve) (1890), *Kyōya Musume* (The Daughter of the Shopkeeper Kyōya) (1890), *Shimoyo no Mushi* (The Cricket on a Frosty Night) (1890), all of which were characterized by a peculiar idealism. Nakamura Kasō (Sō) failed to establish his reputation as a writer because of a premature death, although he had shown extraordinary talent in his works of a strange romanticism, *Hanare-Oshi* (A Solitary Mandarin Duck) (1891), *Sarashi-I* (The Well for Bleaching) (1892), and *Usukeburi* (Faint Smoke) (1897). Thus, there remain no more than a few authors to mention as representing the Ken'yūsha: Ryūrō, Bizan, Sazanami, and Suiin. Since in this group Ryūrō and Bizan displayed their talent not as Ken'yūsha writers but as independent authors of *kannen shōsetsu* (idea novels) and *hisan shōsetsu* (pathos novels), we shall treat them as such. Accordingly, there remain Suiin and Sazanami to mention here.

Emi Suiin (Chūkō), in a sense, had a distaste for Kōyō, and, discontented with the latter's works of commonplace sensuality, produced purer and more elegant ones. Known early for his versatility, he wrote, besides historical novels, even popular fiction such as detective and adventure stories. But his specialty was in short stories of the prose-poem type. In *Tabi Eshi* (The Traveling Artist) (1889), published in the *Bunko*, and in his subsequent works, he manifested his personality. Later, the literary world finally came to recognize his poetic manner of writing, when in 1895 there appeared the collection of short stories entitled *Mizuguruma* (The Water-Mill), which was followed by *Nyōbō-Goroshi* (A Wife Murderer) (1895), *Sumiyaki no Kemuri* (The Smoke of Charcoal-Pits) (1896), *Doromizu Shimizu* (Muddy Water and Clear Water) (1896), and *Zeppeki* (The Precipice) (1896). *Mizuguruma* contained such excellent pieces as *Kabuto no Hoshikage* (The Star on the Warrior's Helmet), *Natsu no Tate* (The Summer Villa), *Yakeyama-Goe* (Crossing Yakeyama), *Dankyō* (The Broken Bridge), *Onsen* (The Hot Spring), and *Kyō-Shijin* (The Mad Poet).

The ideal of Suiin was, above all, the beauty of spotless purity, or purity of heart. That is why he delighted in drawing the beauty of an innocent girl and why he sought beautiful and quiet scenes in nature. Occasionally Suiin delineated an unfortunate artist, poet, or entertainer, altogether in obscurity, stubbornly honest, rustic people, and pitiful women of the lower classes. In so doing, the author showed his infinite compassion for solitary people who despite poverty fought for purity in life and kept themselves unsullied. *Nyōbō-Goroshi* is an excellent work in which this ideal of Suiin is represented. The hero, Kondō Kenkichi, is a serious youth who desires to engage in research in astronomy. Angered by a misdeed committed by his uneducated wife who has a dark past, he kills her and himself in order to save her from the defiling world and to purify their love. This is a manifestation of the author's ideal of purity, his preference for death for the sake of this ideal rather than living by yielding to defilement.

However, this ideal of Suiin had no basis in a profound philosophy of the world, and it was lacking in both romantic passion and intellectual content. It was, as it were, a longing for a vague mood and emotion of purity; indeed, it was rather a kind of poetical emotion. His world was pervaded by a lyricism of simplicity, calmness, and innocence, a world of *mono no aware*, but one different from that of Kōyō.

Iwaya Sazanami was recognized for his works treating the pure, emotional, and pitiful life of youth, such as *Satsuki Koi* (The May Carp), renamed *Hatsu-Momiji* (The First Red

Leaves of Autumn), his maiden work which appeared in *Gara-kuta Bunko* in 1888, followed by *Imosegai* (A Shell of Marriage) and *Yūzenzome* (The Printed Mousseline). *Satsuki Koi* is a romance of the platonic affection of boys and girls and of homosexual feeling among boys, a work of novel taste, although immature in technique. It was rather *Imosegai* that made him famous, a story published in 1890 in *Shincho Hyakushu* (One Hundred Varieties of New Works). Heartbroken because his brother took away his lover, a friend since boyhood, the hero of the story leaves the capital for Kamakura. There the lover, having finally refused the brother's advances, joins him, and finally the two drown themselves in the sea. Especially in the chapter " Spring," the author shows his talent in describing the psychology of boys and girls, a talent which led him to become a specialist in juvenile literature in his later years.

Thus, Sazanami turned to writing juvenile stories where he displayed his genius. He published works for children such as *Koganemaru* (Koganemaru the Faithful Dog) (1891), *Shin-Hakken-Den* (New Edition of The Tale of Eight Loyal Retainers) (1892), and *Otogi Taikōki* (The Children's Biography of Hide-yoshi) (1892), and beside these creative works, he exerted himself in introducing the juvenile literature of the whole world. In contrast with his activities in this field, he made little progress as a regular novelist.

When studied closely, we see that both Sazanami's devotion to the life and feelings of younger people and Suiin's longing for purity basically correspond to the *ninjōshugi* of Kōyō. Herein are to be found both the spiritual composure, founded upon common sense, and the popular quality which were characteristic of the Ken'yūsha writers.

2. *The Beginnings of the Romantic School*

It was Yamada Bimyō (Taketarō) who, armed with Western lyricism, launched into the youthful literature of Romanticism, against the classical sentimentalism of the Ken'yūsha. As already mentioned, Bimyō became famous in the literary world before Kōyō, the leader of the Ken'yūsha, which the former left after a short period of membership.

A precocious genius, Bimyō adopted the ideas expressed in *Shōsetsu Shinzui* as his view of literature. Discontented with the dry expression so common in the translated novels of the time, he held that in a creative work " fact " and " ornamentation " should parallel each other. With this view, in his effort to gain mastery of expression, he first studied Bakin and imitated his style, but later he succeeded in creating a peculiar style of *gembun itchi* (colloquialism) which attracted attention. Bimyō's respect for Bakin apparently contradicted the negative attitude toward this feudal writer stressed in *Shōsetsu Shinzui*. However, in reality, what he valued in Bakin was the splendid style and the grandeur of his romanticism, not his didacticism.

As early as eighteen, Bimyō wrote a fantasy *Tategoto Sōshi* (The Tale of the Harp) (1885), which treated the heroic deeds of King Alfred the Great of England. This story with its florid style and romantic composition was a work far fresher and more poetical than any of the contemporary political novels. As his maiden work we have, then, this novel with its conspicuous romantic flavor which can be regarded as the leading characteristic of all of Bimyō's later works.

In November 1886, his *Chōkai Shōsetsu Tengu* (A Satire on Tasteless Novels) appeared in *Garakuta Bunko*. It is of historical significance as the work where the author for the first time tried to establish his own style, abandoning that of Bakin. This story, left unfinished for some time, was later renamed *Kaki Yamabushi* (The Strolling Monk), and was published with other pieces in the collection of stories *Natsu Kodachi* (The Summer Grove). In July 1887, Bimyō was appointed editor of the magazine *Iratsume* (The Maiden). His *Fūkin Shirabe no Hitofushi* (An Organ Melody), which appeared as a three-part serial beginning with the first issue of the magazine, is notable as a short story describing the psychology of young love. Finally

Bimyō gained fame suddenly when he published *Musashino* (Musashino Province) in the *Yomiuri* in November of that year. This last, a kind of historical novel dealing with the Namboku-chō (Northern and Southern Courts) Era, tells in a lyrical fashion of a tragedy that befell a subordinate of the Nitta family who killed himself to follow that family in death. The autumnal scenery of the Musashino plain depicted here is in harmony with the story's romantic content and makes the reader feel truly delicate emotions, the traditional *mono no aware*. When the work was compiled in the collection *Natsu Kodachi* in August of the following year, it attracted a wider attention. Apart from this work, *Natsu Kodashi* contained five stories : *Kago no Toriko* (The Prisoner in the Cage), *Tamaya no Mise* (Tamaya's Shop), *Hana no Ibara Ibara no Hana* (The Flower of the Thorny Wild Rose), *Kaki Yamabushi*, and *Ada to On* (Vengeance and Benevolence). Except for *Kaki Yamabushi*, a satire on the taste and style of the political novel, these were all short pieces, either lyrical or idyllic, and it was the freshness of style rather than the plot of the stories that the public heeded.

Kochō (Butterfly), published in the special issue of *Kokumin no Tomo* (The Nation's Friend) in January 1889, was an excellent historical novel, better constructed than *Musashino*, and it helped to heighten his reputation as a novelist. The work treats an incident in the fall of the Taira family, wherein a woman named Kochō (Butterfly), torn between her loyalty to the Emperor and her love for her husband, is obliged to kill the latter in the cause of loyalty. When told of the Emperor's death, she then resolves to spend the rest of her life as a solitary nun in tonsure. This work was characteristic not as an exposure of an inhuman aspect of feudal morality, such as sacrifice in the greater cause of loyalty, but as a representation of the pathos of human life arising from man's sincerity. A tragic love story, it successfully portrayed the psychological conflict of the characters, and this, assisted by a fresh, sensitive expression of natural scenery and human manners, makes this piece a distinguished one.

Bimyō continued to publish a few historical novels such as *Ichigo-Hime* (Princess Strawberry) (1889), *Makoto ni Ukiyo* (A Truly Trouble-Filled World) (1891), *Maru Futatsu Hiku Shin-Taiheiki* (A New Edition of Taiheiki) (1891), and *Kabuto-Giku* (The Helmet Chrysanthemum) (1891), although the last two were left unfinished. The most remarkable of these is *Ichigo-Hime*. It is said that the author was inspired to write this work on reading Zola's *Nana*, but of course this does not mean that it is a mere adaptation of the latter work. Bimyō published it in *Miyako no Hana* (The Flower of the Capital) from July 1889 to May of the following year, that is, from the 19th through the 39th issues of the magazine. Ichigo-Hime, or, literally, Princess Strawberry, is born as a daughter of a noble family, and grows up to be a beautiful, talented girl with a seductive body. While she is seeking an opportunity to assassinate Ashikaga Yoshimasa, she falls in love with Uroko Tarō. Once this love wanes, she becomes an adventuress, and brings under her control a number of men, one after another, causing a series of tragedies. Finally, the fatal incident occurs when she unknowingly commits incest. Later she goes mad, and dies by the wayside. Though a touch of Neo-Romantic decadence is discernible in the last scene where a wild dog stares at the corpse of the once wanton woman, the actual objective seems to lie in romantically describing the varied fortunes of the heroine. *Makoto ni Ukiyo*, his next work, was also a rather expert piece. However, Bimyō saw a decline in his historical novels for some time thereafter, with no noteworthy work until his later period when he published such excellent pieces as *Jirō Tsunetaka* (1908), *Kosaishō no Tsubone* (1909), *Taira no Shigehira* (1910), *Taira no Kiyomori* (1910), and others.

Other than the historical novels mentioned above, there is a series of realistic novels of urban life, which include *Hana-guruma* (The Wheel of Flowers) (1888), *Nuregoromo* (Wet

Clothes)(1888), *Kono Ko* (This Child) (1889), and *Kyōshi-Zam-mai* (Devoted to Education) (1890). Most of these are failures, and few have much significance. *Hanaguruma* is the initial work in this series. It relates the love of a young student who has to earn his livelihood, and delineates the psychological process whereby he comes to have affection for a sister of a professor at the law school which he attends. Although somewhat commonplace, the work has a wholesome effect on the reader. *Hakugyokuran* (The White Orchid in Paradise) (1891) is the best of Bimyō's work treating modern life. The hero feels righteous indignation against a young Diet Member for the latter's political infidelity, despite the fact that he has been his supporter and that the politician is his sister's lover. The angry man stabs the Diet Member with a dagger and then kills himself by letting a railway train run over him. Thus, this is a romantic work depicting an earnest desire for purity.

As we have seen above, the hero of *Musashino*, *Kochō*, *Hana-guruma*, and *Hakugyokuran* was, without exception, a man of purity and sincerity, and when the author succeeded in drawing such a character, it meant in most cases that the work was of high quality. Unlike Kōyō, who depicted that classical feeling of love, Bimyō attempted to pursue aestheticism. *Ichigo-Hime* was such a work. Admitting that his aestheticism was superficial as well as immature, at least it can be said that his romanticism was far more modern than the traditional *mono no aware* of the Ken'yūsha writers. Because his character was devoid of composure and perseverance, Bimyō fell into the pit of mannerism and did not sufficiently refine his mode of writing, in spite of his advantage of having had a brilliant beginning. For these reasons and for his lack of power in developing a novel, he was before long removed from the main current of the literary world of the day.

When we speak of Romantics, we cannot afford to overlook Saganoya Omuro and Miyazaki Koshoshi as their forerunners. The works of Saganoya Omuro (Yazaki Chinshirō) are unique in their characteristics of a kind of romantic idealism. He studied Russian at the Tōkyō School of Foreign Languages in the same class as Futabatei, and in his leisure hours read both modern and ancient literature, in which he found Turgenev to be his favorite author. He was introduced to Shōyō through Futabatei, and as Shōyō's pupil he began writing many novels, beginning with *Shusendo no Hara* (A Miser's Mind) (1887). Among them, *Hatsukoi* (First Love) (1889) gained him fame in the world of literature. This is a lyrical piece of strong subjectivism, consisting of an old man's reminiscences of his boyhood when he was secretly in love with his cousin. That pure, platonic love of youthful years, too dear to forget, and the bleak, cruel world that would not allow him to bring that love to fruition, these two things are narrated by the old man with great feeling, thereby making the reader also feel the romantic pathos of the situation.

Such platonic, spiritual love, and regret for its never having been realized, constitute a theme that was often repeated in many of his works which followed, such as *Nozue no Kiku* (The Chrysanthemum in the Field) (1889), *Ruten* (Impermanency) (1889), and *Ikken Hibiki Ari Rakka no Mura* (The Clash of Steel in a Village of Falling Flowers) (1896). In *Nozue no Kiku* a young man marries a girl of a poor family, acting upon his belief that marriage is neither for position nor money and that it should be a union of love and mutual faith. His indignant parents declare that the new couple shall not receive any money from them. The disowned youth shortly afterward commits suicide when he realizes that he is incapable of supporting his new home. However, the bereaved wife decides to spend the rest of her life in solitude, believing that love is eternal, not to be broken because of earthly events, and that man and woman can obtain the happiness of infinite love only in Heaven. Spiritual love here is elevated to a heavenly quality, and the author adores the infinity of such a love. The pure and true affection for Hayashi on the part of O-Tsuyu in *Ruten* resem-

bles that of the boy in *Hatsukoi*, and that of the woman in
Ikken Hibiki Ari Rakka no Mura, who longs for the supreme
happiness of living together with her husband, even to the rejection of the love of her father, and corresponds also to that
of O-Ito in *Nozue no Kiku* with her faith in love.

Naturally, this author, supporting purity of love, took a negative
attitude toward sordid, ugly passion. Such an attitude is made
clear in *Kusare Tamago* (The Rotten Egg) (1889) and *Muko
Erabi* (The Choice of a Husband) (1890), and although rather
different from these two, in *Utsusemi* (A Cicada's Shell) also.
Kusare Tamago is a satire on a mission school woman teacher's
hypocrisy and scandalous behavior. In *Muko Erabi* the author
ridiculed the baseness of those men who do not appreciate the
value of love. *Utsusemi* was intended, according to the author's
comment on the book, to make clear the pitiful serfdom of
women by depicting in detail the circumstances of a particular
woman, who, in the beginning innocent and pure in mind, becomes one of the members of the licensed quarters in order to
help her family, and degenerates little by little under the influence
of environment to become a creature having human shape but
without human heart, or "as empty as a cicada's shell." By
means of this work, the author revolted against the defiling
world, using as his weapon poetical righteousness.

However, the idealism of Saganoya showed its characteristics
more clearly in philosophical and symbolical works than in these
pure, lyrical ones. *Ruten* (1889) and *Mugenkyō* (The Dreamland) (1891) were such works. In the former story there are
two men who are antagonistic to each other in character as
well as in their philosophy of life, Hatano, an optimist who is
subservient and realistic, and Hayashi, a pessimist who is suspicious and idealistic. Beside these two there appears Hatano's
sister, O-Tsuyu, who loves Hayashi. The work is worthy of
note for the reason that the author attempts to explain his
idealistic ideas in the portrayal of the antagonism between the
men. Saganoya here insists that the views of life of these two

are nothing but an illusion, and suggests that the purest sagacity, perfect morality, and infinite love are the idealistic state of man where no antagonism can exist. It is suggested that the affection of O-Tsuyu, also having no opportunity to be realized on this earth, will melt into the infinity of love in Nirvana, and thereby live forever. *Ruten* can be regarded in this way as an idealistic story where the author's desire for such Buddhistic salvation is expressed. The agony of an egoistic idealist and his salvation form the theme of *Mugenkyō*. This is a mystic story with the Christian doctrine of original sin as the foundation, but including also Oriental mythological concepts. The hero's visit to the fairyland and the agony he experiences on a solitary island in the bleak ocean are here represented visually, as well as symbolically, as in the works of Rohan. Because of the shallowness of thought and simplicity of construction, the lyricism pervading this piece of work has nothing in common with the profundity of the symbolical works of the latter. However, the significance of this work as the forerunner of Rohan's novels should be acknowledged.

In a word, Saganoya introduced freshness into the literary world by writing works distinguished for their pure lyricism and a tendency toward idealism.

Miyazaki Koshoshi was first recognized after the publication of his novel *Kisei* (Homecoming) in 1890. This in an autobiographical story in the form of a prose-poem treating the author's homecoming on the occasion of the first anniversary of the death of his father who died while Koshoshi was in Tōkyō for his studies. By relating what he saw and heard and thought in his native place, the author describes his love of his village, his faith in his relatives, his affection for the girl he loves, and the kindness to him of his fellow villagers. All these impress the reader by their pure, warm, and truthful quality. He interweaves into the descriptions of the idyllic country life and the beautiful scenery of the mountain village his deep emotions concerning the vicissitudes of rural life, thereby adding a touch of sadness to the sweet pastoral.

Koshoshi derived this idyllic taste from Wordsworth and T'ao Yüan-ming (365–427 A. D.), and he used verses of the latter, such as *An Ode to My Native Place* and *An Ode to Rurality*, as epigraphs to the chapters of *Kisei*. The Chinese style in which it was written, although tending to make the whole work somewhat formal, sometimes had a delightful effect, and thus it gave the work a fresher quality than the urban literature of the Ken'yūsha writers. The pastoral poetic sentiment in *Kisei*, such as that in the chapter "In the Depth of the Mountains" corresponds to that in the works of Doppo which appeared later, while the truthfulness to his sweetheart depicted in another chapter, "Parting," corresponds to the romantic passions of the members of *Bungakkai* (The Literary World). However, Koshoshi lacked that suspicion notable with Tōkoku. All the chapters of this *Kisei* are full of sadness, and many reasons are given for this feeling, such as the recollection of the dead father and the downfall and misfortune of relatives and acquaintances. It seems to be a pessimistic view that makes the author long for the conservative life of a farming village, where he can enjoy leisure days and turn his back on the bustling city life. In reality, this sadness is no more than sentimentalism, and the longing for rustic life is nothing more than the resistance of a young man to the hypocritical urban scene.

This bright, pastoral romanticism that characterizes the works of Koshoshi is supported by Christian spirituality. In addition to *Kisei*, each of his pieces, such as *Ochimusha* (A Fugitive Warrior) (1891), *Akiya* (The Empty House) (1891), and *Maboroshi* (The Phantom) (1892), is permeated by either a lofty idealism or a pastoral poetic feeling. *Ochimusha* is a story of the chaste wife of a Spartan warrior, while *Akiya* depicts the sad love between a war widow and a pure-hearted youth during the Seinan Civil War (February-September 1877). Of the two, the latter is more successful in representing the pastoral quality in a way even more impressive than *Kisei*. Like Saganoya's

Utsusemi, *Maboroshi*, a more interesting romance, suggested the abolition of licensed prostitution. At that time, *Waseda Bungaku* (Waseda Literature), in its 21st issue, pointed out the influence of *Hamlet* and *Macbeth* in this work of Koshoshi, although he naturally fell far short of the stature of Shakespeare.

In summary, Koshoshi had in common with Saganoya a fresh romanticism and a tendency toward idealism. While Saganoya was skilled in giving shape to ideas, Koshoshi was somewhat superior in the technique of expressing pure, idyllic lyricism. In spite of the efforts of these two writers in developing their own peculiar road to romanticism, they failed to become actually great, and only played the roles of pioneers. In the meantime, with the advent of Ōgai and Rohan, the romantic novel flourished more brilliantly than ever before.

3.   *The Idealistic Romantic School*

In considering the development of the romantic style of writing, we cannot neglect the achievements of Mori Ōgai (Rintarō) during the earlier stage of his literary career. Following his return from study in Germany, Ōgai commenced his literary career by publishing a collection of translated poems entitled *Omokage* (Vestiges) (1889), which was a fresh, up-to-date introduction of the romantic poetry of the Western world. After founding the magazine *Shigarami-Zōshi*, he worked energetically as both critic and translator. He next moved into the field of the novel, his first work being *Maihime* (The Dancing Girl) (1890), followed by *Utakata no Ki* (A Record of a Transient Life) (1890) and *Fumizukai* (The Letter-Bearer) (1891). He drew the immediate attention of the literary world for the elegant and romantic taste displayed in these works. All three novels were based on the author's own experience and observation during his trip abroad, with the action taking place principally in Germany. The common theme was a love-affair between a Japanese youth and a German girl. The romantic sentiments, expressed in a mixed Japanese and Chinese style, were astonishingly new, and together with the exotic flavor, made the works almost indistinguishable from translated novels.

Maihime deals with a young Japanese official, Ōta Toyotarō, who, during his study in Germany, falls in love with a dancing girl named Elise. The hero has to desert his beloved upon his departure for home. As a result, he is overcome by self-reproach and repentance, and the story develops in the form of a recollection written by the hero on the steamship which is taking him home. The author is strongly subjective in dealing with the material, which he adorned with vivid expressions, rich in sentiment. The tragic love-affair described in the story is naturally romantic in mood, and at times even includes pathos. But the author's primary concern is not merely in depicting a tragedy. Rather, the major theme is the hero's repentance for his actions which led the romance to its tragic end, as well as his submission to the fate which required such an ending. And yet the deep melancholy, arising from lost love, and the silent repentance and brooding, compose a kind of peaceful, sentimental world which even pathos cannot disturb—a romantic world, overflowing with lyricism. We may say that it is rather close to that classical world of *mono no aware* in which there is a fusion of the object with subjective feelings.

Utakata no Ki deals with a tragic love-affair between a painter named Kose and his model, Marie. Their affair is intertwined with the tragic death of the insane king, Ludwig II, but the major theme is the strange fate awaiting the tragic heroine, Marie. Since there is a lack of smoothness in the fusion of the two themes, the work, when compared with the other two, can be said to be artistically inferior. Nevertheless, in this work also we find a rich display of that sublime poetic sentiment peculiar to the author.

The primary concern of the author in this piece was, as in the preceding novel, not in the romantic affair between Kose and Marie. Rather, Ōgai attempts to express wonder and resignation at the circumstances which inexorably lead both Marie and the insane king to tragic deaths. In the last section, the author describes the mad monarch who is madly in love with Marie's mother, and out of madness, sees the mother's image in the daughter, and pursuing her, falls from a boat and drowns. Marie, from the shock, also topples from the boat and drowns. This peculiar scene suggests that something like a curse had been cast over Marie and exerted an irresistible power over the insane king. Indeed, a strange mystic power seems to be toying with man. In this work, the reader is deeply moved by the cruelty and mystery of the fate which blots out the dreams of Kose, and the fantasies and even the life of Marie, as if they were all mere "bubbles of water" (*utakata*). Also the work strongly suggests an attitude of resignation at the powerlessness of man. As symbolized by the scenes depicting Starnberg Lake, a world of mystery and melancholy seems to be what Ōgai is seeking in this work.

In *Fumizukai*, the author searches for a deeper poetic mood, rich in both romance and mystery. The story treats of a young Japanese officer, Kobayashi, and his involvement with Ida, daughter of Count Beuro of Dufen Castle. The hero merely serves as a messenger (hence the title) who takes a letter from the girl, whose dream is to serve in the king's castle, to her aunt. Thus, the central character in this story is Ida, and Kobayashi is merely an observer.

Ida dislikes her fiancé and the whole idea of the marriage which her father has forced upon her, and enters the castle in pursuit of a silent, convent-like atmosphere of peace and tranquillity. The heroine is elegant in appearance and in manners, but still there is an air of subtle melancholy about her. In the climax, we see Ida, in order to escape from the stifling atmosphere of the ballroom, standing with her back to a marble shelf on which is arranged a collection of elegant chinaware. Here she divulges her secret to Kobayashi. Her protest against feudal convention, her contempt of "blood and clan" as trivial nonsense, and her dream of finding a convent-like, undefiled life in the world of the aristocracy within the king's castle are pure and elevated feelings. Here is suggested a sublimely tranquil spiritual life, which has been raised to an almost religious plane. The romantic spirit of this work is shown in the unending yearning to attain such a spiritual altitude.

As we have explained, the romanticism displayed by Ōgai in his early days, chiefly through the trilogy we have mentioned, was deeply pervaded by intellectuality and purified by a rigid morality. It has an idealistic tendency, and the romantic sentiment, rather, is extremely restrained and at the same time tinged with pathos. The sentiments are pure and refined but lacking the vitality of youth because of the author's strong rationalism. In this sense, we cannot classify Ōgai as a genuine romantic writer; yet, on the other hand, he was not incapable of perceiving the dreams of youth. Indeed, we can say that the fresh poetical sentiments he could not express in his novels found release in the form of translations.

Ōgai translated numerous Western novels, among which *Umoregi* (The Fossil Wood) (1890–1892) and *Sokkyōshijin* (The Improvisator) (1892–1902) are regarded as superior, and, in the sense of the influence they exerted over the literary world, surpass his original writings. The former work was a translation of the German woman novelist Ossip Schubin's *Die Geschichte eines Genies*, while the latter was translated from the Danish writer Andersen's *Improvisatoren*. The literary style of the two translations was rich in nuance and vivid in romantic color, indicating the author's high artistic standards. This style blended with the romantic nature of the subject matter and raised them to a plane where they became original works. It is important to note also that these translations had an almost unbelievably great influence on the sensitive young readers of the time.

In contrast to the Western-type romanticism of Ōgai, it was Kōda Rohan (Shigeyuki), who, as an author in the Oriental tradition, developed a peculiar romantic style of his own, flavored with subtle idealism, one which was exactly the opposite of that displayed by the Ken'yūsha school. Like Kōyō of this school, Rohan first devoted himself to Saikaku. But contrary to Kōyō who was merely engaged in shallow imitation of the Saikaku style, Rohan grasped the inner working of his predecessor's mind, finally surpassing him to create a peculiar literary world of his own. Rohan was to become, together with Kōyō, the foremost author of the early part of the Meiji twenties. Indeed, his depth of thought, his fertile imagination, and strict literary method of composition, all contributed in raising his art to a plane which was far beyond the reach of writers belonging to the Ken'yūsha school.

His maiden work is actually *Fūryū Zen Temma* (The Romantic Zen Demon of Heaven) (1888). However, the content of this story is unknown to us today because the author used the original manuscript as material for pastework. Therefore, *Tsuyu Dandan* (Immaculate Dewdrops) (1889) has come to be regarded as his first writing, and, incidentally, was the work which brought him his first literary fame. Published in the magazine *Miyako no Hana* (Flower of the Capital), the story had an exotic design, with its setting in both America and China. This, together with an ambitious plot based on a series of fantastic incidents and expressed in a brilliant style, already attested to the fertile imagination and profundity of thought inherent in this author. The theme is the glorification of genuine love which springs up between Lubina*, a daughter of a wealthy man named Bunsame, and a young man Morun-Shingier. The title *Tsuyu Dandan*, or " Immaculate Dewdrops," suggests that the romance, pure and immaculate as dewdrops, will finally lead to a happy and peaceful ending. The undefiled spirit of love-for-love's-sake, as displayed in this work, cannot be

---

*Translator's Note: Inasmuch as the names are given in the Japanese syllabary, it is impossible to know for certain what Romanization, if any, was intended by the author.

found in any previous writings with the exception of works by Saganoya.

As we have pointed out, it is true that this work *Tsuyu Dandan* has its major theme in the love-affair between Lubina and Shingier. If we examine the novel more closely, however, we discover that the author has also expressed an ideal conflicting with this major theme. This ideal, as symbolized by the world in which the two characters Bunsame and Ginchōshi are living, is a spiritual attitude resembling the so-called Oriental attitudes of *muga* (non-egoism) or *shadatsu* (detachment), and one which represents a movement toward a world which belongs to a different dimension from that of love. In fact, it must, of necessity, become a force which denies the ego of love. The author, however, has left the two opposing ideals as they are, and does not go the full length in exposing the contradictions. Instead, he took the easier way of solving the contradictions in the form of a happy ending to the love-affair between Shingier and Lubina. This, evidently, was an indication of the immaturity of the insight of the author, who was just publishing his first work. Nevertheless, by this work Rohan appears to have established the future course of his literary activities which was to take him even higher to a world of detachment and comedy.

His next works were *Issetsuna* (One Instant) (1889), *Fūryūbutsu* (The Elegant Buddha) (1889), *Taidokuro* (Facing the Skull) (1890), and *Dokushushin* (The Brilliantly Painted Lips) (1890). These works, in one way or another, denied love or endorsed a world which transcended love.

Issetsuna is a series of short stories linked together as in the case of some of Saikaku's *ukiyozōshi*. Employing a style patterned after Saikaku, the author dealt with the inner workings of human nature at a certain phase of life. A kind of satire, each of the short stories depicts a world of humor and morality which transcends the world of love. Especially interesting are the third and fourth stories. They relate a sad Ainu tale in which a woman is loved by two men. Here the author gives his approval to love, but at the same time places an even higher value on the moral world wherein willpower and unselfish devotion make it possible for love to be blessed. However, a moral world relying on self-restraint cannot be regarded as the same as a world of non-egoism and detachment.

Fūryūbutsu was the masterpiece which was primarily responsible for elevating Rohan to the first rank of the literary world, side by side with Kōyō. One could say that this superior production deals with the romantic and mystic love-affair between a woodcarver named Shuun and O-Tatsu, daughter of a vendor of *hanazuke*, a kind of pickle. Another view would be that the theme is the woodcarver's passionate love of art. However, in our opinion, it would be more accurate to say that the two themes we have just mentioned are fused together into a fantastic idealist world, and that this work is an artistic expression of this world. Shuun's unlimited love of art is joined to his passionate love for O-Tatsu, and out of this union is born his life-like wooden carving of " The Elegant Buddha," or " Fūryūbutsu." Love, in this work, was to be consummated in a religious and mystic form. " The Elegant Buddha " is an artistic work, a carved Buddhist idol. But at the same time, for the hero Shuun, it is a projection of the image of his beloved O-Tatsu. In this sense, *Fūryūbutsu* symbolized an idealistic world in which beauty, faith, and love are all fused together. This work represented one peak of Rohan's peculiar attitude of transcendence.

Taidokuro (originally entitled *Engai no En*, Ties Without Ties) was another of Rohan's masterpieces. The author in this work seems to have advanced a step further towards perfection in depicting a world of romantic idealism, in comparison with the previous work, *Fūryūbutsu*. The story is a romantic fantasy. A man named Rohan (the same name as the author) meets a beautiful woman deep in the mountains, but, upon waking from his fantasy, he discovers a white skull lying on the ground.

And yet the story is not merely a fantasy, since there is the symbolism here of a religious spirit which transcends the world in which there is conflict between body and soul. The work conjures up an artistic world of great subtlety, in the truest sense of this term. Love, in this work, has been cast down into a world of absolute nothingness. The author, however, is not attempting wholly to deny its existence. Rather, for him, love is a thing which must be purified into a platonic and spiritual existence, or, as an alternative, must be dissolved into a world of detachment. Here we perceive one facet of the author's idealism.

Dokushushin is a satire also based on a Buddhist outlook on life, and in it we find the author assuming a caustic and negative attitude toward the passion of love. It also reflects the author's attitude of detachment, which can be perceived in his other works, such as *Shimbijin* (The Real Beauty) (1890), *Fūjibumi* (The Sealed Letter) (1890), *Kekkōsei* (The Blood-Red Star) (1892), *Shin-Urashima* (The New Rip Van Winkle) (1895), and *Dogū Mokugū* (Clay Idols, Wooden Idols) (1905). All of these works, with the exception of *Shimbijin*, which was closer to a satire, expressed, in a profound and intellectualized symbolism, a world of harmony and conflict in the relation between body and soul. These works displayed a mood of meditation and fantasy, and were testimony to an important phase in the development of the author's romantic idealism.

In addition to this symbolic and fantastic mood in his writing, there is another important facet of Rohan's idealism, namely the bias he shows toward a world of will and morality. In this world, the author praises the intellectual powers and the unrelenting willpower of man. Examples of this are the following novels, which, depicting the staunch attitude of a man of spirit, reveal one of the characteristics of the author. The works are : *Kidanji* (A Man of Courage) (1889), *Ikkōken* (A Sword) (1890), *Tsuji Jōruri* (The Street *Jōruri*-Singer) (1891), *Nemimi Teppō* (A Thunderclap) (1891), *Isanatori* (Fishing) (1891),

Gojū no Tō (The Five-Storied Pagoda) (1891), and *Hige Otoko* (The Man with a Beard) (1896).

Kidanji depicts the courage of a warrior who defies death to uphold his honor. *Hige Otoko* praises the courage and firm attitude of a warrior who stakes his life on his beliefs. *Isana-tori* is a story about a man whose whole life is an example of pride, chivalry, and honesty. In the other novels this manly courage is replaced by the sense of pride of the artist. For example, *Ikkōken* depicts a mediocre village swordsmith, who, through his zealous efforts, his pride, and his immovable faith, finally succeeds in producing a sword which comes to be regarded as the masterpiece of the era. This work had an extremely favorable reception. An artist also plays the most important role in *Tsuji Jōruri* and *Nemimi Teppō* (the latter is the sequel to the former), the hero named Michiya being a master in making pots. Kitamura Tōkoku, in his article " *Kyara Makura and Shin'yō Masshū* " (1892), later pointed out that in this work Rohan came close to the theme of *Kyara Makura*, written by Kōyō. Actually, Rohan, in depicting the erotic life of Michiya, leans towards realistic description, with the result that the work, on the surface, seems different from the world of pride displayed in *Ikkōken*. However, the theme was in the satire of the vulgarity of the hero Nishimura Michiya, and the ultimate ideal of the author was not the brilliant talent of Michiya but the sublime pride of the aging Jōshu, who goes his own artistic way without succumbing to the power of money. As shown in this work, Rohan attempted to emphasize the ideal through the medium of satire, a method he frequently experimented with in other works. Here, we believe, is revealed the idealistic element of the author's character.

Gojū no Tō represents the peak of Rohan's idealistic works. The plot of the story is as follows : An architect nicknamed Nossori Jūbei (Slow-Moving Jūbei), who appears outwardly to have only mediocre talents, accomplishes a superhuman task, on the strength of his willpower and unshakable faith. This courageous and undefiled world of the will provides the main theme of the novel. Against this is contrasted another world of will, one of detachment, which is represented by the open-hearted and candid character of Kawagoe Genta. Jūbei revolts against this latter world and even against the violence of nature, devoting his body and soul to the completion of the pagoda. Thus, this work emphasizes the virtues of willpower, in the deepest sense of the term, and glorifies intense, unselfish devotion to art.

Fūryū Mijinzō (The Elegant Small Idol) (1893-1895) and *Sora Utsu Nami* (The Heaven-Striking Waves) (1903-1905) were both long realistic novels. Although we must not overlook the realistic tendency shown in these works, these two stories, unfinished as they are, seem to have been designed to become works of romantic content. According to what is believed to be the author's own statement, the story in *Fūryū Mijinzō* was to develop like this: The boy, Aoyagi Shinsaburō, and the girl, Mariya O-Sayo, both of whom appear from the first part, entitled "The Boat of Bamboo Grass," grow up as childhood friends, but later are separated for a long time. They meet again in their adolescent days but feel the other to be different, and this leads to complications. The result is a bitterness and sadness, and the two find their only consolation in a world of detachment and tranquillity. Their worlds, however, are separated, although the author's intention was to have them fuse together in the end. (From Yanagida Sen's *Kōda Rohan*). From this synopsis, we receive an impression that the author was striving for a world of transcendence, in which life's tragedy, comedy, and tragicomedy—in other words, all of life—are to be accepted warmheartedly with a fatalistic outlook. If our surmise is correct, this work was also to display an idealistic transcendentalism. Setting aside the question of the whole design of this story, we find, in the part existing now, numerous examples of Rohan's favorite idealistic vision, such as the platonic love-affair between Shinsaburō and O-Sayo in their chilidhood, the world of Zen formed around Saishō Dōjin and Yōshi Gyokuzan, the manly courage of Endō Yukimaru, the chivalrous spirit of the Robin Hood-type Kakizaki Jūrō, and the Amazon-like passions of the female character O-Shizu.

According to the author's own words, the published parts of *Sora Utsu Nami* were only part of the prelude of a gigantic novel. The story was to have its main setting on a desert island in the raging Pacific Ocean. The author's plan was to describe the life on this isolated island shut off from civilization, in order to provide a criticism of modern society. This fantastic plot might have been developed into a spectacular and profound world of idealistic romanticism peculiar to this author. However, as far as we can judge from the published section, this work also displays a Rohan-type idealization, as in the description of the intense agony of the grammar school teacher Mizuno, who becomes involved in a one-sided love-affair with his fellow woman instructor, Iwasaki Isoko, or in the way in which the sense of honor of the female character O-Taki, who falls in love with Mizuno, is described.

In fine, Rohan's literary position was that of an idealistic and romantic writer. But his vision of an idealistic world is intricate and difficult to comprehend, and, in a sense, lofty and unlimited. As a result, it is difficult to translate his manner of writing into a single tendency. However, one thing common in the worlds he envisioned is that they were supported by a spiritual pillar of manliness and fortitude. The sense of a stubborn pride, an unaffected spiritual attitude, a Zen-like mood of detachment, as well as a fertile imagination, a passionate fantasy, and a profound intellectualization of romanticism, these were all the manly attributes of the world envisioned by Rohan. The sincere love and pathos found in *Tsuyu Dandan*, *Fūryū-butsu*, *Dokushushin*, and *Fūryū Satori* (Elegant Enlightenment) merely existed as stages in the course of the purification of the attributes we have just mentioned. This explains why Rohan's romanticism is distinctly different from that of Ōgai, and why there is such a wide gap between him and the *ninjō* (human feeling) world of Kōyō.

Another group belonging to the idealistic romantic school were the woman writers. The principal members of the group were Nakajima Shōen (Toshiko), Tanabe Kaho (Takiko), Kimura Akebono (Eiko), Wakamatsu Shizuko (Iwamoto Kashiko), Tazawa Inafune (Nishikiko), Ōtsuka Kusuoko, Kitada Usurai (Sonko), and Higuchi Ichiyō (Natsuko).

Nakajima Shōen constituted the avant-garde among the women writers. Her literary career started early with the publication of *Zen'aku no Michi* (The Road of Good and Evil) (1887) and *Sankan no Meika* (The Noble Flower in the Valley) (1889). In these works she expressed herself passionately because of her idealistic outlook on life, which was most appropriate to this author who was a fighter in the civil rights movement of the Liberal Party of the day. However, the plots of the stories were not very different from those utilized in political novels, the former work actually being a translated version of a foreign novel. With regard to their poetical sentiment, both of these works still displayed immaturity.

Subsequently, Tanabe Kaho published *Yabu no Uguisu* (The Nightingale in the Bamboo Grove) (1888), while Kimura Akebono published her *Fujo no Kagami* (The Mirror of Women) (1889) the following year. With these works, novels written by women began to show signs of the influence of the new literary movement.

Yabu no Uguisu was Kaho's first work and one worthy of notice in the period which saw the emergence of the romantic novel. This story concerns Shinohara Hamako, daughter of a viscount. She is influenced by the shallow modernism of the day, which saw the awakening of a new civilization, and, while her fiancé Tsutomu is traveling abroad, falls in love with another man. Tsutomu returns home and at first displays anger at her unfaithfulness, but finally condones her romance. Tsutomu himself marries a poor but innocent girl named Matsushima Hideko and finds happiness. As this synopsis indicates, this work was a kind of idealistic domestic novel. The author discovers the true worth of human beings in their nobility of character rather than in learning or talent. She pursued this ideal by selecting love-affairs and family troubles as themes of her novels. Following this work, she wrote such excellent stories as *Tsuyu no Yosuga* (The Ties of Dew) (1895) and *Hagi Kikyō* (The Bush Clover and Chinese Balloon Flower) (1895). The former describes a woman named Tsuyuko, daughter of an aristocrat, who gives up hope of marrying because she is ugly, and instead devotes her whole life to painting. The latter story deals with a woman named Namiko. She also gives up her marriage for the sake of her friend and for a time is lonely, but she eventually finds a good husband and leads a happy life. Both works suggest the even-tempered, idealistic outlook on life held by the author. Kaho has come to be regarded, together with Ichiyō, as the foremost among woman novelists. We must say, however, that her optimistic idealism was decidedly shallow when compared with the serious outlook on life shown by Ichiyō.

Fujo no Kagami, written by Kimura Akebono, describes a woman, of perfect character and beauty, who because of her personality is loved by everyone. After studying at Cambridge, she goes to America and experiences factory life. She returns home, builds a factory to launch a relief movement for slum dwellers, and also engages in the operation of a kindergarten and other social work. The basic tone of this work is Christian philanthropy. More like a biography than a work of fiction, it is an awkward piece, displaying artificiality. However, it is filled with a romantic spirit and pure ideals, and this is what we would expect of the eighteen-year-old author.

Wakamatsu Shizuko earned her first literary reputation for the short story *Wasuregatami* (A Keepsake) (1890), which was a delightful lyric work dealing with maternal love. However, it was for her brilliant translation *Shōkōshi* (Burnett's *Little Lord Fauntleroy*) (1890) that she became famous. This story describes an innocent boy named Cedric and his good-natured and warm-hearted mother, and relates how their naivety and innocence move and purify the minds of the people living around them. This work, which was ranked in a class with Ōgai's famous translation *Sokkyōshijin*, not only impressed and influenced the contemporary readers but also the reading public of later generations. The common subject of her works, whether translation or originals, was the innocence of children and maternal love. The main feature of her works is that they are permeated with an unrestrained lyricism.

In contrast with these writers who held an optimistic position, Inafune and Usurai leaned toward pessimism. Inafune's favorite theme was the pathos of the violation of the innocent and pure. Usurai, on the other hand, frequently depicted the tragic suppression of the innocent. This attitude is displayed typically in the former's *Shirobara* (The White Rose) (1895) and *Godaidō* (The Five Great Halls) (1896, published posthumously), and in the latter's *Oni Sembiki* (One Thousand Demons) (1895) and *Kuromegane* (The Black Eyeglasses) (1895). In the works of Inafune, we see a display of eccentricity in the description of misery and wretchedness, while Usurai showed a tendency to fall into sensationalism in dealing with the world of *ninjō*. However, we must recognize their main characteristics, which are the spirit of revolt against vulgarity shown by Inafune and the romantic pathos of Usurai. An author who commenced her active work in original writing a generation later was Ōtsuka Kusuoko, whose pure and romantic lyricism left a deep impression on her readers.

Higuchi Ichiyō was the writer of greatest talent who shone most brilliantly among the woman writers. She was first known to the literary world for her *Yamizakura* (Cherry Blossoms in the Dark) (1892). A crude short story which was more like an étude than a finished work, this novel dealt with young love between childhood companions, and is filled with a mood of tender sentiment. She next wrote *Umoregi* (The Fossil Wood), which was primarily responsible for giving her a reputation in the literary world. This work dealt with the tragic life of gifted pottery maker and his sister. The hero's passionate love for his art, his stubborn revolt against vulgarity, the beautiful relation between the brother and sister, all attest to the noble idealism inherent in this writer. Ichiyō in this period was devoted to the literary style of Rohan, and *Umoregi* was one example of his influence on her. But Ichiyō's true field was not in the masculine world portrayed by Rohan, and with *Ōtsugomori* (New Year's Eve) (1894) and *Yuku Kumo* (The Passing Cloud) (1895), there was a turning-point in her career. That is, she was now to display an original style in stories like *Takekurabe* (Comparing Heights) (1895), *Nigorie* (The Muddied Stream) (1895), and *Jūsan'ya* (Two Nights Before Full Moon) (1895). *Ōtsugomori* deals with a kind-hearted maid, O-Mine, who, because she needs money to help her uncle, is compelled to steal money from her master. This unfortunate situation is one theme, but another is provided in the spirit of revolt shown by Yamamura Ishinosuke, who protects O-Mine chiefly out of disgust with the egoism of his cruel stepmother. Although this work cannot be regarded as perfect from the viewpoint of literary composition, the author breathed into it a poetical sentiment of justice, revolting against vulgarity and expressing her own critical views on the irrationality of life. This spirit of revolt was to be reproduced in the form of the strong determination displayed by the heroine O-Kyō in *Wakaremichi* (The Parting of the Ways) (1896), in the immorality of O-Machi in *Ware Kara* (On My Own) (1896), and in the decision of O-Ritsu to revolt against family life in *Uramurasaki* (Light Purple) (1896).

The greatest work of Ichiyō is *Takekurabe* (Comparing Heights). This story was serialized in *Bungakkai* beginning with the January issue in 1895. Republished, this time in complete form, in *Bungei Kurabu* (The Literary Club) in the April issue of the following year, the novel was to raise her literary fame to a new height. This work, as we shall explain later, gives a realistic and minute description of the psychology and conduct of boys and girls awakening to sex in a life surrounded by the atmosphere of a prostitute quarter. The major theme, however, is the pure, innocent affection shown by the precocious girl Midori, towards the young priest Shinnyo of the Ryūkaji (The Temple of the Dragon Flower), and the eternal pathos of the world which compels the lovers, living in different circumstances, to be separated forever. The romantic sentiments, expressed in a beautiful and romantic style of the *gazoku setchū* (mixed elegant and colloquial) type, constitute the basic tone of the work, set against the erotic background of the prostitute world of the Yoshiwara. This pure romantic sentiment can be perceived in the tender feelings expressed by O-Seki and Rokunosuke, the lovers who are forced to part, in the novel *Jūsan'ya*. The same sentiment has seeped into the romantic feeling and aspiration displayed by O-Kyō and the boy Kichizō in *Wakaremichi*. Among the works of Ichiyō, *Nigorie* can be regarded as most accomplished, so far as the style of the novel is concerned. Abundant in realistic description, the work, however, can also be regarded as a romantic piece, as evinced by the portrayal of the heroine O-Riki and her gradual sinking into an immorality which leads ultimately to her destruction.

In a word, the basic tone of Ichiyō's writing was the romantic spirit. However, in her case, this spirit did not flare up in the form of passion. Instead, it was bathed in a mild and sentimental pathos, and appeared in the form of a spirit of revolt against vulgarity, or as a mood of eternal pathos of the innocent people oppressed by the vulgar world. In this sense, Ichiyō can be regarded as a conservative writer, but she was free from the artificiality and shallowness which had marred the work of such women writers as Usurai. Indeed, among the group of women writers, she was the best.

4. The Development of Romanticism

The growth of the literary circle as well as the major literary movement in the latter part of the Meiji twenties was in the direction of the development of the genre of romantic novels as a reaction against the conventionality and shallowness of the Ken'yūsha school and in order to undermine the literary style of this latter group. The so-called *kannen shōsetsu* (idea novel) of Izumi Kyōka and Kawakami Bizan, and the *hisan shōsetsu* (pathos novel) of Hirotsu Ryūrō, were the negation of or detachment from the Ken'yūsha style. These novels showed a passionate pursuit of the meaning of life or an aspiration for the extraordinary.

The *kannen shōsetsu* was a form in which the author expressed his own ideas on life and the world, either directly or through suggestion. However, the ideas were not generalized or symbolized, as in Rohan's works, but displayed a tendency toward the specific and the subjective. Thus, in the *kannen shōsetsu* these ideas which were subjective and narrow in compass were not condensed into a generalized outlook on life. Furthermore, they were not assimilated into the body of the work, which gave rise to a certain lack of orderliness. However, the spirit of passionate pursuit of the meaning of life met with an enthusiastic response from the contemporary reader.

On the other hand, the *hisan shōsetsu* found its material in the dark side of life, described the wretchedness of existence, and showed keen interest in giving a penetrating analysis of the mind of the characters. As a result, the author's own ideas or convictions did not have much weight in these works. Consequently, this attitude has some aspects which can be considered as one development of realism. However, the fact that the usual method was to create a strange and abnormal world of eccentricity by use of ugly and mysterious characters indicates that these works belonged to the tradition of the romantic novel. Because of their interpretation of life or their description of the serious state of the world, these *kannen shōsetsu* and *hisan shōsetsu* met the taste of the post-war (the Sino-Japanese War) period, and overwhelmed the literary circle during 1895 and 1896. But because the ideas and plots of the novels were restricted by the limited outlook of the authors, their popularity came to a sudden decline in 1897, to give place to the rising tide of the realistic novel. Only Kyōka was to overcome the weakness of the *kannen shōsetsu* and develop a peculiar romantic world of his own.

Izumi Kyōka (Kyōtarō) was a disciple of Kōyō, but his style was distinctly different from the classic style of the Ken'yūsha school, and it displayed a romantic tendency. In 1893 he wrote his maiden work *Kammuri Yazaemon*, and in the following year, with Kōyō as co-author, he wrote *Giketsu Kyōketsu* (The Blood of Honor) and *Yobihei* (The Reserve Corps), which brought him public notice. In 1895 he published *Yakō Junsa* (The Night-Duty Policeman) and *Gekashitsu* (The Surgery), which drew the attention of the literary world to his peculiar style. These two works, together with Kawakami Bizan's *Shokikan* (The Secretary) (1895) and *Uraomote* (Back and Front) (1895), were hailed as *kannen shōsetsu*. As a result, Kyōka surpassed his master Kōyō as far as reputation was concerned.

Yakō Junsa deals with a policeman with a strong sense of duty, named Hatta. Sacrificing his life and love, he tries to help a worthless and odious man, but in the course of rendering assistance he drowns. This work attempted to expose the contradiction between the sense of duty of a public officer and his human feeling. *Gekashitsu* treats of a man and a woman who have a secret love which they do not wish to be revealed and who die together to protect this secret. This morbid love for purity has something in common with the sense of duty of the policeman Hatta. In the concluding part of this story, we find the following words : " To the religious men of the world we ask, ' Is it impossible for us, burdened with sin, to ascend to heaven ? ' " These words indicate a revolt against the conventional formalism of ethics, a praise of genuine love, and a development in the author of a romantic spirit that revolts against the vulgarity of the world. The ego, which in *Yakō Junsa* was a force in exposing the contradictions of the society, was, in this latter work, elevated and grasped as an absolute imperative.

To sum it up, *Yakō Junsa* and *Gekashitsu* were both regarded as *kannen shōsetsu*, or idea novels, in the sense that the author had presented his outlook and vision of life in a concrete form. This tendency is perceived in his other works which appeared during 1895 and 1896, examples of which are *Shōsei Yahanroku* (Bells Tolling at Night) (1895), *Biwa-Den* (The Tale of the Lute) (1896), *Kaijō Hatsuden* (The Dynamo on the Sea) (1896), and *Bake-Ichō* (The Gingko Ghost) (1896). The theme of *Shōsei Yahanroku* was the indignation against a hypocritical religious character. *Kaijō Hatsuden* was an expression of the poetical sentiment of righteous indignation of the author, who hated misdirected patriotism. *Biwa-Den* and *Bake-Ichō* were, in a sense, sequels to *Gekashitsu*, and in the description of genuine love and the tragic life of a man and woman who both revolt against the prevailing ethical code, they manifest the author's intense spirit of rebellion against convention.

As these examples show, the *kannen shōsetsu* of Kyōka were imbued with the rigid sense of righteousness of the author, in the form of revolt against conventional morality, hatred of the hypocrisy of society, and emphasis on love-for-love's-sake. However, these ideas were extremely subjective and cannot compare with such concepts as that of social justice which cover the whole of life.

Thus, Kyōka, who was never an intellectual, tried to conceal his defects by striking out in a new field in which the subjective ideas of the *kannen shōsetsu* were to be transformed, through the use of imagination, into a poetic and mystic world. This naturally resulted in revealing further the romantic aspect of this author, who went on to create a truly colorful and vivid romantic world.

Ichi no Maki—Roku no Maki (From Scroll One to Scroll Six) (1896), *Teriha Kyōgen* (The Farce of Teriha) (1896), and *Chikai no Maki* (The Scroll of the Vow) (1897) represented the first phase in the development of this romantic style. These works treat of pure love, an affection for an older person of the opposite sex. But in contrast with the sublime and intellectualized love of *Gekashitsu*, *Biwa-Den*, and *Bake-Ichō*, expressed in the form of revolt against the formalistic ethical code of the secular world, love was now freed from ideas and arguments, and shaped into a genuine romantic yearning. It is said that the author wrote *Ichi no Maki—Roku no Maki* and *Chikai no Maki*, both of which portray the adolescent world, under influence of Ichiyō's *Takekurabe*. However, these works, when compared with *Takekurabe*, display much more the author's subjective feeling. *Teriha Kyōgen* was written under inspiration of Ōgai's famous translation *Sokkyōshijin*. It deals with the pure and innocent world of love, and overflows with romantic and poetic sentiment. The affection shown by an older woman towards a young boy in these works was refined further into a kind of maternal love expressing an extremely purified state, with the result that a non-sensual fantasy was created in the following works, namely *Ryūtandan* (The Tale of the Dragon) (1896), *Seishin'an* (The Hermitage of Innocence) (1897), and *Oizuru-Zōshi* (The Tale of the Pilgrim's Cloak) (1898). These works displayed features which are already perceived in *Chikai no Maki*, but elements which in the earlier work are still expressed as real, are in these later works extremely idealized or expressed in an imaginary way.

This aspiration for genuine love is a part of the spirit of love-for-love's-sake. It was common for Kyōka to express this spirit by fusing it with the spirit of revolt against the conventional code of ethics. This spirit was already evident in his *kannen shōsetsu* such as *Gekashitsu*, *Biwa-Den*, and *Bake-Ichō*.

The following works were also an expression of a world of love-for-love's-sake, founded upon poetic justice, hatred of the hypocrisy of society, and revolt against secularity : *Tsuya Monogatari* (Tales of the Funeral Night) (1898), *Fukurō Monogatari* (Tales of the Owl) (1898), *Yushima Mōde* (Pilgrimage to the Yushima Shrine) (1899), and *Onna Keizu* (A Woman's Genealogy) (1907).

However, this spirit of meticulousness and of revolt against secularity is generally, in Kyōka's works, stifled by the evil society. In this sense, Kyōka's world is tragic. For example, a pure, melancholic, but romantic and sad beauty, expressed through suicides, death from insanity, and other tragic episodes, constitutes an important part of his works. Occasionally this beauty flares up and evaporates into a mystic and romantic world in which even the blood of a murder is painted over to give a more brilliant and unreal rouge-like effect. This world was depicted in his early works beginning with *Giketsu Kyōketsu*, *Biwa-Den*, and *Bake-Ichō*, and later in *Tatsumi Kōdan* (The Tatsumi Popular Tale) (1898), *Tsuya Monogatari* (1898), *Zoku Fūryūsen* (The Elegant Line, Continued) (1904), and *Zoku Kōsetsuroku* (The Red Snow Record, Continued) (1904).

Kyōka also displayed a predilection for depicting true love in the prostitute world. This was partly due to his schooling during his younger days and partly to his leaning towards Edo tastes, a result of the influence of his master, Kōyō. And yet Kyōka never portrayed the world of eroticism or the life of the dilettante which were favorite subjects of the Ken'yūsha school. Kyōka loved the geisha and prostitutes who, living like the drifting grasses, still did not lose their ability to experience genuine passion. Kyōka prized these women who had an inner pride and a depth of feeling despite their miserable existence, and to him they appeared like white lotus flowers blooming in a muddy pond. This world was a spiritual one in the deepest sense of the word, a world of pure and innocent love, and it was described in *Fūryū Chōhanagata* (The Elegant Butterfly and Flower Pattern) (1897), *Tatsumi Kōdan, Yushima Mōde,* and *Tsuya Monogatari.* The author's yearning for genuine love was carried on the wings of a spirit of revolt against secularity into a world of romance and fantasy. This is apparent in *Ryūtandan, Seishin'an,* and in *Oizuru-Zōshi.* In addition to these works, the following are also typical examples of his fantastic and romantic style of writing, namely *Sasagani* (The Bamboo Crab) (1897), *Kuroyuri* (The Black Lily) (1898), *Kōya Hijiri* (The Sage of Mt. Kōya) (1900), *Nyosenzenki* (A Fairy Prelude) (1902), *Kusuri-Zōshu* (Medicine Tales) (1903), and *Shunchū* (A Spring Noon) (1906). *Kōya Hijiri* is a supreme masterpiece, and represents the peak of his unique style we have just traced. A priest of Mt. Kōya goes up into the high mountains of the Hida range where he spends one night at the home of a mysterious beauty. During the night he witnesses numerous apparitions, and the work describes this fantasy. It is spun around an ugly idiot youth, who lives with a woman in an isolated house, and a grotesque parade of men turned into animals by the spells cast on them by a sorceress of unearthly beauty. This fantasy unfolds in the deep and silent mountain, and produces an eerie atmosphere of mystery and romanticism. The voluptuous beauty, who, in this isolated house is served by hundreds of grotesque monsters, is the symbol of the genuine beauty which the author was striving to attain through his yearning for purity and his revolt against the secular world.

Another facet of Kyōka's aspiration for beauty appeared in the form of his devotion to art. Frequently the heroes of his stories are artists, as in *Teriha Kyōgen, Hige Daimoku,* and *Tsuya Monogatari,* and in *Sasagani* and *Fukurō Monogatari* craftsmen play the leading roles. The work in which he pursued most conspicuously this theme of devotion to art was *Uta Andon* (Song and the Lamp) (1910), which concerns the love of a *nō*-master for his artistic world. This spirit of art-for-art's-sake was combined with Kyōka's spirit of denial of the vulgar, his longing for the aesthetic atmosphere of the *demi-monde*, and his yearning for genuine love, to form a peculiar world of mystic romanticism, which was, in a sense, an aggregation of all the worlds he envisioned.

The romantic spirit of Kyōka which stemmed from a poetical sense of justice that revolted against vulgarity became realistic whenever the revolt became passionate ; but whenever this spirit of revolt evaporated into a world of sentiment, the romantic spirit passed into a mystic fantasy. *Uta Andon* was a typical example of the latter case, while the former found its ultimate expression in the masterpieces *Fūryūsen* (Elegant Line) (1903) and *Zoku Fūryūsen* (Elegant Line, Continued) (1904).

Although we used the term "realistic" in the foregoing paragraph, the world was a beautified and idealized one of romantic mysticism. Conversely, although we used the word "fantasy" in our explanation in the foregoing paragraph, we still can detect the aura of the romance which exists in this world of actuality, and we can also feel the warmth of the human being living in this world ; for Kyōka's "fantasy" was certainly not a demoniac world, nor was it completely one of sorcery. A more familiar world of faerie—this was precisely the position of fantasy envisioned by Kyōka. In other words, the world as he saw it was a romantic and beautiful one imbued with the mystic and subtle atmosphere of faerie.

In the Ken'yūsha school, Kawakami Bizan (Ryō) was regarded as possessing a special talent. His unique style was shown, albeit slightly, in *Yukioritake* (The Bamboo Bent By Snow) (1890), *Sumizome-Sakura* (The Cherry Dyed Black) (1890), *Shirafuji* (White Wistaria) (1893), and *Shizuhata* (The Rustic Loom) (1893), but these works still failed to establish his literary fame. In 1895, he published *Ōsakazuki* (The Great Saké Cup) and, in the same year, by writing *Shokikan* and *Uraomote*, both of which were so-called *kannen shōsetsu*, he drew sudden attention from the literary world. Bizan, when compared to Kyōka, does not display distinct ideas. The most we can say is that he was possessed of a kind of spirit of revolt against the secular world, but even this was more a part of his personality than a definite tenet.

Shokikan describes a man engaged in the copper business who is even capable of sacrificing the innocence of his beloved daughter for the sake of earning money. A corrupt public official who exploits his own social position to satisfy his sexual desire is placed in the secondary role. Through the activities of these two characters, the author depicts a vulgar world in which virgin purity is sacrificed for the sake of a scandalous relation between bureaucrats and capitalists. At the same time, Bizan praises the noble spirit of a youth, who, deprived of the girl he loves, revolts against the defiling world and devotes his whole life to philosophical research. We can assume that the author expressed his spirit of revolt against the sordid world in the character of this philosophical youth. *Uraomote* describes a reputable gentlemen, known for his charity and virtuous conduct, who, through force of circumstance, breaks into the home of the man his daughter loves, in order to steal a hand-box, but is discovered in the act. The story ends with the father committing suicide after entrusting his daughter to her lover. Here again is displayed the spirit of revolt against a hypocritical society which forces a conscientious man to degrade himself into a culprit.

The germ of the author's spirit can be perceived in his early works which were not yet called *kannen shōsetsu*. For example, in *Yukioritake* he describes a man and woman who revolt against the conventions of society and place a higher value on love than on fame. *Sumizome-Sakura* describes the passion of a girl who, out of love, hurts her benefactor. The principal character in *Shizuhata* is a guard of a mansion, named Yoraku, who because of a hopeless love, retires from the world and reproduces the image of his beloved on a painting, which becomes a famous masterpiece. This character in certain respects may be regarded as the projection of the philosophical student Tsunao in *Shokikan*. The works we have mentioned all dealt with the theme of love, and consequently we must note the author's praise of genuine feeling; but more important is that this unselfish love was supported by a silent resistance to the vulgar world. Indeed, we can consider this to be the main feature of Bizan's writing.

This vague spirit of revolt, in his later works such as *Shira-fuji* and *Ōsakazuki*, shows a slight conceptual tendency. The former was a satire on the frivolous human nature which the author expressed in the saying, " Everyone disperses when there is worry; everyone gathers when there is rejoicing." The latter also expressed a spirit of bitter revolt against the faithless world. However, this spirit was strongly subjective and did not reflect any fully formulated ideas.

On the other hand, we perceive, if not in full degree, some distinct concepts which resemble a sense of justice and of indignation at the wrongs and hypocrisy of society. However, when compared to Kyōka's revolt against the vulgar world which was expressed in poetical justice, Bizan's philosophy did not have any definite goal, and reflected the basic weakness in his thinking. This was the source of the disorder and lukewarmness displayed in his writings, and the main reason why his *kannen shōsetsu* did not develop further.

In later years he displayed to a minor degree a subtle style in such works as *Matsukaze* (The Wind in the Pines) (1896) and *Gensei* (The Humming of the Strings) (1897), but the fatal lack of imagination prevented him from entering a romantic world.

Hirotsu Ryūrō (Naoto) was another writer, who, while belonging to the Ken'yūsha school, displayed a unique style. Even in his earliest work, *Joshi Sansei Shinchūrō* (Women's Participation in Politics Is Just a Dream), written in 1889, we discover this unique style, despite the fact that it was a political novel. In the same year, he wrote *Zangiku* (The Remaining Chrysanthemum), his first official literary work. The penetrating psychological analysis of the heroine who suffers from tuberculosis gave an indication of the method he was to develop in later years. However, his full-scale activity started when he began to write the so-called *hisan shōsetsu*, or pathos novels. Among his works in this genre, the principal ones are *Heme-Den* (The One-Eyed Man) (1895), *Kurotokage* (The Black Lizard) (1895), *Kame-San* (Turtle) (1895), *Kawachiya* (1896), and *Imado Shinjū* (The Imado Double Suicide) (1896).

Heme-Den describes a man with one eye, named Denkichi, who is ugly in appearance but honest in character. He is betrayed by his evil friends, loses his fortune, and finally commits a grave crime, murder. A psychological analysis is given of this profoundly tragic incident. The heroine in *Kurotokage* is also one-eyed, an ugly woman whose face is disfigured by smallpox, but, as the wife of a carpenter, she is virtuous and even-tempered. However, she is violated by her father-in-law in an alcoholic stupor, with the result that she kills him by using a poisonous lizard. She then throws herself into a river and drowns, ending the whole wretched affair. *Kame-San* treats the abnormal relationship between an idiot dwarf nicknamed Turtle and a notorious adventuress known as Python O-Tatsu.

As shown by these examples, Ryūrō had a special interest in using persons who were deformed, either mentally or physically, as characters in his novels. Denkichi in *Heme-Den*, O-Tsuga and her father-in-law, Kichigorō, in *Kurotokage*, and Kamemaro in *Kame-San* are all deformed characters. In some cases, the author contrasts the ugly with the beautiful in order to accentuate the eccentricity. For example, the character in contrast with Denkichi is a beautiful girl named O-Hama, while Turtle is contrasted with the seductive adventuress who has a python tattooed on her beautiful body. The world spun around these characters is eccentricity itself. It can be called a morbid, abnormal one—a world of grotesques. In his predilection for the abnormal and deformed, we see the peculiar characteristics of his romanticism.

As a side-current of the Romantic novel there is the genre of the historical novel. These historical pieces roughly preceded the appearance of the *kannen shōsetsu* and *hisan shōsetsu*, and were born in response to the needs of the readers, who were tired of the limited outlook on life and the conventional plots of the romances written in the Ken'yūsha fashion. At the same time, we can say that the historical novel caught the common people's fancy for biographical works.

The writer who satisfied this kind of public taste and rapidly climbed to the first rank in the literary world was Chinunoura Namiroku (Murakami Makoto). His first work, *Mikazuki* (1891), dealt with the life of a commoner of chivalrous spirit, named Mikazuki Jirōkichi, who, in defiance of the two hundred sixty-odd *daimyō* (feudal lords), conducted heroic resistance against the *hatamoto* warriors (direct Tokugawa retainers). The work, permeated with the stubborn spirit of resistance, depicted the masculine world of honor and bravery, and enjoyed a wide popularity. In the same year he later wrote *Izutsu Menosuke*, which described a fearless youth, his chivalrous activities and tragic love. In *Yakko no Koman* (The Tragedy of Koman) (1892), the author relates the passionate love and sad fate of the heroine Koman. All of the works mentioned here depicted a world of courage, chivalry, and honor, and the author also imbued this world with subtle sentiments, pure, melancholic, and beautiful—a world that captured the heart of the reading public.

As evinced by these works, then, Namiroku portrayed a world of chivalry, and specialized in describing the pride which even dilettantes and ruffians possess. At the same time he praised this passionate moral sense and the unbending spirit of this world. This idealistic and romantic treatment enjoyed a temporary popularity, but he gradually came to display a type of mannerism peculiar to himself, such as that in *Oni Yakko* (The

Devil Servant) (1892), *Yaburedaiko* (The Torn Drum) (1892), *Tasoya Andon* (The Dark Lantern) (1894), and *Hige no Jikyū* (The Bearded Jikyū) (1894). This mannerism exposed the unreality of his biographical plots and his outmoded interpretations of human life. This somewhat vulgar quality caused his works to be tagged as "geisha stories" (literally, *bachibin shōsetsu*, or "novels of plectrum and sidelocks"), and the public very soon tired of his writings.

While Namiroku found his ideal in the common people's code of honor in the Tokugawa Period, the writer who found the ideal of the historical novel in the chivalry of the medieval warriors was Tsukahara Jūshien (Yasushi). His works include *Nagashino Gassen* (The Nagashino War) (1893), *Yamanaka Genzaemon* (1894), *Hōjō Sōun* (1895), and *Yui Shōsetsu* (1897). Also of a similar type were Murai Gensai (Hiroshi), who wrote *Kinugasa-Jō* (Kinugasa Castle) (1892), *Sakura no Gosho* (The Cherry Palace) (1894), *Hinodejima* (The Island of the Rising Sun) (1896), and *Oki no Kojima* (The Small Island Far Out) (1896), and Chizuka Reisui (Kintarō), known for his *Ezo Daiō* (The Great Lord of Ezo) (1892) and *Hangetsu-Jō* (Half-Moon Castle) (1894). These stories dealt exclusively with warriors or persons of a similar nature, and were written as historical biographies which stressed the pride, courage, nobility, and integrity of the characters.

These historical novels were the projection of the author's subjective aim in pursuing the meaning of and gaining lessons from the historical facts. These works not only have a biographical significance but also reflect the passionate attitude of the authors, a fact which is of greater importance to us. This was partly the reason why these historical novels enjoyed popularity and took the place of the so-called geisha stories. At the same time, we must admit, however, that these historical pieces displayed an anachronistic artificiality in plot and were weak in the analysis of the mind and personality of the characters. In this sense, these works cannot escape the criticism of commonness. Nevertheless, the retrospective and idealistic tendency of these works coincided with the spirit of the age which was experiencing a surge of nationalism. These works, together with the stories of Namiroku, engulfed the literary world of 1893 and 1894, the years when other literary production was relatively meagre. This period, meanwhile, saw Takayama Chogyū publish his *Takiguchi Nyūdō* (The Lay Priest Takiguchi), which took first place in a historical novel contest sponsored by the *Yomiuri Shimbun* in 1894 and was warmly received by the reading public. The theme, adapted from the medieval tale *Heike Monogatari*, dealt with a warrior, Saitō Tokiyori, who, failing in love, tires of life, and becomes a Buddhist monk. Later he follows in death Koremori, the son of his lord Shigemori, by self-immolation. Depicting the sorrows of warriors and praising their integrity, this was rather a lyrical epic than a historical novel. It was an expression of melancholy, which was quite natural in the young Chogyū. Although this work cannot escape the criticism of being shallow and superficial in the description of the mind and personality of the characters, the lyrical feeling, expressed in a rhythmical style which was both elegant and beautiful, was memorized by the young readers of the day who were deeply affected by the rising tide of romanticism.

In summary, the historical novels enjoyed a temporary popularity in the wake of the receding geisha stories. However, the subjectivity and superficiality inherent in this genre suggested that some day or other it would have to give way to the *kannen shōsetsu* and *hisan shōsetsu*.

CHAPTER III THE DEVELOPMENT OF REALISM

1. *Shōyō and Futabatei*

In 1885 Tsubouchi Shōyō published *Shōsetsu Shinzui* and *Tōsei Shosei Katagi*, thereby erecting in the Meiji literary world a landmark on the road to realism. However, we do not mean to say that there was no realistic tendency in the period preceding the publication of Shōyō's two works. In fact, the group of *gesaku* writers who were carrying on the tradition of the Edo style began to display, if not voluntarily, a tendency to describe the actual state of the world, as they shifted their theme to the events of the new era.

For example, *Torioi O-Matsu Kaijō Shinwa* (1878), written by Kubota Hikosaku, was a so-called adventuress story (*dokufu-mono*). Yet this story concerning a woman, beautiful but of a low birth, who by force of circumstance meets a tragic death, reflects to a moderate degree the actual atmosphere of the early Meiji years. Okamoto Kisen's *Shimada Ichirō Samidare Nikki* (The Early Summer Rain Diary of Shimada Ichirō) (1879) is a story of revenge, and as the title indicates, deals with the life of Shimada Ichirō. However, this story is actually set in the days after the Seinan War, and mirrors to some extent the actual state of the country during this postwar period. Takeda Kōrai's *Kamuri no Matsu Madono Yoarashi* (The Tempest at Night) is a story of a peasant uprising, and it is a rather a faithful portrayal of an actual event which took place in the village of Shindō in the province of Sagami in 1878, when the leader of the peasants, Kammuri Yazaemon, set fire to the house of a landowning family, the Matsuki. Another love story which was an authentic record was *Nihombashi Ukina no Uta-Hime* (The Lighthearted Singing Queen of Nihombashi) (1883), by Yamada Shuntō. Based on the love tragedy of a Nihombashi geisha named Utakichi, this work attempted a psychological analysis of the lovers as they near their tragic double suicide. This groping for realism is also well represented by Kanagaki Robun's *Agura Nabe*. Only one step forward was needed to reach the world of Shōyō's *Tōsei Shosei Katagi*.

The works mentioned above, though limited, were realistic in the sense that they dealt with actual happenings of the early Meiji years or portrayed the actual state of the world in that period. The political novels, which were to come into vogue next, appeared against a background of political excitement, and at the same time attempted to a certain extent a realistic description of the world of *ninjō*. Especially Suehiro Tetchō's *Setchūbai* and *Kakan'ō* were rather close to the genre of realistic novels. However, just as the *gesaku* writings inevitably became a kind of game or amusement, the political novels too were to degenerate into a vague romantic idealism. In other words, these two literary genres were devoid of that distinct consciousness peculiar to realistic writing. It was precisely in this situation that Shōyō opened up a road to realism, both in the field of literary theory and in actual writing. This work, considering the peculiarity of the situation of the time, was truly an original one.

Shōyō earlier had written about twenty to thirty pieces, but most of them were translations or political essays. *Shumpū Jōwa* (Spring Romance) (1880) and *Taisei Katsugeki : Shunsō Kiwa* (Spring Tales) (1884), which were translations of Scott's romances and poetical tales, attracted attention, but not necessarily for their realistic tendency. However, in the preface of *Kaikan Hifun : Gaiseishi-Den* (1885), a translation of one of Lytton's historical novels, the author explains the meaning of " the real essence of the novel." Stating that " the novel should find its essence in human sentiment and in actuality," he argues that the attribute of a true writer is his depth of penetration into the human mind and his skill at making fictional characters appear as true, living people. A hint of this view is found in the note the author attached to *Shumpū Jōwa*. But it was in the year 1885 that the author assumed a definite position on realism. From February 11 of that year, Shōyō commenced to make a clean copy of his *Shōsetsu Shinzui*, in which he stated explicitly that " in the novel, human sentiments (*ninjō*) come first ; the state and manners of the world (*setai fūzoku*) come next."

The author seems to have had the outlines of both *Shōsetsu Shinzui* and *Tōsei Shosei Katagi* in mind for several years. Although both of these works seem to have taken shape at roughly the same time, the author completed the original manuscript of *Shōsetsu Shinzui* somewhat earlier. The theory expounded in this work was to be gradually reflected in his original writings and to raise *Yūgaku Hasshōnen* (Eight Youths in Pursuit of Knowledge), the work dealing with the author's fellow students and their adventures in Tōkyō which provided the plot for *Tōsei Shosei Katagi*, from the genre of *gesaku* writing and propel it in the direction of realism. It is at the end of this route that we see the appearance of *Tōsei Shosei Katagi*. *Shōsetsu Shinzui* was published in the period from September 1885 to April of the following year. It was completed after *Tōsei Shosei Katagi*, which was published between June 1885 and January of the following year. However, we think it fair to assume that *Shōsetsu Shinzui* provided the theory and that *Tōsei Shosei Katagi* was the materialization of that theory. Incidentally, the author had mapped out the original scheme of *Tōsei Shosei Katagi* at a relatively early period. But since the plot was of *gesaku* origin, it could not have had much success even if it had been written as a realistic novel in conformity with the author's new theory.

Tōsei Shosei Katagi depicted the life at Tōkyō University (in the novel, a certain private school) in about 1881 and 1882. The background of the novel is the school, the students' dormitory, *sukiyaki* houses, and vaudeville stages, which the author himself frequented, and the Yoshiwara prostitute district and the amusement center in Awaji-chō which were the favorite playground of delinquent students. Also forming the background are the geisha houses in Dōbō-chō, a hot spring hotel in Komagome, the home of a kept mistress in Shitaya, and an attorney's office. This setting enabled the author to describe various aspects of the contemporary world, and against this background the life of some ten students of a variety of types. Most of the stories concern the embarrassing experiences of these naive youths. The principal element was comedy, and as Takada Hampō was to point out later, humor and wit. Pathos occupied a minor place in this story. In this sense, this work belonged to the tradition of the *katagi-mono* (" character " works) and *kokkeibon* (humorous books) of the Edo Period, and gave an intellectual and objective treatment of actuality. Here we see the embodiment of the theories of *Shōsetsu Shinzui* which placed emphasis on a realistic description of "the state and manners of the world."

Furthermore, it is evident that the author tried to point out the difference in character among the ten students. However, as the same critic Takada Hampō was to indicate later, Shōyō made much of the external habits of his characters and failed to give a realistic appraisal of the different personalities. So much did the author dwell on these habits and mannerisms that people became curious as to who were the originals of the fictional characters. The hero of the story appeared to be a characterization of the aforementioned critic Hampō himself. But, with the exception of two or three, the characters were not faithful copies of their original models. In general, they were more like products of the author's imagination. However, there is no denying that the author attempted to portray the characters as actual living persons. In other words, it is quite clear that one of the aims of the novel was the realistic expression of human feeling, that is, the faithful copying of human personality. In this sense, the novel can be considered as a by-product of the theories expounded in *Shōsetsu Shinzui*, which advocated the depiction of human sentiment and the state of the world. But as a by-product the novel was incomplete, and there is no denying the fact that there were numerous evidences of romantic artificiality and influence of *gesaku* writing. This is revealed strikingly in the biographical plot composing the core of story, which deals with one of the students, Moriyama Tomoyoshi, and his search for his sister, and it is also revealed in one of the important events in the novel, the love-affair between one of the students, Komachida Sanji, and his childhood sweetheart Tanotsugi, who has become a geisha. The former plot develops in the form of a series of complicated situations similar to those used in *kusazōshi* writing, and has a happy ending with the brother finally meeting his sister. This plot is intertwined with the schemings of a geisha named Kaodori and her mother, and the hero has to overcome numerous misunderstandings to bring everything to a happy conclusion. The whole story also ends when this theme is brought to a close. As to the love-affair between Sanji and Tanotsugi, it also develops along a line similar to that seen in *kusazōshi* writing. In contrast with the positive attitude of Tanotsugi, Sanji, partly under advice from his friends and the warning issued by school authorities, and partly out of his own considerations, attempts to extricate himself from the love-affair. A point different from Edo dramas and novels was that the hero, rather than the heroine, is lukewarm in pursuing love. Thus, this love-affair, rather than the main theme, has significance novel-wise, especially from the viewpoint of portraying human sentiments. However, this story stops abruptly, giving strength to the criticism that the novel was a new style work but without an ending. And yet the fact that the brother-and-sister theme was given a proper solution in the story suggests that this love-affair was merely a secondary plot. Nevertheless, the general impression here is that the novel is without unity.

Despite his efforts, the author failed to give a penetrating analysis of the love-stricken Sanji and Tanotsugi. However, we cannot but feel that if the heroes had been fully developed, they could have become counterparts of the ones in Futabatei's *Ukigumo* and Fūyō's *Seishun* (Youth) and of those in the later works *Sanshirō* and *Higan Sugi Made* (Until after the Spring Equinox) of Sōseki. At any rate, Shōyō attempted to describe the personality and minds of the intellectuals of the contemporary world, a theme which was non-existent in Edo literature. In this sense, this work marked the beginning of the major current of the novel which developed from the Meiji Period onward. And yet this *Tōsei Shosei Katagi* shows the remaining influence of *gesaku* writing in its plots and literary style. Even the fact that the author assumed the pen-name of Harunoya Oboro (Spring Evening Haze) meant that the form of publication was following that of the *kusazōshi* writings. Therefore, it is difficult to treat this work as a strictly Meiji-style novel. However, the realistic elements scattered throughout the novel reflect the desire to portray the image and life of the people of the new age.

After *Tōsei Shosei Katagi* was completed in January 1886, the author in the same month started publication of *Shimmi-gaki : Imotose Kagami* (The Newly Polished Mirror of Marriage). This work was slightly shorter than the previous one but still full-length a novel. The plot of the story was announced beforehand in the last pages of *Tōsei Shosei Katagi*. It begins by portraying the life of the former students, now in their adult life, and deals with the hero, Misawa Tatsuzō, who makes a bad choice in his wife O-Tsuji, the daughter of a fish-dealer; as a result of the unhappy marriage, she commits suicide by drowning. As a parallel development, the daughter of the rich Nanjō family, O-Yuki, who was engaged to Tatsuzō but was forced into another marriage, also falls into an existence even more miserable than that of O-Tsuji. This work also displays a leaning toward the *kusazōshi* taste in that the two parallel plots present unnecessary complications. The theme, as indicated by the title, is more a code of ethics for married life, and the work cannot escape the criticism of reverting to

Bakin-style didacticism. Nevertheless, even in this work we see the author advancing in the direction of realism. It is especially interesting to note that Shōyō in this novel borrowed the method of Western literature in using a separate paragraph for the conversations among the characters.

The same year, Shōyō wrote satirical pieces that showed the influence of the political novel, such as *Naichi Zakkyo : Mirai no Yume* (Too Crowded to Live : A Dream of the Future) and *Fūkai: Kyō Warambe* (A Satirical Remonstrance : The Lad of the Capital). The following year, he turned out short pieces with a slightly realistic color, such as *Tabigoromo* (Travel Dress), *Koko ya Kashiko* (Here and There), and *Tanehiroi* (Collecting Seeds). *Matsu no Uchi* (The New Year Season), published in 1888, is a short story in which the primary interest of the author is in depicting a sensitive student, Kazama Senzaburō, and his reaction to a trifling, but to him significant, incident. This resembles a psychological novel or a detective story. It would appear that Shōyō unconsciously displayed the influence he had received from this type of novel which he had been actively translating at this period. In the following year, 1889, the author indicated his intention to write a full-scale realistic novel, and published a short story entitled *Saikun* (The Wife), which deals with the family difficulties of a public official, Shimokawabe Sadao, who has returned from an overseas trip, and the agony of his wife O-Tane, a normal school graduate, who is troubled by her parents who are always asking for money and by her husband's immoral affairs. The author views these problems through the eyes of the family's maid O-Sono. The story ends with the maid, sent to a pawnshop by her mistress who is pressed with the need of raising money to meet her parents' demands, being robbed of the money on her return home and consequently throwing herself into a well because she feels responsible for the loss. O-Tane divorces her husband, and in her place he brings in the woman with whom he became intimate during his trip abroad. The author, it may be recalled, depicted an inconclusive love affair in *Tōsei Shosei Katagi*. In *Imotose Kagami* he portrayed the tragic consequences of free love and forced marriage. In the work under discussion he deals with the misguided life of a couple after their marriage. Looking at this transition carefully, we perceive in Shōyō a motive that can be compared to that which led the later Sōseki to write *Sanshirō*, *Sorekara* (And Then), and *Kōjin* (The Passerby).

Shōyō, then, attempted in his novels to deal squarely with the marriage problems of the Meiji intellectual. However, restricted by his didactic viewpoint and his *kusazōshi*-style plots, he failed to realize his original objective. In the course of these writings, Shōyō befriended Futabatei and was greatly stimulated by the latter's serious attitude on life and his modern technique of the novel formed by his reading in Russian literature. As a result of this stimulus, Shōyō attempted to discard his *gesaku* attitude and open a real road of realism. But he finally became aware that his ability was not equal to the task, and with *Saikun* as his last work, he stopped writing novels. We know of this attitude from his existing diaries and notes taken from his talks.

Futabatei Shimei (Hasegawa Tatsunosuke), under persuasion from Shōyō, started writing *Ukigumo*, and published the first part in June 1887. This publication bore on its cover the name of Tsubouchi Yūzō as its author, and inside were inscriptions that the co-authors were Harunoya Shujin and Futabatei Shimei. Futabatei at this period was reading the writings of Belinsky, and on his frequent visits to Shōyō's home expressed considerable doubt with regard to the theories expounded in the latter's *Shōsetsu Shinzui*. Moreover, in contrast with Shōyō, whose primary literary influence came from the romantic novels of England, Futabatei, who had read Russian works in the original at the Foreign Language School, was striving for a far more advanced stage, as far as literary methods were concerned. Shōyō to the last could not free himself from the style of Bakin and Shunsui; Futabatei, on the other hand, was working toward the creation of a realistic novel based on an exclusive use of the colloquial style. Therefore, his *Shōsetsu Sōron* (General Theory of the Novel) and *Ukigumo* were far more advanced in the field of realism than Shōyō's respective counterparts, *Shōsetsu Shinzui* and *Tōsei Shosei Katagi*.

Shōsetsu Sōron was published the year before the publication of *Ukigumo* in the *Chūō Gakujutsu Zasshi* (The Central Academic Magazine). This essay was written along the line of Belinsky's "The Essence of Fine Arts," which presented Belinsky's theory of fine arts, the main sections of which Futabatei had already translated, probably with the intention of publishing them in the same magazine. In the final part of his *Shōsetsu Sōron*, Futabatei revealed some opinions which seemed to be his own views on the novel as distinct from those of Belinsky. According to these views, there are two types of novel, the didactic (*kanchō*) and the realistic (*mosha*). However, the true type of novel is the latter, which, he says, is to "reveal the fictional (*kyosō*) by borrowing the garments of the actual (*jissō*)." Furthermore, the actuality is covered with a mist of accidental developments. Therefore, the task of the novel is to extract the essential meaning of actuality from the haphazard phenomena and produce its distinct image through the use of words and with the help of adaptation. In other words, he explains that the objective of the novel is to "perceive directly the real meaning of actuality amid the numerous superficial phenomena. In order to communicate this meaning, the novel must adopt a direct method. But in order to adopt a direct method, the novel must be realistic." Belinsky's ideas displayed attributes originating from Hegel's idealism, and from these ideas, Futabatei had derived his own theories on realism. (We shall refer to this later, in the chapter "The Development of Literary Theory.")

However, in writing *Ukigumo*, rather than these theories, the author seems to have been more influenced by Turgenev's *Father and Sons* and I. V. Gontcharov's *Obryv* (The Cliff). The original aim of Futabatei in studying Russian was a nationalistic one, that is, he was planning to join a movement to prevent the southern expansion of Russia. However, while reading Russian novels, he gradually became influenced by socialism. Futabatei originally was conservative, which position was exemplified, in the literary field, in his deep interest in Edo *gesaku* and chain-style *haikai* (*renku*) poetry. He even showed interest in Edo-style popular songs and in calligraphy. One reason for this change and his subsequent devotion to serious human problems of modern novels was his unaffected character; however, the greatest influence was foreign. This was partly the reason why, despite striving to make his *Ukigumo* approach the genre of the modern novel through use of colloquial style, he could not quite transport himself into a new world.

The theme of *Ukigumo*, similar to that found in Shōyō's works, was a love-affair of an intellectual of the Meiji Period. The hero, Utsumi Bunzō, while lodging at his aunt's home, falls in love with the latter's daughter O-Sei. However, O-Sei, brought up according to modern educational method, is strongly egoistic and refuses to accept the hero's love candidly. The aunt, O-Masa, on the other hand, dislikes the weak character of the hero, and wants to have her daughter marry a talented youth, Honda Noboru, who is filled with personal ambition. O-Sei finally leaves the honest but weak hero and becomes attracted by the optimistic and energetic Noboru. There is no conclusion to this story, but according to the author's statement expressed in *Sakka Kushindan* (The Efforts of a Novelist) and *Ochiba no Hakiyose* (A Gathering of Fallen Leaves), the original plot was to have O-Sei marry Noboru, but this marriage was to fail because Noboru was to desert her. The hero, on the other hand, was to be unable to save his former sweetheart, and out of desperation, was to go insane.

It is clear that Futabatei attempted to depict in the hero

Bunzō a modern intellectual youth, who, because of his intellectuality, becomes retiring and sceptic in character. The author himself, in his later writing *Yo ga Hansei no Zange* (Confessions of Half My Life), states that he was attempting to "put the tendency of the Japanese young men and women of the age, which he had in his mind in abstract form, into concrete form." In other words, he attempted to breathe feeling into these abstract ideas and develop a living human image. However, the characters became mere types and lacked individuality because, despite his aims, he failed to grasp the real personality of his characters, which naturally prevented him from attaining that stage in which universality can be expressed through individuality. Although the heroine O-Sei is depicted as a woman of the new age, who is emancipated and opposed to the feudalism of her mother, she fails to display a really new personality. In many points, she resembles a type of frivolous woman, eager for novelty, who can be found in any period. The feudal-minded O-Masa and the insincere youth Noboru are not very different from O-Sei, so far as lack of individuality is concerned. These two characters are merely given the roles of villains who obstruct the true love of the hero and drive him into a tragic situation, and represent nothing more.

According to the author's words in his later writing *Sakka Kushindan*, he had planned to deal with the contradiction and antagonism between new and old currents of thoughts in Japan, starting from Part III of this work. The stimulus for this plan was alien, that is, the author had found his inspiration in Russian novels. Therefore, we can say that it did not emerge as a result of his own observation or his own experience in the ideological field. The consequence was that the characters O-Sei and Noboru, who were to represent the new ideas in contrast with the feudal O-Masa, did not embody the author's original design, but on the contrary, appeared to be merely frivolous characters. The same thing can be said of Bunzō, who does not seem to indicate on which side he is standing. The combined effect thus was that Bunzō and O-Sei, who were challenging the vulgar world represented by O-Masa and Noboru, betray their original designs, and O-Sei succumbs to the vulgar world while Bunzō loses out because of his own weakness. The whole effect, in this sense, is tragic. Furthermore, while the ideals of O-Masa and Noboru were to attain success in the bureaucratic world, Bunzō and O-Sei at least attempted to maintain spiritual dignity. The author tried to express this spiritual struggle by depicting the inner workings of Bunzō's mind. Despite his resistance, Bunzō finally was to be defeated, but the minute description of Bunzō's mind through the whole course of his losing battle was something which had never been seen in a literary work.

However, it seemed that in shaping Bunzō's character, the author was displaying the influence of *Oblomov* rather than that of Gontcharov's *Obryv*. *Oblomov*, as Futabatei indicated in his *Roshia Bungaku Dan* (Talks on Russian Literature), deals with a type of human being, who, despite being talented, cannot find any task to which he can devote his whole spiritual efforts, and consequently, after groping and fruitless meditation, finally becomes tired of life and sinks into mere indolence. This type was exemplified in Rudin of *Ukigusa* (Drifting Grasses), a translation by Futabatei, and in the hero of Futabatei's own novel *Heibon* (Mediocrity). In *Ukigumo* this same type was exemplified in the young Meiji bureaucrat Bunzō. Thus, this novel announced the birth of a modern personality in this country.

Although *Ukigumo* was, as a novel, far more advanced than Shōyō's *Tōsei Shosei Katagi*, it was essentially a work written under the influence of Russian novels and not one that emerged as an inevitable consequence of the inner development of native literary thought. Therefore, it was impossible to anticipate a constant literary development from this novel. Actually, while Shōyō stopped novel writing with *Saikun* and shifted to critical essays and then to drama, Futabatei himself did not display much activity in the field of the novel, although while writing

Ukigumo he completed translations of Turgenev's *Rendezvous* and *Three Encounters*, and thereby made a significant contribution in this other field. However, in 1906, in response to the *Tōkyō Asahi Shimbun*, he started writing a story entitled *Chasengami* (A Tea Whisk-Style Hairdo), which, dealing with the love-affair of a young and beautiful widow named Yukie, was intended to cast light on the social problem of the chastity of war widows. However, since this task was too much for him, Futabatei discarded the original design and, renaming it *Sono Omokage* (Its Vestiges) (translated into English under the title *An Adopted Husband*), rewrote it as a simple love tragedy. The story concerns a lonely and innocent-minded girl named Sayoko, who fails in marriage and returns to the home of her parents. She falls in love with her sister's husband, Tetsuya, but their love is blocked by the jealousy of the arrogant sister O-Toki. The story ends with the husband escaping to North China to pursue a lonely life, while Sayoko turns to a work appropriate to her Christian outlook, devoting her life to caring for orphans. This novel displayed a certain element of realism but leaned slightly toward romanticism, and for this reason was not very different from the novels which appeared in the wake of *Seishun* (Youth) and *Kobushi* (The Fist). Futabatei by this time had become an ordinary author, moving with the tide of the world.

With the opening of the Naturalistic era, Futabatei was forced to take up novel writing again, principally under persuasion of the *Asahi Shimbun*, and, as an imitation of Katai's *Futon* (The Quilt), wrote *Heibon* (Mediocrity) (1907). However, Futabatei assumed a pose of a confession-making *shishōsetsu* (private novel) writer in this novel, and relied on a loose description of meaningless life, without reaching any proper conclusion. Futabatei was by no means a writer without talent; however, it is ture that he did not have the calibre to become an artist who could create a new age. Essentially a romantic, he did not have the confidence to devote his whole life to literature. But this did not mean that he was equipped with sufficient willpower to carry on activity in a more practical field. In the last phase of his life he went abroad, dreaming of carrying out some great enterprise on a national scale, although the plan he had was rather vague. He died while traveling through the Bay of Bengal.

Shōyō, when compared to Futabatei, displayed a stronger self-confidence in literature. Furthermore, Shōyō was armed with an executive faculty and played the pioneering role in the field of the novel as well as in historical and musical drama. He also carried out the elaborate task of publishing a complete translation of Shakespeare's works. In spite of this, Shōyō also could not move forward from his avant-garde position. When the rear guard appeared, he was forced to step aside into a separate field.

In summary, both of these writers were a step ahead of other authors in absorbing foreign literature, which in the case of Shōyō was English and in the case of Futabatei, Russian. As a result, being endowed with considerable artistic talent, they pointed out to the still immature native literary world, a road leading to the modern Western-style novel. Essentially, however, these two writers were not of the type of Kōyō, Rohan, Ichiyō, or Sōseki, who in their novels conjured up an original world and realized their literary personalities in their respective worlds.

The realism which was later to be achieved in the form of a Japanese Naturalism by writers like Katai, Tōson, and Shūsei, was to have its focus in a sincere attitude based on an honest and penetrating observation of one's own experience of life. This provided a way of perpetuating the expression of life peculiar to the intellectual class of the Meiji Period. On the other hand, the realism advocated by Shōyō and Futabatei strove for objective reproduction of actuality by use of the methods of Western-style fiction. This was a scientific attitude, pursuing the truth of universal life, and consequently did not suit the Japanese climate. However, their attitude of choosing the actual life of

Meiji intellectuals as literary themes was to find a successor in that of the later Naturalists.

2. *Various Phases of the Realistic Novel*

Shōyō and Futabatei appeared to have no successors for the time being, and writers pursuing genuine realistic novels seemed temporarily extinct. On the contrary, the literary world appeared to be dominated by Kōyō's faction which was carrying on the tradition of the Edo *gesaku* writers. However, with the widening of the reading public, the members of this Ken'yūsha school became aware that they could not remain in the realm of *gesaku* writing. As a result, they gradually approached the realistic position originating from Shōyō and Futabatei, and this shift gave rise to a genre called the Ken'yūsha-style realistic novel. These works, on the one hand, bore traces of efforts to endow with a new Meiji character the realism contained in Edo novels. In Kōyō we even perceive a serious effort to revive classics like the *Genji Monogatari* and imbue them with a modern spirit. On the other hand, this Ken'yūsha realism also manifested considerable influence of European realism. Kōyō himself read Zola and Maupassant through English translations and seemed charmed with the minute realistic method displayed in these works. He also made his own adaptations of *The Decameron* and the original works of Molière, and was a co-translator of Tolstoy's works.

However, despite his interests in this direction, the striking feature of his realism was in the minute but superficial description of human sentiments and external phases of life. In other words, his realism was not based on a true attitude of realistic interpretation of human life. His *Ninin Bikuni : Iro Zange* (The Love Confessions of Two Nuns) and *Kyara Makura* (The Perfumed Pillow) show the definite influence of Saikaku. But Kōyō was principally influenced by the latter's unique literary style. As a result, although Saikaku's method in *Kōshoku Ichidai Onna* (The Life of a Voluptuous Woman) was applied in depicting the erotic life and pride of the heroine in his *Kyara Makura*, Kōyō failed to reproduce his master's deep and penetrating observation of human nature. It was the same in the case of his contact with Zola's *La Faute de l'Abbé Mouret* (The Sin of Father Mouret). Kōyō was deeply moved by this work, but his major interest was in its detailed psychological analysis. As a result, Zola's influence was not sufficient to effect any basic change in his outlook on life.

The combined effect of these circumstances was that Kōyō's realism was felt in his vivid expression of the manners of life and in the delicate psychological analysis of love. Although the author failed to produce truly individual characters in *Futari Nyōbō* (Two Wives) and *Sanninzuma* (Three Wives), he tried to concentrate on describing the sufferings of a common man in *Murasaki* (Purple) (1894) and *Tajō Takon* (Tears and Regrets) (1896), thereby coming closer to the literary mode of the later Naturalists. His literary style, adapting itself to the modern content, came to rely on the use of the colloquial language. *Murasaki* deals with the anxiety of a man, who, because of poor memory, fails for three successive times to pass a test to become a doctor. To this main character the author adds in the supporting roles an old woman living in the neighborhood who sympathizes with his misfortune, and the daughter of his teacher. Some parts of the story, such as the scene in which the teacher's daughter presents the hero with a purple cushion as an elbow-rest, or the part where the hero sees his fiancée in a dream, suggest the eroticism peculiar to the author. However, in general, the story is based on a conservative psychological analysis, and the reader's interest is almost completely separated from the events taking place in the story.

This attitude becomes more pronounced in *Tajō Takon*, which is devoted exclusively to describing the loneliness and melancholy experienced by a timid but honest man, following the death of his beloved wife O-Rui. The hero becomes so melancholic that he frowns upon the sister of his deceased wife because she attempts to make him remarry. Another woman, O-Tane, the wife of his friend, also tries to console him, but he refuses to accept such solace. However, as the story develops, he finally begins to respond to the ministrations of O-Tane, with the result that people become suspicious about their relations. Near the end, the hero is driven out of his friend's home because of his suspected relations with the wife, and the final part sees the hero decorating the room of a boarding-house with a portrait of his dead wife and a photograph of O-Tane. Although Kōyō could not free himself from his peculiar world of love, this work tells us that he was attempting to discard plot and external description in favor of psychological description. He now sought also for realization of the beauty of commonplace life, or, to use his own words, " thoroughly to taste the rice cooked in one's own kitchen."

This type of psychoanalysis can also be perceived in *Kokoro no Yami* (The Darkness of the Heart) (1894) and *Iwazu Katarazu* (With Neither Speech Nor Words) (1895), but the process still is pervaded by intense romanticism. In his last great unfinished work, *Konjiki Yasha* (The Gold Demon) (1897), we also see Kōyō attempting to make a minute psychological description of a woman deserted by her lover. He tries to explain how the heroine Miya must suffer because she cast away love in favor of wealth and how the hero Kan'ichi, deprived of true love, turns into a demon obsessed with money. This was fundamentally the same design as that of *Kokoro no Yami*, and Kan'ichi and Miya in a sense represented projections, with certain modification, of the hero Sanoichi and heroine O-Kume in the previous novel. But *Konjiki Yasha* goes slightly further. That is, after Kan'ichi becomes a usurer, the author sets the stage for displaying a world controlled by monetary power, and the story shows a tendency resembling the social novels which were coming into vogue in this period. However, here also Kōyō showed that he was inferior to his master Saikaku, and failed to present a penetrating insight into economic life as the latter had in his *Seken Munazan'yō* (Worldly Expectation) and *Nihon Eitaigura* (The Everlasting Storehouse of Japan). The most Kōyō could do in his *Konjiki Yasha* was to set the stage for romanticism.

Rohan, who in opposition to Kōyō was to become the champion of idealism, was also moving in the direction of realism when he started writing the linked stories of *Fūryū Mijinzō*. The parts written about 1897 reflect the author's personal observation of actual life. Especially the sections *Kiku no Hamamatsu* (Hamamatsu at Chrysanthemum Time) and *Hitorine* (Sleeping Alone), which deal with an everyday affair, that is, the marriage and divorce of the hero Fudeya Shōtarō and his wife O-Hatsu, mirror the author's attitude of observing the happenings of life with a slight smile. In *Yoru no Yuki* (Night Snow) (1898) he describes a boy, Heitarō, who is thrown out of his uncle's home, and explains the decisive psychological factor which prompts him to join a gang of gamblers. In *Karisakagoe* (The Karisaka Mountain Pass) (1903) Rohan makes a psychological observation of the sentimental journey of a youth, who, maltreated by his aunt, runs away without saying goodbye to the girl he loves, and, full of ambition, hikes over the Karisaka Mountain Pass in the direction of Tōkyō. The long work *Sora Utsu Nami*, though unfinished, was not only romantic in certain points, but also displayed powerful realistic touches, as exemplified by the psychoanalysis of the character Mizuno in his troubled love-affair, and by the portrayal of the unique personality of O-Ryū.

In general, novels written in the period represented by Kōyō and Rohan, had, though in varying degrees, a realistic tendency. It would be too troublesome to mention all of them, but one example is Aeba Kōson's *Tōsei Akiudo Katagi* (The Character of the Modern Merchant). Set against the background of the capitalist world, this story described the rising merchant class of the Meiji Period. Essentially an account of worldly success, this work reveals the author's approval of the new economic system. In a sense, there is a similarity with Saikaku's novels dealing with merchant life in the Tokugawa Era. Saitō Ryokuu's *Kakurembo* (Hide-and-Go-Seek) (1891) and *Abura Jigoku* (The Hell of Oil) (1891) both depicted the actual life of prostitutes. Both also display the satirical attitude of the author and his hatred of women. The former deals with a company executive's son who dallies with several geisha, while the latter work, conversely, deals with a serious-minded student who is made a fool of by a geisha. But this author seems to have changed when he came to write *Kado Samisen* (The Samisen at the Gate) (1895). Dealing with a boy and two young girls who fight for his affections, this work is pervaded by the peculiar atmosphere of Tōkyō's downtown district. Since this story was published later in the same year that *Takekurabe* appeared, Ryokuu may have written it under the influence of the latter work. At any rate, the realism of this period was nothing more than a primitive one which merely copied the superficial aspects of life and human sentiments.

In 1895, Kyōka made public *Yakō Junsa* and *Gekashitsu*, while Bizan published *Shokikan* and *Uraomote*. As a result of these successive publications, there arose the genre called *kannen shōsetsu*, or idea novel. This was followed by the appearance of the *hisan shōsetsu*, or pathos novel, and the *shinkoku shōsetsu*, or serious novel, beginning with Ryūrō's *Heme-Den* and *Kurotokage*. In this period we witness an increasing tendency towards romanticism but, paradoxically, realism at the same time also gradually developed.

The "idea novels" were not necessarily turning their backs on the actual world, since they too were casting light on social and individual problems and leaving the solution to the readers. This was a tendency perceived especially in Bizan's writings. But, for Kyōka and his group, it appeared the real objective was not to be found in actual life itself. Rather, for them, actuality had meaning only when it served as a springboard to enhance the romantic spirit and exalt it for an extraordinary effect.

The so-called "pathos novels" and "serious novels" also dealt with actual problems, since they purported to penetrate into the depths of life and cast light on its tragic nature. However, the "pathos" (*hisan*) and "seriousness" (*shinkoku*) are merely the projection of the feeling of astonishment at the eccentricity of life or the subjective expression of a romantic lamentation over the state of the world. In this sense, it cannot be considered genuine realism.

Thus, these new novels which appeared in the romantic current of the day were idealistic and eccentric, and their favorite theme was the dark side of life. Occasionally they dealt with eroticism, and sometimes they depicted immoral relations. Their striking feature was that, to a greater or less degree, they neglected the existence of the wholesome aspects of life. As a reaction, new voices were heard calling for expression of this normal and bright side of life, and this led to the birth of *katei shōsetsu* (domestic novels) advocating pure and moral family life, and to the appearance of social novels whose heroes were usually characters with great willpower who participated actively in the fields of politics and business. These novels, however, were swayed by the contemporary current of thought and failed to establish a definite social outlook. Most of them relied on a religious solution of problems and could be called more accurately "religious novels." At any rate, in contrast with the "dark" stories prevailing since the days of the Ken'yūsha school, these novels possessed a bright and optimistic quality.

Since these works found their themes in actual problems of the home and society, we cannot deny that some realistic elements exist in them. However, generally speaking, they were not established on a definite realistic approach to life. Rather, the writers of these novels relied on ethical principles derived from simple humanitarianism, and through Christian concepts sought to solve the problems of family life and society. For this reason we can say that under a general classification they would belong to an old type of idealism or romanticism. The only thing they have in common with realism is their selection of theme and their method of description; and, in this regard, such realism is not much different from that of the Ken'yūsha writings.

The masterpiece in the *katei shōsetsu* was Tokutomi Roka's *Hototogisu* (The Cuckoo) (1898). This story is about a naval officer's wife who is divorced because she is stricken with tuberculosis. Since this work contains a criticism of the feudal practice of *shūtome-zari* (expulsion of a woman from her home by her mother-in-law), we can say that it dealt with social problems. However, the author's primary concern was in describing the eternal love between the sick young wife and her husband, and the anguish arising from this unfortunate situation. The psychological analysis of the couple is not carried out in a strictly realistic fashion, and this work belongs rather to the romantic mode.

In addition to this, many *katei shōsetsu*, or domestic novels, were read, such as Kikuchi Yūhō's *Ono ga Tsumi* (My Sin) (1899), *Chi-Kyōdai* (Suckled at the Same Breast) (1903), Taguchi Kikutei's *Myōto Nami* (Two Waves) (1903), Nakamura Shun'u's (Kichizō) *Ichijiku* (Figs) (1901), and Yanagawa Shun'yō's *Tomarikyaku* (Guests to Stay) (1903), as well as works by Watanabe Katei (Kurohōshi) and Ōkura Tōrō. But they have no modern significance except in the sense that they were popular reading material. *Ono ga Tsumi* deals with a young medical student and a high school girl who become intimate. A boy is born between them, but the girl deserts this illegitimate child and marries another man; at the end, however, she by chance meets this illegitimate son, and her past sins come to light. Yūhō was following the popular method of using the immoral conduct of high school girls as themes of novels. In this sense, this work could be considered realistic since it dealt with one phase of actual life. However, the keynote was morality, and the emphasis was on the spiritual suffering of the heroine Tamaki and on the love between mother and son. *Ichijiku* deals with a Christian pastor who brings back to Japan an American wife, Emiya, who is not accepted by her husband's family. As far as the story is concerned, this novel was ostensibly to illustrate the social problem called international marriage in the form of a specific family's difficulties. However, Shun'u's concern was primarily religious, as shown by the fact that he first has the hero, the pastor, attempt to commit suicide in order to protect the woman he formerly loved, who has escaped from prison, but later sends him back as a reformed man to his wife Emiya. The fact that the author was pursuing the theme in the light of religious ideas means that this work is closer to the genre of the religious novel. At any rate, the most striking feature of the novel is the intense religious expression of mental agony.

Among the social novels were the following : Uchida Roan's *Kure no Nijūhachinichi* (December Twenty-Eighth) (1898), *Ochibeni* (Wiped Off Rouge) (1899), *Katauzura* (The Forlorn Quail) (1899), and *Shimokuzure* (Melting Frost) (1899) ; Oguri Fūyō's *Seido* (The System) (1899) ; Gotō Chūgai's *Ari no Susabi* (The Ants Amuse Themselves) (1895) and *Funikudan* (The Band of Spoiled Meat) (1900) ; Tokuda Shūsei's *Namakemono* (The Idler) (1899); Tokutomi Roka's *Omoide no Ki* (My Recollections) (1900) and *Kuroshio* (The Black Current) (1901) ; and Kinoshita Naoe's *Hi no Hashira* (The Pillar of Fire) (1904) and *Otto no Jihaku* (The Husband's Confession) (1904).

Kure no Nijūháchinichi deals with a man who first sacrifices the love of his wife to carry out his plan to emigrate to Mexico, but under advice of another woman with whom he is deeply in love, finally awakens to the love of his wife. The author of this work also displays a tendency to rely on a religious solution of the novel's problem. *Hi no Hashira* deals with a man who attempts to carry out social reform from the standpoint of Christian socialism, but for this reason is pursued by the authorities. Although his sweetheart who is a Christian asks him to run away, he refuses, and the story ends with the hero, resigned to his fate, apprehended and taken away in the midst of a snowfall. This work is tinted with the crude romanticism which was often seen in the early political novels. In *Otto no Jihaku* Naoe has become to a certain extent realistic. The hero in this story revolts against the society from a humanistic standpoint, goes to America to establish a communistic farm as well as to meet the woman he loves, and later goes to Russia and dies there. The story, ending with his sweetheart returning home with her lover's remains, was realistic although it still displayed a romantic atmosphere. *Omoide no Ki* is a biographical work deeply colored with Christian humanism.

The works *Kuroshio*, *Seido*, and *Funikudan* were political rather than religious. *Kuroshio* depicted a character who, revolting against corrupt clan politics and the degraded life of the aristocracy, attempts to carry out a reform of the political world. The author was planning to shape this story along the plot of an epic, and depict the transition of the political world from the so-called Europeanization period of early Meiji up to the year which saw the formation of the Social Democratic Party. The story was planned as a long work, composed of six parts, but Roka failed to realize his original design. The works of Chūgai purported to contrast the public life of politicians with their private life. A typical story concerned a wealthy country official who enters the political world, is involved in scandals, and finally ransoms a geisha girl, which incident leads to troubles in his family life. There are some indications that this work was fused with the form of the domestic novel. Fūyō's *Seido* has its theme in the integrity of aging politicians, but he is primarily concerned with the depiction of the personal appearance and personality of the characters. Intertwined with the love-affair and suicide of the only daughter of the main character, the story dealt largely with the characters' private life. It was evident that Chūgai and Fūyō were not writers whose major concern was the social novel. In general, as we explained heretofore, both domestic novels and political stories displayed realistic aspects but, at the same time, reflecting the spirit of the age, were dyed in rich romantic color. However, these novels were gradually enlarging their scope and showed a tendency to cover a wider range of society. Especially the works of Naoe and the later Shirayanagi Shūko not only depicted the society but shed light on problems of socialism. In this sense, we may classify their works separately under the category of socialist novels. This point was commented on by Kaneko Chikusui in his article *Iwayuru Shakai Shōsetsu* (This Thing Called the Social Novel) (1898), which was carried in the magazine *Waseda Bungaku* (Waseda Literature).

The *kannen* and *hisan shōsetsu* (idea and pathos novels) bore strong marks of the psychoanalysis prevailing since the days of Kōyō. This tendency was especially strongly marked in the writings of Ryūrō who was the champion of the *hisan shōsetsu*. There were also many other writers showing keen interest in the genre, such as Bizan, Chūgai, Suiin, Katai, and Ichiyō. Works like *Tajō Takon* and *Fūryū Mijinzō* could also be considered as examples of this tendency. As a general classification, we could list these works as psychological novels. But, among them, the works of the highest artistic value were those of Ryūrō and Ichiyō.

Kawachiya (1896) and *Imado Shinjū* (The Imado Double Suicide) (1896) are regarded as Ryūrō's masterpieces. Compared with his other *hisan shōsetsu*, these two works do not lean excessively toward stark eccentricity. Rather, in these two works which portray the minds of normal human beings there is a suggestion of universality. *Kawachiya* deals with the triangle affair involving Seijirō, who sees the woman originally designed to be his wife become the wife of his elder brother, the elder brother, who, because he weds the sweetheart of the younger, must enter a joyless family life, and finally the heroine herself, who, because she has not married the proper man, suffers excessive maltreatment, and finally must decide to end her life. A triangle affair is a theme dating back to the days of Paolo and Francesca, but Ryūrō applied to this theme a minute literary description that was extremely close to the modern literary technique, and thereby gave a fluid analysis of the inner mind of the three characters. *Imado Shinjū* describes a prostitute of the Yoshiwara who parts with her beloved, but, out of loneliness and grief, accepts the love of a middle-aged man whom she had hated for a long time. However, this man falls into distress, and the prostitute attempts to save him, but the whole affair ends in their double suicide. This double suicide was different from that seen in Chikamatsu's writings. Furthermore, it was by no means a forced affair. The heroine in this work was dying with her new lover with the illusion that she was committing suicide with her first and actually her only true lover. The intricacies of the heroine's feelings were expressed most skilfully by the author.

Ichiyō's works appeared earlier than *Imado Shinjū*, but she was to display a psychoanalysis comparable to that of Ryūrō in a number of works that were published just before her death. *Takekurabe* (Comparing Heights) (1895) gave a vivid description of the local color of the Daionji district near the Yoshiwara prostitute quarter. But more brilliant is her psychological depiction of the sexual awakening among the youngsters Shōtarō, Shinnyo, Midori, and the minor characters. Especially the figure of the heroine Midori of the Daikokuya family, who stands on the threshold of youth, bidding farewell to her adolescent days and preparing for the complicated and troublesome adult life lying ahead, has such freshness that it remains in the reader's mind forever. The reason is that while Ichiyō is presenting this young girl's image nonchalantly and in a simple lyrical mood, she has touched the universal fate of humanity, and this produces a supreme symbolic effect. The heroine Midori is a special type of woman, reared in the world of prostitutes and possessed of a wild character. However, she is not of the abnormal type found frequently in Ryūrō's works but rather is a symbol of common human nature. The same can be said about the other characters in this novel, such as Shōtarō and Shinnyo. Ichiyō's characteristic was pointed out by Ōgai in his article " Three Men's Idle Talks " (fourth issue of the magazine *Mesamashigusa*), in which he commented that she was not concerned with a bestial existence in human form, which had been overworked by Zola and Ibsen and by their imitators, the Naturalists. Instead, Ichiyō had portrayed a " real human being " who laughs and cries with us. Ōgai concludes by praising the technique which enabled Ichiyō to transform her human characters into poetical images, saying, " I would not hesitate in calling her a true poet." The conclusion is that *Takekurabe* was the work of a great poet who possessed the capacity to endow an individualistic character to universal human nature.

Nigorie (The Muddied Stream) (1895) reveals the maturity of Ichiyō's realistic touches, as exemplified in her psychological description of a prostitute O-Riki, living in obscurity in the prostitute district of Kikunoi, and in the portrayal of surrounding life. However, the merit of this work lies rather in the writer's grasp of the particular than of the universal, and the work mirrors her loneliness, agony, resistance, and resignation—feelings and moods which are peculiar to women. In *Jūsan'ya* the writer depicts a woman who was born in a poor feudal warrior family and is married to a public servant, but who must suffer because she cannot divorce her cold-hearted husband. This work describes the universal agony of women, and in certain points seems to reflect Ichiyō's own mental attitude. Deserving special attention, in this connection, is the final part which deals with the heroine's encounter with her former childhood sweetheart who, because he was forced to abandon his love for her, is leading a miserable life. This encounter plunges the heroine into fathomless sorrow, which includes an element of resignation.

Although the dominating mood of Ichiyō's works is passion

and resignation, her works are reinforced, though only to a limited degree, by something which resembles an insight into life. In this sense, her works must be distinguished from the Ken'yūsha-style writings which were merely a superficial reproduction of ways, customs, and sentiments of the human world. Furthermore, from the viewpoint of the essential humanity of a writer, Ichiyō is far more attractive than Ryūrō. This is especially noticeable when we consider that while the insight into life of authors of the *kannen shōsetsu*, domestic and social novels was merely the crude revelation of their own subjective ideas, Ichiyō's insight into life was crystallized into a tender and realistic literary expression.

3. *The Forerunners of Naturalism*

A variety of novels appeared during the romantic period in the Meiji thirties. Among them, the works specifically called *shajitsu shōsetsu* (realistic novels) were represented by the writings of authors like Oguri Fūyō, Kosugi Tengai, and Nagai Kafū, who raised the banner of realism under Naturalistic influence. Although these writers still showed romantic coloring in their writing, they advocated Zolaism as the principle of their literature.   Their significance lay in their efforts to introduce Western realism into the native literature.   The stage they attained must be regarded as far more advanced than the mere entry into nature of the primitive realistic method dating back to Kōyō.

Oguri Fūyō (Katō Isoo) emerged from Kōyō's school, and the general opinion was that he surpassed his master Kōyō in the intensity of his erotic description and in the brilliance of literary style. In 1896, he wrote *Neoshiroi* (The Makeup in Sleep), which dealt with the immoral relations between a brother and sister in a village of the pariah *eta* class, but the publication was banned by the authorities. This work came to be a landmark pointing towards Naturalism. The same year, he wrote *Kikkōzuru* (The Tortoise-Shell Crane) which was based on the life of a *saké*-distiller's family in his native place.   The author displayed a unique style through his accurate and detailed description of the distillery business, as well as in his portrayal of the personality of the family's ignorant servant, who, because of an unsuccessful love-affair, commits suicide by throwing himself into a tub of boiling *saké*. The author's brilliant expression of the hero's seemingly ignorant but obstinate character made the work appear to be a worthy successor of *Gojū no Tō*. For this reason, the author of the latter novel, Rohan, gave his recommendation to this novel, which brought Fūyō his first literary prominence. However, Fūyō, in this period, still displayed a strongly romantic mode, and he was rather close to the *hisan shōsetsu*. In novels like *Rembo-Nagashi* (A Flood of Affection) (1898), and *Katsura Shitaji* (Under the Wig) (1899), both regarded as his masterpieces, the author depicted the tragedy of a talented musician or a female impersonator who falls into distress or goes insane as a result of an unsuccessful love. Although making precise observations of customs through use of a charming style, the author does not display a deep insight into life, and, in this sense, was still inferior to Ryūrō or Ichiyō.

However, Fūyō was to bring himself gradually closer to the mode of Naturalism. The most striking feature of this writer was his sensitive response to the influence of modern Western novels, his readiness to adapt himself to the spirit of the age, and his active interest to absorb anything new. Although this led to a certain lack of originality, his novels, like his brilliant style, were to display a sparkling variety of content. We have mentioned his social novel *Seido* (The System) in the foregoing section. But now the author betrayed Nietzsche's influence in *Sametaru Onna* (The Woman Now Cold) (1901), and showed efforts at imitation of Zola in *Numa no Onna* (The Woman of the Marsh) (1902). And in *Seishun* (Youth) (1905) the author created a personality, peculiar to the modern age, under the influence of Turgenev's *Rudin*. This work, appearing after the publication of Tengai's *Makaze Koikaze* (Winds of Demons and

Love), drew wide attention. However, although it reflected the ways, customs, and thinking of the contemporary age, the defect was that these aspects of life were depicted superficially and were not based on the author's own experience.

The hero of *Seishun*, Seki Kin'ya, indulges in romantic ideas and assumes the pose of a genius. However, the sublime ideas expressed by the hero are actually empty and without the backing of practical acts, and when it comes to carrying out actual work, he becomes egoistic and cowardly. The heroine, a schoolgirl named Ono Shigeru, is charmed by the vague romantic ideas of the hero, accepts his love, and finally conceives his child. However, Kin'ya has no intention of formally recognizing this love, and refuses to marry the girl. The heroine as a result first decides to marry another man but later attempts to solve the relations with the hero by bringing about their marriage. But the hero has already lost his youthful passion and is imprisoned for having caused the abortion of his illegitimate child. Following his release from prison, the hero breaks off relations with Shigeru, and tries to hide himself in his native place, but there he witnesses the suicide of his fiancée whom he had deserted. The hero also decides to commit suicide and sends a letter telling of his decision to Shigeru. However, upon receiving this letter, Shigeru does not believe it and, crying, " He'll never commit suicide," throws a stamped flower, a souvenir of their love, out of the window. The complicated modern personality of the characters is suggested through the development of the plot. But as in the case of *Rudin*, the personality of the characters is explained somewhat in detail through the words of the hero's friend. Furthermore, the author has done a relatively careful piece of work in depicting the nihilistic world during the years of transition from Romanticism to Naturalism. In fact, the hero Kin'ya, infected by egoistic individualism, is a truthful representative of the trend of the day. However, it seems that the author was not depicting the hero out of his own experience but shaping his character along the line of Western novels. Especially, there is ample evidence in the work that the author had been greatly influenced by the hero in *Rudin* which he had read through Futabatei's translation. In this sense, the success of this novel cannot be attributed wholly to Fūyō himself.

After this novel, Fūyō started writing a long work entitled *Tensai* (The Genius) (1907) but failed to complete it. His next works, *Koizame* (Awakening from Love) (1907) and *Ane no Imōto* (Her Younger Sister) (1909), were both banned by the authorities. *Koizame* had a theme similar to that of *Futon* and seems to be an imitation of the latter. The theme of *Ane no Imōto* was the immorality of a wife who engages in prostitution. Since the age had already advanced to the stage of Naturalism, the author in these works seems to be adapting himself to the vogue of the day and shows a general tendency to follow the example of Zola.

It was Tengai who displayed a more distinct design than Fūyō in following the fashion of Zola. Kosugi Tengai (Tamezō) was a disciple of Ryokuu, and first wrote satirical novels like *Kairyō Danna* (The Reformed Husband) (1892) and *Kairyō Wakatono* (The Reformed Prince) (1893). He earned literary distinction by *Hebi Ichigo* (Snake Strawberry) (1899), and finally became the writer of the day by publishing *Hatsusugata* (The New Year Dress) (1900). The heroine of this work, O-Toshi, an actress, was created under influence of Zola's Nana. The fact that the heroine is an illegal daughter of a noblewoman apparently controls her fate. However, O-Toshi enters into a relation of passionate true love with a boy named Ryūtarō, but this genuine love cannot be pursued, and the boy enters the priesthood. The final scenes which see the heroine attend, unnoticed, the ceremonies in which the boy is ordained into the priesthood, and then leave for her own ceremony through which she is to enter a marriage she dislikes, betray the influence of *Takekurabe*. If we are to find Zola's influence, it can be per-

ceived rather in the earlier parts, in the description of the vaudeville theater and in the erotic expression of ways and customs
of the world. It appears that this work, together with the later
works *Koi to Koi* (Love and Love) (1901) and *Nisemurasaki*
(False Purple) (1905), was to become part of a trilogy on the
life of O-Toshi. If we read through these works as a trilogy,
the plot suggests that O-Toshi enters an unhappy marriage and
consequently falls into an extremely degraded life. Some critics
regard this work as the Rougon Macquart of Tengai.

As far as the content is concerned, *Hatsusugata* is not so
near the method of Zola, being rather close to the romantic
style of the day. In the preface the author declares that passion
and subjective ideas will be rooted out from the work and that
it will be written on an intellectual and objective basis. Attention must be paid to the author's words, "Artistic beauty
must move the people as nature moves the sensual feelings of
man. It must be universal and uniform." These words indicate
that there is still a considerable distance between the author
and the determinism (scientism) of Zola, and merely stress
the naturalness of beauty. However, we may say that this
attitude of respecting "nature" was significant in the sense
that it was the forerunner of Naturalism in the midst of the
romantic tide.

While his *Hatsusugata* was written under influence of Zola's
Nana, Tengai in *Hayariuta* (Popular Song) (1901) was evidently
moving yet a step closer towards Naturalism. In the preface of
this work, the author first states that "Nature is nature. It is
neither good nor evil, neither beauty nor ugliness." Then,
declaring that "the novel is a visioned nature," he stresses
that the poet must strictly abstain from mixing his personal
feeling in expressing his imagination and that the images in
literary works must be communicated so that the readers' imagination can feel these images just as if they were experiencing
the natural phenomena with their own senses. Here again
the author is preaching the need of an objective, intellectual,

and realistic attitude, but the difference from his preface in *Ha-tsusugata* is that he has now denied the existence of aesthetic goals and gone a step further in the direction of a science. The only thing separating the author from science was that he allowed for "sensual feeling" and "imagination," in which he recognized the concrete nature of art. In other words, he still allowed the existence of "aesthetic meaning." For this reason, he was not an irrevocable scientist like Zola.

The content of *Hayariuta* is strongly Naturalistic. The story concerns a wife of an important country landowner. As a result of hereditary eroticism, she commits adultery with a handsome medical student in a greenhouse, and her immorality becomes publicly known because it becomes the theme of a popular song. The author employs a rather wide canvas in depicting the feudal family system oppressing the heroine, her husband's dissipated life which finally forces the heroine, swayed by jealousy, to flee to her parents, and the hereditary factor formed as a result of the peculiar family ties. In the last part, portraying the greenhouse scene, the author displays exceptional talent in the expression of eroticism. From the viewpoint of its content, this work was an epoch-making success in the field of realism.

However, Tengai failed to achieve another success comparable to that of *Hayariuta*. He originally lacked a fluid sensibility and rich erotic imagination. His talent was rather in his ability to create an epic-style situation by skilful weaving of plot. In his subsequent works which received wide acclaim, such as the long stories *Makaze Koikaze* (1903) and *Kobushi* (The Fist) (1906–1908), the author showed his peculiar skill in creating plots adapted for newspaper serialization, but, outside of this, he was rather crude in depicting the personality of his characters and in portrayal of the physical surroundings. He was finally to end up as commonplace writer of historical dramas and popular novels.

Makaze Koikaze was published earlier than *Seishun* and,.

dealing with a love-affair of a girl student, moved the readers with its fresh style. According to his own words, Tengai attempted in this work to base himself strictly on an objective standpoint, in opposition to the Ken'yūsha school, which, though holding aloft a banner of realism, actually was merely toying with technique to suit its own individual tastes. Despite his motive, the novel essentially was not new. The only unique feature was that the author shed light on the life and ethical problems of girl students. The heroine, Hatsuno, is portrayed as an independent character with a strong willpower, and could be regarded as the embodiment of the modern ego. However, she appears to be more like a woman with old-fashioned ideas about chastity. Hatsuno resists temptation, and tries to work her way through school, but falls in love with a university student, Tōgo, who is the fiancé of her friend Yoshie. Torn between love and friendship, she decides to sacrifice her love for friendship, but the torment is too great, and she succumbs to illness. Although Tōgo is only vaguely portrayed, the heroine Hatsuno and her friend Yoshie, who is of an entirely different nature, are described distinctly and in an extremely strong moral light which regards love as a *makaze* (a demon wind). There is a rather tragic mood in this work and, in contrast with the modernism of *Seishun*, it has a classic, or a romantic air. But, at the same time, a Naturalistic tendency is perceived in some sections, especially in the description of the erotic life surrounding the girl students.

Kobushi is a massive work that can be compared to *Makaze Koikaze*. The work is threaded through with a passionate praise of the struggles in life, as indicated by the title which represents the power of the will, but still it has a certain classic aroma. The story concerns a student of the Hitotsubashi Commercial High School, who, while aspiring for a life of struggle, falls in love with a duchess, Tagako, as a result of the erotic tendency inherent in the family line of his mother. His life enters a catastrophic stage, and he finally commits *seppuku* in the moonlight. This story was serialized in the *Yomiuri Shimbun*, and the sections in which the hero becomes intimate with Tagako corresponded to the rise of Naturalism in the literary world. As a result, there was a slight change in the author's motives, and he tried to illustrate something like the agony of a Naturalist decadent in the life of the hero. However, the story is concluded in an old-fashioned atmosphere of pathos. The author makes the hero write his will in the following words: " I am not insane, nor am I tired of life. The hereditary power in my blood was the cause of the whole affair, but this power was also the thing which provided the final solution." It seems that the suicide here was an attempt to overcome heredity. It may have been the work of the *kobushi*, that is, the power of the will. As shown by this work, Tengai attempted to introduce the objectivity and the hereditary theories of Naturalism into his writings. Actually, however, he failed to give a thorough and concrete expression to these ideas.

Like Tengai, who, in copying the mode of Zola, had tried to give an artistic expression of the force of heredity but who, because of his lack of power to express it in concrete form, ended by depicting puppets of heredity, Kafū also attempted to deal in his novels with heredity and the animal nature of man. However, in the case of Kafū, too, the original design was not fulfilled and remained merely inchoate.

Nagai Kafū (Sōkichi) first studied Edo *gesaku* writing. After entering the school of Ryūrō, his style approached that of the pathos novel (*hisan shōsetsu*). However, when he started to read French novels, he became a devout follower of Zola. This was illustrated in *Yashin* (Ambition) (1902). This novel deals with the young head of an old established firm who attempts to copy the successful methods of French merchants, and, fired with ambition, tries to renovate his shop into an elaborate department store in opposition to his mother and relatives. Finally, one of his employees who hates him and is engaged to wed his younger sister and take over the store, sets fire to and destroys the new shop which was almost completed. The author has depicted an immature but passionate youth who is swayed by the superficial spirit of reform, but, when faced with harsh reality, sees his ambitious dreams crumble to the ground. The collapse of romantic dreams seems to be the principal theme, and the author apparently borrowed this theme from Zola's *Au Bonheur des Dames*. The actual story, however, is completely different. Zola's novel deals with a man who starts his life penniless, but finally succeeds in establishing a large department store in the center of Paris. In his counterpart, Kafū has the hero's friend express the idea that such ambition as that displayed by the hero is merely a " fever " or " demoniac design."

Jigoku no Hana (The Flower of Hell) (1902) is known to the world for its preface which is the author's declaration of the Naturalistic creed. In this declaration, the author states that there is a bestial side to human nature. This is an inevitable aspect, and if we are to aspire for idealistic life, we must conduct special research in this bestial aspect. " From this standpoint, I am planning to make a daring exposure of the naked desires, brutality, violence, and other dark passions which result from heredity and environment." Actually, heredity is almost neglected in the work itself, which makes only a slight mention of naked desires and violence. The heroine, Tsunehama Sonoko, an English teacher, falls in love with a magazine reporter who is a Christian. However, she discovers that he is on intimate terms with the mistress of the family where she is serving as an English instructor. At the same time, the heroine is violated by her schoolmaster and driven to despair. However, she decides to free herself from conventional ideas, such as respect and honor, and lead a new and unrestricted life. In making this decision, the heroine is influenced by the fact that Tomiko, the daughter of the family where she is serving as an English instructor, has plunged into a new and free life, in order to strike back at the world which made unfair criticism of her family. Thus, Tomiko enjoys a carefree life as a means of resisting the world, but the heroine Sonoko exploits her free situation to return to nature, and attempts to reconstruct her life on the basis of her animal nature, which in the case of Tomiko is despised by the world as a hell of filth. Furthermore, the heroine believes that only by attaining a beautiful moral life in the midst of such defiling life, can one become a person deserving eternal praise. This conclusion is moral, but the point that the heroine returns to nature and to bestial life as a means of challenging the society filled with pretense and vanity displays the strong influence of Naturalism.

Yume no Onna (The Woman of Dreams) (1903) deals with a woman of a samurai family, whose life is ruined by a series of inevitable circumstances. The heroine resembles Saikaku's Ichidai Onna or Zola's Nana. However, the author has shown no effort to shed light on heredity and has merely exaggerated the inevitable power of environment. Furthermore, the heroine Shisō is a normal human being, and the bestiality of human nature can be found only in the erotic desires of the males surrounding her. As a result, the significance of this work, as in his later novels, lay in his beautiful description of the erotic sentiments of the world of prostitutes, with the heroine serving as the pillar of the whole story. In this work, too, we can point to evidence of the influence of Zola, but it was not a display of genuine Zolaism.

It appears that at the time he was writing these works, Kafū was reading Zola's works. Immediately after publication of *Yume no Onna* he compiled *Joyū Nana Kōgai* (An Outline of the Actress Nana), *Kōzui* (The Flood), and *Emīru Zora to Sono Shōsetsu* (Emile Zola and his Novels), and published a book entitled *Joyū Nana* (The Actress Nana). This work tells us of his achievements in his research on Zola but does not contain any remarks advocating Zolaism. It appears to be a serious book of research; however, we can observe that Kafū at this period was studying Zola in order to cultivate a field in Naturalism.

4. *The Position of Doppo*

We are unable to forget the name of Kunikida Doppo (Tetsuo) as a man who, without any relationship to those who tried to transplant French Naturalism of the Zola school, was an admirer of the Wordsworth who is the source of Naturalism, and who from a romantic style opened the way gradually to realism. Indeed Doppo finally must be considered as a pioneer of Naturalism. As Doppo himself says, he was uninfluenced by the works of the Edo Period or those of Kōyō and Rohan, but rather emerged as a lyric poet under the influence of English literature and Christianity. On this point he resembles Tōkoku and Tōson of the *Bungakkai* group. In the matter of having early entered the world of the novel and having opened a new road in realism he is similar to Tōson, but in the matter of having fallen in mid-course he is a genius who reminds us of Tōkoku.

Like the men of *Bungakkai*, Doppo also did not have any interest in dallying in light fiction, but rather faced the serious problems of life, and entered into a solemn introspection, and selected the course of expressing in his works clearly and concisely the struggles and suffering that emerged from it. *Azamukazaru no Ki* (An Undeceiving Diary), which he wrote before he had written any novels, is a record of this spiritual life, and in the latter part his love-affair with Sasaki Nobuko is related in detail, and Doppo's thoughts and feelings which appear in it are foreshadowings of what was to come in his later novels.

If we survey Doppo's works, we find that he started off in 1894 with *Aitei Tsūshin* (Letters to a Beloved Brother). But he was to earn a literary name in 1897 when he published *Doppo-Gin* (Doppo's Poems), *Wasureenu Hitobito* (People I Cannot Forget), and *Gen Oji* (Uncle Gen). *Doppo-Gin* was a collection of his lyric poems. In this collection, as indicated by the poem *Sanrin ni Jiyū Sonsu* (There Is Liberty in the Mountain Forest), the author attempted to transform human life, defiled by hypocrisy and vanity, into a pure, innocent, and natural world, and thereby displayed a romantic aspiration for freedom. This aspiration is felt like a faint echo throughout his works until his last writing.

Doppo started from a Wordsworth-style Naturalism. The human being has a frail, powerless existence in the face of the great universe and the forces of Nature, and, therefore, must frequently suffer under an unhappy star. Human beings, placed under this unhappy star, must bind themselves through love, mingle through mutual sympathy, and cultivate their own fate on their own, with the help of zealous efforts and sincere studies. Poets and novelists must not rely solely on intellectual study but, with a naive feeling of astonishment, must perceive the secrets of the strange universe, and communicate them to all of mankind, with the help of trained observation and expression. These roughly were the ideas inherent in Doppo.

These ideas were reflected by Doppo in about seventy works of fiction which he wrote during a span of twelve years. Thus, after establishing a landmark of short stories in Meiji literature, he died of illness in 1908 at the age of thirty-eight. He was strongly romantic during the years between the publication of *Wasureenu Hitobito* (People I Cannot Forget) (1897) and *Musashino* (1901). As illustrated by *Sorachigawa no Kishibe* (The Banks of the Sorachi River), the works written in this period display to a considerable degree the author's subjective appraisal of the astonishment he feels toward the forces of nature and universe. It is commonly accepted that these years mark the initial stage of his literary career. Subsequently, in *Gyūniku to Bareisho* (Beef and Potatoes) (1901), he expresses " an urge to be surprised," through the words of the hero Okamoto, and gradually assumes a position to discover " this feeling of being surprised " in actual life. Thus, he was to turn out a series of works in which he pointed out the force of fate and the naked face of nature inherent in the lives of unhappy ordinary human beings. This period is regarded as the second stage of his career. Most critics define this stage as a romantic period, albeit with realistic overtones.

Most of Doppo's major works belonged to this second stage. During these years his attitude of penetrating into actuality develops step by step, and with a rather objective attitude, he was to write works which vividly described a certain phase of society. This attitude reached maturity and advanced to the level of Naturalism in the works written in his last year, 1908, namely *Take no Kido* (The Bamboo Wicket) and *Ni-Rōjin* (Two Old Men). Most scholars consider this period as the third phase of his career, or his Naturalistic period. However since his Naturalistic tendency had already been making a gradual appearance in such works as *Gōgai* (Extra) (1906), *Nakiwarai* (Tearful Smiles) (1907), *Hirō* (Fatigue) (1907), and *Kyūshi* (Driven to Death) (1907), some prefer to include these works also in his Naturalistic stage. There are others who distinguish the works written after *Gyūniku to Bareisho* from those written before, and bracket them all into a period of realism.

The works which formed the major portion of his novels and which impressed the readers with effects peculiar to this writer's style belonged to the second stage of Doppo's literary career. Displaying the most striking features in this respect were *Shuchū Nikki* (A Wine-Soaked Diary) (1902), *Ummeironja* (The Fatalist) (1902), and *Jonan* (Troubles From Woman) (1903), which described the life of unfortunate people buffeted by fate. In *Hibon naru Bonjin* (The Uncommon Common Man) (1903), *Ni-Shōjo* (Two Young Girls), and *Haru no Tori* (The Birds of Spring), the author depicted the life of commonplace persons who escape the cruel hands of fate to enter a divine world represented by truth, love, and innocence.

Shuchū Nikki deals with a grammar school teacher, who is

first tormented by his mother and then sees his wife commit suicide, and who goes to a small island where he opens a private school, is loved by the local inhabitants, and finally falls in love with a local girl who gives birth to a child. But before the birth of the child the hero drowns. The story develops in the form of the hero's diary, and shows him trying to forget his troubles by drinking. The author, in the final sections, shows deep sympathy for the hero. *Ummeironja* deals with a man who, by the whim of fate, must regard his mother as the enemy of his father, and who is forced into an abnormal situation in which he must consider and love his own sister as his wife. As a result of his experience, the hero is dissatisfied with the scientific interpretation of life based on the theory of cause and effect, and expressing belief in mystic destiny, indulges in drinking, waiting for fate to strike him. The greater part of this novel is taken up by the words of the miserable fatalist who relates his Oedipus-like sufferings. Also, a considerable part is devoted to conversations on various phases of life, exchanged between this fatalist and a man who has only a scientific view of the world. The major portion of *Jonan* is devoted to confessions of the hero, who, told by a fortune-teller that he would suffer through women, relates his life which developed as the fortune-teller had predicted. Before and after these confessions, the author has added explanatory passages which report that he met the degraded hero who became a miserable-looking, blind *shakuhachi* flutist, and heard him playing a composition so poorly that it was difficult to endure physically to listen to the tune. In these works we have mentioned there is a distinct manifestation of the author's own romantic spirit which is the awesome mystery of fate. All of these works have given a realistic portrayal of the wretched lives of the heroes.

Another work belonging in the same category was *Tomioka Sensei* (Mr. Tomioka), which was further advanced in the realistic treatment of the hero, his personality, and habits. In this work, it appears that the misfortune of the hero seems to have been the result of his obstinate character. Roughly the same thing can be said about his *Gen Oji*, regarded as his maiden work, which suggests that the strange character of the hero seems to have some relation with his unfortunate life. The heroes in these works, as well as those in *Ummeironja*, are all weak-minded but good-natured individuals. They are toyed with by the hand of the unpredictable thing called fate and are made to suffer in the deepest sense of the word.

On the other hand, in *Kamakura Fujin* (The Lady of Kamakura) (1902), *Daisansha* (The Third Man) (1903), and *Koi o Koisuru Hito* (Those Who Love Love) (1907), there are portions in which Doppo seems to have given vent to his feelings arising from his unsuccessful love-affair with Sasaki Nobuko. In this sense, we may say that in these works also are reflected the shadows of a child of fortune. In the works *Shōnen no Hiai* (A Boy's Sorrow) (1902), *E no Kanashimi* (The Sadness of the Picture) (1902), and *Bajō no Tomo* (The Friend on Horseback) (1903), the author relates his childhood recollections. The gypsy woman and his childhood friends appearing in these works seem also to be puppets which are being pulled by the strings of fate. The hero of *Akuma* (Demon) (1903) writes an essay "On Demons," in which he comments on scepticism about the existence of God, the awakening of self-consciousness, and other phases of the anxiety of modern man. This story thus displayed strong marks of the views of the author himself who was treading a path from Christianity to Naturalism. There is a strong feeling in this work of not readily succumbing to fate, but it was unique among Doppo's writings.

In general, works which deal with people tormented by fate showed Doppo's lyrical and melancholic moods. The tragic plot of these works is both serious and straightforward, and for this reason, moves the reader. However, it cannot be denied that the dominating tone was romanticism rather than realism.

In spite of the arguments we have made in the foregoing paragraphs, we do not mean to deny that Doppo not only depicted tragic human beings buffeted about by fate and sunk in unhappiness, but also showed concern for persons who resist and fight back against fate with their human power. Most typical of this latter case is *Hibon naru Bonjin* and its hero Katsura Shōsaku. Katsura is an ordinary man but a person of sincere efforts, inspired by *Saikoku Risshi-Hen* (Biographies of Self-Made Men of Western Countries). He comes to Tōkyō, lives a simple life, devotes his full efforts to his work, and, as a result, does not pay attention to anything else. Such is his personality. His attitude towards life is so sincere and stubborn that the author is compelled in the last part to ask the readers to " drink a toast to this friendly hero." As shown by this character, Doppo's ideal human being was " a man who does his own job, resigned to fate, but who opens a road for himself."

Nishōjo depicts the poor life of two telephone operators. One of the girls is almost persuaded to become a kept mistress but refuses and gains the sympathy of the other. A warm friendship springs up between the two. This warm humanism is implied through a tender realistic expression. *Haru no Tori* deals with a dumb boy who loves birds and who, thinking he can fly like them, jumps down from a castle wall and dies. The author expresses condolence for his sad fate, but, at the same time, seems to be overtaken by something like an aspiration for the innocent life of the boy who lived together with nature. Here is the symbol of Doppo's romantic spirit displayed in the poem *Sanrin ni Jiyū Sonsu* (There Is Liberty in the Mountain Forests).

Gōgai deals with a rather insane baron who complains that he is lonely because there are no more newspaper extras now that the war is over. Naturally, Doppo has no sympathy for such militarism, but states that he had to ask himself, " Isn't there something besides war, something which could make people feel and live the way they did during the war ? " This tells us that although he did not have any definite idea how to achieve it, Doppo's ideal was to have "all mankind fuse together in the same passion." In *Nakiwarai* this ideal seems to take form in the love of a mother. The mother, in this story, is irritated because her child is late in coming home. The child comes home finally and teases his mother who has tears in her eyes but smiles at the same time. The author seems to have perceived in this trivial family affair the sentiment of love expressed in a humorous form. The *ninjō* (human feeling) which he frequently emphasized in *Azamukazaru no Ki* (An Undeceiving Record) seems to have been crystallized and suggested through a realistic expression in this work.

The ideal Doppo wanted to communicate to us is represented by the state of an ego as free as nature itself, by the state of a sincere, moral human being who resigns himself to fate but strives to make his own fortune, or by a feminine mood, in which life is given a tender expression by means of love or human sentiment. Naturally, we cannot expect to have all of these images embodied constantly in a single character. However, it appears that Doppo has harmonized these ideals through a fundamental mood based on truth and sincerity. This corresponds to the realistic standpoint in the sense that both are opposed to vanity or hypocrisy. But Doppo's position was in direct opposition to objective truth based on scientific intellectuality. In this sense, his standpoint coincides with idealism or humanism.

In fact, his works depicting persons living a miserable life, buffeted about by fate, display strong romantic and subjective tendencies, while his works describing persons who have made their own fortunes or harmonized their life with their fate display slight traces of idealism and a moral tendency. But, as he approached his later years, Doppo came closer to Naturalism, and on the basis of an objective attitude, genuine to a considerable degree, depicted the naked life of commonplace persons living unnoticed in society. Traces of his own subjective ideas are almost completely wiped out in writings of this period. Although the work belonged to a relatively early period, Doppo had already assumed an objective attitude in *Junsa* (The Policeman) (1902), but this objective description was limited to the character and life of the policeman who was the hero. However, his methods of sketching which he used in this work met with a favorable response among the readers. It seems that the author himself considered this novel to be a trivial work, which he felt could be written with the help of a memorandum. The author was not assuming a genuine objective standpoint, for Duppo himself shows sympathy for the good-natured policeman, who, despite his attractiveness, seems to live in a sort of a world of nothingness and non-artificiality, standing aloof from the vulgar world. Doppo, in the concluding part, says, " I myself have become very mucd attached to this policeman." As to the works *Gōgai*, *Nakiwarai*, and *Ni-Shōjo*, they could be included under the classification of sketch prose. Although displaying a leaning towards the Naturalistic novel, all of these works betrayed the subjective feelings of the author.

However, a change in mood is perceived in *Hirō*. Here there were no traces of the author's compassion and sympathy for his heroes. The author merely gives a description of a fatigued merchant staying in a hotel at Kyōbashi, and concludes the story with the following sentence describing the hero falling asleep. " The hands fell down to the *tatami* with a thud. Instantly, he began snoring. His face was as pale as that of a dead man." Although it was not the purpose of the author to criticize, from a social standpoint, the obscure life of a merchant working desperately in this society, it seems that the author's design lay in presenting a Naturalistic vision of a corrupted society. The story *Kyūshi* also portrayed the obscure life of a lower-class worker who dies by the roadside because of illness, rain, and poverty. Although superficially this work appears as a Naturalistic writing, depicting a wretched aspect of society, the dominant mood in this piece is the author's compassion towards the hero rather than social criticism. Thus, we perceive in this work a leaning towards humanitarianism.

Among the works of this sort, *Take no Kido* was the most objectively written story, based on accurate description. This story concerns a company clerk who sets up a bamboo wicket between the garden of his home and that of his neighbor, a gardener, so that each can pass into the other's home. However, the gardener's wife utilizes this passage to steal charcoal. Her husband also joins in this stealing, but when their activities are about to be exposed, the wife commits suicide by hanging herself. The author gives a plain description of the family troubles of the office-worker and the irresponsible life of the gardener, who, after the death of his wife, finds another woman and moves to Shibuya. This novel could be regarded as a kind of a tragedy, if the author had attempted to write a story telling of the sad fate of the gardener's young wife, who, because of a trivial social phenomenon like the rise of the price of charcoal must have her life conclude in agony and death. But, compared to the previous work, the author has restrained himself from shedding compassionate tears and from loud weeping.

In *Ni-Rōjin* the author contrasts the life of two elderly men. One is a man with a family, living on a yearly pension of 300 yen, who professes a *laissez-faire* attitude toward life and seems to be satisfied with it. The other, putting his nose to the grindstone, is always looking for a job which is easy and at the same time leads to the most income. This man lives an unsettled life, chiefly because he has embezzled his employer's money, and is always fearful of the police. Although the author seems to assume an objective attitude in writing this story, his compassion apparently is directed toward the former old man. Here we perceive the author's own outlook on life.

As we have seen, Doppo gradually brought himself closer

to the mode of objective and Naturalistic writing. Apparently, one reason was the stimulus afforded by the age. Therefore, if he had not met an early death, he might have taken swifter steps towards humanitarianism, and developed fully in this direction. Once, Doppo, referring to Wordsworth's words, "the still, sad .music of humanity," stated that this sadness came from "God" and that the music was pure, sublime, restrained, and subtle. He said that those who could hear this music represented the ideal type of human being. Also, in *Azamukazaru no Ki* he stated that the essential attribute of a poet was in "perceiving, expressing, and preaching this subtle and sad music which echoes the human feelings through the heart of the living." From here, the ultimate destination could only be humanism.

1. Tōson and Naturalism

The Naturalistic trend, the first hints of which we are able to see in the development of realism, was firmly established by the work of Tayama Katai and Shimazaki Tōson, and since it also led to the development of Naturalistic theory, immediately after the Russo-Japanese War, in 1906 and 1907, we see a rapid growth, and with the successive emergence of such new writers as Tokuda Shūsei, Masamune Hakuchō, Iwano Hōmei, and others, for a time Naturalism occupied the center of the literary world.

Shimazaki Tōson's (Haruki) first work, strictly speaking, was *Utatane* (The Nap) (1897), but, as Tōson himself says in the preface, it was nothing more than the product of relaxation from his main work, poetry, and he had not yet fully entered into the prose form. And yet Tōson, even as a poet, was more a part of the Jinsei-Ha (Life Group) trend than of a purely Romantic one, and after 1899, when he moved to Komoro in Nagano Prefecture, he immersed himself primarily in Ruskin's *Modern Painters*, and while attempting detailed sketches of the nature and human life of the Chikuma River area, earnestly prepared the ground for a prose spirit. These later were published as essays entitled *Chikumagawa no Suketchi* (Chikuma River Sketches) (1912), in which the natural features of the Komoro region, and the poverty of the peasants which is so closely linked to it, are vividly described in an impressionistic manner. Thus, Tōson, who learned this objective method and acquired a grasp of reality, ceased to be an amateur, and resolving to make a second start as a novelist, published several short stories such as *Kyūshujin* (The Old Master) (1902), *Wara Zōri* (Straw Sandals) (1902), *Oyaji* (The Father) (1903), *Rōjō* (The Old Maid) (1903), and *Suisai Gaka* (The Water-Color Painter), and thereby opened up a new road in modern Japanese fiction.

All of these early short stories reflected "the sentiments of the people who live in the mountain villages along the upper reaches of the Chikuma River" (from the preface of the *Ryoku-yōshū*, The Green Leaves Anthology), and they possess local color to such an extent that they can be called "tales of the Chikuma River region." They are works in a Naturalistic manner which find their main theme in the elemental passions of man. In *Kyūshujin* a city-bred young wife who longs for a brilliant social life is very much dissatisfied with her marriage to a man who is much older than she, and finally, bored with the monotonous country life, commits adultery with a young dentist. This work is primarily modeled after *Madame Bovary*, and shows us how deeply Tōson was influenced by Naturalism. The heroine of *Rōjō* through an excess of self-consciousness falls into a state of depression over her heredity, and the male characters of *Oyaji* search for love with all the naturalness of instinct.

The world of these early works is exceedingly Naturalistic, but the method of dealing with these phenomena is not completely so. Love and the elemental passions are certainly not animal qualities which are dealt with in a cold, objective manner. The ending of *Kyūshūjin* consists of a scene wherein the husband, burning with jealousy, uncovers the adultery, but this profound scene is caricatured by the author and disposed of in an almost comic manner. This would indicate the author's humanity which makes him incapable of treating this passion in a cold, detached way. *Wara Zōri* is a horror-filled dramatic piece which depicts the jealousy of a savage man, but again the author brings to bear a deep compassion on this tragedy of passion. That is not all, for in *Oyaji* and *Rōjō* we even see that Tōson, who finds finally he cannot deny passion as the basis of human life, laughs at himself and adopts an attitude of resignation to it. This method of grasping the natural life of man is more assimilative and conforming to nature than it is

Naturalistic and objective. This then is not looking at man in a natural scientific manner but rather a seeking for the basis of human life in nature. We can say that man is not looked upon *as a part of* nature but rather as *in* nature. This natural quality of man in Tōson is on this point close to the nature of Rousseau, and his assimilative thought process is somewhat akin to that of Bashō.

Tōson's admiration of Rousseau is made clear by his reference in *Shinkatamachi Yori* (From Shinkatamachi) to "the self which I discovered in Rousseau's *Confessions.*" That which Tōson learned from the *Confessions* was "the spirit which attempts to look at life truly removed from all restraints" and "the record of one weak human being's life who was discouraged and who despaired." In the same *Shinkatamachi Yori* he states, "when I open the *Confessions,* I discover the ego everywhere." We can say that he interpreted the common, weak, Naturalistic life from the standpoint of Rousseau. Again in the same work he says: "I find Flaubert and Maupassant interesting in that they do not use the dissection method of Zola but follow in the Rousseau tradition of suffering." In another place he says that he finds fascinating the fact that the two writers left the scientific position of Zola and that while Maupassant created his "world of feeling," Flaubert was also both romantic and realistic at the same time. We learn from these words that Tōson was one who did not follow the Zola scientific method. We must say that this is a natural conclusion from Tōson's basic attitude and from his method of *shasei* (realism) which he learned from Ruskin and the painter Millet. Tōson's unique method of human research and self-examination began from this point.

Suisai Gaka (The Water-Color Painter) is a work wherein Tōson depicts his own experience of passion in the person of a water-color artist, and it represents the first step of his principal concern of *ningen tankyū* (human investigation). A young artist named Denkichi suffers when he learns that his wife has a lover, and the work represents that this suffering from passion—the pain of a man who hates a woman's unfaithfulness and the pain of a woman who hates a man's insincerity —is the meaning of human existence. This is a work which strives to find meaning in the love which links man and woman, and rather than a realistic document based on his own experience, it can be thought of as a kind of truth-seeking and as an almost religious expression of sincerity. This spirit of religious self-examination extends through all of Tōson's works. This is Tōson's humanism rather than his Naturalism. To describe human beings in an unreserved manner is a characteristic of Naturalism, but the main feature of Tōson's Naturalism is the addition of his humanism to his search for the fundamental life of human beings. *Suisai Gaka* was a sketch in this Tōson manner, but with the emergence of his powerful work *Hakai* (The Breaking of the Commandment) in 1906, he presented his first full-length novel.

Hakai is not only the first major work which established Tōson's style but is also most significant in the development of Naturalistic literature. This work tells of a young teacher of the outcast *eta* class named Ushimatsu, who suffers from this prejudice and who finally breaks his father's commandment, confessing his *eta* background, determined to clear his life of hypocrisy. He deals with the principal's life from a broad, almost sociological point of view, and the way in which he realizes this in the midst of vivid descriptions of the Nagano Prefecture region is indeed an epoch-making development in realism. The construction of this novel reminds one of Dostoevsky's *Crime and Punishment,* and while one must emphasize the fact that this was written as a true novel, still the form of the confession of the principal is more subjective than objective, and therefore does not represent complete mastery of the fiction form. The spirit behind Ushimatsu's confession is one of battling against his own falseness and is a sincere seeking for truth, so that it is still a continuation of the Rousseau spirit; furthermore, Tōson's own human investigation is reflected in Ushimatsu.

Tōson's second full-length novel which followed *Hakai* was *Haru* (Spring) (1908). This work tells of the suffering and passion of the sincere self-examination of the main character, Kishimoto (who is the author himself), with the atmosphere of the meetings and separations of the youths who gathered around the magazine *Bungakkai* as background, and is thus a kind of autobiographical novel. Of course this autobiographical confessional style was stimulated by the good reception of Katai's *Futon*, but it still must be considered as a natural development of Tōson's method. Ushimatsu of *Hakai* courageously opens a secret door, and Kishimoto of *Haru* also unreservedly opens his heart and reveals the suffering within. *Haru* was Tōson's own " breaking of the commandment." In *Haru* Tōson first ascertained the basis of his own life, and now he proceeded to seek in his family's history the secrets of that life. In *Hakai* Tōson reveals Ushimatsu's origins, and now Tōson confesses his own origins. The novel *Ie* (The Family) must be understood in this sense.

Ie (1910–1911) is again an autobiographical record of the author and his family. It tells of the destiny of the main character, Sankichi (again the author), a member of one of the two old families, linked by blood, whose declining fortunes are traced. Sankichi shares these fortunes, and even after he has formed his own household he encounters fresh difficulties. When one considers how Tōson presents in bold relief the living organism of two old families by tracing painstakingly the fortunes of its members over twenty and more years, with a tight construction and an objective description " that makes literature seem like architecture " (quoted from *Ori ni Furete*, Now and Then, included in *Shisei ni Arite*, In the Streets), then indeed one cannot deny it is the greatest masterpiece of Japanese Naturalism. However, we can see Tōson's deep-rooted humanism in the way in which Sankichi and O-Yuki, the new couple, in their setting up of a new household in a spirit of liberation from family ties, recognize the mystery of the existence of the family as the basis of human life; we can also see this in the probing which determines that in the transmission by blood of the family consists the basis of human life. Of course the attitude of seeking in heredity the causes of the degeneration of the two great families is a purely Naturalistic method, but on the other hand the feeling of love for his own kind, which the author has ascribed to Sankichi, can be interpreted as a transmutation of this degeneracy into a nostalgia for the basis of human life.

In short this Human Life group trend is the thread which runs through all of Tōson's works, and Tōson's view of life is a thing which follows the Rousseau-type Naturalistic tradition. The severity of his search for complete sincerity and the humanism which laments the lack of truth—this harmonious world which is heightened by morality is the stage attained by Tōson's Naturalistic humanism.

Tōson wrote several short stories in the time that he was polishing his long novels *Haru* and *Ie*. These are collected in *Tōson-Shū* (A Tōson Anthology) (1909) and *Shokugo* (After Eating) (1912), and their common characteristic is an acceptance of the pathos of existence and Tōson's ever-present humanism. When we come to his works of the Taishō Era such as *Tabi* (*tabi* are bifurcated Japanese socks) (1912), *Ganseki no Aida* (Among the Rocks) (1912), *Shuppatsu* (The Departure) (1912), and *Tokkan* (The Charge) (1913), which are all collected in *Bifū* (A Gentle Breeze), a bright life as if softened by a gentle breeze is depicted in a realistic manner. This is now a world of complete humanism. This kind of affirmation of life in Tōson's autobiographical works, such as *Sakura no Mi no Jukusuru Toki* (When the Cherries Ripen) (1915–1917) also becomes a bright hope, and after passing through the rigorous moral confession of *Shinsei* (New life) (1918–1919), he arrived at a world of love filled with a deep feeling for life in *Arashi* (The Storm) (1926) and *Bumpai* (The Allotment) (1927).

2. *Katai and Naturalism*

Tayama Katai (Rokuya) is a writer who is even more in the main stream of Naturalism than Tōson. Tōson was never able to take a strong stand in favor of Naturalism, whereas Katai in both his creative writing and criticism earnestly espoused it. In this sense Katai must bear the responsibility for both the virtues and vices of that literary movement.

Katai's emergence as a writer was relatively early, in his mid-twenties, but in his early period he was fascinated by the Romanticism of the pure love novel and love poetry, and had not yet arrived at a complete understanding of the prose medium. Katai's efforts at the establishment of a true prose spirit were stimulated by the trend of the times, and with the publication of *No no Hana* (The Flowers of the Field) (1901) and *Jūemon no Saigo* (The End of Jūemon) (1902) in his mid-twenties, there was promise of a complete change in style. The realistic statement in the preface of *No no Hana* to the effect that " we must write freely even of the secrets of human life and even of the whisperings of the Devil " is of course a positive assertion, but at the same time it is a reflection and judgment on his own previous sentimental romanticizing. It is true that *No no Hana* itself is still a Romantic novel with love as its main theme, but it is not simply a treatment of shallow sentiment, and in his method of seeking the truth of life in the spiritual suffering of the principal character, who is a mild and retiring type of person, we see foreshadowings of realism. *Jūemon no Saigo*, however, is an actual realization of his statement in the preface of *No no Hana*. This work, like Tōson's *Wara Zōri*, describes the instinctive savagery of man, but whereas Tōson pursues this subjectively as man's fundamental life, Katai treats this as *shizen* (nature). This work must thus be called Naturalistic. And yet this also is considerably different from the method of Zola. Needless to say, there is on the one hand something reminiscent of Zola's influence in the process whereby the personality of the hero, who is congenitally deformed and abnormal-minded, becomes perverted and his nature aggravated step by step under the pressure of environment; but on the other, this work exhibits some influence of Nietzsche's thought, and there are indications that its motif was borrowed from *Katzen-Steg* by Sudermann. Therefore, it cannot be said that this work is solely under Zola's influence. The author is not trying to criticize or analyze the inner workings of bestiality here. The wild child of nature is portrayed with an impressionistic touch that vivifies its wildness, and events and their background are all grasped phenomenologically. Here one already discerns the embryo of Katai's matter-of-fact description; yet neither was he the follower of Zola.

However, nature in human beings does not consist in wildness alone. The inner truth in *No no Hana* (The Flowers of the Field) also represents the natural quality in human existence. The pursuit of nature from this viewpoint is shown in such stories as *Umeya no Ume* (The Plum Tree of Umeya) (1902), *Onna-Kyōshi* (The Woman Teacher) (1903), *Nabari Otome* (The Maiden of Nabari) (1905), and *Shōjobyō* (The Maiden's Malady) (1907). They all describe the tragedies of life caused by amorous desires, grasping them as the inevitable result of the instinctive ego which runs counter to worldly common sense and conventional morals and which may be called the nature within. It may be said that this in a sense testifies to the author's comprehension of life from a Naturalistic point of view, though he may not have been fully aware of it. We should add that Katai in the meantime wrote an essay entitled *Rokotsu naru Byōsha* (A Straightforward Description) (1904), and enlarged on and confirmed his previous statement in the preface to *No no Hana* and the method he employed in *Jūemon no Saigo*. Notwithstanding this insistence of his, *Jūemon no Saigo* proved to be nothing more than a mere étude, and the above-listed stories emphasizing amorous desires had not completely outgrown sentimental romanticism. The "straightforward description" which he advocated achieved its more thoroughgoing execution in *Futon* (The Quilt) (1907).

Futon is a bold, unaffected exposure of the inner conflicts which Takenaka Tokio, a middle-aged novelist who has grown weary of his family life, experiences when he encounters Yoko-yama Yoshiko, an attractive young woman who becomes his pupil. This is a kind of a confessional story, with Tokio modeled after the author himself and Yoshiko after Okada Michiyo. The author explains the motive of his writing this work of fiction in his own words in "My Anna Mahr" (a section of *Tōkyō Sanjūnen*). He says that this story was modeled on Hauptmann's *Lonesome People*, and that the author, that is, Tokio, was the simulation of Johannes, and Yoshiko that of Anna Mahr. This was an attempt to "uncover and bring to light" "that which has been concealed and withheld and which it seems to be in danger of devastating one's own spirit to confess," for the purpose of "destroying the traditional pattern" and "opening a new road." This was a revelation of the author's solemn resolution that he would willingly sacrifice both his love and honor in order to write the truth, and was also an indication of the author's love of art which made him devotedly espouse the cause of estab-lishing the new literature holding "straightforward description" as its ideal. With Tōson the spirit of confession was humanism through exploration of life, while with Katai confession was his earnest insistence on and execution of realism.

This means on the one hand that *Futon* marked for Katai the discovery of his method, and on the other, its bold description of sexual life and its method of earnest confession exerted on the literary circle a profound influence in determining the course of Naturalistic literature thereafter. But the descriptions of *Futon* were to some extent colored by the subjectivity inherent in con-fession, making the author's attempt at objective description somehow incomplete. Thus it was not until the publication of the trilogy composed of *Sei* (Life) (1908), *Tsuma* (The Wife) (1908), and *En* (Human Ties) (1910), and of *Inaka Kyōshi* (The Country Teacher) (1909) that Katai's realistic method attained its maturity.

The trilogy of *Sei*, *Tsuma*, and *En* is wholly autobiographical with the main character modeled after the author himself; the minor characters, too, had their model in actuality. Furthermore, this trilogy constitutes a tetralogy together with *Futon*. These works were his experiments in the matter-of-fact description method, which was defined in his own words as " describing things just as you see, hear, or feel them, without adding any subjectivity or any internal explanation or analysis." (From " The Experiment in *Sei*," September 1908). It was because he wished to attain perfection of the rigid, objective attitude that he dared to model characters after his own blood relations. *Sei* presents the picture of complicated human relationship and psychological entanglements among the sick mother, the central figure, her four children, and their respective spouses. Here the author is trying to demonstrate the ugliness of egoism which brings dissension even among blood relations when their interests do not coincide, and the eventual change of the generations from old to new regardless of such antagonisms. The characters in the story are presented as individuals with objective merits, with their psychology and personalities described in realistic detail. *Sei* is one of Katai's masterpieces of matter-of-fact description.

For all that, one of the characters in this story, Sennosuke, who appears to be a copy of the author, is the embodiment of the author's subjectivity, and there are passages where the objective world is explained which are incoherent from the viewpoint of matter-of-fact description. But from the standpoint of fiction, the success of the story with its compact composition is credited to the explanations and analyses. The author, however, in execution of matter-of-fact description, hastening merely to wipe out all subjectivity, goes so far as to discard the insight into and analysis of objective reality. This attitude is also attended by an evil which makes his fiction monotonous and desultory.

Tsuma relates how a young girl becomes a wife and then a mother, and grows gradually domesticated, and at the same time how her husband becomes disillusioned with her. He is weary of life and suffers from the discrepancy between his ideals and reality, but when a young woman pupil appears on the scene, his sensations are stirred afresh. This story is focused on the life of the couple but also relates the lives of the wife's parents and the hero's brothers, the affairs of his friends, and his association with the young woman pupil. The tale of such changing aspects of life is developed in a panoramic fashion, without any relationship of cause and effect among the scenes and without emphasizing any specific theme. This was the practical application of the author's theory which he advocated in "Concerning *Tsuma*" (July 1909), that is, "my idea is to write on nonchalantly from the standpoint that this kind of thing happens, or that that is one way to live life." " I am satisfied if my writings, as a whole, can produce a certain atmosphere." This mode of writing, which lacked both heroes and plot, gave a certain looseness to the novel, which, when compared to *Sei* (Life), seems to lack uniformity. Furthermore, the author's description of the husband, actually a projection of Katai, betrays the sentimental feelings of the author himself. This work represented, in a sense, a return to *Futon*. In it the author seems to have attempted to express, through the daily life of the couple and against the background of passing time, the disillusion, the ennui, and the agony inherent in human life. However, his expression was a trifle subjective, and the ideas he tried to express could not be embodied in concrete form in the novel. The reason was that the novel lacked a central theme, which in the case of *Sei* was the death of the mother.

En (Human Ties) is a sequel to *Futon*. The young student and her sweetheart who appeared in the first novel, in this sequel, marry, have a baby, and become disillusioned as a result of the hardship they undergo in actual life. However, despite their disillusion, the two cling to each other, bound by ties of passionate love. The unfolding of their marriage in this novel is intertwined with the subjective feelings of the hero, an observer in the story but actually the author's projection, and with the affairs of the hero's friends and those of the women he encounters. In this complex state, a series of incidents take place, but the author has not selected any of them as the central subject of the story, and has merely given an objective, and at the same time impressionistic description of them. In *Sei* and *Tsuma* the author has failed to give concrete form to his own projection, which in the former case was Tetsunosuke and in the latter Susumu. In this sense, both of these works lack objective description. However, in the case of *En*, the hero Hattori Kiyoshi assumes a position which is distinctly independent from his creator. We may say that this novel probably represented the ultimate expression of the author's peculiar meditative mood. And, in contrast with *Tsuma*, all of the incidents taking place in the story develop around the same axis, which is the central character Hattori Kiyoshi. As a result, the whole story is united under a common mood and atmosphere. We must say that for Katai this was a success in the objective method. For the first time, the author, in this novel, has succeeded in portraying the fate of human beings bound by strange ties and in suggesting the current of time which sweeps everything with it, by merely giving a superficial description of various phenomena. Naturally, the atmosphere suggested was a vague mood and was not shaped into a concrete symbolic form with ideological content. However, the objective description displayed in *En* was born out of a thorough meditative mood. It is true, on the other hand, that mere enumerating of phenomena has given rise to a certain looseness in the work. This, of course, is counteracted by the compact atmosphere created by the work as a whole. While, this compactness in the atmosphere created by the work attests to the maturity of the author's method, the method itself, which was akin to that of the personal, mental life (*shinkyō*) novels, were ultimately to push the author into a road leading to the triviality of the *shishōsetsu* (the personal novel).

Inaka Kyōshi (The Country Teacher) does not belong to the line of the author's autobiographical novels and is a genuine objective story. This story appeared before *En*. It deals with the solitude, the mental agony, and the loneliness of a country grammar school teacher who has great ambition, but because he is poor cannot study in the capital and must pursue an obscure and unhappy life in the country. On the basis of actual investigations of the hero who actually existed, and with the help of diaries, letters, and rumors, the author sketched the life of this teacher from a thorough objective standpoint. In conducting actual investigations to write this *Inaka Kyōshi*, the author seems to be following the example of Zola's experimental novels. However, Katai was by no means basing his investigation on scientific analysis and dissection. Rather, he was following the impressionistic methods of the Goncourt brothers, and the sole basis of his observation and sketching was his own sensual feeling. The objective description based on this method gave a wholly natural picture of the obscure but passionate school-teacher. It was a success in the best sense of objective description. The author's own sentimental feelings, in this work, have flowed smoothly into his creations, giving a tender and innocent character to the hero's life. The pastoral sentiments expressed through the scenery on the banks of the great Tonegawa are such that they suggest a kind of nostalgic feeling. In this sense, this novel, among his works, displayed the most harmonious combination of the romanticism peculiar to the author and his objective method.

In addition to these, Katai left for us several excellent short stories where his impressive delineation was realized. The representative pieces are *Ippeisotsu* (A Soldier from the Ranks) (1908),

Dote no Ie (The House on the Bank) (1908), *Asa* (Morning) (1910), and *Yōji* (An Infant) (1910). *Ippeisotsu* is an objectively cool sketch of the anxieties and agony of death of a seriously sick soldier who has dropped out of the ranks on the battlefield. That such elaborate description reaches deep into a human mind is indeed exceptional with this author. It is almost unneccessary to say here that this objective attitude corresponds to his method of plain delineation (*heimen byōsha*). *Dote no Ie* describes the sexual secrets of a young maid who works in a restaurant and becomes aware of sex under the stimulus of the circumstances, while *Asa* is an impressionist sketch of a family moving to Tōkyō, where the father will assume a new post, by traveling on a boat down the Tone River. *Yōji* suggests the delicate instinctiveness of an infant by representing impressively the manners of a baby under twelve months of age. All these works are without exception characteristic of the author's dispassionate and contemplative approach.

The method of plain delineation seen in *Inaka Kyōshi* (The Country Teacher), *En* (Human Ties), and other short stories Katai naturally owed to the Goncourt brothers. However, he owed it as well to Matsuura Tatsuo of the Keien school under whom Katai studied as a pupil in his youth. Apart from the problem of whether such a contemplative attitude of Katai was correct or not, the method of writing that rejects any adaptation, draws a phenomenon as it appears, and suggests the meaning of life in a peculiar atmosphere, should be regarded as characteristic of Katai. Nonetheless, the reading public came to lose interest in such monotonous description, and with the decline of Naturalism, Katai was obliged to retire from the forefront of the literary field to try to change his style of writing.

Therefore, from the closing years of Meiji, Katai turned to a realistic style, writing mental life stories called *aiyoku-mono* (love pieces). Thus, again he began showing an inclination to subjectivism. A kind of romantic tendency was conspicuous in the longing for a religious life which overcomes amorous instinct depicted in such works as *Zansetsu* (Lingering Snow) (1917) and *Aru Sō no Kiseki* (The Miracle of a Bonze) (1917). Eventually, powerful "time," which mercilessly sweeps away human efforts, or acceptance of fate was developed as the theme in *Toki wa Sugiyuku* (Time Passes On) (1916) and *Futatabi Kusa no No ni* (Again on the Grassy Field) (1918). Starting from criticism of convention, wherein he even put himself on the operating table, Katai then immersed himself in contemplative impressionism, and after a short period, began to seek the calmness of resignation. This process of Katai was symbolical of the course of Naturalism in this country.

3. *Shūsei and Hakuchō*

Tokuda Shūsei was a more thoroughgoing Naturalist than Tōson or Katai because of the dispassionate quality of his contemplative attitude and of the world of common people narrated in his works. He had no element of Tōson's exclamation and wonder, Katai's sentimentality, or Hakuchō's nihilism. This objective attitude of Shūsei was indeed close to the original Naturalism, but it fell short of the realistic attitude, backed by a scientific spirit, seen in Zola or Maupassant. It was an affirmative acceptance of the actuality wherein Shūsei was obedient to his fate. In this sense, it can be said that Shūsei's Naturalism could not but be a peculiarly Japanese one. Like Tōson and Katai, Shūsei had spent long years as an author before he became a Naturalist. One of the four distinguished pupils of Kōyō, together with Kyōka, Fūyō, and Shun'yō, he started his literary life as the member of Ken'yūsha, and as early as the Meiji twenties Shūsei published his maiden work *Yabukōji* (Spear Flowers) (1896), treating the miserable fate of a girl emerging from an outcast community. Although primitive from a present-day standpoint, this short story contained something not in harmony with the popular style of any other Ken'yūsha writer in the choice of subject as well as in the depth of psychological delineation. In spite of his being Kōyō's pupil,

Shūsei had within himself something antagonistic to the urbanity of the Ken'yūsha, a certain element of the thinking of the common people. For this reason it took him more than ten years after the spectacular début of Kyōka and Fūyō to display his real talent. In the meantime, he gained a certain reputation by publishing a work, *Kumo no Yukue* (The Destination of the Clouds) (1900), which did not yet go beyond the limit of an ordinary novel. However, toward the end of the Meiji thirties, Shūsei's talent as a Naturalist found a soil in which it could flourish. In this connection, stimulated by the movement of Tōson and Katai, he patterned his style after that of Maupassant. The decline of the influence of the Ken'yūsha caused by Kōyō's death was another factor giving him an opportunity for free activity. His novels *Shōkazoku* (A Little Nobleman) (1904), *Ono ga Imashime* (In the Bond of Self) (1906), *Honoo* (The Flame) (1907), and *Chōraku* (Decay) (1907), and short stories in the collections *Hanataba* (The Bouquet) (1905) and *Shūsei-Shū* (A Shūsei Collection)—each of them was a milestone on the course to the eventual flourishing of the author's talent. *Shussan* (The Birth) (1908), which came in the wake of these works, was a short story of pure Naturalism, heralding the next work *Arajotai* (The New Home) with " a non-ideal and no solution " (*murisō, mukaiketsu*) attitude.

By publishing *Arajotai* in 1908, Shūsei established his position as a Naturalist writer of fame. The central figures, the newly married Shinkichi and his wife O-Saku, keep a *saké* shop in suburban Tōkyō. The story depicts their family cares, the disillusionment of their married life, and the process of their yielding to life's inertia, despite their despair, anxiety, and fatigue. The author's skill in a realistic method and construction was fully displayed in this long story. Taking up ordinary and ignorant city-dwellers as the characters, this sketch of a phase of life without any ideal or solution can be said to be a true work of Naturalism.

Ashiato (Footprints) is a story of an uncultured provincial girl, O-Shō, who comes with her family to Tōkyō to live. It describes how the girl comes to awaken to her sensuality and ego as a result of her changing destiny in the midst of a large and decadent city. As the background of the story the author brings forth a large number of men and women having no relation to the life of the heroine O-Shō, such as her family, her aunt and her family, her uncle and his wife, her rival O-Masu, and others. These figures, however, are not necessarily connected directly with the heroine's fate, and they are all treated on the same level. This approach to some extent is like the flat delineation of Katai in *En* (Human Ties). Moreover, in *Ashiato* Shūsei advanced one step beyond Katai's work. In *En* Katai had no intention of seeking the significance of human life as a whole, and contented himself with mere description of phenomena which appeared and disappeared one after another with the process of time, in order to achieve the best work of flat delineation, while in *Ashiato* all the phenomena are presented in a unity as the changeful destiny of O-Shō, and a feminine portrait was given in both body and soul. Thus, the meaning of human life was seized in concrete form. Naturally, however, that meaning was not intentionally pursued as was the case with Tōson, but here only hints of it were given without intention in an absolutely objective sketch of human life. In *En* there was no central figure, and this record of life in the style of a diary or essay could only be given unity through the suggestion of passing time. In contrast with this, the reader of *Ashiato* is able to have a clear image of a woman by following the footprints made by her during the span of her life.

Kabi (Mold), published in 1911, was an autobiographical novel, the hero of which was the author himself. Sasamura, a novelist in obscurity, disillusioned with and tired of married life with an uncultured woman, O-Gin, finally surrenders and inertly comes to bear a dull life with no ideal or light. Shūsei realistically describes this process with cool objectivity in this work, one of his best. With Tōson and Katai, some of their autobiographical works were unsuccessful as novels, because of the religious passion of the former or the sentimentality of the latter, which was an obstruction to a really objective approach to the author himself. And yet in *Kabi* Shūsei succeeded in presenting a pattern for the private life novel (*shishōsetsu*), as he never indulged in sentimentality. In the most emotional scenes, such as the death of the teacher of whom the author was a disciple, and the critical illness of an infant, his child, Shūsei never forgot to objectify his own emotions as the hero's. Herein lies the characteristic of Shūsei's Naturalism.

After *Kabi*, Shūsei wrote *Tadare* (Corruption) (1913) and *Arakure* (Indulgence) (1915), both of which are his representative works. It was in the years of the Taishō Era that these pieces were produced, and this fact suggests that his naturalism flourished the more brilliantly the further Naturalism in general declined. The leading figure of *Tadare* is O-Masu, once a prostitute and now a mistress, juxtaposed by a number of women, the legal wife of Asai, the man who keeps her as mistress, O-Yuki, the heroine's friend in her prostitute days, and O-Ima, O-Masu's sister, who becomes a victim of the amorous Asai. These characters compose the corrupt world of desire related here. His " technique without technique " here is nearer completion than in *Ashiato* (Footprints), and the kaleidoscope of the life of passion is more colorful. *Arakure* presents the portrait of O-Shima who indulges in love, wantonly changing her partners. Despite this plot, almost no element of decadence is perceivable in the energetic life of the heroine, and the reader finds rather something cheerful about the woman. The author casts into relief the woman's manner of life through his unconcerned delineation of sensual scenes and concise, objective style. It may be said that *Arakure* was the culmination of Shūsei's Naturalist works. Although he came to a standstill in his creative activity for a short time, he emerged as an *Ich Roman* (*shishōsetsu*) writer in the latter part of the Taishō Era. His cool and stern objectivity was ever more deepened into an Oriental philosophy of indifference, and thus he attained the maturity seen in his last work, *Shukuzu* (A Miniature) (1941).

Masamune Hakuchō (Tadao) emerged as a rising writer of the Naturalist school in contrast with Tokuda Shūsei. Objectifying the world, Shūsei accepted its mediocrity and absurdity as they appeared to be; quite unconcernedly he mirrored such a world in his mind with no touch of sentimentality. Compared with him, Shūsei had the austerity of an intellectual critic who was able to uncover in an indifferent way the disillusionment of the actual world as well as the agony of a nihilistic *fin-de-siècle* mind, which was the peculiarity of his naturalism. He can be credited as a true realist in that, not allowing himself to be caught in the sentimentality of nihilistic or despairing views, he gave shape through his objects to life's emptiness and man's absurdity by taking a cool, indifferent attitude toward them.

He emerged from among rising young authors by publishing *Jin'ai* (Dust) and *Doko e* (Whither) in 1907 and 1908 respectively. In the former, a short story of city-dwellers' life, Hakuchō told of the misery of these people losing all hope or ideals and who cannot but live like withered trees, "breathing day after day the dust of the Ginza until at last the germs in the dust eat their lives away"; while in the latter work, the author sketched the nihilistic anguish of a modern intellectual who goes wandering and whom "nothing can intoxicate, neither any ism, any book, any woman, nor any talent." This last work is a masterpiece which advances a step further than *Jin'ai*. However, in these works some superficiality is yet recognizable, and his negative mind is as yet lukewarm. This can be proved by the self-despising resignation found in *Jin'ai* and the hero Kenji's finding consolation in the coquetry of Mrs. Katsurada, which might be considered a longing for the romanticism of decadence.

The following works, such as *Bikō* (The Feeble Light) (1910),

Doku (Poison) (1911), and *Doro Ningyō* (The Clay Doll) (1911), are the *chefs-d'oeuvre* showing Hakuchō's further deepened realism and the establishment of his nihilistic philosophy of life. *Bikō* is a kind of objective story belonging to the lineage of *Arajotai* (The New Home) of Shūsei. It depicts the unsettled and dull state of mind of a woman who dares not abandon herself to decadence, though living a slovenly life as either a mistress or a prostitute. Different from Shūsei's feminine characters O-Saku, O-Gin, O-Shō, and O-Masu, who all resignedly approve of their wanton life, Hakuchō's O-Kuni feels restless in finding herself besieged by the ennui and melancholy of a deteriorated life. The author successfully describes her uneasy, vacant mind in this work. *Doku* is a story of a triple love-affair developing around the heroine O-Tayo. Hakuchō tries to pursue a psychology of self-disgust on the part of Katori Gen'ichi, the hero, who, in spite of his hatred of the lasciviousness of O-Tayo and Yuhara his rival, is at last conquered by the impudicity and intensive sensual appeal of the woman. We see here the author's realism more and more controlled by intellect, sensitivity, and technique.

Doro Ningyō (The Clay Doll) is said to have been an autobiographical novel in which the author recorded, for the most part true to the facts, the process of how he got married. Moriya Jūkichi, the central figure, has no regard for women as a result of his having led an abandoned life for a long time. After having met a number of prospective brides without being deeply impressed by or deciding to wed any one of them, he takes a wife in this apathetic state of mind. But he is later mortified at his fate that alienated him from the woman of his choice and made him marry the one he could not love, since he cannot regard his wife as anything but a doll of clay. *Doro Ningyō* portrays such a tasteless, insipid married life in a matter-of-fact style. While Shūsei's *Kabi* (Mold) is the projection of the hero Sasamura's life in despair and disillusionment, *Doro Ningyō* is permeated with the loathing and sarcastic attitude toward the emptiness of life which constituted the author's *Weltanschauung*. Naturally he is distinct from Tōson and Katai in respect to such a nihilistic, idle spectator's view of life. But Hakuchō is also alien to the acceptance of reality which characterized Shūsei, for there is in him an innate, uncompromising criticism of life. This is not any longer accepting reality just as it is, but an objective recognition endorsed by subjectivity. Objectivity in Naturalism, when it reached the limits of its development, had to be surmounted once more by intellectualistic subjectivity. It may not be incorrect to say that the decadent and paranoid tendency perceived in Hakuchō's style prepared the way for the advent of Neo-Romanticism. However, Hakuchō himself dared not describe the world given to nihilism and possessed of paranoiac passions. Here was the limit of Hakuchō as a Naturalist.

In the Taishō Period, Hakuchō's style showed further development in *Irie no Hotori* (Near the Inlet) (1915), *Ushibeya no Nioi* (The Odor of the Cowshed) (1916), and *Shisha Seija* (The Dead and the Living) (1916), and his popularity as an author mounted in spite of the decline of Naturalism. Tatsuo, the hero of *Irie no Hotori*, is the same type as Kenji in *Doko e* (Whither), a paranoid nihilist, but portrayed with more objectivity than Kenji. In *Ushibeya no Nioi* and *Shisha Seija*, Hakuchō describes the conditions of people who, though almost helpless, still persevere in life instinctively. The dispassionate and precise objective description in these stories is even symbolical. At this stage, Hakuchō's objective attitude is not very much different from Shūsei's. This tendency breathes through his later works such as *Dokufu no Yō na Onna* (The Vampire-Like Woman) (1920), *Hito Samazama* (Various People) (1921), and *Umazarishi Naraba* (If She Had Not Borne Him) (1923). When such a style of his degenerated into mannerism he adopted the media of the drama and criticism for the expression of his subjective passion given to negative criticism, thus ending his mission as a Naturalistic writer.

4. The Galaxy of Naturalistic Writers

As the Naturalistic style established itself and gained popularity, a number of new authors appeared one after another, among them Iwano Hōmei, Ikuta Kizan, Chikamatsu Shūkō, Nakamura Seiko, Kamitsukasa Shōken, Mayama Seika, Tamura Toshiko, and Kanō Sakujirō. Naturally they were of different magnitudes as authors, still none of these names can be neglected in discussing the world of Naturalistic literature.

Iwano Hōmei (Yoshie) started his author's career as a poet in the same fashion as Tōson and Katai. The origin of his passionate and serious agony of decadence and his *Weltanschauung* given to impulses can be perceived already in his poetry. It may be said that his novels were the expression of such agony and *Weltanschauung* in the form of prose. In this respect he somewhat resembles Tōson; however, Hōmei's uniqueness consisted in the violent passions of the aimless, instinctive ego, which had only the remotest resemblance to Tōson's sincerity in the pursuit of truth. Hōmei's first story which won him the reputation of an author was *Tandeki* (Indulgence) (1909), the plot of which is as follows: A novelist, who is tired of his family life, becomes attached to a country geisha at a summer seaside resort. He attempts to make an actress of her, but his plan is upset because of the jealousy and conflicts raised by the geisha's patron and the author's wife, and with the passing of time he becomes bored with the woman. Here is the unvarnished presentation of the hero's anguish resulting from his unbridled amorous life. This story describes the love of a man in the prime of manhood as does *Futon* (The Quilt). But in contrast with the standpoint of indifferent observation from which the author of *Futon* viewed objectively even his own inner reality, Hōmei's writing was based in thorough-going egoism and passionate execution. Therefore, Hōmei's confessions were a more subjective outcry of self-fulfilment, which was intrinsically opposed to the introspective attitude displayed by the hero of *Futon*. The world of amorous desires presented here is permeated with the crude, selfish consciousness of the ego which precludes even a trace of tender emotion. And the hero's impulsive and impassioned behavior, effectuated by the simplicity of the style, gives the vivid and even cruel and relentless impression of outrageous reality.

As hitherto explained, *Tandeki* was Hōmei's first attempt at establishing the subjective style which prizes as absolute the impulsive, unthinking execution undertaken by the whole ego, but the objective presentation of such subjectivity was somehow incomplete. The essence of disinterested sincerity which Hōmei pursued with impassioned efforts is given full scope rather in what is called his quintet, which is composed of *Hōrō* (The Wandering) (1910), *Dankyō* (The Broken Bridge) (1911), *Hatten* (Development) (1912), *Dokuyaku o Nomu Onna* (The Lady Who Takes Poison) (1914), and *Tsukimono* (The Possession) (1918). These five novels constitute one long autobiographical work, in which the hero, a writer named Tamura Yoshio, is the shadow of the author himself. Part of this quintet was written in the Taishō Period. The sequence of events constituting the content of these novels is not necessarily consistent with the order of their publication. But the fundamental attitude penetrating through these works comes from the affirmation of the impulsiveness of the whole ego, prizing the burning of subjectivity, which was emphasized also by the author. It may be said that this attitude means the insistence on the impulsive and unthinking self, repudiating all admiration, sentimentality, resignation, and indifferent observation. This was Hōmei's method which distinguished him from Tōson, Katai, Shūsei, and Hakuchō.

Hōrō and *Dankyō* constitute a series linked with the later published *Tsukimono*. They describe the irritation and anguish of the central figure, who, having failed in the canning business which he undertook in accordance with the principle of impas-

sioned execution, stays with his acquaintance at Sapporo pur-
poselessly, and then goes on wandering about in Hokkaidō.
Hatten and *Dokuyaku o Nomu Onna* come in the wake of
Tandeki. They present a lively psychological delineation of
the hero Yoshio, who leads a seemingly scandalous life of
agony, involved in persistent jealousy, hatred, and carnal desire,
arising from his entanglements with his mistress O-Tori and
his wife Chiyoko. It is pathetic and ludicrous, as well as
grotesque, how Hōmei describes the hero's lunatic behavior, his
struggles after self-fulfilment, and the ugly jealousy and wildness
of amorous desires, in his audacious, artless, and plain style. At
this time Hōmei also wrote pleasant, humorous short stories
such as *Bonchi* (The Boy) (1913) and *Hito ka Kuma ka* (A
Man or a Bear) (1913), where anguish and joy, sincerity and
stupidity, are intermingled. Indeed, they are not unrelated to
the world of tragi-comedy of the quintet. This provides an example of the crisis of life in Hōmei's " philosophy of pathos," and
of the optimism of life-for-life's-sake which surmounts such a
crisis. It may also provide a clue to the understanding of his
sympathy with the naturalism inherent in ancient Shintō. In short,
Hōmei's self-fulfilment is somewhat opposed to the mainstream
of Naturalism, and it may be said to have some kinship to the
affirmation of the ego typical of the Shirakaba (White Birch)
school.

Ikuta Kizan (Eigorō) was an author active from the preceding period. A disciple of Iwaya Sazanami, his career itself is
suggestive of the leaning of his style toward romanticism. Kizan's stories in the area of Naturalism include *Fumiko-Hime*
(Princess Fumiko) (1906), *Kyoei* (Vanity) (1907), and *Tokai*
(The Metropolis) (1908). Without exception they unveil the
brutality under the guise of conventional morals, with sensual
aestheticism and romantic emotions heavily breathing through
them. They have some kinship to Hōmei's world in that they
present ego-conscious, unbridled women as heroines, treating of
their impulsive passion. It may testify to the author's decadent

tastes that his books were often suppressed on the charge of expressing rather eccentric ideas.

Chikamatsu Shūkō was an author who had an inclination to anti-Naturalism in his subjective style. *Wakareta Tsuma ni Okuru Tegami* (The Letter to the Divorced Wife) (1910) was his first success. It is in the tradition of stories of the author's personal life, describing the solitude and misery of the hero, who tries to dismiss his loneliness after divorcing his wife through association with a geisha with whom he happens to sleep and in whom coquetry and sincere affection are combined, only to realize that she after all belongs to the unchaste and infamous world, too. His subjective style is seen in the presentation of the tender sentiments of recollection of the divorced wife, or of the sweet sensations of debauchery. *Giwaku* (Suspicion) (1913) is a counterpart to *Wakareta Tsuma ni Okuru Tegami*. The hero's wife elopes with her lover, and he searches for them frantically. The hero's dogged attachment and his serious, self-tormenting hatred are pathetic and lamentable. Later on Shūkō disclosed in his article entitled " The Literary Background of the Period When ' The Letter to the Divorced Wife' Was Written " (*Waseda Bungaku*) (357th Issue, June 1927), that he was rather against the naturalism without ideals, and that *Wakareta Tsuma ni Okuru Tegami* was his protest against the passionless style of Naturalism. This means that his style is characterized by delineations of sentiments and amorous desires, which have closer kinship to decadence than Naturalism. *Maizuru Shinjū* (The Double Suicide at Maizuru) (1915) and *Sumiyoshi Shinjū* (The Double Suicide at Sumiyoshi) (1915), published early in the Taishō Period, are already the literature of romantic sentiments, and in a sense are modern versions of Chikamatsu's works. This period saw the publication of *Aokusa* (The Green Grasses) (1914) and other choice stories of decadence dealing with the prostitutes in the Kyōto and Ōsaka areas. Also *Kurokami* (Black Hair) (1922) was his typical work in the emotional style, narrating the pain of an unquenchable infatuation.

Kamitsukasa Shōken (Nobutaka) also had an emotional style clearly distinct from Naturalism. Following *Kannushi* (The Shintō Priest) (1908), his first success, he wrote in succession such novels as *Kaijin* (The Ashes) (1908) and *Mokuzō* (The Wooden Idol) (1910). But it was not until the beginning of the Taishō Period that his works gained rich flavor. Especially *Hamo no Kawa* (The Skin of a Sea Eel) (1914) is an excellent short story which established his position in the literary circle. In this story of a lovelorn merchant's wife who is deserted by her husband, Shōken exposed her secrets in the light of erotic psychology with such irony and pathos as, harmonized with the delicate atmosphere of the Kamigata area, to give the story a most attractive savor. This author's refined irony and unaffected sincerity had some kinship to the mode of the Yoyū-Ha (The Leisure School).

Nakamura Seiko (Masatame) had his unique gifts recognized by the literary world by the publication of his *Shōnenkō* (The Song of Adolescence) (1907), establishing himself as a new Naturalist writer. The story tells in a plain style of the naive friendship between two youths, one a simple-hearted lad, the other an ill-fated young genius. Their affection tended to homosexuality, and the story is told in the setting of the pastoral atmosphere at the foot of Mt. Fuji. The keynote of his style consisted in the harmony and tranquillity of his simple and smooth portrayal of commonplace events. This disinterested meditation and affirmative view of reality, soon afterwards absorbing the symbolical meaning of human existence into it, paved the way for the world of lyricism typical of the *shishō-setsu*.

Kanō Sakujirō emerged as a writer with *Yakudoshi* (The Critical Age) (1911) at the time when Naturalism was at a low ebb, and his authorship did not reach its height until the middle of the Taishō Period. For this reason his style naturally possessed something beyond the Naturalistic view of reality. In other words, his style has rich emotions with a note of sadness in the realistic description of commonplace, everyday life. This provides his stories with a kind of emotional mood. The essence of such characteristics of his is perfectly displayed by such novels and short stories as *Yo no Naka e* (Into the World) (1918), *Arare no Oto* (The Sound of Hail) (1919), *Kama* (The Iron Pot) (1921), and *Chichi no Kao* (The Face of the Father) (1922).

In conclusion, Shūkō, Shōken, Seiko, and Sakujirō have the same subjective tendency in respect to their lyricism and emotionalism. Such a world of introversive, meditative emotions, which may be termed *mono no aware*, is in contrast with the violent passions of the romantic ego typical of Hōmei. It was not accidental that these authors unexceptionally pursued the meditative state of mind in the form of the *shishōsetsu*, or stories of private affairs, after the beginning of the Taishō Period.

Mayama Seika (Akira) was called the equal of Hakuchō in the early days of his career, and he also displayed a unique style with respect to his subjective and passionate tendency. His representative work, *Minami Koizumi Mura* (The Village of Minami Koizumi) (1907), with its setting in a poor village near Sendai, one typical of the northern part of Japan, describes unreservedly the poverty and ignorance of the peasants, and presents in a way an aspect of social problems, by disclosing the misery of petty peasants whose living is being contaminated by the metropolitan culture. Also *Ahirukai* (The Keeper of the Ducks) creates a serious, heart-rending impression in the portrayal of a narrow-minded, stupid old man who tries in vain to resist the rapid growth of a large town. The world of crude egoism exhibited in these works is indeed monstrous and pathetic, and makes one feel a kind of revulsion. His stories portraying such objective reality have their diametric opposites in his subjective and introspective stories of private life including *Myōgabatake* (The Field of *Myōga*) (1907) and

Haibokusha (The Wreck) (1907). These stories depict the desperate anguish of those who are reduced to destitution and have lost confidence in reality, in much the same manner as the *fin-de-siècle* nihilism of Hakuchō. But Seika's passionate, romantic qualities caused him to shift to drama for their expression. In this respect also he is akin to Hakuchō.

Tamura Toshiko (Toshiko) (with a different Chinese character), a disciple of Rohan and a student of Ichiyō's style, started her writing career with the publication of *Akirame* (Resignation), her first success, under the influence of Naturalistic literature. This work was her attempt to discard the conventional style, and she then went on writing the short story *Ma* (The Demon) (1912), and such romances as *Miira no Kuchibeni* (The Painted Lips of the Mummy) (1913) and *Hōraku no Kei* (Death by Burning) (1914). In these excellent works is exhibited distinctly her Naturalistic inclination.

The plot of *Akirame* is as follows : The heroine so devotedly wishes to make literature her career that she leaves the school where novel-writing is branded as immoral. But she goes home to the country and serves her aged mother, abandoning the enjoyment of the successful première of her own play, because she cannot bear being involved in the entanglements of mortal love and desire. This story describes the heroine's resignation, and the attitude of abandoning herself to fate, it may be said, is still following the tradition of Ichiyō's world. However, delicate feelings inherent in female authors are displayed in the description of love and desire among the heroine's elder sister, her husband, the heroine herself, and the young girl who admires her in a sisterly manner, and in that of the psychology of a girl who is being awakened to sexual instincts.

Ma delineates the psychology of a middle-aged woman who makes sport of her own feelings in her love-affairs with a man younger than she is. *Hōraku no Kei* is a story of masochistic psychology. A wife who has betrayed her husband is, on the one hand, infatuated in "the love which was provoked by her casual flirtation with a man," but, on the other, is unable to dismiss her attachment to her husband, so that out of qualms of conscience she tries to drown herself. *Miira no Kuchibeni* displays the egoism and pathos of the heroine who is bored with marriage as lifeless as a mummy, in which her husband who is unable to understand his wife who loves art, and she who is unable to love her husband's way of life, are united, as it were, merely through painted lips. The female characters in Toshiko's story seem in a way to possess more intellectual qualities than those in Kizan's. In this regard, it may be said that Toshiko was the first woman writer who boldly insisted that women were also human beings. Furthermore, Toshiko chose the course of a woman as a human being like Nora (in *The Doll's House*) in her own real life as well, for she soon went abroad, and was through with the literary world. At any rate, it may be said that there was some affinity between Seika and Toshiko with regard to their dispassionate, penetrating observation and piercing discernment of the internal world of human beings.

In short, Naturalism in Japan included superficial attempts at the imitation of Zola's school, such as those undertaken by Tōson and Katai in their early days. Yet the Japanese Naturalists were in no way concerned with Zola's scientific experimentalism, but passionately leaned to the impressionistic technique of writing employed by Flaubert and Maupassant. It followed that they pursued the method of realism in the prosaic description of personal, everyday impressions, but it had to be reduced to the world of the ego, concentrating on the author's private mental life, and neglecting the broader view of society. The result was that, on the one hand, the social elements were extremely attenuated in their literary art, and, on the other, the ugliness, anguish, despair, and decadence of the ego, fostered by modern individualism, were grasped at the depth of helpless nihilism.

It must be recognized to the credit of Naturalism that it expanded the view of literature into the world of popular mediocrity, that it emancipated humanity from the feudalistic morals outdated in the modern age, and that it cultivated a realistic attitude in trying to grasp the essence of human existence. However, at the same time, Naturalism must face the criticism that, in viewing humanity solely in the light of nature, it not only failed to grasp its value, but also devastated the Arcadia of Beauty by subjugating literary art to Truth. It was from this point that there originated Neo-Idealism as a reaction to Naturalism. On the part of the latter, however, the emergence of Neo-Idealism meant something more than mere reaction. It may be noted that the decadence and diabolism in Neo-Romanticism were the positive, abnormal growth of human instincts grasped by Naturalism as they should be. It also may be said that the consciousness of the ego typical of the Shirakaba-Ha (The White Birch School) was the purified and spiritualized vitality of this instinctive ego. It may further be said that there was only a slight difference between the calm observation represented by Shūsei and the idle spectator's attitude of the Yoyū-Ha (The Leisure School). This means, in other words, that Naturalism was not given full expression of its essential characteristics as it should have been.

In fact, Naturalism itself, unable to observe calm objectivity, drifted toward dreary resignation toward real life, or toward such mentality as could be satisfied with such a hopeless life. For the Japanese Naturalists were not of the stature of Flaubert or Zola. The intellectualist view of reality held by the rising Naturalist writers could not avoid deviation toward emotionalism. This may testify to the fact that Naturalism in its original form can hardly grow in the soil of a Japanese literature which is dominated by such emotionalism.

CHAPTER V   THE RISE OF NEO-IDEALISM

1. *The Romanticism and Idealism around Sōseki*

At about the same time as the rise of Naturalism, the activity of Natsume Sōseki (Kinnosuke), who is the founder of Neo-Idealism, attracted the attention of the literary world. It was in January 1905 that Sōseki's first works, *Wagahai wa Neko de Aru* (I Am a Cat) and *Rondon Tō* (The Tower of London), were made public, and in the same year, Fūyō's *Seishun* (Youth) and Doppo's *Doppo-Shū* (Doppo's Anthology) appeared.   Since *Hakai* (The Breaking of the Commandment) came out in the following year and *Futon* (The Quilt) in the year after that, Sōseki's emergence preceded Naturalism somewhat, and occurred at a time when the afterglow of Romanticism had not yet disappeared. Thus, the fact that the beginning of Sōseki's writing career should have such deep romantic overtones can be said to be one reflection of the current of the time. Another reason Sōseki is considered to be the source of Neo-Idealism is that he was a writer who held an anti-Naturalist position.

After Sōseki was graduated from the English Literature Department of Tōkyō University, he studied in Europe, and when he returned to Japan in 1903, in that same year he began lecturing at Tōkyō University on literary theory. Sōseki is clearly an Akamon (Red Gate, *i. e.*, the symbol of Tōkyō University) writer, and the fact that *Rondon Tō* appeared in *Teikoku Bungaku* (Imperial Literature) testifies to this. Sōseki's Romanticism-Idealism was a continuation of that of the Akamon group which was begun by Bansui and Chogyū. In this sense its starting point was different from that of the Naturalism that stemmed from the Waseda group.

At the same time, Sōseki, together with Shiki, delighted in the *haiku* of the Buson school, and, joining a group of men who were fond of *shaseibun*, wrote his *Wagahai wa Neko de Aru.*

This work was begun as a *shaseibun* étude, and when it first appeared in *Hototogisu* (The Cuckoo), he did not intend to write a full-length novel. Yet its reception was so great that it made Sōseki decide to become a novelist, and it finally caused him to give up his position as a Tōkyō University lecturer and join the *Asahi Shimbun*. This mode of writing called *shaseibun* was a kind of poetic realism. Sōseki entered the literary world after having assimilated both the idealism of the *Teikoku Bungaku* type and the realism (*shajitsushugi*) of the *Hototogisu* type, and in the transition period from Romanticism to Naturalism he came to occupy a strong position.

Wagahai wa Neko de Aru is a *haiku*-type *shaseibun* piece, but its core is the satire and humor derived from English literature, particularly that of the eighteenth century prose writers. On top of this is reared even a scholarly, idealistic superstructure. Disguised as a tomcat, the author criticizes his own life, and satirizes the world of vanity and pretense that surrounds him. This book is certainly the work of an intellect of genius, and underneath it runs a deep current of ethical idealism. We can say that the ideal of his later life, *sokuten kyoshi* (to model oneself after heaven and depart from the self), is already present here in foetal form. Together with violent humor and an almost excessive introspection, there is the evident zeal to penetrate to the very heart of existence.

But this Sōseki, who as a realist turns his penetrating glance at the various aspects of human life, for several years did not develop in a straight line. *Rondon Tō*, which appeared at the same time, can be thought of as a realistic travelogue-like account of his London sightseeing during his stay abroad, but there are many scenes where he calls up the past history of the Tower which are exceedingly romantic in tone. Both *Maboroshi no Tate* (The Phantom Shield) and *Kairokō* (The Song of Evanescence), which next appeared, derived their material from European medieval legend, and giving free rein to his imagination, he attempted to describe in a mystic atmosphere the power of an undivided love. *Koto no Sorane* (The False Sound of the Lute) and *Ichiya* (One Night) have their setting in Japan, but they are still attempts at evoking a fantastic, mystic, and romantic beauty.

All of these works were published in the course of one year, and they tell of the meteoric quality of Sōseki's emergence, but in the following year, *Botchan*, *Kusamakura*, and *Nihyakutōka* (The Two Hundred Tenth Day) further indicate the development of Sōseki's romanticism.

Kusamakura has as its setting the Oama Hot Spring in the vicinity of Kumamoto where he taught before going abroad, and while creating a peaceful Oriental poetic world in the midst of a pastoral nature and Zen adherents, he describes the mind of a painter who is attempting an aesthetic discipline of isolation from the world, and the character of a strange, beautiful girl, Nami, as reflected in this painter's eyes. The author takes on the spirit of the painter and expounds a view of human life called *hi-ninjō* (non-feeling), and he tries to look at this beautiful girl who appears equally capable of madness and of spiritual enlightenment as a mere subject for painting, but this "non-feeling" woman, too, is unable to leave behind completely the past world of feeling even though she has separated from her husband. The climax comes in the last scene where the almost divine feeling of *aware* (compassion) is expressed in her face as she says goodbye to her former husband who leaves to make his livelihood in Manchuria. Thus, there remains the problem of the relationship between *ninjō* (feeling) and *hi-ninjō* (non-feeling).

For *Botchan* Sōseki gathered his material from his teaching experience at a middle school in Matsuyama, and the principal character, a forthright and naive teacher, who is really the author himself, suffers in the corrupt school atmosphere, and finally returns to Tōkyō after having visited a just punishment on a group of sycophants and hypocrites centering around Red Shirt, the nickname that Botchan has given one of the teachers.

Its plot and style, and the fact that it is filled with satire and ethical concern, appear to put it in direct opposition to the aesthetic, transcendental tone of *Kusamakura*; yet both of them deeply reflect the author's subjective spirit, and we can see his strong emphasis on a romantic ideal. *Kusamakura* demonstrates the union of beauty and religion in the union of the painter and Nami, while *Botchan* tries to show, in the conflict of Botchan and Red Shirt, the loneliness that results when the spirit of justice and simplicity has to struggle in vain in a world of injustice and vanity. Both of these works are the reflection of the author's inner spirit, and they are simply expressed as a romantic dream.

Nihyakutōka has a loose, episodic construction based on the conversation of two men, who, as they climb the smoking volcano of Mt. Aso, discourse on their hopes and dreams of socialism. It has a *shaseibun* form and yet it is still filled with romantic ideals.

Nowaki (The Wintry Blast), which appeared in 1907, has a rather true-to-life construction, and comes much closer to being a realistic novel than *Shumi no Iden* (The Inheritance of Tastes), which appeared in the previous year, and yet the main character, Michiya, is still a romantic, burning with ideals of justice. In April of that year, Sōseki joined the *Asahi Shimbun*, and his first work to be printed in it was *Gubijinsō* (The Red Poppy), in which he gives final synthesis and unity to the romantic qualities that had appeared in his works until then. Its main female character, Fujio, is similar to Nami of *Kusamakura* in that she is a woman of strong will, but she demonstrates a personality of rather modern femininity, and the novel is an account of how this proud, egocentric personality and behavior are finally destroyed and how Fujio meets a sudden death. Surrounding her there move Munechika, who is a natural man removed from the self, the philosopher Kōno, who endeavors to depart from the world of vanity and enter into the truth, and the brilliant Ono, who even though he is tempted by Fujio, returns to the world of moral law. The author here shows for the last time his brilliant colors. The construction is also elaborate, with one dramatic scene following another, but the central idea appears to be a kind of idealism that teaches the truth that when the modern ego separates itself from a moral foundation a terrible tragedy occurs. At the same time it indicates that the final destination of the self is nothing other than a truthful and undefiled naturalness which is in the direction of Sōseki's ultimate ideal of *sokuten kyoshi.*

With this work Sōseki's romantic period ends, and in the following year he advanced strikingly toward realism; however, from one viewpoint, he was unwilling to allow these early ideals to remain only in the world of romantic fancy, and seeking them anew in actual life, he embarked upon his career of intense experiment.

At the beginning of 1903 Sōseki first published *Kōfu* (The Miner), attempting, with a detailed realistic method, an analysis of the psychology of a youth who agrees to work in a mine. He approaches the Naturalistic position at the end of the novel, when he looks at the semi-light, semi-dark, indecisive world as the true picture of life. And yet in this novel also there burn the ethical ideals which prize human sincerity.

Sanshirō, which followed, represents the author's characteristic realistic method, and in it he gives a penetrating analysis of the psychology of the late Meiji youth that was awakening to a recognition of self. The main character, Sanshirō, leaves the country and enters Tōkyō student life, where he is perplexed by the new atmosphere and where he is unable to assess the complex personality of a young woman of the new era, Mineko, and is disturbed at not knowing whether he is loved by her or is being made a fool of by her. The author himself calls Mineko an unconscious hypocrite, and as one of the characters, the philosopher Hirota, says, she is the embodiment of the modern woman whose personality is a riddle. Later in O-Nao of *Kōjin*

(The Passerby) he adds even further complexities to the modern woman as a wife, but in *Sanshirō* we are able to see one facet of Sōseki's view of women. Sanshirō is the embodiment of the modern egoism that is in the process of losing all sincerity, and Mineko is his female counterpart, although the process in her case is further advanced.

Sanshirō depicts young men and women who have awakened to the modern ego but who on account of it fall into the evils of individualism, and are unable easily to cast themselves into an altruistic situation. It is a picture of unfulfilled love. Daisuke, the principal of *Sore Kara* (And Then) which appeared in the following year, endeavors to recover Michiyo, the only woman he can truly love, whom he has handed over to his close friend Hiraoka, but since love also is placed in society, he must receive as well the punishment that accompanies this gift. He finally despairs of ever recovering Michiyo from Hiraoka. This work is an account of how even a person who can feel the will of Heaven in the midst of the pretensions of the self is unable to accomplish his love.

Mon (The Gate), which together with the above-mentioned two works constitutes a trilogy, appeared in the following year, 1910. This work is the story of Sōsuke, who has betrayed his best friend to marry his wife and who enjoys this sad love secretly while living with her almost as a recluse in a corner of society; when, however, the friend who has disappeared for awhile reappears, Sōsuke falls into a state of uneasiness, and without telling his wife anything, goes alone to knock at the gate of a Zen Buddhist temple to seek peace of mind. The gate (hence the title), however, does not open, and Sōsuke knows he is fated to stand forever outside it. One who has bravely achieved his love also must bear the burden of a life of anxiety. And yet this trilogy which treats of the spiritual struggle that comes from love, is not a denial of love.

After having produced this trilogy, Sōseki underwent a serious illness, and in 1911 he published only a series of essays entitled

Omoidasu Koto Nado (Random Recollections), which told of his experiences during his illness. This illness, however, further deepened the mind of the author, and after having faced death, his eyes, which searched the patterns of existence, became even sharper. He looked now beyond temporary falseness, and never ceased to seek a religious enlightenment. *Higan Sugi Made* (Until after the Spring Equinox), which appeared in the following year (1912), marks a new starting-point.

This work has a novel construction in that it is made up of several independent stories linked together ; in this group, " Sunaga's Story " is the most significant, and in it he probes most deeply the sickness in the modern ego. The main character, Sunaga Ichizō, is expected to marry his fiancée Chiyoko, but even though he knows that he has only to stretch forth his hand to possess this relatively meek yet passionate woman, he feels a dark shadow on him because of the mystery of his birth, and he turns in on himself, is torn with doubts, and is unable to enter into the natural state of love. Sōseki analyses exhaustively the personality that is weakened and twisted by the modern intellect, and the disease of egoism is completely revealed.

However, Sunaga goes on a trip to cure this evil habit of closing himself in, sees the external world with a clear heart, and tries to learn the method of liberating the self. And yet Sunaga who is strongly introspective is unable to enter into complete enlightenment. In order to pursue further the fate of the egoist who is entangled by his ego, Sōseki continued to write full-length novels after the beginning of Taishō, and finally, by means of his philosophy of *sokuten kyoshi*, he arrived at the threshold of a world of divine purity. These later Meiji works at first glance appear to be Naturalistic, but actually they were stages on the road to his final ideal.

We can consider Sōseki's novels as the fusion of the *shasei-bun* which arose centering around Shiki, on the one hand, and the realism of the Western novel, on the other. *Shaseibun,* the theory of sketching from life which Shiki expounded in his *tanka* and *haiku*, began to be extended to the prose art with the appearance in 1898 of *Shōen no Ki* (The Record of a Small Garden) in *Hototogisu*. From about that time also there began to meet each month an organization for the recitation of *shasei-bun* études called the Sankai (The Mountain Society), and with the publication of *Jojibun* (Descriptive Writing) in the newspaper *Nihon*, *shaseibun* was given its theoretical basis. Those who joined this group were such *haiku* poets as Takahama Kyoshi, Sakamoto Shihōta, Samukawa Sokotsu, Kawahigashi Hekigotō, and Matsuse Seisei, and such *waka* poets as Itō Sachio and Oka Fumoto, and from among these men were produced the *Sunkō-Shū* (compiled by Kyoshi in 1900), *Kangyoku-Shū* (The Cold Gem Anthology) (compiled by Kyoshi in the same year), *Shaseibun-Shū* (A Shaseibun Anthology) (compiled by Kyoshi in 1903), *Hotategai* (A Scallop) (compiled by Shihōta and Kyoshi in 1906), and *Shin-Shaseibun* (New Shaseibun) (compiled by Kyoshi in 1908). Sōseki's *Wagahai wa Neko de Aru* was read before this Sankai, and men like Kyoshi, Takashi, and Sachio also began to move into the area of the true novel form.

Kyoshi's *Fūryū Sempō* (1907) and *Zoku Fūryū Sempō* (Sequel to *Fūryū Sempō*) (1908) already transcend the limits of *shasei-bun*. These works are a brilliant description of the unconstrained life in the Yokawa Main Hall of Hieizan, a night's feast in the Ichiriki restaurant in Gion, a Kyōto inn on a rainy spring night, the moon over Toribeyama, and other Kyōto scenes, but the central theme is the innocent love between the exceedingly handsome acolyte Ichinen and the *maiko* Michitose, and the work is abundantly lyrical. When we come to his *Fūryū Sempō Gojitsu-Dan* (An Elegant Confession: A Tale of Later Days) which he wrote in the Taishō Era, we find he describes how the love of the two loses its strength, and he brings the tale to a rather Naturalistic end. *Ikaruga Monogatari* (A Tale of Ikaruga) (1907) also appears to be a prose-poem about the natural scenes in the vicinity of the Hōryūji, but in the midst of these scenes is sketched lightly the pastoral love of a young priest, Ryōnen, and a weaver girl, O-Michi.

In addition to these, Kyoshi was the author of *Ōuchi Ryoshuku* (The Ōuchi Inn) (1907), *Haikaishi* (The *Haiku* Poet) (1908), *Zoku Haikaishi* (Sequel to *Haikaishi*) (1909), and *Chōsen* (Korea) (1911). As shown by these works, Kyoshi gradually shifted to full-length stories. *Haikaishi* is a lengthy work based on numerous episodes : the hero Haga Sanzō's life as a *haiku* poet, his relations with his masters, Jippū and Ridō, his love-affair with Takemoto Shōkō, a *jōruri* singer, and the last days of his friend Suigetsu. The novel is rather loose, but his way of sketching is quite delicate. In the preface of Kyoshi's *Keitō* (Cockscomb) (1908), Sōseki commented on Kyoshi's novels and used the words " dilettantism, or Leisure school." Sōseki also observed that these modes were based on the Zen spirit. In general, Kyoshi's works displayed such Oriental flavor, and though his work has a Naturalistic tendency it possesses also something substantially different.

Among other sketch prose writers of Kyoshi's group, Shihōta remained as a writer of this genre to the end, Sachio and Takashi turned to the novel, and Terada Torahiko cultivated a new world by writing sketch prose that displayed the characteristics of a novel.

Terada Torahiko (Yoshimura Fuyuhiko, Torahiko, Yabukōji) wrote *haiku*, or sketch prose, under Sōseki from his early days. His first sketch prose piece, which appeared in *Hototogisu*, is *Donguri* (Acorns) (1905), a short work of reminiscences of his late wife. It pictures with affectionate description his wife's falling ill and her long days in bed. He remembers how she liked to gather acorns at the Koishikawa Biological Garden, as he watches his son picking up acorns in the same way. He thinks that the habit may be hereditary, and he deepens anew his sad love for his wife and son. In *Ryūzetsuran* (Agave) (1905), he narrates memories of his boyhood days when he attended his elder sister's wedding celebration. A vase of agave beside a carp pond, Bakin's *Hakkenden* (A Tale of Eight Dogs) which he read in a room of a storehouse, and the lonely face of Kiyoka, a geisha, provide vivid images.

Furthermore, he published the following works in *Hototogisu*: *Arashi* (Storm) (1906), *Mori no E* (A Picture of a Grove) (1907), *Karegiku no Kage* (The Shadow of the Withered Chrysanthemum) (1907), *Yamori Monogatari* (A Tale of a Gecko) (1907), *Shōji no Rakugaki* (Scribblings on the *Shōji*) (1908), *Hana Monogatari* (A Tale of Flowers) (1908), *Gumi* (A Silverberry) (1909), and *Majorika-Zara* (The Majorca Plate) (1909). Torahiko's style of writing has some elements which make it difficult to decide whether his works are sketch prose pieces, essays, or short novels. *Hana Monogatari* is based on his recollections of nine kind of flowers, including bindweed, evening primrose, the chestnut tree blossom, and the great trumpet-flower. It is pervaded by a *haiku* poet-like affectionate feeling towards nature, and the affection is often linked to love of human beings. In *Yamori Monogatari*, which concerns his encounter with a gecko, or wall-lizard, clinging to a street lamp, on his way from his lodging to a public bath, he reflects about his younger days when he had seen a similar creature. He then begins reminiscing about O-Fusa, a maid, and a girl of a kitchenware dealer, and wonders what has happened to them. In his romantic style of writing, imbued with serene grief, we see a scientist-like observation, while at the bottom of his fresh views of life there lies a profound humanism.

Torahiko's works did not attract people's attention at the time of their publication, but after the beginning of the Taishō Era, he gained a large circle of appreciative readers through his jewel-like essays, which were a delicate composite of deep scientific knowledge and rich poetic feeling. *Yabukōji-Shū* (A Yabukōji Anthology) (1923), which was a collection of the prose-style short novels of his early days, was highly esteemed. Torahiko was a success as an essayist, but there is another writer who turned from sketch prose to the novel, Nogami

Yaeko, also an apprentice of Sōseki. She published her maiden work *Enishi* (Fate) (1907) in *Hototogisu*, and thereafter, in succession, *Tanabata-Sama* (The Star Vega) (1907), *Kuroneko* (A Black Cat) (1907), *Shion* (A Michaelmas Daisy) (1908), *Kaki-Yōkan* (Persimmon Candy) (1908), and *Otonari* (A Neighbor) (1908). These works represented her transition from sketch prose to the novel. Her style of writing is somewhat romantic, and yet rather intellectual, devoid of passion, and without any striking characteristics. Since the Taishō Era, she has produced several full-length stories, and at the time of this writing still shows a fertile originality. Sachio and Takashi also started as sketch prose writers, turned to fiction in their early days, and afterwards wrote full-length novels.

Nagatsuka Takashi was originally a *waka* poet, but also devoted efforts to sketch prose writings. He published in the magazine *Ashibi*, *Tsukimi no Yūbe* (An Evening of Viewing the Moon) (1903), *Tsuchiura no Kakō* (The Mouth of the River at Tsuchiura) (1904), *Tonegawa no Ichiya* (An Evening on the Tone River) (1904), and *Kizu no Ato* (The Scar) (1906). His novel *Sumiyaki no Musume* (The Daughter of a Charcoal-Burner) (1906) was also published in the same magazine. It concerns his memory of a charcoal-burning scene which he had seen when he stayed in the Seo valley of Mt. Kiyosumi in Chiba Prefecture. In the novel, he describes O-Aki, the charcoal-burner's daughter, in sketch prose style yet with a dream-like quality. This work is, therefore, of the Sōseki-style Leisure school, and does not yet emerge from the mode of *haiku*-style naturalism. He then published in *Hototogisu Sadogashima* (Sado Island) (1907), the work which established his reputation. It is a sketch prose piece depicting the scenery of Sado Island with some stories of beautiful women who, he states, are " like peony flowers embroidered on gray cloth with strings of gold and silver." *Sadogashima* describes a romantic world, the principal elements of which are its delicacy of sensibility and its beautiful sentiments. In succession, he published *Imohori* (Potato

Digging) (1908), *Kaigyōi* (A Licensed Physician) (1909), *Nano-hana* (Rape-Blossoms) (1909), *O-Fusa* (A Girl Named O-Fusa) (1909), *Kyōshi* (A Teacher) (1909), *Rinshitsu no Kyaku* (A Guest in the Next Room) (1910), and *Tajū to Sono Inu* (Tajū and His Dog) (1910). With Sōseki's recommendation, he published in the *Tōkyō Asahi Shimbun* a full-length story, *Tsuchi* (The Earth), which brought him immortal fame.

Tsuchi describes the local color of his native place, the Kinu-gawa district in Ibaragi Prefecture, through the life of the family of Kanji, a tenant farmer. The maggot-like, miserable life of a peasant against the background of the village is sketched in detail in a Naturalistic and realistic manner. As far as the method is concerned, Takashi seems to have mastered sketch prose writing and succeeded in approaching a realistic plane beyond Naturalism. Through the refined dilettantism of the Sōseki school, he observes objects from many angles so minutely that the reader has difficulty in reading the passages.

The theme of the novel is, however, to bring to light the exceedingly gloomy side of human life such as Kanji's perverse character caused by the serious social problems, and the ugly friction between Kanji and Uhei, his father-in-law. But at the same time he keeps his eyes carefully on the fact that Kanji essentially was not a bad man and was actually a hard worker. Also, the humanistic cordiality which still exists in the heart of Uhei, who is unfriendly to everyone because of his degrading life, the pure love of Kanji's daughter, O-Tsugi, for Uhei, and the sympathy of the neighbors are depicted in a profoundly impressive way. At the end of the work, when Uhei is about to hang himself because it is his fault that the house burned, Kanji's hard feeling towards Uhei finally melts away, and Kanji's family starts a new life in warm light like spring sunshine. The novel by no means penetrated into the miserable aspect of life in a Naturalistic way, but moved rather toward humanistic idealism. The process of the movement from the new romanti-cism to the new idealism, was reflected in the resolving of the difficulties through love. Here we can see the tendency of the sketch prose of the Hototogisu school transformed into novels in the Sōseki manner. In fact, the merits of this work were recognized only through the evaluation of Sōseki.

Itō Sachio is well known as a poet of the Araragi school, but he also had considerable ambition in the field of the novel. His maiden work *Nogiku no Haka* (The Tomb of Wild Chamomile) (1906) in *Hototogisu* obtained a broad reception. Thereafter, in succession, in the same magazine, he published *Tonari no Yome* (A Neighbor's Bride) (1906), *Haru no Ushio* (The Spring Tide) (1906), *Hamagiku* (The Chrysanthemum on the Seashore) (1906), *Kō-Ō Roku* (A Record of Red and Yellow) (1906), *Tsugebito* (An Informer) (1906), *Gumi* (Silverberry) (1909), *Nanako* (A Girl Named Nanako) (1909), *Kagerō* (Heat Haze) (1909), and *Hashi* (Chopsticks) (1909). He also published short novels in *Araragi*, *Shin-Shōsetsu* (The New Novel), and *Chūō Kōron*. Following Takashi's *Tsuchi*, Sachio's full-length *Bunke* (A Branch Family) (1911) was serialized in the *Tōkyō Nichinichi Shimbun*.

Nogiku no Haka is a tragic tale dealing with a genuine love between a naive and innocent girl and boy against a pastoral background. It may be regarded as childish, but in this world the author exposes his own innocent character. Indeed, its simplicity has a strength to touch any reader. *Tonari no Yome* is also a love story of naive farmers. A nineteen-year-old youth falls in love with a girl of the same age. Since the latter is the wife of a neighbor, their romance encounters numerous obstacles. The young man, in the meantime, is sent away to become an adopted son of another family, and their romance is broken off. In this tragic atmosphere, the young woman, who is divorced by her husband, returns to her home. *Haru no Ushio* is a sequel to *Tonari no Yome*. After overcoming numerous difficulties, the two are finally united through the efforts of their sympathetic relatives. His sketching in this work displays a Naturalistic tendency.

Though the plot is rather conventional and his style remains simple, he demonstrates respect for genuine feelings. The two works together may be considered a full-length story, but Sachio really moved into the field of the full-length novel when he wrote *Bunke*. This work also deals with rural life but, lacking variety in style, is not as impressive as the aforementioned *Tsuchi*. In short, Sachio did not possess the extraordinary power of description that Takashi exhibited in *Tsuchi*. Indeed, his best work is still his subjective maiden work which has qualities such as we find in his *waka* poetry.

Suzuki Miekichi is a writer who was stimulated by the romantic qualities displayed by Sōseki in his earlier years rather than by the sketch prose of Kyoshi. His writing was therefore aesthetic and lyrical. While he was a student in the English Literature Department of Tōkyō University, Miekichi gained literary fame by his maiden work *Chidori* (The Plover) (1906) published in *Hototogisu*. It was dedicated to his teacher Sōseki and published together with Sōseki's recommendation. The author began writing *Chidori* when he was recuperating from an illness at his home in Nomijima, Hiroshima Prefecture. He seems to have gained some hints from the locality, but the work is largely fictional and imbued with a rich romanticism. Some critics like Kyoshi's comment : " As sketch prose, there is a lack of sketching. As a novel, the plot is weak." (Kyoshi's letter to Miekichi). However, Sōseki held the work in high esteem as a subtle, lyrical piece. It deals with a young man who has spent a summer at a country-house on an island in the Inland Sea. When he visits it again later, he meets a girl named O-Fuji. There seems to be some progress in their relations, but the girl leaves the island alone without his knowledge A sleeve of her undergarment, which she apparently left as a souvenir, is found in a drawer of his desk. The young man does not seek the girl anymore, believing that their love will be preserved eternally in the sleeve. Against the background of the simple-minded people and the exquisite scenery of the island, the young man's pure love is fully described in a poetic fashion. Miekichi tried, on the whole, to create that beauty which can be seen in Japanese painting and music. His style was fresh, the impressions vivid, and we can even detect some characteristics of the romantic short novels of Western literature.

Miekichi, while studying sketch prose writings, also was influenced by French and Russian novels. He can be said to belong to the Neo-Romantic school of the end of the Meiji Era. After he became a favorite of the literary world by writing *Chidori*, he published in succession lyric short novels which showed his peculiar capabilities, such as *Yamabiko* (An Echo Among the Hills) (1907), *O-Mitsu-San* (A Girl Named O-Mitsu) (1907), *Karasu Monogatari* (A Tale of a Crow) (1908), and *Kurokami* (Black Hair) (1909). *Yamabiko* is a story about his elder sister who became the bride of a wealthy country gentleman in a village deep in the mountains. In the novel the author depicts the traditions of the family, and forecasts an unhappy life for his sister by unfolding the story in the form of an old-fashioned woman's love letters discovered in the attic of the house, the peculiar traditions of the local shrine, and the epitaph on the ancestral gravestone. This work is pervaded by a dark mysticism. The common feature of his works was that he placed himself in a world of fantasy and romanticism, and strove to express the romantic agony of the modern generation.

In the Taishō Period he published *Akai Tori* (The Red Bird), a magazine of fairy-tales, but before this, he wrote full-length novels with a Naturalistic tendency, such as *Kotori no Su* (A Nest of Small Birds) (1910) and *Kuwa no Mi* (Mulberry) (1913). Miekichi was not merely a poet but was also endowed with the penetrating eye of a novelist. *Kotori no Su* is a delicate sketch of the plight of the hero, Jūkichi, a faint projection of the author himself. Jūkichi returns to his native place because of a serious illness. He is overcome by a profound scepticism as a result of the friction with his consumptive and unsympathetic father and his blind grandmother. The author depicts how the hero experiences a *fin-de-siècle* agony through his sad and restless life. This gloomy story is interwoven with a love-affair between the hero and his childhood friend Machiko, who is his cousin. We can see how this novel demonstrated rather faithfully the symptoms of the Naturalism which was then in its last stage.

However, it cannot be said that Miekichi's true field lay in realistic observation and in depiction of decadent agony. He endeavored to probe deep into the profound experience of living in the *fin-de-siècle* world, in accordance with Sōseki's advice that he should not remain long in an effeminate and self-pitying melancholic mood. His true field was, in his early days, romantic lyricism, but toward the end of his life he was to establish himself in the world of fairy-tales.

Like Miekichi, Morita Sōhei appeared in the literary world as one of the ablest disciples of Sōseki, and also treated the *fin-de-siècle* life in his novels. He entered the literary world through his maiden work *Karinesugata* (A Nap) (1903), which he contributed to the *Bungei Kurabu*. In the following year, he read an English translation of D'Annunzio's *Il Trionfo della Morte* under Ueda Bin's suggestion, and was greatly influenced by the work. Later, however, he became a victim of social ostracism as a result of his love-affair with Hiratsuka Raichō (Haruko), a student of the Woman's College Course of which he was a lecturer. But with the help of his *maître* Sōseki, he decided to defend himself by confessing and recording accurately the course of this love-affair. The result was the full-length novel *Baien* (Soot and Smoke) (1909), which was serialized in the *Tōkyō Asahi Shimbun*.

The hero of *Baien*, Kojima Yōkichi, is the author himself. He is an intellectual egoist, but he loses his ambition as a result of disillusionment with his family and its lineage, and falls into a profound and nihilistic loneliness. This decadent and modern youth finds a sweetheart in the person of Manabe Tomoko, a member of the Kon'yō-Kai (The Golden Leaf Society), who is modeled after Raichō. Tomoko is a modern girl with an unusual character, in other words, typical of the new woman who was appearing at that time. Through self-liberation, she tries to live a thoroughly independent life. She assumes the pose of a decadent and pretends to be sexually impotent, thereby avoiding being conquered by her lover. She shows an ardent erotic passion and cold-heartedness at the same time, and confines herself in an emotionless, icy world. Yōkichi feels a new excitement in this girl who entrenches herself behind an ego, and begins to enter into relations with her as an intellectual recreation. She tries to leave him, out of self-preservation, but fails. The hero, tired of ordinary sexual love, tries to "take her up to heaven where nobody can follow" (from the author's review in *Meiji-Taishō Bungaku Zenshū*, The Complete Collection of Meiji and Taishō Literatures), and pursues her with an intricate love technique. The two eventually go to the snowy Obana Pass at Shiobara to die. The heroine wants to have Yōkichi kill her so that she can teach him she has succeeded in protecting her system. She wishes to have the hero feel that it is impossible to conquer her, and to win her victory and crush his life. The hero is interested in transforming her into a sacred woman. They walk in the snow in the moonlight with the intention of enjoying the world of artificial passion. But they give up the idea of dying embracing each other, and go up to the summit of the icy mountain. Thereupon the moonlight fades and day dawns, and suddenly a ray of light shines into their lives.

Towards the end, the author forcibly looked for life's meaning, but since the final part is not the inevitable consequence of the distorted artificial love, the whole volume loses compactness and concludes in confusion and insipidity. Sōseki expressed dissatisfaction that this novel did not grasp the reality of human affection, and said that it was marred by exaggeration and distortion, and was a typical *fin-de-siècle* work. However, it has a historical significance in the sense that the author described faithfully the process of his own strange romance. When it was published, it was received favorably, in contrast with *Tsuchi* which had met with an unfavorable response. This work shows a tendency of moving away from the Sōseki-style Leisure school dilettantism and toward the Aesthetic and Decadent schools. It approaches the method of Tanizaki, displaying traces of Satanism.

In this sense, the work first borrowed the Naturalistic tenet of Sōseki's Romanticism, and this is manifested by the descriptions in the first half; but gradually shifting towards an anti-Naturalistic, Neo-Romantic position, it fell into an Ōgai-style Epicureanism or Aestheticism. Sōhei in his early years was attracted by Ōgai's *Minawa-Shū* (The Water-Spray Anthology). But, at the same time, he could not give up the Sōseki-style intellectual approach to life; as a result, he was unable to adopt a clear-cut attitude. *Jijoden* (An Autobiography) which appeared in the following year is considered as a sequel to *Baien*, but it displays similar faults. In the Taishō Era, apart from *Rinne* (The Transmigration of the Soul), which describes the first half of his life which climaxed with *Baien*, he did not write any other works deserving mention, and finally ended up as a translator.

2. *The Neo-Romantic School—The Decadent School—The Epicurean School*

Naturalism was a literary movement that came to the fore by riding on the tide of the *fin-de-siècle* movement. To put it more accurately, the flow of the *fin-de-siècle* currents in the direction of pure intellectuality, objectivity, and science led to the Naturalist position which regarded life as a field in which the dominant factor was animal instinct. But, at the same time, the mellowing of the *fin-de-siècle* spirit led to somewhat subjective and passionate moods. This situation, which was also seen in the European literary world, produced in the Meiji literary circles the so-called Neo-Romantic, Decadent, and Epicurean schools.

Under a general classification, these schools can be grouped together as a splinter of the Neo-Idealist school; however, they showed a lack of moral and religious ideals. On the contrary, they strove to fulfill their artistic desires in the worlds of eroticism and sentimentality. As a result, the members of these schools, in contrast with the Humanists, could be called Aesthetes. Furthermore, in contrast with the art-for-life's-sake attitude of the Humanists, on frequent occasions they displayed an art-for-art's-sake characteristic. In this sense, these schools can be regarded as of a different nature from the Neo-Idealists. Furthermore, while showing a leaning toward Naturalism, the Neo-Romantics were essentially something new in the romantic field. The Decadents, on the other hand, glorified the sensual and decadent life, which was also a major aspect of the Naturalist mood, and, in an original way, suggested a fusion of Naturalism and Romanticism. The Epicureans also sought satisfaction of demands for decadent beauty but were rather close to the classic world, since they stood for a glorification of the pagan way of life and a naive affirmation of the aesthetic world. Yet in certain cases, the Epicureans based themselves on a rather wholesome vision of life.

But, despite their individual characteristics, there were some things common to all of these schools. Indeed, a definite separation is impossible, and in this chapter we shall deal with them as one group. This group found its representative in Nagai Kafū, who left an impressive mark on the literary world of the late Meiji years.

As mentioned before, Kafū some years earlier had drawn the attention of the literary world for his attempt at the transplantation of Naturalism through his research on Zola. In 1908, Kafū returned from his travels through America and France, and, compiling a number of stories, some of which he had published during his trip overseas, published them under the title of *Amerika Monogatari* (Tales of America) immediately prior to his return to Japan. He then made public a series of stories which were later published under the title *Furansu Monogatari* (Tales of France) (1909). The fresh expressions imbued with rich sentiment, his sympathy for and his penetrating observations on the maturity of the Western civilized countries, were all astonishingly new to his contemporaries. It seemed as if the literary world was witnessing the birth of a new literature.

1909 was the year which saw the Naturalist movement rise to its zenith. The poetical circles saw the appearance of *Jashūmon* and *Haien*, which indicated the ripening of the Symbolist movement. New literary magazines advocating a new Romantic movement, such as *Subaru* and *Okujō Teien*, were published, and made way for the aesthetic and epicurean atmosphere. In this situation, Kafū, who was rather the poet type, and who, though leaning towards Naturalism, also showed a disposition toward Decadent poetry, wrote numerous short stories as a poet-novelist. The stories *Kitsune* (The Fox), *Fukagawa no Uta* (The Song of Fukagawa), *Donten* (Clouded Skies), *Kangokusho no Ura* (Behind the Prison), *Shukuhai* (Toasts), *Kanraku* (Bacchanals), *Botan no Kyaku* (The Guest of the Peonies), and *Shinki-chōsha no Nikki* (The Diary of a Newly-Returned Traveler) were all written in this year. Also written in this year through the next were the medium-length novel *Sumidagawa* (The Sumida River) and the lengthy work *Reishō* (The Sneer).

As shown by the fact that all of the short stories mentioned above were compiled in a volume entitled *Kanraku*, the short story by this name was his representative work of this period. The hero shows interest only in romance and literature. From the age of sixteen he has been involved with numerous women, but each affair merely ends as short-lived sensual pleasure. But with the approach of forty, the hero bids farewell to his past pleasures, and lamenting his departing youth, is overcome by a deep loneliness. The contrast of the sweet pleasures of youth with the resulting decadent and lonesome feelings is expressed in a lyrical style. This contrast, pervaded by a poetical mood, forms the pillar of the story. In the concluding part, Kafū refers to a poem by the hero's favorite poet, Jean Moréas, and advocates a life in which pleasure and bitterness must be thoroughly experienced and one in which one should be satisfied, after that, by reminiscing over the past dreams. This vision of life is appropriate to an epicurean author.

However, it must be noted that at the beginning of the story the author states that he is against old-fashioned romanticism, and that a human being does not necessarily need to devote himself to a single romance. From this standpoint, the author depicts numerous love-affairs. Furthermore, the author cannot resist depicting the ugliness as well as the beauty of women. There is something common here with Naturalism. In addition, from the standpoint of a poet, Kafū expresses vehement resistance against the vulgar society which oppresses and destroys the aesthetic world. The novel, in this sense, marked the beginning of a series of works which were to be imbued with a spirit of criticism of the contemporary civilization. *Shukuhai* deals with a hero who, in his younger days, learns the taste of sensual pleasure. He violates an innocent girl, but because he is fortunate enough to escape from the situation, decides that he must give a toast to his success. (Hence the title.) In this study, the author was expressing his resistance against the religious men and educators who were intimidating students with commandments which did not fit the actual world. This resistance, however, inevitably led toward a feeling of resignation, as exemplified in *Shinkichōsha no Nikki* and *Reishō*.

Kafū, charmed by the beauty of Western civilization, returned home to find that the native culture lay in ruins. Unable to control his anger over the desolate situation, he resisted the militarism which was the principal destructor of culture. However, discovering that his resistance was a puny thing, Kafū sank into a passive, nostalgic mood, gazing back at the culture of the past. At first, Kafū seemed to be a poet glorifying the beauty of Western civilization and turning his back on that of the Orient; however, since he came to understand that it was foolish to seek Western civilization in this country, he turned his attention to the mature culture of the Edo Period. Thus, he complacently sought the remnants of the past in various corners of modern Tōkyō. In the story *Fukagawa no Uta*, he reminisces over the Edo days, while standing in the desolate Fukagawa district. In *Botan no Kyaku*, he relates his pleasure in visiting a peony garden in the Kōtō district with a geisha as his companion. In *Sumidagawa*, the author attempts to find the shadows of the past in the lives of such people as a female instructor of *tokiwazu*, a *haikai* master, the geisha, and stage actors. And, in depicting this complex world, he attempted to evoke the essence of pure Japanese-style romance, with a strong note of loneliness and submission to fate.

When he came to *Reishō*, he drew a conclusion from his philosophical position. In this story, Kafū gives a picture of five eccentric characters such as often appeared in Edo-style *gesaku* stories. They come together, and, in resistance to the vulgar world, make free criticism of the tastelessness of the society, constructing an epicurean life among themselves. Although this work is regarded as representative of the Epicurean school, the author himself thought of it differently. In his article "About My Story *Reishō*," included in *Kōcha no Ato* (After the Tea), he says, "I attempted to depict the epicurean heroes, their motives, the melancholy caused by the stifling atmosphere of the society, and their efforts to enter into a world of resignation symbolized by the *senryū* (comic *haiku*) mood, and into a world of detachment." This vision of life is indicated by the title *Reishō*, which means a sneer, or a sarcastic smile. After writing this work, Kafū became more deeply concerned with expressing "a mood of resignation and detachment" than in making a serious study of "agony and melancholy." In other words, in a mood of resignation and detachment, he sought to unearth the dreams of the past, inevitably moving in a direction of finding beauty in flowers in the shade. All the stories written in 1912, including *Shōtaku* (The Mistress' Home) and the tales contained in *Shimbashi Yawa* (Night Tales of Shimbashi), are attempts to find vestiges of the beauty left by the old indigenous culture.

When Kafū appeared in the center of the literary world, another writer who was more distinctly romantic than he, made his appearance by publishing a story in the second *Shinshichō*. His name was Tanizaki Jun'ichirō, and the magazine he was using as a stepping-stone was issued by literary-minded students of the Literature Department of Tōkyō University. Tanizaki's first work published in the magazine was a historical play, *Tanjō* (The Birth), which was carried in the first issue of September 1910. The following month, he published a scenario entitled *Zō* (Elephant). His literary fame rose suddenly in November when he published a short story entitled *Shisei* (The Tattooing). (It is said that chronologically this *Shisei* was his first work.) *Shisei* was set in the days when the Edo culture had reached maturity. The author depicts a group of persons who still harbor that "noble character" called *gu* (folly), and their search for grotesque beauty in the sensual world. The principal character is a young tattoo artist, Seikichi, who finds a secret pleasure in piercing his customer's skin with a tattoo needle, and who also enjoys it whenever the flesh pierced by the needle swells up, red with blood, and the customer cannot restrain himself from emitting a painful groan. His cherished dream is to find a beautiful woman and to inscribe on her skin a tattoo imbued with his own spirit. After searching for four years, he finally discovers a barefoot girl who has an immaculate white skin. The young artist, to test her sadistic character, shows her a picture of the favorite lady of the infamous Chinese tyrant Chou gazing on the execution of a male-sacrifice. The test produces a favorable reaction, and the artist inscribes a gigantic queen spider on the skin of the girl, saying to her, " I am going to infuse my spirit into the tattoo to make you a true beauty. As of today there will be no woman throughout the whole country who can compare with you. You are no longer a timid person. Every man from now on will become a fertilizer to make you more beautiful..." The morning sun casts its rays on the tattoo. The woman's back seems to glow in resplendent colors.

The epitome of the later literary style of Tanizaki is revealed in this work. The author's indulgence in sensual romanticism, his taste for the grotesque, his aspiration for feminine beauty, his admiration for sadistic women, all of these are fully expressed in this work. This work marked the birth of a new romantic literature which could be compared to Baudelaire's Diabolism or Wilde's Aestheticism. A romanticism based merely on sensuality and sentiment was not new in Japan, since it had been fully expressed in Kyōka's works. But now Tanizaki embarked on an original road, since he displayed, with a certain consciousness, his romanticism in the form of modern decadence. Tanizaki created a unique world in which ideals were to be found especially in unusual physical beauty and in sadistic women. In a sense, we may say that Tanizaki's was a unique literary attitude, an attitude which, in its extreme, called for a discovery of a Nietzsche-like superman world in women.

Therefore, *Shisei* is not merely based on a nostalgia for Edo tastes. It is an attempt to discover the modernism of the Western world in the native beauty. In this sense, this work is comparable to some of the novels written by Kafū. However, Tanizaki was aiming for a more thorough decadent world, and for this reason displays the characteristics of the Neo-Romantic school which appeared after Naturalism. Among other associates of the magazine *Shinshichō*, there were several talented young writers, such as Gotō Sueo, Ōnuki Shōsen, Watsuji Tetsurō, Kimura Sōta, and Koizumi Tetsu, all of whom were baptized by the new romanticism and new idealism. However, none of them displayed a keen aesthetic sense and passion for writing that could be compared to those of Tanizaki. Therefore, among the associates of *Shinshichō*, only Tanizaki was to grow into a full-fledged and great novelist.

In his story *Shisei*, Tanizaki created an image of the ideal type of woman, as he envisioned it. Furthermore, the hero, the young tattoo artist Seikichi, can be considered as a symbol of the process by which Tanizaki created this ideal woman type. Following *Shisei*, Tanizaki published in the next month (December 1910) a story entitled *Kirin* (Prodigy), which deals with Confucius who visits the country of Wei where he engages in a struggle with Nantzu, the consort of Prince Ling, but finally is defeated and departs from the country. In this story, Confucius preaches the way of a true man to the prince, telling him, " If you really wish to obtain an immaculate character as a king, you must first overcome your personal desires." For a moment, the prince shows sign of following his words, but his wife Nantzu distracts him by means of a perfume which she has sprinkled over her beautiful body. The prince is torn between two forces, but in a dramatic meeting between Confucius and the lady, Confucius loses out, resigned to the fact that even his high morality is powerless in the face of her tyranny. The prince returns to the bed of his wife, saying, " I hate you. You are a horrible woman. You are a demon who will finally ruin me, but still I cannot leave you," and falls into her arms. The queen's eyes glitter with the victory of evil. Confucius leaves with these words : " I have not yet seen a person who loves virtue as much as he loves sensual pleasure." The diabolic significance with which Tanizaki first endowed his female characters in *Shisei* became a distinct theme in this story.

From this point on, Tanizaki increasingly inclined towards depicting masochist men who discover pleasure in being tortured and toyed with by such diabolic women. In *Shōnen* (Boys) (1911), he depicts the dream-like awakening of sex during boyhood. Although this story resembled Ichiyō's *Takekurabe*, in the final sections the boys meekly kneel down like cats before the sole girl, Mitsuko, follow her orders faithfully, crawl on all fours if she says, "Become a stool," and, undergoing every kind of physical torture, act like slaves of a queen. In *Hōkan* (The Jester) (1911), he describes the unusual masochism of a professional jester who is satisfied when he is toyed with by a geisha whom he loves. In *Akuma* (The Demon) (1912), the author depicts a youth who licks the handkerchief in which his sweetheart, Teruko, has sneezed. Thus, Tanizaki had come to take up even fetishism as a theme. However, sexual perversion did not occupy the whole of his stories. A considerable realistic element can be perceived in *Shōnen* and *Akuma*. Such works as *Hyōfū* (Whirlwind) (1911) and *Atsumono* (Broth) (1912) were rather close to the genre of realistic novels, and were based in some points on the author's own experience. *The Affair of Two Watches** (1910) and *Himitsu* (The Secret) (1911) composed another separate genre for him, since the dominant theme was a detective story-like curiosity. As indicated by these works, Tanizaki did not lose any of his vitality as a writer with the approach of the Taishō Period. Cultivating an original aesthetic field, and at the same time attempting to depict the unusual psychology of the male who worships feminine beauty, Tanizaki continued to manifest a tenacious and penetrating capacity as a writer, and seemed to be searching into the depth of the human mind. Under the guise of aestheticism, epicureanism, and decadence, which were the typical signs of the *fin-de-siècle* mood, this writer had, deep within himself, a determination to plumb the mysterious depths of human desires.

Osanai Kaoru, who was the editor of *Shinshichō* which was instrumental in introducing Tanizaki to the literary world, came to be known as a poet and a playwright. His activities as a playwright were most conspicuous, and his name was to

---

* *Translator's Note*: The original title is in English.

be known to posterity for his dramatic theory and for his actual application of the theories on the stage. He also was the author of numerous short stories in which he distinguished himself for his penetrating observation and his fresh style. The lengthy work *Ōkawabata* (The Ōkawabata Gay Quarter) (1911) is regarded as his masterpiece. This story was based on the author's own experience when he mingled with stage personnel and frequented the geisha quarters of Ōkawabata with his patron (in the story Fukui), and it depicts the loneliness and discontent of a youth who attempts to pursue a true love-affair in the geisha world.

The youth is called Masao. He first expresses a romantic adoration for a geisha apprentice named Kimitarō who is working in the Yoshichō quarter. After a series of rendezvous with him, Kimitarō becomes a full-fledged geisha and suddenly disappears from the quarter. He next falls in love with a geisha named Kosato, who is the adopted sister of his patron Fukui. The young hero thinks she loves him, but this geisha also leaves him and becomes the mistress of a millionaire. Through these incidents, " Masao finally seems to have awakened from his romantic dreams. Now he thinks that he will pursue love merely as an ornament or a game." But after this decision, he meets another girl, Setsuko. The young hero first thinks that she will easily fall in love with him, but, on the contrary, the girl desires only a brother-and-sister relationship, and refuses to enter into further intimacy. Masao gradually becomes serious and finally proposes to her, but she then runs away from him. Osanai depicts both the external and internal worlds of the geisha, and demonstrates that the actual women living in these worlds are considerably different from the dreamy images held by the youth. Although there are some signs of a Naturalist style in this story, the dominant theme is the pure affection shown by an innocent youth who wanders about trying to realize his dreams, and the dominant mood is found in the contrast between his innocence and the colorful but mysterious atmosphere of the geisha world. In this sense, this work rather should be classified among the works of the Neo-Romantic and the Epicurean schools. This is a rather accurate evaluation if we consider that the author was the editor of the magazine *Shinshichō* which produced writers like Tanizaki.

In contrast with Osanai who sought an epicurean life in the prostitute world, a writer who sought to discover a decadent beauty in the life of traveling stage troupes was Nagata Miki-hiko. Mikihiko earned literary recognition by publishing *Mio* (The Channel) (1911) in *Subaru*, and came into literary pro-minence by publishing *Reiraku* (Ruin) (1912) in *Chūō Kōron*. He was to be ranked, temporarily, together with Tanizaki as the champion of the Decadent novel. *Mio* was based on the author's own experience during his vagabond life in Hokkaidō. The story concerns the love-affair of a handsome young female impersonator (*oyama*), Dennosuke, who is a member of a travel-ing stage troupe, and depicts the lives of these actors whose fate rises and falls like the channel markings of a port. This Dennosuke troupe also appears in *Reiraku*, which, with a sentimental note pervaded by poetical beauty, portrays the de-grading life of the traveling actors. But, the author's literary touch, which first had a certain individual quality, gradually slipped into a method suited to the so-called *taishū-shōsetsu* (popular novels). From the Taishō Period onward, Mikihiko created a peculiar genre called *jōwa bungei* (love-talk literature), and turned out a fantastic number of novels.

Kubota Mantarō was another writer who appeared at roughly the same time as Mikihiko and who also discovered a delicate beauty in the degraded lives of a stage actress and her son. Mantarō was a disciple of Osanai, and in 1911, at the early age of twenty-three, published *Asagao* (The Morning-Glory) in *Mita Bungaku* (Mita Literature). But, in depicting the downtown Tōkyō atmosphere of Asakusa, his native place, he displayed a mature technique, unusual for his age. The hero of this novel who is named Tokumatsu, makes semi-finished leather products. However, the manufacturer stops giving him orders because Tokumatsu sells the raw material entrusted to him, a certain amount of *shōbugawa* (Shōbu leather) valued at a little more than thirty yen, and embezzles the money. His mother tells him to apologize to the firm, but this does not solve the matter. Finally, the hero decides that it might be better if he joined his mother's traveling stage troupe where his childhood sweetheart is also working. The passing of the melancholy days is depicted with a mature technique. The lonely life and melancholic mood of the mother, O-Sumi, who is a traveling actress, the lonely early autumn feeling, symbolized by the withering of the morning-glories, in conjunction with the delicate mood of the hero, create a tranquil atmosphere. Although the restrained description belongs to the Naturalist tradition, the rich display of sentiment belongs rather to the romantic mode. Though depicting the destitute life of a low-caste society, the author was able to conjure up a vision of a beautiful world. There is something naive about this story, and, among the Decadent writers, Mantarō could be considered as having a rather wholesome outlook on life.

Following this novel, Mantarō wrote several dramas, and through these works became known also as a playwright. However, he continued writing novels, such as *Hanabi* (Fireworks), *O-Yone to Jūkichi* (O-Yone and Jūkichi) (1912), and *Hatsunatsu* (The First Summer) (1912). In all of these novels, with a delicate and sensitive touch he depicted scenes pervaded by the *shitamachi* (downtown) atmosphere, and gave sympathetic expression to the nuances of human sentiment. *Fuyuzora* (Winter Skies), written in the Taishō Period, was a sequel to *Asagao*.

Another who was regarded, together with Mantarō, as a member of the Mita school was Minakami Takitarō (Abe Shōzō). Born in Azabu Ward of Tōkyō, Takitarō published, under the name of Abe Shōzō, a story based on recollections of his childhood, *Yamanote no Ko* (A Boy of the Yamanote District) (1911), in the magazine *Mita Bungaku* while he was still a student of Keiō Gijuku University. He gained distinction for the polished style peculiar to a city-dweller, and for his realistic description pervaded by lyricism. However, since the following year he left for study in America, it was not until the Taishō years that Takitarō appeared, together with Mantarō, as the champion of the Mita school.

The Mita school developed through the magazine *Mita Bungaku* whose editor was Kafū. However, it was Ōgai and Ryūson who sent Kafū to Keiō Gijuku.

Ueda Bin (Ryūson) was a close friend of Ōgai and also was friendly with Kafū. On the basis of an understanding of Western civilization common to these three writers, Ryūson established himself as an appreciator of art, and this apparently also was the reason for his forming a group of intellectual epicureans. Although Kafū betrays a rather strong modern decadent temperament, Ōgai and Ryūson display a rather classic personality, and there is no sign of abnormality in them. One thing they had in common was that they all claimed to be dilettantes, although Ryūson substantiated his claim with a theoretical basis.

Ryūson earlier had gained distinction by the strong romantic taste he displayed in *Natsuyama Asobi* (Playing in the Summer Mountains) (1894), published in *Bungakkai,* and by a novel-like essay *Mijikayo* (The Short Night) and *Yoiyami* (Dusk), which were contained in *Miotsukushi* (Channel Markings) (1901). However, it was in the form of a lengthy novel, *Uzumaki* (Whirlpool) (1910), that he revealed the principles of his Neo-Romantic Epicureanism. This novel depicts the hedonist life of a well-educated dilettante named Maki Haruo. It seems that Ryūson had hoped to involve the hero in a modern romance with the heroine Yanagiya Natsuko, but this plan was never realized because the author could not develop the love-affair As a result, the whole fictional plot was not fully developed. Rather, attention is drawn to the author's views on dilettantism which are frequently expressed through the hero.

The hero Haruo's passionate longing for the exotic and for the past is developed, through academic training, into a definite philosophy, namely Epicureanism. His standpoint is to enjoy life and art to the fullest degree, and he strives for a "great enterprise," which, in his words, is "to sharpen the sensibility and sensual organs, to maintain the mind constantly in a fresh state, and thereby to strive to look into every corner of nature's delicate mechanism, or, in other words, to enjoy to the fullest extent all the pleasure of this world." To say it in another way, the hero cherishes the hope of enjoying to the utmost life's one instant which flickers on the road to eternity. Not a superficial attitude, the hero says it is one that requires a passionate desire to understand everything, a broad sympathy, and, in addition, prudence. This attitude suggests the healthiness which is seen in classical Greek literature and is an indication of Ryūson's position. Lacking in both the abnormal decadence and modernism seen in Baudelaire, Ryūson's philosophy was aestheticism, the degree of modernism corresponding to that of W. H. Pater.

The writer who best developed the aestheticism advocated by Ryūson and applied it in the sensual and artistic fields is doubtless Kinoshita Mokutarō (Ōta Masao). Mokutarō was a poet belonging to the *Okujō Teien* school and was also a writer of Symbolist plays. He also published several novels in *Subaru* and *Mita Bungaku*. *Aranuno-Bashi* (1909) and *Rokugatsu no Yoru* (A Night in June) (1909) were more like essays, but in these writings we discover a penetrating interpretation of the epicurean world which is a mixture of the urban atmosphere of Tōkyō and the modern taste. The following works, *Ro* (The Fireplace) (1910), *Garasudon'ya* (The Glass Dealer) (1911), *Sangoju no Netsuke* (The Coral Tree Netsuké) (1912), *Kashi no Yoru* (Night on the Riverbank) (1912), and *Oki no Tatsumaki* (The Waterspout on the Sea) (1912), all display a keen sensibility and a deep romantic coloring. However, these works do not yet indicate any truly profound insight into the core of life. In the Taishō Period Mokutarō wrote works that were more like novels. He was also a cultivated man, a graduate of a medical school, and was rumored, at one time, as the potential successor of Ōgai.

Although we must turn our attention to Ōgai since he was an influential patron of the Neo-Romantics, we must, before that, refer to another writer, who, unusually enough, belonged to the Waseda school. His name is Ogawa Mimei (Kensaku). This writer, while studying at Waseda University, published his maiden work, *Arare to Mizore* (Hail and Sleet) (1905). In 1907, he published the short stories *Shūjin* (A Melancholy Person) and *Ryokuhatsu* (Dark Hair), which were lyrical works that can be considered as a kind of poetical prose. However, his writings began to approach the novel form with such works as those in the collection *Wakusei* (The Planet) (1909). The following works, *Karasugane* (A Loan of Daily Interest) (1909), *Yuki Kitaru Mae* (Before the Snow Came) (1909), *Echigo no Fuyu* (Winter in Echigo) (1910), *Bara to Miko* (The Rose and the Sorceress) (1911), *Mono Iwanu Kao* (The Silent Face) (1911), and *Shōnen no Shi* (A Boy's Death) (1911), all covered the actual world with a tragic tone and, though displaying a slight Naturalistic color, were more inclined towards Neo-Romanticism. In 1908 he founded the Aotori Kai (The Bluebird Society), with the purpose of conducting research in Neo-Romanticism. In 1912 he issued a challenge to the Naturalist school and was commended by the magazine *Waseda Bungaku* for playing an avant-garde role in Neo-Romanticism.

The mood of Mimei's works reflects the climate of his native place, Takada, in the Echigo district, and is pervaded by the grim and melancholy atmosphere peculiar to this northern province. The basic note of his outlook on life is a nihilistic and pessimistic one, tinged with the tragic color of despair, which comes from constant trembling before the merciless power of nature and from constant fear of death. However, at the root of this pessimistic position, we find a pure aspiration, which, aided by a sensibility that feels the secret of a mystic world of eternity, leads to an extremely subjective outlook on life. On the other hand, Mimei, with the innocent mind of a child, sometimes depicts a fairy-tale world. As early as 1906, he edited the *Shōnen Bunko* (The Children's Library) under the guidance of Hōgetsu, and launched a new fairy-tale movement. By publishing a collection of such works entitled *Akai Fune* (The Red Ship) (1910), he became a pioneer in the field of the original fairy-tale written from a genuine artistic standpoint. In the Taishō years, he gained recognition as a writer in this genre.

Mimei's works are all short stories, with the exception of the lengthy novel *Rodon na Neko* (The Stupid Cat) (1912). This work describes the difficult days when he trod a solitary road during the heyday of Naturalism. He gives a rather faithful description of the miserable life which resulted in the death of his two children. From about the time of this publication, he began to show a tendency towards anarchistic humanism, and, in the middle of the Taishō Period, he joined the socialist movement, with the result that his mode of writing, undergoing a violent change, came to show the influence of anarchist ideas. As a member of the Waseda school, he had strong leanings towards Naturalism and, it was almost inevitable that he should have moved towards socialism. However, as far as the style of his early writings in the final years of Meiji is concerned, he must be classified as a member of the Neo-Romantic school.

3. *The Dawning Light of Neo-Idealism and Humanism*

As the patron of the young Romantics, Decadents, and Epicureans clustered around the *Subaru* and *Mita Bungaku*, Mori Ōgai occupied a strategic post in the literary circle of the final Meiji years. However, this did not mean that he was engaging in activity as champion of the *fin-de-siècle* schools. On the contrary, Ōgai was treading alone along his own great literary road. Following the publication of his three-piece maiden work, Ōgai, as an army doctor, participated in the Sino-Japanese and Russo-Japanese Wars. He was also transferred to the garrison in the city of Kokura, and, as a result, he was removed from the literary world. However, following his triumphant return from Manchuria in 1906, he wrote a short novel, *Asane* (Sleeping Late), based on his own observations in that country, and then followed it with several short stories.

But even before this, he had done some work in the literary field. For example, in 1897, he wrote *Somechigae* (The Wrong Dye), a short story depicting chastity in the gay quarters, and written in a Saikaku style. Five years after this, he wrote a play, *Tamakushige Futari Urashima* (The Two Urashimas), and attempted to infuse a new spirit into the dramatic circles by his new dramas. However, his reappearance as a novelist is marked by the aforementioned *Asane*. This story gives a rather humorous description of a war correspondent who becomes involved in an embarrassing situation because he is a late riser. This work can be taken as an indication that Ōgai had cast off his romantic and lyrical garments and was attempting to expose the ugliness in actual life by cultivating a direct, realistic method. The following year, he depicted the scenes in Tōkyō's jammed trolley cars in *Yūrakumon* (Yūraku Gate). In his first novel written with the use of colloquial language, *Hannichi* (A Half-Day), published in 1909, he exposes a woman's instinctive hatred of her mother-in-law, with his own wife (Mori Shige) as the model. The same year he wrote another novel with his wife as model, *Masui* (Dreaded Sleep), in which he analyses the discomfort of a husband who suspects that his wife's chastity has been stained. In the medium-length novel *Ita Sekusuarisu* (Vita Sexualis), he narrates the history of his own sexual experience, while in the works *Niwatori* (Chicken) and *Kinka* (The Gold Coin), he observes the kleptomania of male and female servants and the plight of an alcoholic thief. In these works, Ōgai appeared to be bringing himself closer to the Naturalistic method which was gaining popularity at the time.

However, these works were essentially different from the Naturalist writings. One characteristic of Ōgai was that he often depicted trivial affairs taking place around him with a frank attitude and with use of straightforward colloquial sentences. There was also a certain pure and deep tone about his writing which even made him observe himself as another person. As a result, when he exposes the ugliness in trivial affairs taking place around him, he seems to be standing aloof and gazing down on the world. He never shows concern over the bestiality in human beings, but he nonchalantly sheds light on the stupid world which cannot awaken to reason, gazing through the eyes of rationality which transcends this bestiality inherent in man. Therefore, the animal instincts exposed in Ōgai's works do not represent the whole of man. Rather, such instinct has been presented as a thing which must be gazed upon coldly from a high, idealistic standpoint and as a thing which must be subdued. In this sense, he did not modify his position as an idealist.

Therefore, in the short stories he was to turn out in rapid succession, Ōgai gradually polished the illuminant side of his idealism and cast light on life, thus shaping his works as something distinctly different from the dark, decadent works of the Naturalist school. For example in *Kompira* (The Japanese Neptune), published at the end of 1909, the author analyzed the psychology of himself and his wife as they face the death of their child. His wife attempts to save her child through superstition, but when this fails and the child dies, she gives a passionate display of maternal grief. The husband, on the other hand, believes in the power and knows the limits of science, and thereby remains calm when the child dies. Although the author is opposed to the superstition of his wife, he seems to bow his head to her maternal love ; and though he places confidence in his intellectuality, he cannot hide a feeling of discontent over his unsympathetic, bystander attitude toward the child's death.

In the following year he wrote *Gyūnabe* (The Sukiyaki Pot) in which he depicted the appetite and sexual desires of a man and woman who sit together around a *sukiyaki* pot. On the surface, the author seems to be exposing the ugly nature of man. However, he still maintains the optimistic attitude that man is more advanced than other animals. In *Dokushin* (The Bachelor), written in the same year, he depicts his own bachelor life during the days he was stationed in Kokura. Although the people around him show concern over his unmarried state, the author demonstrates in this work that unsatisfied sexual desire is not such a dreadful thing. In *Ita Sekusuarisu*, he gave a comprehensive account of his own sexual life so that his children could learn something from their father's experience when they grew up. In *Densha no Mado* (The Window of the Trolley Car), published together with *Dokushin*, he depicted a kindly act in a trolley car and, by showing that the kindness which does not expect reward will brighten men's lives, instilled a confidence in human society. The following year, he wrote *Hebi* (The Snake), and hinted that one way to make the world a better place was to crush superstition with the help of science. In the essay-like autobiographical novel *Mōsō* (Delusion), he depicts his own state of mind as he passes into the latter stage of life, and displays the hope that a bright destiny awaits mankind in the distant future. This tendency becomes more distinct in *Hatori Chihiro*, published in August of the following year. In this piece, the author makes public a letter from a youth who is deeply devoted to him and wants to start a career under his guidance; it displays clearly Ōgai's humanitarian attitude.

In this work, the author suggested a road to humanism. It may be that he was betraying somewhat the influence of the Neo-Idealist movement initiated by the Shirakaba school; however, it could also be taken as an indication of the humanistic spirit inherent in Ōgai. In *Shakkuri* (Hiccups), written three months earlier, the author had displayed a deep concern over ethics, and in *Tsuchi Ikka* (One Strike of the Hammer), written in the subsequent Taishō Period, there are signs of a humanistic love based on Christian socialism. Also in the later works *Tenchō* (Heaven's Favorite) and *Futari no Tomo* (Two Friends), there is a rather prominent display of the same humanistic love. This humanistic love and spiritual ideal can be perceived at the root of the plain objective writing in his numerous historical novels and biographies which added luster to the literary world of the early Taishō Period.

However, as he wrote in *Satoimo to Fudō no Me* (The Taro and the Eyes of the God of Fire) (1910), he was not a fanatic who would sacrifice himself for the cause of his ideals. As he repeatedly wrote in *Asobi* (Play) (1910), *Shokudō* (The Dining Room) (1910), *Hyaku Monogatari* (One Hundred Tales) (1911), and *Fushigi na Kagami* (The Strange Mirror) (1912), he was a " bystander," stationed complacently in a " mood of *asobi* (playfulness)." This seems to have some relation with the Epicurean school, but, as Ueda Bin wrote in *Uzumaki*, the " playful mood " does not mean a seeking for pleasure in the sensual world. Rather it means a disposing of oneself calmly and doing what one believes in a carefree way, regardless of what the literary critics say. This mood was expressed by Ōgai in the word " resignation " (*teinen*) in his article " My Position " (1909). It closely resembles Sōseki's *sokuten kyoshi* (to follow heaven and depart from the self), but for Ōgai, endowed with objective intellectuality and an apollonian character, it was relatively easy to enter such a deep spiritual world. And unlike Sōseki, possessed of a dionysian character, Ōgai did not require any apparent ethical effort to attain such a spiritual plane.

Although Ōgai seems to be complacent with his carefree mood (*asobi*) and his position as a bystander (*bōkansha*), he displays a romantic spirit as an " eternal malcontent " (*eien naru fuheika*), as he wrote in *Mōsō*. He expressed a rather strong indignation against the government infringement on personal liberties and against the superficial vogue prevailing in the literary world. This indignation was frequently expressed in the form of satires. In *Fuasuchiesu* (Fasces) (1910) and *Chimmoku no Tō* (The Silent Tower) (1910), he expressed his resistance against the suppression of freedom by public authorities in the form of dialogue and novel. In *Ru Parunasu Ambyuran* (Le Parnasse Ambulin) (1910) and *Fushigi na Kagami* (The Strange Mirror) (1912), he satirized the lack of intellectuality on the part of the literary circle which merely followed the vogue. *Kano Yō ni* (In Such a Way) (1912) was an ideological story which dealt with the tragedy and agony of a young savant who returns from overseas study and decides to rewrite the nation's history from the standpoint of liberalism, but encounters the opposition of his tradition-minded father who tries to protect the world of myths. After writing several stories which were a sequel to this novel, Ōgai endeavored to move in a religious direction.

While writing the short stories we have mentioned above, during the years from the latter part of Meiji to the beginning of Taishō, Ōgai was also writing long stories like *Seinen* (Youth) (1910), *Gan* (The Wild Goose) (1911–1913), and *Kaijin* (Reduced to Ashes) (1911). Partly under the stimulus of Sōseki, Ōgai seemed to have written these works apparently as a trilogy, and attempted to deal with love-affairs, with the youth of the new age as the heroes.

Seinen deals with a youth, Jun'ichi, who comes to Tōkyō to become a writer. But, as in the case of *Sanshirō*, the hero's contact with the urban atmosphere shakes his outlook on life. The author gives a minute description of the youth's psychology, and adds several women to the story. One of them is an innocent girl living next-door, O-Yuki, who is so innocent that the hero cannot enter into sexual relations with her. The second woman is Mrs. Sakai, a voluptuous type, who, the youth learns with disappointment, shows interest only in the fulfilment of sexual impulses. The third woman is O-Kinu, a maid of a hot spring hotel, but though the hero has warm affection for her, he cannot pursue his love further. As a consequence of these experiences, the hero finally learns that he cannot discover a true life in the love of women. Thus, he devotes his whole effort to writing novels based on legends and, for the first time, experiences an urge to live.

Gan deals with a poor girl, O-Tama, who becomes the mistress of a usurer to support her father. But her ego awakens, and she comes to think that she cannot waste her life in such a way. At this propitious moment, she feels a genuine love for a medical student, Okada, who passes in front of her window every day. The girl hopes to escape from her prison-like life as a mistress with the help of Okada, but as a result of the whim of fate, she loses the opportunity of communicating her feelings to him. In contrast with *Seinen*, which is a realistic work resembling in some points an ideological novel, *Gan* displayed rich romantic beauty and seemed a reworking of *Maihime*. The final scenes are extremely lyrical. In these passages we sense a boundless compassion for the unrescued heroine O-Tama and shudder silently at fathomless fate pitted against the sublime.

In reading *Seinen* and *Gan*, we seem to be listening to an elegy to love. But in *Kaijin* we seem to be witnessing the grave-digging and burial of a completely chilled love. The hero Setsuzō is a youth whose heart is glacial and who appears at times to be even cruel. Therefore, although he saves the daughter of the family of his senior, at whose home he is lodged, from the hands of a delinquent boy, a sex pervert, this does not lead to a romance between the hero and the daughter O-Tane. Upon reading through this section, we find the plot is developed as if something cruel had occurred between the hero and the heroine. Ōgai failed to complete the novel, which, in its present form, concludes with the section where the hero is starting to write a story based on a vehement satire. Was it that Ōgai could not endure the idea of pursuing the life of this cold-blooded hero any further? At any rate, the hero Setsuzō seems to be an exaggerated projection of the bystander Ōgai himself. But at the same time the author seemed to be showing a violent reaction against the ego of this complete bystander and to be moving towards "unselfish individualism," which seemed to be the ideological conclusion drawn from *Seinen*.

In this trilogy, Ōgai first passed through the stage of pursuit of love, then to the stage of unsuccessful love, and finally to the burial of love. Yet the common conclusion was the negation of love. This resembles Sōseki's course through *Sanshirō*, *Sorekara*, and *Mon*. The difference between the two authors is that while Sōseki attempted again to analyze love between the sexes from a fresh viewpoint, Ōgai did not return to this subject. Rather, Ōgai was to find his theme in things which transcended romantic love—the relationship of loyalty between a lord and his retainer, friendship, fraternal love, and conjugal affections. In the historical pieces, which became his last writings, Ōgai displayed an admiration for the ancient sages. This led to a temporary resurrection of long stories written in the form of historical biography. But in these stories there was hardly a sign of an artistic motive for writing fiction. Instead, the author strove for a faithful description of the historical facts, with the result that the writings cannot be considered genuine artistic productions. The trilogy depicts a widow faced with sexual temptation, the life of a kept mistress, and the abnormal sexual life of juvenile delinquents, and as such, betrays the influence of Naturalism. However, the general theme was the author's own outlook on love and transcendence of love, and the writings as a whole are pervaded by a romantic and idealistic mood.

While one of Ōgai's major achievements was the development of humanistic ideas, we discover a strong romantic and idealistic element when we trace the whole course of his literary career. In fact, he occupied a position as a patron of the romantic and idealist schools. His literary attitude, described as a "by-stander's position," as a "carefree attitude," or as "resignation," was imbued with a certain culturalism which sought a secluded and retired life in a world of learning and art, and for unrestrained original creation in the cultural field. The author, who disliked fanaticism, lacked active interest in emphasizing the ideals of life and in reconstruction of society. The ethical aspect of Ōgai's humanism appears, in his case, only in a deeply cultivated form.

Ōgai was far more advanced than anyone in transplanting on native grounds Western literature and the ideas which formed its basis. In terms of contribution to the development of literature, he occupied the post of an influential leader of the whole literary world. However, when it came to an ethical outlook on life and its practical application, he lacked the ability to guide the artists engaged in literary work. Rather it was Sōseki who, in this connection, saw numerous followers and admirers come to him to seek his advice. The ripening of the Naturalist idea was now germinating a movement to resurrect human liberty and moral passion among the younger generation. But at this precise moment Ōgai failed to become a leader of this movement, which instead began to develop among the artists clustered around Sōseki.

However, when we survey the writers belonging to the Sōseki school, those who emerged in the earlier period were Aesthetes and Decadents, as illustrated by Miekichi, Sōhei, and others, who displayed a Neo-Romantic style. In the latter period, Sōseki's faction was joined by the so-called Neo-Intellectuals, Kume Masao and Akutagawa Ryūnosuke, who also showed strong Romantic leanings. The disciples who reflected Sōseki's outlook on life in the moral realm were principally scholars who did not move in an artistic direction but instead were inclined to publish their Neo-Idealist theories in the form of critical writings. This explains why there were so many critics advocating Neo-Idealist ideas gathered around Sōseki. In order to find actual writers who displayed Neo-Idealist ideas, we must go over to the Shirakaba school. The writers of this group were not direct disciples of Sōseki, but showed great devotion to him.

The magazine *Shirakaba* (White Birch) was founded in April 1910. The plan to found this magazine first developed four years earlier in 1906, when the magazine's principal figure, Mushakōji Saneatsu, graduated from the Gakushūin (Peers' School) and entered the Sociology Department of Tōkyō Imperial University. In conjunction with Shiga Naoya, Ōgimachi Kinkazu, Kinoshita Toshiharu, all young graduates of the Gakushūin, Mushakōji decided to found a magazine to be entitled *Shirakaba*, and quit school. However, the plan failed, and Mushakōji instead published in the following year a volume entitled *Kōya* (Barren Ground). In the same period, we see the founding of *Mugi* (Barley) by Satomi Ton and Onchi Kin'yuki, and *Tōen* (The Peach Garden) by Yanagi Sōetsu and Kōri Torahiko (Kayano Nijūichi), but these magazines were merged finally and led to the creation of *Shirakaba*. In addition to the aforementioned Mushakōji, Shiga, Ōgimachi, Kinoshita, Satomi, Onchi, and Kōri, the writers participating in this magazine included Kojima Kikuo, Arishima Takeo, Arishima Ikuma, Tanaka Uson, and Kusaka Minoru, and later, Nagayo Yoshio and Yamawaki Nobutoku.

The name Shirakaba school was derived from the writers group which formed around the magazine *Shirakaba*. Since this school was born out of the literary dabblings of the young aristocrats of the Gakushūin, at first it did not display any definite views. Contrary to common supposition, this school was not a society formed to disseminate humanistic ideas. In terms of the unity of its thought this school lacked stability. The only outstanding feature, if we must mention one, was that Mushakōji played an active part as the leader. As to the other members, they displayed a strong tendency to develop their own individual abilities.

Nevertheless, the Shirakaba school occupied a significant position in the literary world, chiefly because it was tinted with the peculiar and rich humanistic coloring born out of the deep passion for morality of Mushakōji, and because one of its influential members, Shiga, turned out works which reflected the steady growth of his refined individualism and the development of his technique as a novelist. As to other writers, such potential luminaries as Arishima Takeo and Nagayo Yoshio were advancing along their individual courses, while Kinoshita in his *waka*, and Satomi in his novels, showed signs of moving towards the Neo-Romantic or Aesthetic schools. The example of these two writers indicates that it would be a mistake to classify all of the members on the basis of a Shirakaba-type morality. And yet this Shirakaba school boldly espoused the ideas of the young aristocrats who aspired for humanistic beauty and individual freedom. There is not the slightest doubt that this school became a motivating force in effecting a wholesale transformation of a world based on the mechanical and scientific views of Naturalism and leaning towards decadence. However, at the same time, there is no denying that the ideals of this school were nothing more than aristocratic and individualistic ones. This inevitably led to a temporary blocking of literary development, which, of necessity, had to move from Naturalism in the direction of socialism and democracy.

Although at the end of the Meiji Period this movement of the Shirakaba school had just got under way, already it was not without some remarkable achievements. Saneatsu had tried to write several stories and plays, out of which he published in the *Shirakaba*, besides three plays, *Umarekuru Ko no Tame ni* (For the Child Coming into Life) (1910), *Perushajin* (The Persians) (1911), *Yoshiko* (A Girl Named Yoshiko) (1911), *Aru Ani no Henji* (An Answer from a Brother) (1912), and *Aru Wakaki Otoko* (A Certain Young Man). Especially the medium-length romance entitled *Omedetaki Hito* (An Innocent) (1911) which was an elaborate work drawn from his personal experiences, distinctly expressed the characteristics of his views of life. It may be said that the seeds of his style that flowered later were sown in this work.

The plot of *Omedetaki Hito* is quite simple. The hero, who has fallen in love with Tsuru, a young girl in his neighborhood, is twice rejected in his proposal, but as her rejections sound insincere, he proposes for the third time through the good offices of a man named Kawaji, only to face the same result. Broken-hearted, he starts on a trip, but in a week his hopes are revived. This change seems so natural to the hero that he senses in it "nature's command, nature's deep, mystic revelation," and he calls himself a "brave man," because he believes unswervingly that he and Tsuru are destined to be married. One day, a year later, he encounters Tsuru in a streetcar, and he is delighted to see her get off at the same stop. He walks in the same direction with her for awhile, but leaves her without exchanging a word. He feels that this is a good omen and relies on Kawaji. However, after half a year he hears that Tsuru has been married happily to a wealthy engineer. He throws himself down in tears, but in no time regains his optimistic mood and feels pity for the girl, thinking that she must have been obliged to marry the engineer on the recommendation of her parents and elders, and that if Tsuru had said to him, "I have never loved you," it was in word only, since she unconsciously had affection for him; at least he tries to convince himself that she felt that way. This novel records the feelings of such an innocent man in the style of the first person as in a journal, with a liberal flow of personal confessions.

This work was a candid expression of the author's views of life which were developed later. The hero gave way to no despair, kept looking forward to the future, believed in life's harmony and God's providence, and never lost the willpower to regain his footing no matter how many times he had fallen. Simplicity, candidness, childish innocence, a tenacious hold on life that seems even absurd, a perfectly optimistic attitude, a spirit of lenient forgiveness, hope for consolation in love, and self-affirmation that appears even vain—the mixture of all these characteristics is, at any rate, contrary to the *fin-de-siècle* mood in Naturalism, and filled with a determination to revive a primitive vitality.

Besides mere primitive simplicity, this work displays also a considerable degree of self-consciousness, self-analysis, and self-satirizing. In a sense, Saneatsu seems to have been presenting such a pointless sort of comedy knowingly. He seems also to have resigned himself to the destiny of human beings who are impressed with their own goodness while satirizing themselves, and obliged to live after all by approving of their behavior just as it is, even though they sometimes try to deny themselves. In comparison with Sōseki's insistence on *sokuten kyoshi*, Saneatsu shows the will to make the self one with fate without abandoning the self. This is possible because with him fate has already been lodged in the self in its innocent state. Furthermore, compared with Ōgai's resignation, Saneatsu seems not to have any need of giving up anything, but rather to be capable of absorbing even a disadvantageous environment under the direction of nature's will. Here one may find the spirit of masculine fortitude comparable to Nietzsche's *amor fati*, but Saneatsu's affirmative attitude has more affinity to the meditative state of mind, typical of the Zen sect, attained by the Oriental sages, of which characteristics are exhibited in his later works.

Saneatsu seems to have learned defiance of fate and belief in the happy conclusion of life's adventures from his study of the teachings of the Zen sect and Ōyōmei (Wang Yang-ming) Confucianism in his youth, but he also appears to have been greatly influenced by Tolstoy and Maeterlinck. His belief, however, does not seem to have been born out of simple optimism but to have been built upon victory over pessimism. Saneatsu's thoughts had not reached any extraordinary depth, nor had they been put to hard tests, yet their implication was not mere childishness. They constitute what might be termed the Neo-Idealism coming in the wake of Naturalism.

Nagayo Yoshio, who like Saneatsu had been influenced by Tolstoy and admired Sōseki, published in the *Shirakaba*, under the name of Hirasawa Nakaji, *Shunshō* (A Spring Night) (1911), *Densha* (The Streetcar) (1911), *Naki Ane ni* (To a Dead Sister) (1912), and *Yōichi no Maboroshi* (Yōichi's Illusion), but his ability was not fully exhibited. Arishima Takeo, who had published only *Aru Onna no Gurimpusu* (The Glimpse of a Certain Woman) (1911) in the *Shirakaba*, also had no noticeable achievement at this time. This work of Takeo was later consummated as a novel entitled *Aru Onna* (A Woman). It attempted to deal with a woman of the new age who consumes herself with an unbridled, instinctive infatuation. The author modeled her after Sasaki Nobuko, who had been in love with Doppo but who afterwards deserted him. Takeo's interpretation of love, that it is the expansion of the ego, was already unfolding in this maiden work. But it is not doing justice to him to regard this piece of the Meiji Period as representing the whole of his work.

Shiga Naoya had already published in the *Shirakaba* before the end of the Meiji Period such short stories as *Abashiri made* (As Far as Abashiri) (1910), *Kamisori* (The Razor) (1910), *Koji* (An Orphan) (1910), *Kare to Muttsu Ue no Onna* (He and a Woman Six Years Older than He) (1910), *Hayao no Imōto* (Hayao's Younger Sister) (1910), *Torio no Byōki* (Torio's Sickness) (1911), *Nigotta Atama* (The Obscure Mind) (1911), *Ippeiji* (One Page) (1911), *Fusuma* (The Paper Sliding-Door) (1911), *Rōjin* (The Old Man) (1911), *Sobo no Tame ni* (On My Grandmother's Behalf) (1911), and *Omoidashita Koto* (Things Remembered) (1911), and in addition to these he had several unpublished stories in manuscript. Although *Abashiri made* had previously been sent to *Teikoku Bungaku* (Imperial Literature) and returned, it was an excellent piece of work which determined Naoya's style. The story deals with a woman who is on the way to Abashiri in Hokkaidō with her children; the hero, who happens to ride in the same train from Ueno Station, deeply sympathizes with her impoverished condition, and treats her as kindly as he can. Such feelings are related succinctly but in detail. Readers were charmed by the author's attitude toward life that keeps a quiet control on liberal goodwill and deep sympathy. This story marked the starting-point for Naoya toward consummation as a mental life novelist (*shinkyō shōsetsuka*) in later years.

All his works, including this one, convey the impression of being dispassionate, composed, and narrative in style, parallel with the Naturalistic matter-of-fact description. But his expression which has attained the apex of refinement and allowed no alteration, seems as if it were the application of the technique of the realistic *tanka* verse form to prose. Moreover, the serenity of his art carries with it the fragrance of humanistic affection that dwells deep in the author's heart. *Kamisori* and *Nigotta Atama* present an exceedingly detailed analysis of the psychology of men who, driven by unusual nervous excitement, commit murder. They are examples of the aspect of the author as a psychologist, who, with severe eyes, penetrates into the mystic functions of moods and sensations of human beings, while *Torio no Byōki* shows another aspect in that, while observing the morbid sentiments of an intimate friend who suffers from a nervous breakdown, the author is in a way holding him in warm affection.

Fusuma deals with a young nurse-maid who falls in love with the hero while staying in the adjacent room of a hotel at a hot spring, and tries to show her childlike affection by opening secretly the paper sliding-door (*fusuma*) between her room and his very late at night. This story is written with some humor, yet it is full of tender affection for the young girl. In *Rōjin*, the hero, who is about seventy, makes a three years' contract with a concubine as young as his granddaughter, but is unable to part with her when the contract has expired. She gives birth to a child, but the old man is aware that it is not by him but by her lover. He overlooks it, and lives as peacefully as ever with her until he dies at seventy-five. The conclusion of the story which describes the young paramour sitting on the old man's cushion after his death has the heartlessness and humor in the tradition of Saikaku, but the whole story is enveloped in the author's warm and tender sympathy with life.

Hayao no Imōto deals with the author's memories of childhood friendship with O-Tsuru, his intimate friend's younger sister, and goes on to relate in an indifferent style the circumstances which led her eventually to marry another man. This story, if compared with *Omedetaki Hito*, is eloquent of the difference in the authors' characters. It may seem that in this work there is only calmness devoid of passion or self-conceit, but in fact it was born out of the same depth of love as *Omedetaki Hito*. *Koji* deals with the marriage and divorce of Toshi, the hero's cousin, who is treated like his own younger sister. Although Toshi is a meek, tender-hearted girl, her character has become somewhat cold and stiff because she was brought up as an orphan, and this factor seems to have been responsible for her divorce. The author contemplates such character and fate as hers with serene resignation. But when he describes the scene where Toshi, who has never cried from sorrow, bursts into bitter tears for the first time in her sleep after dreaming of her deserted baby, he not only shows his excellent skill in plotting a story but creates a deep impression as a humanist. It may be said that this story predicted the author's ability which won him the greatest success among the novelists of the Shirakaba school.

Although Naoya deepened his views on life, as exhibited in the series of excellent short stories based on his sense of justice, and attained consummation as a mental life novelist in the Taishō Period, his achievements by the end of the Meiji Period had reached such a level as has been discussed. This much will be enough to show how the objective description of Naturalism, the abnormal sense of decadence, and the moralistic spirit of humanism were being incorporated into a world of perfect harmony.

PART THREE MEIJI POETRY

CHAPTER I THE ESTABLISHMENT AND DEVELOPMENT OF NEW STYLE POETRY

1. *The Appearance of New Style Poetry and the Poets' Circle in the Early Period*

The word *shi* (poetry) meant, in the early years of Meiji, poetry composed in the Chinese fashion (*kanshi*). The longer poetic form which came into being in Meiji was named *shintaishi* (New Style poetry) to distinguish it from the former, and it was established with the publication of the *Shintaishishō* (An Anthology of New Style Poetry) in 1882. The authors were Inoue Sonken (Tetsujirō), Yatabe Shōkon (Ryōkichi), and Toyama Chuzan (Shōichi), then professors at Tōkyō Imperial University, and it consisted of fourteen translated poems and five original ones. The motivation for the publication of such an anthology can be known from the foreword to Sonken's *Tama-no-o no Uta* (a translation of Longfellow's *The Psalm of Life*), which states that while he had planned for some time to write poetry in the New Style, Shōkon and Chuzan happened to bring him their translations of Hamlet's monologue beginning with " To be, or not to be," and this was the incentive for him to translate Longfellow's *The Psalm of Life* and other poems of a similar nature, as well as to write poems of his own. This account proves that New Style poetry originated from the translating of Western poetry, but if we trace it further back, we find its prototype in the Christian hymns of early Meiji and in the translated Dutch poems which appeared in the latter part of the Edo Era. Nevertheless, it was the authors of the *Shintaishishō* who adopted the style and established it as a new genre of Japanese literature.

The purpose of creating New Style poetry is succinctly expressed in the authors' words : "The poetry of Meiji should not be the poetry of the past but that of Meiji itself. The poetry of Japan should not be that of China but of Japan itself. This is the reason for the creation of New Style poetry." (From Inoue Sonken's foreword to *The Psalm of Life*). "It is regrettable that our countrymen seldom compose poems using the language of the common people. We have worked out a kind of new-styled poetry on the European pattern." (From Yatabe Shōkon's preface to the *Shintaishishō*). They used only the words that were easily "understandable, without any distinction between the old and new, Chinese or European, literary or vulgar." (From Toyama Chuzan's preface to the *Shintaishishō*). They expected that their trial composition would be a poetry of the people, one which would really represent the new age, even though it might be called vulgar. It was to correspond to the temper of the time which endeavored to effect the modernization of Japan by imitating European civilization. They were seeking for new forms to contain the new thought and new feelings, which were difficult to express through the old forms of the *tanka*, *haiku*, and Chinese-style poems.

Their attempt certainly conformed to the trend of the times and proclaimed the beginning of a new poetry, but the poems themselves were far from excellent. The fact that they were not poets but scholars was partially responsible for their inability to put their theory fully into practice. For instance, Shōkon's translation of the aforementioned Hamlet's monologue begins thus :

Nagarō beki ka, tadashi mata
Nagarō beki ni arazaru ka
Koko ga shian no shidokoro zo
Ummei ika ni tsutanaki mo
Kore ni tauru ga masurao ka

Even the best translation achieves no great effect :

Yamayama kasumi iriai no

Kane wa naritsutsu no no ushi wa
Shizuka ni ayumi kaeriyuku
Tagaesu hito mo uchitsukare
Yōyaku sarite ware hitori
Tasogare-doki ni nakorikeri

(The first stanza of Gray's *Elegy*, translated by Shōkon)

As for the form, stanzas were divided as in the original, but the rhythm was mostly in the traditional seven-five-syllable pattern, and the language also was not greatly modernized.

The authors' original works were *Battō Tai* (A Band with Bare Swords) and '*Shakaigaku no Genri*' *ni Daisu* (A Poem Written for "The Principle of Sociology") by Chuzan, and *Kangaku no Uta* (A Song of Encouragement to Study), *Kamakura no Daibutsu ni Mōdete Kan Ari* (On Visiting the Great Buddha of Kamakura), and *Shunkashūtō* (The Four Seasons) by Shōkon, all of which were conceptual and lacked poetic taste. It was only natural that such poetry should have incurred the derision and disdain of the intelligentsia as being "vulgar," "most strange," "crude in the extreme," and "ridiculous."

In spite of such criticism, this crude but free style was welcomed by the general public, especially by the younger generation, and New Style poetry became popular throughout the country. Following this pioneer anthology, *Shintaishiika* (New Style Poems) (1882), compiled by Takeuchi Setsu, *Shintaishisen* (Selected New Style Poetry) (1886), compiled by Yamada Bimyō, *Meiji Shintaishiikasen* (Selected Meiji New Style Poems) (1887), edited by Satō Yūji, and many others were published, but generally the poetry included in them degenerated to the level of war-songs or schoolchildren's songs.

The merit of the *Shintaishishō* lies only in the historical significance of its pioneer role, but the poets who followed showed their individuality and talents in seeking artistic beauty within the form of this New Style poetry. Yuasa Hangetsu (Yoshirō) published *Jūni no Ishizuka* (Twelve Mounds of Stones)

(1885), the first personal collection of poetry in Japan, which was a kind of epic poem on a theme taken from the story of the ephod in the Old Testament.

Chihayaburu kami no shirushi to	In memory of God Almighty
Girugaru no okabe ni sakeru	There stand on the hill of
Yuri no hana no tateru mo takashi	Gilgal
Jūni no ishizuka	As noble as the flowers of the lily,
	The twelve mounds of stones.
	(Part I, Introduction)

Even though the poet went too far in Japanizing the Christian theme, with a graceful diction and eloquent style he advanced beyond the crude and unpolished verse of the *Shintaishishō*.

Hangetsu also wrote *Ametsuchi no Hajime* (The Beginning of Heaven and Earth) (1893), the material for which was taken from *Genesis*, while Togawa Ataka (Zanka) and Isogai Yoshitarō (Umpō) composed descriptive poems based on material from Japanese history. The latter two poets selected famous characters and events from history, adding new interpretations and changing the scene somewhat, but the effect was hardly novel, for they used a rather archaic vocabulary which made their poems appear to be merely Japanese classical *chōka* (long poems). That epic poetry was attempted was another indication of the imitation of European literature ; however, the genius of the Japanese language, which is quite different from that of European languages, was not suitable to long poems of the epic type, and the ones that were attempted on the whole possessed the defect of verbosity, even though they contained some excellent passages. Although these long poems were called *jojishi* (epics), they were quite different from the European epic both in form and content.

It may seem strange that Ochiai Naobumi's *Kōjo Shiragiku no Uta* (The Song of Shiragiku, Filial Daughter) (1888), a translation of Sonken's Chinese poem, won national popularity, but it was not an epic so much as a romantic narrative poem.

It tells how a poor young girl experiences vicissitudes of fortune but finally achieves happiness. Although the story is extremely simple, he described it with clear and graceful diction. It begins as follows :

Aso no yamazato aki fukete	In the mountain village of Aso
Nagame sabishiki yūmagure	On a dreary evening in late
Izuko no tera no kane naramu	autumn
Shogyō mujō to tsugewataru	A temple bell peals out
	That all things are transient.

The worth of this poem lies in the lyric mood which prevails throughout it rather than in the description of the events. There were many other attempts in the field of the epic, but the main current of New Style poetry can be said to have been that of lyric poetry.

Clearly in the realm of lyric poetry is found Miyazaki Koshoshi (Yaokichi) who composed pastoral and rural poems under the influence of nature poets such as Wordsworth. He loved the rural life secluded from civilization, and wrote refined poems with seven-five-syllable metre lines :

Haru no hanano ni kite mireba	I came to a field of spring
Nuruki shimizu mo nagarekeri	flowers
Sono yutaka naru futokoro ni	And found a warm stream
Tsuri suru koto zo omoshiroki	flowing there ;
	Who knows the joy of fishing
	In the rich recesses of its
	waters ?

(The first stanza of *Tsuribito no Uta,* Song of a Fisherman)

He later collected poems of this type in *Koshoshi Shishū* (Poems by Koshoshi) (1893).

Nakanishi Baika (Mikio), who died insane, leaving *Shintai Baika Shishū* (A Collection of New Style Poems by Baika) (1891), was a man of extraordinary temperament. He was a nihilist and lived only for the moment, a rarity among poets of those days, and was noted for his eccentric conduct. He expressed his view of life without affectation in a free style and language, but his poems were largely conceptual and wanting in poetic feeling. His light sense of humor and a certain pathos combined with his decadence make the anthology unique.

By these poets the artistic character of New Style poetry was gradually established, but what gave it fresh life was *Omokage* (Vestiges), an anthology of seventeen poems by the Shinseisha (S. S. S.) group, including Japanese and Chinese translations of the works of such English writers as Shakespeare and Byron, and of German poets such as Goethe and Heine, Japanese translations of the poem of Kao Ch'ing Ch'iu, and Chinese translations of the *Heike Monogatari* (The Tale of the Taira Clan). The translators were Mori Ōgai, Ochiai Naobumi, Koganei Kimiko, Inoue Michiyasu, and Ichimura Sanjirō.

The methods they used in translating were *iyaku* (" meaning translation," which followed the meaning of the original), *kuyaku* (" phrase translation," which followed the meaning and original wording), and *in'yaku* (" rhyme translation," which followed both the versification and meaning of the original), and, as for metre, in addition to the seven-five-syllable one, they used ten-ten, five-five, eight-seven, and eight-six-syllable metres. That they used mainly classical language in translation was contrary to what the *Shintaishishō* had stressed, it would seem, but, nevertheless, the sentiment expressed was far fresher and conveyed admirably the feeling of modern European poetry. Such an attitude on the part of the translators came partly from their intention of answering the call for a classical revival but mainly from the fact that the spoken language was neither endowed with refined poetic beauty nor capable of conveying artistic expression, whatever the content might be. New Style poetry advanced a step closer to more modern poetry in *Omokage* at the same time that it linked itself with traditional verse forms.

Remon no ki wa hana saki kuraki hayashi no naka ni
Kogane iro shitaru kōji wa eda mo tawawa ni minori
Aoku hareshi sora yori shizuyaka ni kaze fuki

Mirute no ki wa shizuka ni raureru no ki wa takaku
Kumo ni sobiete tateru kuni o shiruya kanata e
Kimi to tomo ni yukamashi

(*A Song of Mignon*, the first stanza.)
The above is the Japanese translation of Mignon's song in Goethe's *Wilhelm Meisters Lehrjahre*. Its fluent and elegant diction shows no trace of the crudeness which is found in the translation of Hamlet's monologue in the *Shintaishishō*. Free translation though it be, it communicates the exotic serenity of the original poem most skilfully. The following translation follows the form of the *imayō*, which dates back to the Heian Period, but the translator succeeded in transmitting the fresh romantic sentiment with a note of refined pathos.

Waga ue ni shimo aranakuni
Nazo kaku otsuru namida zo mo
Fumi kudakareshi hanasōbi
Yo wa nare nomi no ukiyo ka wa

(The last stanza of K. Gerok's *Die Rose im Staub*)
The fact that this form was followed by Tōson and the other modern poets is due to the success of this translation. The summer supplement of the *Kokumin no Tomo* in which *Omokage* appeared was published in 1889 in book form under the title of *Moshiogusa* (Seaweed), but it did not gain public attention. Later, all of the poems were included in Ōgai's *Minawashū* (A Water-Spray Anthology), together with *Seikyūshi* (*Ch'ing Ch'iu Tzŭ*) (The Child of the Green Hills) and *Tōkyōkō* (*Tao Hsieh Hsing*) (The Song of the Gallant Thief), and exerted a profound influence on subsequent generations, not only on the translation of poetry but on original poetry as well; in a sense, it represents the beginning of modern Japanese poetry.

The authors of the *Shintaishishō* carried on their literary activity in the magazine *Teikoku Bungaku* (Imperial Literature), but apart from their role of enlightenment, they performed no noteworthy function. Under their guidance, however, Ōmachi Keigetsu (Yoshie), Shioi Ukō (Masao), and Takeshima Hagoromo

(Matajirō) emerged and published *Bibun Imbun : Hanamomiji* (The Red Maple Leaves Anthology of Prose and Poetry) (1896). These poets were called the Daigaku-Ha (University Group), and their poems were of a classic style in seven-five-syllable form, graceful though monotonous. The themes they liked to treat were of the world of the classical romances, and the language they used was therefore neo-classical. This school, with its traditional and classical tastes, appealed to some people, but its adherents were set apart from the main current and did not contribute to the development of a new poetic form.

In opposition to the neo-classicism of the Daigaku-Ha, the poets of *Jojōshi* (Lyric Poetry) (1897) expressed their youthful sentiment simply. *Jojōshi* was a collection of works by Kunikida Doppo (Tetsuo), Matsuoka Kunio, Tayama Katai (Rokuya), Ōta Gyokumei (Harutsuna), Yazaki Saganoya (Chinshirō), and Miyazaki Koshoshi, in whom there was considerable difference of personality yet similarity in the free and frank expression of their emotion. Matsuoka Kunio, particularly, displayed his ability to express fresh and youthful sentiment, as in the following :

Sono no shimizu o kumiagete
Kakine no hana ni kaketsureba
Sanagara tsuyu to narinikeri,
Kimi ga kokoro o kumitorite
Aware to iishi kotonoha zo
Tsui ni koi to wa narinikeru.

When I scooped up the clear water from the garden fountain
And sprinkled it among the hedge flowers,
It turned into dewdrops ;
When I scooped the secret from your heart
And told you that I pitied you,
With the passage of time it turned into love.

(From *Sono no Shimizu*, The Clear Water in the Garden)

A pure and simple love is symbolized in the beauty of nature and expressed with a sentimentality such as we later find in Tōson. Their poems never advanced beyond this kind of naivety and technical simplicity, but *Jojōshi* was like a morning star, foretelling the dawning of modern poetry in Tōson's *Wakanashū* (The Young Herbs Anthology).

It was Kitamura Tōkoku (Montarō) who among the group of early poets epitomizes the spiritual struggles of the time most clearly. The intellectual world of the twentieth year of Meiji (1887) was gradually emerging from the confused stage of imitating Western civilization, and a new movement arose to discover the awakening of the self in Romantic idealism.

Tōkoku was a pioneer in the world of poetry. He sang of the scepticism and rebellion of man who realizes the disparity between the real and the ideal. In *Soshū no Shi* (A Prisoner's Poem) (1889), Tōkoku expressed his thought through the symbol of the suffering of a prisoner. In *Hōraikyoku* (The Song of Fairyland) (1891), he expresses his view of life passionately; the poem relates the inner contradiction and agony in the person of a young man who wanders through both the real and the transcendental worlds. It resembles *Faust* and *The Divine Comedy*, but *Manfred* influenced it most strongly. As its dramatic construction is immature and it wants force, the poem can be called lyric rather than epic. In expression also it is too much the vehicle of ideas, and lacks the natural outflow of poetic feeling. But this poem opened up a new area in modern Japanese poetry in that it was the first time a poet confronted the serious problems of life. Tōkoku is sometimes too quick to give utterance to passion and thought, and artistic refinement often is lacking, but in the *Tōkoku-Shū* (The Tōkoku Anthology) (1894) we can find some excellent lyrics in which the poet vents his melancholy through the symbol of a butterfly or firefly. He killed himself at the age of twenty-seven, defeated in his spiritual struggles, yet he exerted a profound influence on the poets who followed him, and is universally considered to be the founder of Meiji Romanticism.

Among the writers who contributed to the *Bungakkai*, Tōson was the most prominent. He published lyrics, prose, and dramatic poetry continually from the time the magazine was founded.

His dramatic poetry will be discussed later, but with his lyric works such as *Aki no Yume* (Autumn Dreams) (1896), which includes *Akikaze no Uta* (The Song of the Autumn Wind) and eight other poems, and *Usugōri* (Thin Ice) (1896), which includes *O-Yō, O-Kinu, O-Sayo, O-Kume, O-Tsuta*, and *O-Kiku,* both of which are included in his *Wakanashū*, he proclaimed the dawn of modern poetry, establishing definitely the Romanticism that Tōkoku had begun.

We have glanced at the practical side of the New Style poetry group; on the theoretical side, also, investigations were made from various viewpoints. First, the essays on poetry by Yamada Bimyō must be mentioned. Bimyō was one of the most versatile and talented men of his day, and dealt with all sorts of problems in the world of poetry : the compilation of anthologies, the editing of the magazine *Iratsume* (The Maiden), the publishing of poetry in both the colloquial and literary language, poems for children, war songs, narrative poems, and translations from Western poetry. In the field of poetic theory he aroused a controversy with Ningetsu, Roan, and Ōgai by publishing *Nihon Imbun Ron* (A Treatise on Japanese Poetry) in *Kokumin no Tomo* from October 1890 to January 1891. The subjects he treated ranged from that of form to the very nature of poetry.

Bimyō selected the term *imbun* (rhythmical literature) to correspond to poetry, determined its peculiar characteristic to be *sessō* (rhythm), and planned the advancement of Japanese poetry by fixing anew its *inkaku* (rhythmical form). As essential problems in poetry, he argued that it was the poet's function to know the universe intuitively or to listen to the voice of Nature and apprehend the truth, and demanded that the poets achieve sincerity (*seishin*) as the way to adore Nature and to enter into harmony with it. He further contended that in the Western countries people were deprived of this sincerity toward Nature by agnosticism, and that the development of ontology and logic had narrowed imagination and caused the decline of poetry, while in Japan suggestiveness (*yojōshugi*) had weakened "the relation between philosophy and poetry." Japanese poets had come to be overly concerned with elegant and refined phrasing or the mere describing of reality. In opposition to Bimyō, Ōgai contended that the former's view of Western poetry was groundless ; he also contradicted the view that philosophy should be emphasized in poetry, while as for suggestiveness, he felt it should be valued highly in that the reader would "feel the shadow of the greater universe in the picture of the smaller universe" which emerges from the short verse form. Ōgai's position was founded on the aesthetics of Hartmann. (*Bimyōsai Shujin ga Imbun Ron*, Bimyōsai's "Theory of Poetry," 1891).

It is not clear how the defects in Japanese poetry which Bimyō pointed out relate to form, but he nevertheless asserted that it was necessary to make rules on metre in poetry. After having compared the metres in Japanese, Chinese, and Western poetry, he understood the tone of the sounds of Japanese as being dependent on the length, and fixed twelve kinds of metre, such as short-long, long-short, short-short-long, etc., and gave his explanation of each. At this proposal Ōgai was sceptical, and it cannot be denied that it was rather absurd of Bimyō to apply Western prosody to Japanese poetry.

Following *Nihon Imbun Ron*, there were published Ōnishi Sōzan's (Shuku) *Shiika Ron Ippan* (Notes on Poetry) (1890), Isogai Umpō's *Kokushi Ron* (A Treatise on Japanese Poetry) (1892), and Miyazaki Koshoshi's *Imbun Shoken* (Views on Poetry) (1892), which dealt with the same problems that Bimyō had treated. Concerning the problem of rhythm, Ōnishi also contended that the metre in Japanese poetry should be based on the number of sounds in a word, and on the point that the five-seven-syllable pattern was basic, there was almost complete agreement.

Thereafter, with the progress in poetic writing, the problem of metre and vocabulary came under discussion repeatedly. Toyama Chuzan thought emotional oration (*kanjōteki kōen*) was a requisite of New Style poetry, and said that the poet should not adhere to either the seven-five or the five-seven-syllable metre but should use "any and every form of poetry" according to the various ideas and feeling expressed. (From *Shintai Shiikashū*, Introduction, 1895). He accused the University Poets of using too many archaic words, metaphors, and stock epithets, with the result that "the meaning became obscure." (*Shintaishi oyobi Rōdokuhō*, New Style Poetry and the Method of Reciting, 1896). These dissertations were endorsed by Hayashi Onota and Takayama Chogyū, who attached importance to the content of poetry, but were carefully refuted by Shimamura Hōgetsu. Hōgetsu said that metre is absolutely "necessary in the realm of lyric poetry," (*Shintaishi no Katachi ni tsuite*, On the Form of New Style Poetry, 1895) and that it would be "to make a poem prosaic" to require clarity. He further stated that even in an obscure poem a kind of obscure beauty must be recognized. (*Mōrōtai to wa Nan zo ya*, What Is Obscure Style?, 1896). Furthermore, concerning diction, a controversy arose in 1897 between Inoue Sonken, who wished to adopt the colloquial and reject the archaic language, and Takeshima Hagoromo and Ōmachi Keigetsu who opposed him. Thus, discussion of poetic theory became increasingly lively.

We should also say a few words about *kanshi* (Chinese poetry). The word *shi* (poetry) meant Chinese poetry at the beginning of Meiji as has been mentioned above, but at the end of the era it meant New Style poetry, which fact testifies to the vicissitudes of the old and new poetry. Chinese poetry did not occupy a central position in Meiji literature, and yet it did occupy a special place in a corner of the literary world. New Style poetry in its early stage was looked upon as a youngster's sport, while Chinese poetry enjoyed a wide support by people of all ages, and poets' groups, anthologies, magazines, and newspaper columns opened to contributions of Chinese poetry, and maintained its existence throughout the Meiji Era.

Mori Shuntō, who started *Shimbunshi* (New Prose and Poetry)

(1875), introduced the new Ch'ing style of poetry in opposition to the traditional Sung style, while Mori Kainan, his son, formed the Seisha (The Star Society), and exercised a great influence through the Meiji twenties (1887–1896); indeed, father and son were the center of the Chinese poetry world. Among the minor poets who gathered around the Moris, Ono Kozan, Honda Shuchiku, and Kokubu Seigai were the most significant. But in general those who wrote Chinese poems were so steeped in the tradition of Chinese literature that they tried to express old-fashioned feelings in stereotyped phrases which in no way appealed to the modern sense. Only *Kōjo Shiragiku no Uta*, a Japanese translation made by Ochiai Naobumi of the Chinese original written by Inoue Sonken, and the Chinese poems in *Omokage* which were translations of European poetry, were in keeping with the spirit of Meiji literature. It must be noted, however, that Nakano Shōyō, who stood outside of the circle of poets who specialized in Chinese poetry, expressed fresh romantic feelings through the *kanshi* medium and that Mori Ōgai and Natsume Sōseki created an unworldly, elegant mood while retaining an antiquated manner of phrasing. However, in addition to its function as traditional poetry, Chinese poetry also proved a vehicle of political criticism at the beginning of the Meiji Era. It was in this form of literature that Ōnuma Chinzan, in *Tōkyō-Shi* (Song of Tōkyō) (1869), satirized political affairs, and that Narushima Ryūhoku lampooned the society of the day and won popularity. This aspect of Chinese poetry can be seen intermittently throughout the era, and even anthologies were published, but since its followers finally tried too much to win the favor of the journalism of the day, the form came to be called *kyōshi* (comic poetry).

2. The Flowering of Romantic Poetry and Its Development

As the twentieth century approached, the new poetry became fixed in both form and content, and made preparation for the golden age of romantic poetry to come; as Shimazaki

Tōson mentioned later: "At last the age of new poetry arrived. It was like a beautiful sunrise." (From the preface to the *Tōson Shishū*, Poetical Works of Tōson, 1904). Actually, the dawning of this new poetry was nothing other than the appearance of his *Wakanashū* (The Young Herbs Anthology) (August 1897). *Wakanashū* was a collection of poems written in the year preceding the publication, and, as the author wrote in the introduction, expressed turbulent emotions in a free and fresh style; it was this anthology which immediately elevated him to the central position in the poetic world.

Most of his poems are in the seven-five-syllable metre, and in this respect we cannot consider them a new contribution to modern poetry. The content was new but not the form; he expressed his new insights with a serenity that created an unprecedented poetical beauty which revealed "the pathos and suffering of modern life." (Preface to the *Tōson Shishū*). His diction and thought were descended from traditional poetry and songs, such as those in the *Kokinshū*, and yet at the same time were greatly influenced by the Romantic poetry of England and other Western countries. Thus, in him were mingled both Eastern and Western literary techniques; in fact, in the most popular form he created a poetry that was a synthesis of the East and West.

Thus, the *Wakanashū* was the vehicle for the outpouring of the passionate, romantic feeling of Meiji youth in its purest form, and its content was the voice of youthful love crystallized. *Hatsukoi* (First Love) which described the experience of first love with a bashful girl in an apple orchard, the longer poems which relate the joy and sorrow of youth in the persons of O-Yō, O-Sayo, and four other maidens, *Kasa no Uchi* (In the Shade of an Umbrella) and *Yotsu no Sode* (Four Sleeves) which hint at a sensuous temperament—in all of these poems the very heart of the sensitive and dreamy youth seemed to have been poured forth; however, his long poems were weakened by the seven-five-syllable metre, which somehow made them commonplace and wanting in compactness. His long poem *Akikaze no Uta* (The Song of the Autumn Wind) was an exception. The source of the poem was Shelley's *Ode to the West Wind*; it contains the following stanza :

Michi o tsutauru Baramon no	As the Brahman sows the Way
Nishi ni higashi ni chiru gotoku	To the west and to the east,
Fukitadayowasu akikaze ni	The autumn wind blows and
Hirugaeriyuku konoha kana	sows
	The fallen leaves far and wide.

and is recognized as one of the best poems of the book.

Ā urasabishi ametsuchi no	O sad and dreary autumn day,
Tsubo no uchi naru aki no hi ya	In the urn of heaven and earth
Ochiba to tomo ni hirugaeru	Who can tell where the wind
Kaze no yukue o tare ka shiru	goes
	That tumbles with the fallen leaves ?

The above is the last stanza of the same poem, which exquisitely expresses the bleak and dreary autumn atmosphere, and attains an almost perfect symbolism.

After *Wakanashū*, Tōson published *Hitotsubashū* (The One Leaf Anthology) (1898) and *Natsugusa* (Summer Grass) (1898), both of which contain long poems, but the truly excellent pieces in them are few.

His fourth volume, *Rakubaishū* (The Fallen Plum Blossom Anthology) (1901), was his last collection of poems. After *Wakanashū* this collection contained the greatest number of his best poems and showed the deepest poetic insight. The romantic lyric mood that runs through *Wakanashū* is echoed in six poems entitled *Mune yori Mune ni* (From Heart to Heart), although most of the poems deal with the love of a middle-aged man and give the impression that he had become more introspective. This book is significant rather for the poetry of travel which has a note of resignation with regard to the uncertainties of life.

Komoro naru kojō no hotori
Kumo shiroku yūshi kanashimu
Midori nasu hakobe wa moezu
Wakakusa mo shiku ni yoshi nashi
Shirogane no fusuma no okabe
Hi ni tokete awayuki nagaru

At the ruins of Komoro Castle
Clouds float white and the
    traveler feels sad ;
The chickweed has not yet
    come out,
And the young grass is still
    too sparse to stretch him-
    self upon.
Along the slope of the silvery
    mountains
Light snow melts in the sun
    and trickles down.

This poem, *Komoro naru Kojō no Hotori* (At the Ruins of Komoro Castle), which expresses a traveler's sentiment in early spring with the somewhat ponderous five-seven-syllable metre, was loved by the people, together with the poem *Chikumagawa Ryojō no Uta* (Song of a Traveler on the Chikuma River). In contrast with *Akikaze no Uta*, the theme of which was taken from a European concept, here Tōson borrowed much from Tu Fu's *Spring Scenes* and Bashō's *Oku no Hosomichi* (The Narrow Road of Oku), and revealed his attitude of resignation toward the struggles of life and his meditation of eternity. That he felt the evanescence of life keenly was further shown in *Yashi no Mi* (A Cocoanut) and *Hibiki Rin Rin Oto Rin Rin* (Jingling Sounds), and this became his keynote. Thus, Tōson reached an impasse, broke off his career as a poet, and turned to prose to write on more realistic aspects of life, such as he began to develop in *Nōfu* (The Farmer) in *Natsugusa* and *Rōdō Zatsuei* (Songs of Labor in the Field) of the *Rakubaishū*.

Tōson's poetry gave new life to traditional Japanese poetic feeling and was the forerunner of Romantic poetry, but in some quarters he was criticised as a poet of "effeminate," "vague" verses because of his delicate style and excessive sentimentality. The different spirit which was occasioned by the outbreak of the Sino-Japanese War turned from the inner struggle of the modern age and looked forward to some more masculine national poet. In this sense, Tsuchii (Doi) Bansui (Rinkichi), who established another school of Romantic poetry, was favored by the common people.

Bansui began his career as a University poet somewhat later than Tōson, and published his works in *Teikoku Bungaku* and the *Hansei Zasshi* (The Magazine of Introspection). He was introduced into the literary world by his friend Takayama Chogyū, and was known as one gifted with unique and artistic talent among the neo-classic poets. By the time *Tenchi Ujō* (The Sentient World) (1899), a collection of these poems, was published, Bansui had taken his stand as a leading poet, almost abreast of Tōson.

He was also a man of European culture but presented a marked contrast with Tōson on various points. Unlike Tōson who enveloped British Romantic poetry in genuine and graceful Japanese sentiment, Bansui, under the influence of Hugo and Schiller, attempted to approach his ideal by making use of a virile Chinese style; his style was unique in that he alluded to history or legend and composed lengthy historical or narrative poems, proclaiming loudly his ideals with a masculine note, and this gave him the reputation of being an intellectual (*shisō shijin*) and meditative poet (*meisō shijin*). His theme was simple : he sang of the eternity of the universe, deplored the change of things, lamented the vicissitudes of the heroes' fortunes. This attitude of retrospection had always been one of the themes of the Oriental poets, and Bansui did not go beyond it. He said that " poetry should not be the idle talk of an idle man ; poetry should not be simply technique," (from the foreword to *Tenchi Ujō*) and that " it is essential for the advancement of national poetry today to reform the fundamental ideas with regard to poetry." (From the notes to the same book). He put this ambitious opinion into practice, using words of Chinese origin with skill and virility, and thus epitomizing the spirit of the times.

In *Tenchi Ujō, Hoshi Otsu Shūfū Gojōgen* (The Stars Fall and the Autumn Wind Blows on the Field of Gojō) and *Boshō* (The Evening Bell) are the best poems; the former relates with pathos a tale, drawn from ancient Chinese history, about the surviving retainers of a fallen dynasty, and the latter is a meditative work which deplores the vicissitudes of life, hearing the voice of "formless," "boundless" eternity in the bell which "tolls every evening in this defiling world."

Tenchi ujō no yūmagure	On an evening in this sentient world
Waga sanran no yume samete	
Hōrō itsu ka ato mo naku	I awoke from my brilliant dream,
Hana mo nioi mo yūzuki mo	And the Phoenix Pavilion was gone without a trace.
Utsutsu wa moroki haru no yo ya	The blossom and the scent and the evening moon, too—
	Reality is the evanescent world of spring.

This stanza, which is near the end of the poem, is quite unique in its rhythm and the pleasing effect of the Chinese phrasing.

The long poem *Banri no Chōjō no Uta* (Song of the Great Wall of China) and the short *Ōi naru Te no Kage* (The Shadow of a Big Hand) are the outstanding poems of the second collection, *Gyōshō* (The Morning Bell) (1901). In the former, Bansui writes of the vanity of human accomplishment which he felt on viewing the ruins of the Great Wall. Beautiful phrases can be found in the first and second stanzas.

Rakujitsu hikuku kumo awaku	The sun is low and the clouds are sparse
Kanzan misu misu kuren to su	Over the barrier mountain where evening falls;
Seisan uramitodomarite	Regretfully the sturdy horse halts,
Fugyō no yūshi mi wa hitori	As the traveler lingers over the scene.

Zetsuiki hana wa mare nagara	At the far limits the plains
Heibu no midori ima fukashi	are deep green
Haru kenkon ni megurite wa	Though flowers are rare ;
Kasumanu sora mo nakarikeri	Spring returns to the world,
	And no place remains where
	the sky is not curtained by
	mist.

Though the sentiment is old-fashioned, it is expressed compactly and forcefully. But Bansui's poems primarily lacked a modern style and introspection ; therefore, after *Gyōshō* he fell away from the main current of poetry as had Tōson. It is true that he published a volume, *Tōkai Yūshi Gin* (Songs of the Traveler from the East), in 1906, but by that time he was already estranged from the poets' world.

About the time when Tōson and Bansui closed their poetic activity the twentieth century began. From then on, until 1904 –1905, the new Romantic poetry matured, and the Seikin-Ha, or the Star and Violet school (so named because of the poets' habit of referring to stars and flowers in order to express their romantic dreams and longings), flourished and dominated the literary world. In April of 1900 Yosano Tekkan (Hiroshi) began publishing *Myōjō* (The Morning Star), a periodical which led the main current of this Romantic movement. Kambara Ariake, Susukida Kyūkin, and other leading poets of the time contributed their works to this magazine, which at the same time also nurtured a great number of new poets.

Yosano Tekkan, who had made his entry into the poets' circle earlier than Bansui, towers high above his contemporaries both in traditional Japanese poetry (*tanka*) and in the new-type poetry. Most of his collections of poetry contain works in both styles. *Tōzainamboku* (East, West, North, and South) (1896) and *Tenchigen'ō* (The Universe) (1897), the earlier collections, are notable for the author's political consciousness and sentimentality, while *Tekkan-Shi* (Tekkan the Man) (1901) and *Murasaki* (Purple) (1901) reveal the poet's concern with the problem of love. His *Umoregi* (The Fossil Wood) (1902) and *Dokugusa* (Poison Grasses) (1904) contain the best of his poems, the latter being a work of collaboration with his wife. As was the case with Bansui, he followed the style of Chinese poetry, but unlike Bansui, within this compact style he infused a note of melancholy, and as a result created a novel effect. For instance, *Haika* (The Broken Leaves of the Lotus), which begins with :

Yūbe Shinobazu no ike yuku	In the dusk I walk beside
Namida ochizaramu ya	Shinobazu* Pond—
Hasu orete tsuki usuki	How can I restrain my tears ?
	Lotus leaves are broken and
	the moon is dim.

* which means, literally, "cannot be endured"

achieved a success, making use of this style to express the sadness of lost love. *Kogane Higuruma* (The Golden Sunflower) can be called his masterpiece ; it treats of the ultimate state of poetry, the wording being luxuriant and almost exhausting the vocabulary.

Hitomoto mori no kogane higuruma	A brilliant coronet of golden
Shiika no sei naru kimi ni okuru	sunflower
Ō no tabinishi ju no murasaki	I hold to you, an earthly Muse.
Tarete musubite kazashimase	Take it and tie it with the
	purple ribbon
	That you've been given of the
	Sage King of Poetry.

Tekkan's works were characterized by colorfulness and word-painting, and were alive with romantic fantasy ; he actually created a school of romantic poetry of his own, but, on the other hand, he was deficient in knowledge of European literature and lacked the introspective quality necessary to sustain the richness of his language. After *Dokugusa* he returned to his real name of Hiroshi, and endeavored to keep in close touch with the new trends in poetry ; he published *Kashi no Ha* (Oak Leaves) (1910), but historically he belongs to the Romantic stage of Japanese poetry.

Among the younger poets who joined Tekkan's Shinshisha (New Poetry Society), some of whom later left it, were Sōma Gyofū, Maeda Ringai, Chino Bou (Shōshō), Hirano Chōei (Banri), Ishikawa Takuboku, Kitahara Hakushū, Ōta Masao (Kinoshita Mokutarō), and others. Yosano Akiko, wife of Yosano Tekkan, also wrote poems and published them in *Dokugusa* and *Koigoromo* (The Robe of Love) (1905), but her province was the *tanka*, not new poetry. Takuboku, the poet of *Akogare* (Longing) (1905), attracted public attention by his genius, but at this stage he was no more than a young poet who was skilful in imitating his predecessors.

Maeda Ringai (Gisaku), who dissociated himself from the Shinshisha, published the magazine *Shirayuri* (White Lily) in 1903, together with Sōma Gyofū and Iwano Hōmei. He tried eight-seven-syllable metre poetry in his *Natsuhana Otome* (Summer Flower Maiden) (1905) and *Hana-Zuma* (Flower Lady) (1906). He went beyond the *Myōjō* style in his fantastic and luxuriant beauty of language, but his poetry lacked unity of thought.

Outside of the magazine *Myōjō*, in addition to Susukida Kyūkin and Kambara Ariake, there were Takayasu Gekkō, Hiraki Hakusei who showed talent in the epic, Yoshino Gajō who at an early age showed talent in lyric poetry, Iwano Hōmei, Kodama Kagai, and many other poets. Hōmei, who later played an active part in the development of poetic theory, brought out collections of poems such as *Yūshio* (The Evening Tide) (1904) and *Hiren Hika* (Sad Songs of a Sad Love) (1905) at this time, as well as *Kaihōgishi* (The Coast Battery Engineer) (1905), a dramatic poem which displayed his strong will and passionate nature, but he did not achieve much success with any of them. Kodama Kagai, who became famous with his *Shakaishugi Shishū* (A Collection of Socialist Poetry) which was banned, published *Kagai Shishū* (Poems by Kagai) (1904) and *Yuku Kumo* (The Departing Clouds) (1906). All of his poems had a simple note of lamentation, and actually were far from being socialistic, but there was a flow of sincerity which appealed to the reading public.

One of the most significant features of the period was the magazine *Bunko* (The Literary Storehouse). (The title had been changed from the *Shōnen Bunko*, The Boys' Literary Storehouse, which in 1895 had grown out of the *Shōnen-En*, The Boys' Garden.) The magazine was originally published as one to which young boys would contribute, and naturally it was outside of the main current of the poetic world, but the seven-five-syllable type of composition, which was used therein to express simple and pure sentiment, was widely loved and called the *Bunko* style. Among the contributors, Kawai Suimei, Yokose Yau, and Irako Seihaku are noteworthy, and all of them at this time entered the period of their greatest activity.

Kawai Suimei (Matahei) was the editor of the *Bunko* from the time when it was renamed, and it was he who built up the magazine. His poetic style was simple and graceful, yet lacking in individuality. After publishing *Mugenkyū* (The Bow with No String) (1901) and his second anthology *Tōei* (The Shadow of the Pagoda) (1905), he established his own poetic style. *Tōei* (The Shadow of the Pagoda), the title poem, and *Dairi-Bina* (The Doll Emperor and Empress) are particularly fine pieces. The former describes the symmetry of a five-storied pagoda and praises the eternity of art:

Irihi wa nishi ni katamuite	The setting sun inclines toward the west,
Gojū no yane no azayaka ni	While on the grass is reproduced
Kasanari utsuru kusa no ue	Distinctly the fivefold roof;
Tsuki wa hisashi ni ukabiide	The moon emerges from the eaves,
Kokonoe no kage wa mizu ni ari	And the shadow of the spire is cast on the water.

He unerringly and thoroughly expresses the monochrome beauty of the scene. In *Tamamushi* (Iridescence) (1906), an anthology which he published after *Ken'ei* (The Shadow of the Sword)

(1905), the poem *Ochiba o Taku Uta* (The Song of the Burning of Fallen Leaves) is superbly written.

Yokose Yau (Toraju) was an even more prominent figure than Kawai Suimei. He was the author of *Yūzuki* (The Evening Moon) (1899), *Hanamori* (The Gardener) (1905), and *Nijūhasshuku* (Twenty-Eight Relay Stations) (1907). His peculiarity was that sentimental poetic style which is born of physical deformity, and it represented very well a facet of the *Bunko* style. He adopted the diction of Japanese folk songs as in *O-Sai* in the *Yūzuki* anthology, and conveyed a feeling of pathos which was widely loved and caused his poems to be recited by many. He took much of his material from the life of his native Mt. Tsukuba district and won fame as the Tsukuba Poet. *No ni Yama Ariki* (There Was a Hill in the Field) in *Nijūhasshuku* is the most accomplished work of this pastoral elegiac kind.

The characteristics of *Bunko* poetry can be learned from the restrained and graceful style of Suimei and the pastoral sentimentality of Yau, but there was another man who went far beyond them and who demonstrated a rare genius among Meiji poets: Irako Seihaku (Kunzō, Suzushironoya). Irako contributed his poetical works to the *Bunko* while it was still called the *Shōnen Bunko*. He condensed his whole work in single volume, *Kujakubune* (The Peacock Boat), and disappeared from the literary world. This work contains eighteen gems selected from more than a hundred and fifty poems of his, and therefore from the point of density, it belongs to the first rank of Meiji poetry. It is natural that the works showed variety in style, technique, and content. The exact juxtaposition of the words, a clear, intellectual sense, and a mystic fantasy—all these elements of his work represent the characteristics of the post-Romantic poetry of the era. *Hyōhaku* (Wandering Journey), which appeared at the beginning of the book, relates a fantasy of the traveler's dead parents:

Nakihaha wa otome to narite	My mother has become a
Shiroki nuka tsuki ni araware	maiden

Whose white forehead appears
in the moon.

Nakichichi wa warawa to narite
Maroki kata Ginga o wataru

My father has become a boy
Whose round shoulder crosses
the Milky Way.

and in it the feelings in the heart of the traveler, who recalls his childhood, are as the music of a wild pipe. Another poem, *Akiwa no Sato* (The Village of Akiwa), begins with:

Tsuki ni shizumeru shiragiku no
Aki susamajiki kage o mite
Chikuma otome no tamashii no
Nukekaidetaru kokochi seru

A girl of Chikuma
Looks at the bleak autumn
landscape
Where white chrysanthemums
are immersed in the moon-
light
And feels as if her soul were
expressed therein.

and showed his skilful expression of sensation; both works are excellent pieces charged with the traveler's feeling. *Satsukino* (The May Field) depicts a beautiful naked woman who appears at a lake at midday in a hot, southern country. Here his mystic and fantastic feeling is controlled by a compact poetic sense, and made an excellent poem. Among the rest, *Anori no Chigo* (A Boy of Anori) is a masterpiece describing the grandeur and bleakness of the Anori promontory of the province of Shima that he loved. He introduces a boy who faces the crashing waves while sitting in a lonely cottage beside the sea:

Arakabe no koie hitomura
Kodama suru kokoro to kokoro
Chigo hitori osore o shirazu
Hohoemite umi ni kotaeri

In a village of small houses
roughly plastered,
Where heart echoes to heart,
A lad, alone and unafraid,
Smiles and faces the sea.

and thus he realizes something akin to religious benevolence in the poem.

In addition to these men, Takizawa Shūgyō, Hazue Tsuyuko, Shimizu Kisson, Isshiki Seisen, Yamazaki Shikō, Komaki Bochō,

Mizoguchi Hakuyō, Hirai Banson, and Sawamura Koi also contributed poems to the *Bunko*. Koi's *Kohan no Hika* (A Lakeside Elegy) (1907) was a notable collection in which are found *Dan-no-Ura* (first printed in the *Bunko*) and other poems which testified to his talent. Other writers who came from the *Bunko* and are known to the reading public are Kubota Utsubo, who published *Mahiruno* (Midday Field) (1905), Kubota Yamayuri (Toshihiko, Tsukahara Fukuryū, Shimaki Akahiko), Mizuno Yōshū, Kitahara Hakushū, Miki Rofū, and Kawaji Ryūkō. Indeed, the *Bunko* played a most significant role in Meiji literature.

It is natural that the aspiring romantic self seeks for the fulfilment of life in a far-off world, that it discovers a new and rare beauty in legends of ancient and strange lands, and that poets should try to capture in a new poetic form the delicate inner feeling which has become more complicated with the passage of time. Thus, the poetic world that set out with the fancy and longings of the Seikin-Ha (the Star and Violet School) in about 1903 began to make a new attempt at long epics—the *Myōjō* being the center of the movement—or at a new type of poetry beyond the traditional seven-five or five-seven-syllable verses. Succeeding Tōson and Bansui, Susukida Kyūkin (Junsuke) and Kambara Ariake (Hayao) played remark-able roles in the experimentation with new types. The two poets advanced side by side, but the latter contributed to the establishment of Symbolist poetry of the next period, while the former succeeded in perfecting his romantic poems by his unique use of classical language.

Kyūkin's career as a poet began at the end of the Meiji twenties. The years he was writing the poems of *Botekishū* (The Evening Flute Anthology) (1899) and of *Yuku Haru* (The Departing Spring) (1901) constitute a period of apprentice-ship; he then wrote long epics which grow into *Nijūgogen* (Twenty-Five Strings) (1905), and after publishing the poetic anthology *Shiratama-Hime* (The White Pearl Princess) in the same year, he brought out *Hakuyōkyū* (1906) which demonstrated his accomplishment.

Kyūkin studied John Keats from an early age, and tried to translate the latter's sonnets in an eight-six-syllable metre and fourteen lines. He called the form *zekku* (broken off verse). Most of his earlier works possess the same graceful and lyrical quality that is shown in Tōson's poems, but compared with those of the passionate Tōson, his are more intellectual. He had a good command of archaic poetical language, and his inner passion seemed to be controlled considerably by his judicious usage of a classical vocabulary. This tendency came from his liking for archaism, and led to his peculiar manner of writing which emphasized beauty of form by utilizing archaic language with good sense, and thereby establishing another type of romantic poetry than that of Tōson.

His third collection of poems, *Nijūgogen*, displayed his genius most clearly. For the long epics contained therein, he took material from his own fancy or from old romantic legends, and with a grand theme and variegated intellectual imagery or idealistic metaphors he succeeded in creating a brilliant effect. Among the poems were *Raijin no Uta* (Song of the Thunder God), the material for which was taken from a legend of the Kamo Shrine of Kyōto concerning a red arrow, *Kongō-San no Uta* (Song of the Diamond Mountains) that sang of the magnificent view of the Diamond Mountains of Korea, and *Amahasezukai no Uta* (Song of the Messenger-Angel), the story of which was a combined one of the legend of Yomotsuhira Hill about the gods Izanagi and Izanami, and the legends about Amanohashidate and the Hagoromo (the Robe of Feathers). Later, in 1906, Kyūkin published in *Waseda Bungaku* the unfinished *Katsuragi no Kami* (The God Katsuragi) which imitated Aeschylus' *Prometheus Bound*. *Amahasezukai no Uta* was a magnificent long poem. It begins with the description of the god Izanagi who waits for the goddess Izanami :

Yomotsuōto no sotogamae	In the deep of
Karasuguro naru kurayami no	The crow-black darkness
Kami no fukami ni	Outside the gigantic gate of Hell

and it depicts a world similar to that of Greek mythology. These epics were indeed laborious works, but it is undeniable that the monotonous seven-five-syllable metre and the rigid archaic vocabulary hindered the natural development of the narrative. In this regard, *Kōsonjuka ni Tachite* (Under a Gingko Tree) which begins with :

Ā, hi wa kanata	O the sun is far away
Itariya no	Above the ruins of the Seven Hills
Nanatsu no oka no furuato ya	Of the Italian capital

was a successful work. It pictures a great gingko tree that stands on the plateau of Mimasaka as if rebelling against the changes of nature, and from its eternal warfare with the elements the poet tells of human struggles ; with its medium length the poem has a stable beauty.

The fifth anthology, *Hakuyōkyū*, upon publication was highly praised by the leading poets, including Ueda Bin. Now Kyūkin was at his peak. His representative works are *Ā Yamato nishi Aramashikaba* (O to Be in Yamato) and *Bōkyō no Uta* (Song of Homesickness). The former was composed after Browning's poem *Home Thoughts from Abroad* :

Ā, Yamato ni shi aramashikaba	O to be in Yamato
Ima kaminazuki	Now that November is here—
Uwaba chiri suku kaminabi no mori no komichi o	Through the wooded paths of Kaminabi
Akatsukizuyu ni kami nurete yuki koso kayoe	Where the upper leaves have dropped and now are rare,
Ikaruga e. Heguri no ōno, takakusa no	My hair wet with morning dew,

Kogane no umi to yurayuru hi   I would go to the villages of
                                   Ikaruga. The Heguri plain
                                   Where the sea of tall grass
                                   sways and glitters in the
                                   golden sun—

The longing for the old capital of the Tempyō Period noted
for its art is exquisitely expressed with words that have rich associations with ancient matters. The use of this archaic vocabulary to which he seemed to have been addicted proves
advantageous here ; old and new words are well balanced, and
the rhythm which is mainly formed by the alternating of
nineteen-syllable and seventeen-syllable lines conveys a delicate
mood, and helps greatly in making the poem a romantic work.
In *Bōkyō no Uta* is found an echo of that famous song of
Mignon of Goethe. It begins with

Waga furusato wa   My native place is where
Hi no hikari semi no ogawa ni   The sun warms the brook of
uwanurumi   of the cicada
Ariki no eda ni irodori no   And the colored birds warble
nagamegoe suru hinagasa o   the livelong day
                                  Among the branches of the
                                    trees there.

and in the description of the natural scenery of the ancient
city of Kyōto during the four seasons of the year, the poet
expressed his longing for the cultural world of the feudal era.
In this poem his technique really attained perfection.

Kyūkin's propensity for the classical mood was based on a
very limited taste of his own. This is known from the weakness he betrayed in his epics and the failure he had when he
tried to adopt the ballad mode in composing the poems of
Shiratama-Hime. Furthermore, although he was an accomplished poet and had elegance and intellectual clarity, he lacked
the power to express the nuances of modern sentiments, and
this made him estrange himself from the poets' circle of the
day. By the time *Hakuyōkyū* was published, Symbolist poetry
had come into full sway, and in that collection were included

such poems as *Waga Yuku Umi* (The Sea to Which I Go), *Tama no Tokoi* (The Everlasting Well of the Soul), and *Nukago* (The Yam), which approached the realm of idealistic symbolism, although he had to surrender to Ariake in this style. When he completed his masterpieces, the world of Meiji poetry had arrived at its most flourishing period. It was the time when Osanai Kaoru published *Ono no Wakare* (Parting at the Field) (1905) as a special issue of the magazine *Shichinin* (Seven Men) and Kōda Rohan brought out *Kokoro no Ato : Shutsuro* (Traces of the Heart : Emergence from Retirement) (1905). The publication of books of poetry also attained its highest point of the Meiji Era. And yet the completion of the old was merely the signal for the beginning of the new.

3. *The Emergence and Development of Symbolist Poetry*

Meiji poetry underwent a tremendous change in 1905 with the appearance of Symbolist poetry. Originally, the poetry called *shintaishi* was formed after the pattern of the British and American Romantic poets, and therefore it did not possess the modern significance of the post-Naturalistic novels and post-Symbolist poetry of the West. Japan's poetic circle now listened to the new voice from abroad and took the first steps toward a modern poetry. It was the time when the term *shintaishi* was abandoned and *shi* (poem) or *chōshi* (long poem) adopted.

French Symbolist poetry was first transplanted to the soil of Japanese literature with the publication of the *Kaichōon* (The Sound of the Sea Tide), a collection of translated poems by Ueda Bin, but it was Kambara Ariake who actually created Symbolist poetry in Japanese and became its founder in Japan. Ariake appeared some time after Kyūkin, and his subtle style tinged with a meditative mood placed him directly opposite the latter poet. He had devoted himself to D. G. Rossetti for many years, and revealed the influence in his *Kusa-Wakaba* (Young Leaves) (1902) and *Dokugen Aika* (A Single-Stringed Elegy) (1903) with which he rivalled Kyūkin. Ariake, however, was late in becoming conscious of where his talents lay, for in the introduction to his third book, the *Shunchōshū* (The Spring Bird Anthology) (1905), he declared that he would consciously create Symbolist poetry thereafter, that he intended " to select the metre, syllable, diction, and new words to fit the new thought," and that he would " remove the restrictions of language and make it free to express modern ideas." He also declared that he found in Bashō " the most symbolic literature of Japan," and that it was he who fixed the limits of modern symbolism " where the senses of sight and hearing blend," and " the senses of smell and taste feel the incense of the soul."

The *Shunchōshū* marks the influence of Rossetti in its diction, and it includes the masterpieces *Hi no Ochibo* (Gleanings in the Sun), *Shizuka ni Sameshi Tamashii no* (The Soul Wakes Quietly), and *Asa Nari* (It Is Morning). *Asa Nari* especially was widely discussed, for, despite certain faults, it described the dawning waterfront felt by the interwoven senses with fresh, impressionist touches. This volume also cultivated virgin soil in creating long romantic narrative poems equalling those of Kyūkin, among which were *Hime ga Kyoku* (A Song of the Princess), a tale of a southern land, and *Sabi Ono* (The Rusty Axe), which attempted the psychological development of a legend. Both poems follow the technique of the ballad that Rossetti used, and succeeded in creating an exquisite beauty. Nevertheless, the *Shunchōshū*, as can be ascertained from these pieces, is notable for its transitional qualities where Romantic and Symbolist elements are intermixed. Thus, Ariake came to maturity with the subsequent publication of his fourth collection of poems, and with it he reared Japan's greatest monument of Symbolist poetry.

The *Ariake-Shū* (The Ariake Anthology) was published in January 1908 containing forty-eight poems of his own and four translations which he wrote after the *Shunchōshū*. To the inner, subtle feelings that he originally infused in his poems, he added most careful refinements, and as a result an unparalleled style was born. A typical piece is *Hyō no Chi* (Leopard's Blood) placed at the beginning of the volume, eight sonnet-type, four-stanza, fourteen-line linked poems, the scheme of which consists of ponderous seven-five-seven-syllable lines and five-seven-five-syllable lines intermixed. The poet had tried this scheme in *Dokugen Aika* with success, but here he achieved another success-ful result with a different charm. Among the poems, *Chie no Sōja wa Ware o Mite* (A Wise Fortune-Teller Saw Me) and *Matsurika* (The Flower of the Matsuri) are masterpieces. The former symbolizes the mental process from the struggle between reason and amorous desire to the succeeding surrender to the latter. The compressed first stanza, which signifies the voice of reason,

Chie no sōja wa ware o mite kyō shi kataraku,
Na ga mami zo ko wa saga ashiku hinagumoru,
Kokoro yowaku mo hito o kou omoi no sora no
Kumo, hayachi, osowanu saki ni nogareyo to.

The wise fortune-teller saw me and told me today:
" Your features look as ominous as it does before a storm;
You have the weak spirit of one who cherishes a love.
Flee it before clouds and gale visit you."

changes to lamentable love-sorrow,

Ā nogareyo to, taoyageru kimi ga hotori o,
Midorimaki, kusano no hara no uneri yori
Nao yawarakaki kurokami no wagane no nami o,
Ko o ikani kimi wa kikiwaki tamouramu.

Flee from you ! Flee from the bewitching you,
From the tender waves of black hair, tenderer than
The sea of green grass and the verdure of the pasture—
How can you allow me to !

which is followed by the powerful images and compact construc-tion that made the poem nearly perfect.

Matsurika is characterized by its emotional symbolism where instinct and mood are interwoven, in contrast with the former where conceptual symbolism is conspicuous.

Musebi nagekōu
Waga mune no kumori monouki

Sha no tobari shinameki kakage
Kagayaka ni
Aru hi wa utsuru kimi ga omo
Kobi no no ni saku
Afuyō no nue namamekeru sono nioi

Choked with grief
The cloudy melancholy in my breast—
The silken curtain is displayed
Flutteringly—
Your face changes on certain days—
In the field of coquetry there blooms
But nearly withered a poppy with its scent.

This poem in its description of the fantasy of an unrealized love is filled with a modern melancholy and a choking sense of suffering, and constitutes a model of the poetry of Ariake.

Ariake's poems were criticized, as had been Kyūkin's for his use of obsolete words, as being difficult to understand, but this flaw came partly from the modern decadence the poems conveyed and partly from an indefinable religious aspiration, together with the struggle between the two forces; therefore, the ambiguity extended far beyond the sweet and naive lyrical feeling that is based on common sentiment; so much so that in Ariake a unique mode of poetry, which originated from modern Western poetry, was established.

Other excellent pieces in the book, such as *Tama no Hi no Shoku* (The Eclipse of the Soul), *Tsukishiro* (The Whiteness of the Moon), *Aki no Kokoro* (The Heart of Autumn), *Kojaku* (Solitude), and *Isago wa Yakenu* (Sands Are Burning), tell of the spiritual aspiration towards a world of faith that came to the poet after the experience of a decadent life deepened by the struggle between the soul and the flesh. *Kunō* (Afflictions) and *Shingyō* (Absolute Faith) are also filled with religious sentiment.

Ariake's Symbolist poetry reflected the ideological, and belonged to ideological or conceptual symbolism rather than to the emotional symbolism that was common in most of the contemporary poetry. On the other hand, at the time of the *Ariake-Shū*, " free verse " was widely discussed under the influence of Naturalism. This was the reason why the book was censured as merely following the poet's taste, even though it was recognized as highly accomplished. This censure may have been partly responsible for the decrease in his poetical production. He wrote poems after the *Ariake-Shū* which are included in the *Ariake Shishū* (The Collected Poems of Ariake) (1922), but they never excel the pieces he wrote at the prime of his career.

It was Ueda Ryūson's (Bin) *Kaichōon* (The Sound of the Sea Tide), a collection of translated poems, that contributed most to the movement and studies of Symbolist poetry as well as influenced most decisively Japan's poetry thereafter. As regards translation of Western poetry, there appeared Onoe Saishū's *Haine no Shi* (Heine's Poems) (1901) and other works, while Ariake also added some excellent translations, but none of them surpassed those of Ryūson.

Ryūson, before that, had introduced the new thought of the West through the magazines *Teikoku Bungaku* and *Myōjō*, and had enlightened the readers. His career as a translator began towards the end of 1902, and his field of work extended to the British, German, Italian, and French Parnassian and Symbolist poets, in the last of which he took most interest. The *Kaichōon* contained fifty-seven translated poems by twenty-nine original writers, and each was translated into Japanese so beautifully that even the original could hardly equal it. It should be noted that the Symbolist poems of Baudelaire, Verlaine, Verhaeren, and Mallarmé which were contained in it, were, together with the works by the Parnassians, introduced into this country for the first time, and they had a tremendous influence on the development of the poetry of Japan. The most significant was the translation of Verlaine's *Chanson d'Automne*, which the translator entitled *Rakuyō* (Fallen Leaves).

Aki no hi no
Vioron no
Tameiki no
Mi ni shimite
Shitaburu ni
Uraganashi

Thus he transferred the atmosphere of loneliness to a new type
of five-syllable lines, which continued as follows:

Kane no oto ni
Mune futagi
Iro kaete
Namidagumu
Sugishi hi no
Omoide ya

Ge ni ware wa
Uraburete
Koko kashiko
Sadame naku
Tobichirau
Ochiba kana

Even though the translation lacked the original sadness and
decadent mood, still it was successful in transmitting the emotional symbolism. The merit of this book was not restricted
to the translation of Symbolist poems. In addition to the light
German folk songs, the sober, grave pieces of Leconte de Lisle
or Hérédia seemed to have suited the translator. The translations were indeed expertly done, and he stated in the introduction
of the *Kaichōon*: "Presumably on account of my nature, my
sympathy is rather with the Parnassians." The best are *Midi*
and *Sacra Fames* of the former, *Le Récif de Corail* and *Les
Conquérants* of the latter. A double seven-five-syllable line,
i. e., a twenty-four-syllable line, was employed, or else a nineteen-syllable line and seventeen-syllable line were alternated to
create an elegant yet grave mood. His technique affected remarkably the development of the styles of both Susukida Kyūkin and Kambara Ariake.

The introduction of Symbolist poetry was much aided by Ryūson's expositions. He had already discussed the subject in 1896 in the *Teikoku Bungaku*, introducing Verlaine, Mallarmé, and their activities, together with an account of the state of French poetry ; but it was the preface of the *Kaichōon* which was truly an epoch-making event in the history of Japanese poetry, for it introduced both theory and practice. It examined the process before the birth of Symbolist poetry in France, and stated that " the purpose of Symbolist poetry is to produce in the reader a mental state that resembles the poet's idea," and made an explanation with the examples of Régnier's *La Couronne* and Verhaeren's *Parabole*. This was a most significant article in clarifying the theory and practice of Symbolism, together with his article on Mallarmé's poems and *Shōchōshi Shakugi* (An Interpretation of Symbolist Poetry) published in the magazine *Geien* (The Garden of Art) in the following year.

Now " the world of poetry that was warned of the fact that feeling and expression concerning nature and life had changed," (Introduction to the *Shunchōshū*) and heard the voice that cried, " Beware! the Muse's habitation has changed," (Preface to the *Kaichōon*) discussed Symbolism enthusiastically. We have referred to the introduction of the *Shunchōshū* above, but Katayama Koson, who introduced German Symbolist poetry, also discussed *Shinkeishitsu no Bungaku* (Sensitive Literature) in *Teikoku Bungaku* in the same year, and advocated " ideological Symbolism " (*kannen shōchō*), denouncing the " emotional Symbolism " (*jōchō shōchō*) of Volkelt in which the Symbolists of the day took much interest. Soon after there arose a controversy between Katayama and Kakuda Kōkōkakaku who gave the name of *hikyōshi* (comparative interest poetry) to Symbolist poetry. The word *shōchō* (symbol) had already been employed in the translation of Véron's *L'Esthétique* (1878), but with Hasegawa Tenkei's article *Hyōshōshugi no Bungaku* (The Literature of Symbolism) (*Taiyō*, 1905), the word *hyōshō* (also meaning symbol) came to be used generally in referring to Symbolist poetry.

We must not forget that Hasegawa Tenkei also introduced the major work of English Symbolist poetry, Arthur Symons' *Symbolist Movement in Literature*, and through it influenced the Japanese poetic world thereafter.

In Europe, the Symbolist movement was a reaction against Naturalism, but since in Japan both arose almost simultaneously, at this time discussions took place as to the relation between them. Shimamura Hōgetsu in his essay *Torawaretaru Bungei* (Captive Literature) (*Waseda Bungaku*, 1906) defined Symbolism (*hyōshōshugi*, as he called it) as a reactionary aspect of Naturalism which had been imprisoned by knowledge, and concluded that the ultimate point of the tendency was a "religious" (*shūkyōteki*) one. In opposition to him, Iwano Hōmei (Yoshie) advocated a unique theory of Symbolist poetry. As a poet he was most active in the field of poetic theory, and in his *Nihon Kodai Shisō yori Kindai no Hyōshōshugi o Ronzu* (On Modern Symbolism Seen from the Ancient Thought of Japan) in *Waseda Bungaku* (1907) he concluded that the ancient "intense secularism" (*genseishugi*) is the basis of true Symbolism, and advocated "Naturalistic Symbolism." From this standpoint he published "On the Poetry of Naturalistic Symbolism" (*Teikoku Bungaku*, 1907). There are gaps in his logic, and his argument deviates from Symbolism, but the essay was valued highly in the poetical world, as was also his essay *Shintaishi no Sakuhō* (How to Write New Style Poetry) (1907), a detailed study of rhythm. *Yami no Haiban* (Glasses and Plates in the Dark) (1908) is his representative collection of poems, excelling the romantic poems of the *Shirayuri* (The White Lily); but most of the works are too explanatory and as Symbolist poems are still in the stage of experimentation. Among them, *Tsuki to Neko* (The Moon and a Cat) and *Danaē Dokuhaku* (The Monologue of Danae) are good pieces with many well-turned phrases.

That poetic theory, as well as composition, made progress proves that Meiji poetry was gradually entering the stage of reflection on itself, and the poetry of the era was bound to show further development in relation to the trend of Naturalism.

In 1906 Noguchi Yonejirō published *Ayamegusa* (Iris) and *Toyohatakumo* (The Banks of Clouds), which contained Japanese, American, and British poems, for the purpose of having "the flowers of Eastern and Western poetry compete in fragrance," and in the next year Yoshino Gajō edited an anthology, *Meiji Shishū* (An Anthology of Meiji Poetry). The spirit of disposal of things past and the development of a new world are the undercurrent of the poets' circle after the *Kaichōon* heralded the new age. Under these circumstances, early in 1908 the *Ariake-Shū* (Ariake's Poems) was published. In November of the same year the famous *Myōjō* went out of existence after its hundredth issue. In the following year, the magazine *Subaru* (Pleiades) was published by Mori Ōgai, under whose guidance the younger poets who had belonged to the *Myōjō* played an active role in establishing Decadent poetry.

For several years after 1909 the main current of Japanese poetry proved to be a new extension of romanticism in its anti-Naturalistic phase, though it had been not a little influenced by Naturalism in style and on other points. Kitahara Hakushū, Kinoshita Mokutarō, Nagata Hideo, Takamura Kōtarō, and others of the group who were called the Decadent school, and the magazines *Subaru*, *Okujō Teien* (Roof Garden) (first published in 1909), *Zamboa* (Shaddock) (first published in 1911), and *Mita Bungaku* (Mita Literature) (first published in 1910) were the leaders.

Decadent poetry had relation primarily to the realistic feeling of Naturalism, but gradually it was led to the ecstatic world of modern beauty and displayed an essential difference from the latter. Kitahara Hakushū is the representative poet of this school and clearly showed the transition.

Kitahara Hakushū (Ryūkichi) contributed poems to the *Bunko* in his boyhood under the pseudonym of Shasui. Afterwards he joined the Shinshisha group, where, though young, he demonstrated his ability in handling a fresh vocabulary, and cut a figure as the most brilliant poet of the later Myōjō period. A series of his poems, which he called "modern poetry," was filled with a modern sense and startled the poetic world. The poems are *Jashūmon Hikyoku* (Esoteric Music for Heathen Rites), *Shitsunai Teien* (The Indoor Garden), *Akaki Sōjō* (The Crimson Priest), *Akaki Hana no Masui* (Anaesthesia of the Red Flower), and others which are included under the title of *Masui* (Anaesthesia). These poems, together with those under *Shu no Bansō* (Crimson Accompaniment) and *Gaikō no Inshō* (Impressions of Outdoor Light), constitute the essential part of the *Jashūmon* collection. Among the rest, *Jashūmon Hikyoku* and *Akaki Sōjō* are typical of the poet's "modern poetry," particularly in the array of complicated sensual images and morbid sensitiveness. While Ariake's poems are characterized by philosophical ideas and Kyūkin's are filled with retrospective longings, Hakushū's poems are notable for the novelty of material and the grotesqueness and extravagance of association. *Muhon* (Rebellion) in *Shu no Bansō* describes the stream of formless sentiment, and together with the previous *Shitsunai Teien* represents his style of Symbolist poetry. The second stanza is as follows:

Rō no hi to zange no kuyuri
Honobono to, rō izuru shiroki koromo wa
Yūgure ni mono mo naki shūdōme no nagaki hitotsura.
Saare, ima, vioron no, kurushimi no,
Sasu ga goto hinosake no, sono ito no itami naku.
Candlelight and the repentance of confession,
White robes emerging dimly from a corridor,
Of a long line of silent nuns moving in the twilight,
And now each string of the violin pierces their suffering,
Like fire-hot liquor, with its sobbing lament.

But this type of mood-evoking, symbolic work, which avoids treatment of philosophical matters and seeks to express "the subtle rhythm of inmost life" (Introduction to *Jashūmon*) is rather rare. Most works in the book show Hakushū's capabilities as a poet of delicate sense and impressibility, through a multicolored and gaudy array of impressions and through a morbid sensitivity.

It was with the publication of his second collection of poems, *Omoide* (Recollections) (1911), that Hakushū displayed his latent genius and met with an unprecedented favorable reception from the world of poetry. This book, as shown by the title, is an anthology of reminiscences dealing with the pathos, terror, and imagination of the author's childhood, and the peculiar themes and novel technique succeeded in ranking it above any Symbolist work that has ever appeared. The short form adopted here produced the ballad-like effect which had originated with Ueda Bin's *Kaichōon*. Hakushū, furthermore, inserted his native Yanagawa patois in *Rōmaji* (Romanized spelling), which was remarkably effective in creating a new exotic beauty. *Itoguruma* (Spinning-Wheel) affectionately sings of decaying beauty and the mystery of instinct:

Itoguruma, itoguruma,	Spinning-wheel, spinning-wheel,
Shizuka ni fukaki	Quietly and deep,
Te no tsumugi	With my hand do I spin
Sono itoguruma	That spinning-wheel—
Yawaraka ni	Softly
Meguru yūbe zo	As the evening turns—
Warinakere	And we are never separated

and *Aki no Hi* (An Autumn Day) conveys the nostalgia for boyhood days when the poet watched a child acrobatics:

Chiisai sono ko ga akaaka to
Tombogaeri ya, saramawashi ...
Chiisai sono ko wa shinashina to
Karada sorashite sakasama ni,
Ashi o wa ni shite, te ni ukete,
Kao o kakato ni choto hasamu.

That small child brightly—
Somersaults and spinning tricks ...
That small child nimbly—
He turns his body upside down,
His legs make a circle and are caught by his hands,
While his face is caught between his heels.

Shinnetsu (Fever), which describes untraceable terror and hallucination, *Kyōfu* (Terror), *Gannimbō* (A Shaven Head), and *Danshō* (Songs) are all also excellent poems in this collection. Hakushū's many-faceted poetical activities did not stop here. His intense pursuit of modern sensual beauty resulted in his writing a series of poems that described the urban life which he enjoyed together with the members of the Pan no Kai (The Society of the Devotees of Pan), that famous club of young men of letters. The *Tōkyō Keibutsu Shi oyobi Sono Ta* (Scenes of Tōkyō and Other Poems) (1913) included poems which sang of the exotic beauty that emerged from the concourse of the old Edo atmosphere and the modern Tōkyō's charm, and there is in it a deep note of decadence and hedonism. *Okaru Kampei* (O-karu and Kampei) (1910), which caused the magazine *Okujō Teien* to be banned, and the ballad-like *Katakoi* (Unrequited Love) (*Subaru*, 1910) are masterpieces of this type.

Kinoshita Mokutarō (Ōta Masao, Kishino Akashiya) and Nagata Hideo, who dissociated themselves from the *Myōjō* and joined the *Subaru*, then published the *Okujō Teien* with Hakushū, and played important roles in the school; both of these men left noteworthy works of drama, but the former's achievement in poetry also should not be overlooked.

Kinoshita Mokutarō did not publish any separate volumes of collected poetry, but he wrote poems of exotic interest which are included in the *Kinoshita Mokutarō Shishū* (The Collected Poetry of Kinoshita Mokutarō) (1930), and together with other Symbolist poetry that appeared in the same work under the title of *Ryokkin Boshun Chō* (Greenish Gold Late Spring Melodies), showed a poetical genius almost comparable to that of Kitahara Hakushū. With the ballad-type poems which are found in the *Shokugo no Uta* (After-Dinner Songs) (1919), he approached the style of the *Tōkyō Keibutsu Shi*. Thus, in his tendencies he was akin to Hakushū; the difference was that, unlike the former, he always maintained an intellectual and transcendent attitude that never attached itself to things real and worldly. He followed in the path of Ueda's *Kaichōon* when he wrote *Sensōji* (Sensō Temple) (1907) and *Rakujitsu* (The Setting Sun) in the same year in the *Myōjō*, and vied with Hakushū when he published the *Boshun Chō* (Late Spring Melodies), which was later renamed *Ryokkin Boshun Chō* (1908), in the *Chūō Kōron*, and *Hari Don'ya* (The Glass Dealer) (1909) in the *Subaru*. Particularly the former poem that treats of the tedious feeling of late spring exhibits a lucid and intellectual quality entirely different from the excessively flamboyant manner of Hakushū.

> *Hana chiritsu, hana chiritsu,*
> *Hi ni yurete hana chirichiritsu.*
> *Tomo sureba fukamiyuku*
> *Kokoro no modashi uchimidashi*
> *Wakaki hi no kuregata no*
> *Ōboe wa naki koso sagure, . . .*

> Flower petals fall, flower petals fall,
> Branches sway in the light, and petals fall, fall,
> Disturbing the heart
> That deepens with sorrow—
> An oboe groans at the touch
> In the twilight of young day.

Such dilettante attitude develops, after the *Shokugo no Uta*, into *Kimpun Shu* (Gold Powder Wine) (*Mita Bungaku*, 1910), *Ryōgoku* (*Mita Bungaku*, 1910), *Gaitō Shoka* (A Street in Early Summer) (*Subaru*, 1910), and *Serii Shu* (Sherry Wine) (*Subaru*, 1910), and they are representative pieces which show the poet's refined urban taste. In *Kimpun Shu* Mokutarō enjoys the flavor of May in a glass of imported amber brandy and, in *Bā no Onna* (Waitress at a Bar) he sings of silk serge kimono, the sweet smell of the paulownia blossom, a flute, a *samisen*, and the urban sense of season.

> *Ō do ii do Danchikku*
> *Kogane uku sake,*
> *Ō, gogatsu, gogatsu, rikēru-gurasu,*
> *Waga bā no sutēndogurasu*

Machi ni furu ame no murasaki
Eau-de-vie de Dantzick
Liquor with powder gold floating,
O May, it's May, and a liquor glass,
The stained glass of our bar,
The violet of the rain falling in the street.   (the first stanza)

Here his talent is admirably displayed in that the atmosphere of May is exquisitely expressed with the fresh touches of pointillism. Originally he tended to be a dilettante poet, and since, unlike Kitahara Hakushū, he did not care for popularity, he stood aloof from the poets' circle as the Taishō Era began ; however, the Decadent school of the period owed much to him, and his contribution to the literature of the time was significant.

Nagata Hideo was more a dramatist than a poet. He was also an important personage of this school and is noted for an eccentric, decadent style, but his published works are fewer than those of the other two. *In-In* (*Okujō Teien*, 1910) and *Yoru no Gūzō* (Idol of the Night) (*Subaru*, 1909) are excellent.

Takamura Kōtarō appeared in the *Subaru* shortly after Hakushū, showed a unique capability, and enjoyed a lasting fame in poetry. Under the pseudonym of Saiu, he early contributed *tanka* to the *Myōjō*. He began his career as a poet in 1911, the year after he returned from abroad, when he published the poem entitled *Ushinawaretaru Mona Riza* (The Lost Mona Lisa) in the *Subaru*. At this stage he wrote the aforementioned pieces which are found in the anthology *Dōtei* (Process) (1914), *Netsuke no Kuni* (The Land of Netsuké), *Koe* (Voice) (*Subaru*, 1911), and *Shinryoku no Dokuso* (The Poisons of the Fresh Greens) (*Shirakaba*, 1911). Amid the outpouring of Decadent literature he tried to grasp the essentials of lyricism at the root of primitive life, and disclosed his unique characteristic in a rough and bold style of natural poetry. Accordingly, in expression he endeavored to come in touch with the inner life directly, so that he occasionally used the spoken language and free verse styles. For instance, *Koe* begins with :

Yose, yose
Mijinko seikatsu no tokai ga nan da
Piano no kemban ni koshikaketa yō na sōon to
Katamaritsuita parettomen no yō na kondaku to . . .

Stop, stop,
What's this city of insect life ? What's this city of insect life ?
With noises like that of a piano when you sit on the keyboard,
And turbidity like that of a hardened palette . . .

He sang in a rough and coarse manner of the restlessness of
one who is related both to the primeval and urban life. Such
a tendency of his may be attributed to his inborn nature, but
it originated partly from the influence of Rodin under whom
he studied, and it came also partly from intercourse with the
Shirakaba group. From this period began the idealism in
literature which flourished in the Taishō Period.

Other than those mentioned above, Chino Shōshō, Hirano
Banri, and others who had belonged to the *Myōjō*, and Take-
tomo Sōfū, Satō Haruo, and Horiguchi Daigaku who were
active during Taishō belonged to the *Subaru*.

Symbolist poetry at this time took a new turn. The emergence of Miki Rofū, who was influenced by Nagai Kafū's
translations, wrought an epoch-making change.

Ueda Ryūson continued his translation work even after the
Kaichōon (The Sound of the Sea Tide), and introduced the works
of Maeterlinck, Fort, and other Symbolists with mellowed
pen. On the other hand, there appeared another translator
who made an influential contribution in introducing European poetry from a different viewpoint than that of Ryūson,
namely Nagai Kafū. Kafū spent years in Europe and America,
and he was much attached to France. After returning home
in 1908, he contributed translations of modern French poetry
successively to the *Subaru* and the *Mita Bungaku*. These
translations, mostly of Baudelaire, Verlaine, and Régnier, are
contained in the *Sangoshū* (The Coral Anthology) (1913), which
became as well known as Ryūson's work. His was mostly transla-

tion into prose, and the Japanese he used was a mixture of the literary and colloquial languages, which formed a delicate blending of tones and a unique style, such as we find in the translation of Baudelaire's *L'Ennemi*, the first lines of which are, " *Waga seishun wa tada soko koko ni teruhi no hikari nagaretaru Arashi no yami ni sugizariki.*" (*Subaru*, 1909). Compared with Ryūson, who had much in common with the Parnassians, Kafū was temperamentally inclined to the Decadent school, and with his delicate sense, which is found also in his *Furansu Monogatari* (Tales of France), he accomplished a successful translation of Symbolist poetry second only to the *Kaichōon*. Especially *Yoru no Kotori* (Little Birds in the Night) (1909), *Kaeranu Mukashi* (The Irretrievable Past) (1909), and other translations of Verlaine's poetry exerted a powerful influence on Miki Rofū and other poets of the day.

As mentioned before, Miki Rofū (Misao) marked an epoch in the development of Symbolist poetry. He also began his career by contributing poems to the *Bunko*, where he proved his precocity; afterwards he was influenced by Kambara Ariake and Ueda Ryūson, and at the Waseda Poets' Club he was known as an experimenter in free-verse, spoken Japanese poems and in prose-poems. His province was, however, in literary language poetry. Following *Haien* (The Deserted Garden) (1909), he published *Sabishiki Akebono* (Lonely Dawn) (1910) in which a strong influence of Kafū can be traced; thenceforth he turned to Symbolist poetry. *Haien* was his second collection of poems after *Natsuhime* (The Goddess of Summer) (1905). The extravagance and originality of *Jashūmon* can never be found here, but romantic lyricism, with the beauty of tranquillity and solitude, prevails in it, and the book was very favorably received. A number of the poems sing of the meditative world of vain love and memories with a mood of decadence. Herein can be seen the embryo of his symbolism, which grew into the third collection of poems, the *Sabishiki Akebono*, dedicated to Nagai Kafū. The shadow of sad thought that reflects the distress of modern times arising from melancholy scepticism presents a fantastic world that cannot be seen in Hakushū. *Kami to Uo* (God and Fish), at the beginning of the volume, and *Numa no Hotori* (Beside the Marsh) are his typical works. Especially the latter shows perfection of his technique in that the poet caught, in his fantasy of a lurid scene, the spiritual voice in a fusion of thought and emotion.

Ki wa shikabane no gotoku,
Munashiki kaina o kawasu
Sono omote wa yūshū no sufuinkusu,
" Kako " yori kitaru kanashimi no rakuin ari.
Tamashii wa, yuki ni umorete moe,
Araki susurinaki no koe,
Soko yori kikoyu.

Like a skeleton
The tree twists its gaunt limbs—
Its face is of a melancholic sphinx
With a stigma of sorrow impressed by 'the Past.'
A soul burns, buried in the snow,
And a wild voice of weeping
Is heard therefrom.

What brought him fame alongside of Hakushū were the poems that appeared in *Wasurenagusa* (Forget-Me-Not) (August 1912), a special issue of the *Zamboa*. They were *Utsusemi* (The Present Existence), *Tsuki* (The Moon) (the name was changed to *Sagiri no Mine*, Misty Peak, in the *Shiroki Te no Kariudo*), *Sendan* (The Bead Tree), and *Koi no Saezuri* (The Chirping of Love). These poems were later collected in a single volume, *Shiroki Te no Kariudo* (The White-Handed Huntsman) (1913), and achieved fame as genuine Symbolist poetry. In fact, when published in the magazine *Zamboa* they evidently surpassed the thirty-one poems of Hakushū which were printed together with them. Among others, *Utsusemi* is one of the greatest poems written since Ariake's eight-piece *Hyō no Chi* (Leopard's Blood), which is found at the beginning of the *Ariake-Shū*. Two of its stanzas are as follows:

Haru wa ima sora no nagame ni arawaruru
Ari to mo shirenu usugumo ni
Nayamite shinuru ga no kehai.
Negai wa ariya hi wa tōshi, hana wa kasuka ni uchi kunzu.
Yuruki hikari ni tamashii no
Kemuri no gotoku naku gotoku.

Spring now appears in the sky,
Clouds so faint they hardly can be seen,
And the plight of a moth suffering and dying.
If one has a wish the day is far-off;
The flower gives off a faint fragrance.
In the soft light
As if the wraith of a soul were weeping.

Formless melancholy is evoked amid the sorrowful atmosphere of late spring. *Sendan* and *Tsuki* are also filled with spiritual aspiration towards eternity, and are successful pieces. Though Rofū's poems were originally under the influence of Ariake's idealism, he brought about its full development, while as for diction and phrasing he made use of the Japanese classical manner, and in early Taishō he perfected the Oriental, or purely Japanese, Symbolist poetic style together with Hakushū.

Morikawa Kison, author of *Yoru no Ha* (Leaves of the Night) (1912), received a comparatively strong influence from Rofū. He had rather a long poetic career, and was influenced by Yeats and Symons, but we must say that he lacked originality.

4. *The Influence of Naturalism and the Emergence of Free Verse and Colloquial Language Poetry*

Naturalism, which brought a new development in prose literature, gave a critical turn to poetry. It introduced a realistic attitude in the poet and simplification in language in the field of expression, which led to the emergence of free verse and colloquial poetry.

After the publication of the *Shintaishishō*, the most pressing problem in Meiji poetry had been the creation of a new form employing the language of the new age ; there was marked progress in this direction in the Meiji forties (1907–1912). The movement to introduce a realistic trend into poetry is found in the descriptive poems of urban life that Mori Ōgai attempted in the magazine *Myōjō* prior to this period ; Susukida Kyūkin also experimented with colloquial Japanese in his poems. But these attempts were only within the limits of regular and literary poetry, and it was only after the problem of language and form began to be discussed from the point of view of Naturalism that the poets considered this consciously. Naturalism aimed at the establishment of a prose spirit through the direct observation of reality, and when it was applied to poetry, the usage of literary language and the renouncement of traditional poetic forms naturally came to be an issue.

Thus the problem of colloquial poetry was proposed by Shimamura Hōgetsu, a critic in Naturalism, in his *Gendai no Shi* (Modern Poetry) (*Shijin*, 1907), which was followed by Hattori Yoshika and Sōma Gyofū, who both discussed the problem ; Katagami Tengen and Sakurai Tendan joined the controversy ; at the same time, Kawaji Ryūkō, Miki Rofū, and Sōma Gyofū published their experimental works. A new current in the poetic world arose here and began to flow.

The point at issue that Hōgetsu put forth was clarified by Sōma Gyofū in his *Mizukara Azamukeru Shikai* (The Poetic World Which Deceives Itself) and *Shiika no Komponteki Kakushin* (The Basic Revolution in Poetry), and in the latter, three points were stressed : colloquialization of language, renunciation of restriction concerning metre, etc., and liberation from the restriction of line and stanza, all of which were the practical application of the Naturalistic view of literature. However, his opinion did not go beyond the direct application of Naturalism to poetry, and lacked essential observation on poetry itself. On the other hand, Katagami Tengen cast doubts on the nature of poetry with reference to form, and Hattori Yoshika defended the principle of colloquial poetry repeatedly. It was in the same year that Sakurai Tendan, an advocate of German literature, presented a trial translation into colloquial Japanese of the works of D. von Liliencron in his article *Doitsu no Jojōshi ni okeru Inshōteki Shizenshugi* (Impressionistic Naturalism in German Lyric Poetry) (*Waseda Bungaku*), and explained "inner rhythm," as A. Holz called it, giving some suggestions on the problems of rhythm and colloquial language poetry. These discourses indicated the possible course that free verse and colloquial language poetry would follow, and with Hōgetsu's essay *Kōgoshi Mondai* (Problems in Colloquial Language Poetry) (*Yomiuri Shimbun*, 1908) that course seemed to be established. Hōgetsu concentrated on three main points : (1) transference to natural rhythm (*naizairitsu*) based on thought, from artificial and linguistic rhythm ; (2) naturalization of phrasing (*sojihō*) ; (3) application of spoken Japanese grammar. His opinion brought forth many arguments for and against it, but actually it provided the theoretical foundation for the development of colloquial free verse on which later men were to build modern poetry.

Although there was much theoretical contribution, creative work was deplorably meagre, and very few poets made attempts in both the content and form of new poetry ; indeed, most of them can be said to have been groping in the dark.

The movement was advanced through the Waseda Shisha, formed in March 1907, and the magazine *Shizen to Inshō* (Nature and Impression), published by the Jiyū Shisha, which was established in May 1909 as a successor to the above-mentioned group. The progress of Naturalistic poetry was slow, although in the former period the study of the material of realism was rather advanced, and in the latter period free-verse style was considerably popularized. As regards thought itself, however, the new poets were detached from Naturalism.

Actually they were by no means the originators of colloquial language poems. The first attempt was made by Katayama

Koson who translated the poems of German impressionist, such as those of Dehmel and Holz' free-verse *Lyrischer Depeschenstil*, in his essay *Zoku Shinkeishitsu no Bungaku* (The Sequel to " Sensitive Literature ") (*Waseda Bungaku*, 1905). Kawaji Ryūkō also wrote in the new style *Hakidame* (Dustbin) (1907) in the magazine *Shijin* (The Poet), and Sōma Gyofū and Miki Rofū followed his example in the following year. These poems were mostly crude and of little artistic value although they did have historical significance. One example is as follows :

Yakitsuku yō ni hi ga teru.
Kiiroi hokori ga tatte kūki wa museru yō ni kawaite iru.
Mukimiya no mae ni ke no nuketa yaseinu ga iru.

The burning sun shines ;
The choking yellow dust rises in the dry air,
And in front of a store that sells stripped shellfish
Is a lean dog with sparse hair.

(Gyofū's *Yaseinu*, The Lean Dog)

Among the poets of the Waseda Shisha were Sōma Gyofū, Hitomi Tōmei, Katō Kaishun, Noguchi Ujō, and Fukuda Yūsaku, and Miki Rofū also joined it at this period. In the Jiyū Shisha, in addition to Tōmei, Kaishun, and Yūsaku, there were Yamamura Bochō, Mitomi Kyūyō, Imai Hakuyō, and Fukushi Kōu (Kōjirō). Tōmei, the leader of both groups, published *Yoru no Butō* (The Night Dance) (1911), the style of which was a crude decadence and proved to be inferior to that of Kaishun, the poet of *Gokuchū Aika* (Elegy from Prison) (1914). Yūsaku's *Haru no Yume* (Spring Dreams) (1912) revealed a superior talent, as did Kyūyō's works ; but since the author had already been converted to a sensitive lyrical style, it is not proper to mention it here. Thus the poets of this school proved the possibility of employing the spoken language in poetry, but at the same time we can hardly find their works to be of literary value compared to the literary language free verse of the Subaru group. Indeed, the movement was no more than a prelude to that of the Taishō. The names of Kawaji Ryūkō (Makoto) and Ishikawa Takuboku

(Hajime) must be mentioned here, though they are somewhat separated from the main current of the Naturalistic movement. The former's works are characterized by the new form based on "impression rhythm," and the latter's by socialistic thought. Ryūkō emerged from the Bunko group, as had Hakushū and Rofū, and his career as a poet was long. His *Robō no Hana* (Wayside Flowers) (1910) was published in the same year that Rofū's *Sabishiki Akebono* appeared. Therein we can trace the process whereby he proceeded from the pointillism style, as seen in *Arashi no Ato no Kaigan* (The Seashore after the Storm), toward the monotone and melancholy poems of the Verlaine type. His delicate sensitivity is akin to that of Rofū, as in :

Kiesatta yume no natsukashii kage yo,
Hiyayaka na ishi no michi ni otosareta bara no,
Sono hitotsu hitotsu no hanabira yo

Dear shadow of the vanished dream,
Petals of the rose dropped on the cold stone road,
One by one.

(*Gekkō to Bara*, Moonlight and Roses)

Ishikawa Takuboku, who served apprenticeship even after he published his first book of poems, *Akogare* (Yearning), joined the *Myōjo* and then the *Subaru*, but afterward underwent the strong influence of Naturalism. He was converted to the socialistic school and attempted poems in the colloquial language, the most noteworthy work being that published in 1911 in the magazine *Sōsaku* under the title of *Hateshi Naki Giron no Nochi* (After Endless Discussions). It is divided into six parts, and Part Five, which begins with :

Ware wa tsune ni kare o sonkei-seriki,
Shikashite ima mo nao sonkei-su—
Kano kōgai no bochi no kuri no ki no shita ni,
Kare o hōmurite,
Sudeni futatsuki o hetaredomo.

I always respected him,
And respect him even now,
Though two months have already passed

Since he was buried under a chestnut tree
In that cemetery outside the city.

sings of a laborer who lived according to socialism. His poems
of this type employed the traditional literary diction, although
in the manner of expression there was the freedom of new
poetry. He accomplished more in the field of the *tanka* than
in that of new poetry; still, concerning its intellectual content, he
built a watchtower to view the prospects for Taishō poetry.

As we have seen, it can be said that Naturalism in poetry
did not achieve as many results as Symbolism had done, but on
the other hand, it is not too much to say that Decadent poetry
developed from its involvement with this new thought, and in
fact those aforementioned Decadents gradually went the way of
free verse. Naturalism, considered in this light, is in no small
way responsible for the development of modern poetry of Japan.

In connection with the free verse movement, we must give a
glance at the prose-poem which came into existence at this time.
The earliest publication was Ueda Bin's translation of Turgenev
in his *Miotsukushi* (Channel Markings) (1901), which was followed by Iwano Hōmei's of Whitman, under the name of "free
verse," and by Kawai Suimei's book *Kiri* (Mist) (1910); Kambara Ariake also discussed it early, and translated Baudelaire's
prose-poetry using Symons' English translation. He also wrote
*Saboten to Hanabi no Appreciation** (Appreciation of Cactus
and Fireworks) (*Okujō Teien*, 1910). It was at about this
time that the so-called "urban prose-poem" (*tokai sambunshi*)
appeared, under the influence of the prose works of Nagai Kafū,
and the prose-poem became popular at the end of the Meiji Era.
Most of the writers, however, could not distinguish the prose-
poem from free verse, and their works, with the single exception
of Ariake's, were far inferior to the prose works of Kafū or
Hakushū. It remained for the subsequent Taishō poets to achieve
success in this branch of poetry.

---

* *Translator's Note*: The English word was used as such in the title.

CHAPTER II THE REFORMATION OF *TANKA* AND
ITS DEVELOPMENT

1. *The Survival of Edo* Waka *and the Birth of Modern*
Waka

Until 1887, the world of *waka* (thirty-one-syllable poems,
now usually called *tanka*) was ruled by the poets of the Keien
school, who are the descendants of Kagawa Kageki, and the
conservative poets who belonged to the Dōjō (Imperial Court),
Edo, and Ise schools. They were following the ancient tradition
which had been maintained since the foundation of the country,
and there were no signs of developing a tendency favorable to
a fundamental renovation. The Keien school took as its model
the *Kokinshū*, and clung to the traditional views of poetic
composition, but with the consolidation of the Imperial Poetry
Bureau, which had been organized in 1869, this school gradually
came to exert a powerful influence over the Imperial court.
As the rules and regulations of the Bureau were officially decided by the Cabinet, the Keien school was authoritatively
acknowledged as the O-Utadokoro-Ha (The Imperial Poetry
School), and played the leading role among the *waka* poets.
Indeed, it seemed as if the Keien school had recovered the
prosperity that it enjoyed in the Bunka and Bunsei Periods.
It cannot be forgotten also that the Meiji Emperor's favorable
regard did much to extend its influence. The Meiji Emperor
was a poet who was closely related to the Keien school as
regards the mode of composition, but his elevated style, which
arose from his noble personality, placed him above any of the
schools. The names of poets who wrote *waka* before and at
the beginning of the Meiji Era are as follows : Hatta Tomonori,
Kanō Morohira, Ide (Tachibana) Akemi, Ōkuma Kotomichi,
Hiraga Motoyoshi, Inoue Fumio, Nomura Motoni, Ōtagaki Ren-
getsu, Sanjōnishi Suetomo, Kondō Yoshiki, Takasaki Seifū,
Saisho Atsuko, Kuroda Kiyotsuna, Ōkuma Bengyoku, Koide

Tsubara, Fukuda Gyōkai, Sasaki Hirotsuna, Ikebukuro Kiyokaze, and Unagami Tanehira. Especially Suetomo, and the men mentioned after him, played conspicuous roles after the beginning of the Meiji Era.

Nevertheless these poets generally were not conscious of modern literary thought, and adhered to convention. We should rather enumerate the following names as the poets worthy of note before the new school emerged and who were active into the Meiji twenties: Yosano Shōkei (Raigon), Maruyama Sakura, Amada Guan, and Fukumoto Nichinan. Independent men, they published *waka* outside of the poets' circle, and this gave their works a novel and fresh quality. Many such poems can be found in *Guan Ikō* (Posthumous Works of Guan) (1904).

Hito mina no	Eternal day of spring—
Sakura kazashite	While all the people
Asobu chū	Are playing
Nagaki harubi o	Under the cherry blossoms
Yamoi koyaseru	I lie sick in bed.
Awajishima	As I passed through
Mihara matsubara	The pine grove
Asa yukeba	On Awaji Island
Koromo wa nurenu	My clothes became wet
Matsu no shizuku ni	With the morning dewdrops.

His Manyō-style realistic attitude greatly influenced Masaoka Shiki's revolutionary poetic style.

During this period there appeared collections of *waka* that bore the name of the new era, Meiji, in their titles, *e. g.*, *Meiji Kashū* (Meiji Poems) (1876) and *Meiji Genson : Sanjūroku Kasen* (Anthology of the Thirty-Six Meiji Poets) (1877), but they were only imitations of the works of the preceding Edo Era, and there was nothing new in them. Some books of poems showed European influence: in *Yokomoji Hyakunin Isshu* (One Hundred Western-Style Poems of One Hundred Poets) (1873), the poems were printed in Romanized spelling; in *Kaika Shindai Kashū* (Poems on Modern Themes) (1878) the poems were written on the novel themes; and some other books dealt with

Occidental personages and events, but nevertheless their Europeanization was only superficial.

Machite saku	There's something I open
Umegaka yori mo	At the morning window
Ureshiki wa	That gives me more pleasure
Ashita no mado ni	Than the fragrance of the
Hiraku hitohira	plum blossom
	Whose blooming I yearn for.

The newspaper was a novel theme then, and so were the solar calendar, the telegraph, gaslight, governesses, and equality of the sexes. This list indicates the subjects in which the poets felt interest, but their view of poetry and of life was not as changed as it may seem.

As regards critical studies, Unagami Tanehira, who asserted that the *Manyōshū* should be the model, published *Tōkyō Taika : Jūshi Kashū Hyōron* (Criticism of Fourteen Anthologies of Tōkyō Poets) (1884) in which he gave a sharp criticism of the Keien school. Consequently, much discussion took place among the poets, but it was merely a tempest in a teacup, and there was little constructive development. So stagnant was the early Meiji *waka*, that towards the 'nineties, a noteworthy movement arose, namely the New Style poetry movement mentioned in the preceding chapter. Criticism was directed against *waka* from the viewpoint of European poetics. In answer to this criticism from outside, Suematsu Kenchō, from inside the *waka* circle, advocated the improvement of their poetry in *Kagaku Ron* (Essay on *Waka* Poetry) (1884).

Since this advocacy of improvement was primarily founded on an affirmative attitude toward *waka*, it gained strength while the movement of nationalism and revaluation of Japanese classical literature was flourishing about 1887.

Among the advocates were the progressive scholars of Japanese literature at that time : Hagino Yoshiyuki, Konakamura (Ikebe) Yoshikata, Ochiai Naobumi, Sasaki Nobutsuna, Ikebukuro

Kiyokaze, Inoue Michiyasu, and others. A few of them being younger poets who belonged to the Keien school, they were not of the same opinion, but they had almost the same view that poetry should be composed in the language of the times, that the subject matter should be expanded to include common, everyday experiences, and that the form and style of the *chōka* (longer *waka*) and *imayō* should be recovered. A pioneer work entitled *Shōron* (My Opinion) was published by Hagino Yoshiyuki in the *Tōyō Gakkai Zasshi* (Oriental Studies Magazine) in 1887. (It was later contained in his *Kokugaku Waka Kairyō Ron*, On Improving Japanese *Waka* Poetry, 1887.) He discussed the improvement of the theme, style, and material, and criticized the evils of long standing in *waka*, attacked effeminate love poems, and encouraged a masculine and heroic type of poetry. On the other hand, there is no gainsaying his utilitarian position of desiring that literature be a means to promote morality.

Yoshiyuki's opinion created a great sensation. While there were some antagonistic reactions, Mikami Sanji and Takatsu Kuwasaburō expressed constructive criticism on the ground of European poetics. Thus, purely theoretical development was gradually achieved, and with the support of Ikebe Yoshikata and Ochiai Naobumi, it became the main current of the reformation movement. In the following year, Sasaki Takeshi (Nobutsuna) expressed his personal views on the reformation of *waka* in *Waka no Hanashi* (Talks on *Waka*) in the *Jogaku Zasshi* (Women's Academic Magazine), referring at times to European aesthetics. His observations on *waka*, especially on its literary value, were considerably advanced.

That *waka*, because of its formal limitations, was an inappropriate genre of poetry for expressing the complicated thought of modern times was the unanimous opinion since the publication of the *Shintaishishō*. Both Morita Shiken's *Waka o Ronzu* (On *Waka*) (*Kokumin no Tomo*, 1888) and Yamada Bimyō's *Nippon Imbun Ron* (On Japanese Poetry) (*Kokumin no Tomo*,

1890) discussed the problem from the same point of view. Concerning the method of meeting the shortcomings that resulted from the limitation of the length the poem, many reformers thought of reviving the *chōka* style. Sasaki Hirotsuna, in his essay in *Fude no Hana* entitled " Reformation of the *Chōka* " (1888), urged the replacing of *waka* by lengthened seven-five-syllable *imayō*, but his opinion was attacked by Unagami Tanehira, who insisted that only the five-seven-syllable poem of the *Manyō-shū* was the orthodox style. The controversy continued for years, but no constructive results ever came of it. In the same year (1888) there appeared in the *Tōyō Gakkai Zasshi* Hayashi Mikaomi's proposal for *gembun itchika* (colloquial *waka*) and his experimental works on it. It was a by-product of the general tendency of the literary world of the day, and his experiments in a colloquial *waka* were no more than crude specimens. Thus, the *waka* poets began to long for some new style to give expression to new feelings, and this gradually came to be an undercurrent of the poets' circle. Nevertheless, practice did not keep pace with desire until the Meiji twenties (1887–1897).

The general demand for a new type of *waka*, expressed through repeated discussions, was realized with the formation of the Asakasha (The Faint Incense Society) in February 1893. As mentioned before, Ochiai Naobumi had been the leader of the development of the New Style poetry and prose, and published *Shinsen Katen* (A New Code of *Waka* Poetry) (1891) and the magazine *Kagaku* (Poetics) (1892), where he occasionally gave advice on the reformation of *waka* from his particular viewpoint. Since he was fond of young poets and fostered their literary careers, multitudes of rising poets gathered under his leadership. Among them were Ayugai Kaien, Shioi Ukō, Ōmachi Keigetsu, Utsumi Getsujō, Yosano Tekkan, Kubo Inokichi, Hattori Moto-haru, Onoe Saishū, Kaneko Kun'en, and Maruoka Katsura. However, the Asakasha at first held a non-committal attitude on reformation, nor did it have particular periodicals to publish its opinions. The organization became a fruitful nursery for the new *waka* mainly through Naobumi's generous personality and his personal guidance.

Naobumi's *waka* can be found in *Haginoya Kashū* (Poems by Haginoya) (1906):

Hiodoshi no	I think the scarlet-threaded
Yoroi o tsukete	Suit of armor
Tachi hakite	With a sword at its side
Mibayatozo omou	Will become my figure
Yamazakurabana	When I view the mountain cherry-blossoms.
Tamasudare	A butterfly dances,
Yuragu to mo naki	Telling the way
Harukaze no	The soft spring wind wends
Yukue o misete	Which scarcely moves
Mau kochō kana	The jewelled screen.
Hasedera wa	Wetting the stone
Kore yori migi to	Inscribed,
Shirushitaru	" For Hase Temple
Ishi o nurashite	Go Right,"
Yuku shigure kana	The light autumn rain passes on.
Chichigimi yo	How can I die,
Kesa wa ika ni to	When I see my child
Te o tsukite	Bow and ask me,
Tou ko o mireba	" How are you this morning,
Shinarezarikeri	Father ? "

His *waka* were characterized by a refreshing and graceful tone or mild taste. As he grew older, he was influenced by the social trend, and his poetry revealed human affection. But throughout his poetical career he did not rid himself of the attitude of classical harmony.

Against the compromising attitude of his teacher Ochiai Naobumi, Yosano Tekkan represented the positive aspect of the Asakasha, and he made an open declaration of the reformation of the *tanka* (*waka*). He cooperated with Ayugai Kaien, and published in the newspaper *Niroku Shimpō* an essay entitled

Bōkoku no On (Sounds Ruinous to the Country) (May 1894). The essay, with the subtitle of "I Accuse the Present Effete *Waka*," hurled harsh reproaches at the poets connected with the Imperial Poetry Bureau. Doing away with the compromising, lukewarm posture of superficial critics, Tekkan made a frontal attack on them, and called for a fundamental renovation in poetic composition, although he did not indicate any concrete method whereby this could be achieved. His bombastic words, "A single breathing of a true man breathes Heaven and Earth. If a man has magnanimity of mind, what he sings of the Universe is the Universe itself." gave a tremendous shock to the older poets. He also warned that effeminate love poems would endanger the future of the country. His essay was filled with youthful enthusiasm and the nationalistic spirit of the day.

Tekkan's poems of this period were included in his collection *Tōzainamboku* (East, West, South, and North) (1896):

Karayama ni	Among the Korean mountains
Akikaze tatsu ya	Howls the autumn wind.
Tachi nadete	I dare not say,
Ware omou koto	Stroking my sword,
Nakinishimo arazu	That I have no ambition.
Onoe ni wa	How furiously
Itakumo tora no	The tiger roars
Hoyuru kana	In the mountain.
Yūbe wa kaze ni	A storm will surely rise
Naramu to suramu	In the evening.

His was a crabbed and stiff style, and in it the words "tiger" and "sword" appeared so often that he was called the poet of "the Tiger-Sword school." Indeed it cannot be denied that there prevailed in his works a rough and crude diction and a certain childishness, but it should be noted that the romantic and simple spirit of the younger generation of those days is explicitly expressed. Thus the Asakasha, under the guidance of Naobumi, fulfilled its function as the nursery of Meiji *waka*, leading the world from "improvement" to "renovation," from enlightening rationalism to the liberation of the inner life of the Meiji world.

Shortly after Yosano Tekkan put forth his renovation theory, Sasaki Nobutsuna and his Chikuhaku Kai adopted the new theory, and survived long despite the changes in the poetic world. Nobutsuna succeeded to his father Hirotsuna's scholarship in Japanese literature, especially in poetry, and began his career as a poet of the old school, but, as mentioned above, he gradually tended to the new thought, and in about 1896 he published such a poem as:

Fue fuku ka	Who plays the flute?
Ware ka aranu ka	Is it for me or not?
Natsukashiki	The longed-for sound
Koe koso hibike	Echoes
Kumo no hatate ni	Beyond the clouds.

As can be supposed from this example, his works had a slight emotional element of the *shintaishi* (New Style poetry). Nobutsuna was ranked with Tekkan for a time, but, nurtured in the classical literature of Japan, he could not abandon his eclectic position, nor could he hold revolutionary ideas.

The Chikuhaku Kai is supposed to have been organized in April 1899, but the magazine of the association, *Kokoro no Hana*, was first published as early as February of the previous year. At the beginning, old and new *waka* poets, as well as those of the Negishi school, gathered around it, and it was only after 1904 that the magazine was used exclusively for the association activities. Thus, the Chikuhaku Kai school maintained the position of arbiter throughout the period, under the motto of " Widely, deeply, let each one study in his own way." Anthologies, *i. e.*, the *Chikuhakuen-Shū* (The Chikuhakuen Anthology; Vol. I, 1901; Vol. II, 1902, etc.), were successively edited and published, and they did much to popularize *waka*.

Sasaki Nobutsuna's *Omoigusa* (Thoughts and Fancies) (1903), which established his fame, contained well-balanced poems with a mild and even tone :

Ametsuchi no	The sound of the stream
Kakuroegoto o	Is like a murmuring
Wagamune ni	Informing my heart
Sasayaku gotoki	Of the secrets
Mizu no oto kana	Of Heaven and Earth.
Ozasahara	The drops
Tsuyu horohoro to	Drip quietly
Koboreochite	From the bamboo leaves,
Nijūgo bosatsu	And the autumn rain falls
Aki no ame furu	On the images of the twenty-five Bodhisattvas.

These tendencies remained even in later years :

Yuku aki no	A streak of cloud
Yamato no kuni no	Above the pagoda
Yakushiji no	Of the Yakushi Temple
Tō no ue naru	In the province of Yamato
Hitohira no kumo	On a day in late autumn.
Kirakira to	The sea
Umi wa hikarite	Sparkles
Iso no ie	But the noon rain falls
Matsuba-botan ni	On the portulaca
Hiru no ame furu	Near the houses on the beach.

On the other hand, he was also influenced by the Shinshisha school :

Hirogetaru	The autumn sun is cold
Muryōjubon no	On the open
Kindei ni	Gold-lettered scriptures
Aki no hi samuki	Of the old temple
Mine no furudera	On the peak.

These poems prove that he progressed with the transitions in poetical thought. The latter poems were included in his second collection, *Shingetsu* (New Moon) (1912).

Among the *waka* poets who emerged from the Chikuhaku Kai were Ishikure Chimata, Miura Moriji, Kawada Jun, Intō Masatsuna, Kinoshita Toshiharu, Arai Akira, and two women poets, Ōtsuka Kusuoko and Tachibana Itoeko. Kusuoko, who died young, was noted for her poems of superb delicacy, and Itoeko for her pathos-filled works with latent passion. Ishikure Chimata contributed much in the managing of the magazine *Kokoro no Hana* (Flower of the Heart), as well as played an active role in Taishō literature, together with Kinoshita Toshiharu and Kawada Jun.

One of the points that differentiated the reformation movement from the improvement movement was that the former limited the form of *waka* to *tanka* (shorter *waka*). The reason why they forsook *chōka* (longer *waka*) was that the *shintaishi* (New Style poetry) had established itself and left no room for *waka* poets to consider the longer form of poetry as their field. Other reasons were that the leaders such as Ochiai Naobumi, Yosano Tekkan, and Sasaki Nobutsuna were also active in writing New Style poetry and that the *tanka* was beginning to be appreciated as the proper style for lyrical expression.

The reformation movement, which began with the essay *Bōkoku no On*, put primary stress on destroying the old style, but after 1897 it began to study the new-type *tanka* itself. Masaoka Shiki published his famous *Utayomi ni Atauru Sho* (Open Letter to *Waka* Poets) (1898), and *Hyakuchū Jisshu* (Ten Poems from a Hundred) (1898) which were a fine criterion in that sense, while from the end of that year to the beginning of the next, a number of poets' clubs were organized: the Ikazuchi Kai was composed of Kubo Inokichi, Onoe Saishū, Hattori Motoharu, and others who were direct descendants of Ochiai Naobumi; the Wakana Kai was established by Yasugi Sadatoshi and Nunami Takeo; the Akebono Kai by Maruoka Katsura (Tsuki-no-Katsura-no-ya) and Taguchi Shuntō. They were followed by the Kisaragi Kai, the Shinonome Kai, and others. Together with these associations, the Chikuhaku Kai, Negishi Tanka Kai, and Shinshisha contributed greatly in popularizing the new *tanka* poetry.

Next to the Chikuhaku Kai, the Ikazuchi Kai was most active in publication both of criticism and actual poetry, and its romantic and emotional manner of expression was extremely influential among the new poets until the Shinshisha came into existence. Maruoka Tsuki-no-Katsura-no-ya's and Taguchi Shuntō's *Chōran Sekiu* (Morning Storm and Evening Rain) (1900) and Hattori Motoharu's *Kagutsuchi* (Fire God) (1901) were the results of the authors' activities. The former was the pioneer work of new poets, and a forerunner of fascinating, romantic poems :

Hi o keshite	After putting out my light
Yume o matsu ma no	And while waiting for a dream
Makuramoto	I caught the slight sound
Botan kuzururu	Of peony petals falling
Oto shizuka nari	At my pillow.
	(Tsuki-no-Katsura-no-ya)

Hattori Motoharu also wrote fantastic poems that referred to the ancient Heian court life. He may be called a forerunner of such romantics as Yosano Akiko and others, but he did not develop his talents.

Wakayagishi	The youthful voice
Koe rōei to	Began to recite poetry
Narinikeri	Loudly,
Konoezukasa no	With the moon of a spring
Haru no yo no tsuki	night
	On the office of the Imperial Guards.
Yūzukiyo	A moonlit evening—
Fue no ne yamite	The sound of a flute ceases
Chūmon no	As someone seems to approach
Renji no soto ni	The middle gate
Hito no kehai ari	Lattice.

2. The Romantic Reformation and Its Currents

We have already explained that the new poetry of the Meiji Era was brilliantly established with Shimazaki Tōson's *Wakana-*

shū. However, the role of taking over the lyrical inheritance, which had still been weak with Tōson, and of leading it towards a glorious flowering was given to new *tanka* poets and their association: Yosano Tekkan, Yosano Akiko his wife, and the Shinshisha. With their romantic spirit, the reformation of *waka* was successfully achieved.

Tekkan's Shinshisha was organized in November 1899, and its magazine *Myōjō* was first published in April of the following year. From that memorable year until November 1908 when the magazine was discontinued, the whole world of the *tanka* literally followed the leadership of the Shinshisha.

Generally speaking, the reformation of the *tanka* was accomplished by two methods : one was to bring it to the light of European poetry and imbue it with modernity, and the other was to examine it before the historical backdrop of traditional Japanese literature and grasp therein the essence of the *waka* prior to modernizing it. The Shinshisha took the former method. It called the *tanka tanshi* (short poetry), and pursued "the poetry of self," or "the poetry of originality," to establish a new beauty. Such a romantic trend of the Shinshisha was nothing but an adaptation of the spirit of self-emancipation of modern individualism to poetry. In opposition to the reality of the age, it dominated the literary world with its so-called "Star and Violet " poems, protesting the falsehood and ostentation of the vulgar world, and beautifying reality through its poets' imagination and fancy.

Thus the Shinshisha steered the stormy sea of the literary world of the Meiji thirties (1897–1906), its career being divided into three periods, the first of which lasted until 1902. In this period the antagonistic feeling against Tekkan broke out in the form of the scandalous Shōmakyō (Magic Mirror) case (1901), and shortly thereafter Akiko published *Midaregami* (Disheveled Hair), which won her fame as well as gave direction to the world of poetry. The second period lasted until 1906. In this period the society came to represent the viewpoint of the world of poetry at large. Its influence was at its peak; its works were refined, the unbridled passions being now suppressed; the expanded ego was turned to the land of heart's desire, and the essential features of Romanticism were fully developed through imaginative, aesthetic, and structural poetry. The fact that the leadership shifted from Tekkan to Akiko signifies the change in the spirit of the times, that is, from "despotic liberalism" to "individualistic liberalism." But towards the end of this period, the establishment of the ego was accomplished only within the bounds of artistic idealism, and the society began to stand aloof from the reality of the outside world, betraying its dogmatic attitude. In the third period its Parnassianism was manifested. The younger disciples, such as Kitahara Hakushū, Yoshii Isamu, and others, maintained the public approval of the society, but nevertheless the metaphoric, symbolic poetry of the *Myōjō* was on the wane in the face of the attacks from the quarters of Naturalism for its basic lack of realistic appeal. The discontinuance of the *Myōjō* was mainly due to the grave situation that it faced in the last stage, although it was partly because of the secession of the younger members that took place when Yosano Tekkan proclaimed his anti-Naturalist position. Although we recognize that its decline was a historic necessity, it must be remembered that much of the credit for establishing a new romantic beauty and realizing the idea of Meiji poetry goes to the Shinshisha.

The *Myōjō* dealt with general problems of art, but its main interest was poetry, especially the *tanka* and shorter poems, and the leaders in the field were the Yosanos, *i. e.*, Tekkan and Akiko his wife. Of the two the greater was Akiko (Shō), who with her rare genius created variegated romantic poems. She was responsible for *Myōjō* poetry outshining that of all of the other schools.

Midaregami (Disheveled Hair), a collection of *tanka* which she published under the name of Hō Akiko in August 1901, included three hundred ninety-nine poems which she had written in the course of her love-affair with Yosano Tekkan. She sang of youthful ardor in an unprecedented manner, and created a great sensation. Especially her totally affirmative attitude toward humanity, expressed through the emancipation of primitive instinct, was in itself a romantic resistance against conventional morality.

Yo no chō ni	Though once in Heaven
Sasameki tsukishi	She whispered love
Hoshi no ima o	Behind the curtain of Night,
Gekai no hito no	Now on earth is she, alas,
Bin no hotsure yo	With hair disheveled.

The irrepressible passion of youth is sung in a Western manner of delivery. Her affirmation of humanity and eulogy of love are primarily expressed as facets of instinct in such poems as :

Kami goshaku	Five feet of hair—
Tokinaba mizu ni	When combed it is as soft
Yawarakaki	As water—
Otome-gokoro wa	A maiden's heart
Himete hanataji	Is secret and not to be divulged.

Sono ko hatachi	Aged twenty she is,
Kushi ni nagaruru	Black hair
Kurokami no	Flowing under the comb—
Ogori no haru no	What an exuberance of beauty
Utsukushiki kana	She enjoys in the spring.

The flowering of youth is displayed unreservedly by this woman who has emancipated herself from the world of fetters.

Kyō wa nigashi	The sutras are bitter—
Haru no yūbe o	This spring evening,
Oku-no-in no	Accept my poem instead,
Nijūgo bosatsu	O twenty-five saints
Uta uketamae	Of the Inner Temple.

Yawahada no	Not giving a touch
Atsuki chishio ni	To the hot blood
Fure mo mide	Pulsing under the tender skin,
Sabishikarazu ya	Are you not lonely,

Michi o toku kimi	My lord, preacher of the Holy Way ?
Hito no ko ni	Did I commit a sin
Kaseshi wa tsumi ka	To give my arm
Waga kaina	To a son of Man ?
Shiroki wa kami ni	Ought I instead to have en-
Nado yuzuru beki	trusted
	Its whiteness to a god ?

By contrasting Beauty with such ideas as the Holy Way and Sin, she gave a challenge to philistinism in a daring way. In the volume under discussion are found poems that sing of the city of Kyōto which she loved, with the romantic fancy that characterized it.

Kiyomizu e	Everyone I meet is beautiful,
Gion o yogiru	Among the blooming cherry-
Sakurazukiyo	trees
Koyoi au hito	This moonlit night
Mina utsukushiki	On the way from Gion
	To Kiyomizu Temple.
Yūgure o	Even to the soft hair of a
Hana ni kakururu	little fox
Kogitsune no	That hides himself under the
Nikoge ni hibiku	flowers
Kitasaga no kane	At my footsteps
	On this quiet evening,
	Sounds the bell of Kitasaga
	temple.

After *Midaregami*, Akiko published *Koōgi* (The Little Fan) (1904), *Dokugusa* (Poisonous Grasses) (1904), *Koigoromo* (The Robe of Love) (1905), and *Maihime* (Dancing Girl) (1906) successively, and during this period the strong passion of the initial stage gradually calmed down and turned into a quiet longing and fancying. She gathered her material from Eastern and Western literature as well as from things present and ancient, and this made her works richer in theme and more picturesque. In *Koōgi* are found such poems as :

Haru no yūbe	Light rain falling
Sobofuru ame no	On a spring evening
Ōhara ya	In Ōhara—
Hana ni kitsune no	A fox is sleeping among flowers
Nuru Jakkōin	In the precincts of Jakkōin Temple.

Also in *Koigoromo* is found :

Shunjoshō ni	I add " The Tales of Ise "
Ise o kasanete	To a volume " Spring Dawn.''
Kasataranu	Still it does not suffice
Makura wa yagate	For my pillow,
Kuzurekeru kana	Which collapses* before long.

* from the violence of her lovemaking.

Enchanting taste and romantic fantasies are added to the courtly atmosphere, together with her unique romantic description which we find in such a poem as follows :

Miidera ya	At the Mii Temple
Ha waka kaede no	An early summer storm—
Koshita michi	Even the stones cry
Ishi mo naku beki	On the path beneath
Aoarashi kana	The budding maple trees.

On the other hand, Tekkan, close collaborator with Akiko, showed the change in his style from his initial masculine ruggedness into a " Star and Violet " style, full of amorous beauty, when he published *Tenchi Gen'ō* (1897), *Tekkan-Shi* (1901), and *Murasaki* (Purple) (1901). It is generally accepted that Tekkan was inferior to his wife Akiko in delicacy of sense, depth of passion, and versatility of expression.

Soya risō	I weep piteously
Koya ummei no	On a white violet
Wakareji ni	At the crossroad
Shiroki sumire o	Where the way to the ideal
Aware to naku mi	And the way to fate diverge.

Hito no iu	Man says
Botan wa tsui ni	The peony is merely

Chi no hana to	An earthly flower.
Sore omoshiroshi	I do not mind if it is so,
Morote ni dakamu	I shall take it to my bosom.
Ushiro yori	I dressed my love
Kinu kisematsuru	From the back
Haru no yoi	On a spring evening,
Sozoro ya kami no	And her tangled hair
Midarete ochinu	Fell down softly.

Thus, he finally came to keep pace with his wife. After *Murasaki*, he concentrated his energy on writing longer poems, but still during the same period, he published another collection of poems entitled *Umoregi* (The Fossil Wood) (1902) and one with A-kiko entitled *Dokugusa*. The latter contains such superb pieces as:

Chōbō ya	Perhaps this night the Dragon Princess
Ryūnyo mo majiri	
Owasu yo ka	Also listens to the preaching of the Way
Yokawa wa kane ni	At the Yokawa temple
Shiraume no chiru	Where the white plum blossoms
	Scatter with the tolling of the bell.

but gives the impression of following the brilliant development of Akiko's poetry.

The rise and fall of the magazine *Myōjō* were also those of Tekkan and Akiko. Their romantic embers still smoldered after that, but they were losing popularity. Later, Akiko wrote Symbolist poetry and published *Yume no Hana* (The Dream Flower) (1906), *Tokonatsu* (Everlasting Summer) (1908), *Saho-Hime* (The Goddess of Spring)(1909), *Shundeishū* (The Spring Earth Anthology) (1911), and *Seigaiha* (Blue Sea Waves) (1912), and proved her vitality; however, it is undeniable that her works showed mannerism. Tekkan published *Aigikoe* (Love-Making) (1910) under his original name Hiroshi, and *Kashi no Ha* (Oak Leaves) (1910), which proved lacking in originality.

There were not a few younger poets who assisted Tekkan and Akiko in their literary activities. Yamakawa Tomiko, widely known as an unhappy woman poet, was one of them. She demonstrated her brilliant talent, under the pseudonym of Shirayuri (white lily), in rivalry with Akiko, whose *nom de plume* was Shirahagi (white bush clover), in the *Myōjō* in its early stage. She died young, leaving only a small number of poems in the *Koigoromo*. Compared with the expansive and florid poems of Akiko, hers were introspective and melancholic, and made a remarkable contrast with the former poetess, her rival in love.

Kami nagaki	Born a maiden
Otome to umare	With long hair,
Shirayuri ni	I droop my head
Nuka wa fusetsutsu	On a white lily,
Kimi o koso omoe	And think of you.
Wasurejina	Never will I forget you,
Wasure tamawaji	Nor will you forget me;
Sawa iedo	Still my way will be
Tsune no sabishiki	The solitary one
Michi yukamu mi ka	That most women go.

Her introspective mood gave a peculiar strength to her tender-hearted expression. She finally broke with Tekkan, for Akiko's sake, and married another man. Many of her poems of love are touching:

Sore to naku	Having handed over
Akaki hana mina	All the red flowers
Tomo ni yuzuri	To my friend,
Somukite nakite	Alone and with tears
Wasuregusa tsumu	I pick *wasuregusa.**

* the grass of forgetfulness.

She probably was beneath Akiko in capability, but in depth of lyrical spirit, she may have been the greater.

Another woman poet was Chino (Masuda) Masako, who called herself Shiraume (white plum blossom).

Shiraume no	I sensed a white plum blossom
Kinu ni kaoru to	Fragrance on my dress,
Mishi made yo	And no more—
Kimi to wa iwaji	I shall not say it was you—
Haru no yo no yume	The dream of a spring night.
Utsutsu naki	Purple wistaria
Haru no nagori no	Bedecked with dew fell
Yūsame ni	After the departing
Shizurete chirinu	Evening rain
Murasaki no fuji	Of ethereal spring.

She left many graceful poems, although after the *Koigoromo* she tended to be realistic.

Takamura Kōtarō (Takamura Saiu), who afterwards became famous in the realm of longer poems, contributed *tanka*, together with Kubota Utsubo and Sōma Gyofū (Shōji), in the early years of the *Myōjō*, but it was towards the end of the middle period that he demonstrated his ability.

Michisugara	Traveling,
Kyō wa anai ga	I enjoy imitating the guide,
Kuchimane ni	But I would say,
Unebi o koete	" By crossing Mt. Unebi
Rōma ni iramu	One would enter Rome."

Such a poem indicated the romanticism of the youth of that age.

Umi o mite	Under the canopy of Heaven
Taiko no tami no	And at sea,
Odoroki o	I am filled with the wonder
Ware futatabi su	That ancient people
Ōzora no moto	Experienced.
Chi o sarite	Leaving the earth
Nanoka jūnishi	To consider
Rokkyū no	The grandeur of things
Aida ni mono no	Among the constellations
I o omoiori	And the signs of the zodiac.

His style of poetry originated from Tekkan, but as in the above poems, the gravity of his own nature was added to the original mood of the poetry. Kubota Utsubo was noted in the first period, but his talent was fully exhibited after he turned to Naturalism.

Gyofū, too, dissociated himself from the *Myōjō* group together with Maeda Ringai, established the Tōkyō Jumbunsha (The Tōkyō Pure Literature Society), and published the magazine *Shirayuri* (White Lily).   Later he brought out a collection of poems entitled *Suiren* (The Water Lily).

Tamakura no	I pursued your image as far
Yume yori tsuzuku	As the glories of
Yūmoya no	The evening mist
Hatenaru aya ni	That trailed
Kimi o oishi ka	From my idle dreams.

His manner of phrasing was plain and sentimental, but essentially it was still closely related to the *Myōjō* style.

Chino Shōshō (Bou) and Hirano Banri (Chōei) made their appearance in the middle stage of the *Myōjō* school.

Mononoke no	A temple at night
Kurokami kuroki	Dark with the hair
Yo no tera ya	Of evil spirits—
Totose oto naki	Rain is falling on the bell
Kane ni ame furu	That has not been rung these ten long years.

(Shōshō)

Ne no kuni ni	Is that the ship bound
Hatsuramu fune ka	For the country of Ne,
Umi hikuku	That sails low on the sea
Hi teranu kata ni	In the shady side,
Makuro naru ho yo	Hoisting a black sail.

(Shōshō)

Shōshō's poems harbor abstract ideas in a Western style, and Banri was known as a love poet who expressed romantic affection in a simple manner :

Ware o toru	I am sad to find
Kuroki hitomi no	The bewitching black eyes
Waga mae ni	In front of me,
Aru o kanashimi	But I grieve the more
Aranu o ureu	When they are not.

(Banri)

Omme toji	Close your eyes and consider,
Hisoka ni hitori	Alone and secretly,
Waga koi no	How deep
Fukasa o tazune	Is my love for you,
Odoroki tamae	And be surprised.

(Banri)

These two poems are found in his *Wakaki Hi* (Youthful Days) (1907) and are dedicated to Tamano Hanako, a woman poet of the *Myōjō*.

Apart from the above-mentioned poets there were Hiraide Osamu (Roka), who published *Shimpa Waka Hyōron* (A Criticism of *Waka* of the New School) (1901), Mizuno Yōshū (Chōrō), Nakahama Itoko, Kindaichi Kyōsuke (Kamei), and Ōi Sōgo. These people represent the revolutionary group of Meiji poets together with Hakushū, Isamu, and Takuboku.

The existence of an opposition movement against the Shinshisha should not be overlooked. The Ikazuchi Kai early disregarded the old schools, and at the same time doubted Tekkan's crude and revolutionary poems, while "the scenery-sketch poetry" (jokeishi) movement and the Negishi Tanka Kai (Negishi Tanka Association) openly declared their opposition to it. The former movement, led by Onoe Saishū (Hachirō) and Kaneko Kun'en (Yūtarō), unlike the latter, could not rid itself of the romantic current, although it stood its antagonistic ground.

Onoe Saishū was brought up under the instruction of Ōguchi Taiji and Ochiai Naobumi of the Imperial Poetry Bureau School, and then joined the Ikazuchi Kai; he did not comply with the *Myōjō* school in principle from the first, so much so that he finally allied himself with Kaneko Kun'en of the magazine *Shinsei*, who had also been in disagreement with the *Myōjō*. He published *Jokeishi* (Descriptive Poetry) (1902), which contained his own poems and those of his students, in the preface of which he wrote, "What Is Descriptive Poetry?" His opinion was that the poets' function is to follow nature and copy it, never mixing a selfish motive. He stood on the unity of poetry and painting, rejected fanciful, romantic poetry, and advocated realism. However, he and Kun'en actually stopped short of their ideal, and never went beyond a superficial, romantic natural description, in spite of their theoretical assertions :

Sashiwataru *Hagoshi no yūhi* *Chikara nashi* *Biwa no hana chiru* *Yabukage no michi*	The evening sun Shines weakly Through the leaves of the spreading tree. The blossoms of the Japanese medlar are falling On a path in the shade of a grove.

(Saishū)

Tori no kage *Mado ni utsurou* *Koharubi ni* *Konomi koboruru* *Oto shizuka nari*	On a mild autumn day The shadow of a bird Passes over the window— The sound of nuts Falling softly—

(Kun'en)

Introspective, thoughtful, and intellectual observation was Saishū's characteristic ; it was established in the two volumes *Ginrei* (Silver Bells) (1904) and *Seiya* (Silent Night) (1907), and gave fresh air to the world of poetry at the beginning of the last stage of the *Myōjō*. In the former book are found works of resplendent beauty, such as we find in Western painting, and Shinshisha-style fantasy :

Ichijō no *Nōzenkatsura* *Hana hikeba* *Hiru no ame furu* *Shirakashi no mori*	As I pulled off The great trumpet flower Three yards long, The noon rain began to fall In the white oak grove.

On the other hand, he wrote meditative poetry :

Ima no yo wa *Komu yo no kage ka* *Kage naraba*	Is the present life A shadow of the future one ? If so,

Uta wa sono hi no	My poems would be prophecies
Yogen naramashi	Of the coming world.

Such meditative tendencies turned to the melancholy of a delicate psychology when he came to the *Seiya* where his contemplative qualities are particularly prominent.

Natsukashiki	On the days when my heart softens
Omoi waku hi wa	And thinks of my love,
Ichi ni tachi	Even toward the beggar urchins
Mono kou kora mo	Of the marketplace
Shiru hito no goto	My affection turns as toward my friends.
Tōki ki no	With the cloud
Ue naru kumo to	Above the distant trees
Waga mune to	My heart
Tamatama ainu	Has melted casually
Shizuka naru hi ya	This quiet day.
Hiyayaka ni	Some day I can see myself
Namida nagaseru	Coolly meeting
Ware o mite	With another self,
Ware wa arikeri	Weeping,
Tōki yo no sue	In another world of the distant future.

Following these collections, there appeared *Eijitsu* (Long Day) (1909), which proved to have been influenced exceedingly by Naturalism.

Saishū organized the Shazensōsha (The Plantain Society) in April 1905. Under his tutelage emerged Masatomi Ōyō, Wakayama Bokusui, Maeda Yūgure, and Miki Rofū. At this period Masatomi Ōyō published *Natsubisashi* (Summer Gables) (1905) together with another poet, but his work is not of the highest order.

Kaneko Kun'en's poems followed the style of his teacher Ochiai Naobumi in their mildness, but they are nonetheless rather commonplace and weak. His first collection of poems, *Katawarezuki* (Half-Moon) (1901), won him fame.

Akegata no	On a stroll,
Sozoro ariki ni	At peep of dawn
Uguisu no	I heard the first song of the year
Hatsune kikitari	Of the nightingale
Yabukage no michi	On a lane in the shade of a grove.

Hōsenka	The setting sun is shining
Terasu yūhi ni	On a balsam—
Onozukara	Its seeds scatter
Sono mi no warete	Of themselves,
Aki kuremu to su	And autumn is dying.

These pieces were appreciated for the purity of feeling and the skilfulness of technique at that time. In *Shōshikoku* (Little Land of Poetry) (1904), which was published after *Jokeishi*, are found such excellent poems as:

Usuginu ni	Born a ruby flower
Hikari tsutsumeru	Embracing light
Kōgyoku no	With its thin covering,
Hana to umarete	A winter peony blooms
Samushi kambotan	In the cold air.

(Kun'en)

although the collection, as a whole, could not escape the influence of the *Myōjō*. He compiled the works of the members of the Shiragiku Kai (The White Chrysanthemum Society), which he established in October 1903, and published *Reijin* (Bard) (1906). This collection was criticized harshly by the *Myōjō*. Thereafter he approached Naturalism with his succeeding works, *Waga Omoi* (My Thoughts) (1907) and *Sametaru Uta* (Poems of Awakening) (1910); nevertheless, his attitude was lukewarm and assumed a non-committal tone as time went on.

From the Shiragiku Kai arose Oka Tōri, Tanami Mishiro, Yoshiue Shōryō (Aiken), Toki Aika (Koyū), and others. Takeyama Eiko, a younger sister of Kun'en, cut a figure among the group, although she died young, as did Tanami Mishiro.

The name of Ōta Mizuho (Teiichi, Mizuhonoya) must be added here. He played an active role during Taishō, but his début was made at this period. His first volume, *Tsuyukusa* (Gentian) (1902), indicated immaturity, but in the subsequent *Sanjō Kojō* (On Mountain and Lake) (1905), a joint work with Shimaki Akahiko (Yamayuri), he displayed a uniquely elegant, romantic taste in a kind of tenacious style, as in the following :

Waga omoi wa	My thoughts
Nagisa ochiyuku	Take in the sorrow
Unajio no	Of the tide
Urei o hikite	Retreating on the shore,
Tada shizumu naru	And deepen further.
Kurehatete	Night has fallen,
Umi ya sora naru	And the evening star shines
Ochikata no	On the far-off waves
Namima ni oite	Where the sea
Tereru yūzutsu	Meets the sky.

3. *The Realistic Reformation and Its Currents*

Meiji poetry is represented best by the romantic activities of the Shinshisha, but there was another current of realistic tendency which gradually became more powerful, namely that of the Negishi Tanka Kai (Negishi Tanka Society) led by Masaoka Shiki (Tsunenori, Takenosatobito).

As a parallel to the reformation movement led by Tekkan, Shiki published *Utayomi ni Atauru Sho* (An Open Letter to *Waka* Poets) in the newspaper *Nihon* from February to March 1898. (He had begun the work of reformation in the *haiku* several years before this.) This article, which followed Tekkan's *Bōkoku no On*, had a historical significance in the reformation of *tanka*. He made the most harsh criticism of the excessive artifice of the *Kokinshū* on which the old school was modeled, presented a new theory of composition which was founded on realism, and clarified the practical means of renovation. In contrast with Tekkan who solicited help from European poetry, Shiki found the genuine essence of Japanese poetry in the *Manyōshū*, and emphasized that the new *tanka* should begin with the study of the intrinsic nature of the oldest collection of poetry of Japan. His Manyōism was similar to the theory of Amada Guan and Fukumoto Nichinan mentioned before, and to the *Kokka Shinron* (New Theory on Japanese Poetry) (1897) of Suematsu Kenchō, published in the preceding year. It cannot be denied that he was somewhat related to the nationalistic sentiment of the day. However, on the other hand, he held a unique principle of "realistic description" (*shasei*) which developed later into the theory of *shaseiron* and added a new facet to the theory of "return to the *Man-yōshū*." The word *shasei* (copying of life) was borrowed from the technical vocabulary of Western painting, and he utilized it in the wider field of the *haiku*, the *tanka*, and prose, making it his unique theory of realism. This theory of realism was mostly limited to natural description in which he stressed that "impressive and clear" (*inshō meiryō*) aesthetic values should be realized. He did not refer much to the reality of life at large, and the final aim of art was, according to his principle, beauty, so that his theory was not greatly differentiated from that of Yosano Tekkan; the only difference was that Shiki adhered to the concrete method of describing reality, not hazarding to go far into the land of ideals.

The founding of the Negishi Tanka Kai took place in March 1899, when the first gathering was held at Shiki's house in Negishi. Those who joined it were Katori Hotsuma, Oka Fumoto, Kimura Hōu, Akagi Kakudō, Itō Sachio, Nagatsuka Takashi, Warabi Makoto, and others. His outside activities, beginning in 1900, were carried on in the poetry column of the newspaper *Nihon* and the magazine *Kokoro no Hana*. In August of the same year, Shiki sent a letter to Tekkan, and intended to discuss the development of the new *tanka* through the confrontation of romanticism and realism. The plan miscarried, and contrary to his initial idea, it was widely believed that he held the opinion of the incompatibility of his views with those of Tekkan.

1900 was the most fruitful year for the Negishi Tanka Kai.

After the death of Shiki, the school continued its activities by the publication of the magazine *Ashibi* in June 1903 by Itō Sachio, Katori Hotsuma, and Nagatsuka Takashi. But in that golden age of romantic poetry, their poems were apt to imitate the *Manyōshū* superficially and tended to pseudo-classicism; thus, having little relevance to the feeling of the times, they could by no means enter into the main current of the world of poetry. Their anthology, *Takenosatobito Senka* (An Anthology Selected by Takenosatobito, *i. e.*, Shiki), was published in 1904.

Throughout the whole life of Masaoka Shiki, realistic and picturesque impressionistic beauty was his characteristic, but there were some changes in the process of its development. As mentioned before, he published his poetical work *Hyakuchū-Jisshu* together with the *Utayomi ni Atauru Sho* " open letter," and making his new attempt public, he won attention, though his early *tanka* betrayed the masculinity of Chinese poetry, and the mere contrast pattern found in *haiku*.

Ensaki ni	At the edge of the veranda
Tamamaku bashō	The rolled up leaves of the plantain
Tama tokete	Unfurled today
Goshaku no midori	And covered the wash-basin
Chōzubachi o ōu	With two yards of green.
Hito mo kozu	No one comes—
Haru yuku niwa no	Only the petals of the yellow rose
Mizu no ue ni	Scatter
Koborete tamaru	On the pond of my garden,
Yamabuki no hana	As spring departs.
Kanjin no	There is not even a trace
Roba ni muchiutsu	Of the donkeys
Kage mo nashi	That officials drive—
Kinshū Jō-gai	Outside the castle of Chinchou
Yanagi seisei	Willows are deep green.

The novel idea he held can be traced even in these pieces, but he was in his element when he emerged from such a structural manner, selected his material from surrounding objects of daily life, and put it into a picturesque frame. This tendency revealed itself suddenly in 1900, at the peak of the activity of the Negishi Tanka Kai. He attained the ideal of descriptive poetry with a most minute observation of objects, as in :

Shimo-ōi no	The straw cover that has prevented
Wara torisutsuru	frost
Shakuyaku no	Is removed today—
Me no kurenai ni	On the crimson bud
Haru no ame furu	Of the peony
	Falls the rain of spring.
Tomoshibi no	The spring rain pours
Hikari ni terasu	On the peonies
Mado no soto no	Outside the window
Botan ni sosogu	Within the lamplight
Haru no yo no ame	I hold in the night.
Matsu no ha no	Thousands of raindrops
Hosoki hagoto ni	On every needle
Oku tsuyu no	Of the pine-tree,
Chitsuyu mo yurani	Trembling like so many pearls,
Tama mo koborezu	Still cling and never fall.

Then came the third stage. A remarkable degree of lyricism was added to his former attitude, through increased understanding of the spirit of the *Manyōshū* and the consciousness of subjectivity in *tanka* composition. He began freely to collect material from the common objects around his sickbed, and composed a number of poems on the same subject (*rensaku*), which show a mellowed style and a free and easy character. In 1901 he wrote :

Bin ni sasu	The corolla of wistaria
Fuji no hanabusa	I put into the vase
Mijikakereba	Is so short
Tatami no ue ni	It does not reach
Todokazarikeri	The floor.

At the back of the precise description, we notice his mental condition, and in others of his works, such as :

Sahogami no	How sad am I to depart
Wakare kanashimo	From the Goddess of Spring !
Kon haru ni	I doubt if I meet her
Futatabi awan	When she comes
Ware naranakuni	Round again next year.
Ichihatsu no	The iris
Hana saki idete	Has come into flower
Waga me ni wa	And the last spring
Kotoshi bakari no	My eyes shall see
Haru yukan to su	Departs.

he manifested an almost heart-breaking pathos with a flowing style, yet curbing a cheap sentimentality. Descriptive realism in the *tanka*, which is substantially lyric poetry, was a subject of study he left for his school to perform. In Shiki himself, there lay an intense pursuit of beauty at the basis of realistic description. Herein lies a characteristic of *shasei* theory in the Meiji Period. After his death his works were edited by the hands of his disciples to form *Takenosato-Uta* (Poems by Shiki) (1904).

As mentioned above, Masaoka Shiki's *shasei* had significance in its espousal of realism in poetry ; but he did it as a means effective and appropriate, unlike fantastic, idealistic romanticism, and not as a final absolute for composition. Thus, among the members of the Negishi Tanka Kai there were two types of poets : those who thoroughly investigated realism, and those who tended to idealism. Nagatsuka Takashi was the one who went the former way in the purest degree.

Takashi entered the Shiki school when young, and followed Shiki faithfully as he progressed, with a mild and serene method of composition. The essay he contributed to the *Ashibi* was entitled *Shasei no Uta ni tsuite* (On Descriptive Poetry) (1905), and it was the pioneer work which proclaimed the realism in *tanka*, introducing Shiki's objective method in a compact form, and which emphasized the close observation of " the details of a blade of grass and a tree."

Aki no no ni	On the autumn field

Mame hiku ato ni	Among the weeds
Hiki nokoru	That remained
Hagusa ga naka no	After harvesting peas,
Kōrogi no koe	The voice of a cricket.
Kakenameshi	Lonely is the tea tree
Ine no tsukane o	Among the scattered straw
Torisareba	After the rice-plants
Wara no midare ni	Were taken in
Sabishi cha no ki wa	That had been hung on the racks.

These are his early poems, which succeeded in catching the
delicacy of the natural beauty precisely, and penetrated to the
bottom of it. What he aimed at, however, was minute and accurate
presentation rather than the colorful description of Masaoka
Shiki. On this point Takashi did not go exactly the same way
as Shiki; nevertheless, it was significant that the former
provided the means of saving the Negishi school poets from
falling into the mannerism of the *Manyōshū*. Takashi's style
showed a new development from about 1908 :

Sayo fuke ni	The barnyard grass is said
Sakite chirutō	To bloom and fall
Hiekusa no	In a night—
Hisoyaka ni shite	So secretly and silently
Aki sarinuramu	Autumn seems to come.
Umaoi no	Close your eyes and consider
Hige no soyoro ni	Autumn is coming—
Kuru aki wa	It comes touching
Manako o tojite	The trembling antenna
Omoi miru beshi	Of a grasshopper.

In these *tanka*, which reflect the intangible movement of the
season that fills the world the poet perceives, he created a unique
field of poetry. Afterwards he turned to prose and left the
poets' circle, but in 1911 when he began to suffer from larynx
tuberculosis he came back to his former career.

Iki mo shini mo	There was a time
Ten no manimani to	When I thought it
Tairakeku	In the Heavenly Hand
Omoitarishi wa	Either to live or to die—

Tsune no toki nariki   It was a peaceful time.

This is found at the beginning of a series of bedside poems
(*Byōshō Zatsuei*), and it is filled with a feeling of pathos that
touches the reader's heart.

In addition to Nagatsuka Takashi, Shiki's faithful follower
who applied his principle to a delicate and sharp method of
composition, there was another poet who succeeded Shiki, though
in his own way, and made a further extension, namely Itō Sachio
(Kōjirō). He took the name of Shun'en at an early age, started
a career as a classical poet, and later joined Shiki's group at
about the time when Nagatsuka Takashi did. After Shiki died,
he became the actual leader of the *Ashibi* and a merciless critic
of the *Myōjō* school. By nature he was self-assertive, and went
the opposite way from that of Takashi. He emphasized the
content of poetry, but he was prone to " idealistic " and
" formalistic " taste. He also sought to express the lyricism of
the *tanka* in note and accent. He later came to emphasize
these as *gengo no seika* (the transformation of words into sound)
and *sakebi* (exclamation, or ejaculation).

The following poem shows his great ambition when he entered
the Shiki school.

Ushikai ga	When the cowherd
Uta yomu toki ni	Writes a poem,
Yo no naka no	New poems will rise up
Atarashiki uta	Flourishingly
Ōi ni okoru	In the whole world of Japan.

He was a Buddhist, ran a dairy, and was interested in the tea
ceremony and pottery, all of which tastes are reflected in his
poetry. His style was grand, full of lyricism, and consequently
it bore brilliant fruit.

Hito no sumu	Having left
Kunibe o idete	The country of men,
Shiranami ga	White waves
Daichi futawakeshi	Divide the earth in two

Hate ni kinikeri	And extend afar.
Ametsuchi no	Here the fences are
Yomo no yoriai o	The heavens
Kaki ni seru	That hang on every side—
Kujūkuri no hama ni	On the sand of Kujūkuri Beach
Tama hiroi ori	I pick the precious stones.
Takayama mo	At the farthest end of earth
Hikuyama mo naki	The Heaven hangs
Chi no hate wa	Like a curtain before me
Miru me no mae ni	Where there is no hill nor mountain
Ame shi taretari	High or low.

These poems are a part of the series of *tanka* composed on Kujūkuri Beach.   In a grand *Manyōshū* style, the sublimity of nature was admirably copied, and they almost attained perfection.

Sabishisa no	Enduring
Kiwami ni taete	The extreme of loneliness,
Ametsuchi ni	I think deeply
Yosuru inochi o	Of life submitted to
Tsukuzuku to omou	Heaven and Earth.

Furthermore he published an essay, *Zoku Shinkaron* (On the New Waka, Continued) (1902), in the magazine *Kokoro no Hana*. In this article, he discussed *rensaku* (a series of poems on the same subject), and found a new way to extend the area of the *tanka*, which is limited in its length.   This essay exerted a strong influence on the poets that were to come.

4.   *The Naturalistic and Decadent* Waka *Style*

The Meiji *tanka*, which was transformed by the romantic current at the surface, and realistic and descriptive tendency at the bottom, was characterized by the subjective, romantic nature holding " beauty " as its ultimate ideal.   However, after the Russo-Japanese War of 1904–1905, Naturalism became dominant throughout the Japanese literary world, and since the romantic tendency gradually declined, the poets arrived at another turning-point.   Between 1909, the year after the *Myōjō* discontinued publication, and the end of the Meiji Era (1912), various transitional phenomena were seen in connection with the dissolution of Meiji *tanka* and the formation of a new poetry circle. Before this, Mori Ōgai, sympathizer of the new *tanka*, held the Kanchōrō Kakai (Poetical Assembly) at his residence, the Kanchōrō, from March 1907 to the summer of 1909. Through this assembly Ōgai endeavored to unite the poets of the Shinshisha tradition and those of the Negishi school in order to establish a new Japanese poetry. Although Ōgai's effort did not bear as much fruit as he had expected, the poets of both schools had the opportunity to associate with each other, which did much to promote the new poetry movement.

All the poets of this period started from the Naturalistic sentiment of actual life, and their characteristics can be summarized as follows : Concerning content, they changed from a romantic aesthetic tendency to realistic concern with actual life, put more stress on actual truth and the self, and introduced their negative, sceptic view of life into lyricism ; as for expression, they parted with the roundabout, symbolical, and metaphorical taste and pseudo-classic formalism, and made use of plain, direct language, impressive, sensual description, and a prose-like tone. More than that, the prose spirit of Naturalism incited those poets to harbor distrust of the *tanka* itself and a sceptical attitude toward the traditional poetry as a whole. Onoe Saishū published, at this critical moment, October 1910, *Tanka Metsubō Shiron* (A Treatise on the Fall of the Tanka) in the magazine *Sōsaku*. In this essay he stated an exceedingly pessimistic opinion on the future of the *tanka* because of the narrowness of its form and language. Though his attitude was decisive and challenging, it stopped at the application of the prose spirit to the *tanka*, and since it lacked deep perception we cannot see any concrete development thereafter. Nevertheless, his students Wakayama Bokusui (Shigeru), and Maeda Yūgure (Yōzō) materialized, in their creative activities, the Naturalistic tendency.

Wakayama Bokusui, as had Maeda Yūgure, emerged from the

Shazensōsha of Saishū, his first collection of poems being *Umi no Koe* (The Voice of the Sea) (1908), followed by *Hitori Utaeru* (Poems of Myself) (1910). *Betsuri* (Parting) (1910) established his fame with its sonorous note that contained the romantic aspiration of youth.

Ikuyama kawa	How many mountains and rivers
Koesariyukaba	Have I to cross
Sabishisa no	Before I come
Hatenamu kuni zo	To the land of no sorrow ?
Kyō mo tabiyuku	I keep on my pilgrimage this day again.
Shiratori wa	Are you not lonely,
Kanashikarazu ya	White bird ?
Sora no ao	You float without being dyed
Umi no ao ni mo	By the blue of the sky
Somazu tadayou	Or the blue of the sea.

Bokusui's poetry is always tinged with a feeling of wonder and pathos. In a sense it does not belong to the realistic school, but there flows natural simplicity in its tone, and one notices much more sincerity in its artless mode of composition than in the metaphorical poetry of the Shinshisha poets. The title of *Betsuri* connotes his parting from youth.

Ā kuchizuke	Ah, a kiss—
Umi sono mama ni	The sea stops its movement,
Hi wa yukazu	The sun does not go,
Tori mainagara	And flying birds
Use hateyo ima	Die and fall, now !
Hi wa hi nari	The sun is the sun ;
Waga sabishisa wa	My sorrow
Waga no nari	Is also mine.
Mahiru nagisa no	I stand on a sand-dune
Sunayama ni tatsu	At noonday.

The joy and sorrow of love seem to have been sealed in these *tanka*, of which people were very fond. In the next volume, *Rojō* (On the Road) (1911), self-mockery and loneliness are intensified :

Unazoko ni	It is said that

Me no naki uo no	Eyeless fish live
Sumu to iu	At the bottom of the ocean—
Me no naki uo no	These eyeless fish
Koishikarikeri	Are dear to me.
Otoroeshi	It has begun to snow—
Waga shinkeɩ ni	Fluttering
Uchihibiki	In the evening air,
Yūbe shirajira	Jarring
Yuki furiidenu	On my weakened nerves.

He founded the Sōsakusha in January 1911, and began to publish the magazine *Sōsaku* as the periodical of the association. Later he tried free-verse poetry and the poetry of self-confession, and as a Naturalistic poet he was not consistent.

Maeda Yūgure was nearer to Naturalism than Bokusui. He sang of everyday occurrences with a simple attitude. He organized the Hakujitsusha (The Midday Society), the name of which symbolized its opposition to the *Myōjō* (The Morning Star), began publishing *Higuruma* (The Sunflower) and even a pamphlet entitled *Airaku* (Joy and Sorrow), and kept pace with Bokusui's *Sōsaku*. In April 1911 he began publishing *Shiika* (Poetry). His first collection of *tanka*, *Shūkaku* (Harvest) (1910), still contained poetry of a romantic flavor :

Kokoromi ni	Just close your eyes—
Me toji mitamae	You will feel
Haru no hi wa	The spring sun
Shihō ni otsuru	Shedding its beams
Kokochi seraremu	Around you.
Ki ni hana saki	April is still far ahead—
Kimi waga tsuma to	The month when trees
Naran hi no	Are decked with flowers
Shigatsu nakanaka	And you will become
Tōku mo aru kana	My wife.

but about the time when he founded *Shiika*, an unpretentious, realistic tendency made its appearance in place of this early romantic sentimentalism.

Akasabishi	I put in my pocket
Chiisaki kagi o	The rusty

Tamoto ni shi	Little key,
Tsuma to akaruki	And with my wife
Yoru no machi yuku	I walk the lighted street.
Hatsunatsu no	It's sad to see
Ame ni nuretaru	The white nameplate
Waga ie no	On my house
Shiroki nafuda no	Drenched
Sabishikarikeri	By the early summer rain.

These poems were included in *In'ei* (Shadows) (1913).

Kubota Utsubo contributed his works to the *Bunko* and *Myōjō* earlier than the two mentioned above, and at this stage established himself in a Naturalistic mode of composition. As discussed above, Utsubo played an active part in the Shinshisha for a time, but essentially he tended to Naturalism which was in opposition to Myōjōism. In *Mahiruno* (Midday Field) (1905), which won him fame, is found:

Kane narashi	If I should go on a pilgrimage
Shinano no kuni o	To the province of Shinano,
Yuki yukaba	Ringing the hand-bells,
Arishi nagara no	Could I meet with my dear mother
Haha miruramu ka	As she was in this world ?

There is indeed much of romantic spirit, but with the sincere and truthful feeling that pervades it, we should rather link it with the Naturalism of this period. In 1905 he organized the Jūgatsu Kai (The October Society), and then published *Meian* (Light and Dark) in collaboration with Mizuno Yōshū. Afterwards he wrote some novels under the influence of Naturalism. It was in Taishō that he displayed his ability, but even before then he published his works in the *Hakuroshū* (The Silver Dew Anthology) (1907), *Reimei* (Dawn) (1910), and anthologies of the Jūgatsu Kai, and he also brought out a collection of his own poems, *Utsubo Kashū* (Poems by Utsubo) (1912).

Bō to shite	In a land
Ki naru hikari no	Where yellow light
Nijimu kuni	Prevails extensively
Ware ari chiisaki	I stand

Ko o dakite tatsu	With a child in my arms.
	(from *Reimei*)
Mazushikute	" I thought
Ko wa araseji to	I would not have my child
Omoinu to	Live a poor life."
Mimakarinikeru	My father's words
Chichi ga hitokoto	Who is no more.
	(from *Utsubo Kashū*)

These poems demonstrate that he was in his element when he sang of a humble and sober life with his near relatives.

Succeeding Wakayama Bokusui and Maeda Yūgure, Toki Aika (Zemmaro, Koyū) and Ishikawa Takuboku were active as Naturalistic poets, and later as poets with a social consciousness. They held a new outlook on social affairs, and, with an attitude closely linked to the reality of life, endeavored to depart from the Naturalistic mood. Both of them were pioneers of the Seikatsu-Ha, or the Life Group.

Toki came from the Shiragiku Kai of Kaneko Kun'en. He had been influenced by Naturalism while he attended Waseda University. Through his first collection of poems, *Nakiwarai* (A Tearful Smile) (1910), which contained those written in a plain style of three lines in Romanized spelling, he won the favor of Takuboku. It was in his second book, *Tasogare ni* (In the Twilight) (1912), which was written after he became friends with Takuboku, that he gave expression to his social consciousness.

Te no shiroki	Pitiful
Rōdōsha koso	Is the laborer
Kanashikere—	With white hands.
Kokkin no sho o	He was reading the prohibited book
Namida shite yomeri	With tears in his eyes.

On the other hand some of his poems are colored with a mild romanticism.

Yubi o mote	Tracing down farther,
Tōku tadoreba	My finger finds the
Mizuiro no	Dear

Voruga no kawa no　　　Blue line
Natsukashiki kana　　　Of the Volga River.

At other times, a modern sensitive feeling rules his poetry, which is different from Takuboku's sharp, dark feeling towards life.

Rintenki　　　　　　Roar,
Ima koso hibike—　　Rotary press machines !
Ureshiku mo　　　　Isn't it pleasant
Tōkyō-ban ni　　　　To see snow begin to fall
Yuki no furiizu　　　When the Tōkyō edition is coming off
　　　　　　　　　　the press.

In contrast with Toki Aika, who had a somewhat refreshing though realistic tone, Ishikawa Takuboku established the poetry of this school with that passionate feeling which came out of his life's struggle and rough manner of expression. He contributed his poems to the *Myōjō* and *Subaru*, and became known for his precocity. In about 1908 he began to write such symbolic poems as,

Aozameshi　　　　　Only one
Ōi naru kao　　　　Pale
Tada hitotsu　　　　Broad face
Sora ni ukaberi　　　Is hanging in the sky
Aki no yo no umi　　Above the sea of an
　　　　　　　　　　autumn night.

which, at the same time, betrayed the bitter grief of reality. In the first book of three-line poems, *Ichiaku no Suna* (A Handful of Sand) (1910), he sang of the life of a vagabond.

Tōkai no kojima no iso no shirasuna ni
Ware nakinurete
Kani to tawamuru

On the white sand of a small island in the eastern sea,
My face wet with tears,
I play with a crab.

Yamai no goto
Shikyō no kokoro waku hi nari
Me ni aozora no kemuri kanashimo
Feeling homesick,

I look up at the blue sky,
And am sad to find some streaks of smoke therein.

Having freed himself from the *Myōjō* style, he expressed the
sharp pains of life in a simple, unadorned manner, and tried to
give voice to the impulsive feeling that arises from poverty
and self-despair.

Takaki yori tobioriru gotoki kokoro mote
Kono isshō o
Owaru sube naki ka

Isn't there a way of ending life
With the mind of throwing myself
From off a height ?

A feeling of defeat in actual life is positively expressed in the
poem above. In *Kanashiki Gangu* (Sad Toys) (1912), which appeared immediately after his death, the poems have a still more
desperate tone and display a radical impulse which came from
the oppression of life.

Yaya tōki mono ni omoishi
Terorisuto no kanashiki kokoro mo
Chikazuku hi no ari

The sad heart of the terrorists
That I felt far
Comes near to me sometimes.

Or at times he voiced the most stifling nihilistic feelings.

Aru hi futo yamai o wasure
Ushi no naku mane o shiteminu
Tsumako no rusu ni

Sometimes I suddenly forgot my sickness
And mimicked an ox's lowing
While my family was out.

His short life ended in April 1912, together with the Meiji
Era. Towards the end of his life he approached socialism ;
the following poem shows sign of this :

Aki no kaze
Warera Meiji no seinen no kiki o kanashimu
Kao nadete fuku

The autumn wind is blowing,
Stroking the faces of the young men of Meiji
Who feel sorrow at the crisis of the times.

But generally speaking we cannot say that socialistic thought was always present in his poems which he called his " sad toys." The reason he won popularity was that he expressed the young people's sentiment in the form of *tanka* in the most popular manner, and, as a result, he succeeded in making the best use of the sentimental aspect of the nature of *tanka*. On this point we can say that he and Bokusui represent the two directions of the Naturalistic *tanka* poets.

Among the Shinshisha poets, Yoshii Isamu and Kitahara Hakushū were most active. Both of them belonged to the *Myōjō* and are representative younger poets of the school's latter period. After the magazine was discontinued, they joined the *Subaru* mentioned above, and showed a new development in their works. Their poems, also, while being rooted in a Naturalistic feeling, in the matter of developing into the beauty of decadent instinct and of a hedonistic atmosphere, are similar to those of the previously mentioned Decadent poets.

Isamu exhibited his skill in love poetry in the latter period of the Shinshisha, and the first collection of poems *Sakehogai* (The Drinking Party) (1910) established his fame. Though he sang of love and a decadent life, his tone was masculine and free-hearted, and won the greatest reception since *Midaregami*.

Natsu wa kinu	Summer has come
Sagami no umi no	With the southern wind
Nampū ni	Of Sagami Bay ;
Waga hitomi moyu	My eyes burn,
Waga kokoro moyu	My heart burns.
Kimi ga tame	Because of you
Shōsō konan no	These maidens
Otomera wa	Of the Izu region
Ware to asobazu	Are loath
Narinikeru kana	To dally with me.

Izu mo miyu	The shore of Izu
Izu no yamabi mo	Is seen on the horizon;
Mare ni miyu	The mountain fire too
Izu wa mo koishi	Can be seen sometimes—
Waga imo no goto	How I long for Izu, as for my love.

Youthful aspiration is abundantly poured forth in these poems which some critics valued as highly as those of the *Manyōshū*. Singing of the red-lantern quarters:

Ka ni kaku ni	I love Gion
Gion wa koishi	Any way—
Neru toki mo	Even when I lie in bed
Makura no shita o	I hear water
Mizu no nagaruru	Flowing near my pillow.
Waga mune no	The beating of the drum
Tsuzumi no hibiki	Within my breast
Tō tarari	Becomes louder
Tō tō tarari to	And louder
Yoeba tanoshiki	As I drink and am glad.

the gay atmosphere is presented. After that Isamu wrote *Suisōki* (From the Mansion beside the Waters), an essay with poems, in *Sōsaku*, as well as plays, and attained a unique position in the literary world, but few changes were seen in his manner of composition.

Kitahara Hakushū incorporated the delicate and varied modern mood into the *tanka* as he did into longer New Style poems.

Haraisou	A seagull, I
Sono sora yumemi	Ascend to the sky
Kamome ware	Dreaming of Heaven,
Honoka ni noboru	The Paradise,
Umi no kōro ni	From the incense-burner of the sea.
Kuragari o	Into my dream come
Akaki hana shiku	More than a hundred
Kuruma no wa	Wheels
Kazu hyaku amari	That run over
Waga yume ni iru	The red flower in the dark.

He utilized his rich vocabulary, as he did in *Jashūmon*, for some time, and followed the extravagant style of Yosano Akiko.

It was after he joined the *Subaru* that he departed from the symbolistic manner of the *Myōjō* and established his own unique style of modernity. Prior to this, he contributed an essay, *Kiri no Hana to Kasutera* (Paulownia Blossom and Spongecake), to the magazine *Sōsaku* which explained his view of the *tanka*. According to this view, his *tanka* were a by-product of his poetical life, "a little, old, green jewel," and "the essence of sentiment of a pathetic age." He tried to give special light and shade to the *tanka* with delicate sensitivity and modern sentiment, and his goal was attained completely in this volume. An impressionistic composition and rhythmical note conveyed youthful sentiment in :

Haru no tori	Stop singing,
Na nakiso nakiso	Spring bird,
Aka aka to	Stop singing, pray,
To no mo no kusa ni	The crimson sun is setting
Hi no iru yūbe	In the grass outside the window.

Modern sensation moves in :

Hiyashinsu	A hyacinth
Usumurasaki ni	Began blooming
Sakinikeri	Light purple
Hajimete kisu o	On the day
Oboesomeshi hi	I knew my first kiss.
Amaririsu	When the amaryllis
Yume mo fukage ni	Was dreamily
Niou toki	Fragrant,
Futo kuchibiru o	The lips of the two
Sashiateshi kana	Were pressed together.

The fresh mood of :

Iyahate ni	Finally
Ukon-zakura no	The last cherry-blossoms fall
Kanashimi no	And my sorrow
Chirihate nureba	Fades away,
Satsuki wa kitaru	As May arrives.

and the urban sentiment of :

Yuki shiroki	It is morning
Asa no shikiishi	On the snow-covered pavement

Saku saku to	Where a child is walking
Ringo kamitsutsu	Crunching an apple.
Yuku wa tagako zo	Who is he, I wonder ?

were introduced into the world for the first time by Kitahara Hakushū, on which point he brought about a splendid effect in the interrelationship of classical *tanka* and the modern mode of poetry. These poems were included in his first collection, *Kiri no Hana* (Paulownia Blossoms) (1913), which was highly valued by the public and exerted a great influence on the poetic world.

Under these circumstances the effects of the Negishi Tanka Kai must be regarded. The magazine *Ashibi*, first published after Shiki's death, was virtually maintained by Itō Sachio alone, as the result of the dispersion of its leading members. In January 1908 the *Ashibi* was discontinued, and in the following month it was handed over to Mitsui Kōshi's *Akane* (Madder). But this magazine, too, was discontinued because of the discord with Sachio. In October of the same year, Warabi Makoto founded the *Araragi* with Itō Sachio as its head, and began establishing the foundation for the following period.

Although the pseudo-classical poets who had formerly belonged to the *Ashibi*, and Itō Sachio, who was going his own detached way, were out of the mainstream of the times, the younger generation was strongly influenced by it. Those who underwent the influence of the times most sensitively were Shimaki Akahiko (Kubota Toshihiko, Kaki-no-Mura-hito), Saitō Mokichi, Koizumi Chikashi (Ikutarō), Nakamura Kenkichi, and Horiuchi Taku. Tsuchiya Bummei also was publishing his works. Akahiko and Mokichi, at the end of this period, shortly held the leadership of the *Araragi* and showed a new tendency, eliminating Sachio's influence, that is to say, moving from objective description and pseudo-classic Manyōism into a sharp, sensuous Naturalistic trend, which resulted from the their contact with the wider circle of poetry and impressionist painters.

Nevertheless, they did not depart from the realistic method, in spite of such multifarious stimulants, and consolidated their own groundwork for the next period. Their effort was manifested in the theoretical work of Saitō Mokichi which was based upon the studies of Western poetics and scientific observation of the *Manyōshū*. They also tried to take in the spirit of the *Manyōshū* through their experiments at turning "descriptive realism" into "introspective realism."

Shimaki Akahiko was the poet who had published the *Sanjō Kojō* earlier with Ōta Mizuho, and through the local magazine *Himuro* had a connection with the *Ashibi*. Later, in 1909, he merged it with the *Araragi*. His poetry was solid in style.

Kusakare no	The sun shone
Kuni no kubomi ni	On several marshes
Katamareru	Grouped in the low places in the
Numa no ikutsu ni	country
Hi atarinikeri	At this season
	Of withering grass.

His even description can be found in the above poem. On the other hand his sharp sensitivity can be found in:

Asa teru hi no	In the morning sun
Usurashimo	Thin frost
Hiebie to	Melts and soaks
Tade no niguki ni	Chilly
Tokete shimu kana	Into the red stem of the smartweed.

Kenkichi wrote gentle and mild poems, from his *Ashibi* period, and in:

Tani no oku ni	Feeling pitiful and
Aoku kiyubeki	Reminiscing,
Tabi no mi o	I go on a trip
Suzuro hakanaku	And finally vanish away
Kaeriminikeri	In the depth of a valley.

the delicate sense of the writer can be seen in the tendency to sensuousness, reflecting the trend of the time. The poems of the two were later compiled in one volume, *Bareisho no Hana*

(The Potato Blossom) (1913).

Koizumi Chikashi showed the most ordered poems of these three men having Naturalistic tendency. An example of this is:

Machi no ue ni	The smell of
Usuki hokori no	Fine dust rises
Nioi tachi	Over the street
Akehanareyuku .	As today's sadness
Kyō no kanashisa	Departs with the dawn.

Among the younger generation, Saitō Mokichi showed the widest ability by the sharp senses and intense spirit of his realism. He joined Sachio's school at the time of the *Ashibi* and was called an idealist, his style being compared with the realistic manner of Horiuchi Taku. It was from about 1911 that he displayed his unique qualities for which he was gradually becoming noted. A pressing impetus is seen in:

Shirogane no	In a mountain
Yuki furu yama ni	Where the silver snow falls
Hito kayou	A thread
Hosohoso to shite	Of path is seen
Michi miyuru kana	Where people go.
Hitori nomi	All alone
Asa no iihamu	I eat my breakfast—
Aga inochi wa	I think my life
Mijikakaran to	Will not be long—
Moite iihamu	And keep on eating.

An extraordinarily sharp sense and a fresh observation of objects are seen in:

Honoka naru	When I gaze at
Myōga no hana o	The *myōga* blossom
Mamoru toki	With its faint fragrance,
Waga omou ko wa	I think of my beloved child
Haruka naru kamo	Far away.
Neko no shita no	As my hand touches
Usura ni akaki	The pink
Te no furi no	Tongue of a cat
Kono kanashisa o	I know for the first time
Shirisomenikeri	This sadness.

Akanasu no	My steps
Kusarete itaru	Are not very far
Tokoro yori	From the point
Ikuhodo mo naki	Reached by a rotting
Ayumi narikeri	Tomato.

where readers may feel as if they are face to face with a cross-section of consciousness. With these poems Mokichi's name became widely known. His works in this period were included in his first collection of poems, *Shakkō* (Red Light) (1913), which was noted and admired. Thus, the *Araragi* gained an authoritative position in the world of poetry.

The world of the *tanka* in the Taishō Era seemed to be dominated by the *Araragi*, and the secure establishment of symbolic-descriptive poetry (*i. e.*, idealistic realism) was achieved. But the nucleus of this movement is to be found at the end of the Meiji Era.

THE REFORM IN *HAIKU* POETRY AND
ITS DEVELOPMENT

1. *The Remnant of the Edo* Haiku *Poets and the New Style*

For the *haikai* poetry world, the years between the end of
the Edo Period and the beginning of Meiji seemed merely a
continuation of the Tempō Era (1830–1841). The so-called Three
Great Masters of this Tempō Era, namely Sōkyū, Baishitsu, and
Hōrō, had shown concern only in the solidification of their
secular influence as deans of their respective schools, and displayed
a complete lack of refinement. As a consequence, poets who
came under the influence of these masters were swayed by vulgar
fashion. *Haikai* poetry, as far as these poets were concerned,
had degenerated into a sort of game in which the primary
objective was to obtain good marks and the approbation of the
masters.

In spite of this stagnancy, the new age was to usher in certain
developments peculiar to the new civilization. One of such was
the founding of the *Haika Shimbun* (Haiku Poets' Newspaper)
in movable type in 1868, followed by that of the *Haikai Shimbunshi* (Haikai Gazette) by Taibaiu Otohiko in the following
year. The Meiji government, on the other hand, decided to
carry its educational policies into the field of *haikai* poetry for
the purpose of utilizing this literary genre to guide public morality. Under this decision, the government created a post called
the *Haikai* Instructorship in 1874, to which were appointed
such poets as Shunjūan Mikio, Tōkian Tsukihiko, Tsukinomoto
Izan, and Kochikuan Shunko. The same year saw the formation
of the Haikai Kyōrin Meisha (Haikai Culture Society) and the
Meirin Kōsha (Enlightenment Discussion Society) with Izan and
Mikio as their respective presidents. Both societies gave support
to the government's policies and engaged in the task of imple-
menting the enlightenment movement. The latter body, the
Meirin Kōsha, started publication of its organ, the *Haikai* : *Mei-*

rin Zasshi (Haikai Enlightenment Magazine), in 1880. Although these activities helped in arousing the social consciousness of the established *haikai* masters, this did not necessarily mean that they played any important role in raising the artistic consciousness of the masters' group. The new change brought about in the *haikai* world was of a restricted nature, and such activities as the compilation of poems on seasonal themes on the basis of the Western calendar and the borrowing of themes from the emerging new civilization were limited, in the sense that they were merely efforts to adapt *haikai* to the new age superficially, and nothing more.

The most celebrated poet to appear after the closing days of the Edo Period was Izan, a disciple of Baishitsu. Soon after him came Kahōen Tōsai and Shunko. These three became the Three Great Masters of the day. As might be expected of a "master," all three of these poets had accomplished techniques, and their skilfulness gave their verses a certain charm. But this skilfulness was restricted to technique, and this resulted in shallowness of feeling. Naturally, there is no sign of originality in their verses.

The following are some examples of their work:

Afure-i mo	From the gushing spring
Kesa wakamizu no	A pail of new water
Tsurube kana	For this New Year morn
	(Izan)
Asagao ya	A morning glory
Kaki yori ue wa	Higher than the fence
Onore-zaki	Blooms alone
	(Izan)
Kawasemi no	A kingfisher
Kakehi ni kitari	Alights on the bamboo spout
Kesa no aki	This autumn morning
	(Tōsai)
Ake no koe	At dawn
Ichi ichi sayuru	The shrill cries of the plover
Chidori kana	One by one
	(Tōsai)

Nanohana ni	Wave-crests
Iran to suru ya	Threaten to enter
Hashirinami	The field of rape blossoms

(Shunko)

Yuki no hi ya	A snowy day
Torinoko-gami no	Clouded
Usugumori	Like thin *torinoko* paper

(Shunko)

In addition to these masters, Rōsodō Eiki and Shinjūan Mikio headed separate schools, establishing their influence in the Tōkyō *haikai* circles. Eiki was author of verses of such graceful quality as the following:

Hi o daseba	As I shine the lantern
Oboro ugoku ya	The haze moves
Mizu no ue	Above the water

Yūzakura	The evening cherry blossoms
Oshimarenu mi ni	Sprinkle their petals
Furikakaru	Over me whom no one loves

Mikio also wrote poems displaying a serene mood, such as:

Ume sakite	Plum flowers bloom
Yururi to narishi	And the days are
Tsukihi kana	Long and tranquil

Kuru hazu no	As expected
Yō ni kuru nari	There came
Sayo shigure	The fine evening rain

However, both poets showed a tendency to appeal to logic, which gave their verses a mundane quality.

Fuhakken Bainen and Setchūan Jakushi constitute another group of established *haikai* poets. Their representative verses are:

Hito no sumu	Smoke is seen—
Keburi mo miete	A sign of human habitation
Aki no yama	In the autumn mountain

(Bainen)

Yūzuki ya	In the evening moonlight
Nagaruru tsuyu o	Dewdrops trickle down
Manoatari	Before my eyes

(Jakushi)

Kyōto was represented in the *haikai* world by Hananomoto Chōshū who composed such poems as:

Kogarashi no	The winter tempest
Konoha kyoshō ni	Blows dead leaves
Maikominu	Into the temple bell

The *haikai* poets of this period displayed in general a complacent attitude and clung to obsolete styles, unaware of the fact that they were captives of vulgarity.

Signs of a new movement in the *haikai* world are evident from about 1890. One of these was the formation that year of the Murasaki Ginsha (Purple Poetry Society) under the leadership of Ozaki Kōyō. Kōyō had shown interest in *haikai* poetry since his younger days. He called upon Kawakami Bizan, Iwaya Sazanami, and other members of his Ken'yūsha to form a *haikai* poetry circle. His principal motive, however, was to utilize the poetic form as means of polishing a prose style. Therefore, he regarded *haikai* composition as a secondary occupation, and as a result was held in contempt by the established masters of the form. Since they regarded Saikaku as their dean in the field of the novel, the members of this group adopted the Danrin style in their *haikai* composition. This style was the one originated by Nishiyama Sōin who was the *haikai* teacher of Saikaku.

The group members indulged in an extravagant and eccentric style based on jokes and puns. Such a style can be perceived in the following examples:

Nagare-mo ya	Floating duckweed—
Ashi naki kishi ni	On the reedless shore
Tsuke-bin su	False sidelocks
	(Kōyō)

Inazuma ya	A flash of lightning—
Yami o tachiwaru	A sword
Hitogatana	Cleaving the darkness
	(Kōyō)

Shukusei ga	Shukusei observing a fast
Te o dashite miru	Wonders if he could try
Tanishi kana	A mud snail

(Bizan)

Otoko to ya	A *sumō* wrestler—
Hadaka hyakkan no	A man with nothing
Sumō tori	But a powerful body

(Sazanami)

When it came to the creation of a new style in *haikai* poetry, the members of the Murasaki Ginsha displayed a lukewarm attitude. In contrast, the society called the Shii-no-Tomo (Pasania Friends), formed in May of 1891 by Itō Shōu, Mori Saruo, Katayama Tōu, Ishiyama Keizan, and Ishii Tokuchū, displayed a spirit of revolt against the old *haikai* circles and conducted its activities along this line. The following examples reflect the efforts on the part of this society to banish vulgarity from *haikai* poetry.

Minomushi no	A deserted cocoon
Furusu miidashitsu	Of a basket-worm
Koke no hana	Found with the moss flowers

(Shōu)

Kyonen ueshi	A cool breeze blows
Shii no ki nagara	Under the leaves of the pasania
Kaze suzushi	Planted only last year

(In commemoration of the first anniversary of the society)

(Shōu)

Samidare ya	In the early summer rain
Yomogi wa itsu ka	Sagebrush rapidly dissolves
Kurete iru	Into darkness

(Saruo)

Yoiyami no	In the evening twilight
Mizu ni shirakete	Upon the glittering water
Hototogisu	A cuckoo cries

(Tōu)

Masaoka Shiki became an enthusiastic supporter and a member of this society in 1892. The following year, new members were found in Naitō Meisetsu, Ioki Hyōtei, and Fujino Kohaku.

These members, together with Shiki's circle, participated in the society's *haiku* meeting which instituted a new system called *unza* (round-table *haiku*-composing meeting). The society's organ, *Haikai*, inaugurated in March of that year, stopped publication with its second issue, but the fact that a spirit of reform developed from this society deserves attention here.

2. *Shiki's Reform Movement and the Rise of the Nihon School*

The credit for banishing the vulgar fashion prevailing from the days of the Tempō Era and for achieving a reform in this literary field goes to Shiki. Shiki (Dassaishooku Shujin) began composing *haikai* poems in 1885 when he was still a student in the University preparatory school. Two years later, we find him back in Matsuyama, his native place, where he called upon Ōhara Kikai, a member of the Baishitsu school, to receive instruction in *haikai* poetry. Later on, he came to live at the Tokiwa Kai dormitory, where together with the superintendent Meisetsu, and his friends Hyōtei and Niinomi Hifū, he became engrossed in *haikai* and other branches of literature, although he did not display any particular literary consciousness at this time. In 1890, he received a letter from Kawahigashi Hekigotō in Matsuyama asking his advice on *haikai* poetry. The following year, this same Hekigotō introduced another Matsuyama inhabitant, Takahama Kyoshi, to Shiki. Kyoshi also wrote to Shiki asking for his advice. The latter at this time seems to have been inspired by the *haikai* poems of Kohaku, his cousin. Shiki came to show marked interest in *haiku* poetry during the winter of 1891 when he started reading through the *Haiku Bunrui* (Haiku Classification). *Bashō Shichibushū* (Bashō's Seven Part Anthology), especially the *Sarumino* (The Monkey's Straw Raincoat) section, played an important role in enlightening him on the subject.

From 1892 on, Shiki was to devote his life to *haiku* poetry and was filled with an ardor for its reform. In June of that year, he started serializing a column called "The Haiku Talks of Dassaishooku" in the newspaper *Nihon*. He left the university to join this newspaper in December. The following year, he wrote an article entitled "Attacking the Literary World" in this newspaper, and thus fired his first volleys against the old *haikai* masters. Shiki at this time utilized every occasion to publish his views. In an article entitled "Miscellaneous Talks on Bashō," he revealed his revolutionary ideas on *haiku* poetry. As mentioned previously, Shiki had joined hands with the members of the Shii-no-Tomo society and displayed an active interest in writing *haiku* verse. He was connected with the publication of the magazine *Haikai*, and from March 1893 he began to publish his own poems in the literary column of the newspaper *Nihon*. Consequently, Shiki's *haiku* movement was to have its principal vehicle in this newspaper and for this reason his school was to be known as the Nihon school.

The influence of his school spread in proportion to Shiki's achievements in the *haiku* field. Shiki assumed editorship of the *Shō-Nihon* (Small Japan), founded as a parallel publication of the *Nihon* in 1894, and this new publication served in furthering the development of this school. However, it was shortlived, and after it discontinued publication Shiki returned to the *Nihon*. This same year saw Ishii Rogetsu and Satō Kōroku join the staff of the *Nihon*. Also, both Hekigotō and Kyoshi came up to Tōkyō from Matsuyama. The new *haiku* spirit forming around Shiki was now rising like a high tide.

In 1895 Shiki became a war correspondent and participated in the Sino-Japanese War. But, on his return, he suffered a hemorrhage of the lung and became bedridden in Matsuyama. In this city Shiki befriended the author Sōseki, and the two became literary associates. Shiki persuaded Sōseki to join a *haiku* society formed by Yanagiwara Gokudō called the Shōfū Kai (The Pine Wind Society), and helped in arousing local interest in *haiku* composition. The lectures made at this society by Shiki were later compiled and published in the *Nihon*, under the title *Haikai Taiyō* (Outline of Haikai). Shiki's ideas on *haiku* poetry are expressed in a most systematic form in this article. After his return to Tōkyō, his zeal for literature, contrary to his waning health, was intensified. His school's influence began to spread to various districts with amazing speed. In January 1897, a magazine entitled *Hototogisu* was published in Matsuyama by Gokudō. The development of his school at this time is portrayed by Shiki himself in his critical essays " The Haikai World in 1896 " and " Haiku in 1897." Under the guidance of Shiki, Uehara Sansen and Naono Hekireirō cooperated in publishing an anthology *Shin-Haiku* (New Haiku Poetry) in 1898. This was a monumental publication, an accumulation of the achievements of the Nihon school.

Following this temporary success in the reform of *haiku* poetry, Shiki began to invade the *waka* field, although he actually was on his sickbed. He also stressed the necessity of narrative writing, but, despite these other activities, he by no means neglected the *haiku*. In 1898 he had the publication office of the magazine *Hototogisu* moved to Tōkyō, and entrusted the editorship to Kyoshi. Thus, together with the newspaper *Nihon*, the *Hototogisu* was to become the second citadel of Shiki's *haiku* school. In the meantime, Shiki was not sparing any effort to lead the activities of his school. It was through his efforts that the symposiums conducted by his followers, Meisetsu, Hekigotō, Kyoshi, and others, on the subject of *haikai* poetry, were published under the titles *Buson Kushū Kōgi* (Lectures on Buson's Poetic Anthologies) and *Zuimon Zuitō* (Questions and Answers). On the other hand, in the local districts, *haikai* magazines were springing up under the influence of Shiki. Such examples were the *Haisei* (Haikai Star), founded in remote Akita in 1900 by Rogetsu and Shimada Gokū, and the *Takarabune* (Treasure Ship), issued the following year in Ōsaka by Matsuse Seisei, who had previously been an editorial assistant of the *Hototogisu*. As a result of these local publications, the Nihon school attained the zenith of its prosperity.

Meanwhile, Shiki's condition was changing for the worse. He had embarked on an attempt to compile an anthology entitled *Shunkashūtō* (The Four Seasons), which, on the basis of his selections made in the newspaper *Nihon*, was to include the *haiku* written since the appearance of the previously published anthology *Shin-Haiku*. However, his condition was such that after publishing the first part, "Spring," in 1901, he had to entrust the rest of the work to Hekigotō and Kyoshi. (The rest, from the second part, "Summer," was published over the two year period, 1902–1903.) As to his own anthology *Dassaishooku Haikuchō-Shō* (Selections from the Haiku Sketchbook of Dassaishooku), the first part came out in April of 1902, but work stopped there, for Shiki was to succumb to his illness and bring his active life to a close in September.

The question remains : what was his position on the reform of *haiku* poetry and in what direction was he guiding his movement ? Shiki denied the literary value of the *renku* (chain verses) style of *haikai* because both uniformity and orderliness were lacking in it. Instead, he renamed *hokku haiku* and attempted to breathe a modern spirit into this literary genre. This position, of necessity, required Shiki to undertake the urgent task of eliminating the vulgar and banal mode of *haikai* poetry of the past, a mode which he despised as "banality" (*tsukinami-chō*). According to Shiki's views, the principal components of "banality" were intellectual interest and appeal to logic. This, he believed, could not be called literature, since the proper function of literature should be the creation of aesthetic sentiment. "The criterion of beauty is the criterion of literature. This criterion of literature, in turn, is the criterion of *haiku*." (From *Haikai Taiyō*). From this literary consciousness were derived his basic motives—to secure a proper place for *haiku* as a branch of literature and to endow with an artistic character the form which so far had been treated as a tool or a toy by the professional *haikai* masters. Furthermore,

for Shiki, who was baptized and reared in the realistic school
originating from Shōyō and Futabatei, the only solution appeared
to be in guiding *haikai* in the direction of realism.

Shiki himself displayed the banality he despised so much in
his early verses, as illustrated by the following examples :

> *Hitoe-zutsu*   Fall,
> *Hitoe-zutsu chire*   But only one by one,
> *Yaezakura*   O double cherry-blossom

or :

> *Hasu no ha ni*   On the lotus leaf
> *Umaku nottaru*   Perched so skilfully—
> *Kawazu kana*   A frog

Later on, he adopted a Genroku style, as in the following verses :

> *Zukin kite*   I shall be called an old man
> *Oi to yobaren*   With this odd hood—
> *Hatsushigure*   The first autumn rain
>   (composed on the anniversary of Bashō's death)

or :

> *Kogarashi ya*   The wintry wind—
> *Arao kuikomu*   The strings of my grass hat
> *Suge no kasa*   Cut into my face

From about 1892 on, however, Shiki adopted a definite literary
consciousness, that is, of depicting nature as it is.

> *Mozu naku ya*   A shrike cries
> *Ichiban takai*   On the top
> *Ki no saki ni*   Of the highest tree
>
> *Tonari kara*   A leaf of the banana tree
> *Tomoshi no utsuru*   Catches the light
> *Haseo kana*   From the neighboring house
>
> *Hi no ataru*   It is even cold
> *Ishi ni sawareba*   To touch a stone
> *Tsumetasa yo*   Exposed to the sun
>
> *Mo no hana ya*   The duckweed flower—
> *Mizu yuruyaka ni*   In the still water
> *Tenaga-ebi*   A long-legged shrimp

In the above-cited examples, we discover an accurate grasp of the object, a fresh sensibility coupled with objective and concrete expression. These attributes, supported by modern intellectuality, were sufficient to bring about a revolutionary change in the character of *haikai* poetry. Shiki himself considered and proposed this method of realism as the most effective way of banishing subjective worldliness and vulgarity from *haiku* poetry. This standpoint was later to be tagged " sketching " (*shasei*) by his Western-style painter friends, and was to become a characteristic of the Nihon school.

It is to be noted here that Shiki's position, based on sketching and realism, is vitally connected with his devotion to Buson. Discarding his previous Genroku style, Shiki changed to the Temmei style from about 1894. In 1897, he gave a high evaluation of the poetry of Buson in an article entitled "Buson the Poet." When he relies on the use of Chinese expressions or displays an unorthodox style in his poems, Shiki is betraying the influence of Buson. A typical example is:

Shichō karete	My poetic heart dries up
Byōkotsu o gosu	And I nurse my sick bones
Futon kana	In the bedclothes

The deep influence of Buson's classicism can be discovered in the following poems which create a peculiar world of romanticism and aestheticism:

Kinuta uteba	When I strike the fulling-block
Horo horo to hoshi no	The stars
Koborekeru	Gush down
Oboroyo ya	A hazy evening—
Onna nusuman	The plot
Hakarigoto	To steal a maiden
Kagaribi no	A bonfire
Moe ya utsuran	Flares up and spreads—
Shirobotan	To a white peony

This tendency was not a monopoly of Shiki, but rather the common characteristic of the *haiku* style of the *Nihon* school during the period represented by the anthology *Shin-Haiku*.

To quote the words of Shiki, Buson was a poet who had deep "respect for ideals." Therefore, Shiki stressed the need of mastering the method of imaginary as well as realistic description in his *Haikai Taiyō*. In this sense, his realism was not necessarily an absolute position.

We shall now survey some of Shiki's poems which contain a note of realism. In the following example he shows a strong disposition to emphasize the appeal to the color sense through the use of combinations :

Mizu aoku	Blue water
Ishi shiroku ryōgan no	White stones
Momiji kana	And crimson leaves on both banks

The following examples provide a vivid pictorial image :

Suzushisa ya	The coolness—
Matsu no hagoshi no	Through the pine needles
Hokakebune	Sailing-ships
	—At Suma Beach—
Kumo no i no	Cobwebs glistening
Goshiki ni hikaru	In iridescent hues
Harubi kana	In the spring sun
Shimajima ni	The lights are lit
Hi o tomoshikeri	On the islands far and near
Haru no umi	In the spring sea

As illustrated by these examples, the principle objective of what Shiki called " sketching " was to obtain " clear impressions " (*inshō meiryō*). Naturally, the basic aim of sketching is to provide a vivid reproduction of the subject matter in such a way that the reproduced image will appeal to the senses, rather than merely in reproducing a life-like image.

However, in his later " sketch " *haiku* written after 1898, the image of nature described in the poems seems to convey the inner feeling of the poet. For example, the peace and depth of the poet's mind emerges from the following verses :

Kono goro no	These days
Asagao ai ni	The morning glories
Sadamarinu	Bloom always in deep blue

Keitō no	The autumn tempest
Mada itokenaki	Already blows
Nowaki kana	Upon the yet young cockscombs
Bara o kiru	The sound of scissors
Hasami no oto ya	Cutting roses
Satsuki ame	In the early summer rain
Kuroki made	The grapes—
Murasaki fukaki	Their purple is so deep
Budō kana	They appear almost black

In other words, these verses suggest that Shiki has achieved the ideal of " sketching " which, to quote his own words, " implies the exquisite through simplicity." (*Byōshō Rokushaku*, The Six-Foot Sickbed, 1902). Influenced by these examples, the *haiku* composed by members of the Nihon school generally displayed a simplicity and an elegance, a mode which can perceived in the anthology *Shunkashūtō*. Among Shiki's earlier poems, we discover a number of verses expressing the sentiments of a sick man, such as :

	—Viewing the Snow from a Sickbed—
Ikutabi mo	How many times
Yuki no fukasa o	I have asked
Tazunekeri	" How deep is the snow now ? "

or :

Hagi saku ya	The flowers of the bush-clover bloom—
Ikite kotoshi no	My wish is fulfilled
Nozomi taru	To see them again this year

In his later years, Shiki was to write such poems as :

	—About Things—
Imōto no	How late
Kaeri ososa yo	My younger sister stays out—
Itsukazuki	A faint new moon

	—Ten Years on a Sickbed—
Kubi agete	From time to time
Oriori miru ya	Raising my head from the pillow
Niwa no hagi	I look at the bush-clover in the garden

and, passing through this stage, he seems finally to have attained a philosophic maturity, as exemplified in the following *haiku* which was to become one of his three death verses.

Hechima saite	A snake-gourd* is blooming—
Tan no tsumarishi	Clogged with phlegm
Hotoke kana	A dying man
	* which was used as cough medicine

Now let us consider Shiki's eminent followers in the Nihon school. One of them was Kohaku, who, as early as 1891, astonished Shiki with the freshness of his verses, examples of which are :

Kesa mireba	This morning
Sabishikarishi yo no ma no	After a lonely night
Hitoha kana	I saw one fallen leaf
Shūkaidō	The begonia
Kuchiki no tsuyu ni	Blooms in the dew
Sakinikeri	Under the decayed tree

However, this poet's progress ended relatively early because he committed suicide. Hyōtei was another of Shiki's followers who advanced a step ahead of his teacher in striking out a new field in *haiku* poetry. He was skilled in portraying spacious scenes in a laconic style, but later on, preoccupied with worldly matters, he abandoned poetry. The following verses are examples of his style :

Seiran no	The early summer storm
Sue wa	Shaking the green leaves
Bandōtarō kana	Sweeps on to the Bandōtarō River*
	* Tone River
Shiratsuyu ya	The dew is glistening
Jin'ya jin'ya no	With the lights
Hi no utsuri	From the many camps
Kogarashi ni	In the winter tempest
Fuji no takasa yo	Mt. Fuji soars
Shizukasa yo	High and undisturbed

The poet who as the senior member of the Nihon school exerted great influence was Meisetsu (Nariyuki, Rōbaikyo).

Meisetsu became a *haiku* poet in his middle age, but by competing with the young men under Shiki and through arduous effort, he made rapid progress. He had high regard for the anthology *Sarumino*, especially for the verses of Bonchō, and at the same time was impressed by Buson. Consequently, he had a strong leaning towards objectivism and was distinctly classic. His elegant taste and brilliant style are exemplified by the following verses :

Yūzuki ya	The evening moon—
Naya mo umaya mo	Upon the roofs of barn and stable
Ume no kage	The shadows of the plum trees
Hanagiri ya	The blooming paulownia trees—
Nijō watari no	The evening moonlight
Yūzuki yo	In the Nijō district
Hatsufuyu no	The bamboos are green
Take midori nari	In the early winter
Shisendō	Near our Poets' Hall

But, in addition to this sober tone, he could also be witty, as is shown by :

Kagekiyo no	Kagekiyo* has a hard time
Nomi torikanuru	Catching the flea
Yoroi kana	Under his armor
	* a warrior famed for his strength

Furthermore, he had the ability to write artless verses like the following example :

Yaguruma ni	The toy wheel is spinning
Asakaze tsuyoki	In the strong morning wind—
Nobori kana	The carp banner*
	* for the Boys' Festival on May 5th

Hekigotō (Heigorō) and Kyoshi (Kiyoshi) were the twin hopes among Shiki's pupils. Since both of them came from Shiki's native place, they took lessons from him from their boyhood days. They were schoolmates at the Third High School in Kyōto, from which they transferred to the Second High School in Sendai. They quit this school in 1894, and working on the newspaper and doing other jobs, lent their help to Shiki's *haiku* movement. It is of great interest to note that these two poets, in the field of *haiku* writing, were moving in opposite directions. Shiki's observation was that Hekigotō belonged to the realist school while Kyoshi belonged to the idealist school.

Hekigotō earned his reputation early, during the years 1892 and 1893, with verses that were fresh and original as well as skilfully composed. His work during this period included :

Gyōzui o	With used bath water thrown in
Sutete kosui no	The water of the lake
Sasa-nigori	Becomes slightly muddy
Tsuyu fukashi	The deer in the morning
Munage no nururu	Drenches his breast
Asa no shika	In the heavy dew

In 1896 he was praised by Shiki for his orginality in writing verses which corresponded with Shiki's ideal calling for " clear impressions." Such examples were :

Akai tsubaki	A red camellia flower
Shiroi tsubaki to	And then a white one
Ochinikeri	Fall
Suberiotsuru	A firefly
Susuki no naka no	Slips down
Hotaru kana	In the midst of the pampas grass

After this Hekigotō fell into a temporary confusion, but regaining his style, he wrote verses vivid yet laconic in style. These poems shone brilliantly in the anthology *Shunkashūtō*, some examples of which are :

Tsuru no hane ya	The crane's feathers
Shiroki ga ue ni	Gleam whiter
Saekaeru	Than white itself
Ikanobori	The kite is flying
Hyakken no ito o	At the end of a string
Noborikeri	One hundred fathoms long
Ware takaku	The long banner—
Taten to su naru	I shall strive
Nobori kana	To hoist it high

Kono michi no	This road leads
Fuji ni nari uku	Through the pampas grass
Susuki kana	To Mt. Fuji

In dealing with nature, he displayed a keen sensibility and penetrating observation. It is not surprising that he was classified by Shiki as a realist. Indeed, the Shiki school could not have found a better talent than Hekigotō in perfecting its "sketching" style.

Kyoshi, on the other hand, was not as talented as Hekigotō. However, he matched the strides of his rival, step by step, and turning to human interest themes, was able to introduce a novel quality through verses strongly subjective and romantic in flavor. As we mentioned earlier, Shiki respected the aesthetic ideals of Buson, and we can say that Kyoshi, as a member of the idealist school, had inherited Shiki's idealistic tendency. As early as 1893 Kyoshi showed unusual ability with such verses as:

Kyō-onna	The beauties of Kyōto
Hana ni kuruwanu	Are not mad about cherry-blossoms—
Tsumi fukashi	How great their crime

Later on he was to indulge in aesthetic sentiments as displayed in the following verses:

Harusame no	The spring rain—
Ikō ni omoshi	The clothes of love
Koigoromo	Hang languidly on the rack
Hitori sabishi	Alone and sad
Mawaridōro ni	I wish I could enter
Hairubeku	The revolving lantern

In 1896 he created a type of verse which he called *shinsentai* (fantasy style) to express eccentricity in an extravagant way, examples of which are:

Dotō iwa o kamu	Angry billows dash against the rocks—
Ware o kami ka to	I wonder if I am a god
Oboro no yo	This hazy night
Umi ni itte	I shall enter the sea
Umarekawarō	To be reborn
Oborozuki	Under the hazy moon

Furthermore, he drew Shiki's attention by creating *haiku* poems implying a lapse of time, as shown in the following verses :

Nusundaru	A sudden shower falling
Kagashi no kasa ni	Upon the scarecrow's hat
Ame kyū nari	Which was stolen
Sumabayato	I gazed at the moon
Omou haiji ni	At the abandoned temple
Tsuki o mitsu	Where I should like to live

From 1897 onward, Kyoshi was to follow the general trend of the Nihon school and lean towards simplicity. But even in the following verses which belong to the category of "sketches," it is interesting to note that Kyoshi has acquired the refined flavor inherent in nature and has breathed a serene feeling into his poetry.

Chōchō no	The quiet of the sound
Mono kū oto no	Of a butterfly
Shizukasa yo	Taking a meal
Akatsuki no	The deep blue morning-glory
Kon-asagao ya	At dawn
Hoshi hitotsu	Under a solitary star
Enzan ni	On the distant mountains
Hi no ataritaru	The sun is shining—
Kareno kana	A bleak moor

Ranked close to Hekigotō and Kyoshi were Rogetsu and Kō-roku, both native of northern Japan. Rogetsu is known for his idealistic verses such as :

Ei ni hi shite	The Mongolian king fled
Zen'u nigetari	Setting fire to his camp
Fuyu no tsuki	Under the wintry moon
Arataki no	The raging waterfall
Kiri o saku koto	Divides the mist
Gohyakushaku	For five hundred feet
Kinden ya	In the gold pavilion
Haru no yogoto o	They beat the hand drum
Tsuzumi utsu	Every night in spring

In contrast, Kōroku borrowed themes from familiar objects and, as illustrated in the following examples, displayed a mild quality.

Ha ga kurete	Hidden under the leaves
Ringo no akaki	The red of the apples
Nishibi kana	In the western sun
Kariato ni	Heat haze rises
Kagerō tatsu ya	Over the wheatfield
Mugi no hata	After harvest
Kubi agete	The silkworm
Hito natsukashi no	Raises its head
Kaiko kana	As if lonely for man

Seisei, who emerged from Ōsaka somewhat later, had an unusual life, and became known for composing *haiku* which were a cross between "sketching" and the Temmei style, as in the following examples:

Minasoko ni	At the bottom of the stream
Hiru no hiashi ya	A ray of the midday sun—
Yanagihae	A dace
Kagaribi ni	With the light of a bonfire
Shiraha kirameku	The many white arrow plumes
Yakazu kana	Glitter

In discussing the Nihon school, we must not forget the name of the novelist Sōseki. Under the guidance of Shiki, Sōseki made progress in the *haiku* field, as exemplified by the following verse he wrote in 1894:

Kaze ni notte	Riding on the wind
Karuku noshiyuku	Lightly sails
Tsubame kana	The swallow

The following year, the visit of Shiki to Matsuyama intensified Sōseki's interest in *haiku*, and the latter began to demonstrate an exceptional wittiness. The following verses, though airy and humorous, are not in any way touched by vulgarity.

Degawari ya	The change of servants—
Hana to kotaete	The new one answers to the name of Hana*

Chimba nari	Yet she limps
	*which means "flower"

Tatakarete	When beaten
Hiru no ka o haku	The wooden temple gong
Mokugyo kana	Sends forth mosquitoes into noonday

Kanzan ka	Which was stung by a bee
Juttoku ka	Kanzan*
Hachi ni sasareshi wa	Or Juttoku ?*

*two Chinese recluses known for their sagacity

And, in the following verses, Sōseki seems to be breathing in a world of tranquillity.

Hatsufuyu ya	In the early winter
Take kiru yama no	The sound of a hatchet
Nata no oto	Cutting bamboo in the mountain

Sumire hodo na	That I could be reborn
Chiisaki hito ni	As a small man
Umaretashi	The size of a violet

Kusayama ni	On the grassy hill
Uma hanachikeri	Horses are set free—
Haru no sora	The spring sky

3. *The Miscellaneous Peripheral Schools in the Days of Reform*

While the Nihon school was overpowering the *haikai* world and launching a vigorous reform movement, the masters of the old-fashioned schools were still entrenched deeply in their citadels. In between the old and new schools sprang up miscellaneous subsidiary factions.

In October 1894, the Tsukuba Kai (Tsukuba Society) was formed under initiation of Ōno Shachiku, and with the participation of Sassa Seisetsu, Sasagawa Rimpū, Taoka Reiun, and Kokubu Saitō. Later, additional members were found in Numanami Keion and Miyajima Gojōgen. Since these members were connected with Tōkyō Imperial University and published their works in the magazine *Teikoku Bungaku* (Imperial Literature), this group came to be known as the University school, the Imperial

Literature school, or the Akamon school. The main objective of this organization was historical research in *haikai* literature, and in contrast with the Nihon school whose primary concern was *haiku* writing, regarded actual *haiku* composition as a secondary occupation. In the preface of the selection of *haiku* made at its first meeting, entitled *Tsukuba no Fumoto* (At the Foot of Mt. Tsukuba), Seisetsu uses the term "playing at leisure" (*yūyū jiteki no asobi*), which gives us a definite idea of the attitude of this group. Shachiku displays a fanciful taste in the following verses:

Tsubakuro ya	Swallows
Sanjūsangendō	In the rain
No ame	At Sanjūsangendō sanctuary
Risshū no	On the first day of autumn
Taishō tsuku ya	A gaunt priest strikes
Yasehōshi	The great bell

On the other hand, in the verses made by the other members, examples of which we give below, we discover a style resembling that of the Nihon school, but this resemblance is not particularly surprising.

Oboroyo ya	A hazy evening—
Shiratama tsubaki	The white ball of the camellia
Chiran to su	About to fall
	(Seisetsu)
Sammon no	Young leaves
Ni-ō ni semaru	Advancing on the two Deva kings
Wakaba kana	At the temple gate
	(Seisetsu)
Oboroyo ya	In the hazy evening
Dote hatchō no	The singing of *komurobushi*
Komurobushi	Along the riverside promenade
	(Rimpū)
Zangetsu ya	In the morning moon
Koba no tategami	The thoroughbred's mane
Nowaki shite	Blown by the wintry blast
	(Rimpū)

Subsequently, in October 1895, Tsunoda Chikurei joined with

Togawa Zanka, Okano Chijū, and others to found the Shūsei Kai (The Voice of Autumn Society). Transferring to this organization were Kōyō and Sazanami from the Murasaki Ginsha, Shōu from the Shii-no-Tomo, and Shachiku from the Tsukuba Kai, as well as *haiku* poets belonging to the older schools. This meant the amalgamation of all *haiku* groups except the Nihon school, and these intermediate forces, banded together, expressed a spirit of revolt against this reigning Nihon school. This new group at first published news of its *haiku* activities in the *Mainichi Shimbun*, but in 1896 it issued an organ of its own entitled *Haikai : Aki no Koe* (Haiku Poetry : The Voice of Autumn). This periodical discontinued publication in the following year, as the group planned to utilize the magazine *Taiyō* (The Sun) as a substitute organ. However, this also did not last long, and in 1901 the group resumed publication of the *Haisei*. (The name was composed of the first and last characters of *Haikai : Aki no Koe, koe* being *sei* in its Chinese reading.) In 1903 the group discarded this organ and issued its substitute, *Uzue*.

The objectives of this society were explained by Kōyō in his inauguratory article of *Haikai : Aki no Koe* in which he stated : "We, concerned lest in the future there be a decline, hope to effect a renaissance in Meiji *haiku* poetry." Chikurei also revealed the ambitions of the society in this inaugural issue with these words : "Our objective is to regain our position which has been lost in the vicissitudes of the literary storms, and, discarding meaningless formalism, to recreate the true refined taste." (*Chōusō Mango*, Idle Talks by the Rainswept Windows). The truth, however, was that this group did not display any distinct ideal and lacked the unity of the Nihon school. Instead, it was a loose group of dilettantes who enjoyed a high social position and who came together merely to enjoy themselves by writing *haiku* poems. Many of the members devoted themselves to academic research, and, in contrast with the Nihon school where the dominating mode was the Temmei style, this society professed leaning towards the Danrin style or that of the Edo-Za originating from Kikaku. In this sense, this society failed to free itself from the influence of the obsolete style of the past. Chijū perhaps was right when he said this group was a " harmonization of old and new " (*shinkyū chōwa-ha*).

Among the verses written by Chikurei, the following examples displayed a tinge of realism:

Manaita ya	On the chopping-board
Udo nisambon	Some stalks of spikenard
Hi no ataru	Catch two or three rays of sun
Yūdachi ya	A summer shower—
Higoi no odoru	Red carp leap
Kado no kawa	In the river near the gate

However, most of his verses were more like the following examples:

Tsuyu no mi ya	Life as fleeting as the dew—
Tsuyu no tamoto ya	My sleeves wet with dew-like tears—
Tsuyu no yado	This dwelling-place of dew
Hae hitotsu	A single fly
Shusu no obi	On a satin sash
Suberi mo aezu	Yet he does not slip

Zanka's poems, on the other hand, displayed nothing more than vulgar taste, as illustrated in the following:

Toshi no kure	The year is closing—
Dare ka koban o	Won't someone give me
Kuremai ka	A gold coin?
Chōtei senri	The long stretch of the river-bank—
Chō no kokoro to	My soul has become
Narinikeri	A butterfly

As to Kōyō, some of his poems, an example of which is given below, betrayed the influence of traditionalism.

Hototogisu	A happy waking in the night
Atsuraemuki no	Just in time
Nezame kana	To hear a cuckoo

But at the same time he was moving toward simplicity during this period, as is evinced by:

Akisame no	I gazed
Niwa ni hi tomoshite	Holding a light toward the garden
Nagamekeri	In the autumn rain
Nemuritarite	After a good sleep
Shibaraku hae to	For some time
Aitai su	I watched a fly

Sazanami was another member of the society who wrote relatively placid verses such as :

Zukubōshi	The horned owl
Kane tsuku hito ni	Has taken kindly to
Shitashimeri	The man who strikes the bell
Nigirimeshi	I treated a crab
Kani ni furumau	To a bite of a riceball
Shiohi kana	At ebb-tide

The pleasure-loving, non-committal attitude of the Shūsei Kai invited dissatisfaction among its own ranks, and some members left the society to form splinter groups. One case was the formation of the Suzume Kai (The Sparrow Society) about 1898 by Chijū who was known for his critical essays *Haidan Fūbunki* (Reportage from the Haikai World) published in the *Mainichi Shimbun* in September 1895. This new group, joined by Ueda Ryūji, Ōshima Hōsui, Yamaji Hakuu, Murozumi Soshun, and Uchino Mokkyo, issued its own periodical in August 1901, entitled *Hammen* (The Other Side). This Hammen school, which was to call itself the Shinshin-Ha (The Ultra-Modern School), advocated, in opposition to the "sketching" (*shasei-shiki*) of the Nihon school, a method called "designing" (*zuan-shiki*). The society also strove for expression of strong subjectivity with the purpose of creating a new style. The goal of this group was illustrated by Chijū in the following verse :

Kōbai ya	Red plum blossoms—
Waga ie no ku wa	The poems of our school
Nōen ni	Must be as enchanting

Strong subjectivity, mingled with aestheticism, can be perceived in the following verses by members of this society :

Kōsui ni	At the fragrance of the perfume
Tokimeku kokoro	My heart beats—
Uchiwa kana	The fan
	(Chijū)

Kaidō ya	The flowers of the aronia—
Nakaba namida no	If you could cry
Kurenai ni	You would shed red tears
	(Ryūji)

Uta no koi no	With songs and love
Momo no hi momo no	The peach festival is celebrated
Haru nare ya	In the peach-flowering spring
	(Soshun)

Exceptional cases were Hōsui and Hakuu who displayed singular styles, when compared with other members. But their verses, as shown below, can be regarded only as products of eccentricity.

Mono nin to	Just as I wanted to
Omou atakamo	Start cooking
Sumi no okorikeri	The charcoal fire flared up
	(Hōsui)

Ka no koe ya	The buzzing of the mosquito—
Futamoru nabe no	The vapor from the boiling pot
Yuge ni kaze	Drifts in the wind
	(Hakuu)

4. Dissension in the Shiki School and the Neo-Tendency Movement

Hekigotō and Kyoshi, who developed their individual characters under the guidance of Shiki, clashed with each other following the death of their master. Under the circumstances, such antagonism was inevitable. As a result of their alienation, the Nihon school, which so far had formed the core of the new *haiku* movement, broke up into two factions, one led by Hekigotō, and the other by Kyoshi.

In October 1902, Hekigodō took over the *haiku* column in the newspaper *Nihon*. The following year, he became a member of the staff of the newspaper where he established the headquarters of his faction. At first, *haiku* contributors regarded it as a dishonor to have their poems selected by Hekigotō, which naturally led to a decline in the popularity of this column. However, as a result of his zealous efforts, Hekigotō succeeded in developing a number of disciples, namely Ozawa Hekidō, Kidani Rikka, Ōsuga Otoji, and Ogiwara Seisensui, and even in remote districts he was able to find followers such as Hiroe Yaezakura of Izumo, and Sugawara Shichiku and Anzai Ōkaishi, both residents of the Rikuzen district. From 1904 on, Hekigotō initiated a *haiku* group called Haizammai (Contemplation in Haiku), and through these activities opened the golden age of his school. In August 1906, Hekigotō decided to conduct a nationwide tour to increase the number of his supporters, and set out on his journey after entrusting the *haiku* column in the newspaper *Nihon* to Kyoshi. But, prior to and during this tour, he compiled an anthology, *Zoku Shunkashūtō* (The Four Seasons, Continued) (1906–1907), on the basis of his selections made in the *Nihon haiku* column, to sound out public opinion concerning the activities of his school. The so-called Neo-Tendency was germinating during this period, and later developed into a strong movement. We shall refer to this in later paragraphs.

As to Kyoshi, he based himself on the magazine *Hototogisu*, and from 1906 on, he established relations with the newspaper *Kokumin Shimbun* (The People's Newspaper). He found followers in Takada Chōi, Matsune Tōyōjō, Okamoto Hekisansui, and Nakano San'in. Thus, from the spring of 1906, Kyoshi launched and participated actively in a *haiku* group called Haikai Sanshin (Leisure Haikai) in order to compete with the aforementioned *haiku* group Haizammai, organized by the rival Hekigotō school. This did not mean that Kyoshi's primary concern was only *haiku* poetry. He revived the form called *renku* (chain-style *haiku*), the literary value of which had been denied earlier by Shiki, and, recharging it with a consistent poetical meaning, created a style called *haikaishi* (*haikai* verse).

Together with Sōseki and others, he engaged in experiments with this new style. Also, he renewed his efforts in *shaseibun* (sketching prose), which had been of great interest to him for some time, and through this style he moved into the field of the novel.

In accordance with Kyoshi's tendency, the *Hototogisu* started publishing from about 1905, the year of its hundredth issue, *shaseibun* and novels written by the novelist Sōseki and other writers, such as Terada Torahiko, Suzuki Miekichi, and Saka-moto Shihōda. The magazine now displayed the tone of a general literary magazine rather than that of an exclusive *haiku* publication. These developments reached their culmination in August 1908 when Kyoshi announced his intention of abandoning *haiku* in order to concentrate on novels.

Prior to these developments, we find Tōyōjō, who was dis-satisfied with the anthology *Zoku Shunkashūtō* because of its bias toward the Hekigotō school, planning a new anthology. His plan was to compile a work entitled *Shin-Shunkashūtō* (New Four Seasons), which was to include a selection of poems published in the *Nihon*, *Hototogisu*, and *Kokumin Shimbun* during the roughly one year beginning from the middle of 1906. This was published during the years between 1908 and 1914. However, there was no denying that Kyoshi's school was on the decline. While the Hekigotō school was to enjoy a nationwide popularity, Kyoshi's faction was to remain in obscurity until after the comeback of Kyoshi in about 1912.

The antagonism between Hekigotō and Kyoshi, as explained earlier by Shiki, evidently had its roots in the difference of their standpoints, that is, in the difference between the former's realism and the latter's idealism. Their rivalry took form in the following controversy during 1903: Kyoshi published in *Hototogisu* an article entitled "The *Haiku* World Today" in which he criticized the poems in Hekigotō's *Onsen Hyakku* (One Hundred Hot Spring Poems) as leaning toward artificiality, chiefly because the poet, in order to create successful sketching effects, had relied on the excessive use of novelty. Kyoshi demanded that the poems display more harmony. Hekigotō replied to this criticism in an article entitled "Upon Reading Kyoshi's 'The *Haiku* World Today,'" defending his position, which he said was to "describe the actual scenes as they are." Hekigotō, furthermore, noted that, as a poetical instrument, sketching was more advanced than imaginary description. Kyoshi did not underestimate the significance of sketching, but still countered that "we cannot neglect the imaginary description which has been cultivated over the past thousand years." ("The Mood of Sketching and Imagination," 1904). Nevertheless, Hekigotō insisted that "objective research was the foundation of *haiku* writing," (*Kayatsurigusa*, 1906) and later became more active in arguing for the cause of objective sketching.

In order to understand his theory of "sketching," let us look into the following examples:

Takashio no	At high tide
Natsumeku kaze ni	A butterfly fluttering
Chōchō kana	In the summer breeze
Ochichō no	Still hot
Suna ni hane utsu	A dying butterfly
Nao atsushi	Falling on the sand
Tarekubi no	The height of a
Keshi no takasa ni	Hanging poppy
Narinikeri	About to open
No wa karete	The withered moor—
Ashibe sasu tori	Toward the reeds
Hikuki kana	The birds fly low

These poems prove that the poet had now become more rigorous in his attitude towards the subject matter, and his insight deeper, as if it penetrated into the very essence of the object. The careful composition is reinforced by an uncompromising attitude which gives the verses almost a metallic quality. In the previous anthology *Shunkashūtō*, Hekigotō was content with writing verses of a simple and calm mood. But now in the

Zoku Shunkashūtō he attempted to raise his poetry to a higher degree of refinement, as shown in the examples given above.

This anthology *Zoku Shunkashūtō* included many fine verses, each of which, displaying the individual moods of the authors, contributed to the progress of " sketching." Some examples of this are :

Kakimidasu	The boats
Yoshio utsukushi	Escaping the heat at night
Nōryō-bune	Move the beautiful waves
	(Yaezakura)
Yamaguni no	The coldness
Ōki na michi no	Of a broad road
Samusa kana	In the mountain country
	(Yaezakura)
Mammaku no	The tents
Kaze haramiiru	Suck in the wind—
Chōchō kana	A butterfly
	(Shichiku)
Makiwarabi	I add three more
Sambon kaite	Curled brackens—
Haruno kana	The spring meadow sketch
	(Shichiku)
Utan to su	The festival-dolls
Utanu hina no	Seem to strike the hand-drum
Tsuzumi kana	But their hands are fixed
	(Ōkaishi)
Tsuburaka ni	Spring rain—
Hachi tobu sora ya	A bee flying distinctly
Haru no ame	In the sky
	(Ōkaishi)
Asayake ni	In the morning glow
Ōchi no niou	The Ōchi tree fragrance—
Gogatsu kana	The month of May
	(Hekidō)

Yoi yoi ni	We talked on
Kataritsugishi ga	For so many evenings
Yosamu kana	But now the nights are cold
	(Hekidō)

Taiboku no	The giant tree
Eda oroshi-iru	Hanging its branch
Kasumi kana	Into the mist
	(Rikka)

Kutsunugi ni	A crab creeping on the flagstone
Kani kuru yado ya	Of the house
Natsu no tsuki	In the summer moonlight
	(Rikka)

Nami shiro-o	The foaming waves
Higata ni kiyuru	Die on the dried inlet
Akibiyori	This sunny autumn day
	(Otoji)

Hirame naru	The dragon-fly
Ishi ni tombo no	Enjoying the weather
Hiyori kana	On a flat stone
	(Otoji)

On the other hand, Kyoshi himself displayed unusual talent in sketching, examples of which are :

Ōi naru	The large moon
Tsuki o sudare ni	Imprinted on the
Shirushikeri	Bamboo blind

Kiri hitoha	A paulownia leaf
Hiatarinagara	Falls
Ochinikeri	Reflecting the sunlight

In contrast with Hekigotō whose poetical intuition penetrated precisely into the intricacy of nature, Kyoshi faced nature in a tranquil mood, and, reducing the objects into simple images, displayed an elegant taste. His predilection for human interest themes corresponded to his interest in *renku* (chain-style *haiku* poetry). In the following examples, Kyoshi has conjured up an imaginary world, full of romantic appeal :

Horo-horo to	Nuns crying silently
Nakiau ama ya	To each other—
Wasabizuke	The hotness of horse-radish pickles
Kari miru ya	Two faces*
Namida ni nureshi	Looking at wild geese
Kao futatsu	Wet with tears
	* of the nuns in the previous poem

Tōyōjō, in the following poems, displays a poetical mood akin to that of Kyoshi.

Mayuzumi o	Paint your eyebrows
Kō seyo kusa wa	Darker—
Kambashiki	The grasses are so fragrant
Misosazai	The wren
Ishibashi o kuru	Walking over the stone bridge—
Shizuka nari	All is silence

In general, many of the poems collected in the anthology *Shin-Shunkashūtō* were expressions of a mood of seclusion in tranquillity, as illustrated by the following:

Hakuō o	The white sea-gulls
Nosete yo ni iru	Gliding on the spring waves
Haru no mizu	Becoming dark
	(Chōi)
Shu o kobosu	The red ink drips
Uta na senja no	On the charcoal brazier
Hioke kana	As the selector corrects the poem
	(Chōi)
Akegata no	The song of the cricket
Shizuka narikeru	Is so subdued
Kutsuwa-mushi	At dawn
	(San'in)
Sandan ni	Three watermills
Suisha kakaru ya	Standing apart
Aki no kawa	On the autumn river
	(Hekisansui)
Mi ugokeba	If I move
Ugoku nikai ya	The upstair floor also moves
Yowa no fuyu	This winter midnight
	(Hekisansui)

Now to return to the activities of Hekigotō : In contrast with the decline of Kyoshi's school, that of his rival was in its heyday. Hekigotō was to receive a splendid reception at every stop during his tour through northern Japan and Hokkaidō. His diary of this journey was serialized in the *Nihon* under the title *Ichinichi Isshin* (One Letter a Day) and was later published in book form as *Sanzenri* (Three Thousand Miles) (1910).

In the several years following this journey, the *haikai* world seemed to be monopolized by his school. But, Hekigotō himself underwent an inner revolution during this tour, and, dissatisfied with the sketching employed up until that time, began to express doubts on this poetical method. At the end of 1906, the dissolution of the newspaper *Nihon* meant, naturally, the extinction of its *haiku* column, which Hekigotō previously had entrusted to Kyoshi. Hekigotō took this opportunity to reactivate this column in March the following year by shifting it from the defunct *Nihon* to the magazine *Nihon oyobi Nihonjin* (Japan and the Japanese People), and strove for unity among the ranks of his school. However, in December of the same year, he received unexpectedly a letter from Otoji in Nagaoka in Echigo province commenting on the recent trend of the *Nihon haiku* column. This led to the publication of Otoji's article entitled " Concerning the Neo-Tendency in the *Haiku* World," which was carried in the inaugural issue of the magazine *Akane* (Madder) in February of the following year. Stimulated by Otoji and his article, Hekigotō himself now became the champion of this Neo-Tendency Movement.

The substance of Otoji's ideas on Neo-Tendency is as follows. The method of sketching originated by Shiki should be called a " direct narrative style " (*chokujohō*) or an " active expression style " (*katsugenhō*). Whatever the name, this style is useful, he said, only as an elementary and fundamental technique for *haiku* poetry. In order to express subtle and intricate feeling and to communicate the true characteristics of objects, *haiku* poetry must move in the direction of "metaphorical method" (*in'yakuhō*) or "suggestive method" (*anjihō*) through use of "ellipsis" (*shōhitsuhō*). Only this could lead to effective production of symbolic effects of the seasonal themes. His conclusion, thus, was that *haiku* poetry, which so far had to be content with the light, the commonplace, and the plain, through use of the "active expression" style, could now express "the majestic, the implicit, and the profound" through this new style. Otoji found the living examples of the new style among the poems of the Hekigotō school, and praised them as works of a mode he called Neo-Tendency (*shin-keikō*), much to the satisfaction of Hekigotō.

In response to Otoji's theories, Hekigotō published an article in the *Nihon oyobi Nihonjin* in August 1908 entitled "Concerning the Neo-Tendency in the *Haiku* Poetry." The following year, he enlarged upon this subject, and, making his work public, expounded his own theory. He wrote: "Attach importance to real feelings and respect the impressions; that is, efforts to meditate upon poetical thought, derived from personal experience, will inevitably bring us closer to the real life." These views represent an attempt to surpass the method of sketching which heretofore had been concerned with objective reproduction of objects, and, at the same time, they have something in common with the Naturalism which at this period was at its peak in the world of the novel. In contrast with Kyoshi, who was moving in the direction of sketch writing and novels imbued with *haiku* taste, Hekigotō, armed with a keen *Zeitgeist*, was attempting to adapt *haiku* to Naturalism. In late 1907, Hekigotō had to return to Tōkyō temporarily because his mother fell ill, but in April 1909, he again started on a journey to western Japan. Before his departure, he compiled an anthology entitled *Nihon Haiku Shō Dai-Isshū* (First Selection from the *Nihon Haiku* Column) on the basis of poems published in the *Nihon haiku* column (1909). This anthology, developed along the line of *Zoku Shunkashūtō*, signalled the beginning of the Neo-Tendency movement.

Among Hekigotō's verses, Otoji regarded the following as belonging to the Neo-Tendency category :

Insei wa narishikado	I found a place for seclusion
Tammei ya	But the shortness of life—
Ato no tsuki	The remaining moon
Omowazu mo	All of a sudden
Hiyoko umarenu	The chicks were born—
Fuyu sōbi	The winter rose

The novelty of these verses lay in the implication, through exact expression, of subtle feelings which accompany certain situations or scenes. The following verses impress us with the specific features of the locality, by giving crisp, lively impressions of nature.

Hi no utsuru	The burning red
Kitakami kōri	Reflected on
Somenikeri	The forming ice of the Kitakami River
Tera taete	Beyond the temple
Tada ni togareri	Nothing but peaks
Fuyu no yama	In the winter mountain

We may also say that Hekigotō's classicism, nurtured by his devotion to calligraphy of the Han and Six Dynasties Eras, was mirrored in his verses. In the following verse, he expresses a deep tone which keeps his elaborate style within the accepted limit.

Kumo urara	The billowy clouds—
Shikinami o mata	The waves retreat
Sunago kana	And the sand appears again

Sentiment lingers in his following verse :

Haru samushi	I am ashamed of
Ko no aizō ni	My love and hate for my child
Ware o hazu	This cold spring day

The anthology *Nihon Haiku Shō Dai-Isshū* contains a number of good verses, and it is not surprising to discover that most of them were written by the older poets. The following are some examples :

Kogarashi ya	In the winter wind
Uma no hitomi no	The eyes of the horse
Hi to moyuru	Seem to burn
	(Ōkaishi)

Senjū no	The people moved out
Kore o nokoshinu	Leaving in the house
Hikigaeru	This bullfrog
	(Shichiku)

Okubito ya	In the deep mountains
Yama yaite matsu	Men awaiting the salmon,
Nobori-masu	Burn the grasses
	(Yaezakura)

Zansetsu no	The snows unmelted—
Arase hikari ya	The seashore glitters
Mine utsuri	Reflecting the mountain peak
	(Rikka)

Mo o someshi	The duckweed dyed crimson
Yūhi no numa ya	By the evening sun—
Wataru hebi	A snake crosses the pond
	(Otoji)

Iwaya Kuchinashi was a poet who climbed to the top rank by writing verses such as:

Mizu no gotoki	The *sushi*-rice balls are being well
Yo no hitotoki ya	seasoned
Sushi naruru	On this night
	As still as cool waters

or:

Hirame naru	A flat rock
Ishi ya konomi o	Just made
Waru tokoro	For cracking nuts

All of the poets mentioned above kept in harmony with Hekigotō, and this group contributed in molding a majestic and suggestive mode of poetry.

The second journey of Hekigotō, mentioned before, caused repercussions everywhere. New talents were found, namely Nakatsuka Ippekirō, Nakatsuka Kyōya, Shioya Uhei, and Watanabe Hakū, and these men made progress under Hekigotō's guidance. This period, in a sense, marked a new epoch in the Neo-Tendency movement. We are told about its progress in Hekigotō's *Zoku Ichinichi Isshin* (One Letter a Day, Continued), which was published in *Nihon oyobi Nihonjin*, and later as a book entitled *Zoku Sanzenri : Jōkan* (First Part : Three Thousand Miles, Continued). This book contained letters written up to February 1910. The poems written during the years following the publication of the *Nihon Haikushō : Dai-Isshū* up to December 1912, were selected and compiled in the *Nihon Haikushō : Dainishū* (Second Selection from the *Nihon Haiku* Column), published in 1913. In the preface of this publication, Hekigotō wrote about the development of the Neo-Tendency movement, the substance of which follows :

According to Hekigotō, there were two peaks in his *haiku* movement of this period. The first peak was attained in 1909 when he was staying at Kinosaki in the Tajima district. While staying here, he found a new direction for the movement which was to discard conventional seasonal themes, and instead to attempt expression of " actual feelings " (*jikkan*) based on real experience and " psychological description " (*shinri byōsha*), dealing dynamically with the atmosphere of a given instant. The direction, he said, was suggested in the following verses, which include one of his own :

Tare no koto o	Who is the one
Midara ni iku to	The Persimmon Master says
Kakinushi ga	Leads a dissolute life
	(Ippekirō)
Shiki akiraka nari	The time of death is vivid—
Sazanka no	The sasanqua
Sakihokoru	In full bloom
	(Ippekirō)
Kumo o shikaru	There must be a god
Kami aran fuyubi	To scold the cloud so that
Yū togi ni	The sun can light up the winter evening
	(Hekigotō)

The attitude of respecting actual feeling because of a desire to "obtain the truth" belongs, distinctly, to the tradition of Naturalism. The second peak of the movement came in the following year during his sojourn in Tamashima of the Bitchū district. There, on the basis of the following examples, which also included his own, he began to advocate a theory called "non-centralism" (*muchūshin-ron*). The examples of this theory were :

Ame no hanano	Across the rainy field
Kishi o omoya ni	I came to see the flowers
Nagai seri	But stayed too long in the house
	(Kyōya)
Sambō seidan	With elevated talk in the mountain hut
Furuishi ga	I forgot to look at the blossoms
Hanano sudōri su	On the way home
	(Uhei)
Sumō noseshi	The giant wrestler
Binsen no nado	Getting on the ferryboat—
Shike to nari	A tempest
	(Hekigotō)

By the non-centralization, which he found in these verses, he meant the avoidance of artificial concentration of sentiment on a given point and instead the maintenance of a close relation with the natural phenomena themselves ; that is, to quote his words, "to maintain deep contact with the universe." He also explains his theory as "dynamic expression based on an awakening ego."

The followers of Hekigotō seemed to have played the role of avant-garde in putting the poetical ideals of their dean into actual practice. For example, Ippekirō and Uhei, besides the verses given above, displayed a revolutionary style in the following :

Akikaze ya	The autumn wind—
Me ni kyogyo ukabu	A huge fish before their eyes—
Ryō yasumi	The fishermen resting
	(Ippekirō)
Shūjitsu	I cut bamboo all day—
Take o kirishi mimi nari	The buzzing still ringing in my ears

Ginga sumu   Under the Milky Way

(Uhei)

In the following poems by Hekigotō himself, there is a display of a strong Naturalistic tendency cutting deeply into actual life.

Ko o shikaru	A melon hanging on the house—
Samade mo to omou	Don't scold the child
Uri no yado	So severely
Uma taoreshi	Sprinkling water
Ato haku mizu ya	Where the horse died
Higa no tobu	Under the cloud of fire-moths
Gin mashiro	The brightness of the silver coins—
Ushi urishi yo no	On the night of the day the cow was
Nowaki shite	sold
	A wintry blast

However, so eager were they in discarding convention, that Hekigotō and his followers displayed a tendency to lapse into eccentricity. Attempts to create unique style resulted in awkward and ambiguous expression. Contrary to their intentions, their style inevitably led to unnaturalness.

The Neo-Tendency movement, which so far had been carried along under the leadership of Hekigotō, showed signs of discord within its ranks towards the end of the Meiji Era. Otoji, who earlier was instrumental in suggesting the Neo-Tendency movement, now showed discontent with the movement of the Hekigotō school. After 1910, he assumed a critical attitude, and, writing in such magazines as *Kakeaoi* (The Hanging Hollyhock), *Katatsumuri* (Snail), and *Jinsei to Hyōgen* (Life and Expression), he criticized the poetical work of this school. Otoji's belief was that the significance of *haiku* poety lay in the " singing of a sentiment of becoming one with nature." In *Genkon Haiku-Hyō* (Criticism of Contemporary Haiku) (1910), he expressed disfavor with Hekigotō's attempt to ride the tide of Naturalism. He also assailed the school for engaging in "a complicated, meaningless game of words," which, he prophesied, would be the road leading to destruction. ("The Abuse of Words, Which Is Destroying Life," 1912). Otoji was to revert to classicism, and from this standpoint was to call upon *haiku* poetry to return to "the spirit of Bashō."

Meanwhile, on the part of the Neo-Tendency movement, there was an attempt to unify the ranks. This appeared in the form of the publication of *Sōun* (Piled Clouds) in April 1911, by Seisensui with the support of Hekigotō himself. But Seisensui voiced disapproval of Hekigotō's non-centralism, and the two did not get along so well. Starting from the first issue of *Sōun*, Seisensui serialized an article entitled "Comments on Recent Trends in Haiku." In this article, in which he traced the history of *haiku*, Seisensui explained that the Neo-Tendency movement had arrived at a stage of "expressing an atmosphere of actuality and the sentiments of the ego," and had stabilized itself in a distinct 5-5-3-5-syllable pattern style. Thus, he was paving the way for negation of seasonal themes and for the introduction of free verse into the *haiku* field. In actual composition, Seisensui wrote verses like the following:

> *Wasure-namida*
> *Hoho ni teru ko ya*
> *Haru no kaze*
>
> The child has forgotten he cried
> But tears still glitter on his cheeks
> In the spring breeze
>
> *Ugo no akarusa ya*
> *Yūkan uru ko*
> *Akikaze ni*
>
> The brightness after the rain—
> A boy selling evening papers
> In the autumn wind
>
> *Kototoi no akikaze ya*
> *Hi o chirasu*
> *Kawajōki*

The Kototoi Bridge in the autumn wind—
A river-boat
Sputtering up sparks

Hekigotō disapproved the tendency shown by his pupil and broke with Seisensui in 1912. Later on, Hekigotō banded together his followers and inaugurated another magazine *Kaikō* (Sea Crimson) in 1915.

The style called free verse was first experimented with by Ippekirō, one of the most radical in the Hekigotō school. In June 1911, Ippekirō, with the help of sympathizers, published a pamphlet entitled *Shisaku* (Études), and renaming it *Dai-Issaku* (The First Work) the following year, proceeded his own way. Unrestrained by the idea of seasonal themes, and with the help of a free form and expression based on colloquialism, he displayed vivid lyricism, as in the following examples:

Toruko no yō na	I wish I had a Turkish bath
Yu ga hoshii	On the outskirts of town
Basue no aki da	This autumn
Gakutai no	Following a band
Ato kara seifuku de	I walk home in school uniform
Akibi o modoru	In the autumn sun
Omoikiri hashitte	I'd like to run with all my might
Wakaba no yami e	And enter the darkness
Haittemo mitai	Of the young leaves

The attempts of Seisensui and Ippekirō to introduce the free verse style in the *haiku* world seem to be connected with a similar movement in the *waka* and modern poetry fields. But it is not until the Taishō Era and later that we are able to make a proper assessment of this free verse movement.

PART FOUR THE MEIJI DRAMA

CHAPTER I THE REFORM OF *KABUKI* AND THE *SHIMPA* PLAYBOOKS

1. *Mokuami and His Circle*

The most noteworthy event in the whole history of the growth of drama during the Meiji Period is the rise of the new drama inspired by that of the West. The progress toward this new form of literary art, which came into existence during the Meiji forties, was marked by the various movements for reform that arose in the second decade of the era, by the *katsureki* drama (realistic plays based on historical subjects), which was born under stimulus from these movements, and by the *shimpa* (new school) drama, which was initiated as a part of a political movement and then was transformed into a more refined, artistic, dramatic genre on the style of *kabuki*. Furthermore, the activities of men of letters, best represented by Shōyō, both in theory and creative work, and their translation of Western plays, constituted a pioneering achievement in the establishment of the modern drama as a form of literary art.

If it was necessary for the modern drama during the last years of Meiji to abandon various remnants of bygone days for the purpose of qualifying as the dramatic literature of the new age, it was, needless to say, the playbooks of *kabuki* that had to be discarded as an outdated form of playwriting. And among the *kabuki* playwrights, the name of Furukawa Mokuami, who was their monarch from the Kaei Period (1848–1854) through the first half of the Meiji Period, can be mentioned as representative.

Mokuami was born in Tōkyō (then called Edo), his family name was Yoshimura, and he was called Yoshisaburō in his childhood. When he was twenty, he embarked on the career of a playwright, adopting such pen-names as Katsu Genzō and Shiba Shinsuke. In the fourteenth year of Tempō (1843), at twenty-eight years of age, he became the chief playwright of the Kawarazaki-Za (*za* means theatre), and renamed himself Kawatake Shinshichi (the second). (The name of Furukawa Mokuami was adopted after the fourteenth year of Meiji (1884), following his retirement, but has become the one most universally known.) And yet it was not until he joined Ichikawa Kodanji, in the first year of Ansei (1854) when he was thirty-nine, that he began seriously to give full play to his ability.

Originally, the playbooks of *kabuki* had to be written in accordance with the scheme and the atmosphere designated in advance for specific occasions, and with conventional contrivances, all within the carefully prescribed traditional limits. They were written for the actors of a particular troupe to perform, and there was nothing at all of a consciousness of writing a literary work for its own sake, as is the case with modern playwriting, nor any notion of the playwright's artistic freedom. They were mere playbooks, into which actors alone could breathe life. For this reason, it was most desirable for playwrights to work with good actors. Mokuami, by working first with Ichikawa Kodanji, and afterwards with Onoe Kikugorō the Fifth, both excellent *sewa-mono* (realistic domestic drama) actors, was able to demonstrate his gifts as a playwright of *kizewa-mono* (particularly realistic, or pure *sewa-mono*) plays savoring of the refinement and decadence inherent in the last days of the Edo Period.

During a little over a decade, from 1854 to 1866, the year of Kodanji's death, Mokuami wrote about twenty-four *sewa-mono* and a few *oie-mono* (plays based on family feuds in the houses of feudal lords), assigning the leading part to him. Mokuami also wrote a number of plays with Sawamura Tanosuke and Nakamura Shikan as protagonists. The noteworthy plays during this period include : *Tsutamomiji Utsunoya Tōge*

(The Colored Leaves of Vines on the Mountain Pass of Utsunoya) (1856, *Bun'ya-Goroshi**, The Murder of Bun'ya); *Nezumi-Komon Haru no Shingata* (The Little Mouse Pattern for the New Mode of Spring) (1857, *Nezumi Kozō*, Nezumi Kozō the Burglar); *Amimoyō Tōro no Kikukiri* (The Reticulate-Designed Lantern with Chrysanthemum and Paulownia) (1857, *Kozaru Shichinosuke to Tamagiku*, Kozaru Shichinosuke and Tamagiku); *Edozakura Kiyomizu Seigen* (Cherry Blossoms of Edo and Kiyomizu Seigen) (1858, *Kurotegumi no Sukeroku*, Sukeroku of the Black Hand Gang); *Satomoyō Azami no Ironui* (The Colorful Embroidery of Thistles in Vogue in the Gay Quarter) (1859, *Izayoi Seishin*, The Sixteenth Night's Novice); *Sannin Kichiza Kuruwa no Hatsukai* (Three Men Called Kichiza Pay Their First Visit to the Gay Quarter) (1860); *Hachiman Matsuri Yomiya no Nigiwai* (The Night Festivities of the Hachiman Shrine) (1860, *Chijimiya Shinsuke*, Shinsuke the Crêpe Dealer); *Ryō to Mimasu Takane no Kumokiri* (The Dragon-Shaped Clouds over the High Summit) (1861, *Inga Kozō*); *Aoto Zōshi Hana no Nishikie* (The Tale of Aoto with Flowery Colored Illustrations) (1862, *Shiranami Gonin Otoko*, The Five Brigands); *Kanzen Chōaku Nozoki Karakuri* (The Peepshow of Morals Where Vice Is Punished and Virtue Rewarded) (1862, *Murai Chōan*); *Sogamoyō Date no Goshozome* (The Pattern of Splashes for the Soga Brothers) (1864, *Hototogisu-Goroshi to Gosho Gorozō*, The Killing of a Cuckoo and Gosho Gorozō); *Kaidan Tsuki no Kasamori* (The Ghost Story of the Moonlit Woods), (1865, *Kasamori O-Sen*); and *Fune e Uchikomu Hashima no Shiranami* (Foaming Waves under the Bridge Run into the Boat) (1866, *Ikakematsu*).

Now let us take a look at *Sannin Kichiza* in which Kodanji had the leading role and which Mokuami himself personally acknowledged as a satisfactory piece of work. Its outline is as follows: Jūzaburō, a clerk at the Kiya, tries to drown

---

* *Translator's Note*: Since the titles were so unwieldy, the plays came to be known by shorter ones, frequently having no relation to the original.

himself because he is overcome with anxiety at having lost the hundred *ryō* which his master had entrusted to him, but is prevented by Dozaemon Denkichi. Denkichi's daughter O-Tose, who is a prostitute, finds the money, and while looking for Jūzaburō to return it to him is robbed of it by Ojō-Kichiza, a thief in woman's dress. Thence arise a series of entanglements, from which Obō-Kichiza, Oshō-Kichiza (acted by Kodanji), and Ojō-Kichiza emerge as pledged brothers. However, this hundred *ryō* causes Denkichi, Oshō's father, to be murdered by Obō. In addition, Jūzaburō and O-Tose fall in love with each other, without knowing that they are twins. The lovers who have committed incest are killed by their elder brother Oshō, and the three Kichizas, attacked by the police, commit a triple suicide by stabbing one another. Into this main thread of the story, the episodes of a sword called the Kōshin-Maru and the love-affair of Kiya Fumisato (also acted by Kodanji) and Hitoe, Obō's younger sister, are interwoven.

This play draws its inspiration from the world of Yaoya O-Shichi, and is based on the subject of inevitable retribution involving three robbers called Kichiza, with the additional romance of Fumisato and Hitoe, which was borrowed from a *sharehon* entitled *Keiseikai Futasujimichi* (The Dilemma in Visiting Courtesans) by Umebori Kokuga. The story of the three Kichizas belonged to the category of " thief plays," known as *shiranami-mono* (literally, " white waves " pieces), along with *Nezumi Kozō, Benten Kozō*, and *Ikakematsu*; thus, Mokuami, who was talented in writing this sort of play, was also called a *shiranami*-writer. The gruesome scenes of retribution involving blood relations were in the tradition of the school represented by Tsuruya Namboku the Fourth. The play-viewer is filled with horror at the sight of the aged Denkichi who is secretly aware that the series of unfortunate occurrences is nothing but the penalty for his past crimes. Moreover, what one discerns in the minds of the three Kichizas is a sort of nihilistic feeling that makes their lives meaningless, since they feel they are doomed to be arrested and executed sooner or later, and a despair that sees no light at all, either in this or the next world. Such a pessimism can be seen in both *Izayoi Seishin* and *Benten Kozō*. In this kind of drama there is something that does not belong completely to the tradition of rationalistic plays that simply teach the moral that virtue is rewarded and vice is punished.

In contrast with this, Murai Chōan in *Kanzen Chōaku Nozoki Karakuri* is a fiendish rascal with no scruples, who murders his sister's husband to rob him of forty-two *ryō* which he has received for selling his daughter into prostitution, manages to impute the charge to a *rōnin* (a masterless samurai), and then goes so far as to kill even his sister too, and commit fraud, blackmail, and other crimes. He is said to be almost the only absolutely evil person that appears in Mokuami's works, but eventually his past crimes are discovered and he is arrested, so that the *rōnin's* bereaved family and the loyal Kyūhachi are rewarded for their pains with happiness. The play has three scenes of murder, and similarly depicts a dark world. Yet it cannot be called a serious play because its contrived moralizing reveals completely its fundamentally optimistic and rationalistic nature.

In the above-mentioned *Sannin Kichiza*, the plot of the romance of Fumisato and Hitoe was borrowed from a *sharehon*, and *Murai Chōan* was an adaptation of a *kōdan* (a narration based on a historical subject). Most of Mokuami's works written before the Meiji Period had similarly been dramatizations of fiction and *kōdan*. It should be noted, however, that serious individuals with remarkable character, such as Kiya Fumisato, Chijimiya Shinsuke, and Murai Chōan were his own creations. However, this may be accounted for by the unostentatious, realistic style of the performance of Kodanji, to whom these roles were assigned. At any rate, it may be said that Mokuami reorganized the *kabuki* of the past, and at the same time carved out a new field in the *kizewa kyōgen* (the realistic social drama) by collaborating with Kodanji.

Since the beginning of the Meiji Period, Mokuami had written *sewa-mono* plays for such actors as Ichikawa Danjūrō, Ichikawa Sadanji, Iwai Hanshirō, and, above all, Onoe Kikugorō. These plays can be classified into the category of *kizewa kyōgen* that had been transmitted from the Edo Period, and that of the so-called *zangiri-mono* (literally, "cropped hair pieces") that dealt with the new age of Meiji.

The former category includes: *Hototogisu Mizu ni Hibiku Ne* (A Nightingale's Singing Echoes over the Water) (1870, *Totoya no Chawan*, A Totoya Tea-Cup); *Tsuyu Kosode Mukashi Hachijō*) (The Silk Dress Drenched by the Summer Rain) (1873, *Kamiyui Shinza*, Shinza the Hairdresser); *Ōgi Byōshi Ōoka Seidan* (Tales of Trials by Judge Ōoka) (1875, *Ten'ichibō*); *Jitsugessei Kyōwa Seidan* (The Political Topics of Kyōwa in Reference to the Sun, Moon, and Stars) (1878, *Emmeiin*); *Kumo ni Magau Ueno no Hatsuhana* (The Cloudlike First Cherry Blossoms at Ueno) (1881, *Kōchiyama to Naozamurai*); *Shisenryō Koban no Ume no Ha* (Four Thousand Ryō in the Plum Leaf-Shaped Golden Coins) (1885, *Okanegura Yaburi*, The Cracker of the Government Safe); and *Mekura Nagaya Ume no Kaga Tobi* (A Blind Fireman from Kaga Residing in a Tenement) (1886).

The latter category of the *zangiri-mono* includes: *Tōkyō Nichinichi Shimbun* (The Tōkyō Nichinichi Newspaper) (1873, *Torigoe Jinnai*), which was the first specimen of the *zangiri-mono* dealing with masterless samurai of the days of the Shōgunate; *Kurikaesu Kaika no Fumizuki* (The Calendar of Enlightenment) (1874, *Sannin Katawa*, The Three Deformed Persons), which presented many scenes based on the new era; *Fujibitai Tsukuba no Shigeyama* (1877, *Onna Shosei Shigeru*, A Woman Student Named Shigeru), which dealt with a woman student in man's dress; *Kanzen Chōaku Kōshi no Homare* (The Respectable Morals of a Dutiful Son) (1877), dealing with the conditions of penal servitude, with the filial son Zenkichi as the hero ; *Ningen Banji Kane no Yo no Naka* (Money Controls All Human Affairs) (1879), which is said to have been modeled on Lord Lytton's play *Money*; *Hyōryū Kidan Seiyō Kabuki* (The Remarkable Travelogue of Drifting Abroad and the Western Kabuki) (1879), which created the novelty of having all the scenes set in foreign countries, and of staging an interlude performed by hired foreigners ; *Shimoyo no Kane Jūji no Tsujiura* (A Street-Vendor of Fortune-Telling Paper and a Bell on a Frosty Night) (1880), dealing with social aspects accompanying the reforms of the period, such as police protection and a samurai's asking his neighbor to suckle his child ; *Konoma no Hoshi Hakone no Shikabue* (The Starlight through the Trees and the Deer Piper of Hakone) (1880), in which the apparition of a murdered woman is interpreted as a symptom of neurosis; *Shima Chidori Tsuki no Shiranami* (The Island Plovers over the Moonlit Waves) (1881), the greatest success during the period of Kawatake Shinshichi ; *Man-Nijūnen Musuko Kagami* (A Model Son at Twenty Years of Age) (1884), which dealt with the conscription system ; and *Suitengū Megumi no Fukagawa* (The Mercy of the Fukagawa Suitengū God) (1885), presenting with compassion a picture of the samurai class which had been reduced to misery by the Restoration. It may be added that the earliest plan for *zangiri-mono* can be seen in *Tsuki no En Masu no Igakuri* (The Moon-Viewing Party and a Measure of Chestnuts in Burrs) (1872).

In reference to Mokuami's activity during the Meiji Period, it should be particularly noted that the *katsureki* drama was his adaptation of *jidai-mono* to the new currents of the Meiji Period and *zangiri-mono* was that of *sewa-mono*,

We shall consider *Shimachidori Tsuki no Shiranami* as an example :   Shimazō of Akashi and Matsushima Senta break into the Fukushimaya pawn shop and injure the proprietor, who is thereby unable to carry on his business and becomes bankrupt.   Shimazō, upon returning to his native place, finds his son Iwamatsu deformed as a result of an accident which occurred coincidentally at the same hour of the day when he had injured the proprietor of the Fukushimaya. Shimazō becomes penitent, horrified by the retribution of *karma.* He goes back to Tōkyō to return the money to the Fukushimaya, resolved to clear himself by submitting to a trial. Senta tries to tempt Shimazō back to an evil life, but instead is reformed by Shimazō's remonstrances.

This play amply exhibits as its historical background such new professions as that of bank clerk, jinrikisha-puller and waiters at foreign houses; the paraphernalia of civilization, such as finger-rings, *kaban* (brief-cases), *shappo* (*chapeau*) (hats), and pistols (revolvers); and such novelties in the early Meiji Period as jurisprudence, steamboats, telegraph, and the Shōkonsha (The Pantheon for the War Dead) at Kudan. However, the content of the play was not so novel, although its morality, as seen in the reform of five wicked characters into honest men and women, told its departure to some extent from the tradition of the pre-Meiji drama. It should be marked that the play included such preaching of morals and flattery of the Meiji government, as shown in the line in Act Five, " If my repaying the money and giving myself up becomes known to all my fellow burglars, and makes them aware that they are doing evil against human nature that is good, and if any of them comes to forsake his thievery, then I shall have done some service to the Government."

This work was not so greatly different, however, from the conventional drama in respect to the construction of scenes, the rhythm of the speech which consisted of groups of seven and five syllables, or the musical effects. Generally speaking, his *zangiri-mono*, despite their great value from the viewpoint of the history of customs, were incapable of grasping the essential spirit of the new age, much less of breathing a new life into dramatic literature. *Fudeuri Kōbei* (Kōbei the Writing-Brush Vendor) (*Suitengū Megumi no Fukagawa*) and *Shimoyo no Kane* describe the reduced condition of the samurai class with deep compassion. Mokuami must have been deeply impressed by these social aspects of the time, and his feeling at the same time is evidence of his sympathy with the bygone Tokugawa Period. By this token, the touches of his brush show more liveliness and smoothness in the *kizewa-mono* dramatizing the affairs of the common people in the Edo Period than in the *zangiri-mono*. This tendency may be partially accounted for by the fact that he no longer had to be afraid of offending the Shōgu-nate. But for this, he could not have dramatized the subject of cracking the government safe. At the same time, it may have been a result of the protagonist Kikugorō's brilliant style of performance, which was distinct from that of Kodanji. Yet there was no substantial difference in content between the *kizewa-mono* plays written in the pre-Meiji period and those during the Meiji Period, except that in the latter there was an increased tendency toward moralization.

Prior to the Meiji Era, that is, during the years of his collaboration with Kodanji, very few *jidai-mono* (historical drama) and *oie-mono* had been produced by Mokuami, the only noticeable one being *Fuji Tomimasu Suehiro Soga*, or *Soga no Shikigawa* (The Fur Cushion of the Soga Family) (1866). In Meiji he began writing plays for Ichikawa Danjūrō, Ichikawa Sadanji, and other *kabuki* actors. As Danjūrō preferred historical drama, *jidai-mono*, to domestic ones, *sewa-mono*, more of the former were written by Mokuami. At this period of the Meiji Era when military men were gaining influence, and the prevailing atmosphere had something comparable to the initial stage of the establishment of the Tokugawa Shōgunate, the public naturally tended to welcome *jidai-mono* narrating the samurai's life and duties.

Such a tendency led Mokuami to create such *jidai-mono* and *oie-mono* dramas as *Sumie no Ryō Kosui no Nokkiri* * or *Sa-*

---

* *Translator's Note*: Many titles defy English translation and will be given only in Romanization.

manosuke Kosui Watari (Samanosuke Crosses the Lake) (1870), *Kusunoki-Ryū Hanami no Makuhari* (The Cherry-Viewing Excursion of the Kusunoki Family) or (*Keian Taihei Ki*) (1870), *Taiko no Oto Chiyū no Sanryaku* or *Sakai no Taiko* (The Drums of Sakai) (1873), *Hototogisu Date no Kikigaki* or *Date Sōdō* (The Troubles of the Date Family) (1876). However, these pieces added nothing to the tradition of *jidai-mono*, fixed since the closing years of the Edo Era.

In the meantime, from about the twenties of Meiji, various movements for theatrical reform became active in this country. The first one was that started by intellectuals centering around Yoda Gakukai, and they organized themselves into the Kyūko Kai (The Society for Research of Antiquity) in 1884. Gakukai from the beginning played his role as an adviser. For instance, it was on his advice that Mokuami wrote *Matsu no Sakae Chiyoda no Shintoku* for the Shintomi-Za which opened in June 1878. Gakukai and his group were of the opinion that new *jidai-mono* should be written faithful to historical facts and to the ancient practices and manners, as well as language, and he rejected *jidai-mono* of the past for their crudeness and nonsense. Keen reaction to this view came from the promoter Morita Kan'ya and the actor Ichikawa Danjūrō whose love of an elevated tone well matched the belief of Gakukai. Consequently, Mokuami was asked to write *jidai-mono* in accordance with these new rules. The dramas belonging to this lineage are called *katsureki*, meaning, literally, lifelike historical plays.

The term *katsureki* was first employed in 1878 at the time when one of Mokuami's pieces along this line, *Nichō no Yumi Chigusa no Shigetō*, was performed. The plot of this tragedy is as follows: To save the life of Yoshikata Senjō's son, Komaōmaru, Chichibu Shōji Tadayoshi sacrifices his son, Tarō Shigeyasu, and presents his head before the inspector, pretending that it is the required head of Komaōmaru. Saitō Sanemori examines it approvingly, but inwardly he knows it is a substitute and wishes a happy future to the rescued Komaōmaru. When the tragedy was played at the Shintomi-Za, Kanagaki Robun attacked it in the *Kanayomi Shimbun*, and stigmatized it as *katsureki* (the abbreviation for "lifelike historical plays"), which term became popular among theatrical people.

As pioneer works of this genre, we have *Momoyama Mono-gatari* (The Story of Momoyama) or *Jishin Katō* (Katō Kiyo-masa and the Earthquake) (1869, later supplemented in 1873), *Natorigusa Heike Monogatari* (The History of the Heike Family) or *Shigemori Kangen* (The Remonstrance of Shigemori), and representative pieces which appeared thereafter included those written after the author's retirement, *Nidai Genji Homare no Migawari* (1884), *Hōjō Kudai Meika no Isaoshi* (The Merits of the Noble Hōjō Family) (1884), *Yume Monogatari Rosei no Sugatae* (A Dreamlike Story of Rosei) or *Kazan to Chōei* (Wa-tanabe Kazan and Takano Chōei) (1886), *Mibae Genji Michinoku Nikki* (War Diaries of Genji in Michinoku) or *Ise Saburō* (1886), and *Sekigahara Kami no Aoiba* (The Battles of Sekigahara) (1887). Of these, the first three are counted among the eighteen new favorite *kabuki* plays (*shin-kabuki jūhachiban*). The most famous is *Hōjō Kudai Meika no Isaoshi*, in the first part of which Takatoki is played with by a *tengu*, a long-nosed goblin ; the middle part treats the heroic deeds and the death of Homma Yamashiro-no-Kami Naoyuki, and the last part deals with Nitta Yoshisada losing his sword in the sea. It was on the advice of the Kyūko Kai members that Mokuami created this drama. They asked the dramatist to do so after some discussion and even proposed the material for the work. The author is said to have complained of this play both during the time he was engaged in the work and after its completion, saying that the story was not suited to dramatization.

In general, since *katsureki* plays are lacking in dramatic tension and tend to be concerned with outward description, they are consequently monotonous, although unlike the *jidai-mono* of the preceding era they were neither absurd nor obscure. In addition, stage scenes of *katsureki* plays are apt to be dull. The interminable,

difficult dialogues of the main characters, such as the admonish-
ing of Shigemori or the reflective effusions of Watanabe Kazan, made its performance rather difficult, so that only fluent,
steady, and able actors like Danjūrō could play the roles in a
vivid way. Later on, as Morita Kan'ya came to lose interest in
the plays of this genre and left them, Danjūrō became their
only supporter. This sympathy was due to his artistic quality
which accorded with these plays. Although Mokuami tried hard
to create *jidai-mono* of the new era, obeying faithfully the advice
on the part of intellectuals, few of his creations possessed artistic
value because of their simplicity and lack of dramatic situations.
For this failure of the *katsureki* plays, those consulting intelligent people, who were ignorant of the substance or the independence of art and who knew only how to adhere to historical
fact, were mainly responsible. At the same time, the author
himself was to blame for a part of the failure. Mokuami, who
could not but remain an old-fashioned writer, had no deep insight
into the meaning of history, and as a result attempted, on the
basis of common sense, to write *katsureki* plays which he thought
should be realistic only in form.

Other than these, some *shosagoto* (pantomimic dance dramas)
pieces were created by Mokuami, including those notable works
Renjishi, *Tsurigitsune* (one of the eighteen new favorites), *Funa-
benkei* (one of the eighteen), *Momijigari* (one of the eighteen),
Modoribashi (The Drawbridge), *Tsuchigumo*, *Ibaraki*, and *Hito-
tsuya* (The Solitary House), the last four of which are included
the Ten New and Old Plays (*shinko engeki jisshu*). Of these,
Momijigari (October 1887) was an excellent transplantation of
the *nō* drama into *kabuki* form, and related the story of Taira
no Koreshige who conquered a witch in the Togakushi mountains. In *Modoribashi* (October 1889), Watanabe Minamoto
Tsugutsuna meets a beautiful woman at the Ichijō drawbridge,
and recognizing her for the evil demon that she is, cuts her
arm. It can be called a *katsureki* pantomimic dance drama,

and it too is a famous work that was often staged together with *Momijigari*.

According to the biographical notes in a volume attached to the *Mokuami Zenshū* (The Complete Works of Mokuami), his whole work includes one hundred thirty *sewa kyōgen* (love dramas), forty-one pure *jidai-mono* (historical plays), thirty-one quasi-*jidai-mono* (*oie-mono*, *daimyō* familys play, etc.), and eighteen *katsureki* plays, not counting one hundred forty *jōruri* plays. The dramatists of the day in general were prolific, but this was most remarkably true of Mokuami. With his tastes and materials changing in compliance with external conditions, from an artistic standpoint there was no progress, only increasing refinement. Furthermore, as was the case with many other authors belonging to the old era, he had nothing unique in his philosophy of life and thought, and his specialty lay in representing the common sense qualities and feelings of life by his musical dialogues. Through his stage technique of a master of the past theatrical art, Mokuami successfully portrayed these feelings in the afterglow of the Edo *kabuki*.

Prior to the Meiji Era, at the time when Mokuami became an exclusive playwright for the Kawarazaki-Za, and was allowed to name himself Kawatake Shinshichi II, the three major theatres of Edo, the seat of the Tokugawa Shōgunate, had on their staff such dramatists as Mimasuya Nisōji, Namiki Gohei III, Sakurada Jisuke III, and Tsuruya Namboku V. Commonplace writers that they were, they achieved comparatively little, their work remaining in the field either of adaptation and emendation of ancient dramas or that of dramatizing popular stories and novels, including some *kōdan*. Such being the situation, playwrights were in their lowest decline at this period.

Segawa Jokō III, a younger dramatist than Mokuami who entered into contract with the Nakamura-Za in 1848, attained high reputation by writing *Higashiyama Sakura no Sōshi* (The Tale of the Higashiyama Cherries) (1851), a mixture of *Inaka*

Genji and *Sakura Sōgo,* and *Yowa Nasake Ukina no Yokogushi* (The World of Love and the Comb Scandal) (1853), thereby advancing one step ahead of Mokuami. The former work, *Higashi-yama Sakura no Sōshi,* borrowed its plot from Tanehiko's *Nise Murasaki Inaka Genji,* and the latter was an adaptation of Ryōsai's story *Kirare Yosaburō.* After the emergence of Mokuami, Jokō was left behind by the new trends in the Meiji Era, and gradually fell into an impasse. Gohei, Nisōji, and other play-wrights died before the fall of the Shōgunate. Mokuami, who survived, pushed forward in his activity, and thus the authority of playwrights gradually was restored.

After 1865, Mokuami worked for each of the three major theatres of Edo, and in the Meiji Era, until his death, he was the undisputed leader in the circle of theatrical writers. Among his pupils we see such men as Kawatake Shinshichi III, Take-shiba Kisui, Katsu Genzō, Katsu Nōshin, and Furukawa Shin-sui. The works of Shinshichi include *Kagotsurube Sato no Yoizame* (Becoming Sober in the Gay Quarters) (1888), *Ansei Mikumi no Sakazuki* (Three Sets of Winecups) (1893), and *Edo Sodachi O-Matsuri Sashichi* (1898). Kisui wrote *Kami no Megumi Wagō no Torikumi* (The Match in Harmony), commonly known as *Megumi no Kenka* (The Fight of Megumi) (1890). Furukawa Shinsui, as had Morita Kan'ya, did much as an assistant to Mokuami and later became an independent writer as one of his pupils. Shinsui lived until as late as 1901, and Kisui survived until the Taishō Period. Although they occasion-ally wrote plays, they failed to create any work of originality. Then, from without the circle of playwrights, appeared those reformist (Kairyō-Ha) writers such as Gakukai and Ōchi, and they relinquished authority to these talented younger men who succeeded in creating a new phase of *kabuki.*

2. *The Reform of* Kabuki

Since *kabuki* had been originally been fostered by the common people in the Edo Period, it naturally reflected the sentiment and taste of the vulgar audience of Edo. However, the Meiji Restoration, which renamed Edo Tōkyō, caused a shift of political as well as financial power to the hands of those men who came from the country districts, thus changing the taste of the audience. Also, the practical and rationalistic tendencies during the early years of Meiji gave rise to censure of morals and exposure of irrationalities in the traditional drama. In addition, those who had been abroad expressed their opinions in favor of Europeanization. The result was that *kabuki* received interference from scholars, men of letters, and other prominent figures of the time who were outside its tradition. The meddling took the form of a series of movements for the reform of drama that were carried out through the second and the third decades of the Meiji Era.

The dramatic reform movement was initiated by a group represented by Yoda Gakukai. As a historian, Gakukai pointed out that the historical plays staged in those days were fabulous, and maintained that the plays of the new age should be graceful as well as faithful to historical facts, and for this purpose, they should be produced on the grounds of sufficient research into customs, furniture, words, and behavior, in accordance with the knowledge of ancient practices and usages. In European countries, too, such historical realism had become the predominant tendency in the drama of the latter half of the nineteenth century. Therefore, it is said Gakukai felt highly encouraged by the first-hand accounts of persons who had just returned from abroad. His insistence found its sympathizer in Danjūrō and Morita Kan'ya. Kan'ya's reformative enthusiasm was demonstrated at the inauguration ceremony of the newly built Shintomi-Za, in June 1878, when all the actors, proprietors, and playwrights wore Western clothes and observed the ceremony in the Western fashion. On this occasion, they staged *Matsu no Sakae Chiyoda no Shintoku* (The Luxuriance of Pine Trees Symbolizing the Divine Virtue of the Emperor) (by Mokuami) in which Gakukai also had a hand. This play was one of the early examples of the *katsureki*. Gakukai also provided almost the whole plot of Mokuami's *Akamatsu Man'yū Ume no Shirahata* (Akamatsu Man'yū's White Banner with the Plum Blossom Design) and interfered in its staging excessively. This play was the first program of the Shintomi-Za for February 1879, and the second program was *Ningen Banji Kane no Yo no Naka* (Money Controls All Human Affairs) for which Fukuchi Ōchi offered the material.

As discussed before, Mokuami wrote a series of *katsureki* under the guidance of these scholars and intellectuals. In the sixteenth year of Meiji (1883), under Gakukai's leadership, Konakamura Kiyonori, Kurokawa Shinrai, Sekine Shisei, Fukuchi Ōchi, and Kawabe Mitate formed the Kyūko Kai (The Society for Research of Antiquity) to give guidance to Danjūrō and offer material for writing new plays. This tendency was received favorably among some intellectuals, but the traditional *kabuki* audience was greatly dissatisfied. It may be added that the Kyūko Kai lasted until Danjūrō's death, but it was engaged in the dramatic reform movement only during the first two years or so of its existence.

In August 1886, the Engeki Kairyōkai (The Dramatic Reform Society) was formed with Suematsu Kenchō as its advocate, and with Inoue Kaoru, Toyama Shōichi, Yatabe Ryōkichi, Fujita Mokichi, Mori Arinori, Shibusawa Eiichi, Gakukai, and Ōchi as promoters, and the prominent bureaucrats of the time as sponsors, thus mustering celebrities. The prospectus of the society advocated the redemption of the drama from the traditional foul practices, the encouragement of the actual staging of good plays, the elevation of the profession of playwriting to a respectable position, and the building of a stage of ideal structure for the use of plays, concerts, and choruses. Suematsu also published *Engeki Kairyō Iken* (Views on the Reform of Drama), and Toyama *Engeki Kairyōron Shikō* (Private Views on the Reform of Drama), expatiating upon and propagandizing their views.

Regarding the writing of a play, they pointed out that in Japan there was no such systematic dramaturgy as the distinction of a tragedy from a comedy, or the rule of trinity observed abroad, and insisted that the content should be refined and moralistic, that a new play should dispense with the musical element hitherto rendered by *chobo* (the *gidayū* accompaniment), and should depend more on speech. Taken independently, these were remarkable opinions. But as they lacked a grasp of the essence of *kabuki*, they met the opposition of Takada Hampō, Tsubouchi Shōyō, and Mori Ōgai. According to *Engeki Kairyō-ron Shikō* by Toyama, *Shigenoi Shinzaemon* of the Ichimura-Za and *Nakamitsu* of the Shintomi-Za were the plays that were approved by this school.

This movement, with the revision of the unequal treaties close at hand, had also the political purpose of building up rapidly the national prestige and improving Japan's international position. It included, in general, a too drastic insistence on Europeanization. For this reason, aside from its significance from the standpoint of cultural history, it hardly exerted great influence upon the actual drama, in particular playwriting, in spite of its spectacular appearance. In the meantime, conservative tendencies soon emerged; the year 1888 saw a cabinet change and the dissolution of the Kairyōkai less than two years after its birth. The fruit of this movement was the improved position of the drama, as shown in the performance before the Emperor in 1887, and the establishment of copyright and the right of production. The foundation of the Imperial Theater in 1911 may be regarded as an indirect result of its activity.

About the same time that the Engeki Kairyōkai languished, the Nihon Engei Kyōfūkai (The Japan Entertainment Reform Society), headed by Tanabe Renshū, was inaugurated in March 1888, with a view to "reform the evil practices of Japanese entertainment, and promote its gracefulness so as to attain artistic perfection." Okakura Tenshin, Ōtsuki Joden, Takada Sanae, Aeba Kōson, Tsubouchi Shōyō, Yoda Gakukai, and

Fukuchi Ōchi were its committee members. As this society had a too compromising tendency in reaction to the Kairyōkai which was too radical, it was reorganized in September 1889 as the Nihon Engei Kyōkai (The Japan Entertainment Association). Its president was Count Hijikata Hisamoto, its literary committee was composed of Shōyō, Bimyō, Ōgai, Kōyō, Mokuami, and Kōson, while its performance committee was made up of Danjūrō, Kikugorō, Sadanji, and the representatives of various entertainments, and its rehearsal committee of Morita Kan'ya and Tamura Seigi. Under the initiative of Takada Sanae and Okakura Tenshin, the association attempted to improve the national drama while conserving its special qualities, unlike the earlier reformative movements which displayed excessive leanings toward *katsureki*, moralization, and Europeanization. It is noteworthy that it encouraged new authors to write original plays. Although immediate results were not seen, it prepared the ground for the emergence of playwrights other than the writers of *kyōgen*. However, this society, too, was destined to dissolve before its goals were attained.

The first stage of the progress from the traditional *jidai-mono* of Chikamatsu and his followers toward the new historical drama of Shōyō and others was marked by Mokuami's *katsureki*, while the second stage by the works of Gakukai and Ōchi.

Gakukai, who had earlier given advice on Mokuami's plays, eventually undertook writing himself, and produced his maiden play in the style of *katsureki*, *Yoshino Shūi Meika no Homare* (In Praise of an Excellent Poem in the Supplement to the Yoshino Anthology) (1886), in collaboration with Kawajiri Hōshin. The main theme of the play is the love story of Kusunoki Masatsura and Ben no Naishi, a court lady, and Masatsura's death in battle, and romances of other loyal vassals with brave women. Gakukai put into practice his theories by producing historically faithful scenes of Masatsura's archery on horseback and of the debates of the medieval court nobles. But in the matter of speech his views seem not necessarily to have been realized. This play was read aloud at the elocution meetings of the Kairyōkai, and was acclaimed as a refined model of the reformed drama. But it also faced the criticism that there remained some areas yet to be improved. Gakukai exerted himself for the reform of drama long after the establishment of the Kyū-ko Kai. At first he appeared to be a modest, impartial supporter of *katsureki*, but afterwards he gradually inclined to a more radical position, so that he was finally estranged from his friends. His other works include : *Tōsei Futari Muko* (Two Modern Bridegrooms) with the subtitle *Kyakuhon wa Fukkoku* ; *Sekai wa Nihon* (The Best of All Plays Are the French, and the Best of All Nations Is Japan) (1887), and *Mongaku Shōnin Kanjinchō* (Saint Mongaku's Subscription Book) (in collaboration with Hōshin, 1888). Also his *Seitō Bidan Shukujo no Misao* (A Lady's Chastity : A Praiseworthy Anecdote of a Political Party) was performed in 1891 as a reformed play by actors and actresses of the *shimpa* (new school).

Besides Gakukai, Fukuchi Ōchi also participated in the reform of plays as an enlightened intellectual of the time. He first helped Mokuami with the plotting and revision of his playbooks, and was affiliated with various organizations for the reform of the drama. His opinions were moderate in comparison with those of Gakukai ; therefore, they were received favorably by the dramatic circles. In 1889, he collaborated with Chiba Katsugorō in founding the Kabuki-Za, and became its co-proprietor, which work occasioned him to enter theatrical circles. He wrote a large number of plays for Danjūrō and Kikugorō, and when in 1897 he became a chief playwright, this signalled his complete acceptance as a member of the dramatic community. But he gradually demonstrated a weakness in his reformative opinions, so that he was regarded as vulgar by the literary world. His distinguished works include : in the *katsureki*, *Kasuga no Tsubone Kennyo no Kagami* (Lady Kasuga : A

Model of a Wise Woman) (the first edition in 1888 ; the revised edition, *Kasuga no Tsubone*, was staged in 1891), *Sekigahara Homare no Kachidoki* (The Shout of Glorious Triumph on the Field of Sekigahara) (première in October 1892), and *Ōkubo Hikozaemon* (première in September 1893) ; in the dance drama, *Ōmori Hikoshichi* (première in October 1897) and *Shunkyō Kagami-Jishi* (The Vernal Merriment of the Lion Dance) (March 1893) ; and in the *sewa-mono*, *Kyōkaku Harusamegasa* (The Gallant's Umbrella in the Spring Rain) (première in April 1897). *Kasuga no Tsubone Kennyo no Kagami* particularly may be considered one of his representative works. In its first edition it had seven acts, but it was revised into five acts when it was performed. The story goes as follows : Lady O-Fuku is the wife of Inaba Sado-no-Kami, a principal vassal of the house of Kobayakawa. Accredited by Tokugawa Ieyasu to be of good character, she is appointed nurse to Takechiyo, the eldest son of Hidetada, Ieyasu's son and heir. Lady Hidetada, however, is partial toward Kunichiyo, Takechiyo's younger brother, and plots to have him accede to the office of Shōgun. O-Fuku perceives this intrigue in advance, and informs Ieyasu, thereby forestalling the plot. Furthermore, on the occasion of Princess Kazu's marriage to the Emperor, she is appointed guardian, and invested with the second grade of court rank. In the revised edition, the matron Takamado, an attendant of Kunichiyo, is sent as a spy from the Toyotomi family in Ōsaka, so as to make the play more exciting. These events cover a full twenty years in actual history, but are reduced to five years in the play. It was the embodiment of Ōchi's views on *katsureki*, with its material obtained on the basis of careful historical research. It was written with the view of assigning the role of Lady Kasuga to Danjūrō, who played it excellently. However, the criticism of the time was not entirely favorable, for the play presented such flaws as that of verbosity of dry, moralizing lines, and of emphasizing not so much the characters of Ieyasu and Lady Kasuga as the character of Danjūrō. Furthermore, this play magnified the defects of the *katsureki* as well.

3. *The* Shimpa *Playbooks*

Whereas the authors of *katsureki* and *zangiri-mono* ("the crop-hair style drama," which dealt with the crop-haired men of early Meiji), which emerged under the stimulus of the new civilization, had been traditional *kabuki* playwrights and reformists, now a layman's drama came into existence. The latter was called at the time *shin-engeki* (the new performance) and later *shimpa-geki* (the new school drama). This school was inaugurated by Sudō Sadanori, a political canvasser of the Liberal Party, who, following the advice of Nakae Chōmin who had been charged with violating the Peace Regulations and who had fled to Ōsaka, formed the Dai-Nihon Sōshi Kairyō Engekikai (The Greater Japan Political Canvassers' Dramatic Reform Society), and staged *Tainin no Shosei Teisō no Kajin* (The Persevering Students and the Chaste Beauties) and *Kinnō Bidan Ueno no Akebono* (A Royal Episode : Dawn at Ueno) (December 1888) at the Shimmachi-Za in Ōsaka.

Sudō's aim in starting this movement was the promotion of political thought and the relief of political canvassers who were not regularly employed. The call for the utilization of the reformed drama as the medium of promoting political thought had already been voiced in the organ of the Nihon Rikken Seitō (Japan Constitutional Party) issued in June 1883. Further stimulant was provided in those days by the dramatization and performance of *Setchūbai* (Plum Blossoms in the Snow) by Ichikawa Sadanji and others. *Tainin no Shosei* (The Persevering Students), performed by Sudō, was the dramatization of a novel which he published first in the *Shinonome Shimbun* (The Shinonome Newspaper) and afterwards in a book under the title of *Gōtan no Shosei* (The Undaunted Students) (August 1888). This story dealt with two young students from the vicinage of Okayama, their laborious pursuit of education under adversity, their success in becoming a solicitor and an associate judge respectively, both marrying celebrated entertainers of their local district with whom they had been in love, and their paying triumphant visits to their homes. It is very illustrative of the time about the twentieth year of Meiji in that it has students and entertainers as heroes and heroines and in that it eulogizes their success after arduous study, but it cannot be said that it displayed any high degree of political thought. However, its historical significance can be acknowledged in that it was a play written and acted by mere laymen.

In February 1891, Kawakami Otojirō, a political canvasser of the Liberal Party, performed political plays entitled *Keikoku Bidan* (The Noble Tales of Statesmanship) and *Itagaki-Kun Sōnan Jikki* (The Documentary of the Assassination of Mr. Itagaki) at the Unohi-Za in Sakai. Previously he had gained popularity by singing on the stage the so-called *oppekepe-bushi* (a song with a refrain of *oppekepe*) satirizing current events, and had visited Tōkyō with a troupe called Shosei Niwaka (The Student Mimes). He had organized his production so well that by bringing his troupe to Tōkyō and performing at the Nakamura-Za in June of the same year, he attracted the immediate attention of the newspapers and secured himself a principal position in the new theatrical world.

Under impetus from Kawakami and his troupe, a reformed play with the joint participation of actors and actresses was staged under the guidance of Yoda Gakukai in November of the same year at the Azuma-Za. This movement was undertaken by the Seibikan (The House of Sublimity), with Ii Yōhō and others in the leading roles. They staged Gakukai's *Seitō Bidan Shukujo no Misao* (The Chastity of a Lady: A Praiseworthy Anecdote of a Political Party) and Kawajiri Hōshin's *Na mo Ōtaki Urami no Pisutoru* (Ōtaki's Rancorous Revolver). Gakukai's work was a four-act play which had been published serially in the *Miyako no Hana* (The Flower of the Capital). The story goes as follows: A young politician, Tokida Yorikuni, endangers his life in political conflict with Ashino Michiomi, a distinguished bureaucrat, but is saved by Tsuyuko, Michiomi's daughter, who is in love with Yorikuni. Worry causes Tsuyuko's illness, and Michiomi is penitent at her death-bed. The speech in this play smacked of *kabuki* dialogue, and it had no novelty either in the plot or the characters. Yet it was commended for its artistic quality which was rather rare among the new plays of the time.

The years 1892 and 1893 saw the formation of many other dramatic companies. However, in its initial stage the new dramatic movement had almost no plays that were significant from an artistic point of view. Besides those works by men of letters, *Shūi Gojitsu Renji Kusunoki* by Gakukai and *Hirano Jirō* by Ōchi, other adaptations were made by the actors themselves. They were either those of political novels such as *Keikoku Bidan*, or those treating contemporary political affairs such as *Itagaki-Kun Sōnan Jikki*, *Saga Bōdōki* (A Record of the Saga Riots), adapted by Kubota Hikosaku, and *Shimada Ichirō Baiu Nikki* (The Rainy Season Diary of Shimada Ichirō). Though active members of the Liberal Party, both Sudō and Kawakami had only vulgar ideas as regards the value of drama, and were without any strong inclination to a political ideology or any new approach and specific principle in their artistic position. The amateur-like performance of *shosei shibai* (students' plays) was indeed fresh as compared with the standardized acting of *kabuki* ; but this freshness was another indication of its lack of refinement as an art, and therefore it cannot be considered a part of the new drama (*shingeki*) movement differing from *kabuki* in its artistic view. If we are to recognize its value, however, the *shosei shibai* was significant in so far as it was concerned with the current ideas and problems of the new era.

The new theatrical movement took root in Tōkyō in 1892–1893, and in January 1894, when Kawakami and his company staged *Igai* (Surprise) and *Mata Igai* (Surprise Again), both of which were wildly acclaimed, public favor toward the movement became finally established. These dramas took their material from an actual scandal in the family of Count Sōma, and imitated the foreign style. Tazuko, the sister of Count Kuze (actually Sōma), tries to usurp her brother's fortune in conspiracy with a malicious manager; they cast suspicion on the Countess as having poisoned her husband; the plot becomes disclosed before the court and, to make the matter more dramatic, it happens that the judge named Akimoto is a man who once loved Tazuko. This obviously was an imitation of *The Bells* as acted by the famous British actor Henry Irving. The dramas were adapted by Iwasaki Shunka. The reason for the success of these plays was certainly the freshness of the scenes and its up-to-date character. Some expressed the criticism at the time that the imitation of Western drama was so crudely carried out that it became quite unnatural. Detective and court stories of the most contrived type are characteristic of the new school (*shimpa*) dramas in their initial stage, and these two are good examples.

Immediately thereafter, Kawakami mounted *Mata Mata Igai* (Surprise Yet Again), and when the public was beginning to tire of this, the Sino-Japanese War broke out. Being an opportunist, Kawakami took advantage of this occasion and performed some war dramas with overwhelming success, eclipsing traditional plays. They were *Sōzetsu Kaizetsu: Nisshin Sensō* (The Daring and Exciting Sino-Japanese War), *Senchi Kembun Nikki* (Diary on the Front), *Ikaiei Kanraku* (The Fall of Weihaiwei), and others. However, as war enthusiasm declined, his coarse dramas could no longer enjoy popularity, and as a result he was compelled to elaborate them.

The new drama in its early stage can be divided into three groups. The first group contains adaptations of political novels and those of current events. This traces back to the very beginning of the new drama movement. In spite of their extraordinary popularity during the Sino-Japanese War, these works have almost no artistic value. With the passing of time, works of this type faded away, although occasionally there were performed true-story detective plays of urban life, adventures of the polar explorer Captain Gunji, etc., and such a topical play as *Yōkōchū no Higeki* (Tragedies Abroad) (1901), telling of Kawakami's experiences in the United States.

Adaptations of serial stories in newspapers, both fictitious and true, *rakugo* (comic stories), *ninjō-banashi* (stories of human relations), and *kōdan* (entertaining stories) constitute the second group. Dramatists were attentive to these adaptations from the very beginning of the new drama. However, adaptations of *rakugo*, *kōdan*, *gesaku*, etc. were seen already among the traditional plays. The *rakugo* and *kōdan* of the famous story-teller Enchō occupied most of these adaptations in the new era. They are represented by *Matsu no Misao Bijin no Ikiume* (The Beautiful Woman Who Was Buried Alive) (February 1898) and *Nozarashi* (Weather-Beaten) (August 1899). As for adaptations of newspaper stories, there are *Tetsu Sekai* (The Iron World) based on Morita Shiken's serial story in the *Hōchi, Suteobune* (The Small Abandoned Boat), originally Kuroiwa Ruikō's detective novel which appeared in the *Yorozu Chōhō*, as adapted by Iwasaki Shunka, Ihara Seiseien's *Gosunkugi Torakichi* (Torakichi the Carpenter), and Kōdō Tokuchi's comedies, such as *Bukotsu Musume* (An Awkward Daughter) and *Bijutsuka* (The Artist).

After the first period of creation, more poetical beauty came to be demanded of the new dramas, and at last there appeared adaptations of stories by the Ken'yūsha writers. In this connection, the merits of the dramatist Fujisawa Asajirō cannot be overlooked. His earliest work was the dramatization of Kōyō's *Reinetsu* (Cool Fever), acted by Kawakami and his troupe as *Uso to Makoto : Kokoro no Reinetsu* (Falsehood and Truth : Cool Fever in the Heart) (1896). His drama *Kane to Iroyoku* (Money and Desire), performed in the following year, was written after Kōyō's *Natsu Kosode*, itself an adaptation of Molière's *Avare,* and this was the first comedy ever written by a *littérateur.* Apparently, dramatization of the novels by the

Ken'yūsha authors suited contemporary taste. In the Meiji thirties there were dramatized Kōyō's *Konjiki Yasha* (The Gold Demon) and *Kokoro no Yami* (The Darkness of the Heart), and, among the works of Izumi Kyōka, there were such adapted plays as *Taki no Shiraito* (The White Threads of the Waterfall),. an adaptation of *Giketsu Kyōketsu*, *Tatsumi Kōdan*, *Tsuya Monogatari*, and *Kōya Hijiri* (The Sage of Mount Kōya), and in the forties also Kyōka's *Fūryūsen* (The Elegant Line),. *Onna Keizu* (The Destiny of a Woman), *Shirasagi* (The White Heron), and others. All of these afterwards became an essential part of the repertory of *shimpa* (new school) actors. Other than these tragedies which for the most part treated life in the gay quarters, the public favored the following domestic tragedies: Tokutomi Roka's *Hototogisu* (The Cuckoo); Kikuchi Yūhō's *Ono ga Tsumi* (My Crime) and *Chikyōdai* (Weaned from One Breast); and Nakamura Shun'u's *Ichijiku* (Figs).

Ihara Seiseien, in his article *Tsugi no Danjūrō to Kyakuhon* (The Coming Danjūrō and the Playbooks), arguing the need for reform in drama, welcomed this trend of adapting novels in view of the scarcity of playwrights, and in this regard he emphasized that more attention should be paid to the selection of works to be dramatized, which, he pointed out, had until then been made on a vulgar standard. Those adaptators of novels, Iwasaki Shunka, Takeshiba Hyōzō, Kubota Hikosaku, and others, contributed nothing new to the method of drama writing because most of them belonged to the old Kawatake school. However, when compared with the didactic *zangiri-mono* plays of Mokuami and his school, these dramatized novels were more appealing in their human warmth, were largely successful in portraying the sadness of the individual suppressed under circumstances and obligations, and better described the manners of modern life. It was due to the freshness and poetical element attributed to them as new dramas that they were able to attract interest among the public of the time.

Lastly, the third group consists of those works adapted from

Western plays, as well as translated plays. The earliest dramatization of Western novels include *Keikoku Bidan* (Statesmanship
Stories), *Sappho*, and *Le Comte de Monte-Cristo*, known as
Gankutsuō. Of the works belonging to this group, translated
plays are more notable from the historical point of view. They
were mostly translations of Shakespeare's pieces. The first one,
Shiizaru Kidan (*Julius Caesar*), categorized as *seigeki* (orthodox
drama), was played by Kawakami and his company in July 1901.
This was followed by *Hon'an Osero* (*Othello*) by Emi Suiin,
Yami to Hikari (Darkness and Light) by Takayasu Gekkō (an
adaptation of *King Lear*), *Hamlet*, and *Romeo and Juliet*, all
staged in theaters. In addition, we should note such plays as
Ōkan, a translation of Coppée's *Pour la Couronne*, *Sokoku*,
that of Sardou's *Patrie!*, and *Monna Vanna* of Maeterlinck.

As we have seen above, new theatres from the end of the Meiji
twenties to the mid-thirties had very few original plays and
were obliged to rely upon dramatization of popular Japanese
or Western novels as well as upon translated pieces. We may also
note that it was after 1902 that, in accordance with the proposal
of Ihara Seiseien, Ii Yōhō and Kawai Takeo in collaboration
attempted to revitalize the plays of Chikamatsu. With the intention of developing a new area in the dramatic world, they
acted Chikamatsu's plays not as *jōruri* but as reformed plays.

With the death of Danjūrō and Kikugorō, both principal
kabuki actors, Meiji theatrical circles faced a turning-point in
1903, a year worthy of mention in the field of dramatic creation. In January of that year, *Tamakushige Futari Urashima*
(The Two Urashimas of the Jewelled Box) of Ōgai, and in June
Edo-Jō Akewatashi (Edo Surrenders) of Gekkō, were performed
by *shimpa* (new school) actors. The two pieces were not of
the tradition of *shimpa* dramas, and this seems to suggest the
avant-garde position of those concerned with this dramatic
movement. From about this time original dramas began to
appear, replacing novel adaptations until then most prominent.

During this period, the Hongō-Za was the center of the activity of *shimpa* actors.

Hirotsu Ryūrō, one of the Ken'yūsha writers who was famed for his talent in the *shinkoku shōsetsu* (serious novel), in 1905 wrote *Meguro Kōdan*, a drama in four acts and nine scenes. Prior to this, his novel *Chikushōbara* (Giving Birth to Twins) had been adapted by Hanabusa Ryūgai and performed on the *shimpa* stage. The plot of *Meguro Kōdan* is as follows : Son of a prominent family in the Meguro district of Edo, the once wealthy Uehara Shintarō, now ruined as a victim of the plot of a villain, is forced to kill himself as his estates and his sweetheart are taken away by the wicked man. The chivalrous Sakamoto Genji, sympathizing with the hero, kills the villain who has violated the law, and gives himself up to the authorities. That the law favors a wicked man and persecutes a good one is an idea quite characteristic of Ryūrō. However, the motive for Genji's killing the villain is weak, and too much helplessness and ignorance on the part of Uehara make the work superficial. Psychologically, moreover, the hero and his sweetheart's suicides seem unreasonable because Uehara had a supporter in the person of Genji. Their eventual death despite such support may represent the world-philosophy of Ryūrō as the author of *hisan shōsetsu* (pathos novels). In its form, however, this piece is not so different from *kabuki* plays.

In contrast with Ryūrō who wrote only one *shimpa* play, Satō Kōroku, as a dramatist attached to a *shimpa* theater, published many of them. His first work in this field was *Kyōenroku* (A Record of Gallants and Beauties) (first performed in 1906) in seven acts and nine scenes. A wandering count, who has left his home in disgust at family affairs, meets on his aimless journey an actress named Bandō Rikie. They marry and have a child. Unfortunately, on account of the protest of his wife's mother, the count and his child come to be separated from Rikie. Afterward, when the actress is acting *Shigenoi Ko-Wakare* (Shigenoi's Parting from Her Child), she becomes mad from grief. Then it becomes clear that the boy actor in the role of Sankichi, in this play-within-a-play, is actually her son from whom she has been separated for a long time. This work is usually regarded as having been inspired by Oguri Fūyō's *Katsura Shitaji* and Ryūrō's *Rangiku Monogatari*, but the author has declared that this is not true, for he got the idea of the play's construction from *Onna Kamiji* as performed by Takada Minoru and Kitamura Rokurō, and wrote this piece following the advice of these actors. Revised several times, however, this play is nowadays still counted among the *shimpa* repertory. Kōroku's later works include *Hana no Yume* (The Dream of a Flower), *Kumo no Hibiki* (The Sound of Clouds), *Kochi Monogatari* (The Story of the East Wind), *Haru no Uta* (The Song of Spring), *Ushio* (The Tide), and *Haiba* (The Disabled Horse). Of these, *Kumo no Hibiki* appears to have been an attempt at a social play, and *Haiba* is undeniably an imitation of Ibsen's works.

Dramatists of *shimpa* plays, Taguchi Kikutei, Kojima Koshū, and others who were at work during the time when Kōroku was active in this field, left nothing but vulgar pieces of the ordinary *shimpa* type. Sano Tensei's *Dainō* (Extensive Farming), performed by *shimpa* actors in 1907, was written under the strong influence of Ibsen, and *Bokushi no Ie* (The Pastor's House) of Nakamura Kichizō was also a work of this type. The latter was staged in 1909 by the Shin-Shakaigeki-Dan (New Social Drama Company) of which many *shimpa* actors were members. The Hongō-Za actors in these few years gradually transferred from original *shimpa* dramas to modern dramas of Ibsen and others, especially those pieces under the influence of social plays of the West. The *shimpa* drama saw a virtual decline in about the year 1910, and this fact suggests the limit of this form in the history of Meiji drama which took its course toward the establishment of modern drama in this country ; that is, the *shimpa* actors and dramatists could not develop a form to go beyond the scope of a mere Meiji-type domestic tragedy.

CHAPTER II SHŌYŌ'S DRAMAS AND THE NEW *KABUKI*

1. *Shōyō's New Historical Drama and New Musical Drama*

Shōyō was early interested in drama, but it was not until about 1888, according to the chronology written by himself, that he first decided to participate in reform of the theatre and, for that purpose, to present fresh dramatic works of his own. However, he publicly revealed his interest for the first time in his reaction to the activity of the Engeki Kairyō Kai (Society for Dramatic Reform). As regards the movement of the society, not a few critics arose as antagonists. Side by side with Takada Hampō, Mori Ōgai, and others, Shōyō delivered attacks upon it directly in his articles published in the *Yomiuri*, the first one being *Engeki Kairyō Kai no Sōritsu o Kikite Hiken o Nobu* (My Opinions as to the Establishment of the Society for Dramatic Reform) (September 1886), followed by four more essays, while he insinuated a critical attitude toward the movement in four other essays in the same newspaper, beginning with *Kawatake Mokuami-Ō ni Tsugu* (An Open Letter to Kawatake Mokuami) in which Shōyō expressed his sympathy with the Meiji playwright.

His disapproval of the Kairyō Kai and their followers concerned their moralistic and didactic view of reform, their partial interest in the details of customs and facts in the *katsureki* (lifelike historical drama), and their lack of acknowledgement of the national drama (*kokugeki*). Against such views, Shōyō put emphasis upon the artistic nature of drama, and set forth the essentials of vivid description of men and their psychology in history, refuting the trivial and intellectual tendency of the *katsureki*. Fully recognizing the merit of the national drama, he asserted that one should attempt to reform it by adopting opinions of the new era. This assertion of Shōyō may be called one of gradualism.

Despite its spectacular initiation, the reform movement ended without success, and in March 1888 another organization, the Nihon Engeki Kyōfū Kai (The Japan Theatrical Reform Society), headed by Tanabe Renshū, came to be established. However, in September of the following year the younger people who were discontented with the vulgarization of the new society, organized the Nihon Engei Kyōkai (The Japan Theatre Society). In the meantime, Shōyō distinguished himself as a member of both societies and became more and more resolved to exert himself for the renovation of the drama. The Nihon Engei Kyōkai centering around Takada Hampō and Okakura Tenshin purported to promote the national drama as art, preserving its characteristics against the views of the Kairyō Kai and the *katsureki* school. Remarkably enough, this Engei Kyōkai tried to obtain new dramatic works from fresh figures in this field. At that time Shōyō took up his pen, but left the work unfinished.

As the Engei Kyōkai failed, the theatrical reform movement of the early Meiji Era ended. Notwithstanding such unfavorable circumstances, Shōyō did not abandon his original intention, and, as basic preparation for theatrical reform, he then launched into the study of Shakespeare and Chikamatsu, and took part in the training of recitation. This helped the practical studies of drama and dramaturgy, and, more than that, his recitation group made remarkable progress.

From October 1893 to April of the following year Shōyō's article *Wagakuni no Shigeki* (The Historical Drama of Our Country) appeared as a serial in *Waseda Bungaku* (Waseda Literature), and this had as much significance in theatrical circles as had his *Shōsetsu Shinzui* (The Essence of the Novel) in novel writing. In this article Shōyō traced the past and present of the Japanese drama and indicated the future course it should take. In this connection, as regards historical plays in the past, he asserted that Chikamatsu's works were fantastic and legend-based ones where the author introduced historical facts and characters only in order to delineate human feeling (*ninjō*). According to

Shōyō, compared with Chikamatsu's works, those plays of Mokuami in his later years came nearer to being a true historical drama, more or less successfully representing historic facts and persons. In his opinion, Mokuami's historical plays (*jidai-mono*) were inferior to his domestic dramas (*sewa-mono*), although they actually opened the way to historic realism and led to the birth of lifelike historical plays (*katsureki*). As the representative of the *katsureki* school, Shōyō introduced Yoda Gakukai. Though his works had historical background and his characters had dignity, they had little value as plays, Shōyō remarked. As the author became recklessly radical in his views, his works grew unpoetic and prosaic, as seen in the stage scenes of *Kōko Hakuran-jō* (The Archaelogical Museum), and Gakukai was thereby rejected by the theatrical circles.

According to Shōyō the two most influential groups in the dramatic world then were the *katsureki* school of Fukuchi Ōchi in the lineage of Gakukai, and the fantasy play school (*mugen-geki-ha*) which revered Chikamatsu and Mokuami as its masters. Those plays written by Ōchi, who represented the former group, Shōyō wrote, lacked objectivism, were vulgar and utilitarian in thought, poor in variation of character, simple in cause and effect of incident, and wanting in dramatic irony. For these reasons, Shōyō thought it natural that many attacked Ōchi's works. However, before the appearance of the new historical drama, these plays should be recognized as representative historical drama for that period. The fantasy play school was a reaction to this trend, Shōyō insisted. Among the followers of this school there was a group that held that dramas of fantasy were best suited to the purpose of art, which, in their opinion, through blending the real and unreal, could transport the spectator to a land of fantasy. Shōyō, by thus defining the incompatibility of the schools of *katsureki* and *mugen-geki*, regarded the former as having some possibility for future advancement despite its prosaic trend, while the latter was thought to belong to the past, although it had merit in being poetic.

In criticizing the historical dramas of past and present, Shōyō revealed his own inclination toward realistic historical plays. At the same time he did not overlook some of its defects, and, for its improvement, he gave priority to reform in the spiritual field rather than in the technical. He pointed out that "first of all, the dramatist should differentiate the style of an epic from that of a play in verse. Secondly, a play should conform to the unities. Thirdly, men's characters should be the main cause of dramatic actions." In short, he gave first importance to defining clearly the epic and play in verse. Shōyō found no basic and substantial difference between historical plays and others, but he considered the historical play to rely relatively more upon historic facts. Both the historical and non-historical play, in Shōyō's opinion, similarly aimed at suggesting the relation of cause and effect out of the apparent vagueness of the process of the action developed around the characters.

As the initial means of reform, Shōyō insisted on establishing the style of drama, and promised to deal with the technique of plot construction as of second importance, but he failed to fulfill this promise. However, his theatrical views came to be embodied in his piece *Kiri Hitoha* (One Leaf of Paulownia).

Kiri Hitoha, the first historical play of Shōyō, appeared successively in *Waseda Bungaku* from November 1894 to September the following year, and later, in 1896, it was published by Shun'yōdō. The tragedy, consisting of seven acts and fifteen scenes, treated the fall of the family of Toyotomi Hideyoshi. The theme of this work was "the decline and fall of the Toyotomi family gradually caused by complicated and inevitable fate." The main figure of the play, Katagiri Katsumoto, was regarded as a victim of circumstance, and the author found interest in the hero's tragic situation allowing no choice of death or life. (Preface to *Kiri Hitoha*, published after the performance at the Imperial Theatre, 1917).

Finding herself among the Toyotomi family whose fortunes

are declining under the pressure of the Tokugawa, Yodogimi, the widow of Hideyoshi, suffers pangs of conscience before the "murderous tycoon" Hidetsugu, the nephew of Hideyoshi, and his family. But her innate arrogance becomes more and more abnormal, and, spoiled by crafty courtiers, she continues living in her dreams of the past, failing to realize the situation the Toyotomi family is now in. Nobody understands the misgivings of Katagiri Katsumoto as to the future of the family, and its subordinates are deceived by the Tokugawa conspiracy, as the family is headed by such an unstable person as Yodogimi, and as her son Hideyori is yet too young. As a result, the subordinates are suspicious of each other because of their selfishness. Exerting himself alone to keep the enemy in check, Katsumoto fails in all of his efforts. Finally, losing the chance of suicide, he comes to be obliged to retire to his rural residence in Ibaraki. The outline of this tragedy is the development of the suppressed mentality of Katsumoto, intensified by the stories of the death of Katsumoto's beloved daughter Kagerō and the miserable fate of Ginnojō who dearly loved her.

Shōyō wrote this work with the intention of challenging the morality supported by the contemporary upper class and the intellectuals, the fashion of *katsureki* which tended to be too much concerned with complicated ancient practices and usages, and the Western theories of aesthetics which were impractical. With the view of protecting the national drama (*kokugeki*), he took notice of its resemblances to the romantic plays of Shakespeare. Also, the form of a play composed of several anecdotal events in contrast with that of classical drama was here first employed by this ambitious author.

Among the criticism that then arose concerning *Kiri Hitoha*, that of Ōgai's *Shigi no Hanekaki* in *Mesamashigusa* (February 1896) and Chogyū's *Harunoya ga "Kiri Hitoha" o Yomite* (On Reading Shōyō's "A Leaf of Paulownia") (*Taiyō* in April the same year) are noteworthy. Both critics highly appreciated the historical significance of this drama. However, from the point of view of classical tragedy, Ōgai pointed out some defects in the work : its tragic beauty "is nothing but *das Traurig*" ; the characters lack individuality ; the dramatic action proceeds too slowly ; time and space are wasted in telling anecdotes. After enumerating resemblances to *Hamlet*, Ōgai remarked that Shōyō's tragedy was very valuable when seen from the level of contemporary works. Chogyū, on the other hand, acknowledging, with certain reserve, the development of the personality of the characters, felt the tragedy as a whole gave only a vague impression on account of lack of attention to form, although each scene appeared interesting. Also he stated that Katsumoto was not appropriate as a character of a tragedy and that the play was weak in leading to the climax because the author was excessively concerned with historic accuracy.

Now we should like to examine this work in the light of Shōyō's assertions in *Wagakuni no Shigeki* (The Historical Drama of Our Country). In that essay the author expressed his opinion that dramatists should establish a form of drama in verse and that their works should be constructed in such a way that characters themselves would provide the motive for events. Regardless of this, as we stated above, aestheticians criticized the play in that it was not written in the form of a verse drama but in the form of an epic. Although Shōyō took a different stand from the classical view of tragedy, he admitted himself that in writing *Kiri Hitoha* he patterned it after *maruhon* (collections of *jōruri* dramas) in the *kusazōshi* fashion of feudal days where usually many anecdotes were inserted. More than that, morphologically, one thing noticeable in the work is that stage directions were written in *shichi-go-chō*(seven-five-syllable-style) as in *jōruri*, instead of in the ordinary prose for explanatory purposes. Imitation of *maruhon* dramas is seen also as regards the treatment of roles and scenes. For instance, as for roles, Shōyō employs *sabakiyaku* (a role of moral judge), and for scenes, *gochūshin* (the announcement of important events), *michiyuki* (the elopement), and *shosa* (posture dancing) of the traditional drama are seen. Criticism from an aesthetic viewpoint that this play lacked power to lead to a climax and that the intended tragic heroism ended in pathos, shows its insufficiency of content as a drama and its epic character created contrary to the author's will. The failure of dramatic unity resulted partly from its construction modeled after traditional plays which sought to entertain the spectator in each scene on the stage. The characters of the play were alleged to be analogous or, even in the event that their individual personality was acknowledged, their lacking sufficient quality to be tragic heroes was discussed. However, originally, Shōyō created this work as a tragedy of circumstance, which he regarded as having stronger influence in deciding the course of an incident than personality.

Such observation shows that *Kiri Hitoha* emerged with an appearance considerably different from that advocated as the goal of drama in *Wagakuni no Shigeki*. In this regard, the author of the biography *Tsubouchi Shōyō* writes that this was caused by the change of Shōyō's artistic appreciation and finds in this his flexibility in not being attached to one opinion. In a sense, such inconsistency of Shōyō may be considered the result of his gradualism and eclecticism. Further, we may notice its inevitability, considering that at that time Shōyō was wanting in the inner basis for achieving a character play (*seikaku-geki*)—the awakening of the modern ego, and the deep inner comprehension of the world and humanity.

In spite of the many defects that were pointed out, the publication of this work was an epoch-making event in that it signalled the establishment of Japan's modern historical drama. It was all the more remarkable because an author not belonging to the theatrical circles could create a piece of such high quality. Regardless of the sensation with which it was welcomed, it was not until a decade after the publication that this play was mounted on the stage of the Tōkyō-Za (February 1904).

The second historical play by Shōyō, *Maki no Kata* (Lady Maki), intermittently appeared in *Waseda Bungaku* beginning in January 1896 until March the following year, and was performed in May 1905 at the Tōkyō-Za. Later, when published in a separate book, it was changed into a play in seven acts. It is known that the author was interested in the history of crimes committed by the Minamoto Shōgunate during the three genera-tions of its government after the wars in the Hōgen and Heiji years (1156–1159), and this led him to plan a serial historical play consisting of three or five parts treating the life of the Shōgunate family. Herein Maki no Kata, Sanetomo, and Yoshitoki are temporarily treated in a trilogy, the first part of which was realized as *Maki no Kata*. The heroine, the second wife of Hōjō Tokimasa, conspires to have her youngest son Masanori, whom she thinks resembles greatly the Shōgun Sanetomo, appointed as Shōgun in place of the latter. She goes to her conspirators in the persons of Inage Nyūdō and his son and Hiraga Tomomasa, her daughter's husband, who aspires to obtain the supreme position for himself. Masanori kills himself when he comes to know of his mother's plot. While the Hata-keyamas, loyal samurai to Sanetomo, are destroyed, both Lady Maki and her partner Tomomasa are defeated, as the terrible conspiracy is disclosed. In the meantime, Hōjō Yoshitoki suc-ceeds in increasing his influence so as to realize eventually his ambition of coming to power, always disguising himself as the defender of the Minamoto Shōgunate.

This work became part of a trilogy treating Yoshitoki through many years of his life, by the publication of *Nagori no Hoshizukiyo* (The Starry Night) in June 1917 and *Yoshitoki no Saigo* (The End of Yoshitoki) in May 1918, both in the magazine *Chūō Kōron*. Takayama Chogyū, pointing out the incompleteness of the first part, *Maki no Kata*, as an inde-pendent play, expressed his doubt as to the trilogy form of historical drama in general. The critic indicated that in spite of the clearness and unity of Lady Maki's individuality, she was too simple and superficial to become a tragic heroine, causing the deficiency of spiritual greatness of the entire work. In addition, he remarked that unbalanced attention to stage effect had resulted in lack of unity and subsepuent unnaturalness of action, and that too much historical knowledge on the part of the spectator had been expected (*Harunoya Shujin no "Maki no Kata" o Hyōsu*, On Shōyō's "Lady Maki") (*Taiyō*, August 1897).

According to Shōyō, in writing this work, he was, from the beginning, aware of the resemblances between his heroine and Lady Macbeth of Shakespeare. The author stated that he intended to present this character as a commonplace woman of sanguine temperament, often hysterical as well as cruel. (*Kabuki*, 61st issue). Though something like individuality was given to the heroine, her self-sufficiency in a humanistic sense was not recognized by Ōgai in *Mesamashigusa*, nor by Chogyū. One may see here the limit of Shōyō's talent as a dramatist. Also one may feel Chogyū was correct when he estimated the artistic value of this work as inferior to that of the preceding piece *Kiri Hitoha*, considering that the poetical quality was poor throughout the drama despite its excellent stage technique. It is interesting to note that these views of Chogyū as to this play led to the debates exchanged by him and the author Shōyō concerning the interrelation between the artistic and historic qualities of historical plays.

In April 1897, Shōyō published a short historical drama of two acts and five scenes, *Futaba Kusunoki* (A Camphor-Tree in Bud), in the first number of *Shincho Gekkan* (The New Book Monthly). This minor work, half of which was an adaptation, was published in a book entitled *Kiku to Kiri* (Chrysanthemum and Paulownia) in January the following year, together with another drama *Hototogisu Kojō no Rakugetsu* (The Cuckoo and the Setting Moon over the Solitary Castle).

This last play, Shōyō's third work in this field, had earlier been published in a supplement to the magazine *Shinshōsetsu* (The New Novel) (Vol. II, No. 10) in September 1897. The drama was first performed by the Kado-Za in Osaka in May 1905. Consisting of three acts and six scenes, the work was to form the last part of *Kiri Hitoha*. Previously, in the separate volume of *Kiri Hitoha* this had been announced as *Kiri Hitoha Zokuhen : Katsumoto no Matsugo—Zen Ikkan* (The Sequel to "One Leaf of Paulownia " : The Death of Katsumoto—in One Volume) to give the finishing touch to *Kiri Hitoha* to make it a perfect and complete tragedy.

In the castle of Ōsaka, destined to fall sooner or later, disorder prevails as Yodogimi is half mad and the spies from the Tokugawa plot to rescue Sen-Hime (the wife of Toyotomi Hideyori and the daughter of Tokugawa Hidetada). In spite of his serious illness, Katagiri Katsumoto visits the camp of the Tokugawa army to ask Ieyasu to spare the lives of Yodogimi and her son Hideyori. With the permission of the enemy chieftain Ieyasu, Katsumoto goes back to the Ōsaka castle to remove the two. However, Ii Kamon, Honda Sado, and others are on the way to prevent him from doing so. Meantime, the castle catches fire and Yodogimi and her son Hideyori are destroyed. Crying over the destruction, and in deep remorse for his recklessness which led to the failure, Katsumoto dies in despair.

Probably because of the fact that it appeared as the sequel to *Kiri Hitoha,* this work did not create an immediate reaction among critics. It is noteworthy, however, that this was the first play composed purely in dialogue, abandoning both the *jōruri* fashion of *Kiri Hitoha* and the combination of *jōruri* and *heike-biwa* (chanting of the *Heike Monogatari*) of *Maki no Kata.* Furthermore, the unity in dramatic construction suggests the author's progress in creating modern drama.

For the history of Meiji drama the publication of these three reform-motivated, full-scale historical plays during the three years after the end of 1894 had a very deep significance, even if they remained tragedies of circumstance differing from the character drama (*seikaku-geki*) put forward by the author in his article *Wagakuni no Shigeki.* Not quite free yet from the influence of the traditional drama, thus lacking sufficient modern qualities, nonetheless they had great historical meaning as the first attempt at establishing modern drama. In addition, they paved the way for more dramatists to participate with Shōyō in the new movement.

In 1897, Shōyō's essay *Shigeki ni tsukite no Utagai* (Some Doubts as to Historical Drama), which was a rebuttal to Chogyū's views on the drama *Maki no Kata*, appeared in *Waseda Bungaku*. In this article, he insisted that one should not call a drama historical if it does not respect historic facts together with its character as a dramatic poem. He stated that when Chogyū attacked *Maki no Kata*, his charge was naturally based on the historical plays of Shakespeare. Thus, he defended the form employed in *Kiri Hitoha* and *Maki no Kata* on the ground that Shakespeare, in writing serial historical plays, found the epic style better than that of the classical drama, which view more or less varied from his assertion in *Wagakuni no Shigeki*. Against this view, Chogyū answered in the *Taiyō*, emphasizing the need of poetry's independence from historic facts, which were to be introduced only for the purpose of giving plausibility to the work, and thereby contending that history was less important than poetry. In 1899 the debates further extended into the realm of historical painting as to the priority of historic and artistic qualities; they continued until 1901 but with no definite results.

Later, in 1916, Shōyō published an article *Shigeki oyobi Shigeki-Ron no Hensen* (The Changes in Historical Drama and Its Theory) in the magazine *Taikan* to give a survey of his views as regards this genre. At that time he thought he could approve of Chogyū's view as well as his own.

About the year 1894, Shōyō began practicing dancing and acting at his home, and in 1902 he became interested in creating a new dance drama (*shin-buyō-geki*) in preparation for his new work *Shinkyoku Urashima* (Urashima : A New Adaptation), published in November 1904 simultaneously with an essay *Shin-Gakugeki-Ron* (A Treatise on the New Musical Drama). While Shōyō was making a rough outline of his *Urashima*, Ōgai's *Tamakushige Futari Urashima* (The Two Urashimas of the Jewelled Box) happened to appear. But this was sheer coincidence, as admitted by Shōyō himself, who said he was surprised by Ōgai's work.

Shin-Gakugeki-Ron was a brochure of less than one hundred pages where only his introductory views were stated. The purport of this book, though supplemented by a number of essays that followed, was as follows : Ranking among the leading civilized countries of the world after its victory in the Russo-Japanese War, Japan should have its national drama and music for a new age. For that purpose, there is the need for a musical drama where five aspects of art are combined. As musical drama, the Japanese have three variations : *nō*, *kabuki*, and *furigoto* (posture dancing, broader in meaning than *shosagoto* and *keijigoto*). Of these three, the last should be made the foundation of the new musical play. Thus, the *nagauta* would serve as the basis of this new drama, and if this form lacks sublimity, tending to be cheerful, pleasurable, and melodious, *yōkyoku* (*utai*) and *itchūbushi* can compensate for it. For dramatic expression, *tokiwazu*, *tomimoto*, *takemoto*, (types of ballads) etc. are available. In addition, the merits of *takemoto* and *kiyomoto* should be utilized, and in order to bring forth a feeling of strength, activity, greatness, and violence, various Western musical plays are recommended for study. While the Western musical drama consists mainly of songs, so that actors are singers, Shōyō remarks that that of Japan has its characteristic in having its basis in *furigoto*. He named such plays *shin-gaku-geki* (new musical drama).

Shinkyoku Urashima, an embodiment of the opinions in this essay on a new musical drama, has three acts and twelve scenes. Act I : An autumn evening on the beach of Suminoe in Tango province. Urashima who has run away from home meets his old parents who are seeking their son. After the subsequent quarrel, the son attempts suicide, when Oto-Hime, the princess of the Dragon Palace (Ryūgū), the spirit of the turtle once rescued by Urashima, appears. She persuades him not to kill himself and takes him to her undersea kingdom. Act II : Three years have passed. Urashima, meantime, indulging in voluptuous pleasure with the princess, has forgotten the human world. On a moonlit night, he happens to overhear fishermen singing, and he begins to long for his parents and relatives in his native land. He now wishes to return to the world of men. Oto-Hime, in her efforts to retain the youth, assembles graceful dancers to dissipate this longing for human society. However, while the dancing is going on, Urashima sees visions of his old parents, and is thereby degraded from the court. Receiving a beautiful casket as a present from Oto-Hime, Urashima leaves the Dragon Palace for home. Act III : The same beach in Tango province in spring. Urashima realizes he has been in the Dragon Palace not for three years, but for one hundred times as long. Mad with amazement, the unhappy Urashima opens the casket, the princess' souvenir, when white smoke arises out of it to dye his hair and beard a snowy white. Now he finds himself aged more than three hundred years.

As we have seen, the plot for the most part is faithful to the actual legend of Urashima. The curtain goes down on the scene where young men and women sing in chorus with the old Urashima. They sing : " Now comprehend the reality of the earthly life, ye unselfish people who desire eternity. Let us realize eternity in the present world, let us bring eternity in the present world, let us bring eternity in the world some day." The song, a medley of Japanese and foreign melodies, indicates the author's philosophy of seeking harmony between the real and the ideal, as well as indicating allegorically his intention of creating a new national musical drama supported by new music.

According to what Shōyō wrote in an essay *Urashima no Gūi* (The Moral of the Drama *Urashima*) (*Kabuki,* 1905), Urashima represents *yōkyoku* and *itchūbushi,* his parents, *takemoto, tokiwazu,* and *kiyomoto,* and the princess, *nagauta.* The implication is this: as an ideal for national music, harmony between *yōkyoku* (Urashima) and *nagauta* (Oto-Hime) is attempted. As it emerges with little vitality and warmth, popular songs and children's songs (Urashima's parents) are longed for. Urashima returns home to find the world is now inhabited by strange young men and women (Western music). Thus, he stated that with the support of the latter he tried to create a new national music. Considering such a remark, it seems likely that Shōyō composed this play with more concern for artistic problems than for his philosophy of the world.

Scene 4 of Act I of this play was performed by the Bungei Kyōkai in 1907 as the repertory on the occasion of its second public performance. The dancing scene at the Dragon Palace in Act II was acted in 1914 at the Kyōgen-Za headed by Kikugorō VI. The overture (*zenkyoku*) is often performed as a *nagauta.* However, the elaborate staging and the music, a synthesis of various Japanese and foreign schools, naturally make the performance extremely difficult, and the work has been obliged to boast only of its beauty of phraseology as a drama in verse for reading. Truly elegant beauty is seen in the lines of the *zenkyoku* written in *yōkyoku* style, as well as in the words expressing the sadness of Urashima who longs for his parents when he hears the fishers' song at the undersea palace. The whole drama is divided into *utai-mono* (songs) and *serifu* (dialogue), both composed of involved phrases and sentences generally in *shichi-go-cho* (seven-five-syllable pattern), giving a more enchanting effect than *Tamakushige Futari Urashima* (The Two Urashimas of the Jewelled Box) of Ōgai. Having nothing peculiar in content as a dramatic work, one interesting fact is that the author was inspired to write this play by his favorite operas of Wagner. Contrasted with the musical quality of Wagnerian opera, this piece of Shōyō may be regarded as an opera for the display of dancing. It was, however, Shōyō's surprising skill as a rhetorician that most attracted attention among the literary circles. Ueda Bin most enthusiastically recommended Shōyō's style, saying that he wished to appreciate it purely as the lines of a long poem (*Kabuki*, 56th issue). Judging from such enthusiasm, it is quite probable that some of his translations in the collection of translated poems, the *Kaichōon* (The Sound of the Sea Tide), which appeared in the following year, especially those from the Parnassian poets, must have been influenced by this piece of Shōyō.

Chōsei Shin-Urashima (The Long-Lived New Urashima), an abridged adaptation of the original, was rewritten so as to be suitable for performance, but it was not before the Taishō Era that it met with noticeable success on the stage.

Musical plays created by Shōyō in the following years include : *Shinkyoku Kaguya-Hime* (A New Adaptation of Kaguya-Hime) (two acts, fifteen scenes) (1905) ; *Hachikatsugi-Hime* (The Bowl-Bearing Princess) (one act) (1907) ; *Niwaka Sennin* (The Impromptu Hermit) (one act) (1907) ; *Kimmō-Gitsune* (The Golden-Haired Fox) (six scenes) (1908) ; *Ikkyū Zenji* (Ikkyū the Witty Priest) (one act) (1908) ; *O-Natsu Kyōran* (O-Natsu Goes Mad) (one act, five scenes) (1908) ; *Hatsuyume* (The New Year's Day Dream) (one act, two scenes) (1908) ; *Kosode Monogurui* (Kosode the Maniac) (one act) (1908) ; *Wakanoura* (The Sands of Wakanoura) (one act) (1909) ; *Kanzan Juttoku* (Kanzan and Juttoku) (1911) ; *O-Shichi Kichiza* (O-Shichi and Kichiza) (1911) ; *Utamaro to Hokusai* (Utamaro and Hokusai) (one act, two scenes) (1912), etc. Although most of them were performed, all of these plays were nothing more than *kabuki*-fashion pantomimes. With the sole exception of *Kaguya-Hime*, which borrowed music from *yōkyoku*, the plays were molded on musical themes based on Edo-style *zokkyoku* (popular ballads) such as *nagauta* and *tokiwazu*. We cannot perceive even a sign of Shōyō's original design to write a play based on a musical theme which would be a synthesis of Western and native music. When the playwright wrote *Urashima*, he conceived it as the initial model of what he called the people's new drama, and was moving forward with high hopes of realizing this ideal form. However, in the minor dancing plays we have mentioned here, the author's originality was scant, since he merely added a touch of new scenic features to the so-called New *kabuki*. In this respect, however, *O-Natsu Kyōran* was a great success, but this does not hide the fact that these plays signified the limit of Shōyō's capacity as a playwright.

There are some exceptional cases, however. For example, a Japanese-style opera, based on Western music, in which the dominating feature would be ballet, was in the mind of the author when he wrote *Tokoyami* (Eternal Darkness) (1906) for the first repertory of the Bungei Kyōkai, and *Ochitaru Tennyo* (Fallen Angel) (1912), which was part of a play which he had been hoping to write for some time under the title *Shinkyoku Hijiyama no Hagoromo* (A New Play: The Robe of Feathers of Mt. Hiji). Incidentally, this latter play was later retitled *Datennyo* (Fallen Angel) upon its publication. Shōyō himself boasted that these plays were "Japanese-style oil paintings." However, Shōyō was not of a calibre to substantiate his claims, and these works, though actually performed, did not score any noticeable success.

Besides those of Shōyō, there were other attempts to transplant Western-style opera on the native stage. In 1895, a foreigners' group performed Act I of *Faust*. In 1903, Gluck's *Orfeo ed Euridice* was presented on the stage, and this was followed by performances of *Roei no Yume* (Dreams on the Battlefront), with lyrics and music both composed by Kitamura Sueharu, *Reishō* (The Spiritual Bell) by Kobayashi Aio, Gounod's *Faust*, and Mascagni's *Cavalleria Rusticana*. Among opera-style scenarios written during this period, were *Butsuda no Tatakai* (The War of the Buddhas) by Hanafusa Ryūgai, *Fuiderio* (Fidelio) by an unknown playwright, *Kawanakajima* by Shirai Junjō, *Nobe no Kusa* (Grass of the Fields) by Sōma Gyofū, *Shaka* (Shakyamuni) by Hiraki Hakusei, and *Hagoromo* (The Robe of Feather) by Ko-matsu Gyokugan. The most controversial piece was Sugitani Dai-sui's *Yuya* which was performed at the Teikoku-Za in 1912 with a cast including Shibata Tamaki and Shimizu Kintarō. But this performance was received badly, and the failure suggested that transplantation of opera on native ground was almost im-possible.

Still these pioneering efforts in the opera field were directed towards the future and based on an urgent desire to cultivate a new world. However, a contrasting situation was seen in the field of *nō* which occupied a position directly opposite to the modern opera. Here in the *nō* field, about ten new plays appeared since the beginning of the Meiji Era. However, most of them were *kiwa-mono* (topical) productions, written during wartime for example, and failed to display any originality. For this reason, we think it unnecessary to go further into this genre. To sum it up, Shōyō was standing between the two opposite poles, opera and *nō*, trying to create a new world through his musical plays. However, such musical drama failed to score any substantial success and finally became merely a splinter of the *kabuki*.

2. *The New* Kabuki

After publishing *Kiri Hitoha* in 1894, Tsubouchi Shōyō continued his activities as a playwright and turned out, in rapid succession, such plays as *Maki no Kata* and *Hototogisu Kojō no Rakugetsu*. However, these works signalled a temporary halt in his playwright activities in the Meiji years, and Shōyō now began to direct his attention to musical drama.

Shōyō's plays were first staged in 1904. This explains why the activities of other playwrights, who naturally were stimulated by Shōyō, became so conspicuous at about this time. However, plays betraying the influence of Shōyō appeared even earlier, principally the work of playwrights who were close to *Waseda Bungaku*, which was a stronghold of Shōyō. One of the earliest examples is *Noboru Asahi Chōsen Taiheiki* (The Rising Sun in Korea) by Matsui Shōyō (Masaharu, Shō-Ō) (1894), published in the *Yomiuri Shimbun*. The following year saw the publication of *Hitobashira Tsukishima Yurai* (A History of the Human Sacrifice at Tsukishima), a play written by Fujino Kohaku and published in *Waseda Bungaku*. Kohaku died young, but Shōyō wrote another play, *Aku-Genta* (Genta the Villain), which was staged at the Meiji-Za in 1899. This play was composed of two scenes, one dealing with Yoshihira's pursuit of Shigemori in the huge garden of Taikemmon and the other dealing with the capture of Yoshihira at Ishiyama Temple. In the performance, Sadanji I played the role of Yoshihira. This was the first time in the Meiji years that a play written by an author who did not belong to the rank and file of the *kabuki* world was performed on a *kabuki* stage without any modification of the original scenario. Shōyō first wrote his plays for Sadanji I, and then for Sadanji II. The plays which were staged included *Gensammi Yorimasa* (the name of the hero) (1901), *Gotō Matabei* (also the name of the hero), *Tekkoku Kōfuku* (The Surrender of the Enemy Nation), and *Kesa to Moritō* (Kesa and Morito).

However, the new historical plays enjoyed a tremendous popularity in the years before and after the performance of *Kiri Hitoha*. The year before this performance saw the staging of Takayasu Gekkō's *Edo-Jō Akewatashi* (The Surrender at Edo Castle) by the *shimpa* theatrical troupe. The year 1904 saw the performance of Mori Ōgai's *Nichiren Shōnin Tsuji-zeppō* (The Wayside Preaching of St. Nichiren), and the following year saw the staging of Gekkō's *Sakura Shigure* (Showers in the Cherry Blossoms). The same year saw the publication of Yamazaki Shikō's maiden work in historical drama, namely *Uesugi Kenshin* (The Warlord Uesugi). *Kabuki Monogatari* (Kabuki Tales) was staged in 1908, the year which also saw the staging of Okamoto Kidō's *Ishin Zengo* (The Years Before and After the Restoration). In both of these performances Ichikawa Sadanji II played the title role. These examples, we think, are sufficient to explain the great activity in the field of the new historical drama.

In addition to those mentioned above, we can also include in the category of historical playwrights Enomoto Torahiko of the Kabuki-Za, Uda Torahiko of the Teikoku-Za, and other writers who wrote exclusively for their theatres, and also Oka Kitarō, Ihara Seiseien, Okamura Shikō, and others, who, together with Okamoto Kidō, took active part in inaugurating the so-called *bunshi-geki* (drama by men of letters). Among these writers, Enomoto Torahiko, a disciple of the Ōchi school, wrote *Ataka no Seki* (The Ataka Barrier) (première November 1904), which may be regarded as the *katsureki* version of the *kabuki* play *Kanjinchō*, but is actually closer to the new historical drama. This playwright has another work, *Meikō Kakiemon* (Kakiemon the Master Potter), which is regarded as a masterpiece, but it belongs to the subsequent Taishō Period. Ihara Seiseien is known for his *Izumo no O-Kuni* (The Kabuki Dancer O-Kuni) (first performed in June 1910). Oka Onitarō first earned his reputation as a playwright in the early Taishō years. However, already in the Meiji Era, he was known for his energetic efforts as a drama critic, together with Sugi Niseami and the aforementioned Shikō. His works include such comedies as *Futa-Fūfu* (The Two Couples) (1909) and *Ōmisoka* (New Year's Eve) (1910). Both Okamura Shikō and Uda Torahiko did not produce any worthwhile plays. But Shikō's *Migawari Zazen* (The Substitute Zen-Sitter) (1910), which was a dance drama based on the *kyōgen Hanako* (A Girl Named Hanako), is particularly well-known. Torahiko's works include *Kamakura Bushi* (The Kamakura Warriors) (1911). Both of these playwrights continued as authors of dance dramas in the Taishō Period.

Among the historical playwrights we mentioned above, those deserving special attention are Gekkō, Shikō, and Kidō. It was principally through the efforts of these writers that the new historical plays were able to develop and grow as new *kabuki.*

Takayasu Gekkō (Saburō, Shūfū Ginkyaku) was not only versed in Chinese poetry but also showed active interest in the works of the Romantics of Western literature. In the earlier stage of his literary career, he attempted translations of Dostoevsky and Ibsen, and wrote novels and poems. So far as modern cultural background is concerned, he was the most cultivated among the contemporary playwrights with the exception of Ōgai and Shōyō. His maiden work in the dramatic field was *Shigemori*, composed of five acts and twenty scenes, which presented the medieval warlord Shigemori as a romantic and melancholic type. However, weak in dramatic elements, this play may be considered as an emotional drama, strong in lyricism, rather than as a historical piece. Subsequently, Gekkō published *Kugyō* (1897) in the magazine *Shincho Gekkan* (New Book Monthly), and later saw the following plays of his performed on the stages in the Kansai district : *Gesshō* (The Priest Gesshō) (première 1902), *Ōshio Heihachirō* (The Revolt of Ōshio Heihachirō) (1902), and *Yami to Hikari* (Darkness and Light) (première 1902), an adaptation of a foreign work.

As we mentioned before, Gekkō's reputation as a playwright was established when he wrote *Edo-Jō Akewatashi*, which was composed of four acts and fifteen scenes. This play attracted special attention because it played a major role in the theatrical war between Kawakami Otojirō and his antagonists, the actors of the old-fashioned stage. The historical background of this play are the dramatic incidents—the restoration of the Imperial régime and the surrender of the feudal Shōgunate's Edo castle to the Imperial forces—which changed the course of the nation's history. Set against this background, the play is woven around the patriotic activities of Saigō Kichinosuke and Katsu Kaishū, the mental agony of the Shōgun Keiki, the romance.between a young warrior belonging to the *hatamoto* and working for the cause of the Imperial régime and his fiancée, who meets a tragic death, and the chivalrous conduct of the Edo citizens, expressed through the person of the fish-market merchant Sagamiya Buhei. The moral emphasized in this play is that the only way for the individual to cope with the Heavenly Power which moves the current of history is to be just, both to those who try to exploit the tide of history and to those who make a futile resistance against the tide of the times. In the sense that the author attempted to discover a logic in the current of history, this play may be well called a historical one. But, actually, because of the complicated plot, the playwright had to devote most of his effort merely to relating the incidents and failed to back them up with dramatic elements. Poor in dramatic expression, this play lacked poetical flavor when compared to the works of Shōyō. We may also point out that the play was too prosaic and the characters were depicted without consideration as to their respective personalities. But despite these defects, the playwright deserves credit for giving a cohesive description, awkward as it was, of the complicated situation at the time of the Meiji Restoration and for expressing, to a moderate degree, the prevailing spirit of the day. On the basis of this evaluation and in view of its historical significance, this play is regarded as the representative work among Gekkō's historical dramas.

His next work was *Sakura Shigure* (two acts, four scenes) (première December 1905), a dramatic version of tales concerning Haiya Shōyū and Yoshino Dayū. The story deals with Haiya Saburobei and a warlord, Shikō Ōzan, who fight each over the same woman, a geisha named Yoshino Dayū. Saburobei wins out, but because of this quarrel, is disowned by his father Shōyū. The son, Saburobei, with his newly-won sweetheart, moves to an abandoned house where he engages in pottery-making to earn his living. One day, the father Shōyū is caught in a sudden shower and finds shelter under the eaves of the abandoned house, unaware that it is the home of his son. Standing there unperceived, the father looks inside the house and is impressed by the nobility of his son's wife O-Toku (her real name), despite the fact that she was formerly a geisha. The father further learns that his son has repented of his conduct, and he decides to welcome him back. The playwright's chief concern was in tracing the mental growth of Saburobei. Saburobei first lives in a gay world, symbolized by the words " Cherry Flowers " in the title ; but next, he is forced to enter a world of poverty where he experiences a feeling of loneliness, symbolized by the word " Showers " in the title. Breathing the free, Zen-like atmosphere of this world of loneliness, Saburobei matures, which growth is suggested by the incidents in which he demolishes a cracked tea-cup attributed to the famous tea-master Rikyū, and with his own hands molds a crude tea-cup which is a recreation of Rikyū's artistic taste. This incident, as explained in the preface of Volume Three of *Gendai Gikyoku Zenshū* (A Complete Collection of Modern Drama), was an " accidental symbol " of the playwright's own inner life, which, though accepting the traditional spirit, rejected the dead remains of tradition, and instead sought to recreate the subtle flavor inherent in it. Though we cannot wholly accept the evaluation that the play was a " symbol of inner life," the major theme was formed around a certain fixed idea, a quality that was never to be seen in the previous *sewa-mono* plays. The drama, in this sense, had thus grown out of the category of *sewa-mono* and *jidai-mono* plays and reached a new plane which appeared in the course of the development and transformation of new historical plays into the so-called New *kabuki*.

This drama displays a serene and elegant mood, richly imbued with the native literature's traditional poetical sentiment. However, because of its strong inclination to poetic beauty and sentimentality, the play lacks dramatic power. Every dramatic situation has been solved without suffering on the part of the characters concerned. The psychological treatment is scant, and there is no deep reflection on the characters of the *dramatis personae*. The drama relies on the conventional use of *watariserifu* (one speech delivered by several actors in turn) and superfluous phrases, and, accordingly, the mood expressed is nothing more than that perceived generally in Shōyō's works. Indeed, there is no sign of modern taste. In fact, it is astonishing that the cultural background of Gekkō who was so well-versed in Ibsen and other Western literary works, did not exert any influence on his plays. The conclusion is that so far as his activities in the Meiji Period are concerned, there was apparently a limit to his calibre as a playwright, and he could not go beyond the field of the New *kabuki*.

In addition, Gekkō wrote the following dramas during the Meiji Period, namely *Sagano no Tsuyu* (The Dew of the Fields of Saga) (1909), *Gion no Yuri* (The Lily of Gion) (1908), and *Minatogawa* (The Ancient Battlefield of Minatogawa) (1909).

The plays of Yamazaki Shikō (Kosan) were first published in the magazine *Myōjō*. His initial work was *Uesugi Kenshin* (published in *Myōjō*, 1905; its première was in the following year, staged by the *shimpa* troupe), followed by *Nichiren Amagoi* (Nichiren Prays for Rain), *Okehazama* (The Okehazama Battle), *Kamewari Shibata* (Jar-Breaking Shibata), and *Sarasaragoe* (Sarasara Pass), all of which are included in his collection of dramatic pieces entitled *Nanatsu Kikyō* (The Seven Bell-Flowers) (1906). His reputation was established in March 1908, when Ichikawa Sadanji, in his second performance following his return from an overseas trip, staged Shikō's *Kabuki Monogatari* (Kabuki Tales). Upon the request of Sadanji, he then wrote *Hakai Soga* (The Soga Brothers Break the Law). In 1911, his *Yoritomo* (The Shōgun Minamoto Yoritomo) was chosen for the repertory marking the opening of the Teikoku-Za (The Imperial Theatre).

Showing a vehement dislike for the *jidai-mono* of Mokuami and the historical dramas of Ōchi, Shikō respected historical facts. However, careful not to be restricted by them, he attempted to create lines which would be close to the language used in the respective historical periods, but, on the other hand, seemed to be striving to reflect modern ideas in his plays. Accordingly, this author displayed signs of a literary consciousness as a typical historical playwright in the tradition of Shōyō.

His representative work during the Meiji Period is *Kabuki Monogatari*, aptly composed of four acts and eight scenes. The play deals with the second son of the warlord Tokugawa Ieyasu, Echizen Chūnagon Hideyasu, who was also the son-in-law of his father's arch-rival, the great Toyotomi Hideyoshi. Hideyasu experiences a bitter life as his younger brother Hidetada is chosen over him for the position of Shōgun. To make the matter worse, Hideyasu gives protection to his father's rivals, the Ōsaka (Toyotomi) forces, because he himself was once helped by the Toyotomi family. Thus, because of his conduct, the Edo (Tokugawa) forces poison Hideyasu to death. This assassination plot is intertwined with Hideyasu's involvement with an actress named Izumo no O-Kuni, member of an all-female *kabuki* troupe. O-Kuni is torn between her love for Hideyasu and her artistic life. The climax sees O-Kuni, informed of the assassination of her lover, hiding her feelings and going on the stage with the following words, which show her determination to stake her life on art: "Upon entering the stage, the actor becomes a sacrifice to God. Until the curtain falls, he must not leave. Even love is not permitted to interrupt the drama." The theme of Hideyasu's assassination unfolds dramatically, gaining gradual momentum, scene by scene, and the emphasis of the play is, to a considerable degree, placed on this plot. For this reason, the dilemma of O-Kuni, torn between love and art, is not developed as the uniform theme of the play. Nevertheless it is interesting to note here that the playwright, in depicting the troubles of love, did not rely on class struggles, obligations, or political schemes, but instead depicted love in the form of its conflict with art.

As indicated by the fact that he was a contributor to the magazine *Myōjō*, Shikō, among other aspects, was romantic and passionate. This is revealed, for example, in *Kamewari Shi-*

bata by his praise for the romance of the rough-mannered warrior Katsuie, who falls in love with the lady attendant of a youth he has killed with a halberd, and in the scene dealing with the young warrior Kagetora, who kills his own sweetheart and then enters the priesthood, promising that he will never be involved with another woman for the rest of his life. The playwright's passionate tenet is also given a prominent display in the handling of the actress O-Kuni in *Kabuki Monogatari*. Although not quite comparable to the elegance of Gekkō, Shikō's works were pervaded by rich poetic sentiments, and had a satisfactory amount of dramatic power, based on a dramatic composition. But, on the other hand, he still clung to traditional drama methods, as exemplified by his use of the *watari-serifu* and his insertion of *dammari* (pantomime).

The maiden work of Okamoto Kidō (Keiji, Kyōkidō) was *Shishinden* (The Purple Palace) (1902), a historical play dealing with the warrior Genzammi Yorimasa and his capture of a *nue* (a fabulous night bird). Also, with Oka Kitarō as collaborator, he wrote a *kabuki* scenario, *Kogane no Shachihoko Uwasa no Takanami* (The Gold Dolphins and the High Waves of Rumor) (1902). He was also a member of a group of playwrights including Oka Onitarō and Uda Torahiko, who had connection at the time with a sort of New Theater movement which was being carried on by the *bunshi-geki* troupe of the *Tōkyō Mainichi Shimbun*, known as the Wakaba-Kai (The Young Leaves Society). Kidō gained attention when this troupe staged such plays of his as *Temmokuzan* (Tea-Bowl Mountain) (1905) and *Shinra Saburō* (the name of the hero) (1906). His reputation rose when Sadanji performed his *Ishin Zengo* (Before and After the Restoration) (1908). The result was that Kidō now entered a partnership with Sadanji and embarked on a brilliant career in the dramatic world. Kidō was a prolific writer, and among his numerous plays written in the Meiji Period, we can single out from his historical dramas *Shuzenji Monogatari* (The Shuzenji Story), and from his *sewa-mono*-type works *Minowa no*

Shinjū (The Minowa Double Suicide), as the works deserving the most attention.

Shuzenji Monogatari (one act, three scenes; scenario completed March 1909; published in the *Bungei Kurabu* in January 1911; première May 1911, included in a ten-piece drama series entitled *Shōen Gikyoku*, Shōen Dramas) depicts the life of a wooden mask-carver, Yashaō, and his devotion to art. The play is set against a historical background dealing with a medieval warlord, Minamoto Yoriie, who, driven out of Kamakura, the seat of the feudal government, comes to live in the remote town of Shuzenji where he ultimately meets a tragic end. The story is as follows : Yoriie orders Yashaō to carve a mask patterned after the warlord's features. However, no matter how he carves the mask, it displays an omen of imminent death. Yashaō decides that he should not present the unsatisfactory mask, even if the warlord's displeasure should cost him his life. However, as the omen of the mask has foretold, Yoriie is assassinated the same night the mask is finished. Upon learning of the death of the warlord, Yashaō for the first time understands the whole situation. As an artist he feels a deep satisfaction, since the fact that man's destiny, known only to the Almighty, had been reflected in the mask proved that he had been able to enter a deep communion with Nature and that his artistic skill had been perfected almost to the level of the divine creator. For Yashaō, his reputation as an artist was more important than life. And, as such, Yashaō understands the feelings of his elder daughter, who is happy because she is able to serve the feudal lord, though aware that it will be a short-lived happiness which will ultimately cost her life. In the finale, the playwright depicted Yashaō carving the death-mask of the girl. At the time of the première, this final scene met a mixed reaction, some approving it while other criticized it. However, the critics would probably have changed their opinions if they had understood that the scene was meant to symbolize Yashaō's genuine devotion to art which even transcended death.

A similar symbolization can be perceived Shikō's *Kabuki Monogatari*, to which we referred in the early part of this chapter. However, the tragedy of history in *Shuzenji Monogatari* has been pushed into the background, and the principal focus is on Yashaō and his life as an artist. The dramatic composition adopted in this play provided for a concrete image of the artist. The theme can be traced back to the outlook on life displayed by the actress O-Kuni in *Kabuki Monogatari*. However, in the case of Yashaō, the vision of life has been deepened, and, for him, nothing human can interfere with his devotion to art. The sole concern of the playwright Kidō was to depict the psychology of Yashaō as an artist, and we perceive signs of efforts to create a new effect in the form of the dialogue. However, upon looking more deeply for the motive of the playwright, we discover that in writing this play he had taken into account the stage calibre of Sadanji, who played the leading role. Of course the theory that the performance of Sadanji was the major factor in developing the principal character Yashaō, and that in depicting the character of Yashaō, the playwright produced an image of a master-carver but failed to produce a distinct and vivid image of a human personality, is naturally open to discussion and criticism.

Minowa no Shinjū (completed in March 1911 ; première in September the same year) dealt with Fujieda Geki, who belonged to the five hundred-*koku* class of the *hatamoto* (retainers of the Shōgun). He is deeply in love with a woman named Ayagoromo, a prostitute belonging to the Ōbishiya brothel in the Yoshiwara gay quarter. She, however, is caught in a hopeless situation, peculiar to the *demi-monde.* Sympathizing with the fate of his sweetheart and under reproach from higher officials, his relatives, and family, Geki commits double suicide with Ayagoromo at the home of his wet-nurse in Minowa. Although his uncle tries to make the youth commit *seppuku* in order to save the reputation of the family, Geki does not die for the family name. Rather, he dies for himself, and in order to pursue to the end his love for Ayagoromo. The young hero believes that the happiness of obtaining the true affections of a woman is just as important as the joy of a warrior in achieving glorious deeds on the battlefield. The hero, thus, was freeing himself from the bonds of the feudal society and dying with the dream of establishing a new home in the other world. This play displays a mood distinctly different from that of the traditional *shinjū* (double suicide) plays which were pervaded by a dark tone, and suggested a world of no escape under the oppression of society. Rather, the dominant note was "escapism," which expressed itself in the form of the glorification of death. The result was that the drama failed to become a tragedy based on an active ego that stood up against life, and instead remained a sentimental play. The final scene portraying the double suicide is a beautiful sight on the stage, without any trace of grimness or ghastliness.

As shown by the works we have just mentioned, Kidō's plays written in the Meiji Period had already outgrown the category of old-style historical drama and *sewa-mono* plays, and placed major emphasis on the psychology and mood of the individual. As to the content, the plays, to a certain degree, depicted the struggle and transcendence of art and love over the established systems and authority. However, in depicting individual psychology and mood, the playwright failed to raise his drama to the plane of a character play, since the characters were written to be played by specific actors. As to his concern over the transcendence of art over the established society and authority, he failed to reinforce the theme with deep human feeling, and we perceive the lack of self-consciousness on the part of the playwright. To sum it up, the features of his plays were rather the interesting plot, the mood displayed by the stage scenery, and the beautiful dialogue. These features were not necessarily the monopoly of Kidō but rather were the common characteristic of the playwrights of the new historical drama and the New *kabuki*. And, if we are permitted to make a conclusion, these features suggested the limit of the capacity of these playwrights.

THE INTRODUCTION OF THE WESTERN
DRAMA AND THE ESTABLISHMENT OF
THE MODERN DRAMA

1. *The Introduction of Western Plays and the* Shingeki
Movement

Of the Western dramas that were introduced into Japan, the
earliest were the works of William Shakespeare. *Romeo and
Juliet* was adapted into a drama in the Edo Era under the
title *Kokoro no Nazo Toketa Iroito* (Love's Thread Unraveled
the Riddle of the Heart) by Tsuruya Namboku IV, and it was
performed in 1810. In 1871 Nakamura Masanao wrote a short
biography of Shakespeare and translated lines from *Hamlet* in
his book *Saikoku Risshi-Hen* (Biographies of Self-Made Men of
the Western Countries), which was a translation of Samuel
Smiles' *Self-Help*. In the decade between 1877 and 1887 there
appeared the following translations : *Ri-Ō* (*King Lear*) by
Wadagaki Kenzō in 1879 ; *Jinniku Shichiire Saiban* (*The
Merchant of Venice*) by Inoue Tsutomu in 1883 ; *Fukkoku Bōshū
Ryōshu Makichi-Kō Jōwa* (*As You Like It*) by Suiran Sensei
(Fujita Meikaku) in 1883 ; *Shiizaru Kidan : Jiyū no Tachi
Nagori no Kireaji* (*Julius Caesar*) by Tsubouchi Shōyō in 1884 ;
Denkoku Ōji : Hanretta Monogatari (*Hamlet*) by Hagiwara
and Suga in the July and August 1885 issues of the *Chūō
Gakujutsu Zasshi* (The Central Scholarship Magazine) ; *Sakipia
Gikyoku : Rōma Seisui Kan* (*Julius Caesar*) by Kawashima Keizō
in 1886, although the translation had been published as a serial
in the *Nippon Rikken Seitō Shimbun* (The Japan Constitutional
Political Party Newspaper) under the original title *Ōshū Gikyo-
ku : Juriasu Shiizaru no Geki* in 1883 ; *Romyō Juri Gikyoku :
Shunjō Ukiyo no Yume* (*Romeo and Juliet*) by Kawashima Keizō
in 1886 ; *Taisai Kidan : Fuyu Monogatari* (*The Winter's Tale*),
Inga Monogatari (*Measure for Measure*) by Sōkikuyashi (Nita
Keijirō) in 1886. The decade which followed saw a significant

increase in the number of Shakespeare's translations.
It was during these years that Shōyō labored on the translation of Shakespearian works. Giving lectures on the great playwright at a study group and at Waseda University, he published
Shiēkusupiya Kyakuhon Hyōchū Chogen (Commentaries on Shake-
speare's Dramas), *"Makubesu" Hyōchū* (Commentary on *Macbeth*)
(1891), and other works in the *Waseda Bungaku* (Waseda
Literature). Besides, deep interest was manifested among the
associates of the *Bungakkai* (The World of Literature) in
Shakespeare and also in the Elizabethan drama as a whole. A
Japanese version of *Venus and Adonis* under the title *Natsugusa*,
although not a play, was produced by Shimazaki Tōson
(*Jogaku Zasshi*, White-Covered) (1892), and the poet called
Hamlet his " best friend " in one of his writings entitled
Ishiyamadera e "Hamuretto" o Osamuru no Ji (Dedicating a Copy
of *Hamlet* to the Temple at Ishiyama) (1893). We find Kitamura Tōkoku often quoting from *Hamlet*, and we have an ad-
aptation of the same play by Iwano Hōmei, *Higeki : Kommei
Getchū no Yaiba* (A Tragedy : Souls in Distress and Blades in
the Moonlight) (1894).

In the Meiji thirties, publication of a Japanese edition of the
complete works of Shakespeare, the *Sa-Ō Zenshū*, was planned
on the advice of Koizumi Yakumo (Lafcadio Hearn), with
Tozawa Koya and Asano Hyōkyo as collaborators. Translated
by Koya were *Hamlet, Romeo and Juliet, Othello, King Lear*
(all in 1905), *Much Ado about Nothing, Julius Caesar* (1907),
and *The Comedy of Errors* (1908), while the renderings of *The
Merchant of Venice* (1906), *As You Like It* (1908), and *Twelfth
Night* (1909) were done by Hyōkyo. Later, some of the
translations by Shōyō which he had prepared under the title
Sa-Ō Kessaku-Shū (A Collection of the Masterpieces of Shake-
speare) were published. They were *Hamlet* (December 1909),
Romeo and Juliet (September 1910), *Othello* (April 1911), and
King Lear (April 1912).

As for the performance, the Shakespearian play that was first shown on the stage in Japan was *The Merchant of Venice*, adapted by Udagawa Bunkai as *Sakura-Doki Zeni no Yono-naka* (The Season of Cherry-Blossoms in a World Where Gold Rules) and played in 1885 at the Ebisu-Za in Ōsaka. In 1891, at the Gaiety Hall, Yokohama, *Hamlet* and *The Merchant of Venice* were performed by foreign actors, and both Shōyō and Tōkoku were known to have been there among the spectators. In the first half of the first decade of this century, the following plays of Shakespeare were performed in Japan :

TITLE	PERFORMED BY	TRANSLATED BY	ADAPTED BY	YEAR OF PERFORM-ANCE
Julius Caesar (*Shiizaru Kidan*; two scenes)	Ii Yōhō and troupe	Shōyō	Hatakeyama Kohei	1901
Othello	Kawakami and troupe		Emi Suiin	1903
The Merchant of Venice	″	Dohi Shunsho		″
Hamlet	″	Shunsho and Yamagishi Kayō		″
Romeo and Juliet	Ii and troupe		Osanai Kaoru	1904

However, judging only from Ōgai's remarks in a review, *Meiji-Za no Osero* (*Othello* at the Meiji-Za) (*Kabuki*, March 1903), one may infer that those plays were usually performed by actors belonging to the *shimpa* (New School) only for their stories' sake. The first artistically faithful performance of Shakespeare's plays was realized by the Bungei Kyōkai (The Association of Literature and Art), as we shall see later. On one occasion, the Yōgeki Kenkyūkai (The Society for the Study of Western

— 513 —

Drama) (promoters: Sawamura Sōnosuke and Arakawa Shige-
hide) performed *Julius Caesar* in English (May 1907).

Influence of the English dramatist Shakespeare was marked
in Shōyō's early historical plays. For instance, Kagerō, the
beloved daughter of Katagiri Katsumoto in *Kiri Hitoha,*
bears some resemblance to Ophelia in *Hamlet*, and similarities
of scenes are noticeable in certain dramas of Shōyō.
Particularly, his play *Maki no Kata* is said to have been inspired
by the character of Lady Macbeth created by Shakespeare, while
his plan of a series of historical dramas consisting of three or
five pieces had been suggested by Shakespeare's trilogy from
King John to *Richard III* and also by his serial of seven plays
from *Henry IV* to *Henry VIII*. In his later work *Hototogisu
Kojō no Rakugetsu* (The Cuckoo and the Setting Moon over the
Solitary Castle), Shōyō eventually departed from the formalism
of traditional plays and turned to adopt the form of Shakespearian dramas.

We have already mentioned Shimazaki Tōson as an ardent
admirer of Shakespeare. Tōson wrote verse drama such as
Hikyoku: Biwahōshi (An Elegy: The Minstrel Lutist) (*Bungakkai*, 1888), *Hikyoku: Cha no Keburi* (An Elegy: The Smoke
of Roasted Tea Leaves) (the same year; incomplete), and *Shumon no Urei* (The Sorrows of Shumon) (the same). In the form
of traditional drama, he wrote also *Aisomegawa* (The River
Dyed in Indigo) (*Bungakkai*, 1895; incomplete). Tōson's verse
drama had its source in *Hōraikyoku* (The Song of Fairyland)
(1891) by Kitamura Tōkoku. Disposed to dramatic works, Tōkoku
left behind an unfinished piece, *Akumu* (Nightmare), as well as
some critical essays such as *Gekishi no Zento Ikan* (The
Future of Dramatic Poetry) (1893), etc. *Hōraikyoku* had been
composed under the influence of *Manfred*, as stated before, and
also, apparently, of *Faust*. Affected by these verse dramas of
the West, this work was an expression of the *Weltanschauung*
of Tōkoku. With Tōson, too, his dramatic poems were a
representation of the writer's inner life. The hero in *Biwa*

Hōshi, Ikkō, an eccentric, believes in his talent in playing the *biwa*, the Japanese lute. A pure-hearted man who despises selling art for money's sake, he is not accepted in the world, and, as a result, separating himself from his wife and children, he becomes a mendicant priest. However, he always loves his children, and finally his artistic ability comes to be acknowledged. As for *Shumon no Urei*, it shows the strong influence of *Hamlet*. Its hero is like the author himself. Shumon, his loyalty misunderstood by his master, his intimate friend dead, eventually is faced with the fall of his master's family. Consequently, the hero becomes a pessimist with nihilistic views on life, but, at heart, he remains true to his friends and children. Kitamura Shinnosuke in *Cha no Keburi*, created as a representation of the author's mind, is scornful of samurai who do not appreciate a thing of true beauty, despises the so-called heroes and brave men, and advocates love for love's sake. Neither Tōson nor Tōkoku had the least intention of putting their works on the stage, and theirs were no more than poems in the form of drama. In spite of their efforts in elaborating their style, their vocabularies, as yet immature, failed to become sufficiently fresh and elegant for expression in verse. Meanwhile, some influence of *Manfred* is said to exist also in Takayasu Gekkō's work *Shigemori*.

As regards French drama introduced to this country, Corneille's *Le Cid*, adapted by Fukuchi Ōchi, was the first ever performed. In 1887, based on an original of E. Labiche, *Seiyō Engeki Sujigaki : Koimusume Kon'in Jijō* (The Marriage of an Amorous Girl) was published. *Le Médecin malgré Lui* of Molière was then performed as *Niwaka Isha* by Takada Minoru and other actors, and, under the direction of Osanai Kaoru, *L'Amour Médecin* of the same dramatist was produced in 1908 with Ichikawa Sadanji II playing the leading role. We have already referred to Molière's *Avare* as a play occasionally put on the stage under the title *Kane to Iroyoku* (Money and Desire). This adaptation, formerly *Natsu Kosode*, was one of the plays in the repertory of *shimpa* actors. A collection of Molière's dramatic works in three volumes was published in May 1908, but the second volume met immediate suspension by the government before publication. And yet the translator, Kusano Shibaji, had until then continuously made public his renderings of Molière's works. Furthermore, an adaptation of Victor Hugo's *Hernani* was played by Sadanji (then Enshō).

From Germany came, among others, those works of classicism. As early as 1882, Schiller's *Wilhelm Tell* had its Japanese version in *Teru Jiyūdan* (The Story of Tell the Fighter for Freedom) by Shōko Gyoshi, and later two other versions of the famous drama appeared, bearing the titles of *Tokuren Jiyū no Issen* (An Arrow of Freedom) by Nakagawa Kajō (1886) and *Jiketsu Kurui : Kaiten no Gensei* (Words of Blood, Phrases of Tears : An Arrow of Exploit) by Ashida Tsukao (1887). An adaptation was performed by Sadanji (Enshō). Another work of Schiller, *Maria Stuart*, was translated by Ōchi as *Shunsetsu Mari no Gosaigo* (The End of Maria) (1888). Prior to the time when modern dramas were introduced, Ōgai translated Lessing's works *Emilia Galotti* (*Ori Bara*) (1889) and *Philotas* (*Toriko*) (1892). His *Tamakushige Futari Urashima* is known to have been influenced by Goethe's *Faust*. It was mentioned before that he had also translated Calderón's *El Alcalde de Zalamea* in collaboration with Miki Takeji.

With regard to other novelists than Tōkoku and Tōson, Bimyō wrote *Murakami Yoshiteru Nishiki no Hatakaze* (The Loyal Warrior Yoshiteru) (*Meiji Bunko*, series VIII, 1894) with a touch of conventionalism. Rohan's dramatic works include *Manju-Hime* (The Fortune of Manju-Hime) (*Kokkai*, January 1891), *Yūfuku Shijin* (A Lucky Poet) (*Kokkai*, January 1894), *Chinsen-Kai* (A Special Meeting) (*Bungei Kurabu*, January 1904), *Jutsu Kurabe* (A Test of Craft) (*Shinshōsetsu*, January 1905), *Sono Omokage Imayō Hakken-Den* (A Modernized Story of the Eight Loyalists) (*Yomiuri*, March-April 1906), and others. *Chinsen-Kai* and the following two pieces are satirical comedies, while *Manju-Hime*, selecting its subject matter from *Karaito Sōshi* (The Story of Karaito), one of the *otogizōshi* of the Muromachi Era, is a story of a girl Manju-Hime who saves her mother by a graceful dance in the presence of the enemy. *Yūfuku Shijin*, a story of the conflict of two worlds, that of poetry and of money, is based on *Lai Shêng Chai*, a Chinese epic of the Yüan Dynasty which relates the life of a poet named P'ang. These last may be regarded as novels written in the style of drama, and on this point we can see the influence of foreign playwrights.

Japan's modern plays which finally came into existence in the forties of the Meiji Era indispensably owed much to various movements for new-style drama, the *shingeki*, in their preparatory stage. One of the most remarkable was the Bungei Kyōkai whose leader was Shōyō. Formerly the Rōdoku Kai (the Society for Dramatic Reading), founded in 1890 for the study of recitation, it changed its name to the Ekifū Kai (The Ameliorative Society) in 1905, advancing to the study of performance, in view of the turbulent period (1903–1904) in the theatrical world which longed for a new spirit in its activities. In the autumn of 1905, soon after his return from Europe, Shimamura Hōgetsu joined the society, and in January of the following year the society was reorganized into the Bungei Kyōkai as an organization for broad cultural achievement including the work of theatrical reform. Count Ōkuma assumed the first presidency, and Shōyō became an adviser together with Takada Hampō. Those plays performed include *Kiri Hitoha, The Merchant of Venice, Tokoyami, Daigoku-Den* (by Sugitani Daisui), *Hamlet, Shinkyoku Urashima*, etc., yet the organization was timid in taking up any sort of modern drama.

Later the association was reorganized and became the center of the *shingeki* movement, but it fell into financial difficulty. In February 1909, a plan to establish an institute for theatrical studies was decided upon, and, from that time on, Shōyō took entire responsibility for the organization. The students of drama belonging to the association, after occasional private readings, presented their work publicly in Tōkyō, Kyōto, Ōsaka, and Nagoya for a total of fifteen times beginning in May 1911. The repertory, apart from Shakespearian plays like *Hamlet*, *The Merchant of Venice*, *Julius Caesar*, etc., included works of modern north European playwrights, such as Ibsen's *The Doll's House*, Sudermann's *Heimat*, and also Shaw's *A Man of Destiny* and *You Can Never Tell*, Meyer Förster's *Alt-Heidelberg*, dance dramas by Shōyō, such as *Kanzan Juttoku* and *O-Shichi Kichiza*, etc.

Their performances were, on the whole, a success, and particularly *The Doll's House* and *Heimat* stirred up sensational interest not only in the theatrical world but also in the public at large because of their social significance. Moreover, theirs was the first performance of Shakespeare's plays that was reasonably faithful to the originals. The best production was *Hamlet* executed in May 1911 as the first presentation after the establishment of the institute attached to the association. Activities of the association culminated in about the year 1912, but afterward, due to the internal difficulties which occurred and to the double suicide committed by Shimamura Hōgetsu and the actress Matsui Sumako, both chief members of the group, the organization was obliged to face its problems and eventually to dissolve itself after its final performance, *Julius Caesar*, in June 1913. In this connection it must be pointed out that the failure had its underlying cause in the retreat before the rising trend of Naturalism and *l'esprit moderne* on the part of Shōyō who remained an English-type realist and a worker for ethical enlightenment.

This Bungei Kyōkai (The Association of Literature and Art), through its work, contributed much to educating actors and to introducing Shakespearean and modern European drama, but during the period of its existence no original plays were ever created by the members. In spite of such failure, the fact that a cornerstone for the building of modern drama was established by this group must not be overlooked. However, after the dissolution the members of the association organized separately into three groups namely, the Geijutsu-Za (The Art Theater), the Mumei Kai (The Nameless Society), and the Butai Kyōkai (The Stage Association), which together were to contribute to furthering the movement for *shingeki* (new drama).

In the meantime, about two and a half years after the formation of the Bungei Kyōkai, the Jiyū Gekijō (The Free Theater) was established through the joint efforts of Osanai Kaoru and Ichikawa Sadanji. Kaoru who first entered the theatrical world through Ōgai's favor, after 1904 collaborated with the *shimpa* (new school) troupe under Ii Yōhō. His experiences in production with this troupe taught him that the *shimpa* actors were incompetent to bear the artistic burden of performing modern dramas, and he left Ii and other actors in October 1907. In September of that year Kaoru began to edit his own magazine, the *Shinshichō* (usually called the first *Shinshichō*, New Currents of Thought), but he cherished an idea of participating in the new drama movement by organizing what he called the Mukei Gekijō (The Non-Form Theater). Meanwhile, in August 1907, Sadanji returned to Japan after his study in the Western drama under the guidance of Matsui Shōyō, and in the following year he was confronted by difficulties after suffering failure in his reformed public performance. The performance in April 1908 of Molière's *L'Amour Médecin*, adapted as *Kekkon Ryōhō* (Remedy by Marriage), was the occasion when cooperation was finally achieved between Kaoru and Sadanji. In the same year, two other producers, Oka Onitarō and Okamoto Kidō, also united with Sadanji.

In February of the following year, the memorandum for organizing the Jiyū Gekijō was announced, and on November 27 the organization made its début with Ibsen's *John Gabriel Borkmann*. Although admired by some of the members of the Subaru group as delightful, vigorous criticism of the performance came from another side represented by Kusuyama Masao and Naka-mura Kichizō. Yet it must be remembered that this was the first attempt at true stage representation of modern drama. In the first stage of its activities lasting until 1912, when, in the spring, Sadanji and his troupe joined the Shōchiku and when Kaoru left for Europe in December, the Jiyū Gekijō produced seven modern European dramas. They were, in addition to *Borkmann, Der Kammersänger* (*Shuppatsu Mae Hanjikan*) of Wedekind, *The Marriage Proposal* (*Inu,* or *Kekkon Mōshikomi*) of Chekhov, *The Lower Depths* (*Yoru no Yado,* or *Donzoko*) of Gorky, *Le Miracle de Saint Antoine* (*Kiseki*), *La Mort de Tintagiles* (*Tantajiiru no Shi*) of Maeterlinck, and *Einsame Menschen* (*Sabishiki Hitobito*) of Hauptmann. The repertory also included six original plays: Mori Ōgai's *Ikutagawa* (Ikuta River); Yoshii Isamu's *Yumesuke to Sō to* (Yumesuke and a Bonze) and *Kōchiya Yohei* (Kōchiya Yohei the Merchant); Nagata Hideo's *Kanraku no Oni* (The Demon of Pleasure); Akita Ujaku's *Dai-ichi no Akatsuki* (The First Dawn); and Kayano Nijūichi's *Dōjōji* (The Temple of Dōjō).

While the aforementioned Bungei Kyōkai had trained its own actors, the newly-born Jiyū Gekijō, for its performances, relied solely upon those actors already established as professionals. Freely choosing the newest dramas for its repertory, it urged the reform of theatrical art, informed the public about modern Western drama, and also hired some talented dramatists to partic-ipate in its work. These were the chief merits that distin-guished the theater.

The rising *shingeki* (new drama) movement ended its formation period before the closing years of the Meiji Era when several more theatrical organizations were founded and subsequently com-peted with each other in performing modern Western dramas as well as Japanese originals. They were the Shin-Shakai ge-ki-Dan (New Social Dramatic Company), the Shin-Jidaigeki Kyō-kai (New Historical Drama Society), the Engeki Dōshikai (Drama Companions Society), the Doyō Gekijō (Saturday Theater), and institutes for training actors, such as the Tōkyō Haiyū Yōseijo (Tōkyō Actors' School) founded by Fujisawa Asajirō and the Teikoku Joyū Yōseijo (Imperial Actresses' School) founded by Kawakami Sadayakko.

Besides those Western classical and romantic dramatists such as Shakespeare, Calderón, Molière, and Lessing referred to above, among the modern dramatists of the West we find Ibsen, introduced as he was earlier than any of the others, exerting the greatest influence upon the Japan of that day. The first year that saw Japanese translation of Ibsen's work was 1893 when Takayasu Gekkō published a fragment from *The Doll's House* in the magazine *Ittenkō*, and also a part of *The Enemy of The People* (*Shakai no Teki*) in *Dōshisha Bungaku* (Dōshisha Literature). In the following year, Kaneko Umaji's article " Ibsen the Great Norwegian Writer " appeared in *Waseda Bungaku*. Gekkō's translations, finding almost no immediate reaction, were later gathered into a book, *Ibusen Shakaigeki* (Ibsen's Social Drama) (1901). Though himself a pioneer in introducing the Norwegian dramatist, no influence of Ibsen is recognizable in any of Gekkō's writing.

Japan's literary world became remarkable attentive to Ibsen in about 1906, the year when the great dramatist died. On the occasion of Ibsen's death, Shimamura Hōgetsu and others collaborated in writing an essay, "Henrik Ibsen," in *Waseda Bungaku* and in January 1910 the same magazine carried a translation of *The Doll's House.* Earlier, in 1907, headed by Osanai Kaoru, The Ibusen Kai (Society for the Study of Ibsen) was organized with the membership including Yanagida Kunio, Tayama Katai, Iwano Hōmei, Kambara Ariake, Hasegawa Seiya, Shimazaki Tōson, Masamune Hakuchō, and others. The group took up for its study *Hedda Gabler, Vildanden* (*Nogamo*), *Lille Eyolf* (*Osanaki Aiyorufu*), etc., and its studies appeared in succession in the magazine *Shinshichō* (New Currents of Thought). Ibsen's dramas translated in the same year were *Hedda Gabler* (by

Chiba Kikukō and Arai Usen), *Gengangere* (*Yūrei*, by Hashi-moto Seiu), *Når vi döde Vägner* (*Sosei no Hi*, by Kikukō). In 1908 Hōgetsu wrote *Ibusen no Kaiketsu-Geki* (Ibsen's Dramas of Solution) in *Waseda Bungaku* in which, in 1909, was also published Dohi Shunshō's adaptation of *Hedda Gabler* (*Kaburagi Hideko*), followed by Hasegawa Tenkei who wrote a critique of Henrik Ibsen in *Bunshō Sekai* (The World of Writing). In the next year even a bibliographical study came out as Yasunari Sadao compiled in *Waseda Bungaku, Ibusen Eiyaku oyobi Kenkyū Shomoku* (A List of English Translations of Ibsen and a List of Ibsen Studies). In that year, Abe Jirō wrote two articles on Ibsen, *Ibusen no "Kenchikushi Sorunesu"* (Ibsen's *The Master-Builder*) (*Shinshichō*) and *Burandesu no Ibusen-Ron* (G. Brandes' Views on Ibsen) (*Teikoku Bungaku*). These show that studies on Ibsen were at their height during the years immediately after his death.

A similar phenomenon can be witnessed also in the theatrical world. The fact that the Jiyū Gekijō chose Ōgai's translation of *John Gabriel Borkmann* for its first production in November 1909, even if there might have been various reasons forcing them to do so, is still significant enough in the study of Ibsen. In 1911 Ōgai translated *Gengangere* (*Yūrei*) and the Bungei Kyōkai presented *The Doll's House* (*Nora*) while *Yūrei* was played by the Engeki Dōshikai.

Among those Naturalist writers of the Ibsen school, Hauptmann and Sudermann were the earliest introduced by Ōgai. Ōgai discussed the former in his serial review in *Mesamashigusa* entitled *Tonari no Takara* (Treasures in the Neighborhood) (Number Three) (1899), and in November 1906, published "Gerhardt Hauptmann," a detailed critical review and biography of the author. Tobari Shin'ichirō also wrote a review "Gerhardt Hauptmann" (*Teikoku Bungaku*, 1900). Hauptmann was welcomed into Japan almost on the heels of Ibsen, as in 1908 there appeared such articles as Ōgai's *Hauputoman ga Saikin no Nisaku* (Two Recent Works of Hauptmann) (*Kabuki*) and

Koson's *Hauputoman Shinron* (New Views on Hauptmann) (*Shin-shōsetsu*), etc. The following year saw the publication of a Japanese version of *Einsame Menschen* (*Sabishiki Hitobito*) in *Waseda Bungaku* with Kusuyama Masao as the translator. The drama came to be presented on the stage two years later in 1911, while another of Hauptmann's plays, *Vor Sonnenaufgang*, was considered among the very probable dramas to be presented by the Jiyū Gekijō on the occasion of its first public performance in 1909, although it was dismissed in the end. In 1911, the Engeki Dōshikai chose *Elga* (translated by Ōgai as *Sōbō no Yume*) for its first performance in June, and also *Einsame Menschen* was given by the Jiyū Gekijō through Ōgai's translation in October for its fifth presentation.

As for Sudermann, he was first referred to in detail in *Mesamashigusa* in February 1896 in *Doitsu Shin-Gikyoku* (Germany's New Dramas). In 1904, Ōgai pointed out some erroneous comments on the German author published in the *Tōkyō Mainichi Shimbun* in his essay *Zūderuman no Kyakuhon ni tsuite* (On Sudermann's Dramas). The magazine *Myōjō* printed in 1905 *Zūderuman no Kessaku Katsuenshitehi* (*Der Katzensteg*, Masterpiece of Sudermann) by Higuchi Ryūkyō, and in 1908, Chino Shōshō's *Zūderuman no Gikyoku* (Dramas of Sudermann). This *Katzensteg*, rearranged as *Yobihei* (*Reservists*) by Oguri Fūyō, was later played by the *shimpa* (new school) actors. The reputation of Sudermann was further heightened in May 1912 when the authorities suspended the production of *Magda* (translated by Hōgetsu) selected by the Bungei Kyōkai for its third performance.

Arthur W. Pinero was brought before Japan's reading public by Hōgetsu as one of the most eminent dramatists of Britain who was deeply influenced by Ibsen. Hōgetsu's translation of his work *The Second Mrs. Tanqueray* made its appearance in *Shinshōsetsu* in 1906. In that year, Chiba Kikukō published in the *Myōjō* a synopsis of *Lettie* (*Āsū Pinero no Shinsaku " Kyakuhon Retei" no Hanashi, Seigeki Kōgai*) (Arthur Pinero's Recent

Drama *Lettie*). In 1910 the Shin-Shakaigeki-Dan led by Naka-mura Kichizō gave one of Pinero's plays as adapted by Dohi Shunsho under the title *Shōri* (Victory). In the beginning of the Taishō Era, Hōgetsu produced *Paula* which he adapted himself. Such popularity of a second-rate author like Pinero among leaders of the drama movement is noteworthy in rela-tion to their attitude of welcoming Ibsen. Another thing to be noticed in this connection is an attack delivered by Shōyō upon the personality of Nora from a moralistic point of view.

George Bernard Shaw, an author who was under Ibsen's influ-ence in the true sense of the word, had a few of his pieces performed in Japan. First *The Shewing-up of Blanco Posnet*, translated by Ōgai as *Uma-Dorobō* (Horse Thief), was presented in November 1910 by the Shin-Jidaigeki Kyōkai. Then both *Man of Destiny* (translated by Kusuyama Masao) and *Twentieth Century* (translated by Matsui Shōyō) were performed by the Bungei Kyōkai in June and November 1912, respectively.

Maeterlinck and other playwrights belonging to the Symbolism or Neo-Romanticism that constituted another peculiar tendency in the modern dramaturgy of the West were also great contrib-utors to the establishment of modern plays in this country. It was again Ōgai who first introduced Maeterlinck as well as Hofmannsthal. He gave an explanatory review of the fatalism of Maeterlinck in *Kokoro no Hana* (Vol. VI, No. 6) in the essay *Māterurinku no Kyakuhon* (Maeterlinck's Dramas) and also published a summary of *Monna Vanna* (June 1903). In 1906, *Monna Vanna* was put on the stage with Kawakami Otojirō and Ichikawa Enshō (later Sadanji) in the leading roles. This was a memorable event as the earliest performance of modern Western drama in Japan, however crude its produc-tion. In the same year, a lecture on Maeterlinck given by Ueda Bin was printed in the *Myōjō*. In the studies of the Belgian mythologist Sōma Gyofū took part with his reviews and Chino Shōshō also in the field of translation. Osanai Kaoru, whose translation of *Les Aveugles* (*Gummō*) was admired by Ōgai during his student days, made the choice of *Le Miracle de Saint Antoine* for the first trial performance of his Jiyū Gekijō in June 1911. Performed also were *L'Intruse* (translated by Chino Shōshō) and *La Mort de Tintagiles*. The former was acted by those first graduated from the Yūraku-Za Actors' School and the latter on the occasion of the sixth trial perform-ance of the Jiyū Gekijō.

Hofmannsthal's *Oedipus und Sphinx* was reviewed by Ōgai in the magazine *Kabuki* in 1906. Sakurai Tendan published essays on the author, *Hofumansutaru no Shōchōgeki* (Hofmanns-thal's Symbolistic Dramas) in the *Shin-Tenchi* (New World) (1908) and *Hofumansutāru-Ron* (On Hofmannsthal) in *Waseda Bungaku* in 1910. Ōgai's *Saikin Doitsu Kyakuhon Kōgai* (Synopses of Recent German Dramas) in the *Subaru* of Septem-ber 1909 comprised summaries of nine pieces of Hofmannsthal, apart from works of A. Schnitzler, M. Halbe, and Wedekind. Hofmannsthal's *Der Tor und der Tod* (*Chijin to Shi to*), translated by Ōgai, was performed twice, the first time by the Doyō Gekijō in 1911 and, the second, by the Shin-Jidaigeki Kyōkai in 1912. In the meantime, the influence of Maeter-linck and Hofmannsthal was exerted mainly upon those writers of the Subaru school.

Considerable attention was also turned to Wedekind, whose *Frühlings Erwachen*, for instance, was analyzed by Tenkei. Among other Western authors introduced or translated, we find Bahr, Strindberg, D'Annunzio, Rostand, Grillparzer, and Wilde.

During the decade beginning in 1907, the repertories consisted largely of dramas of those authors inclined to Symbolism, such as those of the Irish National Theatre Society, Yeats' *The Hour-Glass*, Lady Gregory's *Hyacinth Halvey*, *Spreading the News*, and *The Workhouse Ward*. These playwrights became known in the Japanese theatrical world again through the efforts of Ōgai and Kaoru. Particularly Osanai Kaoru, under the guidance of Ueda Bin, began, from about the time of his participation in the Masago-Za in 1904, to write on these dramatists in various magazines. This he continued even after the foundation of the *Shinshichō*.

The Western dramas brought to the stage in those days include Bjφrnson's *En Hanske* (*Tebukuro*), Schnitzler's *Der Tapfere Cassian* (*Mosa*), Schmidtbonn's *Mutter Landstrasse* (*Machi no Ko*), and Rilke's *Das Tägliche Leben* (*Kajō-Sahan*).

As for modern Russian plays, Chekhov's *Marriage Proposal* (translated as *Inu*, or " The Dog ") and Gorky's *The Lower Depths* (translated as *Yoru no Yado*, or "The Inn of Night") were presented by the Jiyū Gekijō in 1910. Other pieces performed were *Kuma* (*The Bear*) of Chekhov and *Kensatsukan* (*The Inspector-General*) of Gogol. The magazine *Shinshichō* played a significant role in introducing Russian drama for which Nakazawa Rinsen did much as an anonymous contributor.

In an essay in the form of a letter *Haiyū D-Kun e* (To Actor D) printed in the January 1909 issue of the magazine, Osanai Kaoru expressed his hope of bringing forth " a period of accurate translation," and said that creative works in the field of modern drama should appear only after this period. The activities on the part of Ōgai and Kaoru in translation or introductory work, and also the repertories of various *shingeki* (new drama) organizations make us feel that this hope of Kaoru was at last realized.

The dramatic reviews Kaoru had contributed for several years to many periodicals were collected in *Engeki Shinchō* (New Currents of the Drama) (December 1908) and *Engeki Shinsei* (New Voice of the Drama) (January 1912). These writings by him were as significant in the new drama movement of Japan as had been Shōyō's *Shōsetsu Shinzui* in the novel and *Wagakuni no Shigeki* in the historical drama. There are in them a great number of reviews and opinions on such dramatists as Ibsen, Strindberg, and Bjφrnson, and on Irish drama, fine arts for the theatre, stage directions, etc. With Sadanji as co-author, Kaoru published in November 1912 a book entitled *Jiyū Gekijō*

(Free Theatre) which must be acknowledged as a significant work. In discussing theatrical critics, we should mention, among others, Ōgai's younger brother, Miki Takeji (Mori Tokujirō), who was distinguished for his sensitive, inquiring criticism of *kabuki*, and Kusuyama Masao and Komiya Toyotaka who are significant in the last years of the Meiji Era. Especially, in his *Nakamura Kichiemon-Ron* (A Study of Kichiemon), Toyotaka, standing on Western theatrical theory, ranked the actor Kichiemon as a tragedian qualified to act in all the great tragic works since the Greek drama. This assertion was, in fact, epoch-making in the history of dramatic reviews.

Although in its initial period the new drama movement was busy in importing modern drama from the West, as seen above, at the same time there emerged some Japanese authors, who, under Western influence, began creating their own. We shall try to make a survey of this situation in the following pages.

2. *The Naturalistic and Realistic Drama*

Those dramas written under the influence of modern works of the West at the end of Meiji belong roughly to two different traditions. One is the tradition of Ibsen tending to Naturalistic, realistic dramaturgy, and the other that of such men as Maeterlinck and Hofmannsthal whose works inclined to Neo-Romanticism and Symbolism. Let us first consider the former.

Most of Ibsen's works which were translated, reviewed, or performed in Japan were rather tinted with the Symbolism peculiar to the latter part of the author's literary activity. Notwithstanding this, Japanese pieces written under his influence owed much to his social problem dramas which were generally realistic as well as naturalistic. Among Ibsen's followers we find Mayama Seika, Nagata Hideo, Nakamura Kichizō, and others, and, in a sense, Sano Tensei and Satō Kōroku may be said to have been influenced by him. Mushakōji Saneatsu of the Shirakaba (White Birch) school also appears influenced by this Western playwright as well as by the author of *The Blue Bird*.

Even such a writer as Iwano Hōmei, who seems rather to have accepted French Symbolism, worked in creating social dramas when he employed a method he called "naturalist symbolism" (*shizenshugiteki hyōchōshugi*).

The first drama ever created in Japan based on modern thought is probably Hōmei's tragedy *Honoo no Shita* (The Tongue of Flame), which appeared in *Shinshōsetsu* in 1906. Hōmei early produced an adaptation of *Hamlet*, *Higeki : Kommei Getchū no Yaiba* (A Tragedy : Souls in Distress and Blades in the Moonlight), or its alternate title, *Katsura Gorō*, the name of the hero, (1894), and, in 1905, he wrote a drama in verse, *Meisō Shigeki : Kaihō Gishi* (A Contemplative Poetical Drama : The Sea-Fortress Engineer). In the preface to *Honoo no Shita* the author had this to say : "I shall not force upon the readers my reckless mysticism as is done by certain dramatists of contemporary Europe." He was referring to Maeterlinck and his followers. The present work is a "naturalistic, symbolical drama," which aims at pushing into the world of mystery directly, "through concentrating and emotionalizing thought and reality" on the basis of the Neo-Naturalism held by the author. The subject is a tragic event in society. This is a story of a woman, beautiful but suffering from a terrifying hereditary mental disease that has caused the rupture of her first marriage. Abandoned by her lover, desperate in a lonely life and resolved to kill herself, still she finds a man, and they attempt to burn themselves in the fires of carnal desire. The author stands on his mystic semi-animalism in that he despises religion for its weakness of deceiving nature, and in that he finds a true way of life in continuing to live guided by instinct, in spite of the burden of violent pain man suffers. Disclosing tragic elements in the trifles of everyday life, the author, with his modern thought and method, succeeded in creating an admittedly modern drama. By a fire occurring in the drama, the author seems to be trying to symbolize the conflagration of life that burns human beings into ashes. Regrettably, the drama suffers from a lack of artistic presentation of the intellectual content, is rather rough in treating feeling or mood, and thereby still falls short of becoming a true Symbolist work. Regardless of defects in construction, however, the pioneer quality of the work is worthy of recognition.

In addition to this, Hōmei's dramatic works include *Ono no Fukumatsu* (Fukumatsu the Woodcutter) (1907), *Kagurazaka-shita* (At the Foot of Kagura Hill) (1909), *Sayō Hime* (Sayō-Hime) (1909), *Emma no Medama* (The Eyes of the Devil) (1910), and *Ma no Yume* (A Demoniac Dream) (1911). Hōmei was more skilled in writing novels, but among his dramas, *Emma no Medama* is somewhat better than the others. Depicting in a Naturalistic way the eccentric life of three characters, a dissolute priest, a shameless wife, and an avaricious maidservant, the author leaves the reader in an indescribable mood of bitterness, after causing innocent laughter.

In 1907, the year after *Honoo no Shita* was published, a drama, *Dai-ichininsha* (The First Man), by the Naturalist novelist Mayama Seika appeared in *Chūō Kōron*. The story runs as follows: Dr. Narasaki returns home from an expedition to the North Pole on which all of the other members have perished. Since he is the only survivor of the adventurous journey, there is no one who will believe his account of his great achievements, and he is not even able to publish his memoirs of the expedition. Yūra, his devoted dog, is the sole witness of his deeds in the arctic wilderness and Tetsutarō, his nine-year-old grandson, is the only believer of his story of the venture. One stormy night in late October, the maddened Yūra is killed. The following afternoon, when the drama begins, the doctor's plan of publishing his notes of the journey with the money he had prepared for his younger daughter's dowry, meets rejection from her sister. Desperate, and for a time mad with frustration, he eventually finds consolation in persuading himself that the world of the absolute cannot be admitted into everyday life, being incommunicable to people, that the man who has had a glimpse of the mystery which refuses to make itself known to mankind is punishable, and that it is natural for him to be misunderstood by others. Thus, he reduces his meticulously kept manuscript to ashes, and comes to desire to participate in the life and thinking of an ordinary man.

Though this work is said to have been inspired by *Borkmann*, the hero of the drama, Dr. Narasaki, bears some resemblance to Ibsen's Brand. The perseverance of the proud doctor in trying to tell of his successful exploration of the Pole is somewhat similar to the perseverance on the part of Borkmann, but he seems to resemble more Brand whose efforts in explaining the absolutes of the inner world to others finally meet with failure. However, with Ibsen, the world of Borkmann is an icy, merciless one, while Brand as a man of exceptional character, pursues to the end his way of solitude and persecution. The former dies in desperation, and the latter, too, loses his life by being buried in an avalanche, asking whether man's will is of value before God. And yet they still believe that God is love. Contrasted with this cruel and rigid world of Ibsen, Dr. Narasaki is surrounded by a grandson and daughters who love their father and by nature with its autumnal beauty. Moreover, he resolves to compromise with the secular life, returning to the world of common humanity. This results in softening the tragic element and the conflict in the drama, which relates instead how the sorrows of frustration flow toward a sweet melancholy and resignation. At this point, it should be recognized that Seika fell short of learning Ibsen's austere view of life. Despite such defects, however, the freshness of the material, the ambition of expressing the struggles that confront the modern ego, the dramatic concentration in form, and the bold relief of the hero's personality and psychology, must be pointed out as elements which the author learned from Ibsen. In a word, this is a drama worthy of attention, even if it did not avoid an Ibsen-like exaggeration.

The next drama of Seika, *Umarezarishi Naraba* (If He Had

Not Been Born), published in the following year, 1908, has in its theme something in common with *Gengangere* of Ibsen. Kiyoshi, the only son of a Diet member named Tsuzuki is obliged to have his leg amputated because of a virulent bone disease inherited from his father. The father, himself having fought the cruel destiny of a disabled man, realizes that his son Kiyoshi lacks that spiritual strength yet tries to encourage him to confront the stern reality of life by accepting his fate. He attempts to make his son accept as the symbol of his own life, and not as a mere verse, the line, "If he had not been born," inscribed on the portrait of Judas. Rejecting his wife's request not to do so, the father tells of the necessity of amputation to his frightened son, while a thunderstorm is raging outside. Thus, the drama proceeds on the juxtaposition of three different characters, the father, a man of will, the weak son, and the mother, who is concerned most about worldly trifles such as the selecting of an *obi* (a sash for the *kimono*) or of brooches to wear. Besides the three, there also appears an ominous blind man who predicts man's destiny. Though some exaggeration is seen in emphasizing the catastrophe by having the storm rage and also in the utterances of the father, the piece loses neither dramatic effect nor tension. It differs from *Gengangere* in that the depth of man's guilt is overlooked, although man's destiny is well described.

These works of Seika show us that after all there emerged some dramas of artistic value among those written under the influence of Ibsen. Naturally, Ibsen's influence was conspicuous in the field of dramaturgy as well as recognizable in the choice of materials, but of his thought and the profundity of his inner world they learned very little. Consequently, writers seem to have attempted to intensify the effect of a drama not by the inner profundity of it, but rather by exaggerated outward dramatic situations that would impress the spectator. And yet such failures were perhaps inevitable.

As we have seen before, from about the year 1907, the *shimpa* (new school) actors began to be interested in performing imitations of Ibsen, changing their course to modern plays. In 1907, Sano Tensei won a prize from the *Miyako Shimbun* for his drama *Dainō* (Large-Scale Farming), and subsequently it was performed on the stage of the Hongō-Za with Takada, Fujisawa, and Kitamura playing the leading roles. The play takes place in a farming village on the Tone River immediately after the end of the Russo-Japanese war. The hero, an obstinate individualist, is a large landowner, and a Christian pacifist in faith. Unlike others, he is not ashamed of having been a prisoner of war when sent to the front. In the face of persecution by his father, sister, and villagers, he launches into extensive farming of the type adopted on the continent. The authority of an individual and the victory of the ego are finally achieved as the hero succeeds in carrying out his plan. His work is colored in the fashion of social dramas, and Tensei was probably inspired by Ibsen's *Brand* and other pieces. Over the performance of this prize drama there later arose difficulties with the author, when the theater, afraid of an unfavorable reaction among the public, asked him to make some revisions in the original, although at first the actors had acted it faithfully. After this maiden work, Tensei wrote successively *Ishi* (Will) (1907), treating the strength of a woman in love, *Fushi no Chikai* (The Immortal Oath) (1907), *Kashikoki Hito* (A Wise Man) (1908), *Nihon-Maru* (The Tale of the Nihon-Maru) (1908), *Yui Shōsetsu* (The Last of Yui Shōsetsu) (1908), *Kakushin* (Firm Belief) (1908), and *Kirishitan Korobi* (The Converted Christian) (1909), which concluded his creative activity.

In 1909, Nakamura Kichizō published a drama, *Bokushi no Ie* (The Pastor's House), in the *Asahi Shimbun*, and it was presented in April of the following year by the Shin-Shakaigeki-Dan headed by the author himself. As an exposure of corruption in the religious world, where Kichizō had for a period placed himself as a Christian, this is an example of the social dramas which imitated those of Ibsen. Also in that year there appeared Satō Kōroku's *Haiba* (The Disabled Horse), seemingly an imitation of Ibsen's *Vildanden* and *Fruen tra Havet*. Kōroku then continued to imitate other dramas such as *The Doll's House* and *Gengangere*. *Nami* (The Wave), Kichizō's next work after *Bokushi no Ie*, is also a product of borrowing from Ibsen, in its attempt to disclose the egoism of man toward woman. With Kichizō the influence is more superficial than with Seika or Hideo. This leads us to suspect another influence exerted upon the author by Pinero, a follower of Ibsen. Many well-constructed works were to be created by Kichizō, however, during the subsequent Taishō Era.

While those playwrights mentioned above were generally followers of Naturalism, Nagata Hideo was a writer in the tradition of the *Subaru* group. Despite this fact, his first drama *Kanraku no Oni* (The Demon of Pleasure) (1910), in which the author imitates Ibsen's *Gengangere* and *The Doll's House*, is obviously affected by Naturalism. The heroine, the wife of a scholar, is an egotistic intellectual who has exhausted her feeling in excessive reading of novels and other literary works. Her jurist husband Dr. Endō is an intelligent man of strict morals, and the family lives happily, pending an incident. After their marriage, Mrs. Endō had given birth to a child who was an idiot. And now the peace comes to be broken, as it is proved that the idiot child had been the result of a virus contracted by the husband during his stay overseas. The idiot was the child of guilt, namely "the demon of pleasure," the wife is told. This becomes known when a physician diagnoses the headache the husband suffers. He is now destined to idiocy, madness, or a sudden death from apoplexy. Facing this catastrophe, Dr. Endō wishes to hasten to complete his life-work with the help of his wife whom he asks to forgive his past error. Mrs. Endō refuses this, and her desire turns to a new, greater world where she hopes to live a full life. But drawn by the soul of the dead child who calls her, she decides to remain home as a mother.

Mrs. Endō in the drama represents those women of that day who began to be aware of their new ego and of whom much had been discussed. Her egoism, however, is far less tragic than that of Gunhild in Ibsen's *Borkmann*. The tragedy comes about with her decision to stay at home, which must mean nothing but the frustration of her ego. The author, it appears, does not intend to give tragic emphasis to this point. Rather, he softens the tension by the relief of the scholar husband. We should note the resemblance of such a conclusion to that of the revised version of *The Doll's House* which was necessary for the purpose of performance. Although the writer is very careful in laying a subplot, that is, the reminiscences about the dead child, under the surface of a well-arranged technique of the dramatic process there lies a substantial weakness that makes the piece a shallow one. From the aspect of dramaturgy, however, this work importing Ibsen's method succeeded at least in avoiding the monotony so common in traditional drama.

In the tradition of the *Subaru* was also the chief of *Mita Bungaku* (Mita Literature), Nagai Kafū, a pupil of Ōgai and Bin, who wrote a kind of social drama. His *Furansu Monogatari* (Tales from France) (1909) includes a three-act play *Ikyō no Koi* (Love in a Strange Land). A one-act play, *Taira no Koremori* (the hero's name), was presented as an *entr'acte* on the stage of the Meiji-Za. Another drama, *Aki no Wakare* (The Parting in Autumn) (*Mita Bungaku*, 1911), was a sort of drama in verse, imitating Western opera, and fantastically treating the *P'i-pa-Hsing* (The Lute Song) of the Chinese classical poet Po Chü-i. His social drama *Wakuraba* (Fallen Leaves), a play in three acts, appeared in January of the following year in *Mita Bungaku*. In this play there are a father and his son who cannot understand each other and a man and woman who are bound together only for the sake of money. The story ends in the victory of true love and the son's success in the literary work which the father cannot understand. In the last scene, the successful son telephones his father, telling him the good news of his decoration for his achievement in literature at the very moment the father, abandoned by his mistress, is leading an empty life facing his child's death. Attacking vulgarity as he always does, Kafū could not keep a touch of sensationalism out of this work.

Several dramatic works were also written by Shimamura Hōgetsu, a theorist of Naturalism, who guided the new drama (*shingeki*) movement as a principal member of the Bungei Kyōkai. They were *Taira no Kiyomori* (January 1911), *Ummei no Oka* (The Hill of Destiny) (April 1911), *Kaihin no Hitomaku* (A Scene on the Beach) (July 1911), *Fukushū* (Revenge) (January 1912), *Kyōsō* (The Race) (October 1912), and others, all published in *Waseda Bungaku*. They were rather commonplace works, and only a few of them were actually performed. *Taira no Kiyomori* takes its material from a story in the classic *Heike Monogatari* (The Tale of the Taira Clan). The heroine, Hotoke, who is loved by Kiyomori, deplores her connection with the Taira family as she reads a poem which Giō, Kiyomori's former mistress, now abandoned, wrote on the sliding door on her departure. Meanwhile, Munemori, Kiyomori's father, is anxious about the decline of the family's fortune in view of the threatening political atmosphere. Kiyomori, on the contrary, is eager with his plan to place his government in Fukuhara, a town beyond the reach of riotous Buddhist warriors. In particular, the play depicts the rather solitary but optimistically strong character of Kiyomori. Later, this drama was revised into *Kiyomori to Hotoke-Gozen* (Kiyomori and Hotoke-Gozen) (1916), where Hotoke's character is described as very strong.

Kusuyama Masao contributed a few dramatic works to *Waseda Bungaku*. *Haka* (The Tomb) (April 1910) is a Naturalistic work, the theme of which is the miserable fate of sisters, of whom the elder is a wanton and both of whom have inherited a mental illness. Some influence of Ibsen is discernible in the drama. Another piece, *Seinen to Joyū* (A Youth and an Actress) (1911), is a parody, selecting for its subject the love-affair of an actress abroad with her troupe. His talent, however, was shown less in drama than in drama criticism. Among his articles, *Kikugorō to Kichiemon* (Kikugorō and Kichiemon) (October 1911) is the most remarkable. He also did much for the new drama (*shingeki*) movement, helping Hōgetsu with his Geijutsu-Za.

3. *The Neo-Romantic and Symbolist Drama*

The year 1909 was a memorable one for the Neo-Romantic and Symbolist drama, the second group of modern dramas under the influence of the West, for many representative works appeared one after another during the course of it. They were *Purumūra* (Prumoula), *Kamen* (The Mask), and *Shizuka* of Ōgai; *Nambanji Monzen* (In Front of the Gate of the Southern Barbarian Temple), *Tōdai Chokka* (At the Base of the Lighthouse), and *Onshitsu* (The Greenhouse) of Kinoshita Mokutarō; *Gogo Sanji* (Three O'Clock in the Afternoon), *Asakusa Kannondō* (Asakusa Temple), and *Kamome no Shigai* (A Dead Seagull) of Yoshii Isamu; and *Kinenkai no Zen'ya* (The Eve of an Anniversary Celebration) of Akita Ujaku. Mokutarō also wrote in that year *Ishi Dōban no Kubi* (The Head of Dr. Dauban), but it was published in the following year.

In this group, most of the works of Ōgai, Mokutarō, and Isamu appeared in the magazine *Subaru* founded in the same year. The younger writers of this school may be called, in a sense, disciples of Ōgai, except for Kayano Nijūichi and Mushakōji Saneatsu who both belonged to the Shirakaba group; Ujaku once helped Osanai Kaoru, who enjoyed Ōgai's patronage, with editing the magazine *Shinshichō*; Kubota Mantarō, deeply influenced by Mokutarō, was one of Osanai's students; Tanizaki Jun'ichirō, another young writer collaborating with the *Shinshichō*, was a regular contributor to the *Subaru*. Before the time he began publishing modern dramatic works, Ōgai, as referred to above, had greatly contributed in introducing their models from the West. Besides, during those years he wrote two *kabuki* plays, *Tamakushige Futari Urashima* (The Two Urashimas of the

Jewelled Box) (special issue of *Kabuki,* December 1902) and *Nichiren-Shōnin Tsujizeppō* (The Wayside Preaching of Nichiren the Holy Priest) (*Kabuki,* March 1904). *Tamakushige Futari Urashima,* written for a *shimpa* (new school) actor Yōhō, treats the legend of Urashima who visits a fairyland under the sea. This drama is similar to Goethe's *Faust* as the author chooses for his theme the awakening of Urashima to the importance of man's duty, which leads him to give up his love for Oto-Hime, the princess of the Dragon's palace. As it was written like a musical play, in verse, namely in seven-five-syllable lines, (*shichi-go-chō*), *Tamakushige Futari Urashima* is a drama that may be performed as an opera. As stated by Ōgai himself, it had a new form such as had not been seen before, but the methods of traditional dramaturgy were still employed in stage technique as well as in dialogue. In the first half, the scene in the Dragon's palace, with its sad tone and elegant, lyrical beauty, dancing is predominant. In sharp contrast with this, the latter part, the scene where the old Urashima sees off the young Urashima departing on his expedition to the undersea world, manly vigor and active strength are emphasized.

Nichiren-Shōnin Tsujizeppō appeared immediately after the performance of Shōyō's *Kiri-Hitoha* (One Leaf of Paulownia) and was a product of the period when new historical plays flourished. Written for *kabuki* actors, this drama, although a proof of Ōgai's many-faceted talent, was not one that was able to open up a new phase in the history of the drama.

As a dramatist, Ōgai advanced a step closer to establishing the modern drama in his work *Purumūra,* published in the first issue of the *Subaru* (January 1909). Prumoula is the name of a princess mentioned in the history of Sind (now a province in India). This princess, according to history, sacrificed her life for the sake of her country's revenge. To this classical tragedy, the author Ōgai tried to give a new interpretation, applying psychological analysis. The self-sacrifice on the part of the princess, Ōgai interprets, was committed in revenge of her lover who refused her. In the deadly silence after all the conflicts have terminated and the ruin of Prumoula has become inevitable, the princess in the drama confesses her real intention, thus totally reversing the process of the story of retaliation on behalf of the state. However, in the work, the inner conflicts of the amorous heroine are least depicted so that her confession at the end appears as an unreasonably sudden conclusion. As a result, one of the elements of modern drama, the awakening of the ego, which the author intended to personify in the heroine, was not able to be fully represented here. In addition, its construction adopting a classic, static, and architectural mode, and its style in verse of seven and five syllables (*shichi-go-chō*), were factors which caused the work to fall short of a perfect modern drama. It is interesting to note that the behavior of the Princess Prumoula in the first half of the play resembles that Monna Vanna of Ibsen and of Salomé of Wilde.

Kamen (April 1909) is Ōgai's first work of modern drama. In this play, a doctor, masking himself and transcending conventional morality, advises a tuberculous student to choose a noble, solitary way of living with an austere attitude towards life. Apparently, the doctor here advocates the philosophy of Nietzche. Permeated with the stern atmosphere of a scientist, this piece lacks both in dramatic tension and dionysian passions.

A symbolical approach is seen in Ōgai's next work, *Shizuka* (November 1909), and Ōgai reaches the peak of his dramatic writings in *Ikutagawa* (Ikuta River), which was published in April of the following year. In the field of Symbolist plays, Ōgai is not necessarily the leader, for Kinoshita Mokutarō's *Nambanji Monzen* (In Front of the Gate of the Southern Barbarian Temple) and other pieces are considered to be the pioneering works.

Shizuka, a historical drama based on material from *Gikeiki*

(The Tale of Yoshitsune), is written in a pure, modern Japanese style. Treating events neither significant nor dramatic, the author attempts to give some internal and psychological meaning to them. In the first scene representing Yuigahama, a beach near Kamakura, Adachi Shinzaburō Kiyotsune causes the drowning of Yoshitsune's child by Shizuka, following the instructions of his master Yoritomo. The scene with little dialogue is of a type of play suggestive of a certain atmosphere. In the second scene, Shizuka revisits the house in Kamakura on her return to Kyōto. Conversation is carried on by Adachi, Shizuka, and her mother, revealing the views of life of the former two persons. Both Shizuka, whose child was killed, and Adachi, who drowned the child on his master's order, have arrived at a kind of resignation before destiny. The drama is symbolical because the unfathomable fate of man beyond the influence of will on the part of Shizuka or Adachi is symbolized by a strange fisherman in the first scene and by an ominous girl in the second. These mystic characters belonging to another, unseen world manipulate men, and the attitude of resignation of Shizuka and Adachi is brought about through their unconscious awakening to fate.

Ikutagawa is based on a famous story that appears in the *Manyōshū*, the *Yamato Monogatari*, and other works. A young girl, Ashiya-Otome, is obliged to choose between two men who love her, Unai-Otoko and Chinu-Otoko. She declares she will marry the one who is skilled enough to shoot a white water-bird. However, the two arrows reach their goal simultaneously, and the maiden cannot but choose death as symbolized by the fallen bird. Throwing light on the interior life of the unhappy girl, the mental process of one who becomes aware of man's weakness before destiny, of her own fate at the sight of the dying bird, and who, delivered from worldly passions, is finally led to a religious death, is suggested by the Buddhist prayers *Yuishiki Sanjū Ronshō* chanted by a priest at the end of the drama. Though not suited to be acted on the stage, as a *Lesedrama* this work represents the high point of Ōgai's dramatic ability, being its crystallization, elegant as well as lucid. The Symbolist dramas of Ōgai were quite different in quality from those of Mokutarō who follows in the tradition of Maeterlinck and Hofmannsthal.

Kinoshita Mokutarō's *Nambanji Monzen* (In Front of the Gate of the Southern Barbarian Temple) appeared in the February issue of *Subaru* in 1909, the month after Ōgai's *Purumūra* was published. In 1907, with some of the members of the Shinshisha (The New Poetry Society), Mokutarō traveled on the western coast of Kyūshū in western Japan, and his poems of the journey were later collected in *Amakusa-Gumi* (The Amakusa Rebels). The island of Amakusa* and reminiscences of the so-called Namban** were sung also by the poet Hakushū. This longing for a strange land, symbolized by the foreign civilization introduced in the early years of the Tokugawa Shōgunate, was a general inclination among the members of *Subaru*.

The drama *Nambanji Monzen* has no particular plot nor does it have a definite hero. However, we may call him the hero, the character named Chōjun, who ruins himself in his longings for a strange and remote mystic world, an unknown world of pleasure, of which the symbol is the gate of the church, or, as people call it, Nambanji, namely the Southern Barbarian Temple. His broken-off love-affair with O-Tsuru, later renamed Shirahagi as a courtesan, seems to have urged him to the world of the unknown. Chōjun and O-Tsuru have not been able to make the other believe his or her true love, but in this regard, the author appears to have been not necessarily in sympathy with such reasoning. Nonetheless it is notable that in another piece, *Izumiya Somemono-Mise* (Izumiya the Dyer's), the author treats the same subject as seen here, in the love-affair between Kōichi and O-Ken.

---

* *Translator's Note*: Inhabitants there rioted in feudal days in protest against the Shōgunate's ban on Christianity.
** Literally, southern barbarians, which meant the Occidentals who came from overseas.

As a whole, *Nambanji Monzen*, with its emphasis upon emotion rather than plot, may be regarded as the externalization of the author's interior world. Its symbol, the hero's longing for mystery, has its full expression here, helped by the pictorial and musical effects of the drama where Mokutarō successfully introduced melodies of both East and West. This work of Mokutarō, full of his peculiar romanticism, is the opposite of the symbolical dramas of Ōgai. Contemporary criticism with regard to this drama held that it lacked consistency, but such a view is unjust. Actually, as the author himself boasted, this was a drama written in a completely new form in order to give expression to emotions by means of sensualism. Thus, the whole drama was, as it were, a symbolical epic played on the stage.

In his next work *Tōdai Chokka*, Mokutarō admitted imitating the stage technique of Hofmannsthal. We have sufficient proof that Mokutarō was deeply influenced by Maeterlinck, too, as well as by Hofmannsthal. The longing for things mystic, the pursuit of truth as the source of life, the invitation to pleasure— these are the motifs common in Mokutarō's works such as : *Tōdai Chokka* (Beneath the Lighthouse) (May 1909) ; *Onshitsu* (The Greenhouse) (September 1909) ; *Ishi Dōban no Kubi* (The Head of Dr. Dauban) (January 1910) ; *Indo-Ō to Taishi* (The King of India and the Prince) (May 1910) ; and *Jūichinin no Hemmō* (Eleven Single-Eyed People) (March 1912). These pieces without exception treat the grievance and frustration of a soul incomprehensible to others, a soul wounded in longing. Especially in *Ishi Dōban no Kubi*, an adaptation of an anecdote in *The Arabian Nights*, the author Mokutarō attempts to represent artistically the agony of a man with " a contradictory dualism of nature " to which the author himself was destined. That which introduces beauty and knowledge, thus revealing the fundamental joys of life, will conflict with morals, duty, and other restraints of society. He who searches for the truth of life and he who is able to perceive it together must bear their tragic fate. Such pessimism within the author's mind is successfully symbolized in these works.

All of Mokutarō's dramas mentioned above were written as fantasties, including even those dealing with modern life. On the other hand, *Jikken Jidai* (The Experimental Period) (Spring 1910) is a modern drama written, for the first time, in the method of realism. Mokutarō is seen adopting Ibsen's dramaturgy in this étude. The author presents a hero in his desperate attempt to rid himself of the yoke of human life, namely hereditary disease, sin, and a hypocritical morality, the common subject of Ibsen's dramas. The burdens of pseudo-feudal society, as depicted here, are incomparably heavier than those in Ōgai's *Kamen*. Man's ego undergoes mental suffering when he rebels against the bondage of society, refusing to remain masked.

Izumiya Somemono-Mise was published in *Subaru* in March 1911. Imitating traditional *kabuki* drama such as *Akaneya* and *Horikawa*, but modernizing their tone and atmosphere, the author attempted to write a play of one independent act, singled out of several acts, that would constitute the whole story. The chosen scene is one that describes the old family of the Izumiya, the dyer of a minor city, in the small hours of New Year's Day; the only son Kōichi unexpectedly returns home after long years' absence, but just to bid farewell to his parents. Kōichi who has been taking part in a labor movement as his conscience prompts him, is now being pursued by the police as an accomplice in a certain grave political conspiracy. Kōichi is obsessed with the thought of socialist revolution. This obsession is a variation of that longing for a strange world that characterizes Mokutarō's plays after *Nambanji Monzen*. As the characters in the former play are not understood by people living in the traditional world, so Kōichi who returns to it from "quite a different world" is not appreciated by the people he loves. Unhappily, Kōichi, and something mysterious behind him, impress the people of the old world of the Izumiya as an immeasurable abyss of terror and grief. Intermingling of the new and the old often becomes the theme of Mokutarō's dramatic works. Particularly in this piece, the author successfully embodies the mystic sense of time and man's destiny in the everyday occurrence of the Izumiya family described here. The emotional reaction of the traditional family to the new age is well represented through very deliberate calculation on the part of the author. In the tranquil old family a shadow of apprehension gradually falls among the people. The fear then is realized, and the tension rises to its climax as Kōichi arrives. His departure, in its turn, leaves a stamp of unquenchable sorrow. Such sorrow the author depicts with more effect by juxtaposing those bystanders who unknowingly break the somber atmosphere by their light mood. The author also is very careful that the tempo of conversation to be carried on should correspond to each part of the construction. This meant the emergence of the realistic Symbolist drama which Iwano Hōmei had intended but failed to achieve, a drama quite different from the Symbolist drama of Ōgai, and, more than that, even different from any of the preceding works of Mokutarō. From another point of view, this was a fine example of harmony between Japan's traditional theatrical atmosphere and the Western method of the modern drama.

Although the author himself least expected it, two of the works published in this period, namely *Nambanji Monzen* and *Izumiya Somemono-Mise*, were performed in the Taishō years. However, in his works stage directions are very carefully prepared, indicating that he was concerned about their stage representation.

Compared with this, the works of Yoshii Isamu had been presented on the stage earlier. His *Gogo Sanji* (Three O'Clock in the Afternoon) appeared in the *Subaru* one month prior to the publication of *Nambanji Monzen*. Encouraged by the favorable reaction to this drama, he then continued publishing several pieces. While later in the Taishō Era he was to show his ability in " city-dwellers' drama " (*shisei-geki*), during Meiji, Isamu's works, although demonstrating his talent as a romantic poet, may, in certain aspects, be regarded as an imitation of those of Mokutarō. Nevertheless, several of his plays were performed. They were: *Asakusa Kannondō* (The Temple of Asakusa) (published in June and performed in November 1909); *Yumesuke to Sō to* (Yumesuke and a Bonze) (Jiyū Gekijō, 1910); *Kōchiya Yohei* (Kōchiya Yohei the Merchant) (Jiyū Gekijō, 1911); *Yoru* (Night) (November 1912). All of these are colored with the strong tendency toward exoticism, mysticism, and romanticism that the author seems to have shared with other members of the *Subaru* school.

His customary technique of construction used in his early pieces was to insert a scene of fantasy into that of realism. The same method borrowed from Hofmannsthal was adopted in *Tōdai Chokka* of Mokutarō. To cite an instance, in *Yumesuke to Sō to*, Sandai-Otoko Yumesuke visits Ichidai-Otoko's acquaintance, a priest who lives in his hermitage named "The House of Fantasy" where he worships "Woman." The hermit produces phantoms of true lovers before the visiting youth. Fantastically, there appear O-Shichi and Kichiza who are said to have died a fated death because of love in feudal days. Yumesuke now comes to know that a woman is after all an enigma. In the drama there is reflected some influence of the works of the Tokugawa writer Saikaku such as *Kōshoku Ichidai Otoko* (The Life of a Gallant), *Kōshoku Ichidai Onna* (The Life of a Wanton Woman), *Kōshoku Gonin-Onna* (Five Wanton Women), *Kindai Yasa-Inja* (A Modern Amorous Hermit), etc. Seen from this aspect of thought, this work also follows the *Subaru* school in presenting a priest who advises a youth to admire woman as a riddle or as a mystic being. Despite being a kind of idealistic drama, this work is wanting in thought. *Kōchiya Yohei* appears to have been inspired by Yohei, one of the characters in *Onna-Goroshi Abura-Jigoku* (The Hell of Oil for Woman-Killers) of Chikamatsu. Finding in him a certain melancholy as well as a longing for a land of mystery, the author attributes that longing to a desire for reaching the source of life through women. Thus the hero Yohei is given the soul of a Don Juan. In the drama his deep desire to live in Nagasaki is depicted, but of course the town has a symbolic meaning. In another work, *Nezumi* (The Rat) (January 1912), a boy named Yumemaru tells us that things of mystery should not be known by man and that he who comes to know them will be unhappy. Nonetheless, man cannot help but come to know them, adds the boy.

Treading in the steps of Mokutarō, Isamu could not advance, and his views were far less profound than those of the former. In a word, his intention lay, as he expressed it in *Nezumi*, in drawing "an azure dream," and this romantic world of fantastic melancholy was to be later embodied in works depicting the world of impoverished people of the streets, the subject of his dramas in the Taishō Era.

Kubota Mantarō became a disciple of Osanai Kaoru while he was a student of Keiō University where Kaoru was professor of literature. He made his début in the theatrical world with *Purorōgu* (Prologue) (1911), a prize-winning play in the magazine *Taiyō* (The Sun). Soon after, the author published the sequel, *Zoku-Purorōgu* (Prologue, the Sequel), in *Mita Bungaku*. The hero Yōjirō, a middle school student, is a boy weak in mind as well as in body who lives in resignation and self-pity both characteristic of a depressed city-dweller. The drama unfolds the conflicts between the old and the new centering around the boy, who is the son of an old merchant family in Nihombashi, the traditional business center of Tōkyō. With the method of realism, the author depicts the decaying customs and sentiments before the rise of the modern way of thinking, practical as well as rational. The peculiarity of this drama is a dark, emotional undertone which characterizes the rest of his works which follow. Among them we find *Kuregata* (Twilight), a drama which, according to the author, was inspired by Mokutarō's *Izumiya Somemono-Mise* that had helped him orientate himself. *Kuregata* is a sketch of an evening of festivity in Asakusa, downtown Tōkyō, and the scene takes place in front of an old shop selling *samisen*. By means of conversations exchanged among the people visiting the store, the author poetically describes the rise and fall of the residents of the district and their character. Indeed, this is an elegy for things that are going to ruin. *Yuki* (The Snow) (March 1912) was a sketch of a solitary life in a poor back-street shop.

In dramas as well as novels, his realism has the sentiment of *haiku* poets, so that inconspicuous affairs of life are merged with their background, those elements peculiar to the region and the season. With such a writer as Mantarō, no obvious influence from Western drama is recognizable.

Akita Ujaku (Tokuzō), co-editor of the *Shinshichō* with Osanai Kaoru, published in March 1909 *Kinenkai no Zen'ya* (The Eve of the Anniversary Ceremony) (*Waseda Bungaku*) and in April of the following year *Kaikyō no Gozen* (The Forenoon at the Straits). His works *Dai-ichi no Akatsuki* (The First Dawn), performed in June 1911 by the Jiyū Gekijō, and the simultaneous publication of *Gensō to Yakyoku* (Fantasy and Nocturne), a book of short novels and dramas, established his position in the literary world. He is also the author of *Kyū-hanshu to Kaji* (The Ex-Governor of a Clan and a Fire) (January 1912), *Uzumoreta Haru* (The Buried Spring) (April 1912), etc. Ujaku became influenced by Naturalism in about 1908, but it was not until after the end of the Meiji Era that this influence revealed itself in his dramatic works. Sentimental and romantic tendencies prevail in the works published during Meiji.

In *Dai-ichi no Akatsuki* a young samurai who has gone to Nagasaki for Western studies, once back in the country loses the favor of his master, the head of the clan, because of his far-sighted opinions. Subsequently the unwelcome youth commits murder in madness and, in turn, falls a victim of the fight. Though the young man brought the news of the advent of a certain "great dawn," nobody accepted it. This "great dawn" was symbolical of the heretical ideal which the slain youth was longing for under the influence of Western learning. In his case, too, the efforts on behalf of that ideal, the object of his longing, end in inevitable tragic fate, madness, and premature death. One thing that distinguishes Ujaku from other *Subaru* writers is his belief that the ideal should not be merely the object of longing, but should also be realized on this earth where we live. Thus, he finds ethical value in the madness and death of this unhappy hero. *Uzumoreta Haru* is a drama of the accidental death of a boy and a girl as a result of carelessness of adults. Employing a provincial dialect that gives local color, this work sketches the spring landscape of a northern country with deep compassion for the lost young lives.

When Osanai Kaoru for the second time started his magazine *Shinshichō* (Current of New Thought) in August 1909, Tanizaki Jun'ichirō became one of his collaborators. The author of many novels, Jun'ichirō gained a reputation as an able dramatist by publishing such plays as *Tanjō* (The Birth) (*Shinshichō*, September 1910), *Zō* (An Elephant) (October 1910), *Shinzei* (The Terror of Shinzei) (*Subaru*, January 1911).

This last work takes up the historical personage of the scholar Shinzei and describes the terror of wisdom and the inevitability of fate. Shinzei, a man of clairvoyance, foreseeing the terrible destiny that awaits him, hides himself in the depth of Mount Shigaraki in an attempt to escape from it. Still the inauspicious star that predicts his fate does not cease to watch him. The wise man then desperately begins to live underground. Despite all these efforts to escape, his inevitable fate is that he must die. Neither his profound learning, the like of which cannot be found even among contemporary Chinese or Indian scholars, nor his wide experiences of a life of more than seventy years are of use in escaping his miserable death or in emancipating himself from his attachment to life and his fear of fate. The drama is filled with an extraordinary and gloomy atmosphere. Including this work, the early products of Jun'ichirō usually deal with a decadent cultural life in the past. The stage-setting he designed for his dramas was always too elaborate, but actually the author intended less to have them performed than to write them for reading.

Dramatists belonging to the Shirakaba school were Kayano Nijūichi (Kōri Torahiko) and Mushakōji Saneatsu. The former inclined to mood drama after the fashion of the *Subaru* writers, while the latter wrote humanistic works in common with the members of the *Shirakaba*. Of this group, we have another writer, Arishima Takeo, who is the author of a drama entitled *Rōsenchō no Gensō* (The Fantasy of an Old Captain) (1910).

Kayano Nijūichi became acknowledged as a dramatist from about the time when his *Dōjōji* (The Temple of Dōjō) was acted by the Jiyū Gekijō in 1912. His preceding works consist of *Kanawa* (The Iron Hoop) (*Subaru*, February 1911), *Fuhai Subekarazaru Kyōjin* (A Madman Who Will Not Go to His Ruin) (*Shirakaba*, May 1911), etc. *Dōjōji* was a revision of *Kiyo-Hime* (The Love of Kiyo-Hime) (*Subaru*, June 1911). It is interesting to note, however, that some critics preferred the original to the revision. The story develops in this way : The priest Myōnen of the Dōjō Temple is now under the curse of Kiyo-Hime because he has protected his pupil Anchin from her love. The curse acts upon him and desire for carnal love torments him. To relieve himself of this curse, he has a woman artisan cast a bell for the temple. One day the bell is finished, and on that night Kiyo-Hime, changing herself into a witch, swims across the Hidaka River. The woman who cast the bell is murdered and Myōnen also falls a victim. The entire temple is destroyed by fire. In *Dōjōji* the original is so revised as to exaggerate the cruelty with more elaboration. *Kanawa* is a drama mystically depicting the same passion of jealousy. Generally speaking, fire and blood, passion and mystery are common in the majority of his dramas, such as *Yoshio no Doyomi* (The Roar of the Night Tide) (February 1912) and *Fuhai Subekarazaru Kyōjin*. However,

Chichi to Haha (Father and Mother) (January 1911), treating modern life, is rather a superficial work with some exaggeration in its expression of emotions.

In contrast with Kayano, Mushakōji Saneatsu of the same Shirakaba school tried by means of the drama to express his own thought in a simple way. His talent in theatrical writing was not fully demonstrated before the years of the Taishō Era. Thus, during Meiji he wrote no more than three plays : *Aru Katei* (A Certain Family) (1910), *Momoiro no Heya* (The Rose-Colored Room) (January 1911), and *Aru Hi no Yume* (A Certain Dream) (February 1912).

In *Momoiro no Heya*, there appear two contrasting characters, a young man who lives in a rose-colored room and a woman who lives in a gray one. The man represents an aristocratic humanism that esteems and tries to foster man's ego, and admires love and beauty. "The gray woman" is the symbol of socialism that, in envy of others' happiness, advocates an idea of false equality, asserting that all men should be equal in poverty, evil, unhappiness, etc. Juxtaposing them, the author expresses his view that inequality, misfortune, and the like can be eliminated from human life not by means of equalization but only through the strength of ego grown fruitful and truly great, attainable through protecting man's inner life. This thought of his shows the direction of the course Saneatsu would take in later years. One may regard this piece as an idealistic drama of Symbolism written to advocate such a view. Furthermore, in *Aru Hi no Yume* the author tells us that he who tries to develop his ego must undergo such sufferings as nurturing himself on his own life's blood. Through all of these works we find shining that bright personality of Saneatsu, simple as well as candid. Maeterlinck, Ibsen, and other dramatists are said to have influenced this writer, but he created works peculiar to himself.

In the last five years of the Meiji Era, under various influences of Western works, modern plays began to appear in Japan. True, they were still in bud, but these buds were a promise of the rich efflorescence to come. In early Meiji, the playwrights had started groping for reform in the drama, and, after straying many times on the way, they could finally discern their destination. Indeed, the history of Meiji drama is the changing phases of this groping effort. Such hardships had to be surmounted in order to bring about that colorful age of the drama in the subsequent Taishō Era.

PART FIVE MEIJI NON-FICTION

CHAPTER I ESSAYS, EXPOSITORY WRITING, AND MISCELLANEOUS PROSE

1. *The Essays and Expository Writings of the Authors of the Enlightenment*

We shall begin a general survey of Meiji non-fiction by examining the works of a few writers of the Japanese Enlightenment. Many studies have been made of Fukuzawa Yukichi. We shall limit our review to several of his works which are of considerable importance in the study of Meiji literature.

Gakumon no Susume (Encouragement of Learning) (1872–1876) was the first book of the Enlightenment which gave direction to the people of all classes who were looking for guidance in the period of intellectual confusion at the beginning of Meiji after the abolition of the clans and the institution of the prefectures. The first few lines of the above-mentioned book stated the essence of Fukuzawa's philosophy: "Heaven never created one man above another nor one man below another." Fukuzawa advocated the destruction of the feudal order and the establishment of a new social order wherein all the people would have equal rights as citizens. He denied the vertical alignment of the social classes which was based on Confucian ethics and espoused the liberty and equality which were based on modern Western democracy. He favored progress toward the material civilization of the West and away from the spiritualism (*seishinshugi*) of the East. Fukuzawa was sympathetic toward Anglo-American empiricism and utilitarianism; he was too practical and had too great a desire to instruct the people to waste his time in fruitless academic discussion. Thus, he expounded his philosophy of life whenever he had the opportunity.

According to Fukuzawa, all men are created equal; they

utilize material wealth for their living, and they become independent personalities by associating with others. Their reasoning faculties, which they acquire through education, make their
lives more abundant. Each individual comes to be respected
by others through social intercourse. Herein lies the temporal
progress of man. As man responds to reason he is able to
succeed both economically and socially. Here then is the motive for encouraging learning. Fukuzawa also believed in the
intellectual advancement of society by means of the mutual
association of people. These were the principal ideas on which
his *Gakumon no Susume* was based, and he maintained these
ideas, virtually unchanged, throughout his life. This work indicated that Fukuzawa had attained the highest level of understanding of Western civilization for his time. Its influence was
immense, and it was reprinted seventeen times in the five-year
period after the publication of the first edition. Statistically,
there was one copy of Fukuzawa's book to every one hundred
fifty or one hundred sixty people in Japan. The simplified literary style in which the book was written had much to
do with its popularity. Moreover, he employed a direct and
lucid language which appealed to the common people.

In 1875 Fukuzawa wrote *Bummeiron no Gairyaku* (Outline
of a Critique of Civilization), and by means of it he answered
the criticism of his *Gakumon no Susume.* He particularly
endeavored to clarify and unify his ideas so that he could
challenge the adverse criticism of upper class intellectuals, such
as the conservative scholars of the Chinese classics. In this
book Fukuzawa almost completed his theory of civilization,
which became the foremost exposition of the subject for the
first half of the Meiji Period. *Bummeiron no Gairyaku*, unlike
Gakumon no Susume, was written with a carefully prepared
methodology ; it fixed limits to the discussion and concentrated
on the meaning of civilization. He thought the problem of
wisdom (*chitoku*) should be the focal point of the argument,
and he discussed it not only from the historical but also from

the geographical point of view. Fukuzawa examined the origins of the Japanese as well as the European civilization. He then concluded that Japanese civilization should follow the pattern of that of the West, for he considered this to be the only way that Japan could maintain its independence. In this work the author succeeded in providing a logical basis to his arguments of *Gakumon no Susume*, and established his theory of relative values founded on social intercourse : "The existence of a thing may produce a theory concerning it whereas the opposite can never be true." This was the scientific basis of his philosophy of civilization. Fukuzawa never gave an absolute value to civilization, but rather explained that so-called civilization is the spirit which provides the incentive for the development of human society from a relatively barbaric to a relatively cultural state. Thus, this spirit of civilization should constantly be developing in and with the body of material civilization.

There were some who repudiated this philosophy despite the fact that it was appropriate for his time. In the latter part of his life, Fukuzawa himself wrote in his *Fuku-Ō Hyakuwa* (One Hundred Discourses of Fukuzawa), in which there are traces of Buddhist thought, that "man should not be overly involved in temporal affairs." He also said that "man should consider life in this world to be a mere pastime." If one did so, he felt, one could attain spiritual tranquillity irrespective of what happened in the course of one's life. This appears to contradict Fukuzawa's emphasis on temporal problems. It must be remembered, however, that he had two images of man : one was the concept of man as an economic, rational being ; the other was of man as a religious being.

Kanagaki Robun (Nozaki Bunzō) was the most popular humorous writer of the last days of the Tokugawa, and after the Meiji Restoration he further developed his style, thereby acquiring even more readers. When compared to Fukuzawa, it is true that he cannot escape the criticism of vulgarity, but nevertheless he occupied a unique position in the literary world when

almost everybody was devoting his energy to political writing
and very few were actually interested in works of literature.

He wrote a humorous tale entitled *Agura Nabe*, the Chinese
characters of which mean "A Dish of Relaxation, Foolishness,
and Enjoyment," where he parodied Fukuzawa's books of enlightenment by discoursing in a light vein on civilization.
Kiurizukai, a short work he wrote in 1872, was named after
Fukuzawa's *Kyūri Zukai* (An Illustrated Guide to the Natural
Sciences) (1868), but by a change of characters meant "How to
Use Cucumbers." In it he ridiculed the social classes of his
time by dubbing them variously Fortune, Appetite, Water,
Wind, Cloud and Rain, etc. For example, he changed the
characters which mean atmosphere (*kūki*) to mean "appetite,"
and proceeded to describe a country student who comes to
Tōkyō and who eats in various places, demonstrating a most
prodigious appetite. This type of low comedy could not hold
people's interest for long. Kanagaki seemed to realize this, and
in 1890 he held a large party in which he bade farewell to
the literary world, and retired to his retreat called Kobutsuan,
which means "The Ancient Buddha Hermitage."

Hattori Bushō (Seiichi) was a scholar of Chinese literature
who came to Tōkyō after the Meiji Restoration and wrote
Tōkyō Shin-Hanjōki (A Record of Tōkyō's New Prosperity) in
a simple Chinese style. In this book he described the rapidly
developing areas of the Ginza and Shimbashi, and various at-
tractions, such as a peep-show and a look through a telescope,
which were offered to the public. This was one way for an
old-fashioned scholar of the Chinese classics to keep abreast of
the times, and his work was an imitation of those Edo writers
who described the prosperous streets of Edo under the Tokugawa regime. Later he even wrote about the scandals and
gossip of the red-light districts.

Narushima Ryūhoku (Kinetarō) was also a popular writer in
the Chinese style at that time, but unlike both Robun and
Bushō, he possessed a unique style of great refinement. *Ryū-*

kyō Shinshi Nihen (The Second Volume of Yanagibashi News) (1874) was, as the title indicates, the second volume of *Ryūkyō Shinshi* which had been published at the end of the Tokugawa Period. He wrote about the Yanagibashi gay quarters in a florid but free style, observing detail with the trained eye of a professional, and contrasted it unfavorably with the old Yanagibashi of feudal days. He criticized the officials of the Satsuma and Chōshū clans who did nothing to preserve and improve its traditional spirit under the new regime. Ryūhoku showed how it externally flourished but was losing its former charm.

Ryūhoku was born in a famous Confucian family. From youth he had a carefree nature, and once was put under house arrest for an inadvertent comment he had made. He made use of the opportunity to acquire Western learning. Later, during the last few years of the Tokugawa Shōgunate, he was appointed the acting Director of the Budget Bureau. After the Meiji Restoration he never accepted invitations from the new government, and did not change his attitude towards the Meiji regime even though he was imprisoned for his connection with the *Chōya Shimbun* scandal. Indeed, he was a liberal in its Oriental sense. He looked for a pure element in literature and pleasure which would correspond to an ethic; he interpreted ethics in terms of *fūryū* (elegance); his concept of the independence of literature was based on the establishment of an ethic in literature. Ryūhoku's flowing, elegant style was loved by the upper class which shared his understanding of the Chinese classics; this presented a contrast with Robun whose simple style was admired by the lower class. Ryūhoku's school produced a magazine, *Kagetsu Shinshi* (The Flower and Moon Magazine), and the publication of this organ promoted a new trend in political novel writing in the next generation.

The period of Enlightenment was followed by a period of freedom and popular rights which reached its culmination in 1882.

The latter period produced not only political novels but also much expository prose in four main traditions. In the first place, Katō Hiroyuki became known for his argument in *Jinken Shinsetsu* (New Theories of Civil Rights) (1882); secondly, Taguchi Teiken (Ukichi) wrote *Nihon Kaika Shōshi* (A Short History of the Japanese Enlightenment) (1877–1882); thirdly, Nakae Chōmin (Tokusuke) wrote *Min'yaku Yakkai* (Commentaries on Civil Rights) (1882); fourthly, there developed a system of Christian thought, as indicated by the translation of the New Testament which was completed in 1879.

Katō Hiroyuki, who thought that German education was the most advanced, was a member of the Meirokusha and took an active part in the Enlightenment. He was thereafter appointed president of a university and occupied the highest position in the educational world. His main characteristics were the changing basis and persistency of his polemical attitude. In *Jinken Shinsetsu*, Katō repudiated the popular philosophy of the time, that of the natural rights of man, and then established a new universal theory which governed organic and inorganic creation as well as human beings. He taught that " the vegetable controls inorganic matter. The animal governs the vegetable. According to this pattern, the highly civilized society controls the lower, uncivilized society." His theory was based on evolution which could be developed through natural and artificial selection in terms of heredity and mutation. The natural rights theory was denounced because it was advocated by " a radical dreamer," Rousseau, and supported by " the light-hearted French people."

Hiroyuki completed the exposition of his theory in his *Kyōsha no Kenri no Kyōsō* (The Competition of Strong Men to Win Rights) (1893). In this period, Fukuzawa imitated the English empiricists, and Nakae favored the French revolutionists, whereas Katō looked to German transcendentalism.

The majority of the critics of the time, including disciples of Fukuzawa, attacked Katō on the ground of the latter's changing basis of argument and immature system of thought. They also produced excellent works which exerted a considerable influence upon Meiji literature. Baba Tatsui pointed out contradictions in Katō's theory in his *Tempu Jinken Ron* (The Theory of the Natural Right of Man) (1883). He stated that the fact that the natural right theory does not always contradict evolution was beyond Katō's comprehension, and therefore he confused the facts of the past with things which ought to come in the future. Yano Ryūkei (Fumio) wrote *Jinken Shinsetsu Bakuron* (A Rebuttal to *Jinken Shinsetsu*) (1882), a book which represented the reaction from among the members of the Kaishintō (The Reform Party). Toyama Chuzan (Shōichi) also wrote a book in the same year in which the title sentence stated, " I present a question to the author of *Jinken Shinsetsu* and thereby point out the ignorance of a newspaper man." By this time, Hiroyuki's theory had become discredited, in spite of his several rebuttals, and consequently the writers of the French and English schools had become more popular than those of the German school. At this period, Fujita Mokichi wrote a historical study, *Bummei Tōzenshi* (A History of the Eastward Advance of Civilization) (1884). In the first part of this two-part book he wrote about foreign relations and the importation of Western learning from the Temmon to the end of the Tempō Period, and in Part Two he praised the merits of Watanabe Kazan and Takano Chōei, who in the difficult Tempō Period had endeavored to advocate Dutch learning for the sake of the advancement of the country.

Taguchi Teiken was influenced by English economic theories. He led the theoretical development of the newly emerging citizen class and wrote a history, *Nihon Kaika Shōshi* (A Short History of the Japanese Enlightenment), in imitation of the Western style. He used a free style in organizing his work and did not pay too much attention to the details of chronology ; he merely divided Japanese history into two parts, the first of which was from the ancient period to the medieval period of chivalry, the Sengoku Jidai, (the age of civil wars), and the second from the Sengoku period to the present. Teiken stated that the progress of civilization was based on two factors, the development of "literature" and "monetary wealth." He was interested in giving a rational interpretation to individual historical facts rather than in studying a system of history. In his methodical approach to history he was similar to Fukuzawa.

Nakae Chōmin was the founder of learning of the French type which advocated social revolution. He experienced the Paris Commune while hew as studying in Paris, and after he came back to Japan, he established a school for French learning and discussed his plan for revolution. He published *Seiri Sōdan* (A General Theory of Politics) (1882–1883) at his own expense, and introduced a translation of Rousseau's *Social Contract* in this organ. *Seiri Sōdan* became very popular, so that, in a sense, Nakae became an Oriental Rousseau. His translation of the *Social Contract* was written in a serious Chinese style yet it was a simple and well-summarized translation with notes at the end. "The people possess two kinds of freedom. The first of the two is natural liberty. However, since the people, who are selfish by nature, tend to misuse this liberty, it is therefore necessary for them to have the second, and humanly regulated, liberty. This is a liberty created by the consent of the people who equally surrender their natural rights for a higher and distributive justice." Nakae called this second liberty political freedom.

Nakae's theory was accepted by those who advocated the doctrine of natural rights and civil liberty. Nakae, while engaged in scholarly study of theory, also participated in the civil rights movement and fought against autocratic government. Moreover, he was involved in various business enterprises as well as in the radical schemes of nationalistic expansionists, and, longing for a genuine hero, he went his confused way as a campaigner in the civil rights movement. In the latter part of his life he attempted to organize his own theory of materialism which he called "Nakaenism." When he was told that he was going to die because of his throat cancer, he wrote *Ichinen Yūhan* (One and a Half

Years) (September 1901), which was very popular because of its critical attitude towards every aspect of society. He also wrote *Zoku Ichinen Yūhan* (Sequel to *Ichinen Yūhan*) (October (1901), which showed very clearly the organization of his philosophy.

The last group, consisting of Christians, had its pioneers in the persons of Nakamura Masanao and Niijima Jō. Nakamura was born in a traditional Confucianist family yet later taught Christian doctrine, the core of Western civilization. Niijima established Dōshisha University in Kyōto in 1876 after he had overcome many difficulties. In Sapporo, Hokkaidō, there were two disciples of Clark, Nitobe Inazō and Uchimura Kanzō, who showed promise, while Uemura Masahisa began his evangelical work in Tōkyō with the help of five missionaries who came across the Pacific from the United States. In 1879 the New Testament was translated into Japanese. The completion of this translation was a symbol of the startling growth of the Christian movement. Since then, the Christian religion has had a profound influence upon the development of Japanese civilization, and particularly its literature.

Meanwhile, B. H. Chamberlain of Great Britain completed his translation of the *Kojiki*, entitled *The Kojiki or Record of Ancient Matters*, in 1882. This book indicated that a work of scholarship by an Englishman was far superior to that of any Japanese at that time and that foreigners' study of Japan had attained a high standard. In addition, E. F. Fenollosa, the teacher of Okakura Tenshin, undertook an excellent study in the field of ancient art.

2. *The Expository Writings of Romanticism and Idealism*

As a result of the movement for civil rights and liberty, parliamentary government was established, while in the literary world there emerged such colorful and passionate political critics as Sohō and Setsurei.

Tokutomi Sohō (Iichirō) was a graduate of Dōshisha. He wrote timely articles and published them in the newspaper that was edited by Taguchi Teiken. Sohō advocated the doctrine of a commonwealth in such famous articles as *Dai Jūkyūseiki Nihon no Seinen oyobi Sono Kyōiku* (The Youth of Nineteenth Century Japan and Their Education) (1885), the title of which was later changed to *Shin-Nihon no Seinen* (The Youth of New Japan), and *Shōrai no Nihon* (The Future of Japan) (1886). Sohō, like Yukichi, was interested in Anglo-American relative and concrete value theory rather than in the concept of eternity of German theory or in the French doctrine of revolution.

The cultural policy of the new government was based on the desire for reform and improvement rather than on the passion for revolution or admiration for the past. Sohō had confidence in the youth who would work for the reformation of Japanese culture. He discussed the problems of education and of the future capitalist society in his ambitious writings. "The government has given a parliament to the people. The education of the people through the parliamentary government should result in the prosperity of the nation. Meanwhile, the old feudal society has now been replaced by the new industrial society. Such replacement of the old society by the new is a worldwide tendency and can not be resisted." The content of this theory is similar to that of Fukuzawa. Nevertheless, Sohō had a broader philosophy of the world than Fukuzawa. He was also interested in concrete problems and their actual solution. He organized the Min'yūsha, and published the magazine *Kokumin no Tomo* (The Nation's Friend), which presented many problems to society along the line of orthodox progressivism.

Miyake Setsurei (Yūjirō) established the Seikyōsha (The Society for Political Education) and published his organ *Nipponjin* (The Japanese People). He also wrote *Shinzembi Nipponjin* (The True, Good, and Beautiful Japanese People) (1891), *Giakushū Nipponjin* (The False, Evil, and Ugly Japanese People) (1891), and *Gakan-Shōkei* (My Own Philosophy) (1892). Setsurei's school of writing showed a contrast with that of Sohō. This school represented the nationalistic aspect of the civil rights and liberty movement which reflected the strong desire of the people to emancipate local governments from the autocratic rule of the central government. However, we must pay special attention to the distinction between nationalism in Meiji and the present concept of nationalism. Meiji nationalism was based on the criticism of the superficial Westernization and the discontent over the so-called unequal extraterritoriality treaties which had been concluded between Japan and the Western powers. Setsurei occupied a position between the government and the people, and therefore he could freely lead the people and criticize the government at the same time.

Sohō was interested in historical analysis, whereas Setsurei was known for the depth of his philosophical thought. Setsurei wrote *Uchū* (Universe) (1909) after his *Gakan-Shōkei*. In this later work, he attempted to unite Japanese thought with Western philosophy. A similar attempt has been made by Nishimura Shigeki in his *Nihon Dōtoku Ron* (On Japanese Morality) (1887).

The Ken'yūsha group led the golden age of literature from about 1885, but this leadership reached an impasse by 1893 because of its narrow understanding of Western culture.

Meanwhile, Kitamura Tōkoku (Montarō) and other members of *Bungakkai* produced a new type of critical writing which represented the new realization of man's internal self. Tōkoku shared the zeal of the proponents of the civil rights and liberty movement, but he was also influenced by the broader world-philosophy of Christianity. Since Tōkoku was sensitive enough to absorb all the above-mentioned influence, he was led to a discovery of the basic principle that underlay the modern philosophy of the citizen. By the discovery of this principle, he established his humanistic philosophy of romanticism.

Tōkoku wrote *Enseishika to Josei* (The Pessimistic Poet and Woman) (1892) in which he related his own experience of love. The poet becomes pessimistic since he sees the basic discord of society; he is also unhappy in his married life; however, he can find and pursue the ideal beyond the reality only in the process of love. This was a denial of the present and an aspiration for absolute being; herein we can find the beginnings of romanticism. A new philosophy of love came to be established which was not based on eroticism as had been that of the merchant class of the Tokugawa Era.

Tōkoku applied the above-mentioned Platonic philosophy to his philosophy of the world in *Takai ni taisuru Kannen* (My Conception of the Other World) (1892), wherein he discussed heaven and hell. The ideal beyond this world supplied motives for such concepts as religion, poetry, beauty, and ugliness. He repudiated ancient Japanese literature in that it was too realistic. We recall that Fukuzawa criticized the same literature as being too unrealistic. He also expanded his theory to a philosophy of life in his book which was entitled *Jinsei ni Aiwataru to wa Nan no Iware zo* (It's No Use to Deal with This Worldly Affairs) (1893). In this work, he criticized Yamaji Aizan for discussing problems of this world, such as the success and failure of business enterprises, and never looking beyond them. A poet should look for an absolute ideal in heaven since there is no reward for him in this world of reality. Therefore, he should realize " the sad limit " of this world and seek and pursue an absolute existence in an abstract one.

Tōkoku organized his philosophy of man in *Naibu Seimei Ron* (Discussion of the Interior Life) (1893). We are looking for the absolute existence; however, we have the shadow of this ideal in our mind or internal self, and we call this romantic shadow life. The spirit of the universe (God) can wake the human spirit through the medium of " inspiration." This is the only moment we have to communicate with the universal spirit. As to the relation between the ideal and the human being, life provides a bridge between the two. Life is to be understood as a self which is reproduced rather than as a self-creating self. This romantic theory of Tōkoku was an expression of the Christian philosophy of man. Nevertheless, Tōkoku established his thought merely in the field of literature, and did not try to seek a reinforcement of his theory in religion and philosophy. For him, the momentary inspiration, the extreme and literary emotional passion were more important than the eternal, the absolute and religious moral love. He was only interested in theory to pursue the calling of literature. In a sense this meant the birth of a penetrating modern quality in literature.

Tōkoku succeeded in analyzing the problems of society and life on the basis of Christian philosophy. As a theory of literature, his argument was based on idealism rather than romanticism. He could not establish an idealistic philosophy of the world through his analysis of romanticism because the romantic approach could hardly influence the actual working of society. However, we owe a special debt to Tōkoku, who provided romanticism with a theoretical basis established on the new philosophy of life. He introduced a romantic approach to literature as an analysis of the entire human personality.

Meanwhile, in addition to the above-mentioned works on ethics and religion, Tōkoku wrote some lyrical and subjective works on nature and the universe, wherein he tried to see the projected shadow of his self. He showed a pantheistic tendency in *Matsushima ni oite Bashō o Yomu* (On Reading Bashō at Matsushima) (1892), *Yūkyō no Shōyō* (Wanderings on the Border of Mystery) (1892), *Shūsō Zakki* (Miscellaneous Writings from an Autumn Window) (1892), *Fugaku no Shishin o Omou* (Meditating on the God of Poetry at the Summit of Mt. Fuji) (1893), *San'an Zakki* (Miscellaneous Writings at a Mountain Hut) (1893), and *Bambutsu no Koe to Shijin* (The Voice of the Universe and the Poet) (1893). These works, like those of the Sanrai-Ha, also represent the Oriental view of life.

Hoshino Tenchi (Shinnosuke), Togawa Shūkotsu (Meizō), Baba Kochō (Katsuya), and Hirata Tokuboku (Kiichi) discussed problems of life and literature as members of the *Bungakkai* group together with Tōkoku. Some of them relied upon the quietism of the Japanese feudal era and criticized modern realism. Others were inspired by Western civilization, praised its philosophy of " self," and respected its spiritual freedom. Shimazaki Tōson (Haruki) and Ueda Ryūson (Bin) learned the problems of youth and literature through their own experiences and struggles. They studied these problems with a pure emotional development and provided new material for the consideration of the coming generation.

Uchida Fuchian (Mitsugi) anonymously wrote a book entitled *Bungakusha to Naru Hō* (How to Become a Man of Literature) in December 1893 in which he undertook an extensive criticism of the writers of his time from various points of view. " The man of literature is the happiest and the wealthiest animal. He who wants to be a writer must know the condition of the literary world rather than literature itself. It is more necessary to be handsome and idle than to have an understanding of and sensitivity toward literature. A successful writer must not only have a conspicuous appearance but have a fashionable residence and an exclusive group of friends. He also must advertise himself, despise worldly affairs, and pretend to have a sense of elegance and special expert knowledge. This is the typical attitude of the present famous writers towards life." Uchida found this type of writer among the Min'yūsha, *Jogaku Zasshi*, *Bungakkai*, *Sanrai*, *Yomiuri Shimbun*, *Asahi Shimbun*, Ken'yūsha, *Waseda Bungaku*, and *Shigarami Zōshi* groups. He gave obvious nicknames to the famous writers of his time, such as *Namida no Taika* (Great Sentimentalist), *Gakuyaochi Seizō Taika* (Great Creator of Backstage Passwords), and *Kobun Kirinuki Taika* (Great Plagiarist of the Classics). He even criticized Shōyō, Ōgai, and the Ken'yūsha and *Bungakkai* groups. Shōyō, he contended, not only was a protégé of a tutelary deity, Shakespeare, but also established a place to sell amulets which would help other protégés to misunderstand Shakespeare's works. Ōgai was the foremost intellectual in Japan, and he was an idol who was worshipped by children.

Lastly, the above-mentioned two groups were large groups which consisted of exceedingly conceited authorities; indeed, there were too many so-called great men in the literary world.

Despite the fact that Fuchian's criticism consisted mainly of occasional satire and that he did not directly define his own position, the main theme of his argument was very clear, logical, and consistent. His view of literature developed under Futabatei Shimei's influence, and it belonged to the French and Russian schools. Fuchian taught that the objective of literature should be to explore the truth of human life. If we describe reality, pursue the truth in this reality, and undertake self-criticism, then we should produce a work that is new, beautiful, and moral and which repudiates the old order. His thought started from reality and arrived at the ideal, but it never stood aloof from reality. We should work on the real problems, and through this work we would achieve an internal and an external revolution. The so-called " big " writers seemed to be aloof from the real problems; however, they actually not only strove for applause but truckled to the times. Therefore, they were a band of the most worldly-minded men, in spite of the fact that they were proud of being arbiters of elegance. Of course, the Ken'yūsha was exposed to the main force of his criticism, but even the other schools could hardly escape from this criticism completely.

Prior to the publication of *Bungakusha to Naru Hō*, Fuchian wrote *Bungaku Ippan* (Literature in General) in 1892, and defined literature as the study of various phenomena concerning life. He divided the elements of literature into poetry and philosophy and discussed its social character. This corresponds to the method of analysis which he used in *Bungakusha to Naru Hō*. Fuchian took the attitude that included philosophy, science, and other critical methods into the thinking of literature. This seemed to have established a basis for the realistic as well as the humanistic and socialistic philosophy of literature.

Among the works of the collateral groups which were criticized by Fuchian, there was an introduction to socialism which was written by Sakai Yūzaburō for *Kokumin no Tomo*. Sakai belonged to Nakae Chōmin's socialist school which was somewhat related to Fuchian's French and Russian schools. There was also a Christian group, closely connected with that of the *Bungakkai*, in which the leadership of Kanzō and Masahisa was gradually increasing in importance. Roka and Doppo were also developing in this group for their activities in the forthcoming generation. As a whole, as we can see in the works of Fuchian, the various streams of Western progressive thought were united in this period and formed a broad coalition which consisted of English, French, and Russian thought, as well as socialism and Christianity. Meanwhile, philosophical as well as traditional thought of the German school produced Ōgai and Chogyū, alongside Tōkoku and Fuchian.

Mori Ōgai (Rintarō) was educated under Nishi Amane, and belonged to the German school of Hiroyuki and Tetsujirō. He learned from Nishi Amane's *Hyakuichi Shinron* (One Hundred and One New Arguments) (1874) the distinction between the cultural and natural sciences (psychology and physics), and he also inherited the latter's attitude towards life. Both Ōgai and Nishi Amane were government officials in their public capacity, and they spent their private lives in participating in the move-ment of enlightenment. Ōgai was a military doctor as well as a writer. Having two facets as a writer, intelligence and poetical sentiment, he exerted great influence on the various strata of society for a long time. If we limit our observation of Ōgai to this period, we find that he held a high government position, and reared the German system of philosophy as an important citadel in rivalry with the English and French philosophies of literature which were supported by Shōyō and Fuchian.

Ōgai criticized Setsurei and Shinsen for being too nationalistic. Meanwhile he was not satisfied with English literature which he felt lacked a logical basis, and criticized the actual works by Kōyō and Rohan from aesthetic standards. Since Ōgai repudi-

ated the tendency to express his opinions through the creation
of art (he did not attach any significance to the position that his
writing should influence society, as Fuchian thought important),
he was interested in writing a work which had an artistic value
as a finished and organized work. If we observe Ōgai's system
of aesthetics in comparison with Hartmann's, we find that it
shares the same thinking with realism and copying of life as to
the point that the highest level of beauty can be seen only in " the
individual idea of reason " which possesses intrinsically the character of " a small universe." However, it corresponds to the Oriental
and traditional tendency when it seeks something transcendental
beyond the limit of experience according to the tradition of
German philosophy. On this point Ōgai was in sympathy with
Rohan and Ichiyō. As Ōgai believed in the independence of
art, he was able not only to separate the problem of aesthetic
pursuit from his social life as a military doctor, but also could
stay aloof from the current trend among the famous and lesser
critics of literature who created the golden age of Naturalism.
In 1909 Ōgai announced his position as being one of " resignation," and thereafter began to write about his state of mind in
terms of *asobi* (dilettantism) and *bōkan* (observation). However,
Ōgai had already stated his opinion on literature and social
problems prior to the declaration of this philosophical position.

Shigi no Hane Kaki (The Stroking of a Snipe's Wings) (1896)
contained much criticism against writers of his generation ; *Chie-
bukuro* (A Bag of Wisdom) (1898) was a book on the conduct
of life. After Ōgai moved to Kokura, he wrote *Ōgai Gyoshi to
wa Tare zo* (Who Is this Fisherman called Ōgai ?) (1900), and
showed that he had moved some distance away from the literary
circle of his time. In *Shintōgo* (Words of the Mind) (1900–
1901), *Zoku-Shintōgo* (Words of the Mind, Continued) (1901),
Keigo (Words of Wisdom) (1903–1904), and *Mōjin Mōgo* (A
Blind Man's Blind Words) (1903–1904), Ōgai stated his philosophy
of life, and clearly explained human personality in terms of
German philosophy. Human beings have the objectives of main-

taining an independent personality and achieving its perfection. It is no more advisable to talk too much about one's own strong points than to confess one's weak points to others, since both are basically meaningless. If a master of a household faces an unendurable difficulty, he must meet the other members of his family calmly after he has cried alone and solved the difficult problem by himself. It is foolish to become too friendly with others. A man should not talk unless it does good and is useful to him and the world. He who has a hope for the future and is responsible for his conduct pursues the perfection of his personality as an independent person. This does not conflict with the development and improvement of the society and the world. Rather, we must go ahead towards the permanent values hand in hand. In this context, secular position and status in society should be regarded as things which correspond to the value of his personality. From this position, Ōgai made several many-faceted studies of the reasons for the existence of the social order and cultural values.

As Ōgai's viewpoint was extremely broad, embracing almost all areas of human endeavor and transcending the historical process, he stood outside the mainstream of the literary world, but succeeded, nevertheless, in influencing the latter throughout his entire life. In short, he created in himself the reverse side of literary history. It is interesting to compare Ōgai with the literary theorists of the English, French, and Russian schools who had come into the literary world with fresh new ideas, were corrupted, disappeared into obscurity, and left fragmentary contributions to literary history on the so-called front side.

The impasse of the literary circle was ended by Takayama Chogyū's (Rinjirō) *Takiguchi Nyūdō* (The Lay Priest Takiguchi) in 1894. At the beginning of the same year, *Bungakusha to Naru Hō* was also published. Chogyū was active as a critic of civilization who belonged to the German school; he was different from Ōgai, however, and of course did not have any direct connection with Tōkoku, who was influenced by English Romanticism. Chogyū worked for the first publication of *Teikoku Bungaku* (Imperial Literature) in 1895, wrote a few critical articles about Chikamatsu that made him famous, was put in charge of expository writings of literature for the *Taiyō* (Sun) in the same year, and became the editor-in-chief of the magazine two years later. After he wrote *Takiguchi Nyūdō*, he began to write in an increasingly florid style and gave rise to a trend of romanticism. Chogyū's early thought, which can be known from such writings as *Nihonshugi* (Japanism) (1897), was as nationalistic as that of his friend, Inoue Tetsujirō, and it represented the high tide of the movement toward the realization of the romantic self as a result of Japan's victory over China. This so-called Japanism was different from the nationalism advocated by Setsurei and Sohō. In his theory, Chogyū tried to combine the realization of the individual self seen in Ōgai's thought with the pride of nationalism, and thereby to awaken each person as the possessor of a national characteristic of which he could be proud before the rest of the world. Such a synthesis was in conformity with the spirit of the times, and it was completely different from Ōgai's idealism of the German school which transcended such a spirit.

Soon Chogyū went on to discuss the spirit of the times, presented various new problems to the literary world, and published in 1901 two articles, *Bummei Hihyōka to shite no Bungakusha* (The Man of Letters as a Critic of Civilization) and *Biteki Seikatsu o Ronzu* (Discussing the Aesthetic Life), in which he discussed two kinds of self, one that affirms one's instinct and the other that denies the existence of others. This argument coincided with Neitzsche's thought. As an admirer of Nietzsche, he advocated the idea of a Superman, so that he could transcend the reality of society with a self, and the aesthetic life based on the instinct. Shōyō called this thought dangerous, but Ōgai said that there was nothing to fear since Chogyū's argument was Nietzschean thought "without teeth." By about this time, Japanese literary thought had caught up with that of the Western world.

Chogyū, who experienced the cause of Japan and the spirit of the times and who arrived at a complete philosophy of self, changed his theory for the third time to advocate the principles of Nichiren, and wrote *Kyōgoroku* (1901) and *Nichiren Shōnin to wa Ikanaru Hito zo* (What Kind of a Person Is the Sage Nichiren?) (1902). This is a key to his personality, which had a traditional as well as a modern aspect, for his life in the literary world began with *Takiguchi Nyūdō* and ended with the principles of Nichiren. Chogyū came to know Nichiren under the influence of Tanaka Chigaku, and came to share the latter's sympathy toward this traditional and nationalistic religionist who had a strong ego. This sympathy was most strongly directed toward Nichiren's magnificent and passionate style. Towards the end of his life, Chogyū became rather introspective, and *Mudairoku* (A Titleless Record) (October 1902), which was written immediately before his death, contains the following sentences: "If we wish to know the true aspect of this world, we must transcend this world of affairs. We must separate ourselves from all learning and morality, and thereby observe the world with the pure mind of a new-born babe." In this section of the book, he yearned for a child's mind, which would be "as beautiful as a shining jewel" and also "as translucent as water," and showed his humble intention of returning to nature. However, until the very end he did not lose his innate Dionysian character.

Chogyū also wrote many belletristic essays, such as *Waga Sode no Ki* (A Record of My Sleeve) (1897), *Tsukiyo no Bikan ni tsuite* (On the Sense of Beauty of a Moonlit Night) (1899), *Heike Zakkan* (Miscellaneous Thoughts on the Taira Clan) (1901), and *Seishiroku* (A Record of Quiet Thinking) (1902). All the essays were composed in so beautiful a style that they almost demanded to be intoned with a ringing voice, as did many other essays written by the passionate and sentimental romantics. These essays fascinated the minds of the young people who were looking forward to the reform of Japanese and Chinese poetry. Although they are somewhat crude and empty-sounding, they still have poetical attractiveness because of their incisive thoughts as well as their high-flown style. In *Seishiroku*, which was written in the last year of Chogyū's life, there was no longer any superficial splendor but rather there appeared a note of simplicity and truthfulness. On the whole, Chogyū's belletristic works, which during his lifetime attracted the youth of the entire nation, were carried away by sentimentalism, covered up by rhetoric, and could not describe the naked human personality; however, we can find Chogyū's truthful voice in many of his fragmentary thoughts of *Mudairoku* (A Titleless Record).

Okakura Tenshin (Kakuzō) was contemporary with Chogyū, and also declared the beauty of Japan to the world with a romantic passion. From 1877, under Fenollosa's influence, Tenshin had come to recognize, through his study of Japanese art, the special value of Oriental art in contrast with that of the Occident. He started on a foreign tour in 1901, and completed *The Ideals of the East with Special Reference to the Art of Japan* in India; he wrote in 1902 *The Awakening of the East* and two years later (1904) *The Awakening of Japan* in Boston; he also finished in 1906 *The Book of Tea*. The author wrote all the above-mentioned books in English and praised the Oriental spirituality before the world.

The opening words of *The Ideals of the East*, "Asia is one," express the main theme of Tenshin. Tenshin said that the vast expanse of love, which extended to the extreme and the universal, is a thought that should be the heritage of all the Asian people. He also explained that this thought distinguished the Oriental from the Occidental people who lived around the Mediterranean and the Baltic Seas and tended to be interested in the concrete and to pursue not the object of life but the means of the life, and that this thought resulted in the emergence of all the great religions of the world in Asia. Tenshin praised the various countries of Asia and their different periods, and particularly Japanese art, in his high-flown, compact style. Japan was the museum of Asian civilization ; indeed, it was actually more than the museum. The history of Japanese art was the history of the Asian ideal. Of course there were various errors in historical fact, and the logic of the comparative study was not very sound, but it indicated the extent of Tenshin's insight into the problem as a world citizen that he succeeded in summarizing the characteristics of Oriental civilization and the depth of its religious and spiritual aspect through the study of art. This was an unparalleled achievement at the time.

Koizumi Yakumo (Lafcadio Hearn), who came to Japan in 1890 and became a Japanese citizen five years later, wrote tens of books praising the beauty of Japan, and introduced Japanese culture to the Western world. It was unavoidable that he should have been unable to have a true understanding of Japan and have seen it as a dreamlike world of mystery, in spite of his love for and aspirations with regard to Japan.

Tsunashima Ryōsen (Eiichirō) became a Christian when he was still young. When he grew up, he entered the Tōkyō Semmon Gakkō (later it became Waseda University), became a member of the editorial staff of *Waseda Bungaku* (Waseda Literature), together with Hōgetsu and Chikusui, studied philosophy and ethics under the influence of Ōnishi Sōzan, and influenced greatly the trend of romantic thought after the death of Chogyū. At first he belonged to the orthodox religious group which was guided by Uemura Masahisa and Yokoi Tokio, and then he sought an ethic, went to the expository writings of literature, and became interested in salvation by faith in an outside power which had been advocated by Hōnen and Shinran. However, he continued to pursue the study of Christianity with an earnest and humble attitude, and his study of religion attained its culmination in 1904 when he wrote *Yo ga Kenshin no Jikken* (My Experience of Seeing God). Ryōsen, who had already been suffering from an illness and found solace in " the benevolent persons, men of character, and religionists of this world," vividly describes his experience of seeing God three times : first, sometime in July, when he was sitting on his bed for about an hour in the middle of the night ; secondly, in September when he was on his way to the public bath and looked at the landscape in the light of the setting sun ; thirdly, on a certain night in November when he was about to write something. On all these occasions he saw an unusual, unexperienced glory. For him, this year 1904 was a joyful period of glory and revelation, and particularly the third occasion when " the real self, which until then was holding the writing-brush, in an instant was conscious of being transformed into an existence at the heart of heaven and earth ; the self was submerged, and I felt as if God Himself were actually holding the writing-brush," was " the most astonishing and frightening " experience of his life. It was not that he saw or met God, but that he realized the nature of God and himself, that is, in one moment he became God and God became him. *Byōkanroku* (Record of an Illness) (1905), which contained the section that referred to this experience, and *Kaikōroku* (Record of Revelation) (1907), which contained the essay *Yo wa Kenshin no Jikken ni yorite Nani o Manabitari ya* (What I Have Learned from My Experience of Seeing God), were the most popular collections of his work. In this latter essay, by deducing from his experience, he explained the elevation of faith, the relationship between heaven and man, as well as that between the Father and Son, the spiritual character of God, and his firm belief in eternal life.

Ōnishi Sōzan (Shuku), an excellent scholar of ethics, wrote three essays, *Waka ni Shūkyō Nashi* (There Is No Religion in *Waka*) (1887), *Hiai no Kaikan* (The Pleasure of Sorrow) (1891), and *Yasokyō Mondai* (Problems in Christianity) (1893), in which he stated a logical and dispassionate opinion and showed a·sympathetic attitude toward Christianity. Furthermore, Uemura Masahisa, a Protestant clergyman who contributed much to the establishment of the church belonging to the orthodox group, taught that religion must be familiar with literature, and influenced many men of letters. Nitobe Inazō became a world-famous person by living abroad, and his book *Bushidō* (The Code of the Warrior) (1899), in which he discussed the spirit of Japan, was considered so notable that it was translated into seventeen different languages. However, among the Christian expository writers, Uchimura Kanzō was the most colorful and distinguished figure.

An ardent Christian, Uchimura Kanzō, who studied the natural sciences and had the noble spirit of a *bushi* (warrior), published *Kirisuto Shinto no Nagusame* (The Consolation of a Christian) (1893), *Kyūanroku* (Record of a Search for Peace) (1893), *Yo wa Ika ni shite Kirisuto Shinto to Narishi ka* (*How I Became a Christian*) (1894), *Chijin Ron* (A Treatise on the Earthly Man) (1894) (the original name of the book was *Chirigaku-Kō*, On Geography, and the title was changed to *Chijin Ron* in 1897), *Daihyōteki Nihonjin* (Representative Japanese) (1897) (the original name of the book was *Nihon oyobi Nihonjin, Japan and Japanese*, and the title was changed to *Daihyōteki Nihonjin* in 1908), in English and Japanese after he came back from the United States, despite the *lèse-majesté* affair at the First High School, and showed the originality of his thought. The basis of his philosophy consisted of faith in a sole omnipotent God and the self-realization of the spirit which was responsible to God. Faith and self-realization became the flesh and blood of his thought. As man has no power to save himself, he must pray to God. Such a concept was similar to the thought of Hōnen and Shinran. Kanzō added to these ideas something traditional to the constructive Japanese common sense, that is, as the universe was created by a benevolent Heaven (God), one could be saved without wishing for such a salvation if he lived justly. Therefore, in a lecture entitled *Kōsei e no Saidai Ibutsu*

(The Greatest Legacy Left to Coming Generations) (1894), he taught that, "for the just purpose of making Japan a great nation, everyone should discipline himself and follow the laws of the universe, and that there lay a precious life for one who contributed to others, sacrificing himself in order to follow the teaching of God." In other words, one could not love and pray to God unless one practiced righteousness in this world.

In Kanzō's belief, the criticism of and the actual practice in the society had an important meaning. Such criticism and practice were undertaken surprisingly freely on the basis of the firm belief that one should save the individual eternal soul in the midst of the society. He twice became a reporter of the *Yorozu Chōhō* (1896 and 1900), and meanwhile established two magazines, *Tōkyō Dokuritsu Zasshi* (The Tōkyō Independence Magazine) (1898) and *Seisho no Kenkyū* (A Study of the Bible) (1903). His fiery articles attacked feudal convention, criticized the utilitarian trend of his time, repudiated the worldly influence of the church, and denounced the effeminated literature; indeed, there was almost nothing that escaped his criticism. It is almost needless to say that his was a prayerful attitude and self-abandonment, which was similar to the religious austerities of the small number of upright men who became Bodhisattvas; this was established on the so-called life-giving study of the Bible, the essence of Christianity, and also on the original idea of Christianity without a church, which was similar to the traditional order of Buddhism.

In 1903, immediately prior to the opening of the Russo-Japanese War, there were people who opposed the war along with Kanzō, such as Abe Isoo, a Christian and the author of *Chijō no Risōkoku : Suisu* (The Ideal Country on This Earth : Switzerland) (1904), Kinoshita Naoe, the author of *Hi no Hashira* (The Pillar of Fire) (1904), and also socialists such as Sakai Kosen and Kōtoku Shūsui. Shūsui, a disciple of Chōmin, wrote *Nijusseiki no Kaibutsu : Teikokushugi* (The Monster of the Twentieth Century : Imperialism) (1901) to oppose foreign aggression, relied upon Marxism in *Shakaishugi Shinzui* (The Essence of Socialism) (1903), and became the foremost socialist theorist of the time ; however, he could not completely understand the materialistic dialectic and the materialistic view of history, and ended only by "inciting martyrs and idealists." After he came back from abroad, he became an anarchist and was finally sentenced to death on a charge of high treason. All these thoughts belonged to the English, French, or Russian schools, as opposed to the German school, and responded to the movement of the literature of Naturalism. It was a common characteristic of all of them that the establishment of the self was sought for the individuality which opposed society and corresponded to the absolute.

At that time, although Japan was developing into a world power, it had various social contradictions internally, and also maintained extremely precarious relations with other strong powers externally. This opened a stage for discussion by various thinkers. First of all, Anezaki Chōfū (Masaharu), a close friend of Chogyū, wrote *Fukkatsu no Shokō* (The Dawn Light of Resurrection) (1904), advocated mystic religious thought, and promoted romanticism. Tanaka Chigaku of the Nichiren sect and Shaku Sōen of the Zen sect also advocated the ways of their respective sects, and a Buddhist theorist of the Jōdo sect, Kiyosawa Manshi, published the magazine *Seishinkai* (The Spiritual World) (1901), in which he espoused spiritualism. Even a journalist, such as Kuroiwa Ruikō (Shūroku), wrote *Tenjin Ron* (On the People in Heaven) (1903), and tried to explain the sources of morality in terms of spiritual monism. Philosophers such as Kuwaki Gen'yoku and Nishida Ikutarō planned to establish a new ethic and philosophy, Hatano Seiichi undertook a high level study of Western thought, and Ueda Bin demonstrated a complete appreciation of Western literature and introduced its new ideas. The people exposed themselves to the oppressive society and looked for a higher self in this importation of Western thought.

In addition, Takekoshi Sansa (Yosaburō) advocated internationalism (*sekaishugi*) through his periodical *Sekai no Nihon* (Japan of the World), first published in 1896. He distinguished himself by his original and penetrating criticism of prominent personalities. Yamaji Aizan (Yakichi) quit his job as editor-in-chief of *Gokyō* (Protection of Religious Teaching), a Christian magazine, entered the *Kokumin Shimbun* (The People's Newspaper), and later published the *Kokumin Zasshi* (The People's Magazine) and *Dokuritsu Hyōron* (Independent Criticism). He expressed original views in his historical and literary essays, and took an active part in polemics. Taoka Reiun's (Sayoji) *Reiun Yōei* (Reiun Quiverings) (1899) and *Gegoku-Ki* (Record of Imprisonment) (1901), and Yano Ryūkei's (Fumio) *Shin-Shakai* (The New Society) (1902) were noted for their social criticism. Even such a great writer as Rohan published *Kangen* (Remonstrance) (1901), *Chōgo* (Long Words) (1901), *Shiomachi-Gusa* (Grasses Awaiting the Tide) (1901), and *Katatsumuri-An Yadan* (Night Stories at the Snail Hut) (1907), which are collections of essays, short sketches, and works of research.

3. *The Expository Writings of Naturalism and Neo-Idealism*

During the period of Naturalism, Shimamura Hōgetsu (Takitarō) published the most remarkable expository writings. *Kindai Bungei no Kenkyū* (A Study of Modern Literature) (1909) can be considered the fruit of his works. This book contained very poetic articles such as *Torawaretaru Bungei* (The Captive Literature) (1906) and *Rui Ōke no Yume no Ato* (Traces of the Prosperity of the Royal Family of the Louis) (1906) which were written immediately after the author's return from abroad. Although the above-mentioned works were valuable as literature in themselves, we want here to discuss those articles in which the author dealt with Naturalism as the problem of a philosophy of life. (We shall refer in a later section to Hōgetsu's works in which the author undertook his discussion from the viewpoint of literary theory.) From this point of view, *Jo ni Kaete Jinseikanjō no Shizenshugi o Ronzu* (Instead of a Preface I

Discuss Naturalism from My View of Life) (1909) and *Shizenshugi no Kachi* (The Value of Naturalism) (1908) are significant, and together with these two articles, *Kaigi to Kokuhaku* (Suspicion and Confession) (1909) should also be read.

In *Jo ni Kaete*, the author stated : " I do not have a complete philosophy of life. All the existing philosophies of life have lost their true value before my scholarship." He cursed scholarship and said, " I hereby confess the actual state of my mind as being filled with suspicion and uneasiness." This statement corresponded to the motto which was printed on the cover of the book : art is " the world of contemplation " (*kanshō no sekai*). However, concerning knowledge (or scholarship), he considered the relationship between Naturalism and life, and stated in the concluding part of *Shizenshugi no Kachi* that " Naturalism has connection with general thought on three different levels." The first of the three levels is the destruction of convention and the making of a new departure. On this level, Naturalism is connected with morality. Secondly, a link is established between Naturalism and the experiential sciences by repudiating idealism and emphasizing reality. Thirdly, its religious tendency, which points to one absolute and mysterious being and is not satisfied with any mediocre explanation of religion, is united with the general current of thought which strives to depart from the existing religions. This is " the Oriental tendency to look at the absolute directly in the midst of reality." " The hitherto existing religions represented systems of thought to destroy and reform reality in order to achieve an end," but Naturalism was " a system of thought to enrich and enlarge reality in order to attain an end." Although there were many arguments concerning the realization of Naturalistic thought, the cry, " Let us take back the object of our aspiration to reality and give it the real life once more," represented the true voice of its adherents.

However, if we note that the above-cited *Jo ni Kaete* concluded with the statement which was written later, " For me, the so-called Naturalism in relation to a philosophy of life also means only one aspect of my suspicion," we can say that the author's approval of Naturalism was far from complete, and that he had chosen to confess his everlasting suspicion as to the real self in terms of literature.

In comparison with Hōgetsu, Tayama Katai did not have intellectual doubts, and since he was a writer who contemplated reality exactly as it is, his articles dealt mainly with the methods of describing that reality. As will be discussed in the following section of this book, Katai was satisfied with the world where there was no difference between life and death, or the animate and inanimate, which world he described by the method of impressionistic plane sketching. This gives us the impression that Katai did not go beyond Hōgetsu's first level of Naturalism. We can see Katai's attitude towards this literary movement in *Inki Tsubo* (Ink Bottle) (1909–1910), printed in *Bunshō Sekai* (The World of Writing), in "*Sei*" *ni okeru Kokoromi* (My Experiment in "Life") (1908), "*Tsuma*" *ni tsuite* (Concerning "The Wife") (1909), and *Byōsha Zatsuron* (Miscellaneous Discussions about Description) (1909), carried by *Waseda Bungaku* (Waseda Literature), and also in his criticism of Saikaku.

Hasegawa Tenkei (Seiya), in his essays which were printed in *Shizenshugi* (Naturalism) (first published in 1908), such as *Gemmetsu Jidai no Geijutsu* (The Art of the Period of Disillusionment) (1906), *Genjitsu Bakuro no Hiai* (The Anguish of Exposure to Reality) (1908), and *Shizen-Ha ni taisuru Gokai* (Misunderstanding of the Naturalist School) (1908), emphasized the need of facing reality scientifically and free from all preconceptions, traced the origin of similar attitudes towards art in the history of the West, and defined a kind of barrenness, which had always been experienced together with the destruction of the existing ideal, as "disillusionment" or "the anguish of exposure to reality." This feeling of anguish was understood to be a *fin-de-siècle* thought, and became a profound intellectual affirmation. However, it did not attain Hōgetsu's third level of Naturalism, the religious tendency.

In contrast with Tenkei who advocated a pessimism which denied the existence of any ideal or solution, Iwano Hōmei espoused the optimism of pathetic dogmatism, and explained his position in *Shimpiteki Hanjūshugi* (Mystic Semi-Animalism) (1906), *Shin-Shizenshugi* (Neo-Naturalism) (1909), and *Hitsū no Tetsugaku* (The Philosophy of Pathos) (1910). We can say that he stood on the so-called third level of Hōgetsu, broke through this level relying upon his own philosophy, came down to the second level to destroy scientism, and went as far as the first level as an affirmative action. The phrase " the gate to religion " (*shūkyō no mon*), which Hōgetsu used to represent reality, was meant to establish the reality which was immeasurably different from the absolute ideal, and it created an impassable abyss in the face of the dispassionate subject ; however, Hōmei over-passed this abyss with a passionate subject, and established a new philosophy which united momentarily the reality with the absolute being itself. This was the actual working of a subject which was half human and half animal ; such a philosophy was called Mystic Semi-Animalism.

This was a union of Symbolism and Naturalism which was popular among poets ; phenomena and the real existence, nature and the spirit, the body and the soul, were respectively united metaphysically, and then each unity was organized into one subject by the use of one character, *soku* (to wit). This kind of attitude presented a distinct contrast with that of Hōgetsu which looked for contemplation and confession in dispassionate suspicion, and gave the impression that Naturalism was divided into two schools. Hōgetsu still maintained an attitude of treating Naturalism aesthetically, whereas Hōmei said " art, to wit life," and went directly to reality. Many writers of Naturalism followed a somewhat Oriental tendency which was similar to the thought of Zen or to Tendai *shikan* (enlightenment), but the completely realistic and practical Hōmei sympathized with traditional Shintō, and showed himself to be nationalistic through such books as *Nihon Kodai Shisō yori Kindai no Hyōshōshugi o Ronzu* (Discussing Modern Symbolism on the Basis of Ancient Japanese Thought) (1907).

The above-discussed theories of Naturalism were followed by much favorable and adverse criticism. In the first place, if we observe the basis of Gotō Chūgai (Toranosuke), who published in 1908 an adverse thesis entitled *Hi-Shizenshugi* (Anti-Naturalism), we can see that he understood Naturalism on the level of Katai and Tenkei, criticized it as the presentation of reality without any solution or ideal, and stated that it was an expediency for everyone to enter into the real life which was to come by his own effort. It was, then, nothing more than "the gate of self-help" (*jiriki-mon*), which had to be placed on the opposite side of "the gate of improvement in reliance upon outside help" (*tariki-mon*) by advancing in the direction of a fixed ideal. If the literary art described reality as it was, unless it aimed at the ideal, it was bound to describe something other than reality. Herein lay the idealistic position that regarded the literary art itself as the human activity to achieve the ideal. If Chūgai had applied this theory in its extreme form, Naturalism would not have been admitted even as an expediency, and it would no longer have been regarded even as "the gate of self-help." Although Chūgai pointed out and refuted an important fault of Naturalism, he could not organize a new philosophy of life.

Next, Nakazawa Rinsen (Shigeo) published such books as *Binge-Shū* (Sidelock Flower Anthology) (1905) and explained the evolution from the old to the new civilization. With the passion of genius, the calm mind of the natural scientist, and a profound understanding of Western art, thought, and philosophy, Rinsen endeavored to achieve a logical philosophy as a pragmatist.

Moreover, among the critics of Naturalism, there were people who were not satisfied with a literary movement that could not give any solution to their problems, and took a compromise position by extracting the idealism out of Naturalism. Katagami Tengen (Noburu) of the Waseda school took the above-mentioned position and acquired socialist leanings after the beginning of Taishō. Ikuta Chōkō (Kōji) of the Tōkyō University school also shifted from Naturalism to socialism and later to religion. Tanaka Ōdō (Kiichi) showed his understanding of Naturalism in such articles as *Shosai Yori Gaitō e* (From the Study to the Street) (1911) and *Tetsujinshugi* (The Philosophy of a Wise Man) (1912), and organized various positions of Naturalism to establish a strong idealism under the name of *tetsujinshugi*. He had acquired learning in economics and philosophy, and opened a road for social criticism. Since he thought that the epoch-making development of culture was inevitable, first, he evaluated the validity of Naturalism, and advocated not only an experimental idealism against Hōgetsu's superior experimental realism, but also the philosophy of a wise man against Hōmei's semi-animalism. Therefore, a pattern was produced for Naturalism to move strongly toward a new ideal.

When Naturalism was introduced to Japan, the hitherto existing romanticism and idealism were temporarily destroyed. However, the Japanese writers could not adapt themselves to Western scientism completely, and they were also influenced by lyric and religious elements. This resulted in producing a basis for the emergence of a new romanticism and idealism. Thus, at the end of Meiji, the fact that when Naturalism was hardly established much anti-Naturalist thought arose, indicated not only the reaction to this literary movement but also the internal development of Japanese Naturalism, or at least the tendency to induce such a development.

However, such great writers as Ōgai and Sōseki had firmly maintained a position which was different from Naturalism. The Neo-Idealist critics around these writers, and the writers of the Shirakaba (White Birch) group who organized under their influence also stood clearly against it. The movement of the Shi-

rakaba group saved people from suffocating under the pressure
of reality, and led them to the ideal with artists' passion and will
to work; however, this latter group did not publish any noticeable polemical writing during the Meiji Period. Those who
recovered the romanticism and the idealism from Naturalism,
and established a deeper basis of logic for the Shirakaba group
were Abe Yoshishige, Abe Jirō, Komiya Toyotaka, and Watsuji
Tetsurō, who had matured under Sōseki's influence. They
were all introducers of recent Western literature and philosophy,
and argued freely in the field of the literary art.

It should be noticed that they had steeped themselves in
Western culture and that they observed, contemplated, and
explored the nakedly real world. This was different not only
from the writers of the Enlightenment who had built their own
philosophy, but from their predecessors, Ōgai and Sōseki, who
had imported and pursued substantially the Western literary
art. These younger men had studied mostly German conceptual
philosophy, but since they carried on their activity in the extremely
confused area of the Naturalist movement, they tried to find
their position between these completely contrasting thoughts.
We can see these efforts in Yoshishige's *Jiko no Mondai to
shite Mitaru Shizenshugi Shisō* (Naturalist Thought Seen as the
Problem of the Self) (1910) and *Shizenshugi ni okeru Shukan
no Ichi* (The Position of Subjectivity in Naturalism) (1910), and
in Jirō's *Kyōtan to Shibo* (Astonishment and Aspiration) (1909),
Naiseikatsu Chokusha no Bungaku (A Literature Directly
Describing the Interior Life) (1911–1912), *Dampen* (A Fragment)
(1912), and other articles which were included in *Santarō no
Nikki* (Santarō's Diary) and *Santarō no Nikki Hoi* (Additions
to Santarō's Diary).

These arguments were efforts to uncover the nature of sentiment and emotion, that spiritual reality which had almost
disappeared from sight in the consciousness of Naturalism.
This did not mean to return to the old idealism, but, through
Naturalism, to pursue a road which would lead to a new ro-

mantic world. This was also an attempt to reorganize all of the external world into the pattern of one's own thought by describing one's own internal world. Various articles by Jirō, Toyotaka (Hōryū), Yoshishige (Nōsei), and Sōhei, which were included in *Kage to Koe* (Shadow and Voice) (1911), represented an attempt to look for the new reality and ideal with a strong passion and profound reason. We can see in these articles a wandering of the spirit to search the deep places of life, and clear and serious efforts to organize such wandering into the form of expository writing.

At about this time, the growth of the new thought was helped by the newly advancing schools of Bergson's philosophy, Rudolf Eucken's religious theory and Theodore Lipps' aesthetics; moreover, as Nietzsche's emotionalism was reconsidered, and the literary world was filled by the light of "admiration of life," the haze which covered the Naturalist world of suspicion and indifferenec began to be eliminated. However, it was only in the Taishō Period that this current became the main stream of the literary world. In the realm of philosophy, remarkable works, such as Nishida Ikutarō's *Zen no Kenkyū* (A Study of Good) (1911), were achieved to announce the arrival of Neo-Idealism. However, we can only see the development of the new philosophy in the subsequent generation.

4. *Various Aspects of Travel Literature, Essays, and Diaries*

Japan has produced many excellent accounts of travels, and especially after the beginning of the Meiji Period, it had considerable success in this field of literature. This success resulted from the newly acquired freedom of domestic as well as international travel and also from the use of a fresh style and method of observation.

In the first place, Kōyō and Rohan, who were regarded as the two great luminaries in the literary world, wrote excellent accounts of travels. For example, *Enka Ryōyō* (A Change of Air) (1899), the original title of which was *Hogo Zakkori*

(Waste Paper and Rags), was written by Kōyō on his trip from Hokuriku to Sado for the purpose of recovering his health after the exhaustion of having written *Konjiki Yasha.* Besides this work, Kōyō published other accounts of travel such as *Sado-Buri* (A Trip to Sado), *Zoku Sado-Buri* (A Trip to Sado, Continued), and accounts of trips to Shiobara, Shuzenji, and Chōshi. Rohan felt an internal perturbation in 1890 and went on various travels with severe mental anguish. On these trips, he wrote penetrating accounts of Hakone in works such as *Kyakusha Zappitsu* (Miscellaneous Writings at an Inn), of Chūgoku, Shikoku, and Kyūshū in *Makifude Nikki* (A Diary of Makifude), and of Mt. Akagi in *Jigokudani Nikki* (A Diary of Hell Valley). He published *Chintō Sansui* (Nature at One's Bedside) in 1893, which contained three other accounts of travels, *Ekishin Kōgo* (of travels in Ōu and Hokuriku in 1892), *Tokkan Kikō* (of travels in Ōu), and *Suikyōki* (Record of Drink and Amusement) (of travels in Shinshū and Yashū in 1888), in addition to *Makifude Nikki* and *Jigokudani Nikki.*

The readers of the time were more attracted by a beautiful style than by the elevated thoughts it expressed; moreover, since interest in travel had been increasing ever since the end of the Tokugawa Period, and since, especially after the beginning of the Meiji Era, accounts of travels were very popular, everyone who was interested in writing published accounts of his trips. Ochiai Naobumi's *Shichishushō* (Seven Stumps of Pine) was a record of his visit to his home in the country, but it can be regarded as an account of travel. Ōwada Tateki wrote *Yamato Meguri* (A Trip Around Yamato) and *Senri no Haru* (Spring over a Thousand *Ri*), and Keigetsu, Ukō, and Hagoromo also wrote accounts of travels. These works were similar to Naobumi's, for they were all written in a pure Japanese style. Shiki wrote *Kakehashi no Ki* (Record of Kakehashi), *Kamakura Ikken no Ki* (Record of a Visit to Kamakura), *Hateshirazu no Ki* (Record of the Endless), and *Ōji Kikō* (Record of a Trip to Ōji); Ōhashi Otowa published *Senzan Bansui* (A

Thousand Mountains and Ten Thousand Bodies of Water) (1899). Members of the *Bungakkai*, such as Tokuboku, Shūkotsu, and Kochō, also wrote poetic accounts of travels. The newspaper companies of the time encouraged young writers by asking them to contribute accounts of travels, and this resulted in the emergence of the so-called professional writers of travel literature.

Chizuka Reisui (Kintarō) was known as a novelist, but actually he made his name as a writer of accounts of travel, and published works of poetic beauty, such as *Fuji no Takane* (High Mt. Fuji), *Tsuyuwake-Goromo* (Dew-Dampened Clothing), *Futokoro Suzuri* (A Pocket Inkstone), *Nihon Dōchūki* (Record of Travels in Japan), and *Sansui Kuyō* (A Requiem for a Landscape). Kojima Usui (Kyūta) was also known as a writer of travel accounts, and published many articles including *Sentō Shōkei* (A Small Landscape on the Top of a Fan) (1899). *Fuji-San ni Noboru Ki* (Record of an Ascent of Mt. Fuji) (1903) was an impressionistic and detailed sketch of Mt. Fuji as seen from the Gotemba Entrance in the mist and in the moonlight, and as seen from the Subashiri Entrance in the snow and at sunrise. Usui was one of the founders of the Japanese Mountaineers' Association, and wrote many books such as *Nihon Sansui Ron* (On the Japanese Landscape) (1905) and a four-volume work entitled *Nihon Arupusu* (The Japanese Alps) (1908–1915). Yoshie Kogan (Kyōshō) wrote many books including a travelogue, *Kōgen* (Highland) (1909), and was known as an appreciator of natural beauty. He wrote *Shin-Shizembi Ron* (A Discourse on New Natural Beauty) in the Taishō Period. *Mitake-Yama no Ryōmen* (Both Sides of Mt. Mitake) (1906), written in a simple colloquial style, was unique in its description of the delicate interrelation between the landscape and the psychology of the mountaineer.

The above-mentioned *Nihon Sansui Ron* and *Shin-Shizembi Ron* were accounts of landscape rather than of travel, whereas Shiga Shinsen (Jūkō) organized his travel experiences in the large volume *Nihon Fūkei Ron* (On the Japanese Landscape) (1894), and pointed out three characteristics of Japanese scenery superior to that of the rest of the world from the scientific viewpoint of geography and geology. These were *shōsha* (elegance), *bi* (beauty) and *tettō* (forcefulness). He described the Japanese landscape quite objectively, yet with deep poetical sentiment and love of his native land.

In addition, Bizan's *Futokoro Nikki* (A Pocket Diary) (1901) and Katai's *Nansen Hokuba* (South Ship and North Horse) (1899) and *Nikkō* (1900) were filled with the deep emotion which the authors experienced through their trips. Katai by nature liked travel ; moreover, he became an assistant to the compilers of *Dai-Nihon Chishi* (A Geographical Description of Japan), and took a nationwide trip, so that the first volume of his complete works is devoted to the accounts of his travels.

There were other accounts of travel which had specific characters. Yanagida Kunio's *Yūkaitōki* (A Record of Travel on Sea and Islands) (1901) was a fluent article which described with love the geographical features and the customs of the regions he visited on a trip between Ise and Shima ; it is considered that trips of this kind provided an incentive for the study of folklore which later became very popular throughout Japan. *Nochi no Kari Kotoba no Ki* (1908) was a product of his one hundred-day trip to Kyūshū and Shikoku ; after writing this book, he became interested in the mountain villages, and realized the importance of the local belief in mountain gods. The poet Hekigotō's *Sanzenri* (Three Thousand *Ri*) (1909) was different from other accounts of travel, and Tokutomi Roka's *Junrei Kikō* (Record of a Pilgrimage) (1906), in which the author described his visits to Jerusalem and to see Tolstoy, was also an interesting work of travel.

There were many travelogues such as those of Roka. Sugimura Sojinkan's (Kōtarō) *Daiei Yūki* (Record of a Trip to Great Britain) (1908) and *Hankyū Shūyū* (A Trip around the Hemisphere) (1909), and Shibukawa Genji's *Yabuno Mukujū :*

— 587 —

Sekai Kembutsu (Yabuno Mukujū's Sightseeing Trip of the
World) (1910) were very popular because of the inclusion of
the interesting foreign experiences of these journalists. Anezaki
Chōfū's (Masaharu) *Hanatsumi Nikki* (A Diary of Flower-
Gathering) (1909) and Sōseki's *Rondon Shōsoku* (News from
London) (1901) were popular among the intellectual class because of the writers' academic attitude towards their experience
abroad. *Rondon Shōsoku* was regarded as a diary, but it consisted of letters which Sōseki sent to Shiki from London. If
we had dealt with the letters of Meiji writers as a part of the
literary art, we could have found abundant material for such a
study. However, we could not expand our study to include
the field of authors' letters in this book.

In the mind of the authors of travel journals there existed
not only the traditional love of nature but also the desire to
take a rest apart from that human society wherein they could
not have sufficient satisfaction for their free self. The same
thing can be said about essays. Essays, above all, enjoyed a
free style, doing away with all formalities; indeed, there were
so many kinds of essays that they can hardly be classified into
definite categories. Now, however, we wish to consider some
kinds of miscellaneous prose, such as so-called elegant prose
(*bibun*), short pieces (*shōhimbun*), and sketches (*shaseibun*).

Elegant prose was the pseudo-classical style of writing of the
scholars of Japanese classical literature. The first work of this
type was written by Ochiai Naobumi under the title of *Haginoya Ikō* (Posthumous Works of Haginoya) (published for the
first time in 1905), while *Bibun Imbun Hanamomiji* (A Belletristic
and Metrical Composition: Flowery Red Maples) (1896), which
was written by Shioi Ukō, Takeshima Hagoromo, and Ōmachi
Keigetsu, is typical of this elegant prose. According to Keigetsu's
introduction, an elegant prose piece was a poem without any
style. Literature was composed of metrical compositions, dramas,
and novels. The novel was one kind of elegant prose, but the so-

called elegant prose here meant "belletristic writings." It was something like today's prose-poem, as we can see from the title of such books as Ōwada Tateki's *Sambun Imbun : Yuki Tsuki Hana* (Prose and Metrical Composition : Snow, Moon, and Flower) (1897), and *Sambun Imbun : Miyama-Zakura* (Prose and Metrical Composition : Cherry Blossoms in the Deep Mountains) (1899), the elegant prose or belletristic writings were sometimes called "prose" (*sambun*). Elegant prose was born in the transition period of the years of Meiji during which the beautiful style of the Ken'yūsha novel was very popular, and the next romantic generation of the Meiji thirties was about to be begun by Chogyū's *Takiguchi Nyūdō*. After the victory in the Sino-Japanese War, the increasing nationalist passion produced "Japanism," and those belletrists who belonged to *Teikoku Bungaku* together with Chogyū, drawing on their training in the national literature, expressed the romantic poetical sentiment of the time in a classical manner.

Hagoromo excelled in his use of metrical composition by which he showed the delicacy of the traditional Japanese style. Keigetsu used a style similar to that of the Chinese classics by means of which he expressed the feeling of both splendor and sadness. Despite these differences, they wrote about faint sadness in terms of the old-fashioned sentiment of elegy and lament, love of blood relationship, and sentiment toward nature, but they could not overcome monotony and shallowness ; they merely showed the regularity and beauty of the pseudo-classical style. In addition, Ukō later wrote "Belletristic and Metrical Composition" *Ankō Soei* (A Sweet Smell Floats in the Darkness) (1901), while Keigetsu was a very capable prose writer ; he made his name by writing "Belletristic and Metrical Composition" *Kigiku Shiragiku* (Yellow and White Chrysanthemums) (1898), and also established himself as a literary critic. On the whole, elegant prose writing suited the taste of the time and became very popular, but it was only a small flower that decorated the Meiji literary world temporarily.

The origin and scope of the short piece are not clear, but the term had been used since an earlier period. It referred to a special kind of essay with an emphasis on description and style ; as to its content, it was something like unorganized fragments of a novel concerning daily happenings. Elegant prose pursued beauty of expression and showed indifference to social meanings, whereas the short piece was satisfied with the description of personal problems, and also had a tendency to confine itself to a small world apart from society. It possessed something in common with the mental life and private novel.

If we study the origin of short pieces, we can find Tokutomi Roka's *Shizen to Jinsei* (Nature and Life) (1900) in an intermediate position between elegant prose and this new form He did not pursue literature in terms of beauty of style, but tried instead to find an ideal in the concise perfection of the work. The author tried to understand the object correctly, to have his subjective attitude penetrate into the object freely, and to enjoy the complete music of thought and literature on the basis of the harmony of subjectivity and objectivity. Roka began this tendency already in *Seizan Hakuun* (Blue Mountains and White Clouds) (1898) and *Seiro-Shū* (The Green Reed Anthology) (1902), but created a unique style in *Shizen to Jinsei* by the pure sensibility that accompanied his Christian thought, as well as by his fluent phrasing patterned on Western models. This book contained some short stories and critical writings, but the eighty-six articles which were included in *Shizen ni taisuru Gofundoki* (Five Minutes Facing Nature), *Shasei-Chō* (A Sketchbook), and *Shōnan Zappitsu* (Shōnan Miscellaneous Writings) represent the best of the essay-style short pieces of the Meiji Period. The section of *Shōnan Zappitsu* where the author looked up at Mt. Fuji from Suruga Bay and described vividly, with an abundant vocabulary, the kaleidoscopic scenery of the mountain shining in the changing light of the sinking sun, was the essence of nature observation ; moreover, occasional inserted sentences of the author's impressions, which had a fresh but grave tone, consisted of meditations on God and reflections on society, and created the self-portrait of the author who had a passion for life. This was a refined prose piece containing abundant lyrical sentiment.

Roka began to live on a farm in Kasuya Chitose-Mura, Tōkyō in 1907, and six years later published an essay, *Mimizu no Tawagoto* (The Nonsense of an Earthworm), which showed the deepening of his thought.

Roka advanced with the group of new writers, such as Doppo, Katai, and Tōson, in the Meiji thirties, and put his mark on Meiji literature as a serious pursuer of the modern self. We must here recall the fact that in 1898 Doppo wrote *Musashino* under the title of *Ima no Musashino* (The Present Musashino) and published it as an independent volume one year after the publication of *Shizen to Jinsei*. After the beginning of the twentieth century, Tōson described thoroughly the changes of nature and various aspects of the agricultural life in his home in Komoro in Shinshū, and completed twelve chapters of *Chikumagawa no Suketchi* (Chikuma River Sketches) (first published in 1912). Since this was a collection of short pieces, it indicated progress in this field. However, Roka and Doppo could not recover the self from nature. Since they attempted to solve the problem of self by the evolving self, their attitudes became contemplative and religious, and they went back to nature to seek for God. This meant a revival of nature and also a self-development in nature, but this was neither a method of scientifically finding the self in human relations nor was it the standpoint of a Naturalist who identifies nature with man. Even if there are traces of Naturalism in *Musashino*, it is the Naturalism of the Wordsworth school. When we come to Tōson, we approach the true territory of Naturalism, and *Chikumagawa no Suketchi* had significance as the groundwork for *Hakai* (The Breaking of the Commandment). Therefore, the so-called short pieces created a trend which opened up a new world for literature in the age of Naturalism.

The term " a short piece " (*shōhin*) came to be used popularly about the time when Naturalism was established. This was the time when *Bunshō Sekai* (The World of Writing) established a special column for short pieces, undertook a study of them, and carried the discussion concerning them by Tayama Katai and Maeda Bokujō (Akira). Mizuno Yōshū, Kubota Utsubo, and Yoshie Kogan became known as writers of short pieces, and there were also many written by such Naturalist writers as Katai, Hakuchō, and Seika, which were highly regarded. During the latter part of Meiji, books were published to teach the form and method of writing short pieces.

There were some works of the idealist writers which can properly be called " short pieces." These works showed the depth of the author's thought. They are represented by Natsume Sōseki's *Bunchō* (A Java Sparrow) (1908), *Yume Jūya* (Ten Nights of Dreams) (1908), *Eijitsu Shōhin* (Short Pieces of Long Days) (1909), *Shiki no E* (Paintings of Shiki) (1911), and *Kēberu Sensei* (Dr. Koeber) (1911). *Bunchō* and *Yume Jūya* are especially excellent pieces of short work.

Bunchō is a story about a person who casually comes to keep a Java sparrow. He recalls in the Java sparrow's beautiful figure the affection which he had for a girl a long time before ; however, he kills this bird by neglecting to feed it, and thereafter his son digs a grave for it. It was neither especially exciting reading nor did it express profound thought, but it vividly pictured the scenes of the story by its plain description, and it also succeeded in painting the self-portrait of the author's personality. In *Yume Jūya* the author tried to refresh his memory of the romantic feelings of youth, and we find therein deep observation on life and a reflection on himself. There are not only the dream of the death of an innocent and beautiful girl and a white lily as a rebirth of this girl, but also the dream of the extraordinary decision of a high-minded warrior who studied and practised the doctrine of the Zen sect at the risk of his life ; if he could not achieve spiritual enlighenment, he would kill himself, whereas if he could, he would kill the Buddhist priest. The dream of the seventh night seemed to express Sōseki's own philosophy of life. Most of the dreams are composed of two main personalities ; the author becomes either a hero or a spectator, and the pieces show a brilliant dramatic development.

Sōseki gradually recovered from the illness of the modern self by the deepening of his philosophy of life in the world of the novel, and, as a result, he came to believe devoutly that man can reach heaven by departing from the self. In 1910 he became seriously ill at Shuzenji, wavering for awhile between life and death, and after such an experience he left the incomparable short piece of contemplation *Omoidasu Koto Nado* (Things Which I Recall). This work was published in the *Asahi Shimbun* between October 1910 and February 1911. In it the author found a way to establish the spirit of departing from the self and reaching heaven, *i. e.*, the reduction of one's self into nature, by tracing the thought on his sickbed. It meant that although it was an oasis produced by the leisure on the sickbed, the Oriental tradition of elegance had provided the image for the philosophy of leaving the self and reaching heaven. This was the ultimate level of attainment of the essay in the Meiji Period. He was not satisfied with the simple world of romanticism that existed prior to the age of Naturalism, but produced a world of Neo-Idealism in competition with the hitherto existing Naturalism. This world of Neo-Idealism was developed to the level which was attained by *Garasudo no Naka* (Inside My Glass Doors) (1915).

Besides Sōseki, Nagai Kafū, too, competed against Naturalism by advocating his criticism of civilization from the aesthetic point of view. This attitude towards literature which was a severe criticism of the imitative civilization of Meiji had begun with Ryūhoku and was maintained by the writers of the Meiji

Period through Ryokuu. It possessed something in common with the Rohan-style concept of the supremacy of art which was espoused by Ōgai. Kafū's work, which was entitled *Kōcha no Ato* (After a Cup of Black Tea), made public between 1910 and 1911 and published in book form in 1911, was an essay rather than a short piece. Kafū selected scenes from his daily life, such as the Shiba mausoleum, theatres, *ukiyoe* prints, an airing of clothes, and the Ginza, one by one, and expressed his poetical sentiment of grieving over the departed Edo culture. Among the works of the Epicurean school, *Waga Oitachi* (My Personal History), the introduction to Kitahara Hakushū's collection of poems *Omoide* (Recollections) (1911), was a remarkable work. In this introduction, the poet wrote about the southern landscapes of his home in Yanagawa on the island of Kyūshū, and of his youth passed therein, with the fresh sense of the modern age. This had a strong fragrance of art; it was not a short piece in the context of Naturalism but rather a new type of belletristic work in contrast with that literary movement.

According to Shiki's *Jojibun* (Descriptive Writing) (1900), *shaseibun* (sketch writing) repudiated the embellished style which was adorned by classic and elegant phrases, as well as the tendency of the writers to state cleverly their own ideals and to parade the novelty of them. The writers of the sketching school had to copy the things which appeared in this world, both that of nature and of man. It meant a sketching and a description of reality, but he felt it was necessary also to make a good selection of the material to be treated. The scene had to be made to live by "emphasizing the most beautiful and impressive part of it." Yet the best part could often be found in the half-concealed places under the surface rather than in the broad and conspicuous places on the surface of the scene. Thus the writers were required not only to be objective but also to grasp the core of the scene which was not yet discovered by others but filled with a new beauty. This was the extension of the realism by which he attempted to reform the *haiku* and *tanka*, and it was also related to his repudiation of conventional styles. Shiki called this kind of style *shaseiteki no shōhimbun* (the style for realistic short pieces) or *shajitsuteki shōhimbun* (the style for descriptive short pieces) in such books as his *Byōshō Rokushaku* (The Six-Foot Sickbed), and Shiki's followers tried to establish a new form based on this sketch writing.

Shiki's sketch writings began with *Shōen no Ki* (A Record of a Small Garden) (1898), which was followed by *Shajō Shoken* (My Impressions on a Train) (1898), *Natsu no Yo no Oto* (The Sounds of a Summer Night) (1899), and *Izari-Guruma* (Wheelchair for a Cripple) (1899), and this kind of writing attained its final form in *Meshi Matsu Ma* (While Waiting for a Meal) (1899). We can consider it to be a revival of that poetic prose style known as *haibun*. We have already referred to the collections of sketch writing which were edited by poets and prose writers of the Shiki school. Kyoshi edited *Kangyoku-Shū* (The Cold Gem Anthology) (1900) while Shiki was still alive. In this collection, Sokotsu's *Shinshūjin* (The New Prisoner), in which he described in detail his experience as a prisoner, was considered to be a remarkable work. Among the works written after the death of Shiki, we can consider the collection of Shihōta and Kyoshi, *Shaseibun-Shū : Hotategai* (A Collection of Sketches : A Scallop) (1906), to be the perfection of the sketching style. When Shihōta, with his terse and compact style, wrote *Yume no Gotoshi* (Like a Dream) (1906), he said that he was able by this essay to escape from the complicated spiritual condition of the present and return to the pure and innocent emotions of his boyhood in a fishermen's village along the coast of the Japan Sea. In 1907, the sketching style attained its maturity, but such works as Nagatsuka Takashi's *Sadogashima* (Sado Island) and Kyoshi's *Fūryū Sempō* (Elegant Enlightenment) had already advanced into the area of the novel; and this indicated the tendency of all the writers except Shihōta to depart from the field of the sketching style.

Sōseki, a close friend of Shiki, encouraged the above-mentioned poets and prose writers, and provided a logical basis for the sketching style after the death of Shiki. Sōseki created an idealism of internal reflection in the field of short pieces. Also, in the field of sketch-writing, he expanded the thesis which was established by *Jojibun*, and created an original theory based on this thesis. We referred to this in the previous section entitled "The Romanticism and Idealism around Sōseki."

In Sōseki's short essay *Shaseibun* (The Sketching Style) (1907), the characteristics of this style were explained. Such a style dealt with the author's state of mind, and it always pictured his personality. This would seem to suggest that it was based on subjectivism, but the main purpose of sketching was to copy an object, and its content was "the attitude of an adult in looking at a child," or the attitude "of describing others who are crying without crying over them oneself." This did not mean a cold attitude but "a smiling sympathy toward others." Because of this characteristic, Sōseki was considered to be of the Yoyū-Ha (Leisure school). He hoped that even if he established a certain distance between the object and himself, his calm and artistic subjective thoughts, rather than his objectivity, would penetrate the object. *Shaseibun* would seem to have something in common with Naturalism which looked at phenomena objectively and scientifically; but actually it took an opposite position. We have dealt with the early essays of Terada Torahiko, but now we can consider them as short pieces of the sketching style from the viewpoint of the Yoyū-Ha. The sketching style was developed into the novel by Takahama Kyoshi, Natsume Sōseki, Nagatsuka Takashi, Itō Sachio, and Suzuki Miekichi. The novels of these authors, who had passed through the stage of the sketching style, came to have an Oriental character which distinguished them from the works of Naturalism.

Japan has traditionally produced diaries of high artistic value.

By the modern awakening of the self, diaries became more important than ever before as a record of an individual's self-reflection. Many writers left behind them diaries, such as Kōyō's *Tochimandō Nichiroku* (The Diary of Tochimandō), and these records were often published in book form after their death. Indeed, since there are too many diaries to be covered in this book, we shall mention only the especially significant ones, such as those of Ichiyō, Shiki, Doppo, and Takuboku. Higuchi Ichiyō continued to write diaries under the various titles of *Chiri no Naka* (In the Dust), *Mizu no Ue* (Above the Water), and *Shinobugusa* (A Hare's Foot Fern) during the period between 1891 and 1896. Ichiyō, who published many excellent short novels in *Bungakkai* (Literary World) as its regular contributor, wrote about her modest but active daily life, and left a record of her brief twenty-five years. She managed a household of an impoverished former samurai class with her mother and a younger sister, worried about debts, and ran a small business. In this austerity, she learned not only the poetry of the Heian style at Nakajima Utako's private school together with children of the wealthy class, but also the techniques of novel-writing from her respected teacher, Nakarai Tōsui. When she published a novel, she worried about what people would say about her work, but also, with a hidden self-confidence, expressed her discontent at society. Indeed, we can see the naked personality of Ichiyō in her diaries.

Although Ichiyō used the style of the Saikaku school for her novel-writing, she wrote her diaries in a proficient classic style. We feel as if we are hearing Ichiyō's original voice when we read at various places in the context of her delicate writing her clearcut opinions. In the world of the novel, this voice of the growing self of one who lived in an obscure corner of the city came to appeal to the public as a sign, albeit feeble, of resistance to society. Meanwhile, in the world of the diary, although Ichiyō was restrained by the established relationships such as exist between members of a household and between a teacher and

a student, she still spoke very frankly and openly in the newly
created field of literary criticism. It seemed that at this time
Ichiyō was in agony internally, and experienced her " self "
not as a human being but through her art. This indicated the
trend of the time. However, when the high tide of Romanticism
came towards the end of her life, the yearning for her internal
self was constricted into a somewhat empty-sounding description
of psychology. In spite of her experience of love, she never
attained peace of mind concerning the above-mentioned problem.
This indicated the history of the intellectual development of those
who belonged to *Bungakkai* (The Literary World), such as
Tōkoku and Tōson. Her diary was a woman's description of one
phase of the development of such a mind.

Shiki produced several essays of the diary style. The important ones were daily records of his sickbed, such as *Shōra
Gyokueki* (Shōra Jewel Liquid) (1896), *Bokujū Itteki* (One Drop
of India Ink) (1901), *Byōshō Rokushaku* (The Six-Foot Sickbed)
(1902), and *Gyōga Manroku* (Leisurely Records of the Sickbed)
(1901-1902). All of these except *Gyōga Manroku* were carried
in *Nihon* (Japan), had a public character, and can be considered
as essays. Although he suffered from an incurable disease, Shiki
maintained high spirits and wrote until two days before his death.
He found a life worth living by keeping abreast of society
through the publication of his works. At the age of thirty,
Shiki wrote his first essay, *Shōra Gyokueki*. This was the time
when he had completed the reform of the *haiku* and was working
hard writing his severe criticism of a wide variety of things,
such as religion, society, the novel, the theatre, painting, books
of research, newspapers, and various personalities, in order not
to surrender to his illness. Four years had passed since the publication of his first book when Shiki published *Bokujū Itteki*.
Although he was actively advocating the reform of the *tanka*
and the adoption of sketch-writing, he could no longer hope for
recovery from his illness and stayed in one room. Still he
sometimes went out in a rickshaw. He also fought, as a literary

critic, against the Myōjō school, discussed Hiraga Motoyoshi, and directed the current trend of *haiku* composition ; meanwhile he came to realize he was a sick man, treated small things around his bed, and composed pure, jewel-like series of *haiku* concerning such things as a carp in a tub, wistaria flowers in a vase, and yellow roses on a bamboo fence. He faced the suffering of his disease and his forthcoming death, sometimes thought of drinking poison, at other times tried to beautify death by the dream of a white rabbit, but finally became a simple and innocent child who tried to bring this world into the other world, and hoped to have a momentary freedom and a good meal rather than to have eternal life.

However, he spent six years on his sickbed before he wrote *Byōshō Rokushaku*, and in this book he spoke of the pain rather than of death. Spiritual enlightenment no longer meant " not to fear death " but " not to fear to live." He said that although religion was of no use to him he could at least listen to some interesting religious stories. The disease was painful ; was he a fool to endure this pain ? He did not care any more about persons who laughed at him. " Those who were laughing at him would be laughed at by others when they were buried under the ground." We can hear in these words a pathetic voice which might be called the pride of a sick man. It was his sole consolation to sketch the flowers and fruit by his bedside, but it was not enough to make him forget the extraordinary experience of his incurable disease. He then came to a stage where he wanted to get the most out of his remaining life and to have the most complete medical treatment. This did not mean his attachment to life but his enjoyment of disease ; he did not fear death but hoped for complete treatment. In this way, it seemed that Shiki had attained the enlightenment of a patient. It was a complete physiological philosophy of life, one commonly held by those who are in the midst of social intercourse, and thus it represented a thoroughly secular outlook. *Gyōga Manroku* consisted of fragments, such as menus of his meals, sketches of small things around the bed. It is a frightening experience to read parts of the record where he wondered how to kill himself by looking at a sharp blade, and also where he complained of his physical pain and of the fact that there was nothing but food to mitigate it. This was a private record which the recorder had no intention of having published after his death, so that he expressed his true feelings with pathos.

Azamukazaru no Ki (An Undeceiving Record) was published in 1908 after Doppo's death. This confession was Doppo's diary between February 1893, when he was twenty-three, and May 1897, when he became twenty-seven. The beginning of the diary was devoted to a record of Doppo's maturing mind which ambitiously questioned various problems of life, pondered over them reflectively, and pursued the solution of them. The middle part was a private record of his passionate love-affair with his future wife Nobuko, and also of his self-reflection. The latter part traced his calm and steady prayerful attitude after the failure of his love-affair and marriage. He became a Christian as a young man and was influenced directly by Uemura Masahisa and Uchimura Kanzō; he sought God, reflected on love, sought beauty, and pursued seriously his own "self" at the risk of his life, as did both Roka and Koshoshi. Therefore, this book was based on a plan of making all people feel beauty, and thereby let them achieve eternity, while defending, by means of strength and virtue, the light and hope given by God.

However, he admitted in his honest confession that he could not always achieve his faith, and he pursued a naked self with suspicion as a human being and with anguish as a poet. He then tried to clarify all the concepts beyond the limit of their established definitions. These concepts included not only the new Western ones, such as life, duty, rights and obligations, but also time, history, the universe, and man. He questioned these concepts in terms of what, why, and whence, by departing from all preconceived notions in an attempt to find a way to live in this world, and began treading an extremely complicated road of self-analysis. Is it possible to find significance by looking at reality, or will truth appear only at one's death ? This painful approach to truth was not through the wisdom of the philosopher, but rather through the emotion, tears, and humanity common to many people. Indeed, this human feeling is the container of beauty, and herein a poet could find his philosophy.

His pursuit of beauty was replaced by his pursuit of the emotions ; the philosopher, by a member of the common people ; his desire to be a great man, by his desire to share his sympathy with all the rest of mankind. Therefore, the attitude of pursuing the image of God produced the profound attitude of desiring to approach nature. Of course, Doppo did not lose his faith in an absolute God, but, in the latter part of his life, he became more interested in the approach to nature. Finally, his warm sympathy towards the common people was poured into nature which he came to love more than human beings. Thus, Doppo's increasing realization of his own duty shifted his interests to the beautiful and pure, but also the cold and horrible nature in his pursuit of absolute truth. In this way, his pursuit of " self " was first based on the problems of the Christian God, secondly turned to human society, and thirdly came to find the original pattern of the self in nature. Nature was a second god, and he felt it could save the self from the social life.

It took thirty-five years before Ishikawa Takuboku's diary, which had been treasured at Hakodate Library, came to be published. This diary consisted of ten different kinds of a total of thirteen note-books. It covered the period between 1902, when Takuboku was seventeen, and 1912, when he became twenty-seven. Four note-books covered every one of the 365 days of 1908. He did not leave any diary for 1903 and 1905, and we can find only fragmentary records for the rest of the years.

Unlike other diaries we have hitherto mentioned, Takuboku did not want to publish his at all, and actually wanted it burned after his death. For Takuboku wanted to maintain his "self" only through the publication of essays, poems, and *tanka*. The diary was nothing but an impression of his daily life, or at most a memorandum of his writing prior to its publication. The *Myōjō* movement of Romanticism drew Takuboku's attention; he became more interested in New Style poetry than in the *tanka*, and thus was a so-called progressive young man. The third diary, *Shibutami Nikki* (A Diary of Shibutami), covered the period when Takuboku, as the best assistant teacher in Japan, began a somewhat settled but nonetheless distressing life at home; from this period on he became rapidly interested in the Naturalist movement. After the difficult days of Hokkaidō, he moved to Tōkyō for the last time. This period of his life was described in the most complete fifth diary of 1908, and it was in this work that his Naturalist tendency came to its culminating point. Although Takuboku left his family in Hokkaidō and came to Tōkyō alone, he still suffered from dire poverty. Thus, he was forced to make short poems with the scheme which he originally intended to use for his novel. During his Naturalist period, he had not yet become a popular writer. In 1909, he was invited by the *Subaru*, which was supported by Ōgai, to participate in a New Art movement, and gradually deepened his understanding of Naturalism; thereafter, he invited his family to come from Hokkaidō to Tōkyō, and continued an endless life of distress. The seventh diary, which was written in Roman letters, described vividly his self-confidence and his dreary, depraved life at that time.

Takuboku then became a selector for the *tanka* column of the *Asahi Shimbun*, discovered the discrepancy which lay between Naturalism and himself, and so arrived at a new intellectual position. Since he was so completely occupied explaining his new position, his diary was discontinued here and there. It seemed that Takuboku, when he considered the

Kōtoku Shūsui's grand treason case, came to the conclusion that socialism was the only ideology to solve the difficulties of society. In 1911, the ninth diary was written on his sickbed. This fragmentary record also indicated that his socialist thought was losing its strength. Therefore, Takuboku began his career in the Romantic period of poetry, grew in the Naturalist development, although he was allied originally with the anti-Naturalists, and finally came to plunge into socialism. He died at this point without having contributed too much to the socialist movement. These diaries can be regarded as the mirror of late Meiji thought of the new generation.

CHAPTER II   THE DEVELOPMENT OF LITERARY THEORY

1. *Early Concepts of Literature and the Introduction of Literary Theory*

Since the Edo Era, such literary forms as the *yomihon*, *kusazōshi*, *kokkeibon*, and *ninjōbon* were usually referred to as *gesaku*, "works of entertainment" or light fiction. This name suggests how this kind of writing was regarded at that time. *Gesaku* meant those works written for the sake of pleasure and relaxation on the part of authors who wished to entertain the common people. Such authors even referred to themselves self-deprecatingly as *gesaku* writers. On the other hand, it should be noted that the novel form called *haishi-shōsetsu* which was influenced by its Chinese prototype was then regarded as the means for promoting justice (punishment of vice and reward of virtue) based on a Confucian feudal morality.

These trivial and utilitarian concepts of literature were continued in Meiji by surviving *gesaku* writers. However, these writers could not remain completely indifferent to the social movements of the new era. In 1872 the Education Ministry proclaimed "three principles of education" on the basis of piety (*keishin*) and patriotism (*aikoku*). Accordingly, Kanagaki Robun and Sansantei Arindo (Jōno Saigiku) said that they would work thereafter in compliance with these principles, and would change their method of writing. On this occasion the two men assumed the responsibility for "guiding the uneducated," and remained unchanged in their humble attitude of admitting their occupation to be "mean and humiliating." Later, in 1884, in a work entitled *Chōtori Tsukuba Suso Moyō*, the author Takahata Ransen wrote the following: "By informing the youth and women of the importance of loyalty, filial piety, and fidelity, it is the author's sole desire to assist in any way possible in the punishing of vice and the promoting of virtue."

Although translations of Western novels that appeared along with the rising tendency toward Europeanization led new currents into the literary world, we find in them too some utilitarian consciousness in the sense of didacticism and enlightenment. For example, Niwa (Oda) Jun'ichirō, who published *Karyū Shunwa* (A Spring Tale of Flowers and Willows) (a translation of Bulwer-Lytton's *Ernest Maltravers* and *Alice*) in 1878, later stated in referring to the translation that he had intended to introduce to his countrymen who were ignorant of them " those manners and feelings in modern Britain fully detailed in the original books." (From the preface to *Tsūzoku Karyū Shunwa*, the popular edition of the above-mentioned book, 1884). While in *Fukkoku Kakumei : Nishinoumi no Chishio no Koarashi* (The French Revolution : A Bloody Whirlwind in the West), translated by Sakurada Momoe in 1882, it was stated that " the author (*i. e.*, the translator) would be overjoyed if his fellow countrymen should gain their individual liberty in the manner of those courageous foreigners, who, as related in the present work, revolted in the midst of their sufferings." This statement indicated a political utilitarianism in that the translator hoped that his work would contribute in some way to the movement for liberty and civil rights.

As emphasized in the *Nippon Rikken Seitō Shimbun* (The Japan Constitutional Party Newspaper) on June 9, 1883, this movement for civil rights aimed at " reforming the novel and the drama... so that they might become the means of sowing and nurturing the seeds of freedom in the soil of this country," and thus it necessitated the participation of politicians themselves in the writing of novels and plays in an easily understandable form for the common people, wherein they would advocate freedom and civil rights in place of the " promote-virtue, reprove-vice " ideas of feudal works. It hardly needs to be said that the so-called political novels of those days, produced under such circumstances, were permeated with a political consciousness. Nevertheless, the *gesaku* concept of literature still remained in the mind of some writers such as Yano Ryūkei, who, rejecting the utilitarian view, declared that "the main function of the novel is to guide the reader into a dreamland of pain and pleasure," and that "it is nothing more than a vessel for simple enjoyment like other realms of' art such as music and painting." (From the preface to *Keikoku Bidan*, A Noble Tale of Statesmanship, 1883–1884).

Generally speaking, on the occasion of a great turning-point in history such as this period following the Meiji Restoration, empiricism and utilitarianism are likely to be given priority, since the promoting of material civilization is regarded as foremost, and literature and the other arts are rejected as either non-profitable or harmful. In *Saikoku Risshi-Hen* (Biographies of Self-Made Men of Western Countries) (a translation of Samuel Smiles' *Self-Help* by Nakamura Keiu), we find a chapter devoted to the "harm of romantic novels," and we can imagine that this way of thinking was common among most scholars and intellectuals of the time. For them, *bungaku*, or literature, usually meant not such vulgar works as *gesaku*, but poetry, expository prose, and learning in general. An even more severe view of literature was given by the philosopher of the Enlightenment Fukuzawa Yukichi, who insisted that "reading difficult ancient texts as well as finding pleasure in composing *waka* and Chinese poetry" meant nothing more than engaging in "fruitless *bungaku* (literature)," and that "it should not be respected too highly." (From *Gakumon no Susume*, The Encouragement of Learning, first series, 1872). It is significant that in spite of the prevailing tendency to despise the literary art, there was one journalist who favored poetry and the novel. This was Fukuchi Ōchi, who wrote on December 2, 1874, in the *Tōkyō Nichinichi Shimbun* where his articles on literature often appeared, that "poems and novels express the thinking of man, immortalize his words, depict interesting scenes, dissipate pain and gloom, and thus indeed become an indispensable pleasure of an enlightened people."

One of the scholars of the Enlightenment was Nishi Amane.
He introduced knowledge of the literary art of the West as well as
that of various branches of its science. Educated in Holland in
the latter years (the Bunkyū and Ganji Eras) of the Edo Period,
he began in 1870 a series of lectures which he entitled *Hyakugaku Renkan* (Chain of a Hundred Studies). In these lectures
he gave to literature a Japanese equivalent of *bunshōgaku* or
bungaku, establishing its place in the academic system. According to him, poetry was to be included within this literature
parallel with such subjects as grammar, the study of ideographs,
rhetoric, and etymology. He placed poetry also within the criterion of " art " (*geijutsu*) or " liberal arts " (*gagei*), along with
music, painting, sculpture, and calligraphy, and regarded it as
one of the objects to be treated in " aesthetics " (*kashuron*) as a
province of philosophy, while the " romance " (*haishi*) and " fable"
(*shōsetsu*), unlike poetry, belonged to the field of " history "
(*rekishi*). In his *Chisetsu* (Treatise on Intellect), published in
1874, Nishi gave a general term *littérature* (*bunshōka*) to all of
these three. His rather utilitarian attitude may be perceived by
the following statement which appeared in this treatise : " Poetry
is a tool for elevating the human mind and beautifying manners ;
therefore, it is of no small merit." In 1872, in his notes for
the lecture he delivered in the presence of the Meiji Emperor
which were later published under the title *Bimyōgakusetsu*
(Aesthetic Theory), he attempted to survey *esthétique* (*bimyō-
gaku*), which he contended constituted the basic principles of
" fine art " (*bijutsu*) that includes both " poetry " (*shiika*) and
" prose " (*sambun*). Later, he translated *Mental Philosophy* by
J. Haven (1878), who had adopted Hegelian aesthetics, and he
early had come in contact with the thought of Immanuel Kant.
Nevertheless, on the whole, he chose for his academic position
the positivism of the Auguste Comte school.

However, Nishi's theories had no particular relation to the

main current of the literary world. In 1879 Kikuchi Dairoku's translated work *Shūji oyobi Kabun* (Rhetoric and Belles-Lettres), published by the Education Ministry as a part of its *Hyakka Zensho* (Encyclopaedia), introduced the British theory of literature with its basis in rhetoric. In 1883 and the following year there appeared a Japanese edition, translated by Nakae Chōmin, of *Esthétique* (Aesthetics) by the French empiricist E. Véron, under the title *Ishi Bigaku*. But neither of these imported theories was immediately received favorably by the Japanese literary world. Meanwhile, in 1882, Professor Fenollosa, an American who had been invited to Japan to teach at Tōkyō University, gave a series of lectures on painting, based on Hegelian aesthetics. These lectures, later published as *Bijutsu Shinsetsu* (Truth about Fine Arts), had a tremendous effect among Japanese intellectuals, inasmuch as they included remarkable insights into the nature of art and even of literature.

Furthermore, Fenollosa's student, Ariga Nagao, in his work *Bungakuron* (On Literature), published in 1885, attempted to treat art on the principle of *hogō* (synthesis), which he thought characteristic of Chinese culture in general. The main thesis of the work lay in his affirmation of " the restoration of moral discipline through synthesis," and when he wrote that " what we call literature is the study of synthesis," he was speaking from a Confucian standpoint, and demonstrated his antagonism toward Western ideas.

2. *The Establishment of a Realistic Theory of Literature*

About the year 1885, under the influence of heated discussions regarding " reform " (*kairyō*) in various areas of Japanese culture, the literary world, too, was urged to reconsider its theoretical foundation. The rising reformative movement in literature tended to seek on the Western model a way appropriate to the new era, and stood in criticism of Japan's traditional literature. In these efforts a tendency toward *shajitsushugi* (realism) is discernible.

Such a movement was first seen in the field of poetry. In 1882, even prior to the emergence of so-called reformative opinions, the earliest attempt at a new poetical expression took the form of the publication of the *Shintaishishō* (An Anthology of New Style Poetry). As already mentioned in one of the preceding chapters, these poems were products of those who insisted upon introducing into poetry " ordinary words " to give proper expression to modern thoughts and feelings. For that purpose the authors adopted the Western form of the long poem, rejecting that narrow and obsolete or classical vocabulary that had been common in *waka* and *kanshi* (Chinese poems). This anthology, it appears, had a considerable influence upon such men as Tsubouchi Shōyō. Shōyō also took notice of the above-mentioned *Shūji oyobi Kabun* and *Bijutsu Shinsetsu*. He then framed his own theory of the novel, aided by the Western literary reviews, histories of English literature, and studies of rhetoric, in all of which he had read widely. For his theory he also took consideration of Motoori Norinaga's *Genji Monogatari Tama no Ogushi* (Comments on " The Tale of Genji "). From September 1885 until some time in the following year, his *Shōsetsu Shinzui* (The Essence of the Novel) was published in finished form. Fragments of the book had already been made public in several places, such as in the preface to his translation *Kaikan Hifun: Gaiseishi-Den* (Heroic Biographies) (1885). The author's intention was to contribute to the " reform and development of our novel."

Shōyō made an attempt to explain the nature of the novel on the basis that it belonged to an area of art (*bijutsu*). In his opinion, the novel, together with music, poetry, and drama, belonged to " non-concrete art " (*mukei no bijutsu*), while painting, sculpture, and architecture belonged to " a concrete art " (*yūkei no bijutsu*), so that he had, first of all, to clarify the general characteristics of art as a whole. In this regard, Fenollosa had lectured that " art aims at entertaining the human mind and eyes, as well as elevating the personality," while

another critic saw in art "the best means for cultural development." However, according to Shōyō, it was improper to place
true art on the same level with practical art (*jitsuyōgi*), by putting
them in the same mold (*igata*). "Cultural development," and,
for him, *jimbun hatsuiku*, the said moral purpose of "elevating
the personality," were nothing more than the "natural effect"
of art. The essential objective of art should be "to make man
feel as if he were living in a world of fantasy," and to entertain, in this sense, the "human mind and eyes." Functionally
different from other kinds of art that appeal to the eye or
ear, the novel, however, was thought, like poetry and the
drama, to "appeal exclusively to the human mind."

The purpose of the art of the novel, although in another
way explained as "offering entertainment to people," was distinct from that of the *gesaku* for women and children. On the
contrary, he meant apparently the aesthetic significance of
novels when he wrote that the novel was to appeal to the
"delicate sentiment" or "literary mind" of those readers who
"rejoice in romantic fantasy and are fond of elegant phenomena." It is likely that, taking into consideration the British view
that regards the novel as "a record of human life," the critic
found its characteristic in the pleasure to be realized through
criticism of the human world.

Despite his seemingly aesthetic viewpoint, however, according
to Shōyō, "to entertain the human mind" was interpreted as
a "direct benefit" of a novel, and, in contrast with this, he
pointed out what he called the "indirect benefits." He enumerated four of them, when he stated that a novel should always:
(1) help dignify the personality; (2) be instructive in the distinction between right and wrong; (3) become supplementary
to authentic history; (4) set an excellent example for literary
writing. It is to be remarked that such effects, obviously
practical and utilitarian, were expected, albeit indirectly, from
the novel. As to *Tōsei Shosei Katagi* (The Character of the
Modern Student), a novel where Shōyō carried into practice

his theories of *Shōsetsu Shinzui*, the author revealed that he secretly intended to help rectify students' manners which were either too effeminate or too coarse. (*Shōsetsu o Ronjite Shosei Katagi no Shui ni Oyobu*, On the Novel: What I Intended in My Novel about Students, 1885–1886). It is evident enough that a concept of moral utility still remained in the mind of Shōyō. Although he was the first to open the way toward recognizing the aesthetic autonomy of literature, he did not succeed in establishing it.

The contents of *Shōsetsu Shinzui*, beginning with general remarks on the novel, included its historic changes, subject matter, variations, benefits, rules, etc. Through all of these chapters, the author's emphasis was placed on two points: first, a novel should take up humane sentiments and social manners; second, in their depiction a method of *mogi* or *mosha* (copying) should be used. This method, which he called *shajitsushugi* (realism), was proposed in opposition to that feudalistic reprove-vice-and-promote-virtue theory of the novel, and he tried to theorize this proposition. When he ruled that "the main subject of a novel is human sentiment," he induced it from the viewpoint that a novel should, above all, appeal to the heart. Though he prescribed that "social manners and affairs are second in importance," little attention was paid to any social aspect of a work. Rather, assuming that a human being is "an animal of passions," he felt that novels should treat more those instinctive, natural desires of an individual. Shōyō's giving preference to those natural, human sentiments becomes the more significant when we see in it an implied criticism of feudal, Confucian morals under which they were suppressed at all times, a fixed idea of good and evil being the only rule. Significantly, however, even in the Edo Era, there were pioneers in this theory, such as Norinaga, who pointed out that *mono no aware* was the essence of a tale. The quotation from Norinaga's *Genji Monogatari Tama no Ogushi*, where this matter was deliberated, appearing in *Shōsetsu Shin-*

zui, makes us surmise that Shōyō received some influence from the feudal scholar.

Furthermore, Shōyō emphasized the making of a story "true to life," and, to attain this goal, he asserted that a novelist should always rely fully upon "copying" in his description of life and men in the world. According to Shōyō, a true novel should be an "artistic novel," strictly differentiated from the "romance" consisting of absurd fiction, or the "fable" and "allegory" both existing for allegorical purposes, or the "didactic novel" molded on moralistic views. However, he admitted some adaptation is natural, for unlike an authentic record, a novel is a product of "fantastic imagination," as a kind of "fictitious story." From this viewpoint, base matters and obscene passions are to be avoided, or, if inevitable, such material should be treated in a dispassionate, objective way. In short, a writer should create a personality on the principles of psychology, and, considering this person a living man in the real world, the novelist should be completely objective in depicting his feelings, thus keeping himself from obtruding his opinions as to right and wrong. To seize and express human feelings in their "true, natural state," through an approach graphical as well as objective, was the end set by Shōyō in his *shajitsushugi* (realism).

Such assertions of Shōyō, having, on many points, a certain coincidence with the modern realism of the West, should have been an epoch-making proposition at the time. Unfortunately, Shōyō was as yet lukewarm in his attack against that once prevailing concept of considering literature as a plaything (*gesaku*); worse than that, he knew nothing of the Naturalism arising at that time in the West, particularly in France, and, lastly, his theoretical background was principally derived from the English literature of the early half of the nineteenth century. It is likely that these defects resulted in a certain limitation of Shōyō's realism.

It is significant that, motivated by his reading of the much discussed *Shōsetsu Shinzui,* Hasegawa Futabatei came to have intercourse with the author. In their association, Shōyō was not infrequently enlightened on some important points by his pupil. Like Shōyō, Futabatei had chosen a way to realism, though it was under the influence of modern Russian literature, its novels and literary theories. Thus, his realism, in its basis, was noticeably different from that of Shōyō.

Futabatei's essay *Shōsetsu Sōron* (General Remarks on the Novel), a review of Shōyō's *Tōsei Shosei Katagi,* was published in April 1886, through the kindness of the author, in the *Chūō Gakujutsu Zasshi* (Central Academic Magazine). In this essay, on the premise that "art should deliberate idea with the help of feelings," he remarked that "a novelist should perceive what is the just natural state (idea) out of various phenomena (forms) visible in the world." Undoubtedly Futabatei owes this remark to the Russian philosopher V. G. Belinsky, and particularly to his essay translated by Futabatei himself as *Bijutsu no Hongi* (Substance of Art). Belinsky holds, according to the translation, that "art is the direct contemplation of truth, *i.e.,* it proposes idea through form." What Futabatei calls *i* or *ishō,* namely idea, originates from the idealism of Hegel who influenced the Russian critic. It is characteristic of Futabatei that at the same time that he supported such idealism, he should also have been a supporter of realism. It came about in this way: the idea, once captured directly, in a novel was to be communicated to the reader again by a direct method. For such a method, he put forward *mosha* (copying), thus rejecting instructive novels as nothing but "propaganda for Buddhistic doctrines." "Copying" is defined as "drawing a fictitious phase (*kyosō*) through a real phase (*jissō*)." This meant to actualize the universal absolute idea (*kyosō*) through concrete, special form (*jissō*), that is, through various aspects of the phenomenal world. Thus, the supreme stage of "copying" was found in "creating something true to nature, perfectly endowed with both idea and form."

The realism of Futabatei varied from that of Shōyō in that

the former attached importance to " idea " as such, while the latter aimed at something akin to a psychological analysis of human feelings caught in their " natural, untempered state." It may be said that this was a natural course to take for Futabatei who was born with a philosophical, idealistic temperament. Nevertheless, there is room for doubt as to whether, without any knowledge of Hegelian philosophy, Futabatei could rightfully have comprehended Belinsky's thought.

Meanwhile, the philosophical views of Belinsky were also taken up by Shōyō through his pupil Futabatei. For instance, in his novel *Naichi Zakkyo : Mirai no Yume* (A Dream of the Future) Shōyō had this to say : " ' The poet, with the power of his senses, exquisitely finds out truth' was well said by a Russian aesthete." In another place Shōyō echoed this remark in defining art as " activities seeking truth with the help of one's feelings." (*Bijutsu Ron*, On Art, 1887). Later, apparently influenced by Véron's *Esthétique*, which he came to study through translation, Shōyō often employed such terms as " beauty " (*bi*) or " supreme thought " (*myōsō*) in place of the " truth " he had used before. When we note that Shōyō even began using " idea, namely *ishō*," to correspond to " truth " or " supreme thought," we may suspect his conversion to idealism. Actually, however, Shōyō used this term " idea " to mean nothing more than " inexplicable states of mind." (*ibid.*). Thereafter, the comprehension of such inexplicables by an empirical method of " direct observation " (*chokusetsu no kansatsu*) was proposed. (*Shōsetsu no Shudan*, Methods of the Novel, 1887).

Such were the changes in viewpoint which the author of *Shōsetsu Shinzui* underwent after its publication. Meanwhile, the reaction to the thoughts revealed in that book was ever widening its circle. The influence was evident in the novelist Yamada Bimyō, one of the members of the Ken'yūsha, who with his peculiar taste for *gesaku*, regarded literature as " pleasure " (*kairaku*). Echoes to *Shōsetsu Shinzui* were also heard among those critics who took the Christian position. One of them, Iwamoto Zenji, discontented with Shōyō's realism that "solely aims at tracing sentiment," argued in the *Jogaku Zasshi* that true realism should be "helpful to moral instruction" by "delineating the world as it is." (*Joshi to Shōsetsu*, Women and the Novel, 1886). On the other hand, Tokutomi Sohō, chief editor of the *Kokumin no Tomo*, also expected a novelist "to copy changing aspects of society," thus playing his part as "the mirror of the world" and "the prophet" in the domain of knowledge. (*Kinrai Ryūkō no Seiji-Shōsetsu o Hyōsu*, Some Criticism of Political Novels Recently in Vogue, 1887). It is to be noted that these critics were unanimous in trying to turn the attention of novelists to the significance of society in writing. In contrast with Shōyō who was little interested in society, Futabatei, himself very familiar with the Russian literature that had a strong socialistic concern, stated that seeking truth was the duty of a poet, and that in order to fulfil this duty, he should "show national character, manners, and aims, outline the general trends of the nation, and also vividly depict the actualities of living people." (*Ochiba no Hakiyose*, The Gathering of Fallen Leaves, 1889); while his friend, Yagasaki Saganoya, in discussing the responsibilities of a novelist, enumerated these three : "display of truth," "explanation of human life," and "criticism of society." (*Shōsetsuka no Sekinin*, A Novelist's Responsibilities, 1889).

3. *The Literary Theory of Romanticism and Idealism*

About 1890, stimulated by the growing influence of the Ken'-yūsha led by Ozaki Kōyō, and also by the advent of Kōda Rohan, which made the literary world flourish, there was considerable activity in the domain of criticism. Ishibashi Ningetsu (Tomokichi), with his knowledge in German studies, emerged as a prominent critic in such magazines as the *Jogaku Zasshi* and the *Kokumin no Tomo*. Mori Ōgai discussed the idealistic aesthetics brought from Germany in his brilliant essays which appeared in *Bungaku Hyōron : Shigarami-Zōshi* founded by himself in October 1889. In opposition to Ōgai, there was

Shōyō, who became in October 1891 the chief editor of *Waseda Bungaku*. Discussions by these great writers brought about more serious and deepened criticism of art and literature.

In an essay, *Sōjitsuron* (On Imagination and Reality) (1890), Ningetsu gave a definition to poetry. He said, " Poetry is an artistic materialization of man's *Seelenleben* and *Geistesleben* through the exercise of words." On the assumption that *Seel* eventually becomes *jitsu* (*shinkei*) (reality, or true scene), and *Geist, sō* (*kyoshō*) (imagination, or emptiness), Ningetsu asserted that " harmonizing these two elements is the source of the immortal life of poetry (art and literature)." Thus, denying both the Risō-Ha (idealists) and Shajitsu-Ha (realists), he took his own position. According to him, to aim at " exterior greatness " in elegance, style, and construction was too superficial a goal, and he indicated the importance of " interior greatness," that is, the broadening of " mind," or " poetical heart."

From such a point of view, Ningetsu admired Rohan for his " interior greatness " (*Ikkōken ni taisuru Yo no Iken*, My Opinions on the Novel " One Sword," 1890), and this caused the author to be even more highly regarded. In another essay, criticizing the works of Ōgai, Ningetsu charged the novelist with being overly interested in " external things," and doubted if " in its interior, his work was really an expression of sound, immortal, and mysterious mind (*Geist*)." (*Utakata no Ki*, 1890). Immediately Ōgai retorted, saying that " *yūgen*, or the *Mysterium* (mystery) of concrete beauty, is usually concealed in the darkest of reasoning." Beauty, he argued, could not exist without a concrete exterior, and Ningetsu's view of seeking it in the interior was wrong, for such a view was apt to regard art and literature as the means to " practicing virtue " (*sakuzen*) or " seeking truth " (*kyūshin*), thus falling into the danger of losing sight of beauty itself. (*Ningetsu Yūgen o Ronzuru ni Kotauru Sho*, My Answer to Ningetsu's Essay on Mystery, 1890). Ōgai's emphasis upon the concreteness of beauty stood on the concrete idealism which he had borrowed from the German philosopher

Hartmann. Armed with the aesthetics of this German philosopher who synthesized the thought of Schopenhauer and Hegel into a philosophy of unconsciousness, Ōgai also vehemently attacked the then-prevailing realism and didacticism.

Though admitting the merits of realism (*jissaishugi*, or *shajitsushugi*) in exploring a new realm through the "method of psychological observation," Ōgai blamed extreme Naturalists like Zola for being contented with "imitation of nature," and he contended that "the dirt of nature should be cleared off by means of the imagination of the novelist, who, in composing, should rely upon imagination stimulated by the joy in working." (*Gendai Shoka no Shōsetsu-Ron o Yomu*, On Reading Contemporary Writers' Studies of the Novel, 1889). On the other hand, he also rejected those novelists in favor of analogical, abstract ideals as expressed in the *yomihon* of the Edo Era. Warning them that they were out of the middle-of-the-road of art (*ibid.*), Ōgai held that the poet could give birth to beauty only through materializing a concrete world by means of imagination, while his *Idee*, or ideal, acted upon things and facts found in nature ; also, in this regard he differentiated artistic beauty from scientific truth and moral virtue. Thus, by stressing that beauty should be concrete and ideal, Ōgai made an attempt to establish the autonomy of art and literature of which beauty was the substance.

Such a position of Ōgai was made more distinct in the course of his debates with Shōyō which followed. In December 1890, in his article published in the *Yomiuri Shimbun*, Shōyō, reviewing recent novels, divided novelists of the day into three groups according to their tendencies, the Koyū-Ha (phenomenal study group), Setchū-Ha (eclectic group), and Ningen-Ha (human study group), and analyzed the differences in quality among them. The first group, it appeared to Shōyō, composed their works mostly of specific events, relying upon some principle. The second group put an emphasis upon delineating disposition and feelings of men, taking up events for that purpose, and the third chose for their plots the causal relation of men, who were treated as the cause, and events, as the effect. In the following year, he developed his argument on two kinds of poets, the "lyrical poet," (Risō-Ha) (Idealists) and the "dramatist" (Zōka-Ha) (Naturalists), in an essay published in the same newspaper, *Baika Shishū o Yomite* (On Reading *Baika Shishū*). Despite the "inductive criticism," borrowed from R. G. Moulton, that he applied in these essays, Shōyō, conscious of value, had a secret desire to rank the "humanity group" and the "dramatist" the highest. The attack from Ōgai, armed with Hartmann's aesthetics, was delivered just at this point. According to Ōgai's *Sambō Rombun* (Essays Written at a Mountain Cottage), which appeared serially in the magazine *Shigarami-Zōshi*, the correct method of criticism must lie in value judgment deduced from an "aesthetic idea" as the standard. Each of the three groups assumed by Shōyō corresponds to the *Gattungsidee, Individualsidee*, and *Mikrokosmismus* of Hartmann respectively, and that area of poetry which he calls "lyrical" is equivalent to lyrics, and that which he calls "dramatic," to epics. Each of these three shows the degree of concreteness of beauty from the viewpoint of concrete idealism, and consequently each means a grade of value. (*Shōyō-Shi no Shohyōgo*, Some Remarks on Shōyō, 1891).

To put this matter under examination, if the works belonging to the so-called Ningen-Ha (human study group) are to be characterized as "particular in appearance, but general in substance" (Shōyō), such definition may be regarded as corresponding to the idea of *Mikrokosmismus* that holds that an individual constitutes a concrete microcosm. The two novelists seem to agree in that both of them acknowledge this idea to be most significant, with Shōyō approving of it tacitly, and Ōgai candidly. However, in reality, the issue for them was not resolved in so simple a manner, and for some time there were to follow more violent debates between them on this problem.

Waseda Bungaku, presided over by Shōyō, published from

its first appearance an annotated text of Shakespeare's dramatic works in each issue, and such editing was very much suited to this literary magazine disposed toward public enlightenment. In his note which appeared in the initial number, Shōyō, as the annotator, wrote to the effect that since in Shakespearian drama there was "submerged idealism" (*botsu-risō*), it was useless to make a commentary on it in the light of any ideal. Also, on the occasion of the magazine's beginning to review contemporary literary works in a new column, Shōyō wrote that a critic's prior duty was "reporting of facts," while judgment should be left to the reader. (*Ware ni Arazu Shite Nanji ni Ari*, It's up to You, Not to Us, 1891), Immediately thereafter, in *Waseda Bungaku no Botsu-Risō* (The "Submerged Idealism" in *Waseda Bungaku*) (1891), in his *Sambō Rombun*, Ōgai attacked Shōyō for those remarks. Thus, there broke out repeated polemics between the two men.

In their debates, discontented with Shōyō's method of merely "reporting facts" (*kijitsu*), which depended on Anglo-Saxon common sense, Ōgai advocated against it the necessity of "theorization" (*danri*), through the mouth of an imaginary person named Uyū Sensei (Dr. Non-Existence), namely the philosopher Hartmann. Their controversy was a consequence of the difference in the method they adopted for their criticism, inductive for Shōyō, and deductive for Ōgai. Although both men equally recognized the significance of the two methods, their opinions uncompromisingly differed as to which method was of more importance. In this regard, Shōyō said that their difference lay in the question as to whether the great ideal has not yet, or has already, been attained. (*Uyū Sensei ni Kotau*, My Answer to Dr. Non-Existence, 1892). If so, their opposition was over their difference of conception as to "the ideal." For Ōgai, from his position of *yū-risō* (possessing ideal), namely idealism, attacked sharply Shōyō who adhered to his *botsu-risō*, or submerged idealism.

What does Shōyō mean by his submerged idealism? He does

not mean an absolute absence of the ideal, and the ideal as he understands it is different from Ōgai's *Idee*. In a word, according to Shōyō, submerged idealism stands for the invisibility of the author's ideal, or the supreme good. (*Sono I wa Tagaeri*, Difference of Views, 1892). Metaphysically, Shōyō holds that "the vastness of Nature embraces all of the ideals of the past and present, and yet has space for more." (*Botsu-Risō no Gogi o Benzu*, A Discussion of Submerged Idealism, 1892). We can give the name of Great Ideal to this vast aggregation of ideals, but "so long as we cannot demonstrate what this Great Ideal truly is," we are obliged to name it submerged idealism, as a means for cognition of nature. (*ibid.*). Naturally, such a theory of cognition could not be admitted by Ōgai. Following the philosophy of unconsciousness of Hartmann, Ōgai stressed that the world was full of a certain "ideal *a priori*" (*senten no risō*), that is, absolute *Idee* that is active. (*Waseda Bungaku no Botsu-Risō*, 1892). Shōyō did not go further than answering that there was no way of defining the existence of such ideal. (*Uyū Sensei ni Kotau*).

This concept of submerged idealism, when applied to literature, is used "to represent its purpose, namely one of the aspects of the substance of a drama," Shōyō asserted. (*Botsu-Risō no Gogi o Benzu*). In the same essay, this assertion is paraphrased as, "a drama is the work where the author successfully depicts a variety of personalities, apart from his own self." In some ways, this corresponds to the Human school (Ningen-Ha) in novel-writing. It was this view that Ōgai attacked by stating that "Shōyō apparently confounds *Individualsidee* and *Mikrokosmismus* in regarding them as equivalent." (*Waseda Bungaku no Botsu-Risō*). Here Shōyō values highly an author, who, expressing none of his view of life or of the world, is able to present what is individual or peculiar to him in his works. Undoubtedly this should have been a point acceptable to Ōgai. However, Ōgai's *Idee*, the fundamental of things concrete, was beyond the scope of Shōyō's thought.

Idea, as Hegel meant it, had been imported through Belinsky

by Futabatei in his "theory of copying" (*moshasetsu*), as we stated above. And now the literary theory of idealism on the model of Hartmann came to be established by Ōgai. At the end of the controversy he published his version of Hartmann's aesthetics and studies of it in his essays *Shimbi Ron* (Theory of Aesthetics) (1892–1893) and *Shimbi Kōryō* (Rules of Aesthetics) (1899). As Ōgai tells us, he was not satisfied with Hartmann's philosophy, and had no intention of "retailing" his aesthetic views. Thus, his interest was diverted to the empirical psychology of Wundt and his school. (*Gessōjo*, 1896)

On the other hand, Shōyō must not be regarded as a mere realist; moreover, it should be noted that Ōgai was incorrect when he identified submerged idealism with Zolaism. (*Emiru Zora ga Botsu-Risō*, The Submerged Idealism of Emile Zola, 1892). In *Biji Ronkō* (An Essay on Rhetoric) (1893), published shortly after the debate ended, Shōyō, enlarging upon his submerged idealism, called belles-lettres "the second nature" (*daini no shizen*) which "contains an infinite number of ideals." He established what he called "extreme purity" (*shijun*) as an essential element of "unchanging reality," such as truth, goodness, and beauty.

The vehement arguments exchanged by these two notable writers were followed by the activity of the younger generation, represented by Kitamura Tōkoku and others, which added animation to the circle of criticism. A contributor to the *Jogaku Zasshi* (Women's Academic Magazine) for a time, Tōkoku then became connected with *Bungakkai* (The World of Literature), founded in January 1893 as an independent magazine in the tradition of the former periodical. There, with other contributors to the new magazine, he developed new views on literature from a romantic standpoint.

Contemplation of the traditional classic literature on the basis of the knowledge they acquired from Western studies is a tendency common to the members of this school. In an essay appearing in the July 1892 issue of the *Jogaku Zasshi, Toku-gawa-Shi Jidai no Heiminteki Risō* (The Plebeian Ideal of the Tokugawa Era), Tōkoku regretted that under the yoke of feudalism the common people of the Tokugawa Era were forced to lose their " spiritual nature " (*reisei*) and to narrow and distort their ideals of *iki*, or *sui* (fine taste), and *otokodate*, or *kyō* (gallantry). In another essay, he blamed Rohan and Kōyō for following the feudal writers of the Genroku Era (1690–1703) who could but depict the erotic side of " extreme brutality," and who were ignorant of true love, the " expression of the exquisite spiritual life of mankind." (" *Kyara Makura* " *oyobi* " *Shin'yō Masshū,*" " The Perfumed Pillow," and " A Final Collection of New Leaves," 1892). Under the influence of Christian thought, he held love to be " the key to the secret of life " (*Ensei-Shika to Josei,* The Poet of Pessimism and Woman, 1892), and stated that even if it may be a burden throughout his life, it is the duty of a poet to copy that " beauty contained in love." (*Uta-Nembutsu o Yomite,* On Reading *Uta-Nembutsu,* 1892). When Tōkoku spoke of " copying " (*shajitsu*), he differentiated it from that of the Jissai-Ha (the school of actuality), and his emphasis was placed upon such matters as spiritual nature and beauty. Also, a strong inclination toward romanticism is recognizable in one of his arguments : " Copying tends to become copying for copying's sake, unless it is based upon the author's passion." (*Jōnetsu,* Passion, 1894).

His romanticism finds its clearer expression in the concluding words of his article *Jinsei ni Aiwataru to wa Nan no Ii zo* (What Is the Real Attitude to Life ?), published in *Bungakkai* in February 1893. He says : " With a lofty ideal, look upon the truly spacious structure, the truly magnificent state, and the truly grand enterprise. Then seek, casting your longing to the extremity of the sky." He wrote this essay in opposition to Aizan who expounded the utilitarian position in his essay *Rai Noboru o Ronzu* (On Rai Noboru the Historian) (1893), carried in the *Kokumin no Tomo* (The Nation's Friend). Aizan argued that "writing is itself man's work," and that if it is of no benefit to life and has no direct relation to life, it is only a vain thing. Tōkoku criticized this as violation of "the sovereignty of literature," and advocated that literature should pursue the countless mysteries in the world. Admiring Bashō, the *haiku* poet, for his "attaining what is absolute, namely Idea" beyond the border of reality, Tōkoku found the real object of literature in such an idealistic and romantic world. Sohō attacked such an attitude of Tōkoku as "indifferent to society" and as "keeping aloof." (*Shakai ni okeru Shisō no San-Chōryū*, Three Currents of Thought in Society, 1893). The young critic retorted by asserting that only the thought that keeps aloof from society can communicate humanity. (*Kokumin to Shisō*, The People and Thought, 1893).

For art, "Humanity is the one and only purpose." These words of Tōkoku appear in *Bambutsu no Koe to Shijin* (The Voice of Creation and the Poet) (1893). If its characteristic consists, as emphasized in his *Naibu Seimei Ron* (On the Inner Life), in inner life, the mission of the poet will be defined as relating that inner life. Meanwhile, the inner life is "eternally unchangeable and immovable unless through the agency of God." Thus, it cannot be an object of observation; it can be observed only through studying various aspects of its expression. In this study, those who employ objectivism are called the Shajitsu-Ha (the school of realism). Tōkoku's interest, however, was rather attracted by the Risō-Ha (the school of idealism) whose method is subjectivism. This latter school, according to Tōkoku, "analyzes reality by means of idea," or, in other words, it makes the supreme good become concrete on the ground of reality. Furthermore, in order to grasp that inner life which is providential, one should rely upon inspiration, "a sort of correspondence between the spirit of universe, namely God, and the spirit of man, namely the inner life," as Tōkoku defined it. Man's "eye of life will be recreated" after such tacit correspondence, and only this eye is able to find out and observe idea which has its concrete form in Nature and in all creation.

This attitude of Tōkoku of searching for idea in concrete reality may correspond to Ōgai's concrete idealism. However, Tōkoku had a noticeable inclination toward pantheism, as shown by his hearing the voice of "Nature's soul" in the whole creation. (*Bambutsu no Koe to Shijin*). Moreover, the essay *Emaruson* (On Emerson) (1894), which appeared after his death, shows his dependence upon this American transcendentalist. One may also notice in him a certain influence of Sohō, who explained inspiration as " divine power " (*Insupirēshon*, Inspiration, 1888), and who wrote that " it is the duty of a poet to observe humanity (*jinsei*) and human feelings (*ninjō*) which are mysterious." (*Kansatsu*, Observation, 1893).

As for other members of *Bungakkai*, we have first Hoshino Tenchi who admired Arihara no Narihira, the ancient poet and author of the *Ise Monogatari* (Tales of Ise), " for his divine talent in the expression of pathos " and " for having immersed himself in divine beauty." (*Narihira Ason Azuma Kudari no Sugata*, On Narihira's Travel to East, 1894). *Haiku* poets in the feudal era were lauded by another member, Togawa Shūkotsu, who longed for their kind of life " in a world separated from and indifferent to worldly vicissitude " (*Haijin no Seikō o Omou*, The Life and Temper of the *Haiku* Poet, 1893), and Hirata Tokuboku yearned after Kenkō Hōshi, a monk and man of letters who lived at the end of the Kamakura Shōgunate, who desired " a perfumed world of delicacy." (*Yoshida Kenkō*, 1893). In all of them the romantic tendency is conspicuous. In the face of the popularity enjoyed by inferior and unwholesome literature during the Sino-Japanese War (1894–1895), Tokuboku insisted that the true writer should aim at " the eternity of poetry and the infinity of art." (*Nijūshichinen o Okuru*, Farewell to the Twenty-Seventh Year of Meiji, 1894). Meanwhile, such romantic opinions held by the members of *Bungakkai* were not impervious to the changes which resulted from the outbreak of the war and the suicide of Tōkoku. One of the most remarkable of these changes is seen in Shūkotsu's essay *Kien Izuku ni ka Aru* (Where Is Our High Spirit of the Past ?) (1895), in which, in place of Christian thought, he turned his attention to Greek philosophy that " gives more importance to this life, regarding it as a pleasant thing to be enjoyed," and also expressed his interest in the Renaissance. In the same year, Ueda Ryūson (Bin), who had joined the group a short time after its foundation, showed an inclination to aestheticism and the contemplative view by explaining the sense of beauty in the following manner : " It (the sense of beauty) helps man to dream of a different world by disclosing to him every shade of beauty in everyday feeling." (*Bijutsu no Kanshō*, Appreciation of Art, 1895).

During the decade after the end of the war, there was a most active critic in the person of Takayama Chogyū, who collaborated with Ryūson in *Teikoku Bungaku* (Imperial Literature) and took charge of the literary columns in the magazine *Taiyō* (The Sun). Emulating Ōgai and Shōyō, the young critic took full advantage of his unusual talent and entered upon a period of great activity.

First he emerged as an idealist when he demanded of literary works that " they demonstrate and realize an idealistic condition that does not actually exist in ordinary society." (*Sakka no Dōnen to Kannen*, The Morals and Concepts of the Writer, 1896). From this standpoint, he recognized the significance of idealistic novels and valued highly the representative writer of this genre, Izumi Kyōka, for his " reaching the ultimate of idealization." (*Seinen Shōsetsu o Yomu*, On Reading Novels for Youth, 1896). These views of Chogyū published in *Taiyō* were then attacked by Ōgai in an article entitled *Shigi no Hanekaki* (A Shaking of the Snipe's Feathers) in *Mesamashigusa* (Grasses of Awakening). According to Ōgai, the idealistic novels belong to the *Tendenz Roman* (tendency novel), and " the ultimate point attained by Kyōka is not a concrete but an abstract one." For this reason, Ōgai concluded, Chogyū who supported such works was merely adhering to abstract idealism. As a matter of fact, Chogyū and Ōgai had much in common in their attitude to idealism. In addition, as the author of *Kinsei Bigaku* (Modern Aesthetics) (1899), Chogyū, well-versed in this field of philosophy, advocated the necessity of " knowledge of aesthetics " (*shimbigaku no chishiki*) as the essential standard for criticism (*Wagakuni Genkon no Bungeikai ni okeru Hihyōka no Hommu*, The Duty of the Critic in the Literary World of Present-Day Japan, 1897), and Ōgai concurred in this opinion. Nevertheless, Chogyū was critical of the concrete idealism of Hartmann and his school. He insisted that consciousness of beauty has two sides, that of the abstract and the concrete, and asserted that " especially in the present day an accurate understanding of the value and significance of abstract beauty is most necessary." (*Bigakujō no Risōsetsu ni tsuite*, On Aesthetic Idealism, 1900). What then in reality was Chogyū's ideal ? In short, it possessed a deep moral consciousness.

In theorizing upon art, Chogyū occasionally stressed " the concept of a moral ideal " (*dōtoku no risō chō kannen*). Even though art is not subjugated to morality, he asserted, ultimately morality should rule as the guide of humanity. (*Yorokobu-Beki Bundan no Ichi-Keikō*, One Welcome Tendency in the Literary World, 1895). Such a view, of course, encountered opposition from Ōgai who was meticulous in distinguishing beauty from goodness. However, Chogyū, admitting " the difference between these two as actual phenomena," believed " in their union as ideals." (*Zen to Bi no Kankei*, The Relation between Good and Beauty, 1896). Further, in protesting against the view of the autonomy of literature, he contended that literature should be put under the restriction of the state and society. In arguing this point, he stated that literature should nourish human activities, and vice versa. " If such a reciprocal relation does not exist between life and literature, the result will be only superfluous or morbid literature." (*Bungaku ni taisuru Kom-*

ponteki Gokai, Basic Misunderstanding with Regard to Literature, 1897). At that time, what he regarded as useful and sound literature was one which had its basis in the national character, namely what he called *Nipponshugi* (Japanism).

Finding himself one of a nation awakened to its pride under the stimulus of its victory in the Sino-Japanese War, Chogyū became interested in the traditional art of this country, and in May 1897 he published an article entitled *Nipponshugi* (Japanism). This doctrine, as he expounded it, was " a moral principle which has its foundation in the spirit of self-dependence as the basic characteristic of the nation, and which makes it a goal to exhibit the ambition cherished by the nation on the occasion of the establishment of this country." Applying this doctrine to literature, Chogyū charged that contemporary novels were devoid of moral ideas and incapable of satisfying the national sentiment. Thus, he labelled them as " un-nationalistic literature " (*hi-kokuminteki bungaku*). (*Shōsetsu Kakushin no Jiki*, The Time for Reform of the Novel, 1898). In his opinion, didactic works were commendable, because they were " the clearest reflection of the national character that tends to be realistic as well as moralistic." (*Kyokutei Bakin*, The Edo Novelist Bakin, 1898).

Such moralistic idealism, however, underwent an important change when the critic came to know of Nietzsche. In January 1901, in an essay entitled *Bummei Hihyōka to shite no Bungakusha* (The Man of Letters as a Critic of Civilization), Chogyū declared his affinity to the individualism of this German poet and philosopher, and stressed that men of letters should become, as had Nietzsche, critics of civilization. In August of that year, he admired the natural instinct of human beings in another essay, *Biteki Seikatsu o Ronzu* (On the Aesthetic Life). This time he abandoned as valueless morals which he had previously valued most highly, and emphasized beauty and instinct. He wrote : " Aesthetic beauty is of absolute value, and the satisfaction of instinctive desires is the purest of aesthetic values."

Led by his passionate temperament, he came to revere Nichiren in the last years of his life. He then urged a strong subjectivism that would even risk extremism or partiality in order to introduce vitality into the world of art by exhibiting the ideal, both divine and individual. (*Anezaki Chōfū ni Atauru Sho*, A Note to Anezaki Chōfū, 1901). In the same work he expressed his "hope for the rise of romanticism rather than the rise of the ethical movement of moralists." We may suppose, it was with this strong subjectivism that Chogyū himself worked for the realization of that hope. Unlike Tōkoku who esteemed spiritual nature, Chogyū, standing on the same ground of humanity in the *Bungakkai* tradition, in his romanticism gave importance to what was natural and instinctive. This clarifies his position as a predecessor of the Naturalists.

4. *The Literary Theory of Naturalism and Anti-Naturalism*

From about the beginning of the twentieth century, when the romantic current of thought was at its height, as represented by the writings of Chogyū, in the area of the novel, Naturalism began to emerge. As mentioned earlier, such writers as Kosugi Tengai, Nagai Kafū, and Tayama Katai began publishing their views in their efforts to theorize this new ideology.

In the preface to his novel *Hatsusugata* (The New Year Dress) (1900), Tengai insisted that artistic beauty should give the reader the feeling he receives from natural phenomena. Thus, he wrote that "the author has attempted to impress the reader's senses (by the novel) as they are impressed by worldly matters." This indicates that his intention was to copy nature, which he regarded as valuable in itself. In the foreword to his *Hayariuta* (A Popular Song) (1902), Tengai explained that nature exists beyond any definition of good and evil, beauty and ugliness, etc., and asserted that "the novel constitutes an imaginary nature." It is true that he insisted that the novel should reject "the slightest subjectivism" (*ichigō no watakushi*) of the author in description, and that it should only copy things just as they are (*ari no mama ni utsusu beki*). But his naturalism was as yet unreal, at least in that he thought a novel consisted of the world of imagination. Though Tengai is said to have had some knowledge of Zola, his views were not so distant from those expressed in Shōyō's *Shōsetsu Shinzui.*

It was rather Kafū who first made it clear what Zolaism was. In the epilogue to *Jigoku no Hana* (Flowers of Hell) (1902), Kafū stated that "mankind certainly has, in certain of its aspects, something brutal," and declared that he would draw without reserve the dark side of human life resulting from heredity and circumstance. Evidently, he owed the declaration to Zola's *Le Roman Experimental.* From this time on, writers began to transplant actively the literary theory of Naturalism, which had been rejected by Ōgai.

Katai, according to the preface to *No no Hana* (Flowers of the Field) (1901), modeled himself upon those French writers, such as Maupassant and Flaubert, who, without the least subjectivism, successfully described the details of human life in their world where one can feel the presence of nature. In February 1904, Katai in an essay, *Rokotsu naru Byōsha* (Candid Description), emphasized the rejection of technique in description, and opened the way to Naturalism by urging the following of the example of Continental literature. He proposed that "every description should be frank, true, and natural."

It was after the year 1906 that Naturalism flourished with remarkable vigor and became the object of animated discussion. Several magazines began carrying reviews treating this movement. *Bunshō Sekai* (The World of Writing), founded in 1906, was headed by Katai who advocated Naturalism through it. *Taiyō* had Hasegawa Tenkei, while *Waseda Bungaku* became, as it were, the fortress of the movement with such critics as Shimamura Hōgetsu, Sōma Gyofū, and Katagami Tengen. There was also Iwano Hōmei, who very early set forth his peculiar Naturalism. It goes without saying that the appearance of the various theories of these Naturalists met much criticism from those who had different standpoints. We shall attempt a survey of the situation.

Naturalism, as held by Hōmei, is distinguishable in that it was based upon what he called "mystic semi-animalism" (*shimpiteki hanjūshugi*). Under this motto, he fervently developed his theory in June 1906. Hōmei, sympathizing with Swedenborg, Emerson, and Maeterlinck in their mysticism, believed in the existence of a mystic quality in the depth of nature. Despite this sympathy, he was not satisfied with their method of grasping the relation between nature and spirit. In his opinion, they apprehended this relation either in a fixed way or by means of reasoning. With such a view, he stipulated that "nature is equal to soul" on the basis of the formal logic of "conversion of symbols" (*hyōshō no tenkan*). According to Hōmei, "the symbol of one thing can be that of another," and the whole creation exists among these interchanging, "purposeless symbols" (*mumokuteki hyōshō*). Man cannot live without relying upon "the intuition of symbols" (*hyōshō no chokkan*). Man is regarded "as a symbol that lives by eating its symbol and, in return, gives birth, through pain, to the same symbol." In the opinion of Hōmei, man is "a miserable soul that is incarnated." Thus, his proposition that nature equals the soul corresponds to the understanding of man as the unification of flesh and soul. Here is the basis for his "semi-animal-and-semi-spiritualism" (*hanjū-hanreishugi*), or, in short, his "semi-animalism" (*hanjūshugi*).

From such a standpoint, he demanded that literature should "represent as much as possible the greatness and profundity of the world of symbol and mystery that undergoes changes every moment," that is, "it should bring forth on the stage this fleshly soul of pain and sorrow in the rise and fall that it faces at every moment." In such a case, Hōmei asserted, the activity of flesh and soul should be "grasped by means of intuition" and be "directly traced in writing." He called this method "a kind of realism in an advanced stage," and espoused it as Naturalism.

It is clear that the Naturalism of Hōmei differs on many points from the ordinary understanding of Naturalism, since Hōmei himself calls it "Neo-Naturalism" (*shin-shizenshugi*). In the first place, what was peculiar to his Naturalism was his neglect of that scientific attitude which should be its backbone. Instead, he was interested in mysticism. Taking note of the natural and brutal sides of man, he criticized European Naturalism for its shallowness. In his view, it was inclined to the material side and gave especial importance to objectivism, thereby tending to "abuse the spontaneity of subjectivity." (*Bungaku no Shinkeikō*, The New Tendency of Literature, 1908). Hōmei held that nature and spirit can attain union through the medium of the concept of symbol. From this standpoint, his Neo-Naturalism is also called "Naturalistic Symbolism" (*shizenshugi-teki hyōshōshugi*). Here it comes to have some relation to the Symbolist poetry of the West, but Hōmei was dissatisfied with the latter as "it obscures itself by abstract idea." (*ibid.*). What Hōmei intended was to "exert the whole might of the nervous system of man, namely passionate energy." (*ibid.*). Unlike the majority of Naturalists, Hōmei regarded Naturalism not only as a problem in the world of art but also "as a problem of human life in modern civilization." (*ibid.*). However, finding something similar to Naturalism in ancient Japan, he looked back upon his ancestors, who, "deeply interested in mundane affairs, lived energetically from moment to moment with fervent love of life." (*Nihon Kodai Shisō yori Kindai no Hyōshōshugi o Ronzu*, Modern Symbolism in the Light of Japan's Ancient Thought, 1907).

Because of such eccentric views, Hōmei's Naturalism was difficult for the public to accept, so that it was Tenkei who primarily orientated Naturalism in this country. Although at first Tenkei was suspicious of Naturalism, in October 1906, with his article *Gemmetsu Jidai no Geijutsu* (Art in the Age of Disillusionment) in *Taiyō*, he launched into activity as a Naturalist. In this review, he made it plain that truthful and correct imagination should be discovered in place of the old illusive one destroyed by the Reformation, the French Revolution, and the progress of science. For that purpose he taught that there had to emerge anew an "unornamental art (*mushoku geijutsu*) which would draw truth," and which would be foreign to art for pleasure and opposed to superficial delineation.

Furthering this view, Tenkei asserted that both the philosophical and religious ideal are nothing but "the result of playful logic," and that realism is a kind of idealism in that "it regards scientific research as the supreme ideal." Thus, he thought none of these was sufficient to rely upon for reaching the truth of reality. One thing important, he urged, was to demolish all ideals and to display reality instead. Naturalism should make it its duty "to look directly at reality and thus find new meanings in it." In such a case, "absolute indifference" (*munen musō*) is required. (*Ronriteki Yūgi o Haisu*, Against Playful Logic, 1907). This act of discovering the new meaning of reality naturally is accompanied by the sorrows and sufferings of frustration, Tenkei pointed out in the essay *Genjitsu Bakuro no Hiai* (The Sorrow of Exposing Reality) (1908). If Western Naturalism risks depicting ugly things, trivia, and immoral or sensual matters, it is merely because it finds in them uncovered reality, he explained, and affirmed that such attempts are made against a background of deep sorrow.

Although Tenkei set forth these opinions as to Naturalism with the background of his thorough knowledge of the literature of the West, we cannot but notice a peculiar retouching in the Naturalism which he introduced. He mistakenly concluded that Naturalism, devoid of both ideals and values, stands upon nihilism, which, he believed, resembles the *nihil* and *nil admirari* (*kyomu tentan*) of the ancient Chinese philosophers Laotzu and Chuangtzu. (*Shizen-Ha ni taisuru Gokai*, Some Misunderstandings as to Naturalists, 1908). The attitude of Naturalists, Tenkei pointed out, resembles that of the Zen Buddhists or the pupils of the Laotzu and Chuangtzu school, for the attitude of the former as well as the latter remains unresolved as to the confused reality confronting it. (*Mukaiketsu ka Kaiketsu ka*, Unresolved or Resolved?, 1908). In grasping reality, they, the Naturalists, will face " the actualities before their eyes " — the green of the willows, the scarlet of the flowers, etc. — in the capacity of onlookers, not as intellectuals armed with scientific knowledge. (*Futatabi Shizenshugi no Rikkyakuchi ni tsuite*, What Is the Standpoint of Naturalism?, Continued, 1907). Such a view has some affinity to the Leisure school, which will be discussed later. Obviously, on this point, Tenkei was different from Hōmei, who tried to pour fervent energy into what he called a being of soul and flesh. Therefore, as a matter of course, his Naturalism, which was characterized by its indifferent, contemplative attitude, should have been a purely "artistic theory," unrelated to the practical world. (*Mukaiketsu ka Kaiketsu ka*).

The most systematic study of Naturalism was developed by Hōgetsu who stood comparatively close to Tenkei's position. Earlier, in January 1906, he published an essay, *Torawaretaru Bungei* (Captive Literature), a survey of the literary tendencies of the West. Reinforced by his acquirements during his stay abroad, he declared in that essay that Naturalism was too much concerned with scientific knowledge. Instead, he suggested that a new direction of literature should be found in the rising Symbolism and mysticism which took interest in the emotional and the mystic. Naturally, such a view was not acceptable to the literary world, considering the actual circumstances of that day. Thus, finding himself surrounded by the high tide of Naturalism in the current of literary thought, he was obliged to change his views, and thereafter he turned into an active supporter of Naturalism.

In June 1907, Hōgetsu wrote *Ima no Bundan to Shinshizenshugi* (The Present Literary World and Neo-Naturalism). In this article he stressed the importance of pure Naturalism, which, in his opinion, should " regard a phenomenon as the fusion of matter and ego " (*jishō ni butsuga no gattai o miru*). With this view, he demanded, as did Tenkei, an attitude of " absolute indifference" (*munen musō*) like the serenity of water. Hōgetsu expected that the phenomena with which the ego is fused would be the source of " fresh feelings " (*seishin no jōmi*), and he attempted to ladle out new vitality of nature therefrom. Such was the thought peculiar to Hōgetsu. In the following year, he published *Bungeijō no Shizenshugi* (Naturalism in Art), *Shizenshugi no Kachi Ikan* (What Is the Value of Naturalism?), etc., and furthered his theorization based on the historical facts of the literature of Japan and the West and aided by his knowledge of aesthetics. Dividing Naturalism into two types, " original Naturalism," purely objective as well as realistic, and " impressive Naturalism," which is subjective, he asserted that a harmony of the two was the best. Here the critic introduced truth as the common goal to be reached by both types of Naturalism. According to Hōgetsu, aesthetic subjectivism is classified into three kinds, lyrical, sentimental, and emotional. However, both lyricism and sentimentalism should be rejected since they hinder truth. Thus, he proposed that the duty of Naturalism consists in drawing the true aspects of nature, through faithful representation of " the fusion of intellect and feeling " (*chi-jō yūkai*) which includes emotional subjectivism.

For the purpose of revealing the truth of life, Naturalism, applying scientific knowledge, will go so far as to treat social and moral problems, thereby daring to depict candidly the ugly side of reality. In such a case, if Naturalism tends to a " moral or practical objective," it would run a risk of endangering the independence of literature. In spite of such fear, however, Hōgetsu believed that " beauty is the only goal of literature." According to him, the attempts to find what is true in reality would give profound significance to literature. " Truth is, after all, one of the ways to achieve beauty," Hōgetsu insisted. Thus, so long as it is approached from an artistic viewpoint, this truth will help specify the content of beauty, and " become a facet of it." (Each quotation from *Shizenshugi no Kachi Ikan*).

Contrary to those Naturalists who in general so far appeared to neglect aesthetic value in literature, Hōgetsu in this way openly supported it as the essential point in his effort to theorize Naturalism. This indicated his point of view as an aesthetician, which Hōgetsu actually was. To look back upon his past, Hōgetsu, who was one of Shōyō's pupils, also respected Ōgai for his aesthetic views, and had studied under philosophers and aestheticians such as Ōnishi Shuku (Sōzan) and Koya (Ōtsuka) Yasuharu. As a result of such experiences, his critical reviews on literature always were based on aesthetics as "the philosophy of literature." Yet as to Hartmann's aesthetics, he criticized its theory of imagination as "incompatible with the art of modern times which tries to discover beauty in reality itself." In this connection, Hōgetsu interpreted beauty as follows: "Beauty is a kind of particular mood that arises when man faces and contemplates reality." (*Bigaku Gairon*, Outline of Aesthetics, 1909).

Although Hōgetsu approved of Naturalism as a principle of an "unresolved and a non-idealistic" attitude toward reality, he himself did not necessarily adhere to it. He said the Naturalists reject ideal and solution as they regard them to be "mean, shallow, and restricted." Taking this into consideration, he could not help asking, "Does it not vitalize Naturalism to search for something ultimate and absolute in the depth of them (ideal and solution)?" Further, for Hōgetsu, a view which held Naturalistic literature as specifically concerned with the description of brutalism and the satisfaction of instinctive desires was very erroneous. Rather, he asserted that through description true to nature, Naturalistic literature moves the reader to "meditative emotions" (*meisōteki jōshu*), and stirs in him "the unlimited desire to seek after truth infinitely." In this way, literature can lead the reader to "the entrance to religion" (*shūkyō no mon*), or as Hōgetsu also said, to "the height of beauty or the substance of life," which should be the goal of Naturalism. (Each quotation is from *Shizenshugi no Kachi Ikan*). Such Naturalism is also explained as a Zen-type literature where earthly affairs are put under contemplation of "the cold self" (*sameta jiko*). (*Sameta Jiko*, The Cold Self, 1908). Basing himself upon Kant's theory of indifference, in another essay Hōgetsu defines Naturalism as "the art of contemplation" (*kanshō no geijutsu*). (*Geijutsu to Jisseikatsu no Kai ni Yokotawaru Issen*, The Borderline between Art and Actual Life, 1908). We may recognize some reflection of Oriental thinking in that the critic sees in reality what is religious and absolute. Since, in his view, art can be born only in a world of contemplation, a borderline dividing art from real life inevitably exists. He succinctly expressed this in the following words : "So long as a man is occupied with the practical things of life, he cannot appreciate what life really is." (*ibid.*).

Hōgetsu, who until that time had been studying Naturalism principally as a literary problem, then came to feel it necessary to reinforce his Naturalism in relation to his philosophy of life. He first attempted this in an essay which took the place of a preface in his collection of critical essays entitled *Kindai Bungei no Kenkyū* (Studies of Modern Literature), published in June 1909, *Jo ni Kaete Jinseikanjō no Shizenshugi o Ronzu* (In Place of a Preface I Discuss Naturalism as a Philosophy of Life). He suggested that a desolate desert begins where all meditation ends, and he himself tried to find the pleasure of life in "the contemplation of reality, namely in literature and the arts," which "represent to us real life and make us desire the matter of greatest importance." (*Kaigi to Kokuhaku*, Suspicion and Confession, 1909).

In contrast with Hōgetsu's Naturalism, characterized as academic and theoretical, Katai set forth his views on Naturalism mainly in the field of technique—especially the problem of depiction—relying upon his creative experience as a novelist. On the occasion of publishing his novel *Sei* (Life) in 1908, Katai told of his method of "plain delineation" (*heimen byōsha*) adopted in writing that work. This was merely a further development of what he had earlier called "candid description" (*rokotsu naru byōsha*). This so-called plain delineation meant a method of relating, "with no subjectivism, the author's experiences in the real world just as they had been when he had seen, heard, and felt them," that is, in the "impressive" way that is seen in the works of Maupassant or the Goncourt brothers. (" *Sei* " *ni okeru Kokoromi*, My Trial in the Novel "Life "). Katai enlarged upon this subject in his articles published in *Bunshō Sekai* (The World of Writing) and other periodicals.

Of this plain delineation, the first thing to be pointed out is that it is an effort to write true to the facts in the author's experience. Katai rejected imagination with the statement that "it cannot be true to nature" (*Shōsetsu Shinron*, A New Theory of the Novel), and, on the contrary, he believed that any fact, however unnatural and strange it may appear, will find natural expression if it undergoes sufficient observation. (*Bunshō Shingo*, Fresh Views on Writing). Furthermore, he insisted that although facts are multitudinous, confused, and complicated, the writer ought to esteem them, "since they are natural phenomena," and should not be allowed to tamper with them. (*Takujōgo*, Table Talk). He strongly demanded of a writer an objective attitude toward facts, calling it "an attitude of objectifying things." Thus Katai emphasized transforming subjectivism into, as it were, "a transparent lens," in an effort to achieve "full objectivity." (*Inki Tsubo*, Ink Bottle, 1909). Impressionism that was to be attained in this way was the charactic element of his Naturalism. Thus, differing from Hōgetsu who tried to season his Naturalism with emotion, Katai proterisposed "a literature of objectivism" in the pure sense of the word. (*ibid.*). On the other hand, like Tenkei and Hōgetsu, he favored discriminating practice and art. It was from this viewpoint that he criticized Hōmei's novels for "lack of objectivity," and declared that "when one is immersed in the whirl of practical activities, one cannot know the true state of things." (*ibid.*). In short, to draw in an objective and impressionistic way natural facts as they impress the author, while keeping his subjectivism always immanent, that is, "the representation of phenomena—their simple representation " (*Takujōgo*) was the basic method of Katai's Naturalism.

One must note that the view that holds art as the "reflection of nature" underlies the method of delineation set forth by Katai. To seek after what is "nature-like" (*shizenrashisa*) or to depict things "pressing on nature" (*shizen ni semaru*) was proposed as the aim of an artistic work, and given the same meaning as "pressing on truth" (*shin ni semaru*). This stemmed from his belief that "nothing is more extensive than Nature and also nothing is more intricate and complete." He then expanded the discussion to treat the affinity of art to religion, by asserting that art, "in a way, resembles Zen or *shikan* (the perception of universal truth by suppression of evil thoughts)." (*Shōsetsu Shinron*, A New Theory of the Novel). On this point, he may be said to agree with the view of Hōgetsu.

Lastly, we should consider the theory of Tengen, who, as the rear-guard of Naturalism, suggested the turning for its new course. With him, too, "Naturalistic literature is unresolved toward life," for "it should not go further than representing honestly, as well as candidly, the results of thorough contemplation" of life, which basically is not resolvable. (*Mikaiketsu no Jinsei to Shizenshugi*, The Unresolved Life and Naturalism, 1908). Nevertheless, Tengen could not endure to leave life in this undetermined state forever. Tengen stated that Naturalistic literature has within it profound sadness, because "a Naturalist tries to communicate his feelings arising from the failure of his efforts to provide a solution to life." "The agony expressed in literature is, after all, an image of the inquiring spirit," he contended. (*ibid.*). Such sadness and even agony are attributed to "actual contradictions that vitiate the establishment of life, the basic demand of humanity." (*Shinkō Bungaku no Igi*, The Significance of the New Literature, 1908).

Tengen's exposition of Naturalism as being based on the "inquiring spirit" (*motomuru kokoro*) and the demand of "establishing life" (*sei no juritsu*) varied from that of Tenkei or Hōgetsu, who either reduced it to nihilism, or regarded it as comparable to Zen contemplation. From this point of view, he criticized Katai for his lack of "inquiring spirit" and for his being satisfied with the objective reality. (*Tayama Katai-Shi no Shizenshugi*, The Naturalism of Tayama Katai, 1908). "Pure objectivism and pure realism" emphasized by other Naturalists could not in themselves satisfy him. Approving of these as the basis for Naturalist literature, he simultaneously gave importance to a work which, "penetrated with subjective emotions, would, on the whole, make the reader imagine a kind of troubled mind." (*Inshō-Ha no Shōsetsu*, The Novel of the Impressionist School, 1908). Thus, Tengen proposed emphatically that Naturalism should enter upon a new phase by enriching "its content with strong, fresh, creative subjectivism." (*Seishin Kyōretsu naru Shukan*, Strong and Fresh Subjectivism, 1909). We can discern a romantic as well as an idealistic tendency in this proposition.

In an article entitled *Shizenshugi no Shukanteki Yōso* (Subjective Elements in Naturalism) (1910), he discussed in detail the subjectivism needed for Naturalism. According to him, Naturalism in literature is subjected to "the mechanical and materialistic" philosophy which views the world by applying "objectivity as the sole standard." The Naturalist, Tengen asserted, should place emphasis upon "the perturbation and agony on the part of that subjectivism which desires freedom of the spirit in face of the oppression of such a world view." Although an objective method of description may be adopted as effective in expressing them, what should be basic for the author are such subjective elements. It is noteworthy that the critic himself recognized "the romantic spirit" in this assertion.

Furthermore, we can hear idealistic overtones in his following statements in *Sei no Yōkyū to Geijutsu* (Demands of Life and Art) (1912): "What we demand from literature are fullness and tension of life, and life's activity." He welcomed the emergence of the Shirakaba school and such writers as Kafū, Mimei,

Sōhei, and Miekichi, who together introduced a new style in the literary world, because, in his opinion, they were "seekers after a full and tense real life." (*Kinchō Jūjitsu o Hossuru Bungaku*, Literature Desirous of Tension and Fullness, 1912). Tengen acknowledged that this view deviated from the true course of Naturalism. However, he apologized for it by stating that "this is, after all, a branch of Naturalism, or, at any rate, its keynote is basically Naturalistic." (*ibid.*). It is true this was a far-fetched explanation, as pointed out by Abe Yoshishige who will be mentioned below. Nevertheless, it does not lose its significance as a barometer showing the crisis which Naturalism then faced.

There were also some in a bystander position who sympathized with Naturalist thinking. Such a critic as Ikuta Chōkō regarded Naturalism as inseparable from modern civilization, the basic elements of which were the "utilitarian mind," "liberalism," and "individualism." Because it answered the demands of the spirit of the times, he stated that "we cannot but recognize its great original value, even though it may also have some defects." With such reservation, he admitted he was a Naturalist. (*Shizenshugi Ron*, On Naturalism, 1908). Shortly afterward, however, with the rise of Neo-Idealism and Symbolism, Chōkō began to be dissatisfied with the nihilistic view and materialistic philosophy of Naturalism, and wanted rather "to look up at the heaven of mysticism through the window of Symbolism." (*Shizenshugi yori Shōchōshugi*, From Naturalism to Symbolism, 1908).

Gotō Chūgai, who appeared in the literary world together with Hōgetsu, at the time of the rise of Naturalism repeatedly delivered attacks on it in the magazine *Shinshōsetsu* (The New Novel). He criticized Naturalists as being preoccupied with reality, and pointed out that "they were bent on eulogizing the power of the flesh," thus "totally neglecting the undeniable faith in the power of the soul." (*Zuikanroku*, A Record That Follows Feeling, 1907). Instead he stated that he "desired a literature which transcends reality." (*Majime Nare*, Be Serious, 1908). He compared Naturalism to the Buddhist cult of self-reliance (*jiriki mon*), and considered that both philosophies " have neither the power to work out salvation nor to provide an adequate solution to the problems of life." Instead, as the cult of salvation by faith (*tariki mon*) in literature, he recommended one that " apart from the real world . . . or by purifying reality . . . absorbs the reader's soul into a different world of beauty." (*Bungeijō no Jiriki Mon to Tariki Mon*, Cult of Self-Reliance and Cult of Salvation by Faith in Literature, 1908). Moreover, in an essay, *Shizenshugi Hikaku Ron* (A Comparative Study within Naturalism) (1908), Chūgai charged the Naturalist critics with contradictions and inconsistency. In addition, Higuchi Ryūkyō, who organized the Bungei Kakushin Kai (Literary Reform Society), together with Chūgai, Sasagawa Rimpū, and others, also participated in the anti-Naturalist campaign, although they were not so influential as to change the course of literature.

The rivals of the Naturalists were the group called the Haikai-Ha (Haikai school) or Yoyū-Ha (Leisure school) centering around Kyoshi, and they continued to reveal their unique stand in *Hototogisu* (The Cuckoo). In this magazine, Natsume Sōseki and his pupils Abe Yoshishige, Abe Jirō, Komiya Toyotaka, etc., also took part. These critics were also active in the *Tōkyō Asahi Shimbun* literary columns edited by Sōseki. In some cases, they were in concert with the Shirakaba school of Mushakōji Saneatsu, with their Neo-Idealist assertions.

Kyoshi and his school advocated *shaseibun* (sketch-writing) with a view to " delineate a faithful sketch of the object," following the fashion of *haiku* (*Haikai Hitokuchi-Banashi*, Short Commentaries on *Haiku*, 1907), and they tried to apply this method to the novel. Such an objective manner of drawing real things just as they are may appear to correspond to Naturalism. Though admitting a probable tendency to subjectivism, Kyoshi advised "the maintaining of an objective attitude (toward reality) supported by passion." (*Shin-Shaseibun*, New Sketch-Writing, 1908). Such objectivism was the peculiar attitude of "sketch-writing" that aimed at "supermundane dignity" (*chōdatsu-shita fūkaku*) based on "the taste of unworldly *haiku*." (*Haiku Hitokuchi-Banashi*). While Naturalism attempted to reveal the truth of life, Kyoshi and his group tried to represent the supermundane joys of beauty and taste.

We may say that Sōseki employed this method of sketching when he described the world of "non-feeling" (*hi-ninjō*) in *Kusamakura* (The Grass Pillow) (1906), which he defined as "a novel resembling *haiku* in which beauty is the vital element." (*Yo ga "Kusamakura,"* My "Grass Pillow"). Sōseki, appreciating the works of "sketch" writers, made it clear that he "finds a placid mood in them..." and "feels relaxed while reading them..." (*Shaseibun*, Sketch-Writing, 1907). Notwithstanding this, he was not totally in conformity with their method. This is clear in his monitory remarks: "There are those who are so proud of such (old-fashioned) methods as to be contemptuous of other schools. Yet we must remember that nowadays it is the twentieth century." (*ibid.*).

Writing a preface to Kyoshi's collection of stories *Keitō* (Cockscomb) (1908), Sōseki tagged the works of Kyoshi and his school as *yoyū no aru shōsetsu* (leisure novels), and explained their characteristics in contrast with the *yoyū no nai shōsetsu* (leisureless novels), which have no "leisurely" or "easy" elements, and which, "treating the vital problems of life, show the seriousness of destiny." Also, the former "leisure novels" are otherwise named *semaranai shōsetsu* (novels which do not press) or *furenai shōsetsu* (not touching novels). Sōseki pointed out that these "leisure novels" are characterized by their *teikai shumi* (rambling taste), *Zen-mi* (Zen taste), not harassed by life and death, and *haimi* (*haiku* taste). The words *teikai shumi* arise from his remark which can be paraphrased as follows: "When one thing or other attracts the attention of an author, he thinks about it from his own point of view, or indulges in associating imagination. He looks upon the object from this angle or that, and is reluctant to leave it."

In this preface, Sōseki intended solely to show, in Kyoshi's favor, the significance of "leisure novels." But some critics raised their voice against these remarks, regarding them as an apology for Sōseki's own position. Hōmei criticized the statements as the "intention of reviving old *gesaku*-style novels" (*Bunkai Shigi*, A Private View of the Literary World, 1908), and Tenkei charged the obscurity of the "leisure novels" supported by Sōseki. (*Iwayuru Yoyū-Ha Shōsetsu no Kachi*, The Value of the So-Called Leisure School Novels, 1908). However, as mentioned above, Tenkei, as well as Hōgetsu and Katai, regarded Naturalism as inclined to religion rather than to science, and from such a position valued an indifferent and contemplative attitude. If we take this into consideration, their Naturalism with its Oriental characteristic naturally had a similarity to "sketch-writing."

Sōseki had early made some attempts at a purely theoretical study of literature in his lectures at the university, collected under the title *Bungaku Ron* (On Literature) (delivered 1903–1905 ; published 1907). The content of literature was thought "to consist mainly of emotion," and its form was defined as "the unification of cognitive element (F) and emotional element (f)." Sōseki owes this view to the theory of Spencer and other philosophers, and thus stands on an empirical and psychological basis. Later, in several lectures, including *Bungei no Tetsugakuteki Kiso* (The Philosophical Basis of Literature) (1907), where, in addition, value judgment was introduced, he discussed the fundamental problems of literature, partly with an intention of analyzing and confronting Naturalism.

In *Bungei no Tetsugakuteki Kiso*, Sōseki attacked the Naturalists for valuing truth too highly as the objective of literature, by asserting that "they give excessive importance to truth, to the detriment of beauty, goodness, and sublimity." In the following year, in another lecture, *Sōsakka no Taido* (The Attitude of the

Creative Writer), he explained the necessity of the emergence of *kishin bungaku* (literature that reveals the truth) of the Naturalist type to replace *jōsō bungaku* (literature of emotion) of romanticism and idealism. Furthermore, in another lecture entitled *Bungei to Dōtoku* (Literature and Morality) (1911), he regarded romantic morals as belonging to the past, and Naturalism as having " the virtue of honesty " in " its frank expression of the true state of things without affectation."

In these lectures, Sōseki reviewed the historical and relative relations between Romanticism-Idealism and Naturalism, and it is noteworthy that he attempted to find moral values in Naturalism which was generally thought to be an amoral philosophy. Such a view of Naturalism must have stemmed from his belief that "literature could not transcend morality" and "should foster a desire for things ethical." (*Kyōiku to Dōtoku*, Education and Morality, 1911). This reveals the ethical tendency of Sōseki himself. On the other hand, however, he was obviously interested in the aesthetic world of the Leisure school (Yoyū-Ha). It was toward the end of his life that these two different elements of his thinking were unified into the concept of *sokuten kyoshi* (to follow heaven and depart from the self).

Since Naturalism was the literary philosophy having historical necessity, as recognized by Sōseki, it was an urgent problem for the younger generation to know in what way they could penetrate it. Abe Jirō emphasized " the romantic elements of Naturalism," and tried to trace its movement toward romanticism. He stated that " the value of Naturalism lies in its description of the miserable state of human life, which, separated from nature, has lost the deep emotion of wonder, and also in that it never fails to make the reader feel within his heart a romantic, sentimental yearning for some unknown state." (*Kyōtan to Shibo*, Admiration and Longing, 1909). Jirō attacked *Waseda Bungaku* (Waseda Literature) for its admiration of Kafū, who had appeared as an Epicurean, which contradicted its advocacy of Naturalism. (*Mizukara Shirazaru Shizenshugi-sha*, Naturalists Ignorant of Themselves, 1910). In this essay he stated his congeniality with the Dionysian elements of Naturalism, elements of which Naturalists themselves were ignorant. By Dionysian literature, he meant "literature which directly depicts man's inner life," wherein "the self would invite and dance together with the whole universe." He approved, on the other hand, of the Apollonian "literature of objective description," too, in so far as it was motivated "purely by the self." (*Naiseikatsu Chokusha no Bungaku: Futatabi*, Literature of Direct Description of Inner Life, Continued, 1912).

Abe Yoshishige who confessed having previously been "a practicing Naturalist" became disappointed with "the sensitive, passive, and material self," and, driven by an irresistible "longing for things of primary importance," came to hold an attitude similar to Jirō. (*Jiko no Mondai to shite Mitaru Shizenshugi Shisō*, Naturalist Thought as a Problem of the Self, 1910). He blamed Tengen for his inconsistency of adhering to Naturalism in spite of the emphasis he placed upon the importance of subjective and romantic elements in Naturalist literature. (*Shizenshugi ni okeru Shukan no Ichi*, The Position of Subject in Naturalism, 1910). He began to pay attention to the Neo-Idealist philosopher Eucken who advocated a spiritual life, which he interpreted as a philosophy "founded upon the demand of man for regaining his self conquered by Nature." (*Gendai no Junkyōsha*, Modern Martyrs, 1910).

It was from the same position as Jirō and Yoshishige that Komiya Toyotaka declared that he "liked the literature of *werden* that is desirous of stimulus as means." (*Shigeki ni Ikin to suru Bungei*, Literature That Strives to Live on Stimulus). Toyotaka also set forth the idea of "renaissance of illusion" (*maboroshi no fukkatsu*), and said that "a true Naturalist should be a true idealist and, in addition, he should be a true illusionist." (*Dampen-Go*, Fragmentary Words).

The idea of "for the sake of self" (*jiko no tame*) mentioned by Jirō was strongly advocated by Mushakōji Saneatsu as well. Saneatsu held that "the present age can no longer be satisfied with Naturalist objectivism; it is too individualistic." ("*Jiko no Tame*" *oyobi Sono Ta*, "For the Sake of Self" and Other Articles, 1912). He stressed that personality and individuality should be esteemed and that inner desires arising therefrom be given an opportunity for expression. His belief was this: "I should like to do good for society and humanity only if in so doing I do good for myself." (*Jiko no Tame no Geijutsu*, Art for the Sake of Self, 1911). With this belief, Saneatsu led the Neo-Idealist movement as the head of the Shirakaba school. The way to the predominance of the Neo-Idealist view of literature, the keynote of the subsequent Taishō Era, was prepared in such a manner.

INDEX

INDEX

Certain authors are listed under their pen-name as well as their surname. In such cases, the page entries, however, are given only under their pen-name. While selection has perforce been arbitrary, it is hoped that such an arrangement will facilitate use of this index.

L

CENTENARY CULTURAL COUNCIL SERIES

JAPANESE LITERATURE
IN THE
MEIJI ERA

Published
by
ŌBUNSHA
Tōkyō, Japan
Akao Yoshio, President

First Impression 1955

PRINTED IN TŌKYŌ, JAPAN